READINGS IN SOCIAL PSYCHOLOGY

Second Edition

READINGS IN
SOCIAL PSYCHOLOGY

Classic and Contemporary Contributions

EDITED BY

LETITIA ANNE PEPLAU
University of California, Los Angeles

DAVID O. SEARS
University of California, Los Angeles

SHELLEY E. TAYLOR
University of California, Los Angeles

JONATHAN L. FREEDMAN
University of Toronto

Prentice Hall, Englewood Cliffs, New Jersey 07632

Library of Congress Cataloging-in-Publication Data

Readings in social psychology.

   Bibliography: p.
   1. Social psychology. I. Peplau, Letitia Anne.
HM251.R368 1988   302   88-2422
ISBN 0-13-761081-5 (pbk.)

Editorial/production supervision and
  interior design: *Hilda Tauber*
Cover design: *Ben Santora*
Manufacturing buyer: *Ray Keating*

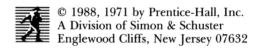

© 1988, 1971 by Prentice-Hall, Inc.
A Division of Simon & Schuster
Englewood Cliffs, New Jersey 07632

Printed in the United States of America

10 9 8 7 6 5 4 3 2 1

ISBN 0-13-761081-5   01

PRENTICE-HALL INTERNATIONAL (UK) LIMITED, *London*
PRENTICE-HALL OF AUSTRALIA PTY. LIMITED, *Sydney*
PRENTICE-HALL CANADA INC., *Toronto*
PRENTICE-HALL HISPANOAMERICANA, S.A., *Mexico*
PRENTICE-HALL OF INDIA PRIVATE LIMITED, *New Delhi*
PRENTICE-HALL OF JAPAN, INC., *Tokyo*
SIMON & SCHUSTER ASIA PTE. LTD., *Singapore*
EDITORA PRENTICE-HALL DO BRASIL, LTDA., *Rio de Janeiro*

CONTENTS

4

Judgment Under Uncertainty: Heuristics and Biases   *35*

Amos Tversky and Daniel Kahneman

5

Friendship and the Development of Self-Schemas: The Effects of Talking About Others   *48*

Francine M. Deutsch and Mary Ellen Mackesy

PART II   Attitudes and Attitude Change

6

Cognitive Consequences of Forced Compliance   *55*

Leon Festinger and James M. Carlsmith

7

Effects of Fear-Arousing Communications   *64*

Irving L. Janis and Seymour Feshbach

8

Communication Modality as a Determinant of Persuasion: The Role of Communicator Salience   *79*

Shelly Chaiken and Alice H. Eagly

9

The Effects of Involvement on Responses to Argument Quantity and Quality: Central and Peripheral Routes to Persuasion   *96*

Richard E. Petty and John T. Cacioppo

PART III *Interpersonal Attraction and Relationships*

PART IV *Aggression and Prosocial Behavior*

PART V   Social Influence and Behavior in Groups

PART VI *Applied Social Psychology*

PART VII *Reflections on Ethics and Methods in Social Psychology*

PREFACE

This collection of 31 articles presents a selection of outstanding social psychological research from the past four decades. We have included classic works from the 1950s by such founders of modern social psychology as Solomon Asch, Albert Bandura, Leon Festinger, Irving Janis, Harold Kelley, Stanley Schachter, and Muzafer Sherif. Other selections represent the heyday of laboratory experimentation in social psychology during the 1960s and 1970s, including the obedience studies of Stanley Milgram, experiments on interpersonal attraction by Elaine Hatfield and her associates, and work on helping behavior by John Darley and Bibb Latané. Half the articles present the very latest contemporary research on the major topics in social psychology today. Together, these articles provide a balanced picture of the nature of social psychological research, and how it has changed over time.

The topics covered in this collection represent the core research areas in social psychology. Parts I to V are devoted to basic issues in the field: social cognition and attribution, attitudes and attitude change, interpersonal attraction and relationships, aggression and prosocial behavior, and social influence and group behavior. Part VI deals with applied social psychology and includes recent articles on school desegregation, sex roles, environmental psychology, health psychology, and political psy-

chology. Part VII considers ethical and methodological issues in social psychological research. Articles presenting both sides on the ethical debate on the Milgram obedience studies are followed by excerpts from current U.S. Federal Regulations for the Protection of Human Research Subjects. The final selections raise critical questions about laboratory methods and the extensive use of college students as research subjects in social psychology. These selections span a wide range of theoretical orientations and methodologies. The research in this volume uses laboratory experiments, field experiments, self-report questionnaires and surveys, content analyses, and behavioral observations.

This book is designed primarily for use in undergraduate courses on social psychology. As editors, we have been concerned to select articles that convey to students a sense of the excitement and diversity of the field. To assist student readers, the book begins with a short introductory chapter on reading research reports in social psychology. Since most of the articles in this volume are from psychological journals, this chapter discusses the general format of journal articles, explains some commonly used statistical terms, and offers general advice on reading research reports. In addition, each selection in the book is preceded by a brief introduction intended to put the article into context, to highlight key findings, and to raise questions for students to consider about the methods or implications of the study.

We are grateful to the authors of the papers collected here for their permission to reprint their work. We would like to express our appreciation to Hilda Tauber, our Production Editor, to Susan Finnemore, our Psychology Editor, and to the staff at Prentice Hall for their able assistance with this project. In putting together this collection, we have been fortunate in having the help of Susan Campbell, Carolyn Drago, Steven L. Gordon, Leigh Anne Locke, Julie Verette, Monique Watson, and Gail Van Winkle. Finally, we want to thank the reviewers for this edition: Charles S. Carver, University of Miami; Susan T. Fiske, University of Massachusetts; Reid Hastie, Northwestern University; Charles M. Judd, University of Colorado; Bonnie Klentz, University of West Florida; and Philip Tetlock, University of California, Berkeley.

INTRODUCTION

Reading Research Reports in Social Psychology

LETITIA ANNE PEPLAU

This book contains 31 professional research reports written by social psychologists. These reports provide an insider's view of how social psychologists go about their work: how we formulate hypotheses, design empirical research, analyze data, and interpret our findings. Included are both classic articles from the early days of modern social psychology in the 1950s and very recent articles on topics at the leading edge of social psychology today. We believe that these selections provide an exciting glimpse of social-psychological researchers in action.

Reading a professional article in psychology is somewhat different from other reading that you do. In this brief introduction, we offer some advice for those who are reading research reports in social psychology for the first time.

FORMAT OF JOURNAL ARTICLES

Most journal articles in psychology follow a standard organization based on the *Publication Manual of the American Psychological Association*. A typical article has five main sections: abstract, introduction, method, results, and discussion.

Abstract. The abstract provides a quick overview of the research problem, the methods used, the main findings, and the conclusions to be drawn from the study. The abstract is probably the single most important paragraph in the article, and deserves special attention. If you read the abstract carefully (and perhaps more than once), it will be easier to follow the rest of the article.

Introduction. The introduction sets the stage for the study by describing the central issue of interest, and briefly reviewing previous research on the topic. The introduction also presents the rationale for the research, that is, the reasons for undertaking this particular study. The introduction specifies the goals of the research, and the research strategy to be used. In some articles the research problem will be stated in the form of specific hypotheses. After reading the introduction, you should be able to answer these questions: Why is this study important? What questions will this study answer? How does this study build on previous research?

Method. The method section describes in detail how the study was conducted. This section usually begins with a description of the subjects who participated in the research. Next, the materials used in the study such as questionnaires or standardized laboratory tasks are described. The method section also includes a step-by-

1

step description of the specific procedures used in the research. In reading the method section, try to imagine what it was like to be a participant in the study. After reading the method section, you should be able to describe from start to finish what the researcher did and how he or she did it.

Results. The results section describes the data that were collected and the ways in which the data were analyzed. Statistical analyses are presented here. Because space in professional journals is limited, authors must juggle the need to be clear and detailed against the need to be concise. Tables and figures are often used to summarize information efficiently, and you should be sure to look at them carefully. After reading the results section, you should be able to answer these questions: What were the main findings? Did the results support the original hypotheses? Were there any important but unexpected results?

Discussion. The discussion section evaluates and interprets the results. This is where the researcher can consider the implications of the study, and compare its findings to results from previous research. Authors sometimes also comment on limitations or special features of their research that may have affected the results, or propose directions for future studies. After reading the discussion section, you should be able to answer these questions: What have we learned from this research? How have these findings helped to understand the original research problem identified in the introduction?

There is no single "right" way to read a journal article. As you read the articles in this book, you will need to develop an approach that works well for you. Some people find it easiest to get a clear overview of a study before tackling the details of methods and statistics. So they carefully read the introduction and conclusion sections first, and then go back to read the methods and results to fill in the details. Others prefer to read an article from front to back in sequence. You may want to try these or other approaches to see which you person-

ally prefer. As you read an article, try to summarize in your own words the research problem or hypotheses, the specific findings for each hypothesis, and the overall conclusions to be drawn. Don't be surprised if you need to read some articles more than once in order to understand them fully.

GOALS IN READING RESEARCH REPORTS

Before you begin, it's a good idea to think about what you want to get out of this reading. Here are some things to look for in this collection of research reports.

1. *Specific research results.* Obviously, a main goal in reading research reports is to learn about important findings from social-psychological research. The articles in this book provide a sampling of some fascinating information about human behavior on such diverse topics as aggression, interpersonal attraction, social cognition, sex roles, and health psychology.

2. *How social psychologists learn about human behavior.* The research methods used by social psychologists are diverse, and the selections in this book illustrate a wide range of approaches. Many of the studies in this volume use experimental research designs in which subjects are randomly assigned to one of several conditions controlled by the researcher. In the first selection, for example, Kelley induces college students to expect that a guest lecturer will be either "warm" or "cold," and studies how these experimental manipulations affect their impressions of the lecturer. Other articles use correlational designs to investigate naturally occurring relationships among variables. For example, are dating couples who are highly matched in intelligence or physical attractiveness more likely to stay together than couples who differ in these characteristics? In selection 12, Hill, Rubin, and Peplau use correlational analyses to examine the links between similarity and breaking up in college-age couples.

The studies in this collection also vary in

whether they take place in the laboratory or in the field. In selection 14, Bandura, Ross, and Ross bring children into the laboratory to investigate the impact of aggressive adult models on children's aggressive behavior. In selection 24, Baum and Davis conduct a field experiment on a college campus. They use an architectural intervention to change the physical layout of college dormitories to see whether students assigned to smaller living groups have a better social life than those in larger living groups. Finally, the studies in this book also illustrate a number of different methods of data collection, including behavioral observation, self-report questionnaires, and archival research. As you read each article, think about the types of research design and methods of data collection that are used.

3. *Ethical issues in social-psychological research.* Over the years, psychologists have become more sensitive to ethical issues in research. Selection 29 presents current guidelines, developed in 1983 by the U.S. government, to protect the welfare of research subjects. Articles 27 and 28 debate ethical issues in research. As you read the articles in this collection, consider not only the benefits derived from the results of the work, but also the risks that may have existed for research participants.

What are the possible risks of social-psychological research? Often the risks are relatively minor—subjects might find a questionnaire boring and tedious, or feel that a study wasted half an hour of their time. In other cases, however, research may expose people to more serious harm, such as public embarrassment, loss of self-esteem, or the invasion of privacy. To protect human subjects, psychologists should make every effort to minimize possible risks. And, when risks cannot be eliminated, subjects should be given clear information about the study in advance, so that they can judge for themselves whether they want to participate and can give "informed consent."

A particularly sticky issue in psychological research has been the use of deception. In the early days of social psychology, it was fairly common for experimenters to stage elaborate hoaxes involving confederates who posed as naïve subjects. This book includes studies that exposed subjects to deceptions ranging from innocuous to extreme. Subjects were: asked to play with a "boy baby" who was actually a girl (selection 23); confronted with a group of peers (actually confederates) who disagreed with their judgments (18); exposed to fake emergencies (16); and led to believe that they were administering painful electric shocks to a research partner (19). As you read these and other studies, consider how harmful these deceptions actually might have been to subjects, and whether you think the deception was justified. Remember, however, that most of these studies are from an earlier time when many people considered deception an acceptable and sometimes necessary aspect of psychological experiments. As you read studies using deception, see if you can think of ways to investigate the same issues without deception. Today, ethical guidelines place severe limits on the use of deception in psychological research.

4. *Historical changes in social psychology.* Because the articles in this collection span 40 years, they offer a view of how our research questions and methods have developed over time. Perhaps the most obvious change is in the complexity of current techniques for data analysis. Dramatic advances in computers and statistics make it possible for researchers today to test complicated conceptual models involving many variables simultaneously. Whereas the older studies in this collection use t-tests to compare mean scores between two groups of subjects or simple correlations to look for the association between two variables, some of the newer studies describe complex analyses of variance and multiple regression equations.

A second and perhaps less obvious change concerns the issue of gender. Most of the early studies in social psychology, including the classic articles in this book, were published by men. Today, women are much better represented among psychological researchers, and nearly half of the doctorates awarded in social psychology go to women. Many of the early studies in social psychology had only male subjects—

in part because researchers studied college students, and they were disproportionately male. Today, the college sophomores who are often research subjects are evenly divided between women and men, and researchers pay more attention to the sex of research subjects and to possible sex differences in social behavior. Even the language used by psychologists has changed. The *Publication Manual of the American Psychological Association* requires authors to avoid sexist language in professional publications. For example, it is no longer considered appropriate to use the terms "man" or "mankind" to refer to people of both sexes.

A FEW WORDS ABOUT STATISTICS

For many people, the most intimidating aspect of reading professional articles in psychology is confronting the statistical analyses of data in the results section. Such terms as "log-linear analysis" or "analysis of covariance" may seem mysterious and perplexing. For students with advanced training in research design and statistics, the articles in this collection provide an opportunity to see how particular techniques are actually put to use in research. But how should students with little or no background in statistics handle this issue?

Readers cannot be expected to understand the specifics of sophisticated data analyses that go beyond their level of training. And this should not be necessary. In an essay on how to write a good journal article, Daryl Bem offers this advice to psychologists:

No matter how technical or abstruse your article is in its particulars, intelligent nonpsychologists with no expertise in statistics or experimental design should be able to comprehend the broad outlines of what you did and why. They should understand in general terms what was learned. (1987, p. 174)

In other words, even articles with the fanciest of statistics should also state the key findings in plain English. Our suggestion to students is to read the results section carefully. Try to understand what each particular analysis is designed to accomplish and how specific results are interpreted. Some of the basic abbreviations and statistical terms you will encounter are explained on page 5. But do not worry that you need to be a statistician to understand the results reported in professional articles. The goal for students lacking an advanced background in statistics is to be a thoughtful consumer of psychological research.

One reason you can safely overlook the finer points of complex data analysis in reading journal articles is that each article is subjected to a careful professional review before publication. The leading psychology journals require that articles submitted for publication be evaluated by two or three psychologists with expertise in the subject matter. Reviewers are asked to judge both the overall significance of the study and the adequacy of its methodology. Further, the competition to have an article accepted for publication is often fierce. The *Journal of Personality and Social Psychology*, which initially published many of the articles reprinted in this book, currently rejects as many as 9 out of 10 articles submitted. So there is some assurance that articles published in major journals meet the methodological standards of the day.

We hope that these suggestions will help you get started reading the articles in this book. We believe that the research reported here represents some of the most interesting and important work in social psychology. As you read psychologists describing their own work, you will gain a better appreciation of the excitement and the challenges of our quest to understand social behavior.

REFERENCES

American Psychological Association. (1983). *Publication manual of the American Psychological Association* (3rd ed.). Washington, DC.

Bem, D. J. (1987). Writing the empirical journal article. In M. P. Zanna & J. M. Darley (Eds.), *The compleat academic: A practical guide for the beginning social scientists* (pp. 171–201). New York: Random House.

COMMON STATISTICAL TERMS AND ABBREVIATIONS

analysis of variance A statistical procedure that uses an F-test to assess the degree of difference between the mean scores of two or more groups.

ANOVA Abbreviation for analysis of variance.

chi square A measure of the degree of association between two categorical variables, abbreviated as χ^2. [A categorical variable has named categories, not numerical values; religion is a categorical variable with such categories as Catholic, Jewish, Protestant, etc.]

correlation A measure of the degree of relationship between two variables (e.g., intelligence and income), sometimes abbreviated as r. A correlation can range between -1 (perfect negative relationship) and $+1$ (perfect positive relationship); $r = 0$ means there is no relationship between the variables.

factor analysis A statistical procedure for uncovering common dimensions or factors that link variables together; a researcher might use this to see if a 20-item questionnaire has distinct subscales.

F or F-test The F statistic is obtained from an F-test used to assess the degree of difference between the mean scores of two or more groups.

log-linear analysis A statistical procedure for determining the degree of association between categorical (named) variables.

M Abbreviation for the mean or average score.

N or n Abbreviation for the number of subjects in a study or subgroup.

ns Abbreviation for not statistically significant.

p Abbreviation for probability or significance level. This refers to the likelihood that a pattern of results could have occurred by chance; $p = .01$ means that there is only a 1% probability that the observed result occurred by chance.

r Abbreviation for correlation (see above).

regression analysis A statistical procedure that allows the researcher to predict the value of one variable given the value of one or more other variables.

reliability Refers to the degree to which test scores are reproducible and consistent over time.

S or Ss Abbreviations for subject and subjects.

SD Standard deviation. This refers to how much scores vary around the mean score; a large SD means that there is much variation in scores.

statistical significance A result, such as a difference in scores between two groups, is said to be statistically significant if it is unlikely to have occurred by chance. For example, if a group difference is significant at the ".05 level," the probability is only 5% that a difference of this size occurred by chance.

t or t-test The t statistic is obtained in a t-test used to assess the degree of difference in mean scores between two groups.

validity Refers to the degree to which a test or instrument measures what is is intended to measure.

1

The Warm-Cold Variable in First Impressions of Persons

HAROLD H. KELLEY

The central idea of this paper is that our expectations about another person's traits determine our behavior toward that person, no matter what traits that person actually has. As Kelley points out, this idea helps to explain the power of stereotypes about the members of various social groups, which are themselves expectations about the characteristics of group members. The study itself shows that merely describing a discussion leader as "warm" or "cold" has far-reaching effects on the traits that students attribute to the leader—in part reflecting the familiar "halo effect." Perhaps the most impressive finding, however, is that the students' expectations about the discussion leader's personality even influenced their behavior toward him—how much they participated in a discussion with him—not just their perceptions of him or their attitudes toward him. This successful use of a behavioral dependent variable, along with the more usual paper-and-pencil rating scales, is one of the reasons this paper has become a classic.

This experiment is one of several studies of first impressions (Kelley, 1948), the purpose of the series being to investigate the stability of early judgments, their determinants, and the relation of such judgments to the behavior of the person making them. In interpreting the data from several nonexperimental studies on the stability of first impressions, it proved to be necessary to postulate inner-observer variables which contribute to the impression and which remain relatively constant through time. Also some evidence was obtained which directly

Reprinted from the *Journal of Personality*, 1950, *18*, pp. 431–439. Copyright 1950 by Duke University Press. Reprinted by permission.

demonstrated the existence of these variables and their nature. The present experiment was designed to determine the effects of one kind of inner-observer variable, specifically, *expectations* about the stimulus person which the observer brings to the exposure situation.

That prior information or labels attached to a stimulus person make a difference in observers' first impressions is almost too obvious to require demonstration. The expectations resulting from such preinformation may restrict, modify, or accentuate the impressions he will have. The crucial question is: What changes in perception will accompany a given expectation? Studies of stereotyping, for example, that of Katz and Braly (1947), indicate that from an ethnic label such as "German" or "Negro," a number of perceptions follow which are culturally determined. The present study finds its main significance in relation to a study by Asch (1946) which demonstrates that certain crucial labels can transform the entire impression of the person, leading to attributions which are related to the label on a broad cultural basis.

Asch read to his subjects a list of adjectives which purportedly described a particular person. He then asked them to characterize that person. He found that the inclusion in the list of what he called *central* qualities, such as "warm" as opposed to "cold," produced a widespread change in the entire impression. This effect was not adequately explained by the halo effect since it did not extend indiscriminately in a positive or negative direction to all characteristics. Rather, it differentially transformed the other qualities, for example, by changing their relative importance in the total impression. Peripheral qualities (such as "polite" versus "blunt") did not produce effects as strong as those produced by the central qualities.

The present study tested the effects of such central qualities upon the early impressions of *real* persons, the same qualities, "warm" vs. "cold," being used. They were introduced as preinformation about the stimulus person before his actual appearance; so presumably they operated as expectations rather than as part of the stimulus pattern during the exposure period. In addition, information was obtained about the effects of the expectations upon the observers' behavior toward the stimulus person. An earlier study in this series has indicated that the more incompatible the observer initially perceived the stimulus person to be, the less the observer initiated interaction with him thereafter. The second purpose of the present experiment, then, was to provide a better controlled study of this relationship.

No previous studies reported in the literature have dealt with the importance of first impressions for behavior. The most relevant data are found in the sociometric literature, where there are scattered studies of the relation between choices among children having some prior acquaintance and their interaction behavior. For an example, see the study by Newstetter, Feldstein, and Newcomb (1938).

PROCEDURE

The experiment was performed in three sections of a psychology course at the Massachusetts Institute of Technology. The three sections provided 23, 16, and 16 subjects respectively. All 55 subjects were men, most of them in their third college year. In each class the stimulus person (also a male) was completely unknown to the subjects before the experimental period. One person served as stimulus person in two sections, and a second person took this role in the third section. In each case the stimulus person was introduced by the experimenter, who posed as a representative of the course instructors and who gave the following statement:

Your regular instructor is out of town today, and since we of Economics 70 are interested in the general problem of how various classes react to different instructors, we're going to have an instructor today you've never had before, Mr. ———. Then, at the end of the period, I want you to fill out some forms about him. In order to give you some idea of what he's like, we've had a person who knows him write up a little biographical note about him. I'll pass this out to you now and you can read it before he arrives. *Please read these to yourselves and don't talk about this among yourselves until the class is over so that he won't get wind of what's going on.*

Two kinds of these notes were distributed, the two being identical except that in one the stimulus person was described among other things as being "rather cold" whereas in the other form the phrase "very warm" was substituted. The content of the "rather cold" version is as follows:

Mr. ——— is a graduate student in the Department of Economics and Social Science here at M. I. T. He has had three semesters of teaching experience in psychology at another college. This is his first semester teaching Ec. 70. He is 26 years old, a veteran, and married. People who know him consider him to be a rather cold person, industrious, critical, practical, and determined.

The two types of preinformation were distributed randomly within each of the three classes and in such a manner that the students were not aware that two kinds of information were being given out. The stimulus person then appeared and led the class in a twenty-minute discussion. During this time the experimenter kept a record of how often each student participated in the discussion. Since the discussion was almost totally leader-centered, this participation record indicates the number of times each student initiated verbal interaction with the instructor. After the discussion period, the stimulus person left the room, and the experimenter gave the following instructions:

Now, I'd like to get your impression of Mr. ———. This is not a test of you and can in no way affect your grade in this course. This material will not be identified as belonging to particular persons and will be kept strictly confidential. It will be of most value to us if you are completely honest in your evaluation of Mr. ———. Also, please understand that what you put down will not be used against him or cause him to lose his job or anything like that. This is not a test of him but merely a study of how different classes react to different instructors.

The subjects then wrote free descriptions of the stimulus person and finally rated him on a set of 15 rating scales.

RESULTS AND DISCUSSION

1. *Influence of warm-cold variable on first impressions.* The differences in the ratings produced by the warm-cold variable were consistent from one section to another even where different stimulus persons were used. Consequently, the data from the three sections were combined by equating means (the standard deviations were approximately equal) and the results for the total group are presented in Table 1. Also in this table is presented that part of Asch's data which refers to the qualities included in our rating scales. From this table it is quite

clear that those given the "warm" preinformation consistently rated the stimulus person more favorably than do those given the "cold" preinformation. Summarizing the statistically significant differences, the "warm" subjects rated the stimulus person as more considerate of others, more informal, more sociable, more popular, better natured, more humorous, and more humane. These findings are very similar to Asch's for the characteristics common to both studies. He found more frequent attribution to his hypothetical "warm" personalities of sociability, popularity, good naturedness, generosity, humorousness, and humaneness. So these data strongly support his finding that such a central quality as "warmth" can greatly influence the total impression of a personality. This effect is found to be operative in the perception of real persons.

This general favorableness in the perceptions of the "warm" observers as compared with the "cold" ones indicates that something like a halo effect may have been operating in these ratings. Although his data are not completely persuasive on this point, Asch was convinced that such a general effect was *not* operating in his study. Closer inspection of the present data makes it clear that the "warm-cold" effect cannot be explained altogether on the basis of simple halo effect. In Table 1 it is evident that the "warm-cold" variable produced differential effects from one rating scale to another. The size of this effect seems to depend upon the closeness of relation between the specific dimension of any given rating scale and the central quality of "warmth" or "coldness." Even though the rating of intelligence may be influenced by a halo effect, it is not influenced to the same degree to which considerateness is. It seems to make sense to view such strongly influenced items as considerateness, informality, good naturedness, and humaneness as dynamically more closely related to warmth and hence more perceived in terms of this relation than in terms of a general positive or negative feeling toward the stimulus person. If first impressions are normally made in terms of such general dimensions as "warmth" and "coldness," the power they give the observer in making predictions and specific evaluations about

Table 1 Comparison of "Warm" and "Cold" Observers in Terms of Average Ratings Given Stimulus Persons

Item	Low End of Rating Scale	High End of Rating Scale	Average Rating		Level of Significance of Warm-Cold Difference	Asch's Data: Percent of Group Assigning Quality at Low End of Our Rating Scale*	
			Warm N = 27	Cold N = 28		Warm	Cold
1	Knows his stuff	Doesn't know his stuff	3.5	4.6			
2	Considerate of others	Self-centered	6.3	9.6	1%		
3†	Informal	Formal	6.3	9.6	1%		
4†	Modest	Proud	9.4	10.6			
5	Sociable	Unsociable	5.6	10.4	1%	91%	38%
6	Self-assured	Uncertain of himself	8.4	9.1			
7	High intelligence	Low intelligence	4.8	5.1			
8	Popular	Unpopular	4.0	7.4	1%	84%	28%
9†	Good natured	Irritable	9.4	12.0	5%	94%	17%
10	Generous	Ungenerous	8.2	9.6		91%	08%
11	Humorous	Humorless	8.3	11.7	1%	77%	13%
12	Important	Insignificant	6.5	8.6		88%	99%
13†	Humane	Ruthless	8.6	11.0	5%	86%	31%
14†	Submissive	Dominant	13.2	14.5			
15	Will go far	Will not get ahead	4.2	5.8			

* Given for all qualities common to Asch's list and this set of rating scales.

† These scales were reversed when presented to the subjects.

such disparate behavior characteristics as formality and considerateness is considerable (even though these predictions may be incorrect or misleading).

The free report impression data were analyzed for only one of the sections. In general, there were few sizable differences between the "warm" and "cold" observers. The "warm" observers attributed more nervousness, more sincerity, and more industriousness to the stimulus person. Although the frequencies of comparable qualities are very low because of the great variety of descriptions produced by the observers, there is considerable agreement with the rating scale data.

Two important phenomena are illustrated in these free description protocols, the first of them having been noted by Asch. *Firstly*, the characteristics of the stimulus person are interpreted in terms of the precognition of warmth or coldness. For example, a "warm" observer

writes about a rather shy and retiring stimulus person as follows: "He makes friends slowly but they are lasting friendships when formed." In another instance, several "cold" observers describe him as being ". . . intolerant: would be angry if you disagree with his views . . ."; while several "warm" observers put the same thing this way: "Unyielding in principle, not easily influenced or swayed from his original attitude." *Secondly*, the preinformation about the stimulus person's warmth or coldness is evaluated and interpreted in the light of the direct behavioral data about him. For example, "He has a slight inferiority complex which leads to his coldness," and "His conscientiousness and industriousness might be mistaken for coldness." Examples of these two phenomena occurred rather infrequently, and there was no way to evaluate the relative strengths of these countertendencies. Certainly some such evaluation is necessary to determine the conditions under which behavior which is contrary to a stereotyped label resists distortion and leads to rejection of the label.

A comparison of the data from the two different stimulus persons is pertinent to the last point in so far as it indicates the interaction between the properties of the stimulus person and the label. The fact that the warm-cold variable generally produced differences in the same direction for the two stimulus persons, even though they are very different in personality, behavior, and mannerisms, indicates the strength of this variable. However, there were some exceptions to this tendency as well as marked differences in the *degree* to which the experimental variable was able to produce differences. For example, stimulus person A typically appears to be anything but lacking in self-esteem and on rating scale 4 he was generally at the "proud" end of the scale. Although the "warm" observers tended to rate him as they did the other stimulus person (i.e., more "modest"), the difference between the "warm" and "cold" means for stimulus person A is very small and not significant as it is for stimulus person B. Similarly, stimulus person B was seen as "unpopular" and "humorless," which agrees with his typical classroom behavior. Again the "warm" observers rated him more favorably on these items, but their ratings were not significantly different from those of the "cold" observers, as was true for the other stimulus person. Thus we see that the strength or compellingness of various qualities of the stimulus person must be reckoned with. The stimulus is not passive to the forces arising from the label but actively resists distortion and may severely limit the degree of influence exerted by the preinformation.

2. *Influence of warm-cold variable on interaction with the stimulus person.* In the analysis of the frequency with which the various students took part in the discussion led by the stimulus person, a larger proportion of those given the "warm" preinformation participated than of those given the "cold" preinformation. Fifty-six percent of the "warm" subjects entered the discussion, whereas only 32 percent of the "cold" subjects did so. Thus the expectation of warmth not only produced more favorable

early perceptions of the stimulus person but led to greater initiation of interaction with him. This relation is a low one, significant at between the 5 percent and 10 percent level of confidence, but it is in line with the general principle that social perception serves to guide and steer the person's behavior in his social environment.

As would be expected from the foregoing findings, there was also a relation between the favorableness of the impression and whether or not the person participated in the discussion. Although any single item yielded only a small and insignificant relation to participation, when a number are combined the trend becomes clear cut. For example, when we combine the seven items which were influenced to a statistically significant degree by the warm-cold variable, the total score bears considerable relation to participation, the relationship being significant as well beyond the 1 percent level. A larger proportion of those having favorable total impressions participated than of those having unfavorable impressions, the biserial correlation between these variables being .34. Although this relation may be interpreted in several ways, its seems most likely that the unfavorable perception led to a curtailment of interaction. Support for this comes from one of the other studies in this series (Kelley, 1948). There it was found that those persons having unfavorable impressions of the instructor at the end of the first class meeting tended less often to initiate interactions with him in the succeeding four meetings than did those having favorable first impressions. There was also some tendency in the same study for those persons who interacted least with the instructor to change least in their judgments of him from the first to later impressions.

It will be noted that these relations lend some support to the autistic hostility hypothesis proposed by Newcomb (1947). This hypothesis suggests that the possession of an initially hostile attitude toward a person leads to a restriction of communication and contact with him which in turn serves to preserve the hostile attitude by preventing the acquisition of data which could correct it. The present data indicate that a restriction of interaction is associated with unfavorable preinformation and an unfavorable perception. The data from the other study support this result and also indicate the correctness of the second part of the hypothesis, that restricted interaction reduces the likelihood of change in the attitude.

What makes these findings more significant is that they appear in the context of a discussion class where there are numerous *induced* and *own* forces to enter the discussion and to interact with the instructor. It seems likely that the effects predicted by Newcomb's hypothesis would be much more marked in a setting where such forces were not present.

SUMMARY

The warm-cold variable had been found by Asch to produce large differences in the impressions of personality formed from a list of adjectives. In this study the same variable was introduced in the form of expectations about a real person and was found to produce similar differences in first impressions of him in a classroom setting. In addition, the differences in

first impressions produced by the different expectations were shown to influence the observers' behavior toward the stimulus person. Those observers given the favorable expectation (who, consequently, had a favorable impression of the stimulus person) tended to interact more with him than did those given the unfavorable expectation.

REFERENCES

Asch, S. E. (1946). Forming impressions of personality. *Journal of Abnormal and Social Psychology, 41*, 258–290.

Katz, D., & Braly, K. W. (1947). Verbal stereotypes and racial prejudice. In T. M. Newcomb & E. L. Hartley (Eds.), *Readings in social psychology*. New York: Holt, pp. 204–210.

Kelley, H. H. (1948). *First impressions in interpersonal relations*. Unpublished doctoral dissertation, Massachusetts Institute of Technology, Cambridge, Mass.

Newcomb, T. M. (1947). Autistic hostility and social reality. *Human Relations, 1*, 69–86.

Newstetter, W. I., Feldstein, M. J., & Newcomb, T. M. (1938). *Group adjustment: A study in experimental sociology*. Cleveland: Western Reserve University.

2

Videotape and the Attribution Process: Reversing Actors' and Observers' Points of View

MICHAEL D. STORMS

Jones and Nisbett had suggested that there is an "actor-observer bias" in attributions, such that people tend to see their own behavior as controlled by the situation they are in, but see the behavior of other people as controlled by such internal dispositions as their personalities, values, and attitudes. In this study, Storms tests one explanation of this bias—that it is merely due to the difference in the perspectives of actors and observers. The most interesting aspect of the experiment is the demonstration that the attributional bias can be reversed simply by reversing the visual perspectives of actors and observers. To show this, Storms had two people interact, with two observers looking on. Then he showed them a videotape of the interaction from one of two perspectives—the same view as they had originally, or a reversal, in which they view it from the other person's perspective. Table 1 shows that the usual actor-observer difference is found when people viewed the interaction from their original perspective, but it is reversed when they viewed exactly the same interaction from the other person's perspective. Thus, the study both replicates the original actor-observer bias, and explains it by showing that it is a simple function of perspective.

ABSTRACT. Two actor subjects at a time engaged in a brief, unstructured conversation while two observer subjects looked on. Later a questionnaire measured the actors' attributions of their own behavior in the conversation either to dispositional, internal causes or to situational, external causes. Similarly, each observer attributed his matched actor's behavior. Videotapes of the conversation, replayed to subjects before the attribution questionnaire, provided an experimental manipulation of visual orientation. Some actors and observers saw no videotape replay, while other subjects saw a tape that merely repeated their original visual orientations. As predicted for both of these conditions, the actors attributed relatively more to the situation than the observers. A third set of subjects saw a videotape taken from a new perspective—some actors saw a tape of themselves, while some observers saw the other participant with whom their matched actor had been conversing. With this reorientation, self-viewing actors attributed relatively more to their own dispositions than observers. The results indicated the importance of visual orientation in determining attributional differences between actors and observers. Pragmatically, the theoretical framework and results of the study had relevance to the use of videotape self-observation in therapy groups.

When an individual observes a behavior and attempts to understand its causes, he is concerned with the relative importance of personal dispositions of the actor and the surrounding social and environmental context. Both an observer who wishes to explain another's behavior and an actor who tries to understand his own behavior attempt to make the appropriate

Reprinted from the Journal of Personality and Social Psychology, 1973, 27, pp. 166–175. Copyright 1973 by the American Psychological Association. Reprinted by permission of publisher and author.

causal attributions. There is reason to believe, however, that actors and observers do not always arrive at the same explanation of the actor's behavior. Jones and Nisbett (1971) have argued that when actors seek to explain their own behavior, they are inclined to give considerable weight to external, environmental (i.e., situational) causes. Observers, on the other hand, place considerably more emphasis on internal, personal (i.e., dispositional) causes of the actor's behavior.

Several studies (Jones & Harris, 1967; Jones, Rock, Shaver, Goethals, & Ward, 1968; McArthur, 1970, 1972; Nisbett, Caputo, Legant, & Marecek, 1973) have been cited in support of this general proposition, and Jones and Nisbett have discussed a variety of factors which might lead to such attributional differences between actors and observers. These factors include (a) differences in information about the event, behavior, and context which is *available* to actors and observers and (b) differences in how information is *processed* by actors and observers. Actors may have private information about some aspects of the event, including their own feelings and the historical context in which the event transpires, while observers may have more complete information about the behavior itself. Furthermore, in the interests of controlling events and predicting the future, actors may attend more to situational variables in an event, and observers may attend more to variations in the actor's behavior.

The present study examines a fundamental difference between actors and observers which may lead, in turn, to some of the information differences postulated by Jones and Nisbett (1971). Perhaps the most obvious difference between actors and observers is that they have, quite literally, different points of view. Actors cannot see themselves act; physically they cannot observe much of their own behavior. They may watch the antecedents of their own behavior, or its consequences, or both. But they do not normally view the behavior itself. In addition to the physical difficulty of watching oneself, there are temporal restrictions which contribute to a lack of self-observation. There may not be enough time or mental capacity to contemplate past behavior, monitor present behav-

ior, and plan future behavior all at once. Finally, there are motivational reasons for avoiding an excess of self-observation. In the interest of acting unself-consciously and maintaining control over the immediate events taking place, the actor may learn that it is dysfunctional to be overly concerned with his own present and past behavior. Instead, it is reasonable to assume that most actors focus on the situation in which they find themselves. They look at, attend to, and think about various changing aspects of the environment in which and to which they must respond.

While the actor is watching the situation in which he finds himself, the observer is probably watching the actor. It is usually interesting and often important to watch the behavior of other people. Consequently, observers are often visually oriented toward the actor. Although an observer can take his eyes off the actor and view other aspects of the situation, he probably sees less of the situation than the actor does. As with actors, the observer's scope is also limited by time. Observers cannot simultaneously watch the actor and observe as much of the situation as the actor can. Moreover, observers may find it more efficient in terms of controlling and predicting the ongoing event to concentrate on the actor's behavior rather than on the actor's situation. Finally, the actor is, after all, part of the observer's situation. For the same reason that an actor focuses on his own situation, the observer focuses on the behavior of the actor, which is part of his (the observer's) situation.

Thus, we postulate that there is a simple difference between actors and observers. Actors watch their environment (which includes the behavior of other people) more than they watch their own behavior. Observers watch the behavior of the actor more than they watch the actor's situation.

If it is true that attributions are largely influenced by point of view, it should be possible to change the way actors and observers interpret a behavior by changing their visual orientations.

A test of this hypothesis requires some means of changing actors' and observers' orientations. Fortunately, modern technology provides a simple and interesting means to accomplish this change—namely, the use of videotape. Videotapes of an event, taken from various camera angles, can be replayed to actors and observers to redirect their attention to other aspects of the event. Of particular interest is the case in which videotape presents a new visual orientation, that is, when actors are shown a tape of their own behavior from the observer's perspective and when observers are shown a tape of some key aspect of the actor's situation from the actor's perspective. Such reorientation should affect actors and observers so as to weaken (or even reverse) their original attributional biases. Actors who see themselves should make more dispositional attributions about their own behavior. Observers who see another aspect of the actor's situation should become more situational in attributing the actor's behavior.

Thus, the question to be answered by this study is whether actors' and observers' attributions can be significantly influenced, perhaps even reversed, by changing their visual orientation toward an event. The implications of such a question may go beyond immediate theoretical concerns. Discrepancies between actors' and observers' perceptions and interpretations of behavior are of paramount concern to therapists, group relations consultants, and other group leaders. Often such practitioners must attempt to bridge the interpretational gap between actor and observer, patient and therapist, and individual and group.

METHOD

Overview

The hypothesis was tested in an experiment that featured a simple interpersonal event, namely a brief getting-acquainted conversation between two strangers (actors). In addition, two other subjects (observers) were told to watch the conversation but not to participate in it.

Videotape replays of the conversation provided the experimental manipulation. The design made it possible to compare the effects of three orientation conditions: (*a*) one in which

no visual reorientation was attempted (no videotape), (*b*) one in which videotape was used simply to repeat the subject's original orientations (same orientation), and (*c*) one in which videotape reversed the orientation of actor and observer (new orientation). In one set of conditions, actors and observers saw a videotape from essentially the same orientation as they had had in "real life." Actors saw a videotape replay of the other participant with whom they were conversing (actor—same orientation), and observers saw a videotape of the same actor they had been observing and about whom they would later answer questions (observer—same orientation). In another set of conditions, actors and observers received an entirely new orientation on videotape. Actors saw a videotape of themselves in the conversation (actor—new orientation), and observers saw a videotape of the other participant with whom their target actor had been conversing (observer—new orientation). In addition, a set of actors and observers were run with no videotape replay.

Subjects

One hundred and twenty Yale undergraduate male volunteers participated in 30 groups of 4. Subjects were solicited by sign-up sheets which specified that people who volunteered for the same session should not be previously acquainted.

Procedure

When each group of four subjects arrived at the experiment, they were told,

This is a study in an area of social psychology called "interpersonal dynamics." More specifically, I'm interested in what I call "getting acquainted"—that is, what happens when two strangers meet for the first time and initiate their first conversation. Two of you in this study will be having a short, first conversation with each other. In addition, this study calls for two observers.

Subjects were randomly assigned to the role of actor (actually referred to as participant in the script) or observer. Two subjects were assigned to be actors and to have a getting-acquainted conversation together. Each of the remaining two observer subjects was assigned to observe his matched actor during the conversation.

The experimenter then mentioned,

There is one thing I would like to add to the procedure today. I've gotten hold of some video-tape equipment and I will be taping your conversation. My thought was that it might be useful to you in answering the questionnaires to see the conversation replayed on tape.

Subjects were then seated in the experimental room as shown in Figure 1. Actors sat at one end of the table, across from each other, with one camera focused on each. Observers sat at the other end of the table, diagonally across from and facing their matched actors. The experimenter reiterated that the conversation would last about 5 minutes, that the actors could talk about anything they wished, perhaps starting with their names and where they lived, and that observers should silently watch their matched actors.

After adjusting the equipment, the experimenter signaled to the participants to begin their conversation. Five minutes later, he asked them to stop and wait silently while the tapes were rewound. At this point, the experimental manipulation was performed. A random number table was consulted to determine whether the session would be a control session, in which

case the subject would not see any tape, or an experimental session. If an experimental session was indicated, the experimenter continued, "I'm afraid only one camera was working very well and the other one is just too poor to see anything. So we'll only be able to see one of you on the videotape." Experimental subjects were always shown the tape of Actor 1.

Thus one actor, Actor 2, saw a tape of the same participant he had just seen in real life (Actor 1) and was the actor–same orientation subject. The other actor, Actor 1, viewed the tape of himself and was the actor–new orientation subject. Similarly, one observer, Observer 1, saw a tape of the same actor he had been observing in the conversation (Actor 1) and was the observer–same orientation subject. The other observer, Observer 2, saw a tape of the participant whom he had not been observing previously (Actor 1) and was the observer–new orientation subject. Thus each experimental session yielded one subject in each of the four experimental cells.

If a control session was indicated, the experimenter said the following instead: "I'm afraid this is lousy equipment. It just didn't take a good enough picture to be worth our while looking at it. So we'll just have to skip the tapes and go on to the questionnaire." These no-videotape control sessions produced two actor–no-videotape subjects and two observer–no-videotape subjects.

At this point, for control subjects, and after the videotape replay for experimental subjects, the experimenter introduced the questionnaire, stressing that it was confidential and that the subjects would not see each other's responses. When the subjects completed the questions, they were debriefed. At this time, the experimenter raised the issue of experimental deception, but no subject indicated suspicion that the videotape had been a deliberate manipulation or even an essential part of the experiment.

Measures

On the postexperimental questionnaire, actor subjects answered mostly questions about themselves, and observer subjects answered

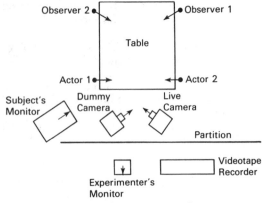

Figure 1.   Setup of the experimental room.

questions about their matched actor. After a few introductory filler items, a page of instructions and the key dependent measures of attribution were presented. The instructions informed subjects that in the next part of the questionnaire they would be asked to describe their own (their matched actor's) behavior along four standard dimensions: friendliness, talkativeness, nervousness, and dominance. Then, for each of the four behaviors, subjects were to indicate how much influence they thought the following two factors had in causing that behavior:

(A) <u>Personal characteristics</u> about yourself (your matched participant): How important were your (his) personality, traits, character, personal style, attitudes, mood, and so on in causing you (him) to behave the way you (he) did?

(B) <u>Characteristics of the situation</u>: How important were such factors as being in an experiment, the "getting acquainted" situation, the topic of conversation, the way the other participant behaved and so on in causing you (him) to behave the way you (he) did?

Thus, on each of the next four pages, three questions were presented. The first asked about the perceived level of behavior on one of the four dimensions, for example, "To what extent did you (your matched participant) behave in a friendly, warm manner?" The question was followed by a 9-point scale labeled extremely friendly (9) to extremely unfriendly (1). Presented next were the two attribution questions: "How important were <u>personal characteristics</u> about you (your matched participant) in causing you (him) to behave that way?" and "How important were <u>characteristics of the situation</u> in causing you (him) to behave that way?" Each of these questions was followed by a 9-point scale labeled extremely important (9) to extremely unimportant (1).

These last two questions, repeated over the four behavioral dimensions, provided the principal and most direct measure of subjects' attributions. These four dimensions were not selected on the basis of any particular theoretical or empirical considerations, but simply because it was anticipated that subjects would manifest behaviors along each of these dimensions and that subjects would be able to make judgments about them. Since the hypothesis was concerned with the relative strength of dispositional versus situational attributions and made no distinctions among the four behavioral dimensions, the appropriate measure was the difference between perceived importance of personal characteristics and perceived importance of situational characteristics in causing the actor's behavior, summed over all four behaviors. This difference score was referred to as the dispositional–situational index. A higher value on this index indicated that a subjects' attributions were relatively more dispositional and less situational. It is important to note this dual meaning of the dispositional–situational index. When an effect is described as "relatively more dispositional," it is equally valid to say "relatively less situational."

A second, less direct measure of the subjects' attributions appeared later in the questionnaire. The subjects were asked to report their estimates of the actor's level of behavior in *general* on each of the four behavioral dimensions, for example, "How friendly a person are you (is your matched participant) in general?" Responses were made on a scale from very friendly (9) to very unfriendly (1). It was then possible to compare these answers to the subjects' previous answers about the actor's level of behavior in the conversation. If a subject had perceived that the actor's behavior in the conversation was due to a stable personal disposition, then the subject would likely have predicted that the actor behaved the same way in general. Thus, dispositional attributions would lead to a low discrepancy between the subject's perception of the actor's behavior in the conversation and his behavior in general. On the other hand, if the subject had thought that the actor's behavior was caused by the situation, he would more likely have reported that the actor behaved differently in general. Thus, situational attributions would lead to greater discrepancy between the subjects' perceptions of the actor's present and general levels of behavior. The simplest measure of this discrepancy was the absolute value of the difference between the present level-of-behavior scores and the general level-of-behavior scores, summed over all four behaviors. This measure was referred to as the present-behavior–general-behavior index. The higher the value of this discrepancy index, the more a subject made situational (or the less he made dispositional) attributions.

The remainder of the questionnaire contained items not directly related to present concerns.

RESULTS

Dispositional versus Situational Attributions for Behavior

The main hypothesis of the present study concerns the effects of videotape reorientation on actors' and observers' causal attributions of the actor's behavior. Before considering the effects of reorientation, however, it is helpful to examine the evidence pertinent to the original Jones and Nisbett (1971) hypothesis that actors are characteristically inclined to attribute causality to aspects of the situation, while observers tend to attribute causality to the actor's disposition. Evidence for this proposition is

found in two conditions of the present experiment: the no-videotape cells in which the subjects did not receive any videotape replay, and the same-orientation cells in which the videotape merely repeated the subjects' original visual perspectives.

The relevant data are presented in Table 1. The key dependent measure, the total dispositional–situational index, reflects the relative strength of dispositional and situational attributions; a higher value on this index indicates relatively more dispositional (less situational) attributing. A comparison of the dispositional–situational means for actors and observers in the no-videotape and same-orientation cells reveals that, in both of these conditions, actors attributed relatively more to situational causes than did observers ($p < .12$, $p < .05$, respectively).[1] It is further noted from these data that a videotape which merely repeated the subjects' original orientation had little effect on either actors or observers. Dispositional–situational scores for actors in the same-orientation condition did not differ from those for actors in the no-videotape condition ($q = 1.79$, ns), and scores for observers in the two conditions were also similar ($q = 1$, ns). Thus, under conditions of no videotape and under conditions of repeated videotape orientation, the subject's role as actor or observer was an important determinant of attributions. Actors attributed their own behavior relatively more to situational causes, and observers attributed the behavior relatively more to dispositional causes.

The main hypothesis of the present study can be examined with the data presented in the last column of Table 1. It was anticipated that actors who saw themselves on videotape would become relatively less situational (more dispositional) in attributions of their own behavior, while observers who saw a videotape of the other participant with whom the actor

Table 1 Dispositional, Situational, and Dispositional Minus Situational Attribution Scores Totaled Over All Four Behaviors

Attribution	Same Orientation	No Videotape	New Orientation
Actors' attributions of own behavior			
Dispositional	26.10	27.35	27.50
Situational	25.95	25.10	20.70
Dispositional–situational	.15[a]	2.25[ab]	6.80[c]
Observers' attributions of matched actor's behavior			
Dispositional	27.10	27.30	25.75
Situational	22.20	22.50	24.15
Dispositional–situational	4.90[bc]	4.80[bc]	1.60[ab]

Note. Dispositional–situational means not sharing the same superscript are significantly different at the .05 level or beyond by Newman-Keuls tests.

[1] These comparisons, and all two cell comparisons in the present study, are based on the q statistic from the Newman-Keuls procedure for testing differences among several means (see Winer, 1962). The degrees of freedom, taken from the overall analysis of variance, equal 114; n equals 20 per cell. The Newman-Keuls is a more stringent test than the usual two-tailed t test.

had been conversing would become relatively more situational (less dispositional) in their attributions of the actor's behavior. Since opposite effects of videotape reorientation were predicted for actors and observers, the hypothesis was properly tested by the interaction between subjects' roles (actor or observer) and videotape orientation. The predicted Role × Videotape Orientation interaction was obtained at beyond the .001 level of confidence ($F = 9.72$, $df = 2/114$, $p < .001$). Neither the main effect for role, nor the main effect for videotape orientation was significant. The interaction reflected a complete reversal of the relative perspectives of actor and observer in the new-orientation condition. In the same-orientation and no-videotape conditions, the actors' attributions were more situational than the observers'. In the new-orientation condition, in contrast, the actors were relatively more dispositional than the observers. This reversed effect was significant in itself ($p < .05$).

Examining the simple dispositional and situational scores also presented in Table 1, it is apparent that reorientation had a stronger influence on the subjects' evaluation of situational factors than on their evaluation of dispositional factors. The array of means for attributions to dispositional causes was in the direction of the predicted interaction, but the effect did not reach significance ($F = 1.38$, $df = 2/114$, ns). The situational attribution scores showed the expected reverse pattern, and the interaction was significant ($F = 5.78$, $df = 2/114$, $p < .005$).

The hypothesis is thus strongly supported. Visual orientation has a powerful influence on the attributions of actors and observers. Indeed, the data in Table 1 suggest the strongest possible conclusion: Under some circumstances actual role as actor or observer is unimportant, and visual orientation is totally determinative of attributions.

Two other aspects of the dispositional–situational data are noteworthy. (*a*) Repetition on videotape of essentially the same information which had been presented in real life had little effect on either the actors or the observers. Actors in the same-orientation condition were only slightly and nonsignificantly more situa-

tional than no-videotape actors, and same-orientation observers were only slightly and nonsignificantly more dispositional than no-videotape observers. (*b*) The predicted experimental effects were not obtained with equal strength for all four·of the behaviors on which the total dispositional–situational index was based.

The fact that videotape in the same-orientation cells had little effect on the subject's attributions suggests that mere repetition of information and the addition of time to review the event did not affect the subject's perceptions of the event. The subjects appear to have absorbed all relevant data about the event during its real-life occurrence. Of course, one would not necessarily expect this to be true of all events. If the episode were more complex or of longer duration, subjects could easily miss important information in vivo. A videotape replay would fill in these informational gaps and could, quite possibly, produce different attributions.

The most noteworthy difference among the four behavioral dimensions was the failure of the dominance dimension to contribute to the experimental effects. Considering each behavioral dimension separately, the Role × Videotape Orientation interaction was significant for friendliness, talkativeness, and nervousness, each at the .025 level of confidence, but was trivial for dominance ($F < 1$). Comments by subjects during the debriefing suggest a possible reason for the failure of dominance to contribute to the experimental effects. Subjects complained that dominance was a difficult dimension on which to judge people in the context of a simple, 5-minute getting-acquainted conversation. While friendliness, talkativeness, and nervousness are dimensions with concrete behavioral counterparts (such as smiling, talking, and fidgeting), apparently dominance is a more abstract dimension and requires a higher order of inference.

When the dominance question was excluded from the analysis, each of the experimental effects was strengthened. Across the remaining three dimensions, the interaction test of videotape reorientation was strengthened from an F of 9.72 to an F of 13.89 ($df = 2/114$, $p <$

.001). Tests for the Jones and Nisbett (1971) hypothesis were also strengthened; the contrast between actors and observers in the no-videotape condition was significant at the .05 level, and the contrast between actors and observers in the same-orientation conditions was significant at the .01 level.

Perceived Level of Behavior and Perceived Discrepancy from General Behavior

In addition to the two attribution questions, the subjects also answered questions about the perceived level of behavior on each dimension. Past experiments in this area have typically created a specific, standardized behavior for subjects to attribute. The present experiment, with its unstructured conversations, did not furnish all subjects with the same behavior. This flexibility was desirable, in that it provided a more general test of the attribution hypotheses over several, naturally occurring behaviors. But it also created the possibility that perceptions of the perceived level or intensity of behavior could differ among experimental conditions and thus account for the different attributions. This does not appear to have been the case, however. There were two ways of calculating perceived level of behavior: (a) by taking the direct value from the 9-point scale for each level-of-behavior response and (b) since the scales were bipolar (for example, 9 = very friendly to 1 = very unfriendly), by taking the deviation of the subject's response from the midpoint of the scale (5). Neither of these measures yielded significant comparisons between any cells in the experiment, either for each behavior considered separately or for all four behaviors totaled. Furthermore, the overall correlations between the total dispositional–situational measure of attributions and the two measures of perceived level of behavior were trivial and nonsignificant ($r = -.049$, for the direct score; $r = -.021$, for the score of deviation from midpoint). Thus, it is apparent that differences in perceived level of behavior could not account for the attribution differences.

Since there were no significant differences in perceived level of behavior, it is meaningful to examine the second measure of subjects'

Table 2 Present Behavior Minus General Behavior Discrepancy Scores Summed over All Four Behaviors

Subjects	Same Orientation	No Videotape	New Orientation
Actors	7.15	5.00	4.25
Observers	5.45	4.90	5.90

attributions, the present-behavior–general-behavior discrepancy scores. This index reflected the absolute difference between the subjects' perceptions of the actor's *present behavior* (in the conversation) and the actor's *general behavior*, summed over all four behaviors. A small discrepancy would indicate that a subject expected the actor's present behavior to generalize and was thus making a dispositional attribution. A greater discrepancy would indicate less generalization of the actor's behavior and thus a situational attribution.

The results of the present-behavior–general-behavior discrepancy measure, presented in Table 2, corroborated the findings on the dispositional–situational measure of attributions. The effects of videotape reorientation, as tested in the Role × Videotape Orientation interaction, reached significance at $p < .05$, ($F = 3.38, df = 2/114$). Again, neither the main effect for role nor the main effect for orientation was significant. Although the direction of differences between the actors and observers in the various conditions was as expected, none of the individual comparisons between cells reached significance on the present-behavior–general-behavior measure, even with the exclusion of the dominance dimension. It appears that the results for the present-behavior–general behavior measure followed the same pattern as, but were generally weaker than, the results for the dispositional–situational measure. The two measures were, incidentally, significantly correlated (overall $r = .361, p < .01$).

DISCUSSION

The present study demonstrates that visual orientation has a powerful influence on the inferences made by actors and observers about the causes of the actor's behavior. When videotape was not presented and subjects were left to assume their own orientations, or when videotape reproduced subjects' original orientations, actors attributed their behavior relatively more to situational causes than did observers. This finding supports the Jones and Nisbett (1971) hypothesis that actors' attributions are typically more situational than observers'. But under conditions of reorientation, when subjects saw a new point of view on videotape, the attributional differences between actors and observers were exactly reversed. Reoriented, self-viewing actors attributed their behaviors relatively less to situational causes than did observers. This effect was obtained on two very different measures of attribution across a variety of behavioral dimensions in an unstructured situation.

Mechanisms of Videotape Reorientation

Two important issues arise concerning the possible mechanisms by which video orientation affected attributions. The first issue, one crucial to any laboratory social psychology experiment, concerns experimenter demand characteristics. Demand characteristics could have influenced the results of the present study if the hypotheses had been communicated to subjects either by the experimenter's behavior or by the fact the subjects viewed only one videotape. Both of these possibilities depend on subjects' developing the expectation that videotape had importance for how they should respond. The possibility of communicating the hypotheses was avoided by leading subjects to believe that videotape was not an essential part of the experiment and that the experimenter had wanted to show both tapes but could not, due to circumstances beyond his control. During debriefing, subjects were questioned on their reactions to this hoax; they reported no suspicion that the videotape breakdown had been intentional or important. Moreover, if subjects had been responding to the attribution questions out of desire to support the experimenter's hypotheses, it is unlikely they could have produced the results of the indirect present-behavior–general-behavior measure. This index was derived from the absolute value of

the difference between the four level-of-behavior questions and the four general-behavior questions. These questions were widely separated in the questionnaire, and subjects would have had to perform a rather elaborate calculus to produce these results deliberately. Thus, it does not seem likely that the reorientation effects can be accounted for by experimenter demand characteristics.

The second issue involves the possible mechanisms by which videotape caused the predicted attributions. This study was designed to demonstrate that a global manipulation (visual orientation) affects actors' and observers' attributions of the actor's behavior. The study was not designed to separate out the many possible mechanisms by which this might occur. However, some informed speculation is possible.

Jones and Nisbett (1971) proposed several factors that contribute to attributional differences between actors and observers, including differences in the information available about an event and differences in how that information is processed. These two categories are not mutually exclusive, and videotape orientation may have affected aspects of both information availability and information processing. When actors or observers saw a videotape of an event from a different point of view, they may have received some totally new information. The actor may have realized, for the first time, some new aspects of his own behavior; the observer may have seen new aspects of the situation or of the other participant. These new facts could have contributed to changes in subjects' inferences about the cause of behavior. Second, the salience of already available information may have changed for reoriented subjects. Changes in the salience of information have been shown to affect people's perceptions of the reasons for their behavior. For example, Kiesler, Nisbett, and Zanna (1969) found that subjects tended to adopt as explanations of their own behavior motives that were made salient by a confederate. Similarly, subjects in the present study might have formulated their attributions about the actor's behavior on the basis of potential causes which had just been made salient by the videotape. Finally, videotape reorientation may have produced new responses sets for subjects. Actors who viewed themselves on tape may have been put into a "self-discovery" frame of mind and thus led to think about their own personality as revealed in their behavior. Similarly, observers who saw a videotape from the actor's point of view may have developed an "empathic" set, imagining themselves to be in the actor's shoes.

It is also of interest to consider the exact nature of the attributional changes evoked by videotape. Changes on the key dependent variable, the dispositional–situational index, were accounted for mostly by changed evaluations of situational causes. Actors assigned a great deal of causality to the situation unless videotape forced them to look away from the situation and toward their own behavior. Observers originally assigned less causality to the situation unless videotape impressed situational factors on them. Differences in attribution to dispositional causes, although in the expected direction, were much weaker than these differences in attribution to situational causes. It may be that the relatively greater amount of change on the situational dimension reflects people's general way of viewing the role of dispositions in causing behavior. People may characteristically assign fixed and fairly high importance to personal responsibility for behavior. Consequently, they may be left with only one means of modifying their relative assignment of causality and responsibility, namely by varying their evaluations of the situation. In line with this possibility, there may have been a ceiling effect for dispositional attributions in the present study; the overall mean importance assigned to dispositional causes equaled nearly 7 out of a possible 9 scale points. Subjects were thus left with little room to express enhanced dispositional influences.

Up to this point, discussion has been limited to information-related variables which may be modified by video exposure and may in turn affect attributions. Undoubtedly, motivational variables, such as the need to maintain self-esteem and particular self-concepts, could also be affected by videotape observations. One might expect the self-viewing actors in particular to be influenced by such motivations. It is

important to note, however, that the present findings were obtained in a situation which was, in many respects, low-key. The behaviors elicited in the getting-acquainted conversations were routine and probably not highly relevant to actors' self-concepts, the interaction between subjects was fairly unemotional, and actors and observers did not have the opportunity to discuss their potentially opposing views of the actor's behavior. It is therefore important to consider whether the present findings would generalize to situations where actors and observers are more emotionally involved, such as in psychotherapy and in other experiential or encounter groups. These are sometimes called training groups or "T Groups" because they are designed as learning experiences for group members. There is reason to believe that the present findings have some applicability to the use of videotape even in such emotionally charged settings.

Videotape in Therapy and T Groups

There has been a recent and dramatic increase in the application of videotape feedback in therapy and human relations training. Alger and Hogan (1966a) asserted that "videotape recording represents a technological breakthrough with the kind of significance for psychiatry that the microscope has had for biology [p. 1]." In clinical practice, videotape is frequently used to increase a patient's knowledge of his own behavior (cf. Bailey & Sowder, 1970; Holzman, 1969), and this apparently leads to therapeutic gain. Reivich and Geertsma (1968) reported increased accuracy in patients' knowledge of their own behavior after videotape self-observation. They measured the disparity between a patient's self-ratings on clinical scales and the ratings given him by psychiatric nurses. After videotape self-observation, the ratings of the actor patient came to agree more with the ratings of the observer nurses. Alderfer and Lodahl (1971) found that videotape playback in T groups increased subjects' "openness." Openness was defined as willingness to explore the internal meaning of and accept personal responsibility for an attitude or behavior. Finally, case studies in marital therapy (Alger

& Hogan, 1966a; Kagan, Krathwohl, & Miller, 1963) have reported that one or both marriage partners are more willing to assume the blame for a poor relationship after seeing themselves on videotape.

On the other hand, some negative consequences of self-observation have also been reported. For instance, Carrere (1954) used videotape to show alcoholics how they behaved when intoxicated, but he found it necessary to edit the more shocking scenes. The full presentation of their behavior when drunk was too stressful for many of his patients. Parades, Ludwig, Hassenfeld, and Cornelison (1969) similarly reported the lowering of alcoholic patients' self-esteem after viewing their own drunken behavior on tape. Leitenberg, Agras, Thompson, and Wright (1968) gave behavioral feedback (although not video) to phobic patients undergoing behavior modification. These authors found that feedback to patients about successful progress speeds their cure, but information about temporary setbacks interferes with the therapy. Finally, Geertsma and Reivich (1965) reported that some self-viewing depressive patients become more depressed, some schizophrenic patients engage in more bizarre behavior, and some neurotics show an increase in the symptoms characteristic of their particular disorder.

Research to date on the use of videotape in therapy is insufficient to indicate how and with whom it is a beneficial therapy adjunct. It may be possible, however, to apply the findings and the theoretical framework of the present study to the issue of videotape use in therapy. The present study demonstrates that self-observation can change the causal interpretation a person gives to his own behavior. The self-viewing actor (and possibly the self-viewing patient) is more likely to accept personal, dispositional responsibility for his behavior and is less likely to deflect responsibility to the situation.

This attributional consequence of self-observation may help to account for some of the effects of videotape in therapy. For example, the increased openness of T group participants after self-observation may reflect a tendency for each group member to assume more personal, dispositional responsibility for his behavior in the group. Similarly, in marital therapy, the husband or wife who sees himself or herself on videotape may realize for the first time his or her own behavioral contribution to the marital conflict and may be more willing to place a dispositional blame on himself or herself. Finally, the reported increase in agreement between a patient's clinical self-ratings after videotape self-observation and the ratings of observing psychiatric nurses closely parallels the present findings. Self-observation increases an individual's dispositional attributions, thus bringing him more in agreement with the observer's built-in bias for dispositional attributions.

It seems likely that this increase in dispositionality of a patient's attributions would prove to be sometimes therapeutic and sometimes distherapeutic. Successful therapy no doubt usually involves making a patient aware of his own behavior and convincing him to accept personal responsibility for that behavior. Self-observation apparently aids this process and, to that extent, should be therapeutic. However, two potentially negative outcomes of this process might be suggested. First, in becoming more dispositional about their own behavior, individuals who see themselves on videotape may actually underestimate real and viable situational explanations for their behavior. Actors in the present study who saw their own behavior on videotape had a higher mean for dispositional attributions and a lower mean for situational attributions than any other group of subjects. This suggests the possibility that self-viewing actors may have been "undersituational" in attributing their own behavior. That is, videotape may have reoriented these actors so much that they perceived situational causes for their behavior to be even less important than did others who viewed them. And if, as Jones and Nisbett (1971) have suggested, observers are themselves inclined to underattribute to the situation, this poses a disturbing possibility for therapy. Ironically, the therapist and the self-viewing patient could reach complete agreement about the patient's behavior, yet this agreement could result from a mutual underestimation of the importance of the patient's situation in causing his behavior. This collaborative illusion between patient and therapist could be especially harmful if the patient blames himself for behavior that is in fact due to some aspect of his environment.

Past research on attribution processes has uncovered another area where attributions to the self can have distherapeutic results. Storms and Nisbett (1970) and Valins and Nisbett (1971) have suggested that negative self-labeling which results from attributing uncomplimentary behaviors to dispositions within oneself often lead to a loss of self-esteem and an actual increase in the pathological behavior. For example, insomniacs who attribute their sleeplessness to some negative state within themselves may increase their anxiety and thus aggravate their original condition. Storms and Nisbett proposed that such exacerbation may result whenever self-attributions of a negative disposition increase the individual's anxiety and when anxiety is an irritant to the pathology, such as in impotence, stuttering, and other neurotic conditions. This exacerbation phenomenon may be occurring in some of the therapy cases where negative results have followed the use of videotapes. The finding that self-observation lowers the self-esteem of alcoholic patients might be an instance of this. An alcoholic patient who sees a tape of his own drunken behavior may become quite upset and depressed about himself. Such a traumatic experience may only increase the likelihood that the patient will drink to excess. Whenever a pathology is caused or influenced by a poor self-concept, self-observation of extremely uncomplimentary behavior may serve to retard therapeutic progress.

Research on attribution processes may help to create a theoretical framework for the area of videotape self-observation in therapy settings. The present study suggests that self-observation increases an individual's dispositional attributions of his own behavior and that this brings interpretation of his behavior more in line with an observer's interpretation. In most cases, this should be advantageous to the therapy process, but in certain cases self-attributions could lead to an exacerbation of the original pathology. Therapists would therefore be

well advised to look critically at the potential consequences of self-observation. It seems especially important to consider whether a personal, dispositional attribution of the pathological behavior aids the patient to become aware of his problem and to deal with it, or whether self-attribution increases the patient's anxiety to the point of exacerbating his problem.

REFERENCES

Alderfer, C. P., & Lodahl, T. M. A quasi experiment on the use of experiential methods in the classroom. *Journal of Applied Behavioral Science*, 1971, 7, 43–69.

Alger, I., & Hogan, P. The use of videotape recordings in conjoint marital therapy. Paper presented at the meeting of the American Psychoanalytic Association, Atlantic City, N.J., May 1966. (a)

Alger, I., & Hogan, P. Videotape: Its use and significance in psychotherapy. Paper presented at the meeting of the Society of Medical Psychoanalysts, New York Academy of Medicine, New York, September 1966. (b)

Bailey, K. G., & Sowder, W. T. Audiotape and videotape self-confrontation in psychotherapy. *Psychological Bulletin*, 1970, 74, 127–137.

Carrere, M. J. Le psychochoc cinématographique. *Annales Médico-Psychologiques*, 1954, 112, 240–245.

Geertsma, R. H., & Reivich, R. S. Repetitive self-observation by videotape playback. *Journal of Nervous and Mental Disease*, 1965, 141, 29–41.

Holzman, P. S. On hearing and seeing oneself. *Journal of Nervous and Mental Disease*, 1969, 148, 198–209.

Jones, E. E., & Harris, V. A. The attribution of attitudes. *Journal of Experimental Social Psychology*, 1967, 3, 1–24.

Jones, E. E., & Nisbett, R. E. *The actor and the observer: Divergent perceptions of the causes of behavior.* Morristown, N.J.: General Learning Press, 1971.

Jones, E. E., Rock, L., Shaver, K. G., Goethals, G. R., & Ward, L. M. Pattern of performance and ability attribution: An unexpected primacy effect. *Journal of Personality and Social Psychology*, 1968, 10, 317–340.

Kagan, N., Krathwohl, D. R., & Miller, R. Stimulated recall in therapy using videotape: A case study. *Journal of Counseling Psychology*, 1963, 10, 237–243.

Kiesler, C. A., Nisbett, R. E., & Zanna, M. P. On inferring one's beliefs from one's behavior. *Journal of Personality and Social Psychology*, 1969, 11, 321–327.

Leitenberg, H., Agras, W. S., Thompson, L. E., & Wright, D. E. Feedback in behavior modification: An experimental analysis of two cases. *Journal of Applied Behavioral Analysis*, 1968, 1, 131–137.

McArthur, L. Appropriateness of the behavior and consensus and distinctiveness information as determinants of actors' and observers' attributions. Unpublished manuscript, Yale University, 1970.

McArthur, L. A. The how and what of why: Some determinants and consequences of causal attribution. *Journal of Personality and Social Psychology*, 1972, *22*, 171–193.

Nisbett, R. E., Caputo, G. C., Legant, P., & Marecek, J. Behavior as seen by the actor and as seen by the observer. *Journal of Personality and Social Psychology*, 1973, *27*, 154–164.

Parades, A., Ludwig, K. D., Hassenfeld, I. N., & Cornelison, F. S. A clinical study of alcoholics using audio-visual self-image feedback. *Journal of Nervous and Mental Disease*, 1969, *148*, 449–456.

Reivich, R. S., & Geertsma, R. H. Experiences with videotape self-observation by psychiatric inpatients. *Journal of Kansas Medical Society*, 1968, *69*, 39–44.

Storms, M. D., & Nisbett, R. E. Insomnia and the attribution process. *Journal of Personality and Social Psychology*, 1970, *16*, 319–328.

Valins, S., & Nisbett, R. E. *Some implications of attribution process for the development and treatment of emotional disorders*. Morristown, N.J.: General Learning Press, 1971.

Winer, B. J. *Statistical principles in experimental design*. New York: McGraw-Hill, 1962.

3

Attributions in the Sports Pages

Richard R. Lau and Dan Russell

This study tests the idea that attributions are biased in the direction of enhancing one's own self-esteem. Such "self-serving" attributional biases result in internal attributions for success and external attributions for failure. This study is a particularly interesting demonstration of self-serving biases because it uses a form of archival data—explanations for the outcomes of major sports events as reported in newspapers. The main finding, shown in Table 1, is that players and coaches are more likely to attribute their wins to internal factors, and their losses to external factors, than are sportswriters describing exactly the same events. Presumably this occurred because players and coaches are more ego-involved in the events, and therefore have more self-esteem at stake in how the outcomes are interpreted. This research also shows that the attributional process tends to be triggered more by unexpected events than by expected ones (Table 3)—people evidently feel no great need to try to develop elaborate explanations for the occurrence of expected outcomes.

ABSTRACT. The present investigation extended the generality of attribution research by exploring several important issues in a highly involving real-world setting in which attributions naturally occur: athletic competition. Newspaper accounts of baseball and football games were coded for attributional content. These data supported a motivational or self-enhancement explanation for the tendency to make internal attributions for success and external attributions for failure. No support was found for Miller and Ross's contention that this tendency is mediated by expectancies. It was also found that more attributions were made after unexpected, as opposed to expected, outcomes. And in accordance with Weiner's attribution model, there was a tendency for relatively more stable attributions to be given after expected outcomes. The advantages and disadvantages of studying attributions in archival data and the possibility of attribu-

Reprinted from the *Journal of Personality and Social Psychology*, 1980, *39*, pp. 29–38. Copyright 1980 by the American Psychological Association. Reprinted by permission of publisher and authors.

tions justifying behavior rather than explaining behavior are discussed.

An important motivator of human thought is the desire to understand the determinants of behavior. Like the psychologist, the average person is assumed to test "causal theories" concerning the reasons behind his or her own actions and the actions of other people. Such causal knowledge is highly adaptive, yielding to lay attributors an understanding of (and consequently the ability to predict and control) many situations in which they find themselves.

The desire to achieve an understanding of the causes of human behavior has always been considered the chief motivation underlying the attribution process (e.g., Jones & Davis, 1965; Kelley, 1967, 1971). Rather than studying attributions in important human situations, however, most attribution research has asked some captive population (typically college undergraduates) to give causal explanations for their own or some other person's behavior in hypothetical or fairly trivial situations. These attributions are almost always recorded on forced-choice, closed-ended scales. Therefore, the type of attributions that can be made (and even whether or not to make attributions at all) is generally determined by the experimenter.[1]

But how relevant are the results of such laboratory-based experiments to real-world settings in which attributions occur? Causal explanations that are made in the course of everyday human interaction may serve purposes beyond understanding the determinants of behavior. For instance, Kelley's research has led him to ask, "What if the person learns and is motivated to make attributions not for some abstract understanding of the world, but rather, to explain his own actions and to attempt to control the actions of his close associates?" (Orvis, Kelley, & Butler, 1976, p. 379; see also Kelley, Note

1). Certainly attributions serve a variety of motivations, and the determinants or consequences of the attribution process could be very different when attributions are serving different purposes. It is therefore important to explore the generality of the findings from laboratory-based attribution research in real-world settings.

The sports pages are a natural setting where explanations for behavior are frequently given by players, coaches, and sportswriters. There are several good reasons why the sports pages are an excellent site to study the attribution process. First, as noted above, the typical laboratory experiment gathers attributions on forced-choice, closed-ended scales. In the sports pages, on the other hand, the players, coaches, and sportswriters have a much greater range of possible responses available to them. They are, of course, constrained by plausibility and the norms or conventions of that setting, but certainly the scope of possible explanations is much greater in such free responses than is usually the case in the laboratory.

Second, athletic events are highly involving. Avid sports fans "live and die" with their teams every game, and players and coaches are even more involved. They spend a great deal of time, energy, joy, and suffering to win games. Moreover, a string of bad performances could possibly cost professional athletes or coaches their jobs. Such high levels of involvement are rarely achieved in the laboratory.

The current study examined explanations for the outcomes of sporting events given in the sports pages. The actual explanations were coded for attributional content. Using these data, several important questions in the attribution area were addressed.

A good deal of research has documented the tendency to make internal attributions for success and external attributions for failure. A recent controversy concerns whether this tendency (often called "hedonic bias") reflects a motivational bias or not (see reviews by Bradley, 1978; and Snyder, Stephan, & Rosenfield, 1978). A motivational interpretation of hedonic bias is consistent with the notion that attributions frequently serve self-presenta-

---

[1] Such a preclusion, of course, is not inherent in closed-ended scales. For instance, subjects could be offered a wide variety of possible attribution scales and explicitly instructed to respond to only those scales that they thought were relevant. But in practice this is rarely done.

tional purposes. Such a motivational interpretation predicts that the general tendency for success to be attributed internally and failure to be attributed externally should increase with the ego-involvement of the attributor, a prediction that has been tested in other investigations of hedonic bias (Harvey, Arkin, Gleason, & Johnston, 1974; Miller & Norman, 1975; Snyder, Stephan, & Rosenfield, 1976). In the present context, a motivational hypothesis would predict that coaches and players would show a greater tendency to attribute success internally and failure externally in comparison with sportswriters, since the former should be more ego-involved with the outcome.

Miller and Ross (1975) contend that most support for a motivational or self-enhancement interpretation of hedonic bias has come from fairly trivial experiments, and they see the case as far from proven. As an alternative, Miller and Ross offer a nonmotivational explanation for the phenomenon. They argue that people typically expect and intend to succeed; hence, success is attributed internally, and unexpected and unintended failures are attributed externally. For instance, Feather and Simon (1971a, 1971b) found that unexpected success or failure was more likely to be attributed to external factors than was expected success or failure. In the current investigation, this nonmotivational explanation would predict that expected success should result in more internal attributions than unexpected success, whereas unexpected failure should result in more external attributions than expected failure. The ego-involvement of the attributor should be irrelevant.

There are several aspects of the setting being investigated here that could affect the motivational hypothesis. One is the fact that these attributions are given publicly, and there is an informal norm among athletes to be humble about their successful performances and to accept blame for their failures. This factor could mute evidence of a hedonic bias for players and coaches. On the other hand, the involvement of players and coaches in the outcome is much greater in this study than is true in most laboratory experiments, and this could

accentuate a hedonic bias (if the motivational interpretation is correct). Evidence for or against a motivational bias in the current study must be considered in light of the above aspects of this setting.

A second question addressed in the current study concerns *when* attributions occur. Little research to date has directly investigated this question (Wong & Weiner, Note 2, is the only exception we know of). Indeed, the use of closed-ended rating scales to gather attribution data (as is typically done in attribution research) generally precludes the possibility of participants either simply not making causal attributions or varying the number of attributions made. Kelley (1971) has suggested that unexpected events will evoke cognitive processing by the individual, since prior explanations that underlay the person's expectations would be called into question. For example, if a bad team defeats a good one, a wide variety of explanations become plausible (such as weather, luck, very high motivation on the part of the underdog or low motivation for the favorite, injuries). But if the favorite wins as expected, the relative abilities of the two teams are clearly the most plausible explanation. Thus unexpected events may prompt an "attributional search" (assuming the event is of some importance to the individual) in which a variety of explanations are tested both for their plausibility and for their satisfaction of the individual's needs and motives. So it is hypothesized that unexpected outcomes will lead to a greater number of causal attributions being made.

Finally, based on Weiner's (1974, 1979) attribution model, it is hypothesized that expected outcomes of games should result in stable causal explanations irrespective of whether the outcome is successful or unsuccessful. On the one hand, this hypothesis seeks to replicate prior laboratory research supporting Weiner's model (e.g., Feather & Simon, 1971b; Frieze & Weiner, 1971; Weiner, Frieze, Kukla, Rest & Rosenbaum, 1971). But given that (a) the setting is so involving, (b) the explanations are coded from free responses, and (c) the attributions may be serving self-presentational purposes, the current situation is in many ways very different from the typical context in which Weiner's model has been tested.

METHOD

Procedure

Articles covering 33 major sporting events in eight daily newspapers during the fall of 1977 were analyzed for attributional content. These events included the six games of the World Series and a variety of college and professional football games. For the most part, articles from the city of one of the teams involved in the game were used, because only these articles were long enough to contain explanations for the results of the game. (Shorter articles about games of less interest to the readers of a newspaper are most often limited to descriptions of the game rather than including explanations for the outcome.) A total of 594 explanations from 107 articles were identified.

Eight advanced undergraduates collected the attributions. These students were all thoroughly trained to identify any explanations offered for the outcome of a game. They worked in pairs, with one member of each team serving as a "check" on his or her partner to ensure that all explanations were recorded from each article.

Each explanation was written on one side of a 3 × 5 card. The game, newspaper, and source of attribution—player, coach, or sportswriter—were recorded on the back of the card. This procedure was designed to allow for "blind" coding of the attributions, although the source of the attribution was sometimes obvious from the explanation itself.

Coding

The content coding of attributions from an archival source is a new procedure to attribution research. Coding systems for open-ended causal explanations have been developed (e.g., Elig & Frieze, 1975), but only for attributional content derived in settings very different from the current one. Therefore, a new coding system was devised.

To test the hypotheses, it was necessary to code the causal explanations in terms of two causal dimensions: stability and locus of causality. These dimensions were coded directly from the attributional statements, based on the definitions of the two causal dimensions given by Weiner (1974). The following definitional criteria were used by the coders.

Stability. The stability of an attribution was defined temporally; an explanation was considered stable if it would predict the same outcome recurring in future games. Unstable attributions referred to factors that could vary over time, such as a great effort by a team or a bad call by an umpire or referee.

Locus of causality. For the locus of causality dimension, it was simply noted whether the attribution referred to something about one team or the other, or to the particular situation. For players and coaches, attributions referring to one's own team were categorized as internal, whereas attributions to the other team or to the particular situation were categorized as external. Likewise, attributions to the sportswriter's home team were categorized as internal, whereas attributions to the other team or to the situation were categorized as external. Such a categorization scheme was necessary so that the coding along the internal–external dimension would be comparable for players and coaches, on the one hand, and sportswriters, on the other. The coding of the locus dimension will be discussed at greater length below.

The following examples illustrate the coding scheme. After the fourth game of the World Series, a game won by the Yankees (giving them a 3–1 lead in the series), Yankee manager Billy Martin said of Lou Piniella, the star of the game, "Piniella has done it all." This statement refers to something about the Yankees, and it was said by a Yankee, so it was coded as internal. The verb tense of the statement ("has done") suggests that Martin was not referring simply to the one game, but to the course of the entire season. Hence the statement also seems to refer to a stable attribute of the individual in question (ability or stable effort) and was coded as stable along the stable–unstable dimension. After the same game, Ron Cey, a member of the losing Dodgers, said, "I think we've hit the ball all right. But I think we're unlucky." This is clearly an attribution to bad luck, and was coded as external (circumstances) and unstable. The next two statements were made by Dodger manager Tommy Lasorda after the Dodgers had lost the last game of the series. "It took a great team to beat us, and the Yankees definitely are a great team." This is an attribution to the Yankee's ability, and as it was said by a Dodger, it was coded as external and stable. Finally, of Reggie Jackson's performance in the sixth game, Lasorda said, "You're supposed to keep the ball in on him. Well, we didn't." Here the attribution is something "we" did, something "we" presumably could have done better, but did not. Hence it was coded as internal and unstable.

The two coders (the authors) initially agreed on 88% of the two dimensions coded for each attribution. Disagreements were discussed by the coders, and when a reconciliation could not be reached within 1 minute, the attribution was discarded. Over 96% of the original explanations were successfully coded into the two dimensions.

As described above, attributions to a player's or coach's team were coded as internal. For example, attributions to both one's own ability and to a teammate's ability were coded as internal. We decided on this coding for several reasons. The first is practical: Attributions to "my own ability" (effort, etc.) or "self" attributions were viable responses only for players, and therefore, it would be sensible to make this distinction only for players. But if we had tried to break down the attributions of players (about 22% of our total sample) by locus of causality, stability, or expectancies, the cell sizes would have become simply too small for analysis.

Second, both football and baseball are *team* sports. It is not clear how meaningful an attribution to one's own effort or ability is in determining the outcome of the game as a whole. And certainly attributions to a teammate are much more internal than attributions to the other team or to a cause such as luck. Moreover, there is some indirect evidence supporting this coding system. Iso-Ahola (1977) had 150 Little Leaguers attribute the outcome of a game to the coach, ability, effort, task diffi-

culty, and luck with reference to their team and to themselves individually. These nine ratings were factor analyzed, and two clear factors resulted. The external factor involved high loadings for team luck, self-luck, team task difficulty, and personal task difficulty. The internal factor was defined by attributions to team effort, self-effort, team ability, self-ability, and to the coach. Hence subjects apparently did not discriminate between their coach, their team (and by implication, their teammates), or themselves in attributing causality for the outcome of a game (see also Ross & Sicoly, 1979).

Additional Measures

A further datum was recorded with each attribution. If there had been a clear favorite for a game, the result was categorized as expected or as unexpected, depending on the outcome. Games in which there had been no clear favorite were placed in a third category, regardless of outcome. Because the World Series is a series of games, it was difficult to say that there were clear expectancies for one of the teams to win any given game, although at the outset the Dodgers were expected to win most of the games. Football games are more discrete events, with teams usually meeting once or twice a season. Hence, only attributions taken from football games were used in analyses involving expectancies.

The odds established by Harrah's Reno Race Sportsbook as reported in the newspaper were used to determine favorites. If a team was favored by two points or less, however, the game was categorized as having "no clear favorite." In addition, if the result of a game was highly discrepant (more than 10 points) from the predicted outcome, even if the favorite still won, the result of the game was also categorized as unexpected. That is, if (a) the favorite lost the game, (b) a big favorite won by a very small margin, or (c) a slight favorite won by a very big margin, the result of the game was categorized as unexpected.

Clearly we were *not* measuring the "subjective" expectancies of our attributors. Moreover, players and coaches would probably rarely admit to expecting to lose. But certainly players, coaches, and sportswriters are not unaware of the roles of favorite or underdog in any game. Our more objective measure is a rough but probably valid indicator of subjective expectancies, particularly since we are only making a dichotomous distinction. In any case it was the only measure of expectancies available.

Finally, the number of attributions from each article and the length of each article in inches were recorded. The number of attributions per inch was used as a measure of the frequency of attributions in an article.

RESULTS

Hedonic Bias

The data were first analyzed for evidence of success–failure differences in the locus of causality. The percentage of internal and external attributions for winners and losers (combining the attributions of players, coaches, and sportswriters) were compared. As expected, clear evidence of a tendency to attribute success internally was found: 74.9% of the attributions from the perspective of the winning team were internal, while only 54.9% of the attributions from the losing team were internal. A log-linear analysis (Bishop, Fienberg, & Holland, 1975) on the 2 × 2 table formed by crossing locus of causality of the attribution with the outcome of the game indicated that this interaction was highly significant, $\chi^2(1) = 21.84$, $p < .001$.[2]

Given this evidence of a success–failure difference in causal explanations, further analyses

Table 1 Test of the Motivational Bias Hypothesis

Attribution	Players and Coaches		Sportswriters	
	Win	Loss	Win	Loss
Internal	80.3	52.8	68.5	57.1
External	19.7	47.2	31.5	42.9
n	132	144	111	140

Note. Figures are in percents.

compared the motivational versus expectancy explanations for this difference. To test for a motivational basis for the success–failure difference in locus of attributions, the attributions of coaches and players were compared to those of sportswriters. A motivational explanation predicts that the success–failure difference in attributions will be greater for coaches and players in comparison with sportswriters, based on the greater ego-involvement of the former group with the outcome.[3] Thus the perspective of the attributor should interact with the outcome in producing the resultant attribution.

To test for this effect, the loci of the attributions made by players and coaches versus sportswriters for winning and losing outcomes were compared, again using log-linear analysis. The percentages are shown in Table 1. As predicted by the motivational bias hypothesis, the 3-way interaction was significant, $\chi^2(1) = 4.47$, $p < .04$. Players and coaches showed greater evidence of a motivational bias, making more internal attributions for success and fewer internal attributions for failure, relative to sportswriters. It should be pointed out, however, that the evidence for a motivational bias here is only relative, since for both winning and losing (and for players, coaches, and sportswriters) the majority of the attributions were internal.

A closer examination of Table 1 suggests that differences in attributing causality between players, coaches, and sportswriters occur chiefly after wins. Players and coaches are

---

[2] All chi-squares are likelihood ratio (rather than Pearson) chi-squares. Log-linear analyses were used because this technique allows one to consider more than two variables simultaneously and to have a separate significance test for each effect (i.e., association). We should note that the use of chi-square is not entirely appropriate here, because some observations (those made by the same person about the same game) are not completely independent. No one knows exactly how much bias any degree of dependence between observations causes in the use of chi-square, however. We assume that the degree of dependence in the current data is small enough, relative to the sample size, to not be a serious problem.

[3] Players and coaches were initially analyzed separately, but as the results were very similar, the two groups were combined and contrasted with sportswriters.

much more likely to attribute a good outcome to internal causes than are sportswriters, but only slightly less likely to attribute a bad outcome to themselves than are the writers. When the data in Table 1 were rearranged to explicitly test this difference, players and coaches differed from sportswriters in locus of attribution only after wins, $\chi^2(1) = 3.88$, $p < .05$, but not after losses, $\chi^2(1) = .38$, *ns*. This finding is consistent with previous work that has found evidence of self-serving biases chiefly after success but not failure (see Miller & Ross, 1975).

The expectancy explanation proposes that expected events will be attributed internally, whereas unexpected outcomes will be attributed externally. Since players and coaches typically expect and intend to succeed, the argument goes, their successes are attributed internally. In the current data, there are games that a losing team should clearly expect to lose, as well as games that a winning team should clearly expect to win; both of these cases would be predicted to produce internal attributions. Cases in which the winning or losing outcomes are unexpected should, on the other hand, produce external attributions. So the expectancy hypothesis predicts an Expectancy × Locus (Internal–External) interaction.

Table 2 presents the percentage of internal and external explanations for expected and unexpected outcomes separately from the perspective of winning and losing teams. Clearly, more internal attributions were made for wins than for losses, $\chi^2(1) = 11.54$, $p < .001$. But just as clearly, expectancies did not mediate this effect. Both the Expectancy × Locus and Expectancy × Locus × Win–Loss interactions were trivial, $\chi^2(1) = .21$, *ns*, and $\chi^2(1) = .03$,

ns, respectively. Expanding this analysis to compare the attributions of players and coaches to sportswriters provides no additional evidence for the importance of expectancies. All interactions involving expectancies and source of attribution (players and coaches or sportswriters) were nonsignificant.

Frequency of Causal Attributions

A second set of analyses concerned when the attributions occurred, with the number of attributions per inch of newsprint serving as an index of how frequently causal explanations were made for a particular game. It was predicted that unexpected outcomes would elicit a greater number of attributions, regardless of whether the outcome was a win or a loss. A 2 × 2 analysis of variance (ANOVA), crossing expected and unexpected outcome with win–loss, was conducted to test this hypothesis. Because the number of attributions typically reported in each article differed between newspapers, the number of attributions per inch for each article was centered (by subtracting the mean) for the different newspapers separately, and then these centered measures were analyzed. Such a centering procedure is preferable to standardization because it removes mean differences while retaining the variances. The only significant effect found was for expected versus unexpected events, $F(1,62) = 4.42$, $p < .04$, with unexpected outcomes eliciting a greater number of attributions per inch (see Table 3). Thus as hypothesized, unexpected outcomes produced a greater number of explanations.

Table 2 Test of the Expectancy Hypothesis

Attribution	Winners		Losers	
	Expected	Unex-pected	Expected	Unex-pected
Internal	78.7	79.7	63.0	62.3
External	21.3	20.3	37.0	37.7
n	89	69	54	130

Note. Figures are in percents.

Table 3 Frequency of Attributions as a Function of Expectedness of Outcomes and Win–Loss

Outcome	Win	Loss
Expected	−.027	−.032
n	22	10
Unexpected	.036	.032
n	12	22

Note. Cell entries are a centered measure of the number of attributions per inch of newsprint. Negative entries indicate fewer attributions than average, positive entries indicate more attributions than average.

Expectancy and Stability

Finally, based on Weiner's (1974, 1979) attribution model, it was predicted that expected outcomes would elicit more stable causal attributions than unexpected outcomes. The relevant data are shown in Table 4. There was a tendency for this hypothesis to be supported, although the results did not reach conventional levels of significance, $\chi^2(1) = 3.03$, $p < .09$. Also notable in Table 4 is the preponderance of unstable attributions. Fully two thirds of all attributions were coded as unstable. This indicates the strong preference for explanations involving effort (such as great concentration or making a spectacular play) on the part of their team or the other team by attributors. Other research has also indicated that effort is the most frequent attribution in achievement settings (e.g., Elig & Frieze, 1979).

Table 4   Stability and Expectancies

Condition	Expected	Unexpected
Stable	37.8	29.0
Unstable	62.2	71.0
n	164	186

Note. Figures are in percents.

DISCUSSION

The results from the current study support a variety of predictions from attribution research in a real-world setting. The empirically well-established success versus failure difference in the locus of causal attribution was found in the current context. The results supported a motivationally based explanation for this success–failure difference, in contrast to a nonmotivational explanation based on expectancies. Attributions were also found to be more frequent following unexpected outcomes, as predicted. Finally, some support was found for the prediction from Weiner's (1974, 1979) attribution model that expected outcomes lead to more stable causal explanations.

The causal accounts gathered here were freely given by the attributors (although the attributions were sometimes given in response to "why" questions from the sportswriters) and were less constrained in form and content than those generated in laboratory settings. The causal attributions made by the attributors were also very public, and may therefore serve more to justify performance (by the athletes and coaches) or to justify predictions for a specific game (by the sportswriters) than to reach an abstract causal understanding of the events.

This raises a question concerning whether these public statements differ from the private explanations made by the attributors. Do the causal attributions collected in the present study reflect the attributions "really" made by the players, coaches, and sportswriters? Although we have no means of assessing private attributions, the answer to this question is most certainly *no* in some instances and *yes* in others. For example, norms concerning social behavior (e.g., humility or bravado) may affect the public explanations offered by the attributor, but not the private ones really believed. On the other hand, one could argue that the attributor, to maintain consistency, brings his or her private attributions in line with his or her public statements.

The only research we know of that addresses this question of public and private attributions found only one instance in which the two differed. Folkes (1978) examined the differences between the public explanations given by people when refusing a date and the actual (private) reasons for their refusal. Her findings indicate that only when the real reason for the refusal had something to do with internal characteristics of the person being rejected (e.g., he or she was physically unattractive) did people give some other (external) public explanation for their refusal. Folkes' subjects did not "lead on" the person being rejected by inaccurately communicating the permanence (stability) of their rejection, however.

Do possible differences between public and private attributions (about which we can only speculate) make our findings irrelevant to previous attribution research? As mentioned above, research conducted by Kelley and his colleagues (Orvis, Kelley, & Butler, 1976) has suggested that the attribution process may often serve impression management or self-presentational purposes. Attributions as *justifications* rather than as *explanations* for behavior may be more prevalent in highly involving real-world settings such as the present one. The relevance of the present study to previous research lies in extending the findings of laboratory-based investigations to a situation in which public attributions are quite possibly serving self-presentational purposes.

The present study supported a motivational basis for the success–failure differences in the locus of causal attribution over an explanation relying on expectancies. As noted above, however, more internal attributions were made for both success *and* failure, although the frequency of internal explanations was much higher for success. Miller and Ross (1975) have argued that evidence for a self-serving bias in attributions requires evidence of both internal causal ascriptions for success (self-enhancing attributions) and external ascriptions for failure (self-protective attributions). The present results do not provide evidence for a self-protective bias.

One could argue, however, that the typical or base-rate attribution for sports performance in general is internal and that any self-protective or self-enhancing attributional bias must influence this modal attribution. The work of Weiner (1974, 1979) and others on causal explanations in achievement contexts has found that explanations for achievement outcomes are typically internal for both success and failure (see also Scanlon & Passer, Note 3). Any attributional bias must operate within the context in which attributions are being made, and the effect of the bias will always be relative to the modal attribution for this situation. Placing self-serving biases in this perspective, it seems more reasonable, as Bradley (1978) suggests, to see both self-protective and self-enhancing biases as reflecting a general tendency to view oneself positively, and to consider the modal locus of causality used to explain events in the situation under study when predicting how an attributional bias will reveal itself.

Another issue we have addressed is the "when" of attribution. As was pointed out earlier, the sports pages are a real-world setting in which attributions frequently occur. The ef-

fect of one variable, whether the result of the game was expected or not, was found to have a significant influence on the prevalence of causal explanations. As a cautionary note on interpreting the finding that more attributions are made following unexpected events, we should note that the results most appropriately apply only to the sportswriters. They make as many attributions as they want in their stories. The sportswriters also serve as gatekeepers in that they decide which statements by players and coaches to print. The writers are of course limited by what the players and coaches say, but they certainly do not print every word uttered. Therefore, although there is every reason to expect players and coaches as well as sportswriters to make fewer attributions after expected events than after unexpected events, these data are most germane to the writers.

The current findings clearly demonstrate the usefulness of archival data to attribution research. It is possible, and we might argue more appropriate, to study the attribution process in natural settings. Such settings are almost always more involving than laboratory experiments, and questions of external validity are easily addressed.

Of course there are problems with coding free-response data. A particularly difficult issue that we faced involved the coding of attributions to one's team or teammates along the internal–external dimension. We finally decided to code such attributions as internal. In general, the issue of what is internal and what is external is not always evident. For instance, as Monson and Snyder (1977) suggest, most internal statements can be rephrased into external statements, and vice versa. Steve Garvey's statement that "They played better than us," for example, could be just as easily restated as "We played worse than them." These two statements are semantically equivalent, but would be coded as external and internal to the Dodgers, respectively, in the current coding scheme. Ross (1977), in discussing the distinction between situational and dispositional explanations for behavior, also addresses this problem. According to Ross, the above two statements are identical in content, but differ in form, and the comparable content argues for not distinguishing them in terms of locus of causality.

In defense of the current coding scheme, evidence of logical or semantic comparability does not necessarily imply that the two statements are psychologically identical. The fact that Garvey chose to say that the Yankees played better than the Dodgers may indeed imply that he was making an attribution to the Yankees. Simple logical analyses such as that done by Ross are not sufficient to resolve these difficulties in understanding the meaning of different causal explanations to the attributor, and further research is needed as an aid in coding attributions. We would like to suggest that the results of the current investigation provide construct validity for the coding system we devised (Cronbach & Meehl, 1955).

Despite these problematic issues, the current study will hopefully encourage future researchers to investigate the attribution process in the real-world contexts where it naturally occurs by using archival data or assessing ongoing thought processes.

REFERENCE NOTES

1. Kelley, H. H. *Recent research in causal attribution.* Address at the meeting of the Western Psychological Association, Los Angeles, April, 1976.
2. Wong, P. T. P., & Weiner, B. *When people ask why questions and the temporal course of the attribution process.* Unpublished manuscript, University of California, Los Angeles, 1979.
3. Scanlon, T. K., & Passer, M. W. *Self-serving biases in the competitive sport setting: An attributional dilemma.* Unpublished manuscript, University of California, Los Angeles, 1978.

REFERENCES

Bishop, Y. M. M., Fienberg, S. E., & Holland, P. W. *Discrete multivariate analysis: Theory and practice.* Cambridge: MIT Press, 1975.

Bradley, G. W. Self-serving biases in the attribution process: A reexamination of the fact or fiction question. *Journal of Personality and Social Psychology*, 1978, *36*, 56–71.

Cronbach, L. J., & Meehl, P. E. Construct validity in psychological tests. *Psychological Bulletin*, 1955, *52*, 281–302.

Elig, T. W., & Frieze, I. H. A multi-dimensional scheme for coding and interpreting perceived causality for success and failure events: The Coding Scheme of Perceived Causality (CSPC). JSAS *Catalog of Selected Documents in Psychology*, 1975, *5*, 313.

Elig, T. W., & Frieze, I. H. Measuring causal attributions for success and failure. *Journal of Personality and Social Psychology*, 1979, *37*, 621–634.

Feather, N. T., & Simon, J. G. Attribution of responsibility and valence of success and failure in relation to initial confidence and task performance. *Journal of Personality and Social Psychology*, 1971, *18*, 173–188. (a)

Feather, N. T., & Simon, J. G. Causal attributions for success and failure in relation to expectations of success based upon selective or manipulative control. *Journal of Personality*, 1971, *39*, 527–541. (b)

Folkes, V. S. *Causal communication in the early stages of affiliative relationships.* Unpublished doctoral dissertation, University of California, Los Angeles, 1978.

Frieze, I. H., & Weiner, B. Cue utilization and attributional judgments for success and failure. *Journal of Personality*, 1971, *39*, 591–605.

Harvey, J. H., Arkin, R. M., Gleason, J. M., & Johnston, S. A. Effect of expected and observed outcome of an action on differential causal attributions of actor and observer. *Journal of Personality*, 1974, *42*, 62–77.

Iso-Ahola, S. Effects of self-enhancement and consistency on causal and trait attributions following success and failure in motor performance. *Research Quarterly*, 1977, *48*, 718–726.

Jones, E. E., & Davis, K. E. From acts to dispositions: The attribution process in person perception. In L. Berkowitz (Ed.), *Advances in experimental social psychology* (Vol. 2). New York: Academic Press, 1965.

Kelley, H. H. Attribution theory in social psychology. In D. Levine (Ed.), *Nebraska Symposium on Motivation* (Vol. 15). Lincoln: University of Nebraska Press, 1967.

Kelley, H. H. Attribution in social interaction. In E. E. Jones et al. (Eds.), *Attribution: Perceiving the causes of behavior.* Morristown, N.J.: General Learning Press, 1971.

Miller, D. T., & Norman, S. A. Actor–observer differences in perceptions of effective control. *Journal of Personality and Social Psychology*, 1975, *3*, 503–515.

Miller, D. T., & Ross, M. Self-serving biases in the attribution of causality: Fact or Fiction? *Psychological Bulletin*, 1975, *82*, 213–225.

Monson, T. C., & Snyder, M. Actors, observers, and the attribution process: Toward a reconceptualization. *Journal of Experimental Social Psychology*, 1977, *13*, 89–111.

Orvis, B. R., Kelley, H. H., & Butler, D. Attributional conflict in young couples. In J. H. Harvey et al. (Eds.), *New directions in attribution research* (Vol. 1). Hillsdale, N.J.: Erlbaum, 1976.

Ross, L. The intuitive psychologist and his shortcomings: Distortions in the attribution process. In L. Berkowitz (Ed.), *Advances in experimental social psychology* (Vol. 10). New York: Academic Press, 1977.

Ross, M., & Sicoly, F. Egocentric biases in availability and attribution. *Journal of Personality and Social Psychology*, 1979, *37*, 322–336.

Snyder, M. L., Stephan, W. G., & Rosenfield, D. Egotism and attribution. *Journal of Personality and Social Psychology*, 1976, *33*, 435–441.

Snyder, M. L., Stephan, W. G., & Rosenfield, D. Attributional egotism. In J. H. Harvey et al. (Eds.), *New directions in attribution research* (Vol. 2). Hillsdale, N.J.: Erlbaum, 1978.

Weiner, B. Achievement motivation as conceptualized by an attribution theorist. In B. Weiner (Ed.), *Achievement motivation and attribution theory*. Morristown, N.J.: General Learning Press, 1974.

Weiner, B. A. theory of motivation for some classroom experiences. *Journal of Educational Psychology*, 1979, *71*, 3–25.

Weiner, B., Frieze, I., Kukla, L. R., Rest, S., & Rosenbaum, R. M. Perceiving the causes of success and failure. In E. E. Jones et al. (Eds.), *Attribution: Perceiving the causes of behavior*. Morristown, N.J.: General Learning Press, 1971.

4

Judgment Under Uncertainty: Heuristics and Biases

Amos Tversky and Daniel Kahneman

We make many decisions every day. Some are small decisions such as what to have for dinner, and others are more substantial, such as deciding what career to pursue. In this groundbreaking study, Tversky and Kahneman point out that decisions must often be made with incomplete information. You may have to pick one graduate school from several, without having visited any of the campuses and knowing only a little about the faculty. You may decide on a vacation spot based on a brief conversation with a travel agent you just met. Kahneman and Tversky suggest that under conditions of uncertainty, people use shortcuts called "heuristics" that guide and, in some cases, bias their decisions. This article describes three common heuristics: representativeness, availability, and adjustment from an anchor. In using these heuristics, decision-makers often ignore well-established rules of inference that might lead them to very different conclusions. The findings of Tversky and Kahneman have had a major impact on the thinking of not only psychologists, but also physicians, lawyers, business people, economists, and others who must make complex inferences with incomplete information. As you read this article, try out the examples on yourself. Are you prone to some of the same errors and biases in judgment that the decision-makers in this study demonstrated?

Many decisions are based on beliefs concerning the likelihood of uncertain events such as the outcome of an election, the guilt of a defendant, or the future value of the dollar. These beliefs are usually expressed in statements such as "I think that . . .," "chances are . . .," "it is unlikely that . . .," and so forth. Occasionally, beliefs concerning uncertain events are

Reprinted from *Science*, 1974, *185*, pp. 1124–1131. Copyright 1974 by the American Association for the Advancement of Science. Reprinted by permission.

expressed in numerical form as odds or subjective probabilities. What determines such beliefs? How do people assess the probability of an uncertain event or the value of an uncertain quantity? This article shows that people rely on a limited number of heuristic principles which reduce the complex tasks of assessing probabilities and predicting values to simpler judgmental operations. In general, these heuristics are quite useful, but sometimes they lead to severe and systematic errors.

The subjective assessment of probability resembles the subjective assessment of physical quantities such as distance or size. These judgments are all based on data of limited validity, which are processed according to heuristic rules. For example, the apparent distance of an object is determined in part by its clarity. The more sharply the object is seen, the closer it appears to be. This rule has some validity, because in any given scene the more distant objects are seen less sharply than nearer objects. However, the reliance on this rule leads to systematic errors in the estimation of distance. Specifically, distances are often overestimated when visibility is poor because the contours of objects are blurred. On the other hand, distances are often underestimated when visibility is good because the objects are seen sharply. Thus, the reliance on clarity as an indication of distance leads to common biases. Such biases are also found in the intuitive judgment of probability. This article describes three heuristics that are employed to assess probabilities and to predict values. Biases to which these heuristics lead are enumerated, and the applied and theoretical implications of these observations are discussed.

REPRESENTATIVENESS

Many of the probabilistic questions with which people are concerned belong to one of the following types: What is the probability that object A belongs to class B? What is the probability that event A originates from process B? What is the probability that process B will generate event A? In answering such questions, people typically rely on the representativeness heuristic, in which probabilities are evaluated by the degree to which A is representative of B, that is, by the degree to which A resembles B. For example, when A is highly representative of B, the probability that A originates from B is judged to be high. On the other hand, if A is not similar to B, the probability that A originates from B is judged to be low.

For an illustration of judgment by representativeness, consider an individual who has been described by a former neighbor as follows: "Steve is very shy and withdrawn, invariably helpful, but with little interest in people, or in the world of reality. A meek and tidy soul, he has a need for order and structure, and a passion for detail." How do people assess the probability that Steve is engaged in a particular occupation from a list of possibilities (for example, farmer, salesman, airline pilot, librarian, or physician)? How do people order these occupations from most to least likely? In the representativeness heuristic, the probability that Steve is a librarian, for example, is assessed by the degree to which he is representative of, or similar to, the stereotype of a librarian. Indeed, research with problems of this type has shown that people order the occupations by probability and by similarity in exactly the same way (Kahneman & Tversky, 1973). This approach to the judgment of probability leads to serious errors, because similarity, or representativeness, is not influenced by several factors that should affect judgments of probability.

Insensitivity to Prior Probability of Outcomes

One of the factors that have no effect on representativeness but should have a major effect on probability is the prior probability, or base-rate frequency, of the outcomes. In the case of Steve, for example, the fact that there are many more farmers than librarians in the population should enter into any reasonable estimate of the probability that Steve is a librarian rather than a farmer. Considerations of base-rate frequency, however, do not affect the similarity of Steve to the stereotypes of librarians and farmers. If people evaluate probability by representativeness, therefore, prior probabilities will be neglected. This hypothesis was tested in an experiment where prior probabilities were manipulated (Kahneman & Tversky, 1973). Subjects were shown brief personality descriptions of several individuals, allegedly sampled at random from a group of 100 professionals—engineers and lawyers. The subjects were asked to assess, for each description, the probability that it belonged to an engineer rather than to a lawyer. In one experimental condition, subjects were told that the group from which the descriptions had been drawn consisted of 70 engineers and 30 lawyers. In another condition, subjects were told that the group consisted of 30 engineers and 70 lawyers. The odds that any particular description belongs to an engineer rather than to a lawyer should be higher in the first condition, where there is a majority of engineers, than in the second condition, where there is a majority of lawyers. Specifically, it can be shown by applying Bayes' rule that the ratio of these odds should be $(.7/.3)^2$, or 5.44, for each description. In a sharp violation of Bayes' rule, the subjects in the two conditions produced essentially the same probability judgments. Apparently, subjects evaluated the likelihood that a particular description belonged to an engineer rather than to a lawyer by the degree to which this description was representative of the two stereotypes, with little or no regard for the prior probabilities of the categories.

The subjects used prior probabilities correctly when they had no other information. In the absence of a personality sketch, they judged the probability that an unknown individual is an engineer to be .7 and .3, respectively, in the two base-rate conditions. However, prior probabilities were effectively ignored when a description was introduced, even when this description was totally uninformative. The responses to the following description illustrate this phenomenon:

Dick is a 30 year old man. He is married with no children. A man of high ability and high motivation, he promises to be quite successful in his field. He is well liked by his colleagues.

This description was intended to convey no information relevant to the question of whether Dick is an engineer or a lawyer. Consequently, the probability that Dick is an engineer should equal the proportion of engineers in the group, as if no description had been given. The subjects, however, judged the probability of Dick being an engineer to be .5 regardless of whether the stated proportion of engineers in the group was .7 or .3. Evidently, people respond differently when given no evidence and when given worthless evidence. When no specific evidence is given, prior probabilities are properly utilized; when worthless evidence is given, prior probabilities are ignored (Kahneman & Tversky, 1973).

Insensitivity to Sample Size

To evaluate the probability of obtaining a particular result in a sample drawn from a specified population, people typically apply the representativeness heuristic. That is, they assess the likelihood of a sample result, for example, that the average height in a random sample of ten men will be 6 feet (180 centimeters), by the similarity of this result to the corresponding parameter (that is, to the average height in the population of men). The similarity of a sample statistic to a population parameter does not depend on the size of the sample. Consequently, if probabilities are assessed by representativeness, then the judged probability of a sample statistic will be essentially independent of sample size. Indeed, when subjects assessed the distributions of average height for samples of various sizes, they produced identical distributions. For example, the probability of obtaining an average height greater than 6 feet was assigned the same value for samples of 1000, 100, and 10 men (Kahneman & Tversky, 1972). Moreover, subjects failed to appreciate the role of sample size even when it was emphasized in the formulation of the problem. Consider the following question:

A certain town is served by two hospitals. In the larger hospital about 45 babies are born each day, and in the smaller hospital about 15 babies are born each day. As you know, about 50 percent of all babies are boys. However, the exact percentage varies from day to day. Sometimes it may be higher than 50 percent, sometimes lower.

For a period of 1 year, each hospital recorded the days on which more than 60 percent of the babies born were boys. Which hospital do you think recorded more such days?

The larger hospital (21)

The smaller hospital (21)

About the same (that is, within 5 percent of each other) (53)

The values in parentheses are the number of undergraduate students who chose each answer.

Most subjects judged the probability of obtaining more than 60 percent boys to be the same in the small and in the large hospital, presumably because these events are described by the same statistic and are therefore equally representative of the general population. In contrast, sampling theory entails that the expected number of days on which more than 60 percent of the babies are boys is much greater in the small hospital than in the large one, because a large sample is less likely to stray from 50 percent. This fundamental notion of statistics is evidently not part of people's repertoire of intuitions.

A similar insensitivity to sample size has been reported in judgments of posterior probability, that is, of the probability that a sample has been drawn from one population rather than from another. Consider the following example:

Imagine an urn filled with balls, of which ⅔ are of one color and ⅓ of another. One individual has drawn 5 balls from the urn, and found that 4 were red and 1 was white. Another individual has drawn 20 balls and found that 12 were red and 8 were white. Which of the two individuals should feel more confident that the urn contains ⅔ red balls and ⅓ white balls, rather than the opposite? What odds should each individual give?

In this problem, the correct posterior odds are 8 to 1 for the 4:1 sample and 16 to 1 for the 12:8 sample, assuming equal prior probabilities. However, most people feel that the first sample provides much stronger evidence for the hypothesis that the urn is predominantly red, because the proportion of red balls is larger in the first than in the second sample. Here again, intuitive judgments are dominated by

the sample proportion and are essentially unaffected by the size of the sample, which plays a crucial role in the determination of the actual posterior odds (Kahneman & Tversky, 1972). In addition, intuitive estimates of posterior odds are far less extreme than the correct values. The underestimation of the impact of evidence has been observed repeatedly in problems of this type (Edwards, 1968; Slovic & Lichtenstein, 1971). It has been labeled "conservatism."

Misconceptions of Chance

People expect that a sequence of events generated by a random process will represent the essential characteristics of that process even when the sequence is short. In considering tosses of a coin for heads or tails, for example, people regard the sequence H-T-H-T-T-H to be more likely than the sequence H-H-H-T-T-T, which does not appear random, and also more likely than the sequence H-H-H-H-T-H, which does not represent the fairness of the coin (Kahneman & Tversky, 1972). Thus, people expect that the essential characteristics of the process will be represented, not only globally in the entire sequence, but also locally in each of its parts. A locally representative sequence, however, deviates systematically from chance expectation: it contains too many alternations and too few runs. Another consequence of the belief in local representativeness is the well-known gambler's fallacy. After observing a long run of red on the roulette wheel, for example, most people erroneously believe that black is now due, presumably because the occurence of black will result in a more representative sequence than the occurence of an additional red. Chance is commonly viewed as a self-correcting process in which a deviation in one direction induces a deviation in the opposite direction to restore the equilibrium. In fact, deviations are not "corrected" as a chance process unfolds, they are merely diluted.

Misconceptions of chance are not limited to naive subjects. A study of the statistical intuitions of experienced research psychologists (Tversky & Kahneman, 1971) revealed a lingering belief in what may be called the "law of small numbers," according to which even small samples are highly representative of the populations from which they are drawn. The responses of these investigators reflected the expectation that a valid hypothesis about a population will be represented by a statistically significant result in a sample—with little regard for its size. As a consequence, the researchers put too much faith in the results of small samples and grossly overestimated the replicability of such results. In the actual conduct of research, this bias leads to the selection of samples of inadequate size and to overinterpretation of findings.

Insensitivity to Predictability

People are sometimes called upon to make such numerical predictions as the future value of a stock, the demand for a commodity, or the outcome of a football game. Such predictions are often made by representativeness. For example, suppose one is given a description of a company and is asked to predict its future profit. If the description of the company is very favorable, a very high profit will appear most representative of that description; if the description is mediocre, a mediocre performance will appear most representative. The degree to which the description is favorable is unaffected by the reliability of that description or by the degree to which it permits accurate prediction. Hence, if people predict solely in terms of the favorableness of the description, their predictions will be insensitive to the reliability of the evidence and to the expected accuracy of the prediction.

This mode of judgment violates the normative statistical theory in which the extremeness and the range of predictions are controlled by considerations of predictability. When predictability is nil, the same prediction should be made in all cases. For example, if the descriptions of companies provide no information relevant to profit, then the same value (such as average profit) should be predicted for all companies. If predictability is perfect, of course, the values predicted will match the actual values and the range of predictions will equal the range of outcomes. In general, the higher the predictability, the wider the range of predicted values.

Several studies of numerical prediction have demonstrated that intuitive predictions violate this rule, and that subjects show little or no regard for considerations of predictability (Kahneman & Tversky, 1973). In one of these studies, subjects were presented with several paragraphs, each describing the performance of a student teacher during a particular practice lesson. Some subjects were asked to *evaluate* the quality of the lesson described in the paragraph in percentile scores, relative to a specified population. Other subjects were asked to *predict*, also in percentile scores, the standing of each student teacher 5 years after the practice lesson. The judgments made under the two conditons were identical. That is, the prediction of a remote criterion (success of a teacher after 5 years) was identical to the evaluation of the information on which the prediction was based (the quality of the practice lesson). The students who made these predictions were undoubtedly aware of the limited predictability of teaching competence on the basis of a single trial lesson 5 years earlier; nevertheless, their predictions were as extreme as their evaluations.

The Illusion of Validity

As we have seen, people often predict by selecting the outcome (for example, an occupation) that is most representative of the input (for example, the description of a person). The confidence they have in their prediction depends primarily on the degree of representativeness (that is, on the quality of the match between the selected outcome and the input) with little or no regard for the factors that limit predictive accuracy. Thus, people express great confidence in the prediction that a person is a librarian when given a description of his personality which matches the stereotype of librarians, even if the description is scanty, unreliable, or outdated. The unwarranted confidence which is produced by a good fit between the predicted outcome and the input information may be called the illusion of validity. This illusion persists even when the judge is aware of the factors that limit the accuracy of his predictions. It is a common observation that psychologists who conduct selection interviews often experience considerable confidence in their predictions, even when they know of the vast literature that shows selection interviews to be highly fallible. The continued reliance on the clinical interview for selection, despite repeated demonstrations of its inadequacy, amply attests to the strength of this effect.

The internal consistency of a pattern of inputs is a major determinant of one's confidence in predictions based on these inputs. For example, people express more confidence in predicting the final grade-point average of a student whose first-year record consists entirely of B's than in predicting the grade-point average of a student whose first-year record includes many A's and C's. Highly consistent patterns are most often observed when the input variables are highly redundant or correlated. Hence, people tend to have great confidence in predictions based on redundant input variables. However, an elementary result in the statistics of correlation asserts that, given input variables of stated validity, a prediction based on several such inputs can achieve higher accuracy when they are independent of each other than when they are redundant or correlated. Thus, redundancy among inputs decreases accuracy even as it increases confidence, and people are often confident in predictions that are quite likely to be off the mark (Kahneman & Tversky, 1973).

Misconceptions of Regression

Suppose a large group of children has been examined on two equivalent versions of an aptitude test. If one selects ten children from among those who did best on one of the two versions, he will usually find their performance on the second version to be somewhat disappointing. Conversely, if one selects ten children from among those who did worst on one version, they will be found, on the average, to do somewhat better on the other version. More generally, consider two variables X and Y which have the same distribution. If one selects individuals whose average X score deviates from the mean of X by k units, then the average of their Y scores will usually deviate from the mean of Y by less than k units. These observations illustrate a general phenomenon known as regression toward the mean, which was first documented by Galton more than 100 years ago.

In the normal course of life, one encounters many instances of regression toward the mean: in the comparison of the height of fathers and sons, of the intelligence of husbands and wives, or of the performance of individuals on consecutive examinations. Nevertheless, people do not develop correct intuitions about this phenomenon. First, they do not expect regression in many contexts where it is bound to occur. Second, when they recognize the occurrence of regression, they often invent spurious causal explanations for it (Kahneman & Tversky, 1973). We suggest that the phenomenon of regression remains elusive because it is incompatible with the belief that the predicted outcome should be maximally representative of the input, and, hence, that the value of the outcome variable should be as extreme as the value of the input variable.

The failure to recognize the import of regression can have pernicious consequences, as illustrated by the following observation (Kahneman & Tversky, 1973). In a discussion of flight training, experienced instructors noted that praise for an exceptionally smooth landing is typically followed by a poorer landing on the next try, while harsh criticism after a rough landing is usually followed by an improvement on the next try. The instructors concluded that verbal rewards are detrimental to learning, while verbal punishments are beneficial, contrary to accepted psychological doctrine. This conclusion is unwarranted because of the presence of regression toward the mean. As in other cases of repeated examination, an improvement will usually follow a poor performance and a deterioration will usually follow an outstanding performance, even if the instructor does not respond to the trainee's achievement on the first attempt. Because the instructors had praised their trainees after good landings and admonished them after poor ones, they reached the erroneous and potentially harmful conclusion that punishment is more effective than reward.

Thus, the failure to understand the effect of regression leads one to overestimate the effectiveness of punishment and to underestimate the effectiveness of reward. In social interaction, as well as in training, rewards are typically administered when performance is good, and punishments are typically administered when performance is poor. By regression alone, therefore, behavior is most likely to improve after punishment and most likely to deteriorate after reward. Consequently, the human condition is such that, by chance alone, one is most often rewarded for punishing others and most often punished for rewarding them. People are generally not aware of this contingency. In fact, the elusive role of regression in determining the apparent consequences of reward and punishment seems to have escaped the notice of students of this area.

AVAILABILITY

There are situations in which people assess the frequency of a class or the probability of an event by the ease with which instances or occurrences can be brought to mind. For example, one may assess the risk of heart attack among middle-aged people by recalling such occurrences among one's acquaintances. Similarly, one may evaluate the probability that a given business venture will fail by imagining various difficulties it could encounter. This judgmental heuristic is called availability. Availability is a useful clue for assessing frequency or probability, because instances of large classes are usually reached better and faster than instances of less frequent classes. However, availability is affected by factors other than frequency and probability. Consequently, the reliance on availability leads to predictable biases, some of which are illustrated below.

Biases Due to the Retrievability of Instances

When the size of a class is judged by the availability of its instances, a class whose instances are easily retrieved will appear more numerous than a class of equal frequency whose instances are less retrievable. In an elementary demonstration of this effect, subjects heard a list of well-known personalities of both sexes and were subsequently asked to judge whether the list contained more names of men than of women. Different lists were presented to different groups of subjects. In some of the lists the men were relatively more famous than the women, and in others the women were relatively more famous than the men. In each of the lists, the subjects erroneously judged that the class (sex) that had the more famous personalities was the more numerous (Tversky & Kahneman, 1973).

In addition to familiarity, there are other factors, such as salience, which affect the retrievability of instances. For example, the impact of seeing a house burning on the subjective probability of such accidents is probably greater than the impact of reading about a fire in the local paper. Furthermore, recent occurrences are likely to be relatively more available than earlier occurrences. It is a common experience that the subjective probability of traffic accidents rises temporarily when one sees a car overturned by the side of the road.

Biases Due to the Effectiveness of a Search Set

Suppose one samples a word (of three letters or more) at random from an English text. Is it more likely that the word starts with r or that r is the third letter? People approach this problem by recalling words that begin with r (road) and words that have r in the third position (car) and assess the relative frequency by the ease with which words of the two types come to mind. Because it is much easier to search for words by their first letter than by their third letter, most people judge words that begin with a given consonant to be more numerous than words in which the same consonant appears in the third position. They do so even for consonants, such as r or k, that are more frequent in the third position than in the first (Tversky & Kahneman, 1973).

Different tasks elicit different search sets. For example, suppose you are asked to rate the frequency with which abstract words (*thought, love*) and concrete words (*door, water*) appear in written English. A natural way to answer this question is to search for contexts in which the word could appear. It seems easier to think of contexts in which an abstract concept is mentioned (*love* in love stories) than to think of contexts in which a concrete word (such as *door*) is mentioned. If the frequency of words is judged by the availability of the contexts in which they appear, abstract words will be judged as relatively more numerous than concrete words. This bias has been observed in a recent study (Galbraith & Underwood, 1973) which showed that the judged frequency of occurrence of abstract words was much higher than that of concrete words, equated in objective frequency. Abstract words were also judged to appear in a much greater variety of contexts than concrete words.

Biases of Imaginability

Sometimes one has to assess the frequency of a class whose instances are not stored in memory but can be generated according to a given rule. In such situations, one typically generates several instances and evaluates frequency or probability by the ease with which the relevant instances can be constructed. However, the ease of constructing instances does not always reflect their actual frequency, and this mode of evaluation is prone to biases. To illustrate, consider a group of 10 people who form committees of k members, $2 \leq k \leq 8$. How many different committees of k members can be formed? The correct answer to this problem is given by the binomial coefficient $\binom{10}{k}$ which reaches a maximum of 252 for $k = 5$. Clearly, the number of committees of k members equals the number of committees of $(10 - k)$ members, because any committee of k members defines a unique group of $(10 - k)$ nonmembers.

One way to answer this question without computation is to mentally construct committees of k members and to evaluate their number by the ease with which they come to mind. Committees of few members, say 2, are more available than committees of many members, say 8. The simplest scheme for the construction of committees is a partition of the group into

disjoint sets. One readily sees that it is easy to construct five disjoint committees of 2 members, while it is impossible to generate even two disjoint committees of 8 members. Consequently, if frequency is assessed by imaginability, or by availability for construction, the small committees will appear more numerous than larger committees, in contrast to the correct bell-shaped function. Indeed, when naive subjects were asked to estimate the number of distinct committees of various sizes, their estimates were a decreasing monotonic function of committee size (Tversky & Kahneman, 1973). For example, the median estimate of the number of committees of 2 members was 70, while the estimate for committees of 8 members was 20 (the correct answer is 45 in both cases).

Imaginability plays an important role in the evaluation of probabilities in real-life situations. The risk involved in an adventurous expedition, for example, is evaluated by imagining contingencies with which the expedition is not equipped to cope. If many such difficulties are vividly portrayed, the expedition can be made to appear exceedingly dangerous, although the ease with which disasters are imagined need not reflect their actual likelihood. Conversely, the risk involved in an undertaking may be grossly underestimated if some possible dangers are either difficult to conceive of, or simply do not come to mind.

Illusory Correlation

Chapman and Chapman (1969) have described an interesting bias in the judgment of the frequency with which two events co-occur. They presented naive judges with information concerning several hypothetical mental patients. The data for each patient consisted of a clinical diagnosis and a drawing of a person made by the patient. Later the judges estimated the frequency with which each diagnosis (such as paranoia or suspiciousness) had been accompanied by various features of the drawing (such as peculiar eyes). The subjects markedly overestimated the frequency of co-occurrence of natural associates, such as suspiciousness and peculiar eyes. This effect was labeled illusory correlation. In their erroneous judgments of the data to which they had been exposed, naive subjects "rediscovered" much of the common, but unfounded, clinical lore concerning the interpretation of the draw-a-person test. The illusory correlation effect was extremely resistant to contradictory data. It persisted even when the correlation between symptom and diagnosis was actually negative, and it prevented the judges from detecting relationships that were in fact present.

Availability provides a natural account for the illusory-correlation effect. The judgment of how frequently two events co-occur could be based on the strength of the associative bond between them. When the association is strong, one is likely to conclude that the events have been frequently paired. Consequently, strong associates will be judged to have occurred together frequently. According to this view, the illusory correlation between suspiciousness and peculiar drawing of the eyes, for example, is due to the fact that suspiciousness is more readily associated with the eyes than with any other part of the body.

Lifelong experience has taught us that, in general, instances of large classes are recalled better and faster than instances of less frequent classes; that likely occurrences are easier to imagine than unlikely ones; and that the associative connections between events are strengthened when the events frequently co-occur. As a result, man has at his disposal a procedure (the availability heuristic) for estimating the numerosity of a class, the likelihood of an event, or the frequency of co-occurrences, by the ease with which the relevant mental operations of retrieval, construction, or association can be performed. However, as the preceding examples have demonstrated, this valuable estimation procedure results in systematic errors.

ADJUSTMENT AND ANCHORING

In many situations, people make estimates by starting from an initial value that is adjusted to yield the final answer. The initial value, or starting point, may be suggested by the formulation of the problem, or it may be the result of a partial computation. In either case, adjustments are typically insufficient (Slovic & Lichtenstein, 1971). That is, different starting points yield different estimates, which are biased toward the initial values. We call this phenomenon anchoring.

Insufficient Adjustment

In a demonstration of the anchoring effect, subjects were asked to estimate various quantities, stated in percentages (for example, the percentage of African countries in the United Nations). For each quantity, a number between 0 and 100 was determined by spinning a wheel of fortune in the subjects' presence. The subjects were instructed to indicate first whether that number was higher or lower than the value of the quantity, and then to estimate the value of the quantity by moving upward or downward from the given number. Different groups were given different numbers for each quantity, and these arbitrary numbers had a marked effect on estimates. For example, the median estimates of the percentage of African countries in the United Nations were 25 and 45 for groups that received 10 and 65, respectively, as starting points. Payoffs for accuracy did not reduce the anchoring effect.

Anchoring occurs not only when the starting point is given to the subject, but also when the subject bases his estimate on the result of some incomplete computation. A study of intuitive numerical estimation illustrates this effect. Two groups of high school students estimated, within 5 seconds, a numerical expression that was written on the blackboard. One group estimated the product

$$8 \times 7 \times 6 \times 5 \times 4 \times 3 \times 2 \times 1$$

while another group estimated the product

$$1 \times 2 \times 3 \times 4 \times 5 \times 6 \times 7 \times 8$$

To rapidly answer such questions, people may perform a few steps of computation and estimate the product by extrapolation or adjustment. Because adjustments are typically insufficient, this procedure should lead to underestimation. Furthermore, because the result of the first few steps of multiplication (performed from left to right) is higher in the descending sequence than in the ascending sequence, the former expression should be judged larger than the latter. Both predictions were confirmed. The median estimate for the ascending sequence was 512, while the median estimate for the descending sequence was 2,250. The correct answer is 40,320.

Biases in the Evaluation of Conjunctive and Disjunctive Events

In a recent study by Bar-Hillel (1973) subjects were given the opportunity to bet on one of two events. Three types of events were used: (i) simple events, such as drawing a red marble from a bag containing 50 percent red marbles and 50 percent white marbles; (ii) conjunctive events, such as drawing a red marble seven times in succession, with replacement, from a bag containing 90 percent red marbles and 10 percent white marbles; and (iii) disjunctive events, such as drawing a red marble at least once in seven successive tries, with replacement, from a bag containing 10 percent red marbles and 90 percent white marbles. In this problem, a significant majority of subjects preferred to bet on the conjunctive event (the probability of which is .48) rather than on the simple event (the probability of which is .50). Subjects also preferred to bet on the simple event rather than on the disjunctive event, which has a probability of .52. Thus, most subjects bet on the less likely event in both comparisons. This pattern of choices illustrates a general finding. Studies of choice among gambles and of judgments of probability indicate that people tend to overestimate the probability of conjunctive events (Cohen, Chesnick, & Haran, 1972) and to underestimate the probability of disjunctive events. These biases are readily explained as effects of anchoring. The stated probability of the elementary event (success at any one stage) provides a natural starting point for the estimation of the probabilities of both conjunctive and disjunctive events. Since adjustment from the starting point is typically insufficient, the final estimates remain too

close to the probabilities of the elementary events in both cases. Note that the overall probability of a conjunctive event is lower than the probability of each elementary event, whereas the overall probability of a disjunctive event is higher than the probability of each elementary event. As a consequence of anchoring, the overall probability will be overestimated in conjunctive problems and underestimated in disjunctive problems.

Biases in the evaluation of compound events are particularly significant in the context of planning. The successful completion of an undertaking, such as the development of a new product, typically has a conjunctive character: for the undertaking to succeed, each of a series of events must occur. Even when each of these events is very likely, the overall probability of success can be quite low if the number of events is large. The general tendency to overestimate the probability of conjunctive events leads to unwarranted optimism in the evaluation of the likelihood that a plan will succeed or that a project will be completed on time. Conversely, disjunctive structures are typically encountered in the evaluation of risks. A complex system, such as a nuclear reactor or a human body, will malfunction if any of its essential components fails. Even when the likelihood of failure in each component is slight, the probability of an overall failure can be high if many components are involved. Because of anchoring, people will tend to underestimate the probabilities of failure in complex systems. Thus, the direction of the anchoring bias can sometimes be inferred from the structure of the event. The chain-like structure of conjunctions leads to overestimation; the funnel-like structure of disjunctions leads to underestimation.

Anchoring in the Assessment of Subjective Probability Distributions

In decision analysis, experts are often required to express their beliefs about a quantity, such as the value of the Dow-Jones average on a particular day, in the form of a probability distribution. Such a distribution is usually constructed by asking the person to select values of the quantity that correspond to specified percentiles of his subjective probability distribution. For example, the judge may be asked to select a number, X_{90}, such that his subjective probability that this number will be higher than the value of the Dow-Jones average is .90. That is, he should select the value X_{90} so that he is just willing to accept 9 to 1 odds that the Dow-Jones average will not exceed it. A subjective probability distribution for the value of the Dow-Jones average can be constructed from several such judgments corresponding to different percentiles.

By collecting subjective probability distributions for many different quantities, it is possible to test the judge for proper calibration. A judge is properly (or externally) calibrated in a set of problems if exactly 11 percent of the true values of the assessed quantities falls below his stated values of X_{11}. For example, the true values should fall below X_{01} for 1 percent of the quantities and above X_{99} for 1 percent of the quantities. Thus, the true values should fall in the confidence interval between X_{01} and X_{99} on 98 percent of the problems.

Several investigators (Alpert & Raiffa, 1969; Staël von Holstein, 1971b; Winkler, 1967) have obtained probability disruptions for many quantities from a large number of judges. These distributions indicated large and systematic departures from proper calibration. In most studies, the actual values of the assessed quantities are either smaller than X_{01} or greater than X_{99} for about 30 percent of the problems. That is, the subjects state overly narrow confidence intervals which reflect more certainty than is justified by their knowledge about the assessed quantities. This bias is common to naive and to sophisticated subjects, and it is not eliminated by introducing proper scoring rules, which provide incentives for external calibration. This effect is attributable, in part at least, to anchoring.

To select X_{90} for the value of the Dow-Jones average, for example, it is natural to begin by thinking about one's best estimate of the Dow-Jones and to adjust this value upward. If this adjustment—like most others—is insufficient, then X_{90} will not be sufficiently extreme. A

similar anchoring effect will occur in the selection of X_{10}, which is presumably obtained by adjusting one's best estimate downward. Consequently, the confidence interval between X_{10} and X_{90} will be too narrow, and the assessed probability distribution will be too tight. In support of this interpretation it can be shown that subjective probabilities are systematically altered by a procedure in which one's best estimate does not serve as an anchor.

Subjective probability distributions for a given quantity (the Dow-Jones average) can be obtained in two different ways: (i) by asking the subject to select values of the Dow-Jones that correspond to specified percentiles of his probability distribution and (ii) by asking the subject to assess the probabilities that the true value of the Dow-Jones will exceed some specified values. The two procedures are formally equivalent and should yield identical distributions. However, they suggest different modes of adjustment from different anchors. In procedure (i), the natural starting point is one's best estimate of the quality. In procedure (ii), on the other hand, the subject may be anchored on the value stated in the question. Alternatively, he may be anchored on even odds, or 50–50 chances, which is a natural starting point in the estimation of likelihood. In either case, procedure (ii) should yield less extreme odds than procedure (i).

To contrast the two procedures, a set of 24 quantities (such as the air distance from New Delhi to Peking) was presented to a group of subjects who assessed either X_{10} or X_{90} for each problem. Another group of subjects received the median judgment of the first group for each of the 24 quantities. They were asked to assess the odds that each of the given values exceeded the true value of the relevant quantity. In the absence of any bias, the second group should retrieve the odds specified to the first group, that is, 9:1. However, if even odds or the stated value serve as anchors, the odds of the second group should be less extreme, that is, closer to 1:1. Indeed, the median odds stated by this group, across all problems, were 3:1. When the judgments of the two groups were tested for external calibration, it was found that subjects in the first group were too extreme, in accord with earlier studies. The events that they defined as having a probability of .10 actually obtained in 24 percent of the cases. In contrast, subjects in the second group were too conservative. Events to which they assigned an average probability of .34 actually obtained in 26 percent of the cases. These results illustrate the manner in which the degree of calibration depends on the procedure of elicitation.

DISCUSSION

This article has been concerned with cognitive biases that stem from the reliance on judgmental heuristics. These biases are not attributable to motivational effects such as wishful thinking or the distortion of judgments by payoffs and penalties. Indeed, several of the severe errors of judgment reported earlier occurred despite the fact that subjects were encouraged to be accurate and were rewarded for the correct answers (Kahneman & Tversky, 1972; Tversky & Kahneman, 1973).

The reliance on heuristics and the prevalence of biases are not restricted to laymen. Experienced researchers are also prone to the same biases—when they think intuitively. For example, the tendency to predict the outcome that best represents the data, with insufficient regard for prior probability, has been observed in the intuitive judgments of individuals who have had extensive training in statistics (Kahneman & Tversky, 1973; Tversky & Kahneman, 1971). Although the statistically sophisticated avoid elementary errors, such as the gambler's fallacy, their intuitive judgments are liable to similar fallacies in more intricate and less transparent problems.

It is not surprising that useful heuristics such as representativeness and availability are retained, even though they occasionally lead to errors in prediction or estimation. What is perhaps surprising is the failure of people to infer from lifelong experience such fundamental statistical rules as regression toward the mean, or the effect of sample size on sampling vari-

ability. Although everyone is exposed, in the normal course of life, to numerous examples from which these rules could have been induced, very few people discover the principles of sampling and regression on their own. Statistical principles are not learned from everyday experience because the relevant instances are not coded appropriately. For example, people do not discover that successive lines in a text differ more in average word length than do successive pages, because they simply do not attend to the average word length of individual lines or pages. Thus, people do not learn the relation between sample size and sampling variability, although the data for such learning are abundant.

The lack of an appropriate code also explains why people usually do not detect the biases in their judgments of probability. A person could conceivably learn whether his judgments are externally calibrated by keeping a tally of the proportion of events that actually occur among those to which he assigns the same probability. However, it is not natural to group events by their judged probability. In the absence of such grouping it is impossible for an individual to discover, for example, that only 50 percent of the predictions to which he has assigned a probability of .9 or higher actually come true.

The empirical analysis of cognitive biases has implications for the theoretical and applied role of judged probabilities. Modern decision theory (de Finetti, 1968; Savage, 1954) regards subjective probability as the quantified opinion of an idealized person. Specifically, the subjective probability of a given event is defined by the set of bets about this event that such a person is willing to accept. An internally consistent, or coherent, subjective probability measure can be derived for an individual if his choices among bets satisfy certain principles, that is, the axioms of the theory. The derived probability is subjective in the sense that different individuals are allowed to have different probabilities for the same event. The major contribution of this approach is that it provides a rigorous subjective interpretation of probability that is applicable to unique events and is embedded in a general theory of rational decision.

It should perhaps be noted that, while subjective probabilities can sometimes be inferred from preferences among bets, they are normally not formed in this fashion. A person bets on team A rather than on team B because he believes that team A is more likely to win; he does not infer this belief from his betting preferences. Thus, in reality, subjective probabilities determine preferences among bets and are not derived from them, as in the axiomatic theory of rational decision (Savage, 1954).

The inherently subjective nature of probability has led many students to the belief that coherence, or internal consistency, is the only valid criterion by which judged probabilities should be evaluated. From the standpoint of the formal theory of subjective probability, any set of internally consistent probability judgments is as good as any other. This criterion is not entirely satisfactory, because an internally consistent set of subjective probabilities can be incompatible with other beliefs held by the individual. Consider a person whose subjective probabilities for all possible outcomes of a coin-tossing game reflect the gambler's fallacy. That is, his estimate of the probability of tails on a particular toss increases with the number of consecutive heads that preceded that toss. The judgments of such a person could be internally consistent and therefore acceptable as adequate subjective probabilities according to the criterion of the formal theory. These probabilities, however, are incompatible with the generally held belief that a coin has no memory and is therefore incapable of generating sequential dependencies. For judged probabilities to be considered adequate, or rational, internal consistency is not enough. The judgments must be compatible with the entire web of beliefs held by the individual. Unfortunately, there can be no simple formal procedure for assessing the compatibility of a set of probability judgments with the judge's total system of beliefs. The rational judge will nevertheless strive for compatibility, even though internal consistency is more easily achieved and assessed. In particular, he will attempt to make his probability judgments compatible with his knowledge about the subject matter, the laws of probability, and his own judgmental heuristics and biases.

SUMMARY

This article described three heuristics that are employed in making judgments under uncertainty: (1) representativeness, which is usually employed when people are asked to judge the probability that an object or event A belongs to class or process B; (2) availability of instances or scenarios, which is often employed when people are asked to assess the frequency of a class or the plausibility of a particular development; and (3) adjustment from an anchor, which is usually employed in numerical prediction when a relevant value is available. These heuristics are highly economical and usually effective, but they lead to systematic and predictable errors. A better understanding of these heuristics and of the biases to which they lead could improve judgments and decisions in situations of uncertainty.

REFERENCES

Alpert, M., & Raiffa, H. (1969). Unpublished manuscript.

Bar-Hillel, M. (1973). *Organizational Behavior and Human Performance, 9*, 396.

Chapman, L. J., & Chapman, J. P. (1967). *Journal of Abnormal Psychology, 73*, 193.

Cohen, J., Chesnick, E. I., & Haran, D. (1972). *British Journal of Psychology, 63*, 41.

De Finetti, B. (1968). In D. E. Sills (Ed.), *International encyclopedia of the social sciences*, Vol. 12. pp. 496–504. New York: MacMillan.

Edwards, W. (1968). In B. Kleinmuntz (Ed.), *Formal representation of human judgment*, pp. 17–52. New York: Wiley.

Galbraith, R. C., & Underwood, B. J. (1973). *Memory and Cognition, 1*, 56.

Kahneman, D., & Tversky, A. (1973). *Psychological Review, 80*, 237.

Kahneman, D., & Tversky, A. (1972). *Cognitive Psychology, 3*, 430.

Savage, L. J. (1954). *The foundations of statistics.* New York: Wiley.

Slovic, P., & Lichtenstein, S. (1971). *Organizational Behavior and Human Performance, 6,* 649.

Tversky, A., & Kahneman, D. (1971). *Psychological Bulletin, 76,* 105.

Tversky, A., & Kahneman, D. (1973). *Cognitive Psychology, 5,* 207.

von Holstein, C. A. S. (1971) *Acta Psychologica, 35,* 478.

Winkler, R. L. (1967). *Journal of the American Statistical Association, 62,* 776.

5

Friendship and the Development of Self-Schemas: The Effects of Talking About Others

Francine M. Deutsch and Mary Ellen Mackesy

Many people have clear impressions of their own attributes, including how smart, independent, or friendly they are. The cognitive structures that organize and summarize this information about the self have been termed "self-schemas." In this article, Deutsch and Mackesy describe some ways in which people develop their self-schemas. The authors suggest that when we talk to our friends about other people, we become aware of the dimensions our friends use to describe other people, and eventually we use these dimensions to think about ourselves. The evidence offered by Deutsch and Mackesy is important for showing how schemas about the self and others develop, and also for the methods the authors used. The first study shows that schemas of friends are more similar to each other than those of nonfriends. The second study demonstrates the same phenomenon experimentally by showing that two people who are initially strangers will, through their conversation, come to be similar in the dimensions they use for describing others. This combination of naturalistic and experimental evidence provides especially strong support for Deutsch and Mackesy's arguments.

ABSTRACT. *Two studies were conducted to examine a model proposed to explain similarity in the self-schemas of friends. According to this model, in the ongoing conversation of friendship, each person becomes aware of the dimensions used by the friend for describing people. Over time each incorporates some of the friend's dimensions for organizing information about others and ultimately for describing the self. In the first study the self-conceptions of friends and nonfriends were compared. As predicted, friends, as compared to nonfriends, had more similar self-schemas, and more readily adopted each other's self-schema dimensions for describing a target. In the second study two unacquainted partners discussed their impressions of a target person. Subsequently, the pairs shared more similar self-schemas and incorporated dimensions from each other's self-schemas for self-description and for description of the target person. Thus, the results of both studies are consistent with the model proposed. Directions for future research are discussed.*

Reprinted from *Personality and Social Psychology Bulletin,* 1985, *11*(4), pp. 399–408. Copyright 1985 by the Society for Personality and Social Psychology, Inc. Reprinted by permission of Sage Publications, Inc. and the authors.

Since Markus (1977) used the term "self-schema" to define cognitive structures that summarize and organize information about the self, research on this topic has focused primarily on the information-processing effects of these self-schemas. For example, studies have shown that individuals who possess self-schemas in a particular domain are faster to endorse self-descriptive characteristics than are aschematic persons (Kuiper, 1981; Markus, 1977; Markus, Crane, Bernstein, & Siladi, 1982), can retrieve more behavioral evidence to support the self-description, show better recall for schema-consistent information, and are more resistant to contradictory information about the self in that domain (Markus, 1977; Markus et al., 1982).

Little attention had been given to the social consequences of these individual differences in information processing, but in a recent study (Deutsch, Kroll, & Goss, 1984) the self-schemas of friends were shown to bear a systematic relation to one another. Not only did friends tend to share self-schema dimensions, but when judging the self-descriptiveness of traits, individuals rated traits higher and endorsed them more quickly if they were included among their friends' self-schema dimensions than if they were not.

This cognitive similarity between friends is consistent with earlier research based on Kelly's (1970) theory of personal constructs. Kelly argued that individuals habitually use a finite number of dichotomous dimensions (constructs) for processing information about reality. The particular dimensions used vary among people, but the total set of constructs used by any particular individual is that person's "personal construct system." Furthermore, Kelly's theory states that similarity in personal construct systems is important in social relationships for two reasons. First, in order for individuals even to enter relationships, they must be cognizant of each other's personal construct systems. Second, within social relationships individuals seek to validate and elaborate their own personal constructs. In line with Kelly's theory, Duck (1972; 1977) hypothesized and found that friends possess more similar personal construct systems than do nonfriends.

Although neither Kelly nor Duck discusses self-knowledge explicitly, the parallel between the findings that friends possess similar personal construct systems (Duck, 1972; 1977) and also share self-schema dimensions (Deutsch et al., 1984) provides evidence of a connection between self-knowledge and knowledge about others. Moreover, previous research has shown that dimensions central to an individual's self-conceptions are used for describing others (Shrauger & Patterson, 1974) and for processing information about others (Markus & Smith, 1981). Thus, the cognitive similarity between friends extends to the dimensions friends use to classify, describe, and evaluate information about others as well as about the self.

Two alternative explanations might account for cognitive similarity between friends. Individuals may choose to become friends with others who share their style of organizing information about people. This choice would provide for ease of communication and would enable them to validate their own system of personal constructs. Alternatively, friendship may provide a context in which an individual's personal construct system may evolve and grow. Friendship creates the opportunity for personal constructs to be elaborated and extended, allowing new ways of viewing the self.

We propose that the ongoing conversation that occurs between friends provides a mechanism by which friends become more similar in both their conceptions of others and of themselves. Duck (1973) found that people are aware of the constructs that their friends use in making evaluations of others. This awareness probably arises from conversations in which observations and evaluations of others are exchanged. In such conversations each friend presumably uses his or her own self-schema dimensions or constructs, allowing the friend to become aware of those habitually used. Subsequently, each might begin to use the friend's dimensions to describe other people and ultimately to describe the self. This process would account for friends' similarity in describing others (Duck, 1972, 1973, 1977) as well as the similarity of friends' self-schemas (Deutsch et al., 1984).

Two studies were conducted to examine some of the assumptions and implications of this model. In the first study we compared friends' and nonfriends' self-schemas and their descriptions of target persons. We predicted that, as compared to nonfriends, friends would use more similar trait dimensions for self-description and would be more likely to use each other's self-descriptive traits for describing a target person. In the second study we examined the effects of conversation on the similarity that emerged between two unacquainted partners who discussed and evaluated a character sketch of a target person.

STUDY 1

METHOD

Subjects

Sixteen pairs of female friends who were undergraduates at Mount Holyoke College were recruited to voluntarily participate in this study.

Procedure

Pairs of friends came to the lab together, but were separated and performed all tasks individually. The only explanation they were given for the procedure was that they were participating in a study of personality factors in friendship. Subjects read one of two character sketches. These sketches, designed to be roughly equivalent, described two different target persons, both female college students residing in dormitories. Modeled after the essays reported by Higgins, King, and Mavin (1982), the sketches were composed of descriptions of behaviors characteristic of 20 preselected personality traits (e.g., creative, concerned, opinionated). They were designed to depict two individuals, equally likable, to whom the same descriptive dimensions could readily be applied.[1]

In order to identify their self-schemas, subjects were asked to list 10 self-descriptive traits. Half listed their traits before reading the character sketch and writing their impressions; the other half listed them afterwards. The order in which this self-description was obtained was counterbalanced across the character sketch conditions. Finally, subjects rated themselves on 40 9-point bipolar scales describing traits. Nineteen of these traits had been used in the character sketches, and the remaining 21 traits are frequently used for self-description.

RESULTS AND DISCUSSION

Similarity of Friends' Self-Descriptions

In order to compare similarity between friends and nonfriends, one person in each friendship pair was randomly designated as the *primary subject*, the other as the *friend*. For statistical analyses each primary subject was also randomly paired with a nonfriend, a subject in the same experimental conditions who had been designated a *friend* of another *primary subject*.

The primary subjects' self-schemas were scored for overlap with the self-schemas of their friends and their nonfriends. A trait was considered overlapping if the two subjects listed identical traits, synonyms, or antonyms. The analysis of variance on this overlap measure included two factors: a repeated-measures factor, type of pair (friend/nonfriend); and a between-subjects factor, time of self-description (before/after reading target description). As predicted, the only statistically significant

---

[1] The two targets were described as exhibiting different behaviors characteristic of various traits. For example, behaviors characteristic of unreliability were included in the description of that target person. One was described as a person who habitually convinces others to participate in projects that she then abandons. "When it comes to doing anything herself, she never has the time. She sometimes makes commitments and then backs out." The other target's unreliability is described in terms of her course work. "She sometimes says that she will help others, but frequently backs out of it later. She often fails to return borrowed books and notes." For a few traits the targets were described as exhibiting opposite behavior. For example, one description suggests that the target is messy. "Her room is cluttered and her bed is carelessly made. Her desk is usually hidden under a pile of books and papers." The other description implies the target's neatness. "Her room is carefully coordinated, her books neatly shelved."

effect was a main effect of type of pair on overlap, $F(1,14) = 12.47$, p < .005. Consistent with previous research (Deutsch et al., 1984), friends generated more overlapping traits in their self-descriptions ($M = 2.31$) than did nonfriends ($M = 1.44$). Apparently, in this subject population there is a baseline of approximately 14% overlap in traits used for self-description between randomly paired individuals, whereas between friends the overlap is approximately 23%. Because the time of self-description showed neither a main effect, $F(1, 14) = 1.38$, $p > .25$, nor an interaction with type of pair, $F(1, 14) = 0, p > .99$, on overlap, the similarity measured between pairs cannot be attributed to exposure to the target description. Friends were more similar than randomly paired individuals at the outset of the study.

Use of Friends' Self-Schema Dimensions

The model of change that we are proposing asserts that this similarity arises because friends adopt each other's self-schema dimensions for describing people—both other people and themselves. In order to test this prediction, we compared the proportion of friends' self-schema dimensions used by primary subjects in describing the target person with that of nonfriends. A Wilcoxon test for correlated samples showed that primary subjects used a greater proportion of their friends' ($M = .20$) than their nonfriends' ($M = .12$) dimensions to describe the target person, $W_{obs}(9) = 7$, $p < .05$. This is a particularly striking result, because friends never discussed the target person, nor did they discuss the dimensions they used for self-description in this study. Despite the absence of explicit discussion, this result suggests that the constructs used by friends take on a special importance to each other.

The numbers of similar dimensions in the descriptions of friends and nonfriends were also compared. Surprisingly, friends' descriptions of the target person were no more similar ($M = 1.18$) than were the descriptions of nonfriends ($M = 1.25$). Apparently, with the low absolute number of dimensions used, it was possible for friends to use each other's self-schema dimensions without necessarily using

the same dimensions. If we think of dimensions from the individual's self-schema and the friend's self-schema as a pool of accessible constructs (Higgins et al., 1982) available for use in descriptions, it is clear that when a small sample of dimensions from the pool is used by two friends, the particular sample may not overlap. Presumably, if more descriptions were included, similarity in the descriptions of friends would emerge.

STUDY 2

The model of self-concept development that we are proposing is largely cognitive. Through conversations about people, friends become cognizant of each other's constructs or dimensions for understanding the social world and eventually adopt these dimensions for self-description. Although conversations about third persons typically occur between friends, we expected that an analogous process would occur if strangers were brought together and specifically instructed to discuss other people. In Study 2 we examined the similarity that emerged between two unacquainted subjects who discussed and evaluated a character sketch of a target. We hypothesized that partners will give more similar self-descriptions after a discussion of a target person. We also hypothesized that subjects will use an increased number of dimensions from their partners' self-schemas to describe a target person and to describe themselves.

METHOD

Subjects

Forty female undergraduates at Mount Holyoke College were recruited for voluntary participation in this study. Subjects were run in groups.

Procedure

After a group of subjects was assembled at the laboratory, members were randomly assigned partners—with the provision that all pairs were previously unacquainted. The only explanation given to subjects about the nature of the experiment was that it was a study of personality and social interaction. In the first part of the study all activities were carried out independently. First, subjects were instructed to list 10 self-descriptive traits that were used to identify their self-schemas. These lists were collected, subjects read a paragraph depicting one of two target persons (TP1), and were given 3 minutes to write their impressions of that person. After their descriptions were collected, they individually read descriptions of a second target person (TP2). The order of presentation of the two target persons was counterbalanced. Subsequently, subjects discussed their impressions of the second target person with their partners and then *independently* wrote their descriptions in the 3 minutes allotted. They were in no way directed to pay attention to the dimensions used by their partners. Finally, subjects again individually listed 10 self-descriptive traits and rated liking for their partners, their partners' liking for them, similarity to their partners, and the likelihood that they would become friends. During debriefing there was no indication at all that the subjects were aware of the focus of the study.

RESULTS AND DISCUSSION

Similarity in Partners' Self-Descriptions

The major hypothesis of this study was that similarity in the self-schemas of partners will increase after discussion of a target person. Following the procedure used in Study 1, the numbers of traits used as self-descriptive by both partners, before and after the discussion, were calculated. As predicted, there was significantly more self-schema overlap after the discussion of a target person ($M = 2.05$) than before that discussion ($M = 1.3$), $t(19) = 3.29$, $p < .004$. It is interesting to note that the 13% trait overlap found between unacquainted partners in this study is very close to the 14% overlap found between the randomly paired subjects in Study 1. Moreover, the 20% overlap in the self-descriptions of the pairs after they have discussed a target person is only slightly less than the 23% trait overlap found between friends in Study 1.

Use of Partners' Self-Schema Dimension

If, as we propose, this similarity develops because through conversations about people subjects learn to adopt to each other's self-schema dimensions for describing people, two predictions follow. First, subjects will use a greater number of their partners' self-schema dimensions to describe the target person whom they had discussed (TP2) than the target person whom they had not discussed (TP1). Second, after discussion, subjects would use an increased number of their partners' dimensions for self-description.

In order to test the first prediction, an analysis of variance was conducted with two repeated-measures factors: source of dimension (own/partner's self-schema) and target person (TP1, not discussed/TP2, discussed). Because partners were not independent of one another, their data were averaged. As predicted, a significant interaction between source of dimension and target person was obtained, $F(1, 19) = 17.92$, $p < .001$. Individual comparisons show that subjects used more of their partners' self-schema dimensions to describe TP2 who had been discussed ($M = 1.23$) than to describe TP1 who had not been discussed ($M = .731$), $F(1, 19) = 14.91$, $p < .01$, whereas they used fewer of their own self-schema dimensions to describe TP2 ($M = 1.05$) than to describe TP1 ($M = 1.33$), $F(1, 19) = 4.67$, $p < .05$. Thus we can conclude that the discussion led subjects to use each other's self-schema dimensions for describing a target person.

In order to test the second prediction, that subjects adopted their partners' self-schema dimensions for self-description, the number of dimensions newly listed in the subject's self-description at the end of the study that had been listed as self-descriptive by the partner at the beginning of the study was calculated. As predicted, after the discussion of the target person, subjects had adopted a significant number of dimensions ($M = .75$) used initially in their partners' self-descriptions, $t(19) = 7.55$, $p < .001$.

THE EFFECT OF LIKING

In order to determine whether or not liking could account for the similarity in self-schemas developed between partners, partner-pairs were grouped according to the degree of change they exhibited in self-schema overlap. Pairs whose self-schema overlap either did not change or decreased were designated low changers, whereas pairs whose overlap scores increased were designated high changers. A total liking score for each pair was obtained by averaging their ratings for liking, perception of partner's liking, perceived similarity, and perceived potential for friendship. High and low changers were compared on this composite score, but no significant difference was found between the two groups, $t = 1.18$, $p < .25$. Apparently, similarity of self-schemas developed independently of the partners' degree of affection for one another.

This striking absence of an effect of liking is consistent with our assertion that the process that occurs in conversation is cognitive rather than motivational. Individuals may adopt new dimensions, even without desiring to emulate their partners or friends, simply because these dimensions have been made salient as viable constructs for describing people. This analysis does not imply that liking has no impact at all. In real life relationships the degree of liking will affect the amount and type of social interaction that occurs. The type of conversation elicited in this study would most likely occur between people in positive social relationships. In that context we would expect this process of self-schema change to occur. Also, in friendship, individuals may consciously desire to become more similar. Consequently they are attentive to their friends' characteristic ways of processing social information and actively try to emulate them. Although these affective components of friendship may facilitate the development of similarity, our results are notable because they show that similarity can develop

on a cognitive level without the emotional aspects of friendship.

SUMMARY AND CONCLUSIONS

Taken together, the results of Studies 1 and 2 are consistent with the model of change that we propose. In Study 1 we showed that friends do indeed share more self-schema dimensions than do nonfriends and that friends tend to use each other's self-schema dimensions for describing a target person. In Study 2 we found that after discussing a target person, unacquainted partners would adopt each other's self-schema dimensions for describing the target person and themselves and would develop more similar self-conceptions. It seems reasonable to assume that if strangers adopt each other's constructs, even temporarily, then the repeated exposure friends experience leads them to more lasting changes.

Previous writers have argued that the self is the central cognitive structure that serves as a referent for processing all kinds of information (Kuiper, 1981; Kuiper & Rogers, 1979). One interesting implication of this model is that processing information about others may serve as a referent for the self.

In future research it would be useful to trace the changes in self-conception that accompany the development of real friendships. According to our model, it should be possible to predict the nature of these changes by identifying the self-schemas of each friend in the incipient stages of the relationship. If conversation about others is the critical component for this process of change, then friendships that develop without this conversation should be less likely to produce changing self-descriptions. For example, a previous study found that conversation is a more central aspect of women's than of men's friendships. Close women friends are more likely to discuss a wide variety of topics including intimate relationships and to discuss those topics in depth than are their male counterparts (Aries & Johnson, 1983). The present research used only female subjects. Male friends might be less likely to spontaneously develop similar self-conceptions, but if given a task similar to that used in Study 2 (discussion of a target person) we would expect an increased use of similar constructs between male partners, paralleling the findings for female partners.

Another useful methodological extension would be to repeat the paradigm used in Study 2 in multiple sessions in order to examine the stability of the changes obtained. Moreover, given that partners would probably show increased variability in liking in multiple sessions, the effects of liking could be assessed more carefully in that context.

Finally, it might be interesting in future research to study the relation between the constructs used by parents to describe people and the developing self-conceptions of their children. The process we have proposed may account not only for change but also for the dimensions initially adopted as central to self-conception.

REFERENCES

Aires, E. J., & Johnson, F. L. (1983). Close friendship in adulthood: Conversational content between same-sex friends. *Sex Roles, 9,* 1183–1196.

Bailey, R. C., Finney, P., & Helm, B. (1975). Self-concept support and friendship duration. *Journal of Social Psychology, 96,* 237–243.

Deutsch, F. M., Kroll, J.F., & Goss, R., (1984) *Shared selves: The influence of friendship on self-schema.* Manuscript submitted for publication.

Duck, S., (1972). Friendship, similarity and the reptest. *Psychological Reports, 31,* 231–234.

Duck, S. (1973). Similarity and perceived similarity of personal constructs as influence on friendship choice. *British Journal of Social and Clinical Psychology, 12,* 156–165.

Duck, S. (1977). Inquiry, hypothesis and the quest for validation: Personal construct systems in the development of acquaintance. In S. Duck (Ed.), *Theory and practice in interpersonal attraction* (pp. 379–404). New York: Academic Press.

Fiedler, F. E., Warrington, W. G., & Blaisdell, F. J. (1952). Unconscious attitudes as correlates of sociometric choice in a social group. *Journal of Abnormal and Social Psychology, 47,* 790–796.

Higgins, E. T., King, G. A., & Mavin, G. H. (1982). Individual construct accessibility and subjective impressions and recall. *Journal of Personality and Social Psychology, 43,* 35–47.

Kelly, G. A. (1970). A brief introduction to personal construct theory. In D. Bannister (Ed.), *Perspectives in personal construct theory* (pp. 1–29). New York: Academic Press.

Kuiper, N. A. (1981). Convergent evidence for the self as a prototype: The "inverted-U RT effect" for self and other judgments. *Personality and Social Psycholgoy Bulletin, 7,* 438–443.

Kuiper, N.A., & Rogers, T. B. (1979). Encoding of personal information: Self-other differences. *Journal of Personality and Social Psychology, 37,* 499–514.

Markus, H. (1977). Self-schemata and processing information about the self. *Journal of Personality and Social Psychology, 42,* 38–50.

Markus, H., Crane, M., Bernstein, S., & Siladi, M. (1982). Self-schemas and gender. *Journal of Personality and Social Psychology, 42,* 38–50.

Markus, H., & Smith, J. (1981). The influence of self-schemata on the perception of others. In N. Cantor & J. F. Kihlstrom (Eds.), *Personality, cognition, and social interaction* (pp. 233–262). Hillsdale, NJ: Lawrence Erlbaum.

Miller, N., Campbell, D. T., Twedt, H., & O'Connell, E. J. (1966). Similarity, contrast, and complementarity in friendship choice. *Journal of Personality and Social Psychology, 32,* 205–213.

Shrauger, J. S. & Patterson, M. B. (1974). Self-evaluation and the selection of dimensions for evaluting others. *Journal of Personality, 42,* 569–585.

Thompson, W. R., & Nishimura, R. (1958). Some determinants of friendship. *Journal of Personality, 20,* 305–314.

6

Cognitive Consequences of Forced Compliance

Leon Festinger and James M. Carlsmith

This study is a classic example of both experimental research in social psychology and of research on cognitive dissonance theory. Like many studies in the dissonance theory tradition, it tests a nonobvious prediction—that the less people are paid for carrying out a task, the more they will like it. This rather simple, if counter-intuitive idea, is tested using an extraordinarily elaborate experimental procedure, with multiple deceptions. This research requires considerable ingenuity, and even acting ability, on the part of the experimenters. It relies on creating a powerful experience in the experimental situation itself, called "experimental realism," as opposed to simulating some particular real-life situation, called "mundane realism." This complex experimental manipulation of the independent variable is perhaps the most interesting and distinctive feature of the study. This complexity is, incidentally, a marked contrast to the very simple paper-and-pencil measures of the dependent variable, and the very simple statistical analysis used. But, consistent with dissonance theory, as shown in Table 1, the students who were paid $1 for performing a counter-attitudinal act—telling another student that a boring task is in fact interesting—wound up liking the task better than did students paid $20 for performing the same act. The simple dependent variable and analysis did the job.

What happens to a person's private opinion if he is forced to do or say something contrary to that opinion? Only recently has there been any experimental work related to this question. Two studies reported by Janis and King (1954; 1956) clearly showed that, at least under some conditions, the private opinion changes so as to bring it into closer correspondence with the overt behavior the person was forced to per-

Reprinted from the *Journal of Abnormal and Social Psychology*, 1959, *58*, pp. 203–210. Copyright 1959 by the American Psychological Association. Reprinted by permission of publisher and authors.

form. Specifically, they showed that if a person is forced to improvise a speech supporting a point of view with which he disagrees, his private opinion moves toward the position advocated in the speech. The observed opinion change is greater than for persons who only hear the speech or for persons who read a prepared speech with emphasis solely on elocution and manner of delivery. The authors of these two studies explain their results mainly in terms of mental rehearsal and thinking up new arguments. In this way, they propose, the person who is forced to improvise a speech convinces himself. They present some evidence, which is not altogether conclusive, in support of this explanation. We will have more to say concerning this explanation in discussing the results of our experiment.

Kelman (1953) tried to pursue the matter further. He reasoned that if the person is induced to make an overt statement contrary to his private opinion by the offer of some reward, then the greater the reward offered, the greater should be the subsequent opinion change. His data, however, did not support this idea. He found, rather, that a large reward produced less subsequent opinion change than did a smaller reward. Actually, this finding by Kelman is consistent with the theory we will outline below but, for a number of reasons, is not conclusive. One of the major weaknesses of the data is that not all subjects in the experiment made an overt statement contrary to their private opinion in order to obtain the offered reward. What is more, as one might expect, the percentage of subjects who complied increased as the size of the offered reward increased. Thus, with self-selection of who did and who did not make the required overt statement and with varying percentages of subjects in the different conditions who did make the required statement, no interpretation of the data can be unequivocal.

Recently, Festinger (1957) proposed a theory concerning cognitive dissonance from which come a number of derivations about opinion change following forced compliance. Since these derivations are stated in detail by Festinger (1957, Ch. 4), we will here give only a brief outline of the reasoning.

Let us consider a person who privately holds opinion "X" but has, as a result of pressure brought to bear on him, publicly stated that he believes "not X."

1. This person has two cognitions which, psychologically, do not fit together: one of these is the knowledge that he believes "X," the other the knowledge that he has publicly stated that he believes "not X." If no factors other than his private opinion are considered, it would follow, at least in our culture, that if he believes "X" he would publicly state "X." Hence, his cognition of his private belief is dissonant with his cognition concerning his actual public statement.

2. Similarly, the knowledge that he has said "not X" is consonant with (does fit together with) those cognitive elements corresponding to the reasons, pressures, promises of rewards and/or threats of punishment which induced him to say "not X."

3. In evaluating the total magnitude of dissonance, one must take account of both dissonances and consonances. Let us think of the sum of all the dissonances involving some particular cognition as "D" and the sum of all the consonances as "C." Then we might think of the total magnitude of dissonance as being a function of "D" divided by "D" plus "C."

Let us then see what can be said about the total magnitude of dissonance in a person created by the knowledge that he said "not X" and really believes "X." With everything else held constant, this total magnitude of dissonance would decrease as the number and importance of the pressures which induced him to say "not X" increased.

Thus, if the overt behavior was brought about by, say, offers of reward or threats of punishment, the magnitude of dissonance is maximal if these promised rewards or threatened punishments were just barely sufficient to induce the person to say "not X." From this point on, as the promised rewards or threatened punishment become larger, the magnitude of dissonance becomes smaller.

4. One way in which the dissonance can be reduced is for the person to change his private opinion so as to bring it into correspondence with what he has said. One would consequently expect to observe such opinion change after a person has been forced or induced to say something contrary to his private opinion. Furthermore, since the pressure to reduce dissonance will be a function of the magnitude of the dissonance, the observed opinion change should be greatest when the pressure used to elicit the overt behavior is just sufficient to do it.

The present experiment was designed to test this derivation under controlled, laboratory conditions. In the experiment we varied the amount of reward used to force persons to make a statement contrary to their private views. The prediction [from 3 and 4 above] is that the larger the reward given to the subject, the smaller will be the subsequent opinion change.

PROCEDURE

Seventy-one male students in the introductory psychology course at Stanford University were used in the experiment. In this course, students are required to spend a certain number of hours as subjects (Ss) in experiments. They choose among the available experiments by signing their names on a sheet posted on the bulletin board which states the nature of the experiment. The present experiment was listed as a two-hour experiment dealing with "Measures of Performance."

During the first week of the course, when the requirement of serving in experiments was announced and explained to the students, the instructor also told them about a study that the psychology department was conducting. He explained that, since they were required to serve in experiments, the department was conducting a study to evaluate these experiments in order to be able to improve them in the future. They were told that a sample of students would be interviewed after having served as Ss. They were urged to cooperate in these interviews by being completely frank and honest. The importance of this announcement will become clear shortly. It enabled us to measure the opinions of our Ss in a context not directly connected with our experiment and in which we could reasonably expect frank and honest expressions of opinion.

When the S arrived for the experiment on "Measures of Performance" he had to wait for a few minutes in the secretary's office. The experimenter (E) then came in, introduced himself to the S and, together, they walked into the laboratory room where the E said:

This experiment usually takes a little over an hour but, of course, we had to schedule it for two hours. Since we have that extra time, the introductory psychology people asked if they

could interview some of our subjects. [Offhand and conversationally.] Did they announce that in class? I gather that they're interviewing some people who have been in experiments. I don't know much about it. Anyhow, they may want to interview you when you're through here.

With no further introduction or explanation the S was shown the first task, which involved putting 12 spools onto a tray, emptying the tray, refilling it with spools, and so on. He was told to use one hand and to work at his own speed. He did this for one-half hour. The E then removed the tray and spools and placed in front of the S a board containing 48 square pegs. His task was to turn each peg a quarter turn clockwise, then another quarter turn, and so on. He was told again to use one hand and to work at his own speed. The S worked at this task for another half hour.

While the S was working on these tasks, the E sat, with a stop watch in his hand, busily making notations on a sheet of paper. He did so in order to make it convincing that this was what the E was interested in and that these tasks, and how the S worked on them, was the total experiment. From our point of view the experiment had hardly started. The hour which the S spent working on the repetitive, monotonous tasks was intended to provide, for each S uniformly, an experience about which he would have a somewhat negative opinion.

After the half hour on the second task was over, the E conspicuously set the stop watch back to zero, put it away, pushed his chair back, lit a cigarette, and said:

O.K. Well, that's all we have in the experiment itself. I'd like to explain what this has been all about so you'll have some idea of why you were doing this. [E pauses.] Well, the way the experiment is set up is this. There are actually two groups in the experiment. In one, the group you were in, we bring the subject in and give him essentially no introduction to the experiment. That is, all we tell him is what he needs to know in order to do the tasks, and he has no idea of what the experiment is all about, or what it's going to be like, or anything like that. But in the other group, we have a student that we've hired that works for us regularly, and what I do is take him into the next room where the subject is waiting—

the same room you were waiting in before—and I introduce him as if he had just finished being a subject in the experiment. That is, I say: "This is so-and-so, who's just finished the experiment, and I've asked him to tell you a little of what it's about before you start." The fellow who works for us then, in conversation with the next subject, makes these points: [The E then produced a sheet headed "For Group B" which had written on it: It was very enjoyable, I had a lot of fun, I enjoyed myself, it was very interesting, it was intriguing, it was exciting. The E showed this to the S and then proceeded with his false explanation of the purpose of the experiment.] Now, of course, we have this student do this, because if the experimenter does it, it doesn't look as realistic, and what we're interested in doing is comparing how these two groups do on the experiment—the one with this previous expectation about the experiment, and the other, like yourself, with essentially none.

Up to this point the procedure was identical for Ss in all conditions. From this point on they diverged somewhat. Three conditions were run, Control, One Dollar, and Twenty Dollars, as follows:

Control Condition

The E continued:

Is that fairly clear? [Pause.] Look, that fellow [looks at watch] I was telling you about from the introductory psychology class said he would get here a couple of minutes from now. Would you mind waiting to see if he wants to talk to you? Fine. Why don't we go into the other room to wait? [The E left the S in the secretary's office for four minutes. He then returned and said:] O.K. Let's check and see if he does want to talk to you.

One and Twenty Dollar Conditions

The E continued:

Is that fairly clear how it is set up and what we're trying to do? [Pause.] Now, I also have a sort of strange thing to ask you. The thing is this. [Long pause, some confusion and uncertainty in the following, with a degree of embarrassment on the part of the E. The manner of the E contrasted strongly with the preceding un-

hesitant and assured false explanation of the experiment. The point was to make it seem to the S that this was the first time the E had done this and that he felt unsure of himself.] The fellow who normally does this for us couldn't do it today—he just phoned in, and something or other came up for him—so we've been looking around for someone that we could hire to do it for us. You see, we've got another subject waiting [looks at watch] who is supposed to be in that other condition. Now Professor———, who is in charge of this experiment, suggested that perhaps we could take a chance on your doing it for us. I'll tell you what we had in mind: the thing is, if you could do it for us now, then of course you would know how to do it, and if something like this should ever come up again, that is, the regular fellow couldn't make it, and we had a subject scheduled, it would be very reassuring to us to know that we had somebody else we could call on who knew how to do it. So, if you would be willing to do this for us, we'd like to hire you to do it now and then be on call in the future, if something like this should ever happen again. We can pay you a dollar (twenty dollars) for doing this for us, that is, for doing it now and then being on call. Do you think you could do that for us?

If the S hesitated, the E said things like, "It will only take a few minutes," "The regular person is pretty reliable; this is the first time he has missed," or "If we needed you we could phone you a day or two in advance; if you couldn't make it, of course, we wouldn't expect you to come." After the S agreed to do it, the E gave him the previously mentioned sheet of paper headed "For Group B" and asked him to read it through again. The E then paid the S one dollar (twenty dollars), made out a hand-written receipt form, and asked the S to sign it. He then said:

O.K., the way we'll do it is this. As I said, the next subject should be here by now. I think the next one is a girl. I'll take you into the next room and introduce you to her, saying that you've just finished the experiment and that we've asked you to tell her a little about it. And what we want you to do is just sit down and get into a conversation with her and try to get across the points on that sheet of paper. I'll leave you alone and come back after a couple of minutes. O.K.?

The E then took the S into the secretary's office where he had previously waited and where the next S was waiting. (The secretary had left the office.) He introduced the girl and the S to one another saying that the S had just finished the experiment and would tell her something about it. He then left saying he would return in a couple of minutes. The girl, an undergraduate hired for this role, said little until the S made some positive remarks about the experiment and then said that she was surprised because a friend of hers had taken the experiment the week before and had told her that it was boring and that she ought to try to get out of it. Most Ss responded by saying something like "Oh, no, it's really very interesting. I'm sure you'll enjoy it." The girl listened quietly after this, accepting and agreeing to everything the S told her. The discussion between the S and the girl was recorded on a hidden tape recorder.

After two minutes the E returned, asked the girl to go into the experimental room, thanked the S for talking to the girl, wrote down his phone number to continue the fiction that we might call on him again in the future and then said: "Look, could we check and see if that fellow from introductory psychology wants to talk to you?"

From this point on, the procedure for all three conditions was once more identical. As the E and the S started to walk to the office where the interviewer was, the E said: "Thanks very much for working on those tasks for us. I hope you did enjoy it. Most of our subjects tell us afterward that they found it quite interesting. You get a chance to see how you react to the tasks and so forth." This short persuasive communication was made in all conditions in exactly the same way. The reason for doing it, theoretically, was to make it easier for anyone who wanted to persuade himself that the tasks had been, indeed, enjoyable.

When they arrived at the interviewer's office, the E asked the interviewer whether or not he wanted to talk to the S. The interviewer said yes, the E shook hands with the S, said good-bye, and left. The interviewer, of course, was always kept in complete ignorance of which condition the S was in. The interview consisted of four questions, on each of which the S was first encouraged to talk about the matter and was then asked to rate his opinion or reaction on an 11-point scale. The questions are as follows:

1. Were the tasks interesting and enjoyable? In what way? In what way were they not? Would you rate how you feel about them on a scale from -5 to $+5$ where -5 means they were extremely dull and boring, $+5$ means they were extremely interesting and enjoyable, and zero means they were neutral, neither interesting nor uninteresting.
2. Did the experiment give you an opportunity to learn about your own ability to perform these tasks? In what way? In what way not? Would you rate how you feel about this on a scale from 0 to 10 where 0 means you learned nothing and 10 means you learned a great deal.
3. From what you know about the experiment and the tasks involved in it, would you say the experiment was measuring anything important? That is, do you think the results may have scientific value? In what way? In what way not? Would you rate your opinion on this matter on a scale from 0 to 10 where 0 means the results have no scientific value or importance and 10 means they have a great deal of value and importance.
4. Would you have any desire to participate in another similar experiment? Why? Why not? Would you rate your desire to participate in a similar experiment again on a scale from -5 to $+5$, where -5 means you would definitely dislike to participate, $+5$ means you would definitely like to participate, and 0 means you have no particular feeling about it one way or the other.

As may be seen, the questions varied in how directly relevant they were to what the S had told the girl. This point will be discussed further in connection with the results.

At the close of the interview the S was asked what he thought the experiment was about and, following this, was asked directly whether or not he was suspicious of anything and, if so, what he was suspicious of. When the interview was over, the interviewer brought the S back to the experimental room where the E was waiting together with the girl who had posed as the waiting S. (In the control condition, of course, the girl was not there.) The true purpose of the experiment was then explained to the S in detail, and the reasons for each of the various steps in the experiment were explained carefully in relation to the true purpose. All experimental Ss in both One Dollar and Twenty Dollar conditions were asked, after this explanation, to return the money they had been given. All Ss, without exception, were quite willing to return the money.

The data from 11 of the 71 Ss in the experiment had to be discarded for the following reasons:

1. Five Ss (three in the One Dollar and two in the Twenty Dollar condition) indicated in the interview that they were suspicious about having been paid to tell the girl the experiment was fun and suspected that that was the real purpose of the experiment.
2. Two Ss (both in the One Dollar condition) told the girl that they had been hired, that the experiment was really boring but they were supposed to say it was fun.
3. Three Ss (one in the One Dollar and two in the Twenty Dollar condition) refused to take the money and refused to be hired.
4. One S (in the One Dollar condition), immediately after having talked to the girl, demanded her phone number saying he would call her and explain things, and also told the E he wanted to wait until she was finished so he could tell her about it.

These 11 Ss were, of course, run through the total experiment anyhow and the experiment was explained to them afterwards. Their data, however, are not included in the analysis.

Summary of Design

There remain, for analysis, 20 Ss in each of the three conditions. Let us review these briefly: 1. *Control condition.* These Ss were treated identically in all respects to the Ss in the experimental conditions, except that they were never asked to, and never did, tell the waiting girl that the experimental tasks were enjoyable and lots of fun. 2. *One Dollar condition.* These Ss were hired for one dollar to tell a waiting S that tasks, which were really rather dull and boring, were interesting, enjoyable, and lots of fun. 3. *Twenty Dollar condition.* These

Ss were hired for twenty dollars to do the same thing.

RESULTS

The major results of the experiment are summarized in Table 1 which lists, separately for each of the three experimental conditions, the average rating which the Ss gave at the end of each question on the interview. We will discuss each of the questions on the interview separately, because they were intended to measure different things. One other point before we proceed to examine the data. In all the comparisons, the Control condition should be regarded as a baseline from which to evaluate the results in the other two conditions. The Control condition gives us, essentially, the reactions of Ss to the tasks and their opinions about the experiment as falsely explained to them, without the experimental introduction of dissonance. The data from the other conditions may be viewed, in a sense, as changes from this baseline.

How Enjoyable the Tasks Were

The average ratings on this question, presented in the first row of figures in Table 1,

Table 1 Average Ratings on Interview Questions for Each Condition

	Experimental Condition		
Question on Interview	Control (N = 20)	One Dollar (N = 20)	Twenty Dollars (N = 20)
How enjoyable tasks were (rated from −5 to +5)	−.45	+1.35	−.05
How much they learned (rated from 0 to 10)	3.08	2.80	3.15
Scientific importance (rated from 0 to 10)	5.60	6.45	5.18
Participate in similar exp. (rated from −5 to +5)	−.62	+1.20	−.25

are the results most important to the experiment. These results are the ones most directly relevant to the specific dissonance which was experimentally created. It will be recalled that the tasks were purposely arranged to be rather boring and monotonous. And, indeed, in the Control condition the average rating was −.45, somewhat on the negative side of the neutral point.

In the other two conditions, however, the Ss told someone that these tasks were interesting and enjoyable. The resulting dissonance could, of course, most directly be reduced by persuading themselves that the tasks were, indeed, interesting and enjoyable. In the One Dollar condition, since the magnitude of dissonance was high, the pressure to reduce this dissonance would also be high. In this condition, the average rating was +1.35, considerably on the positive side and significantly different from the Control condition at the .02 level[1] ($t = 2.48$).

In the Twenty Dollar condition, where less dissonance was created experimentally because of the greater importance of the consonant relations, there is correspondingly less evidence of dissonance reduction. The average rating in this condition is only −.05, slightly and not significantly higher than the Control condition. The difference between the One Dollar and Twenty Dollar conditions is significant at the .03 level ($t = 2.22$). In short, when an S was induced, by offer of reward, to say something contrary to his private opinion, this private opinion tended to change so as to correspond more closely with what he had said. The greater the reward offered (beyond what was necessary to elicit the behavior) the smaller was the effect.

Desire to Participate in a Similar Experiment

The results from this question are shown in the last row of Table 1. This question is less directly related to the dissonance that was experimentally created for the Ss. Certainly, the more interesting and enjoyable they felt the tasks were, the greater would be their desire

---

[1] All statistical tests referred to in this paper are two-tailed.

to participate in a similar experiment. But other factors would enter also. Hence, one would expect the results on this question to be very similar to the results on "how enjoyable the tasks were" but weaker. Actually, the results, as may be seen in the table, are in exactly the same direction, and the magnitude of the mean differences is fully as large as on the first question. The variability is greater, however, and the differences do not yield high levels of statistical significance. The difference between the One Dollar condition (+1.20) and the Control condition (−.62) is significant at the .08 level ($t = 1.78$). The difference between the One Dollar condition and the Twenty Dollar condition (−.25) reaches only the .15 level of significance ($t = 1.46$).

The Scientific Importance of the Experiment

This question was included because there was a chance that differences might emerge. There are, after all, other ways in which the experimentally created dissonance could be reduced. For example, one way would be for the S to magnify for himself the value of the reward he obtained. This, however, was unlikely in this experiment because money was used for the reward and it is undoubtedly difficult to convince oneself that one dollar is more than it really is. There is another possible way, however. The Ss were given a very good reason, in addition to being paid, for saying what they did to the waiting girl. The Ss were told it was necessary for the experiment. The dissonance could, consequently, be reduced by magnifying the importance of this cognition. The more scientifically important they considered the experiment to be, the less was the total magnitude of dissonance. It is possible, then, that the results on this question, shown in the third row of figures in Table 1, might reflect dissonance reduction.

The results are weakly in line with what one would expect if the dissonance were somewhat reduced in this manner. The One Dollar condition is higher than the other two. The difference between the One and Twenty Dollar conditions reaches the .08 level of significance on a two-tailed test ($t = 1.79$). The difference between the One Dollar and Control conditions is not impressive at all ($t = 1.21$). The result that the Twenty Dollar condition is actually lower than the Control condition is undoubtedly a matter of chance ($t = 0.58$).

How Much They Learned From the Experiment

The results on this question are shown in the second row of figures in Table 1. The question was included because, as far as we could see, it had nothing to do with the dissonance that was experimentally created and could not be used for dissonance reduction. One would then expect no differences at all among the three conditions. We felt it was important to show that the effect was not a completely general one but was specific to the content of the dissonance which was created. As can be readily seen in Table 1, there are only negligible differences among conditions. The highest t value for any of these differences is only 0.48.

DISCUSSION OF A POSSIBLE ALTERNATIVE EXPLANATION

We mentioned in the introduction that Janis and King (1954; 1956) in explaining their findings, proposed an explanation in terms of the self-convincing effect of mental rehearsal and thinking up new arguments by the person who had to improvise a speech. Kelman (1953), in the previously mentioned study, in attempting to explain the unexpected finding that the persons who complied in the moderate reward condition changed their opinion more than in the high reward condition, also proposed the same kind of explanation. If the results of our experiment are to be taken as strong corroboration of the theory of cognitive dissonance, this possible alternative explanation must be dealt with.

Specifically, as applied to our results, this alternative explanation would maintain that perhaps, for some reason, the Ss in the One Dollar condition worked harder at telling the waiting girl that the tasks were fun and enjoyable. That is, in the One Dollar condition they may have rehearsed it more mentally, thought

up more ways of saying it, may have said it more convincingly, and so on. Why this might have been the case is, of course, not immediately apparent. One might expect that, in the Twenty Dollar condition, having been paid more, they would try to do a better job of it than in the One Dollar condition. But nevertheless, the possibility exists that the Ss in the One Dollar condition may have improvised more.

Because of the desirability of investigating this possible alternative explanation, we recorded on a tape recorder the conversation between each S and the girl. These recordings were transcribed and then rated, by two independent raters, on five dimensions. The ratings were, of course done in ignorance of which condition each S was in. The reliabilities of these ratings, that is, the correlations between the two independent raters, ranged from .61 to .88, with an average reliability of .71. The five ratings were:

1. The content of what the S said *before* the girl made the remark that her friend told her it was boring. The stronger the S's positive statements about the tasks, and the more ways in which he said they were interesting and enjoyable, the higher the rating.
2. The content of what the S said *after* the girl made the above-mentioned remark. This was rated in the same way as for the content before the remark.
3. A similar rating of the over-all content of what the S said.
4. A rating of how persuasive and convincing the S was in what he said and the way in which he said it.
5. A rating of the amount of time in the discussion that the S spent discussing the tasks as opposed to going off into irrelevant things.

The mean ratings for the One Dollar and Twenty Dollar conditions, averaging the ratings of the two independent raters, are presented in Table 2. It is clear from examining the table that, in all cases, the Twenty Dollar condition is slightly higher. The differences are small, however, and only on the rating of "amount of time" does the difference between the two conditions even approach significance. We are certainly justified in concluding that

Table 2 Average Ratings of Discussion Between Subject and Girl

	Condition		
Dimension Rated	*One Dollar*	*Twenty Dollars*	*Value of* t
Content before remark by girl (rated from 0 to 5)	2.26	2.62	1.08
Content after remark by girl (rated from 0 to 5)	1.63	1.75	0.11
Over-all content (rated from 0 to 5)	1.89	2.19	1.08
Persuasiveness and conviction (rated from 0 to 10)	4.79	5.50	0.99
Time spent on topic (rated from 0 to 10)	6.74	8.19	1.80

the Ss in the One Dollar condition did not improvise more nor act more convincingly. Hence, the alternative explanation discussed above cannot account for the findings.

SUMMARY

Recently, Festinger (1957) has proposed a theory concerning cognitive dissonance. Two derivations from this theory are tested here. These are:

1. If a person is induced to do or say something which is contrary to his private opinion, there will be a tendency for him to change his opinion so as to bring it into correspondence with what he has done or said.

2. The larger the pressure used to elicit the overt behavior (beyond the minimum needed to elicit it) the weaker will be the above-mentioned tendency.

A laboratory experiment was designed to test these derivations. Subjects were subjected to a boring experience and then paid to tell someone that the experience had been interesting and enjoyable. The amount of money paid the subject was varied. The private opinions of the subjects concerning the experiences were then determined.

The results strongly corroborate the theory that was tested.

REFERENCES

Festinger, L. *A theory of cognitive dissonance.* Evanston, Ill: Row Peterson, 1957.

Janis, I. L., & King, B. T. The influence of role-playing on opinion change. *Journal of Abnormal and Social Psychology*, 1954, *49*, 211–218.

Kelman, H. Attitude change as a function of response restriction. *Human Relations*, 1953, *6*, 185–214.

King, B. T., & Janis, I. L. Comparison of the effectiveness of improvised versus non-improvised role-playing in producing opinion changes. *Human Relations*, 1956, *9*, 177–186.

7

Effects of Fear-Arousing Communications

Irving L. Janis and Seymour Feshbach

This study tests a counter-intuitive idea derived from psychodynamic theory—that the more fear a mass communication arouses, the less successful it will be in producing attitude or behavioral change. The idea is that more frightening communications arouse too much anxiety, and so lead to avoidance and inattentiveness. The study itself attempts to present subjects with a situation much like that they encounter when exposed to real-life mass communications—that is, it presents them with "mundane realism." The independent variable is a relatively simple manipulation of fear-arousing content in a mass communication. But the authors measure a number of different dimensions of subjects' response other than simply their conformity to the recommendations of the communication, in an effort to obtain a refined portrait of their responses, with direct evidence about the psychological process it evoked. The main finding is, then, that high fear produced less conformity to the recommendations of the communication (Table 6) and less protection against later counter-propaganda (Table 7), despite inspiring more worry (Tables 2 and 3) and being appraised more favorably (Table 4). The reason, presumably, is that the high fear communication inspired more avoidance (Table 8) because of its gruesome content.

It is generally recognized that when beliefs and attitudes are modified, learning processes are involved in which motivational factors play a primary role. Symbols in mass communications can be manipulated in a variety of ways so as to arouse socially acquired motives such as need for achievement, group conformity, power-seeking, and the more emotion-laden drives arising from aggression, sympathy, guilt, and anxiety.

The present experiment was designed to study the effects of one particular type of motive-incentive variable in persuasive communications, namely, the arousal of fear or anxiety by depicting potential dangers to which the audience might be exposed. Fear appeals of this sort are frequently used to influence attitudes and behavior. For example, medical au-

thorities sometimes try to persuade people to visit cancer detection clinics by pointing to the dangerous consequences of failing to detect the early symptoms of cancer; various political groups play up the threat of war or totalitarianism in an attempt to motivate adherence to their political program. Our interest in such attempts is primarily that of determining the conditions under which the arousal of fear is effective or ineffective in eliciting changes in beliefs, practices, and attitudes.

Implicit in the use of fear appeals is the assumption that when emotional tension is aroused, the audience will become more highly motivated to accept the reassuring beliefs or recommendations advocated by the communicator. But the tendency to accept reassuring ideas about ways and means of warding off anticipated danger may not always be the dominant reaction to a fear-arousing communication. Under certain conditions, other types of

Reprinted from the *Journal of Abnormal and Social Psychology,* 1953, *48,* pp. 78–92. Copyright 1953 by the American Psychological Association. Reprinted by permission of publisher and authors.

defensive reactions may occur which could give rise to highly undesirable effects from the standpoint of the communicator.

Clinical studies based on patients' reactions to psychiatric treatment call attention to three main types of emotional interference which can prevent a person from being influenced by verbal communications which deal with anxiety-arousing topics.

1. When a communication touches off intense feelings of anxiety, communicatees will sometimes fail to pay attention to what is being said. Inattentiveness may be a motivated effort to avoid thoughts which evoke incipient feelings of anxiety. This defensive tendency may be manifested by overt attempts to change the subject of conversation to a less disturbing topic. When such attempts fail and anxiety mounts to a very high level, attention disturbances may become much more severe, e.g., "inability to concentrate," "distractibility," or other symptoms of the cognitive disorganization temporarily produced by high emotional tension (4).

2. When exposed to an anxiety-arousing communication, communicatees will occasionally react to the unpleasant ("punishing") experience by becoming aggressive toward the communicator. If the communicator is perceived as being responsible for producing painful feelings, aggression is likely to take the form of rejecting his statements.

3. If a communication succeeds in arousing intense anxiety and if the communicatee's emotional tension is not readily reduced either by the reassurances contained in the communication or by self-delivered reassurances, the residual emotional tension may motivate defensive avoidances, i.e., attempts to ward off subsequent exposures to the anxiety-arousing content. The experience of being temporarily unable to terminate the disturbing affective state elicited by a discussion of a potential threat can give rise to a powerful incentive to avoid thinking or hearing about it again; this may ultimately result in failing to recall what the communicator said, losing interest in the topic, denying or minimizing the importance of the threat.

The above reaction tendencies, while formulated in general terms, take account of three specific types of behavior observed during psychoanalytic or psychotherapeutic sessions (1, 2, 3). The first two refer to immediate reactions that often occur when a therapist gives an interpretation which brings anxiety-laden thoughts or motives into the patient's focus of awareness: (a) attention disturbances, blocking of associations, mishearing, evasiveness, and similar forms of "resistance"; and (b) argumentativeness, defiance, contempt, and other manifestations of reactive hostility directed toward the therapist. The third refers to certain types of subsequent "resistance," displayed during the later course of treatment, as a carry-over effect of the therapist's disturbing comments or interpretations.

Although the three types of defensive behavior have been observed primarily in clinical studies of psychoneurotic patients (whose anxiety reactions are generally linked with unconscious conflicts), it seems probable that similar reactions may occur among normal persons during or after exposure to communications which make them acutely aware of severe threats of external danger. Nevertheless, it remains an open question whether such sources of emotional interference play any significant role in determining the net effectiveness of fear-arousing material in mass communications, especially when the communications are presented in an impersonal social setting where emotional responses of the audience are likely to be greatly attenuated.

The present experiment was designed to investigate the consequences of using fear appeals in persuasive communications that are presented in an impersonal group situation. One of the main purposes was to explore the potentially adverse effects which might result from defensive reactions of the sort previously noted in the more restricted situation of psychotherapy.

METHOD

The experiment was designed so as to provide measures of the effects of three different intensities of "fear appeal" in a standard communication on dental hygiene, presented to high school students. The influence of the fear-arousing material was investigated by means of a series of questionnaires which provided data on emotional reactions to the communication and on changes in dental hygiene beliefs, practices, and attitudes.

The Three Forms of Communication

A 15-minute illustrated lecture was prepared in three different forms, all of which contained the same essential information about causes of tooth decay and the same series of recommendations concerning oral hygiene practices. The three (recorded) lectures were of approximately equal length and were delivered in a standard manner by the same speaker. Each recording was supplemented by about 20 slides, which were shown on the screen in a prearranged sequence, to illustrate various points made by the speaker.

The three forms of the illustrated talk differed only with respect to the amount of fear-arousing material presented. Form 1 contained a strong fear appeal, emphasizing the painful consequences of tooth decay, diseased gums, and other dangers that can result from improper dental hygiene. Form 2 presented a moderate appeal in which the dangers were described in a milder and more factual manner. Form 3 presented a minimal appeal which rarely alluded to the consequences of tooth neglect. In Form 3, most of the fear-arousing material was replaced by relatively neutral information dealing with the growth and functions of the teeth. In all other respects, however, Form 3 was identical with Forms 1 and 2.

The fear appeals were designed to represent typical characteristics of mass communications which attempt to stimulate emotional reactions in order to motivate the audience to conform to a set of recommendations. The main technique was that of calling attention to the potential dangers that can ensue from nonconformity. For example, the Strong appeal contained such statements as the following:

If you ever develop an infection of this kind from improper care of your teeth, it will be an extremely serious matter because these infections are really dangerous. They can spread to your eyes, or your heart, or your joints and cause secondary infections which may lead to diseases such as arthritic paralysis, kidney damage, or total blindness.

One of the main characteristics of the Strong appeal was the use of personalized threat-references explicitly directed to the audience, i.e., statements to the effect that "this can happen to you." The Moderate appeal, on the other hand, described the dangerous consequences of improper oral hygiene in a more factual way, using impersonal language. In the Minimal appeal, the limited discussion of unfavorable consequences also used a purely factual style.

The major differences in content are summarized in Table 1, which is based on a systematic content analysis of the three recorded lectures. The data in this table show how often each type of "threat" was mentioned. It is apparent that the main difference between the Strong appeal and the Moderate appeal was

Table 1 Content Analysis of the Three Forms of the Communication: References to Consequences of Improper Care of the Teeth

Type of Reference	Form 1 (Strong Appeal)	Form 2 (Moderate Appeal)	Form 3 (Minimal Appeal)
Pain from toothaches	11	1	0
Cancer, paralysis, blindness or other secondary diseases	6	0	0
Having teeth pulled, cavities drilled, or other painful dental work	9	1	0
Having cavities filled or having to go to the dentist	0	5	1
Mouth infections: sore, swollen, inflamed gums	18	16	2
Ugly or discolored teeth	4	2	0
"Decayed" teeth	14	12	6
"Cavities"	9	12	9
Total references to unfavorable consequences	71	49	18

not so much in the total frequency of threat references as in the variety and types of threats that were emphasized. The Minimal appeal, however, differed markedly from the other two in that it contained relatively few threat references, almost all of which were restricted to "cavities" or "tooth decay."

One of the reasons for selecting dental hygiene as a suitable topic for investigating the influence of fear appeals was precisely because discussions of this topic readily lend themselves to quantitative and qualitative variations of the sort shown in Table 1. Moreover, because of the nature of the potential dangers that are referred to, one could reasonably expect the audience to be fairly responsive to such variations in content—the teeth and gums probably represent an important component in the average person's body image, and, according to psychoanalytic observations, the threat of damage to the teeth and gums can sometimes evoke deep-seated anxieties concerning body integrity. In any case, by playing up the threat of pain, disease, and body damage, the material introduced in Form 1 is probably representative of the more extreme forms of fear appeals currently to be found in persuasive communications presented via the press, radio, television, and other mass media.

The fear appeals did not rely exclusively upon verbal material to convey the threatening consequences of nonconformity. In Form 1, the slides used to illustrate the lecture included a series of eleven highly realistic photographs which vividly portrayed tooth decay and mouth infections. Form 2, the Moderate appeal, included nine photographs which were milder examples of oral pathology than those used in Form 1. In Form 3, however, no realistic photographs of this kind were presented: X-ray pictures, diagrams of cavities, and photographs of completely healthy teeth were substituted for the photographs of oral pathology.

Subjects

The entire freshman class of a large Connecticut high school was divided into four groups on a random basis. Each of the three

forms of the communication was given to a separate experimental group; the fourth group was used as a control group and was exposed to a similar communication on a completely different topic (the structure and functioning of the human eye). Altogether there were 200 students in the experiment, with 50 in each group.

The four groups were well equated with respect to age, sex, educational level, and IQ. The mean age for each group was approximately 15 years and there were roughly equal numbers of boys and girls in each group. The mean and standard deviation of IQ scores, as measured by the Otis group test, were almost identical in all four groups.

Administration of the Questionnaires

The first questionnaire, given one week before the communication, was represented to the students as a general health survey of high school students. The key questions dealing with dental hygiene were interspersed among questions dealing with many other aspects of health and hygiene.

One week later the illustrated talks were given as part of the school's hygiene program. Immediately after the end of the communication, the students in each group were asked to fill out a short questionnaire designed to provide data on immediate effects of the communication, such as the amount of information acquired, attitudes toward the communication, and emotional reactions. A follow-up questionnaire was given one week later in order to ascertain the carry-over effects of the different forms of the communication.

RESULTS

Affective Reactions

Evidence that the three forms of the illustrated talk differed with respect to the amount of emotional tension evoked during the communication is presented in Table 2. Immediately after exposure to the communication, the students were asked three questions concerning the feelings they had just experienced

Table 2 Feelings of Worry or Concern Evoked During the Communication

Questionnaire Responses	Strong Group (N = 50)	Moderate Group (N = 50)	Minimal Group (N = 50)
Felt worried—a "few times" or "many times"—about own mouth condition	74%	60%	48%
Felt "somewhat" or "very" worried about improper care of own teeth	66%	36%	34%
Thought about condition of own teeth "most of the time"	42%	34%	22%

"while the illustrated talk was being given." Their responses indicate that the fear stimuli were successful in arousing affective reactions. On each of the three questionnaire items shown in the table, the difference between the Strong group and the Minimal group is reliable at beyond the .05 confidence level.[1] The Moderate group consistently falls in an intermediate position but does not, in most instances, differ significantly from the other two groups.

Further evidence of the effectiveness of the fear-arousing material was obtained from responses to the following two questions, each of which had a checklist of five answer categories ranging from "Very worried" to "Not at all worried":

1. When you think about the possibility that you might develop diseased gums, how concerned or worried do you feel about it?

2. When you think about the possibility that you might developed decayed teeth, how concerned or worried do you feel about it? Since these questions made no reference to the illustrated talk, it was feasible to include them in the pre- and postcommunication questionnaires given to all four groups.

---

[1] All probability values reported in this paper are based on one tail of the theoretical distribution, since the results were used to test specific hypotheses which predict the direction of the differences.

Systematic comparisons were made in terms of the percentage in each group who reported relatively high disturbance (i.e., "somewhat" or "very worried") in response to both questions. The results, presented in Table 3, show a marked increase in affective disturbance among each of the three experimental groups, as compared with the control group. Paralleling the results in Table 2, the greatest increase is found in the Strong group. The difference between the Moderate and the Minimal groups, however, is insignificant.

In order to obtain an over-all estimate of the relative degree of emotional arousal evoked by the three forms of the communication, a total score was computed for each individual in each experimental group, based on answers to all five questions: two points credit was given to each response specified in Tables 2 and 3 as indicative of high disturbance; one point credit was given to intermediate responses on the checklist; zero credit was given for the last two response categories in each check list, which uniformly designated a relative absence of worry or concern. Hence individual scores ranged from zero to ten. The mean scores for the Strong, Moderate and Minimal groups were 7.8, 6.6, and 5.9 respectively. The Strong group differs reliably at the one per cent confidence level from each of the other two groups ($t = 2.3$ and 3.6). The difference between the Moderate and Minimal groups approaches reliability at the .08 confidence level ($t = 1.4$).

In general, the foregoing evidence indicates that after exposure to the communications, the Strong group felt more worried about the condition of their teeth than did the other two groups; the Moderate group, in turn, tended to feel more worried than the Minimal group.

Information Acquired

Immediately after exposure to the illustrated talk, each experimental group was given an information test consisting of 23 separate items. The test was based on the factual assertions common to all three forms of the communication, including topics such as the anatomical structure of the teeth, the causes of cavities and of gum disease, the "correct" technique of toothbrushing, and the type of toothbrush

Table 3 Percentage of Each Group Who Reported Feeling Somewhat or Very Worried about Decayed Teeth and Diseased Gums

	Strong Group (N = 50)	Moderate Group (N = 50)	Minimal Group (N = 50)	Control Group (N = 50)
One week *before* the communication	34	24	22	30
Immediately after the communication	76	50	46	38
Change	+42%	+26%	+24%	+8%

Table 4 Percentage of Each Group Who Expressed Strongly Favorable Appraisals of the Communication

Appraisal Response	Strong Group (N = 50)	Moderate Group (N = 50)	Minimal Group (N = 50)
The illustrated talk does a very good teaching job.	62	50	40
Most or all of it was interesting.	80	68	64
It was very easy to pay attention to what the speaker was saying.	74	36	50
My mind practically never wandered.	58	46	42
The slides do a very good job.	52	20	22
The speaker's voice was very good.	66	56	58
The illustrated talk definitely should be given to all Connecticut high schools.	74	58	70

recommended by dental authorities. No significant differences were found among the three experimental groups with respect to information test scores. Comparisons with the Control group show that the three forms of the dental hygiene communication were equally effective in teaching the factual material.

Attitude Toward the Communication

The questionnaire given immediately after exposure to the illustrated talk included a series of seven items concerning the students' appraisals of the communication. From the results shown in Table 4, it is apparent that the Strong group responded more favorably than the other two groups.[2]

These findings imply that interest in the communication and acceptance of its educational value were heightened by the Strong appeal. But this conclusion applies only to relatively impersonal, objective ratings of the communication. Additional evidence presented in

Table 5, based on questions which elicited evaluations of a more subjective character, reveals a markedly different attitude toward the communication among those exposed to the Strong appeal.

One of the additional questions was the following: "Was there anything in the illustrated talk on dental hygiene that you disliked?" Unfavorable ("dislike") answers were given by a reliably higher percentage of students in the Strong group than in the Moderate or Minimal

---

[2] The Strong group differs significantly ($p < .05$) from the Minimal group on five of the seven items and from the Moderate group on three items; the Moderate group does *not* differ reliably from the Minimal group on any of the items.

Table 5 Percentage of Each Group Who Expressed Complaints about the Communication

Type of Complaint	Strong Group (N = 50)	Moderate Group (N = 50)	Minimal Group (N = 50)
Disliked something in the illustrated talk.	28	8	2
The slides were too unpleasant ("horrible," "gory," "disgusting," etc.).	34	2	0
There was not enough material on prevention.	20	2	8

groups (first row of Table 5). A tabulation was also made of the total number of students in each group who gave complaints in their answers to either of two open-end questions which asked for criticisms of the illustrated talk. The results on complaints about the unpleasant character of the slides are shown in row two of Table 5; the difference between the Strong group and each of the other two groups is reliable at the .01 confidence level. Similarly, a reliably higher percentage of the Strong group complained about insufficient material on ways and means of preventing tooth and gum disease (row three of Table 5). The latter type of criticism often was accompanied by the suggestion that some of the disturbing material should be eliminated, as is illustrated by the following comments from two students in the Strong group: "Leave out the slides that show the rottiness of the teeth and have more in about how to brush your teeth"; "I don't think you should have shown so many gory pictures without showing more to prevent it." Comments of this sort, together with the data presented in Table 5, provide additional evidence of residual emotional tension. They imply that the Strong appeal created a need for reassurance which persisted after the communication was over, despite the fact that the communication contained a large number of reassuring recommendations.

The apparent inconsistency between the results in Tables 4 and 5 suggests that the Strong appeal evoked a more mixed or ambivalent attitude toward the communication than did the Moderate or Minimal appeals. Some of the comments, particularly about the slides, help to illuminate the differentiation between the individual's *objective* evaluation of the communication and his *subjective* response to it. The following illustrative excerpts from the Strong group were selected from the answers given to the open-end question which asked for criticisms and suggestions:

I did not care for the "gory" illustrations of decayed teeth and diseased mouths but I really think that it did make me feel sure that I did not want this to happen to me.

Some of the pictures went to the extremes but they probably had an effect on most of the people who wouldn't want their teeth to look like that.

I think it is good because it scares people when they see the awful things that can happen.

Such comments not only attest to the motivational impact of the Strong appeal, but also suggest one of the ways in which the discrepancy between subjective and objective evaluations may have been reconciled. In such cases, the ambivalence seems to have been resolved by adopting an attitude to the effect that "this is disagreeable medicine, but it is good for us."

Conformity to Dental Hygiene Recommendations

The immediate effects of the illustrated talks described above show the type of affective reactions evoked by the fear-arousing material but provide little information bearing directly on attitude changes. The questionnaire administered one week later, however, was designed to measure some of the major carry-over effects of fear appeals, particularly with respect to changes in dental hygiene practices, beliefs, and preferences. The results provide an empirical basis for estimating the degree to which such communications succeed in modifying attitudes.

Personal practices were investigated by asking the students to describe the way they were currently brushing their teeth: the type of stroke used, the amount of surface area cleansed, the amount of force applied, the length of time spent on brushing the teeth, and the time of day that the teeth were brushed. The same five questions were asked one week before the communication and again one week after. These questions covered practices about which the following specific recommendations were made in all three forms of the illustrated talk: (*a*) the teeth should be brushed with an up-and-down (vertical) stroke; (*b*) the inner surface of the teeth should be brushed as well as the outer surface; (*c*) the teeth should be brushed gently, using only a slight amount of force; (*d*) in order to cleanse the teeth adequately, one should spend about three minutes on each brushing; (*e*) in the morning, the teeth should be brushed after breakfast (rather than before).

Each student was given a score, ranging from zero to five, which represented the number of recommended practices on which he conformed. Before exposure to the communication, the majority of students in all four groups had very low scores and the group differences were insignificant. By comparing the score that each individual attained one week after the communication with that attained two weeks earlier, it was possible to determine for each group the percentage who changed in the direction of increased or decreased conformity.

The results, shown in Table 6, reveal that the greatest amount of conformity was produced by the communication which contained the least amount of fear-arousing material. The Strong group showed reliably less change than the Minimal group; in fact, the Strong group failed to differ significantly from the Control group, whereas the Minimal group showed a highly reliable increase in conformity as compared with the Control group. The Moderate group falls in an intermediate position, but does not differ reliably from the Strong or Minimal groups. Although there is some ambiguity with respect to the relative effectiveness of the Moderate appeal, the data in Table 6 show a fairly consistent trend which suggests that as the amount of fear-arousing material is increased, conformity tends to decrease. In contrast to the marked increase in conformity produced by the Minimal appeal and the fairly sizable increase produced by the Moderate appeal, the Strong appeal failed to achieve any significant effect whatsoever.

One cannot be certain, of course, that the findings represent changes in overt behavioral conformity, since the observations are based on the Ss' own verbal reports. What remains problematical, however, is whether the verbal responses reflect *only* "lip-service" to the recommendations or whether they also reflect internalized attitudes that were actually carried out in action. The results, nevertheless, demonstrate that the Strong appeal was markedly less effective than the Minimal appeal, at least with respect to eliciting verbal conformity.

Beliefs Concerning the "Proper" Type of Toothbrush

The illustrated talk presented an extensive discussion of the "proper" type of toothbrush recommended by dental authorities. Four main characteristices were emphasized: (*a*) the bristles should be of medium hardness, (*b*) the brush should have three rows of bristles, (*c*) the handle should be completely straight, and (*d*) the brushing surface should be completely straight. Personal beliefs concerning the desirability of these four characteristics were measured by four questions which were included in the precommunication questionnaire as well as in the questionnaire given one week after the communication. The main finding was that all three experimental groups, as compared with the Control group, showed a significant change in the direction of accepting the conclusions presented in the communication. Among the three experimental groups, there were no significant differences with respect to net changes. Nevertheless, as will be seen in the next section, the fear-arousing material appears to have had a considerable effect on the degree to which the students adhered to such

Table 6 Effect of the Illustrated Talk on Conformity to Dental Hygiene Recommendations

Type of Change	Strong Group (N = 50)	Moderate Group (N = 50)	Minimal Group (N = 50)	Control Group (N = 50)
Increased conformity	28%	44%	50%	22%
Decreased conformity	20%	22%	14%	22%
No change	52%	34%	36%	56%
Net change in conformity	+8%	+22%	+36%	0%

beliefs in the face of counteracting propaganda.

Resistance to Counteracting Propaganda

In addition to describing the four essential characteristics of the "proper" toothbrush, the illustrated talk contained numerous comments and illustrations to explain the need for avoiding the "wrong" kind of toothbrush. Much of the material on cavities and other unpleasant consequences of tooth neglect was presented in this context. *The importance of using the proper kind of toothbrush* was the theme that was most heavily emphasized throughout the entire communication.

The key questionnaire item, designed to determine inital attitudes before exposure to the communication, was the following:

Please read the following statement carefully and decide whether you believe it is true or false.

It does not matter what kind of toothbrush a person uses. *Any sort of toothbrush* that is sold in a drugstore will keep your teeth clean and healthy—if you use it regularly.

Do you think that this statement is true or false? (Check One.)

One week after exposure to the communications, the question was asked again, in essentially the same form, with the same checklist of five answer categories (ranging from "Feel certain that it is true" to "Feel certain that it is false"). But in the post-communication questionnaire, the question was preceded by the following propaganda material which contradicted the dominant theme of the illustrated talk:

A well-known dentist recently made the following statement:

Some dentists, including a number of so-called "experts" on dental hygiene, claim it is important to use a special type of toothbrush in order to clean the teeth properly. But from my own experience, I believe that there is no sound basis for that idea. My honest opinion, as a dentist, is that it does not matter what kind of toothbrush a person uses. Any sort of toothbrush that is sold in a drugstore will keep your teeth clean and healthy—if you use it regularly.

That this propaganda exposure had a pronounced effect is revealed by the attitude changes shown by the Control group. A statistically reliable change in the direction of more agreement with the counterpropaganda was found in the Control group.

How effective were the three forms of the illustrated talk in preventing students from accepting the propaganda to which they were exposed one week later? Did the fear appeals augment or diminish the students' resistance to the counteracting progaganda? A fairly definite answer emerges from the results in Table 7, which shows the percentage of each group who changed in the direction of agreement or disagreement with the counterpropaganda statement.

Before exposure to the illustrated talk, the group differences were negligible: approximately 50 per cent of the students in each of the four groups agreed with the statement that "it does not matter what kind of toothbrush a person uses." But two weeks later (immediately after exposure to the counterpropaganda) there were marked and statistically reliable differences which indicate that although all three

Table 7 Effect of the Illustrated Talk on Reactions to Subsequent Counterpropaganda: Net Percentage of Each Group Who Changed in the Direction of Agreeing with the Statement that "It Does Not Matter what Kind of Toothbrush a Person Uses"

Type of Change	Strong Group (N = 50)	Moderate Group (N = 50)	Minimal Group (N = 50)	Control Group (N = 50)
More agreement	30	28	14	44
Less agreement	38	42	54	24
No change	32	30	32	32
Net change	−8	−14	−40	+20
Net effect of exposure to the illustrated talk	−28	−34	−60	

Table 8 Types of Refutation Given by Students Who Disagreed with the Counterpropaganda

Type of Refutation	Strong Group (N = 30)	Moderate Group (N = 29)	Minimal Group (N = 39)	Control Group (N = 18)
Explicit reference to the illustrated talk as an authoritative source for the opposite conclusion	7%	14%	18%	0%
One or more arguments cited that had been presented in the illustrated talk	43%	38%	59%	28%
One or more arguments cited that contradicted the content of the illustrated talk	0%	0%	0%	22%
No answer or no specific reason given	50%	52%	36%	50%

forms of the illustrated talk had some influence, the Minimal appeal was most effective in producing resistance to the counterpropaganda. Thus, the results suggest that under conditions where people will be exposed to competing communications dealing with the same issues, the use of a strong fear appeal will tend to be less effective than a minimal appeal in producing stable and persistent attitude changes.

Some clues to mediating processes were detected in the students' responses to an open-end question which asked them to "give the reason" for their answers to the key attitude item on which the results in Table 7 are based. A systematic analysis was made of the write-in answers given by those students who had disagreed with the counterpropaganda. In their refutations, some of the students made use of material that had been presented one week earlier, either by referring to the illustrated talk as an authoritative source or by citing one of the main arguments presented in the illustrated talk. From the results presented in the first two rows of Table 8, it is apparent that such refutations were given more frequently by the Minimal group than by the other experimental groups. The comparatively low frequency of such answers in the Strong and Moderate groups was not compensated for by an increase in any other type of specific reasons, as indicated by the results in the last row of the table.[3]

Although the group differences are not uniformly reliable, they reveal a consistent trend which suggests an "avoidance" tendency among the students who had been exposed to the fear appeals. Apparently, even those who resisted the counterpropaganda were inclined to avoid recalling the content of the fear-arousing communication.

DISCUSSION

The results in the preceding sections indicate that the Minimal appeal was the most effective form of the communication in that it elicited (a) more resistance to subsequent counterpropaganda and (b) a higher incidence of verbal adherence, and perhaps a greater degree of behavioral conformity, to a set of recommended practices. The absence of any significant differences on other indicators of preferences and beliefs implies that the Moderate and Strong appeals had no unique positive effects that would compensate for the observed detrimental effects. Thus, the findings consistently indicate that inclusion of the fear-arousing material not only failed to increase

[3] On the first type of reason (reference to the illustrated talk), the only difference large enough to approach statistical reliability was that between the Minimal group and the Control group ($p = .08$). On the second type of reason (arguments cited from the illustrated talk), the difference between the Minimal group

and the Control group was found to be highly reliable ($p = .03$) while the difference between the Minimal and Moderate groups approached statistical reliability ($p = .08$). The Control group differed reliably from each of the experimental groups (at beyond the .10 confidence level) with respect to giving arguments which contradicted those contained in the illustrated talk (row three of the table). None of the other percentage differences in Table 8 were large enough to be significant at the .10 confidence level. (In some columns, the percentages add up to more than 100 per cent because a few students gave more than one type of refutation.)

the effectiveness of the communication, but actually interfered with its over-all success.

The outcome of the present experiment by no means precludes the possibility that, under certain conditions, fear appeals may prove to be highly successful. For instance, the Strong appeal was found to be maximally effective in arousing interest and in eliciting a high degree of emotional tension. The evocation of such reactions might augment the effectiveness of mass communications which are designed to instigate prompt audience action, such as donating money or volunteering to perform a group task. But if the communication is intended to create more sustained preferences or attitudes, the achievement of positive effects probably depends upon a number of different factors. Our experimental results suggest that in the latter case, a relatively low degree of fear arousal is likely to be the optimal level, that an appeal which is too strong will tend to evoke some form of interference which reduces the effectiveness of the communication. The findings definitely contradict the assumption that as the dosage of fear-arousing stimuli (in a mass communication) is increased, the audience will become more highly motivated to accept the reassuring recommendations contained in the communication. Beneficial motivating effects probably occur when a relatively slight amount of fear-arousing material is inserted; but for communications of the sort used in the present experiment, the optimal dosage appears to be far below the level of the strongest fear appeals that a communicator could use if he chose to do so.

Before examining the implications of the findings in more detail, it is necessary to take account of the problems of generalizing from the findings of the present study. The present experiment shows the effects of only one type of communication, presented in an educational setting to a student audience. Until replications are carried out—using other media, topics, and fear-eliciting stimuli, in a variety of communication settings, with different audiences, etc.— one cannot be certain that the conclusions hold true for other situations. The results from a single experiment are obviously not sufficient for drawing broad generalizations concerning

the entire range of fear-arousing communications which are currently being brought to the focus of public attention. Nor can unreplicated results be relied upon for extracting dependable rubrics that could be applied by educators, editors, public relations experts, propagandists, or other communication specialists who face the practical problems of selecting appropriate appeals for motivating mass audiences.

Nevertheless, the present experiment helps to elucidate the potentially unfavorable effects that may result from mass communications which play up ominous threats, alarming contingencies, or signs of impending danger. For instance, the findings tend to bear out some of the points raised concerning the need for careful pretesting and for other cautions when warnings about the dangers of atomic bombing are presented in civilian defense communications that are intended to prepare the public for coping with wartime emergencies (6). Moreover, despite our inability to specify the range of communications to which our conclusions would apply, we can derive tentative inferences that may have important theoretical implications with respect to the dynamics of "normal" fear reactions.

We turn now to a central question posed by the experimental findings: Why is it that the fear-arousing stimuli resulted in less adherence to recommended practices and less resistance to counterpropaganda? Although our experiment cannot give a definitive answer, it provides some suggestive leads concerning potential sources of emotional interference.

In the introduction, we have described three forms of "resistence" frequently observed in psychotherapy that might also occur among normal personalities exposed to mass communications which evoke strong fear or anxiety: (a) inattentiveness during the communication session, (b) rejection of the communicator's statements motivated by reactive aggression, and (c) subsequent defensive avoidance motivated by residual emotional tension. We shall discuss briefly the pertinent findings from the present experiment with a view to making a preliminary assessment of the importance of each of the three types of interfering reactions.

1. Our results provide no evidence that a

strong fear appeal produces inattentiveness or any form of distraction that would interfere with learning efficiency during the communication session. The three forms of the communication were found to be equally effective in teaching the factual material on dental hygiene, as measured by a comprehensive information test given immediately after exposure to the communication. Beliefs concerning the desirable characteristics of the "proper" type of toothbrush were also acquired equally well. One might even surmise (from the results of Table 4) that the Strong appeal may have had a beneficial effect on attention, because a significantly higher percentage of the Strong group reported that (a) it was very easy to pay attention to what the speaker was saying and (b) they experienced very little "mind-wandering."

The absence of any observable reduction of learning efficiency is consistent with numerous clinical observations which imply that normal personalities can ordinarily tolerate unpleasant information concerning potential threats to the self without manifesting any marked impairment of "ego" functions. Our findings definitely suggest that the use of fear-arousing material of the sort presented in the illustrated talks would rarely give rise to any interference with the audience's ability to learn the content of the communication.

It is necessary to bear in mind, however, that in the present experiment the communication was given to a "captive" classroom audience. When people are at home listening to the radio, or in any situation where they feel free to choose whether or not to terminate the communication exposure, the use of strong emotional appeals might often have drastic effects on sustained attention. Consequently, the tentative generalization concerning the low probability of inattentiveness would be expected to apply primarily to those fear-arousing communications which are presented under conditions where social norms or situational constraints prevent the audience from directing attention elsewhere.

Even with a "captive" audience, it is quite possible that under certain extreme conditions a strong fear appeal might interfere with learning efficiency. For instance, the same sort of temporary cognitive impairment that is sometimes observed when verbal stimuli happen to touch off unconscious personal conflicts or emotional "complexes" might also occur when a mass communication elicits sharp awareness of unexpected danger, particularly when the audience immediately perceives the threat to be imminent and inescapable. Hence, the inferences from our experimental findings probably should be restricted to fear appeals which deal with remote threats or with relatively familiar dangers that are perceived to be avoidable.

2. The fact that the Strong group expressed the greatest amount of subjective dislike of the illustrated talk and made the most complaints about its content could be construed as suggesting a potentially aggressive attitude. But if the aggressive reactions aroused by the use of the Strong fear appeal were intense enough to motivate rejection of the conclusions, one would not expect to find this group giving the most favorable appraisals of the interest value of the illustrated talk, of the quality of its presentation, and of its over-all educational success. Thus, although the possibility of suppressed aggression cannot be precluded, it seems unlikely that this factor was a major source of emotional interference. In drawing this tentative conclusion, however, we do not intend to minimize the importance of aggression as a potential source of interference. In the present experiment, the communication was administered as an official part of the school's hygiene program and contained recommendations that were obviously intended to be beneficial to the audience. Under markedly different conditions, where the auspices and intent of the communication are perceived to be less benign, the audience would probably be less disposed to suppress or control aggressive reactions. The low level of verbalized aggression observed in the present study, however, suggests that in the absence of cues which arouse the audience's suspicions, some factor other than reactive hostility may be a much more important source of interference.

3. Subsequent defensive avoidance arising from residual emotional tension seems to be the most likely explanation of the outcome of the present study. We have seen, from the data

on immediate affective reactions, that the disturbing feelings which had been aroused during the illustrated talk tended to persist after the communication had ended, despite the reassuring recommendations which had been presented. The analysis of complaints made by the three experimental groups (Table 5) provides additional evidence that the need for reassurance persisted primarily among the students who had been exposed to the Strong appeal. Such findings support the following hypothesis: *When a mass communication is designed to influence an audience to adopt specific ways and means of averting a threat, the use of a strong fear appeal, as against a milder one, increases the likelihood that the audience will be left in a state of emotional tension which is not fully relieved by rehearsing the reassuring recommendations contained in the communication.* This hypothesis is compatible with the general assumption that when a person is exposed to signs of "threat," the greater the intensity of the fear reaction evoked, the greater the likelihood that his emotional tension will persist after the external stimulus has terminated.

Whether or not the above hypothesis is correct, the fact remains that "unreduced" emotional tension was manifested immediately after the communication predominantly by the group exposed to the Strong appeal. Our findings on subsequent reactions provide some suggestive evidence concerning the consequences of experiencing this type of residual tension. In general, the evidence appears to be consistent with the following hypothesis: *When fear is strongly aroused but is not fully relieved by the reassurances contained in a mass communication, the audience will become motivated to ignore or to minimize the importance of the threat.* This hypothesis could be regarded as a special case of the following general proposition which pertains to the effects of human exposure to any fear-producing stimulus: Other things being equal, the more persistent the fear reaction, the greater will be the (acquired) motivation to avoid subsequent exposures to internal and external cues which were present at the time the fear reaction was aroused. This proposition is based on the postulate that fear is a stimulus-

producing response which has the functional properties of a drive (2, 7).

In the context of the present experiment, one would predict that the group displaying the greatest degree of residual fear would be most strongly motivated to ward off those internal symbolic cues—such as anticipations of the threatening consequences of improper dental hygiene—which were salient during and immediately after the communication. This prediction seems to be fairly well borne out by the evidence on carry-over effects, particularly by the finding that the greatest degree of resistance to the subsequent counterpropaganda was shown by the group which has been least motivated by fear. The use of the Strong appeal, as against the Minimal one, evidently resulted in less rejection of a subsequent communication which discounted and contradicted what was said in the original communication. In effect, the second communication asserted that one could ignore the alleged consequences of using the wrong type of toothbrush, and, in that sense, minimized the dangers which previously had been heavily emphasized by the fear-arousing communication.

The results obtained from the students' reports on their dental hygiene practices could be interpreted as supporting another prediction from the same hypothesis. It would be expected that those students who changed their practices, after having heard and seen one of the three forms of the illustrated talk, were motivated to do so because they recalled some of the verbal material which had been given in support of the recommendations, most of which referred to the unfavorable consequences of continuing to do the "wrong" thing. In theoretical terms, one might say that their conformity to the recommendations was mediated by symbolic responses which had been learned during the communication. The mediating responses (anticipations, thoughts, or images) acquired from any one of the three forms of the illustrated talk would frequently have, as their content, some reference to unpleasant consequences for the self, and consequently would cue off a resolution or an overt action that would be accompanied by anticipated success in warding off the threat. But defensive avoidance of the mediating responses would reduce the amount of conformity to whatever protective action is recommended by the fear-arousing communication. Hence the prediction would be that when rehearsal of statements concerning potential danger is accompanied by strong emotional tension during and after the communication, the audience will become motivated to avoid recalling those statements on later occasions when appropriate action could ordinarily be carried out. An inhibiting motivation of this kind acquired from the illustrated talk would tend to prevent the students from adopting the recommended changes in their toothbrushing habits because they would fail to think about the unpleasant consequences of improper dental hygiene at times when they subsequently perform the act of brushing their teeth.

Much more direct evidence in support of the "defensive avoidance" hypothesis comes from the analysis of spontaneous write-in answers in which the students explained why they disagreed with the counterpropaganda (Table 8). Those who had been exposed to the least amount of fear-arousing material were the ones who were most likely to refer to the illustrated talk as an authoritative source and to make use of its arguments. The relative absence of such references in the spontaneous answers given by those who had been exposed to the Moderate and Strong appeals implies a tendency to avoid recalling the content of the fear-arousing communication.

Although the various pieces of evidence discussed above seem to fit together, they cannot be regarded as a conclusive demonstration of the defensive avoidance hypothesis. What our findings clearly show is that a strong fear appeal can be markedly less effective than a minimal appeal, at least under the limited conditions represented in our experiment. Exactly which conditions and which mediating mechanisms are responsible for this outcome will remain problematical until further investigations are carried out. Nevertheless, so far as the present findings go, they consistently support the conclusion that the use of a strong fear appeal

will tend to reduce the over-all success of a persuasive communication, if it evokes a high degree of emotional tension without adequately satisfying the need for reassurance.

SUMMARY AND CONCLUSIONS

The experiment was designed to investigate the effects of persuasive communications which attempt to motivate people to conform with a set of recommendations by stimulating fear reactions. An illustrated lecture on dental hygiene was prepared in three different forms, representing three different intensities of fear appeal: the Strong appeal emphasized and graphically illustrated the threat of pain, disease, and body damage; the Moderate appeal described the same dangers in a milder and more factual manner; the Minimal appeal rarely referred to the unpleasant consequences of improper dental hygiene. Although differing in the amount of fear-arousing material presented, the three forms of the communication contained the same essential information and the same set of recommendations.

Equivalent groups of high school students were exposed to the three different forms of the communication as part of the school's hygiene program. In addition, the experiment included an equated control group which was not exposed to the dental hygiene communication but was given a similar communication on an irrelevant topic. Altogether there were 200 students in the experiment, with 50 in each group. A questionnaire containing a series of items on dental hygiene beliefs, practices, and attitudes was administered to all four groups one week before the communications were presented. In order to observe the changes produced by the illustrated talk, postcommunication questionnaires were given immediately after exposure and again one week later.

1. The fear appeals were successful in arousing affective reactions. Immediately after the communication, the group exposed to the Strong appeal reported feeling more worried about the condition of their teeth than did the other groups. The Moderate appeal, in turn,

evoked a higher incidence of "worry" reactions that did the Minimal appeal.

2. The three forms of the illustrated talk were equally effective with respect to (a) teaching the factual content of the communication, as assessed by an information test, and (b) modifying beliefs concerning four specific characteristics of the "proper" type of toothbrush. The evidence indicates that the emotional reactions aroused by the Strong appeal did not produce inattentiveness or reduce learning efficiency.

3. As compared with the other two forms of the communication, the Strong appeal evoked a more mixed or ambivalent attitude toward the communication. The students exposed to the Strong appeal were more likely than the others to give favorable appraisals concerning the interest value and the quality of the presentation. Nevertheless, they showed the greatest amount of subjective dislike of the communication and made more complaints about the content.

4. From an analysis of the changes in each individual's reports about his current toothbrushing practices, it was found that the greatest amount of conformity to the communicator's recommendations was produced by the Minimal appeal. The Strong appeal failed to produce any significant change in dental hygiene practices, whereas the Minimal appeal resulted in a reliable increase in conformity, as compared with the Control group. Similar findings also emerged from an analysis of responses which indicated whether the students had gone to a dentist during the week following exposure to the illustrated talk, reflecting conformity to another recommendation made by the communicator. The evidence strongly suggests that as the amount of fear-arousing material is increased, conformity to recommended (protective) actions tends to decrease.

5. One week after the illustrated talk had been presented, exposure to counterpropaganda (which contradicted the main theme of the original communication) produced a greater effect on attitudes in the Control group than in the three experimental groups. The Minimal appeal, however, proved to be the most effective form of the illustrated talk with respect to producing resistance to the counterpropaganda. The results tend to support the conclusion that under conditions where people are exposed to competing communications dealing with the same issues, the use of a strong fear appeal is less successful than a minimal appeal in producing stable and persistent attitude changes.

6. The main conclusion which emerges from the entire set of findings is that the overall effectiveness of a persuasive communication will tend to be reduced by the use of a strong fear appeal, if it evokes a high degree of emotional tension without adequately satisfying the need for reassurance. The evidence from the present experiment appears to be consistent with the following two explanatory hypotheses:

a. When a mass communication is designed to influence an audience to adopt specific ways and means of averting a threat, the use of a strong fear appeal, as against a milder one, increases the likelihood that the audience will be left in a state of emotional tension which is not fully relieved by rehearsing the reassuring recommendations contained in the communication.

b. When fear is strongly aroused but is not fully relieved by the reassurances contained in a mass communication, the audience will become motivated to ignore or to minimize the importance of the threat.

REFERENCES

1. Alexander, F., & French, T. M. *Psychoanalytic therapy.* New York: Ronald, 1946.
2. Dollard, J., & Miller, N. E. *Personality and psychotherapy.* New York: McGraw-Hill, 1950.
3. Fenichel, O. *Problems of psychoanalytic technique.* New York: Psychoanalytic Quarterly, 1941.
4. Hanfmann, E. Psychological approaches to the study of anxiety. In P. H. Hoch and J. Zubin (Eds.), *Anxiety.* New York: Grune & Stratton, 1950. Pp. 51–69.
5. Hovland, C. I., Lumsdaine, A. A., & Sheffield, F. D. *Experiments on mass communication.* Princeton: Princeton University Press, 1949.
6. Janis, I. L. *Air war and emotional stress.* New York: McGraw-Hill, 1951.
7. Mowrer, O. H. *Learning theory and personality dynamics: Selected papers.* New York: Ronald, 1950.

8

Communication Modality as a Determinant of Persuasion: The Role of Communicator Salience

Shelly Chaiken and Alice H. Eagly

This study compares the persuasive effects of mass communications presented through video, audio, or written media. Previous studies had produced rather uninformative results, but Chaiken and Eagly hoped to bring fresh light to the problem by applying recent concepts about social cognition. They suggest that two processes might affect reactions to media persuasion: a "systematic process" in which subjects actively process communication arguments, and a "heuristic process" in which they do not, and use simple decision rules instead. Written communications are hypothesized to stimulate more systematic processing than audio or video communications. Thus simpler cues having little to do with the content of persuasive arguments, such as communicator likability, should be more effective in the audio or video media than in the written media. The prediction, then, is to an interaction of communicator likability and type of media. As can be seen in Tables 1 and 2, communicator likability affects opinion change with video and audio communications, but not when they are written. This paper is a good example of contemporary research on attitude change because it uses more cognitive theorizing and because it tests more complex interaction predictions about the impact of two independent variables at once, rather than the simple effects of one variable. The study also attempts to obtain direct evidence on the processes at work, measuring the number of communicator-related thoughts, using the "thought-listing" technique. This technique has been criticized as simply providing another index of the dependent variables—the subject's opinion following the communication—rather than an independent index of whatever mental processes had produced that opinion. This paper, however, distinguishes between thoughts focused on communicators and messages, giving more insight into the presumed mediating processes.

ABSTRACT. In two experiments, a likable or unlikable communicator delivered a persuasive message via the written, audiotaped, or videotaped modality. In both studies, the likable communicator was more persuasive in videotaped and audiotaped (vs. written) conditions, whereas the unlikable communicator was more persuasive in the written modality. Because of these opposing effects of modality on the persuasiveness of likable and unlikable communicators, communicator likability was a significant determinant of persuasion only in the two broadcast modalities. Additional findings suggested that subjects engaged in more processing of communicator cues when exposed to videotaped or audiotaped, compared to written, messages and that communicator-based (vs. message-based) cognitions predicted opinion change primarily within videotape and audiotape (vs. written) conditions. It was concluded that the videotaped and audiotaped modalities enhance the salience of communicator-related information with

Reprinted from the *Journal of Personality and Social Psychology*, 1983, *45*, pp. 241–256. Copyright 1983 by the American Psychological Association. Reprinted by permission of publisher and authors.

the consequence that communicator characteristics exert a disproportionate impact on persuasion when messages are transmitted in videotaped and audiotaped (vs. written) form. The relevance of the findings to understanding "vividness" phenomena is also discussed.

Previous research on media effects in persuasion has proven largely inconsistent. Although the modal finding in this literature appears to be that live or videotaped messages induce greater opinion change than do audiotaped messages (Frandsen, 1963), which, in turn, induce greater change than do written communications (Cantril & Allport, 1935; Haugh, 1952; Knower, 1935, 1936; Wilke, 1934), a number of studies have obtained either no differences in persuasiveness as a function of communication modality or greater opinion change with written messages (McGinnies, 1965; Tannenbaum & Kerrick, 1954; Werner, 1978; Werner & Latané, 1976).

In an earlier article (Chaiken & Eagly, 1976), we suggested that at least some of the inconsistency in the modality literature might be explained in terms of message comprehensibility. Based on research indicating that good comprehension of persuasive argumentation often facilitates opinion change (e.g., Eagly, 1974; Eagly & Warren, 1976) and research suggesting that written (vs. videotaped or audiotaped) messages enhance comprehension, especially for complex material (e.g., Beighley, 1952; Harwood, 1951; Westover, 1958; Wilson, 1974), we predicted and found that modality differences in persuasion favored the written mode with inherently difficult-to-understand material, whereas the more usual advantage of videotaped and audiotaped modalities was found with easy material.

Although the Chaiken and Eagly (1976) study demonstrates that message comprehensibility can moderate the persuasive impact of modality, two facts suggest that comprehensibility differences alone cannot fully explain inconsistencies in this literature. First, the slope of the function relating message comprehension to persuasion is relatively flat (Calder, Insko, & Yandell, 1974; Insko, Lind, & LaTour, 1976). Thus, a fairly large difference in com-

prehension would be required to exert a detectable effect on persuasion (Eagly, 1978). Second, message comprehension may be an important determinant of opinion change only in persuasion contexts that maximize the tendency for recipients to focus attentively on persuasive argumentation and to base their opinions on such content cues (Chaiken, 1978, 1980; Chaiken & Eagly, 1976; Miller, Maruyama, Beaber, & Valone, 1976).

To further explore media effects in persuasion, the present research examined the idea that the persuasive impact of communication modality is contingent on the valence of a communicator's personal characteristics or "image."[1] The persuasive impact of communicator characteristics should be affected by modality because nonverbal communicator-related cues are present in videotaped and audiotaped messages but are absent in written messages. Because these nonverbal cues (e.g., the communicator's physical appearance and/or voice) may draw message recipients' attention to the communicator, his or her personal characteristics may be more salient and therefore exert a disproportionate impact on persuasion when messages are transmitted in videotaped or audiotaped rather than written form. This idea is consistent with research on the salience of persons, which indicates that salient individuals are remembered better, viewed as more casually prominent, and have their personal attributes rated more extremely (McArthur, 1981; Taylor & Fiske, 1978; Taylor & Thompson, 1982). Whether the greater persuasive impact of communicator cues in videotaped and audiotaped modalities is positive or negative should depend on whether the communicator cues made salient are themselves positive or negative. For positive cues conveying, for example, that a communicator is likable or expert, increased salience should enhance persuasiveness. However, for negative cues

---

[1] To exclude message reception from consideration as a mediator of persuasion, the present research employed relatively easy-to-understand messages (Chaiken & Eagly, 1976) and a cover story ("people's reactions to speeches") that we hoped would not lead subjects to focus excessively on persuasive argumentation (Chaiken, 1978, 1980).

conveying that a communicator is unlikable or inexpert, increased salience should decrease persuasiveness.

Assuming that communicators with positive attributes are generally chosen to deliver messages in persuasion experiments, the communicator salience argument implies that the modal finding in past literature should be (as it is) greater persuasion for videotaped and audiotaped (vs. written) messages. Further, in studies employing communicators whose attributes differ markedly, the persuasive effect of media should depend on the valence of these attributes. Consistent with this expectation, Andreoli and Worchel (1978) found that a newscaster and a former politician (presumably trustworthy sources) were more persuasive on television than over the radio or in a newspaper story, whereas a political candidate (a presumably untrustworthy source) was more persuasive in a newspaper story or over the radio than on television. Similar though weaker findings were obtained by Worchel, Andreoli, and Eason (1975).

Other researchers have discussed media differences in terms compatible with our communicator salience argument. For example, Keating and Latané (1976) argued that a "live speaker's" persuasiveness decreases progressively with televised, oral, and written presentations because the media become "less rich and transmit less information." Worchel et al. (1975) and Andreoli and Worchel (1978) suggested that television is more "involving" than radio or newspaper and, further, that the more-involving media highlight communicator characteristics. Also, Short, Williams, and Christie (1976) argued that the media vary in "social presence," which they defined as the salience of the other person (e.g., the communicator) and the consequent salience of interpersonal relationships. According to these authors, social presence is greatest in face-to-face communication, followed by videotape, audiotape, and written communications. Although the notions that media differ in richness, involvement, and social presence are quite global, they are consistent with the idea that the persuasive impact of modality is contingent on the valence of communicator characteristics.

Another approach to understanding the effects of communication media stems from recent theorizing and research on "vividness" efects. Vivid information is information that presumably attracts and holds people's attention because it is, for example, concrete and imagery-provoking or proximal in a sensory, temporal, or spatial way (Nisbett & Ross, 1980). By this definition, videotaped and audiotaped modalities present information more vividly than does the written modality. Because vividly presented information is hypothesized to exert a greater impact on judgments than nonvividly presented information (Nisbett & Ross, 1980; Taylor & Thompson, 1982), it might be predicted, as Taylor and Thompson (1982) recently suggested, that the more vivid videotaped or audiotaped modalities should effect greater persuasion than the less vivid written modality. Yet, according to our analysis, in many persuasion settings, it is not the persuasive message itself that is made more vivid in videotaped and audiotaped (vs. written) modalities, but, rather, information about the communicator. Given this clarification, our ideas about the greater salience and thus the greater persuasive impact of communicator characteristics in the broadcast media are, in fact, consistent with the general hypothesis that vivid (vs. nonvivid) information exerts a disproportionate impact on people's judgments.

To develop the communicator salience explanation more thoroughly, it is useful to employ Chaiken's (1978, 1980, Note 1) heuristic versus systematic analysis of persuasion. In the systematic view of persuasion, message recipients focus primarily on persuasive argumentation in forming their opinion judgments, whereas in the heuristic view, recipients engage in little, if any, detailed processing of message content and, instead, tend to employ simple decision rules often (though not exclusively; Chaiken, 1980, Note 1) based on cues such as the communicator's identity in judging message acceptability. In the initial test of this analysis, Chaiken (1980) found that high (vs. low) levels of response involvement or issue involvement tended to foster systematic (vs. heuristic) information processing: In two experiments, the opinions of high-involvement subjects were more strongly influenced by the amount of argumentation contained in a persuasive message than by the communicator's likability (vs. unlikability), whereas the opinions of low-involvement subjects were more strongly affected by the communicator's likability than by the amount of argumentation he or she provided. As further specified by Chaiken's analysis, opinion change was found to be mediated primarily by message-based (vs. communicator-based) cognitions for high- (vs. low-) involvement subjects. More recent findings reported by Petty, Cacioppo, and Goldman (1981) also supported the heuristic versus systematic processing distinction.

Of primary interest here is the idea that, aside from a motivational variable like involvement, contextual features of a persuasion setting, such as communication modality, may influence the degree to which recipients process and utilize communicator cues in making their opinion judgments. As argued earlier, the broadcast modalities may increase the salience of communicator cues, with the consequence that communicator characteristics should exert a greater (positive or negative) persuasive impact when messages are transmitted in videotaped or audiotaped, rather than written, form. The heuristic versus systematic analysis implies further that recipients of videotaped or audiotaped messages should predicate their opinions primarily on their reactions to the communicator and less on their reactions to message content. In contrast, recipients of written messages (for whom communicator cues may be less salient than message content) should show a greater tendency to predicate their opinions on their evaluation of message content.[2]

To test these ideas, subjects in two experiments were exposed to a videotaped, an audio-taped, or a written persuasive message from a likable or unlikable communicator. We anticipated that with a likable communicator, videotaped and audiotaped messages would be more persuasive than written messages, whereas with an unlikable communicator, videotaped and audiotaped (vs. written) messages would be less persuasive. Because the video and the audio modalities both differ from the written modality by the addition of nonverbal communicator-related cues, and because prior research has typically not found large or systematic persuasion differences between the two broadcast modalities (e.g., Chaiken & Eagly, 1976), we predicted similar findings for videotaped and audiotaped messages. The present research also attempted to obtain relatively direct evidence that recipients pay more attention to the communicator (and perhaps less attention to message content) with videotaped and audiotaped (vs. written) messages. To accomplish this goal, a thought-listing task (Brock, 1967; Osterhouse & Brock, 1970) was included in both experiments, and subjects' cognitive responses were classified according to whether they were communicator oriented or message oriented. Finally, Experiment 2 also explored opinion persistence. Based on the heuristic versus systematic analysis of persuasion and research indicating that opinion change persists longer to the extent that it is bolstered by topic-relevant cognitions (Chaiken, 1980; Cook & Flay, 1978), we hypothesized that, regardless of communicator likability, the presumably source-mediated opinion change manifested by subjects within videotaped and audiotaped modalities would show less persistence than would the presumably content-mediated opinion change manifested by subjects within the written modality.

EXPERIMENT 1

METHOD

Subjects

Subjects were 109 psychology students from the University of Toronto who received extra credit toward their course grades for participat-

---

[2] The current predictions are expected to hold primarily for moderately involving message topics such as the ones employed in the present research. As suggested by the heuristic versus systematic analysis, when involvement is extremely high, recipients may attend primarily to message content (vs. communicator cues), regardless of modality. And, when involvement is extremely low, recipients may attend primarily to communicator cues, regardless of modality.

ing. Data from three subjects were discarded because they questioned the cover story ($n = 2$) or failed to indicate their opinions ($n = 1$).

Procedure

At a mass testing session held early in the academic year, all introductory psychology students completed a large set of questionnaires. One of these questionnaires solicited students' agreement with a pool of opinion items that included the target statement, "The University of Toronto should switch to a trimester system." A list of students who disagreed with this statement and who were under 25 years of age was compiled, and experimental subjects were recruited by phone from this list.

Participating in groups of three to nine persons, subjects learned during the laboratory session that the experiment concerned "people's reactions to speeches." The experimenter stated that subjects would read (listen to, view) and give their reactions to a "randomly selected" speech on one of a variety of campus issues.

After this introduction, the experimenter announced the topic (see below) of the speech and distributed written transcripts of a "background interview" with the speaker that contained the communicator-likability manipulation (see below). Within each session, subjects were randomly assigned to likability conditions.

Next, the experimenter distributed written transcripts or played an audiotape or videotape of the speech (persuasive message, see below). Afterwards, subjects completed a questionnaire that assessed their "reactions" to the speech (dependent variables, see below). Finally, subjects were debriefed and excused.

Topic and Persuasive Message

The position advocated in the persuasive message was "The University of Toronto should switch to the trimester system of instruction." The message was approximately 700 words long, contained five supportive arguments, and was designed to be relatively easy to understand (see Footnote 1).

Independent Variables

Communicator likability. In the "background interview," the speaker (communicator) was portrayed as a male University of Toronto (U of T) administrator whose work involved scholarship coordination and bursaries and who had recently come to U of T from the University of British Columbia (UBC) where he had held a similar position. Communicator likability was established by the communicator's response to the interviewer's question, "How do you like being at U of T compared to UBC?" The communicator's response to this question appears below. Phrases common to both likability conditions appear without parentheses or brackets, and phrases that appear only in the likable or the unlikable version are enclosed in parentheses or brackets, respectively.

Well, it's interesting that you asked that question. . . . To tell you the truth, I really (prefer being here at U of T and living in Toronto to being out west) [preferred being out west to being here at U of T and living in Toronto]. For one thing, the people who I've met both in my work and other contexts, including colleagues, students, faculty, and other staff, strike me as (being much friendlier and nicer than) [not being really as friendly and nice as] the people I knew at UBC. . . . Also I think that in terms of the overall ability of the students and faculty here, that U of T is a much (higher) [lower] quality institution than UBC. I feel that U of T students particularly are (especially bright individuals) [really overrated]. . . . I guess that in general, too, I find life here in Toronto to be a lot (more) [less] pleasant. (There's so much more to do here—movies get here sooner, and there are more and better theater groups and the restaurants and night life are really much better) [While there are plenty of things to do here—movies, theaters, restaurants, night life—I really don't think that their overall quality is very high in Toronto compared to other places]. For me, I guess U of T and Toronto has (been a really) [not really been a very] good place to be.

Communication modality. A 35-year-old male colleague of the first author was trained to deliver the persuasive message. The speaker's final performance was videotaped for use in the videotape conditions, and the audio portion of the tape was played in the audiotape conditions. These versions of the message lasted approximately 5 minutes, and subjects in written conditions were given 5 minutes to read the written transcript of the message.

Dependent Variables

Opinions. At the pretest, subjects indicated their agreement with the statement, "The University of Toronto should switch to a trimester system," by marking a 15-point scale anchored by "agree strongly" and "disagree strongly." In the laboratory, subjects wrote down the communicator's topic and the overall position he advocated ("The University of Toronto should switch to the trimester system of instruction") and then indicated their agreement with this position by marking the same 15-point scale described above.

Comprehension. Subjects were asked to summarize each of the communicator's arguments. An argument was scored as correct if, in the opinion of two independent raters ($r = .79$), it accurately summarized an argument contained in the message. As noted above, subjects were also asked to write down the message's topic and overall position.

Cognitive responses. Subjects were given 3 minutes to list their "thoughts and ideas" about "the speaker and his speech." Statements were scored by two independent raters as either message oriented (M) or communicator oriented (C) and as either positively (+), negatively (−), or neutrally (0) valenced. Examples of statements placed in each of the above categories (along with interrater reliability coefficients) are C+ ($r = .82$), "Speaker has good voice"; C− ($r = .79$), "He seems unfriendly"; C0 ($r = .68$), "Seems like a nature lover"; M+ ($r = .83$), "The economic advantages of the trimester seem reasonable"; M− ($r = .82$), "I'm not sure students would benefit so much from the new system"; M0 ($r = .73$), "He said that many U.S. schools are on the trimester."

Source perception. Subjects rated the communicator on 12 bipolar-adjective scales. Positive poles of these 15-point scales were likable, knowledgeable, modest, intelligent, approach-

able, competent, warm, trustworthy, pleasing, sincere, friendly, and unbiased.

Other measures. On 15-point scales, subjects rated how *distracted* they felt from the content of the speech, how *difficult* it was to understand the speech, the relative amount of time they had spent *thinking* about the communicator's arguments (vs. his personal characteristics), and the *importance* of the message topic. Also on 15-point scales, subjects indicated how much *effort* they had expended and how *pleasant* they had found the experience of reading (listening to, viewing) the speech. Subjects also indicated their age and sex and, just prior to the debriefing, their written interpretations of the experiment. Answers to this open-ended question were coded for suspicion.

RESULTS

The design included three levels of communication modality and two levels each of communicator likability and subject sex. Because preliminary analyses revealed no significant effects that involved sex on subjects' opinions, the reported analyses ignored this variable.

Check on Communicator Likability Manipulation

A factor analysis of subjects' source ratings yielded two rotated factors, labeled Attractiveness (likable, friendly, approachable, pleasing, modest, warm, and unbiased) and Expertise (knowledgeable, intelligent, and competent). These factors accounted for 49.2% and 12.3% of the variance, respectively. Analyses of variance (ANOVAS) on subjects' factor scores indicated that the likable (vs. the unlikable) communicator was perceived as more attractive, $F(1, 100) = 41.72, p < .001$, and more expert, $F(1, 100) = 5.55, p < .025$. Other source-perception findings are reported below.

Opinions

An ANOVA revealed no significant effects on subjects' premessage (i.e., pretest) opinions (all $Fs < 1.00$). Nevertheless, to control for extremity of initial opinions and for the slight differ-

Table 1 Dependent Variables as a Function of Modality and Communicator Likability: Experiment 1

| | COMMUNICATOR LIKABILITY | | | | | |
| | Likable | | | Unlikable | | |
Dependent Variable	*Written*	*Audiotape*	*Videotape*	*Written*	*Audiotape*	*Videotape*
Opinion change	3.66	4.82	4.87	3.43	1.47	.48
Communicator-oriented thoughts	1.05	1.72	2.12	1.00	1.41	1.44

Note. Higher numbers indicate greater opinion change and more communicator-oriented thoughts. Cell *ns* range from 16 to 19.

ences between experimental conditions with respect to these scores, subjects' opinion-change scores (postmessage minus premessage opinions) were treated by an analysis of covariance, using premessage opinions as the covariate. Mean opinion-change scores (adjusted on the basis of premessage opinions) for the various experimental conditions are shown in Table 1.

As expected, the Modality × Likability interaction proved significant on opinion change, $F(2, 99) = 3.74, p < .03$. Planned comparisons indicated that, compared to subjects in written conditions, videotape and audiotape subjects (combined) agreed somewhat more with the likable communicator's message ($p < .15$) but agreed significantly less with the unlikable communicator's message ($p < .005$). A second set of contrasts revealed that the likable (vs. unlikable) communicator was significantly more persuasive within both videotape ($p < .001$) and audiotape ($p < .005$) conditions but only negligibly more persuasive within written conditions ($F < 1.0$).

In addition, the analysis of opinion change also revealed a significant overall tendency for the likable (vs. unlikable) communicator to elicit greater persuasion, $F(1, 99) = 16.39$, $p < .0001$ ($Ms = 4.43$ vs. 1.88, respectively). Finally, the modality main effect was nonsignificant on opinion change ($F < 1.0$).

Cognitive Responses

The number of thoughts expressed by each subject in each thought category (M+, M−, M0, C+, C−, C0) was calculated and used to form a number of indexes. The ANOVA findings on these variables are most efficiently pre-

sented in terms of four summed indexes: (a) total communicator-oriented thoughts, (b) total message-oriented thoughts (regardless of valence), (c) total positive thoughts, and (d) total negative thoughts (regardless of orientation).

On the communicator-oriented thought index (see Table 1), the modality main effect approached significance, $F(2, 100) = 2.73, p < .07$: As expected, subjects expressed fewer communicator-oriented thoughts as modality changed from videotape to audiotape to written, $Ms = 1.79$ versus 1.57 versus 1.03, respectively; $F(1, 100) = 5.10, p < .05$, for linear trend. There were no significant effects on the message-oriented thought index. On the remaining two thought indexes, analyses indicated that subjects expressed more positive thoughts in response to the likable (vs. unlikable) communicator ($p < .005$) and expressed more negative thoughts as modality changed from written to audiotape to videotape ($p < .05$).

Source Perception

As noted earlier, the likable (vs. the unlikable) communicator was perceived as significantly more attractive and expert. In addition, perceived communicator expertise increased as modality changed from videotape to audiotape to written ($p < .05$).

Other Measures

The modality main effect was significant on subjects' self-reports of the relative amount of time they had spent thinking about the communicator's arguments versus the communicator's personal characteristics ($p < .05$) and on their self-reports of the extent to which they were distracted from the content of the persuasive message ($p < .05$): Compared to subjects in written and audiotape conditions (who differed little on these measures), videotape subjects reported more time thinking about the communicator's personal characteristics and greater distraction from message content. A likability main effect on the pleasantness ratings ($p < .01$) indicated that subjects exposed to the likable (vs. the unlikable) communicator regarded their experience of reading (listening to, viewing) the message as more pleasant.

All subjects demonstrated satisfactory recall of the message topic and all but two (retained in the analyses) correctly recalled the message's overall position. No significant effects were obtained on subjects' recall of the message's arguments or on their ratings of effort expended, difficulty understanding message content, and topic importance.

Correlational Analyses

To explore the relative influence of message-based cognitions versus source-based cognitions on opinion change, two multiple-regression analyses were performed, one employing data from subjects in written conditions ($n = 38$) and one using data from subjects within videotape and audiotape conditions combined ($n = 68$).[3] Both analyses predicted opinion change from the following variables: premessage opinions, arguments recalled, positive minus negative message-oriented thoughts, positive minus negative communicator-oriented thoughts, Attractiveness factor scores, and Expertise factor scores. For subjects in written conditions, the only significant predictor of opinion change other than premessage opinions ($p < .001$) was the positive minus negative message-oriented thoughts index, $\beta = .47$, $F(1, 31) = 9.39$, $p < .005$: Greater opinion change was associated with a greater number of positive (vs. negative) message-oriented thoughts. In contrast, within videotape and audiotape conditions, the only significant predictors of opinion change (aside from premes-

sage opinions, $p < .001$) were heightened perceptions of communicator attractiveness, $\beta = .31$, $F(1, 61) = 6.21$, $p < .025$, and a greater number of positive (vs. negative) communicator-oriented thoughts, $\beta = .24$, $F(1, 61) = 4.98$, $p < .05$.

EXPERIMENT 2

In order to extend the generality of our argument that media differences in the salience of communicator cues affect persuasion, a second study was conducted. This experiment employed an opinion-only control group in lieu of assessing subjects' premessage opinions. In addition, the design of Experiment 2 incorporated an internal replication by using two new message topics, and it also featured a delayed telephone posttest of opinions. Aside from these differences, the methodology of Experiment 2 was virtually identical to that of the first experiment.

In accord with Experiment 1, we expected that videotape and audiotape (vs. written) subjects would show more initial (postmessage) agreement with the likable communicator but less agreement with the unlikable communicator. We anticipated, however, that the Modality × Likability interaction would not be obtained on subjects' delayed opinions. Instead, based on the systematic versus heuristic analysis of persuasion, we expected that greater delayed opinion change would be manifested by subjects originally exposed to written (vs. videotaped or audiotaped) messages.

METHOD

Subjects were 179 psychology students from the University of Toronto. Subjects were eliminated if they suspected an influence attempt ($n = 5$), doubted the cover story ($n = 4$), failed to indicate their opinions ($n = 2$), or were over 25 years of age ($n = 5$).[4] Thirty-five additional students served as opinion-only control sub-

---

[3] When the videotape and audiotape conditions were examined separately, the regression analyses yielded similar findings for the two conditions for both Experiments 1 and 2.

[4] By including the nine suspicious subjects and the five subjects who were over 25 years old in the opinion-change analyses, results virtually identical to those reported in the text were found.

jects. All subjects received extra credit toward their course grades or $2.50 for participating.

Procedure

Participating in groups of two to six persons, subjects attended a laboratory session that was identical to the Experiment 1 session except that subjects were not debriefed before being excused. Approximately 10 days later, subjects were telephoned by an experimenter (blind to experimental condition). Under the guise of conducting a campus opinion survey, the experimenter solicited subjects' agreement with various statements, two of which corresponded to the positions advocated in the messages presented at the laboratory session (see below). After probing for suspicion regarding the relationship between the posttest and the laboratory session, the experimenter thanked subjects for cooperating in the telephone survey. At a later date, each subject received a debriefing letter.

Independent Variables

Message topic and position advocated. Subjects were exposed to a persuasive message concerning the topic of tuition fees or Ontario Student Assistant Program (OSAP) grants. The positions advocated in the two messages were "Tuition at the University of Toronto should be increased" and "OSAP grants should not be made available to graduate students," respectively. Pretesting with opinion-only control subjects ($n = 35$) indicated that University of Toronto undergraduates disagreed to about the same extent with these opinion statements, Mtuition $= 12.77$, and MOSAP $= 12.89$, on a 15-point scale where $15 =$ disagree strongly. Each message was approximately 780 words long, contained five supportive arguments, and was designed to be relatively easy to comprehend.

Communicator likability. The two versions of the "background interview" that manipulated communicator likability were identical to those employed in Experiment 1.

Communication modality. A 28-year-old male amateur actor was trained to deliver both persuasive messages. The videotaped and audio-taped version of each message lasted approximately 5.5 minutes, and subjects in written conditions were allotted 5.5 minutes to read written transcripts of the messages.

Dependent Variables

Except for the deletion of the premessage opinion measure and the addition of the delayed postmessage opinion measure, the measuring instruments were identical to those used in Experiment 1. The two raters who scored the comprehension and thought data of Experiment 2 showed adequate agreement: argument recall, $r = .83$; M+, $r = .88$; M−, $r = .87$; M0, $r = .81$; C+, $r = .83$; C−, $r = .80$; and C0, $r = .74$. During the delayed telephone posttest, subjects indicated their agreement with the positions advocated in the persuasive messages (see above) by responding orally to 5-point scales anchored by "strongly agree" and "strongly disagree." Subjects were also asked whether they had been in any "similar" opinion surveys. Answers to this open-ended question were coded for suspicion regarding the relationship between the phone call and the laboratory session.

RESULTS

The design included three levels of communication modality and two levels each of communicator likability, message topic, and subject sex. For the sake of brevity, sex and topic effects obtained on measures other than opinions are described only when relevant to the main hypotheses.

Check on Communicator Likability Manipulation

A factor analysis of subjects' source ratings yielded two rotated factors that closely paralleled those factors obtained in Experiment 1. The Attractiveness factor (likable, friendly, pleasing, approachable, warm, and modest) accounted for 41.2% of the variance, and the Expertise factor (knowledgeable, intelligent, competent, and trustworthy) accounted for 14.1%. Analyses on subjects' factor scores indicated that the likable (vs. the unlikable) communicator was perceived as more attractive, $F(1, 139) = 5.10, p < .025$. Other source-perception findings are reported below.

Opinions

Initial postmessage opinions in all treatment groups differed significantly from the opinion-only control group in the direction of greater agreement with the persuasive message ($ps < .05$ using Dunnett's test). In order that opinions appear on a scale comparable to Experiment 1's difference scores, initial opinion-change scores (see Table 2) were calculated by subtracting the mean opinion expressed by control subjects from each subject's postmessage opinion.

As in Experiment 1, the Modality × Likability interaction was significant on initial opinion change, $F(2, 139) = 3.48, p < .05$. Planned comparisons yielded stronger findings than those obtained in the first study: Compared to subjects in written conditions, videotape and audiotape subjects (combined) agreed significantly more with the likable communicator's message ($p < .05$) but agreed significantly less with the unlikable communicator's message ($p < .005$). Our second set of contrasts showed that the likable (vs. the unlikable) communicator was more persuasive within both videotape ($p < .06$) and audiotape ($p < .05$) conditions but was nonsignificantly less persuasive within written conditions, $F(1, 139) = 2.12$, ns.

Two main effects also attained significance on initial opinion change: Greater agreement occurred for subjects who received an OSAP (vs. tuition) message ($p < .001$) and for male (vs. female) subjects ($p < .05$). Unlike Experiment 1, in which the likability main effect was significant on opinion change, the likable (vs. the unlikable) communicator proved only slightly more persuasive on an overall basis ($p = .13$). Finally, as in Experiment 1, the modality main effect was nonsignificant on initial opinion change ($F < 1.0$).

To explore our hypothesis regarding opinion persistence, a repeated measures ANOVA, which employed time of posttest (initial vs. delayed) as an additional design factor, was performed. The analysis utilized data from only 132 of the 163 subjects, because 20 subjects could not be contacted for the telephone posttest, 4 subjects refused to participate in the telephone survey, and 7 subjects were assessed as being suspicious of the association between the delayed posttest and their earlier laboratory participation.

Although opinion change tended to dissipate over time, the time of posttest main effect was nonsignificant, $F(1, 108) < 1.0$. Further, the time of posttest did not interact on a significant basis with any other experimental variable. Although the predicted Time × Modality × Likability interaction proved only marginal in this analysis, $F(2, 108) = 1.96, p < .15$, it did describe the expected pattern of opinion-change findings. The initial opinion-change findings for the reduced sample replicated those findings obtained with the larger sample (i.e., significantly greater/lesser opinion change given the likable/unlikable communicator among videotape and audiotape subjects). In contrast, subjects' delayed opinion-change scores showed no evidence of this Modality × Likability interaction pattern, $F(2, 108) = 1.14$, ns. Instead, the dominant trend on delayed opinion change was, as expected, due to communication modality alone, $F(2, 108) = 1.95, p < .15$: Regardless of communicator

Table 2 Dependent Variables as a Function of Modality and Communicator Likability: Experiment 2

| | COMMUNICATOR LIKABILITY | | | | | |
| | Likable | | | Unlikable | | |
Dependent Variable	Written	Audiotape	Videotape	Written	Audiotape	Videotape
Opinion change	5.65	7.08	6.95	6.90	4.83	5.22
Communicator-oriented thoughts	1.04	1.44	1.42	1.14	1.71	2.32

Note. Higher numbers indicate greater opinion change and more communicator-oriented thoughts. Cell ns range from 25 to 28.

likability, delayed opinion change tended to be somewhat greater for subjects originally exposed to written versus audiotaped versus videotaped messages, Ms = 6.62 versus 6.11 versus 5.72, respectively, $F(1, 108)$ = 1.83, ns for linear trend.

Cognitive Responses

On the communicator-oriented thought index (see Table 2), the modality main effect approached significance, $F(2, 139)$ = 2.94, $p < .06$: Paralleling Experiment 1, subjects expressed fewer thoughts about the communicator as modality changed from videotape to audiotape to written, Ms = 1.89 versus 1.58 versus 1.09, respectively, $F(1, 139)$ = 5.69, $p < .025$ for linear trend. As in the first experiment, there were no significant effects on the message-oriented thought index.

Subjects generated more positive thoughts in response to the likable (vs. unlikable) communicator ($p < .05$). Unlike Experiment 1, the Modality × Likability interaction attained significance on this index ($p < .025$) and also on the negative thoughts index ($p < .05$). Videotape and audiotape (vs. written) subjects expressed more positive thoughts (Ms = 2.72 vs. 1.78, respectively) and fewer negative thoughts (Ms = 2.09 vs. 2.43, respectively) given the likable communicator, but they expressed fewer positive thoughts (Ms = 1.48 vs. 2.00, respectively) and more negative thoughts (Ms = 3.12 vs. 1.82, respectively) given the unlikable communicator.

Source Perception

In addition to the likability main effect noted earlier, the analysis of subjects' Attractiveness factor scores revealed more positive communicator ratings as modality changed from videotape to audiotape to written ($p < .005$). In addition, both the Modality × Likability and the Modality × Likability × Topic interactions were significant on this variable ($ps < .025$ and $< .005$, respectively). Paralleling the findings obtained on the positive and negative thought indexes, the two-way interaction revealed an overall tendency for videotape and audiotape subjects to rate the likable com-

municator more positively and the unlikable communicator more negatively than written subjects. The three-way interaction, however, indicated one reversal to this overall tendency: Videotape and audiotape subjects exposed to the likable communicator's tuition message rated the source slightly more negatively than did written subjects.

Other Measures

The modality main effect approached significance on subjects' distraction ratings ($p = .08$) and on their self-reports of the relative amount of time they had spent thinking about the communicator's arguments versus his personal characteristics ($p = .07$): Paralleling the Experiment 1 findings (in which the modality main effect attained significance on both measures), videotape subjects reported greater distraction from message content and more time thinking about the communicator's personal characteristics than did subjects in either written or audiotape conditions.

As in Experiment 1, subjects exposed to the likable (vs. the unlikable) communicator rated their experience of reading (listening to, viewing) the message as more pleasant ($p = .05$). All subjects correctly recalled the message's topic and overall position. Finally, analyses on subjects' recall of persuasive arguments and ratings of topic importance, effort, and difficulty understanding message content yielded no significant effects that involved the primary experimental variables.

Correlational Analyses

Two multiple-regression analyses were performed, one using data from written subjects ($n = 56$) and one using data from videotape and audiotape subjects ($n = 106$). Both analyses predicted initial opinion change from arguments recalled, positive minus negative message-oriented thoughts, positive minus negative communicator-oriented thoughts, Attractiveness factor scores, and Expertise factor scores. These analyses yielded findings that were slightly different from, yet generally compatible with, the results obtained in Experiment 1. For written subjects, the only significant predictor of initial opinion change was the positive minus negative message-oriented thoughts index, $\beta = .58, F(1, 50) = 25.32, p < .001$: Greater opinion change was associated with a greater number of positive (vs. negative) message-oriented thoughts. For videotape and audiotape subjects, significant predictors of opinion change were heightened perceptions of communicator expertise, $\beta = .31, F(1, 100) = 9.12, p < .005$, and a greater number of positive (vs. negative) message-oriented thoughts, $\beta = .41, F(1, 100) = 19.51, p < .001$. Although the positive minus negative message-oriented thoughts index thus contributed significantly to the prediction equation for both the written and the videotape/audiotape subject samples, it was, nevertheless, a slightly better predictor of opinion change within written (vs. videotape/audiotape) conditions, $t(158) = 1.09$, ns.

DISCUSSION

The present analysis of the persuasive impact of communication modality suggested taking into account the valence of communicator attributes and the effect of modality on the salience of these characteristics. Based on the assumption that nonverbal communicator-related cues in videotaped and audiotaped messages draw recipients' attention to the communicator, we hypothesized that communicator characteristics should be more salient and thus exert a greater (positive or negative) persuasive impact when messages are transmitted in videotaped or audiotaped, rather than written, form.

The two experiments, which utilized three different persuasion topics, provided fairly strong support for this hypothesis. On a marginal basis in Experiment 1 and a significant basis in Experiment 2, the likable communicator was more persuasive when his message was transmitted by videotape or audiotape rather than when transmitted in written form. In contrast, in both experiments, the unlikable communicator was significantly more persuasive when his message was transmitted in written form rather than when transmitted by videotape or audiotape. As a consequence of these opposing effects of modality on the persuasive

impact of communicator likability, the likable communicator proved significantly more persuasive than his unlikable counterpart only when subjects received videotaped or audiotaped (vs. written) messages. Communicator likability, then, proved a more powerful determinant of persuasion in the broadcast media than in the written modality.

The findings also proved generally consistent with our underlying assumption that recipients of videotaped or audiotaped (vs. written) messages would show heightened attention to, and thus greater processing of, communicator cues. In both experiments, subjects emitted more thoughts about the communicator as modality changed from written to audiotape to videotape. In addition, although audiotape and written subjects did not differ reliably in terms of their self-reports of the time they spent thinking about the communicator (vs. message content) and the degree to which they felt distracted from message content, videotape subjects in both experiments tended to report greater thought about the communicator and greater distraction from message content.

Based on Chaiken's (1978, 1980, Note 1) heuristic versus systematic analysis of persuasion, we expected that heightened attention to communicator cues in the broadcast media might occur at the expense of attention to message content with the result that persuasion would be primarily determined by communicator-based (vs. message-based) cognitions in the broadcast media (vs. the written modality). The results on the distraction measure, as well as the (nonsignificant) tendency in both studies for videotape (vs. written or audiotape) subjects to generate fewer message-oriented thoughts, provided suggestive evidence for this hypothesis. Stronger support was provided by our regression analyses, which examined the relative influence of subjects' communicator-based and message-based cognitions on opinion change. In Experiment 1, communicator-based, but not message-based, cognitions significantly predicted opinion change for videotape and audiotape subjects, whereas message-based, but not communicator-based, cognitions significantly predicted opinion change among written subjects. Paralleling these findings, in Experiment

2, subjects' perceptions of the communicator proved to be a significant predictor of opinion change within videotaped and audiotaped, but not written, conditions. Also, although message-based cognitions significantly predicted opinion change for all Experiment 2 subjects, these cognitions tended to be a slightly better predictor of persuasion among written (vs. videotape and audiotape) subjects.[5]

Persistence of Opinion Change

Based on findings that opinion change persists longer to the extent that it is bolstered by topic-relevant cognitions (Chaiken, 1980; Cook & Flay, 1978) and the expectation that recipients of written (vs. videotaped or audiotaped) messages would predicate their (initial) opinion judgments primarily on the basis of message content (vs. their perceptions of the communicator), we hypothesized that, regardless of communicator likability, greater delayed opinion change would be manifested by subjects originally exposed to written (vs. videotaped or audiotaped) messages. Although the Time of Posttest × Modality × Likability interaction implied by this hypothesis proved only marginal ($p < .15$) in the repeated-measures analysis of the Experiment 2 opinion data, it did describe the anticipated pattern of findings.

---

[5] The finding that, along with communicator-based cognitions, message-based cognitions significantly predicted opinion change for videotaped and audiotaped subjects in Experiment 2 but not Experiment 1 may be due to the different persuasion topics employed. Although none of our three topics were rated extremely in terms of personal importance, the Experiment 2 topics (OSAP grants and, especially, tuition increases) were considered somewhat more important than the Experiment 1 trimester topic. The greater processing of message cues that occurred among videotape and audiotape subjects in Experiment 2 may have been due, then, to the greater personal importance of the topics employed. This reasoning is consistent with the heuristic versus systematic analysis, which suggests that higher issue involvement increases the persuasive impact of message content. Because this analysis also suggests that higher involvement decreases the persuasive impact of noncontent cues (see text), the fact that communicator likability exerted a weaker overall effect on opinion change in Experiment 2 ($p = .13$) than in Experiment 1 ($p < .001$) may also be a product of differences in topic importance.

Whereas the immediate persuasive impact of modality was, as already discussed, contingent on communicator likability, with the result that modality alone exerted no overall impact on initial opinion change ($F < 1.0$), delayed opinion change was, as expected, somewhat greater for subjects originally exposed to written, compared to audiotaped or videotaped, messages ($p < .15$).

The failure to obtain stronger evidence in support of our persistence hypothesis may be a product of two factors. First, the repeated-measures analysis of opinion change may have lacked adequate statistical power because, due to subject attrition (see above), it was based on 20% fewer observations than the main analysis of initial opinion change was. Second, and probably more important, unlike their Experiment 1 counterparts, videotape and audiotape subjects in Experiment 2 tended to base their initial opinion judgments at least partially on their reactions to message content (see above). Thus, the main requirement underlying our persistence hypothesis—that recipients of videotaped or audiotaped (vs. written) messages would show little, if any, tendency to process message content—was not fully met in Experiment 2 (see Footnote 5). Further research on media effects should address itself more seriously to the issue of opinion persistence. Although the present findings can be considered only tentative, they do suggest that, whereas the immediate impact of a persuasive message can be maximized by utilizing an electronic medium and a communicator with positively valenced personal attributes, a relatively enduring change in opinions may be more likely to occur when the written modality is employed.

Communicator Likability and Opinion Change

The present research was less informative about the mediation of the persuasive impact of communicator likability. Although in both studies subjects responded with more positive thoughts (regardless of orientation) when they received a message from a likable (vs. an unlikable) communicator, the effects of modality on this difference in cognitive responding were inconsistent across the two studies: In Experiment 2, but not in Experiment 1, subjects' positive (and also negative) thoughts were more polarized in videotaped and audiotaped (vs. written) conditions. Thus, it seems unlikely that the greater persuasive impact of communicator likability in the broadcast modalities can be viewed simply as a product of how positive subjects' thoughts were as they listened to the message. A similar point can be made in relation to subjects' communicator ratings. Although in Experiment 2, perceptions of communicator attractiveness were more polarized in the videotaped and audiotaped (vs. written) modalities, this effect was not obtained in Experiment 1.

The absence of consistent covariation of opinion change with either cognitive responses or perceived communicator attractiveness is not problematic in terms of our assumptions about the cognitive mediation of persuasion. We assumed that people process communicator cues more thoroughly when their attention is drawn to the communicator. Because people think more about the communicator, his or her attributes exert a greater persuasive impact, regardless of whether their image of the communicator or their cognitive responses become more positive (for the likable communicator) or more negative (for the unlikable communicator). As suggested by the heuristic view of persuasion (in which simple rules or cognitive heuristics mediate persuasion), the persuasive impact of communicator likability may reflect recipients' use of a simple schema such as "people generally agree with persons they like" (Chaiken, 1980). In this regard, it is important to note that the likability manipulation had no impact in either experiment on measures presumed to reflect subjects' processing of message content (e.g., message-oriented thoughts, argument recall, and time spent thinking about persuasive argumentation vs. time spent thinking about communicator characteristics). These findings are consistent with previous research (e.g., Chaiken, 1980; Norman, 1976; Snyder & Rothbart, 1971) and the heuristic view of persuasion in that they indicate that communicator characteristics such as

likability often directly affect recipients' tendencies to accept or reject a message's overall conclusion without necessarily influencing recipients' processing of message content.

Vividness and Persuasion

In a recent review paper, Taylor and Thompson (1982) concluded that, despite the intuitive appeal of the hypothesis that vivid (vs. nonvivid) information is more impactful, empirical evidence is equivocal. These authors suggested that some failures to demonstrate vividness effects might be attributed to researchers' failures to specify exactly what is being made more vivid by their particular vividness manipulations. A simple application of the vividness logic to the modality-persuasion literature, for example, predicts that the more "vivid" broadcast modalities should effect greater persuasion than the less vivid written modality. This is, in fact, the logic applied to this literature by Taylor and Thompson, and they concluded, as we would, that much research fails to support it. Our analysis, however, suggested that it is not necessarily persuasive message content that is made more vivid in the broadcast modalities but, rather, communicator-related information. Given this clarification, the present finding that communicator likability exerted a greater persuasive impact when videotaped or audiotaped (vs. written) messages were transmitted provides good evidence in support of the vividness hypothesis.[6]

Our research also lends credence to Taylor and Thompson's (1982) speculation that vividness effects, like the conceptually similar sa-

---

[6] Although our experiments represent a relatively clear demonstration that vivid information is more impactful, they provide little information (nor were they designed to) regarding the cognitive mediation of vividness effects. Indeed, our findings are consistent with any number of mechanisms that have been postulated to underlie vividness effects (e.g., differential verbal and/or visual recall, differential ease of recall [availability] of vivid information). For elaborated discussions of retrieval-based explanations for vividness effects as well as the idea that vividness effects may occur directly at the encoding (vs. the retrieval) stage of information processing, see Taylor and Thompson (1982) and McArthur (1980).

lience effect, may occur primarily under conditions of differential, rather than absolute, attention. According to Taylor and Thompson, most vividness studies have exposed subjects to *either* vivid or nonvivid information (but not to both). In contrast, the present persuasion research dealt with a situation in which two main sources of information—communicator cues versus message content—competed for subjects' attention. Under this relatively naturally occurring condition of differential attention, we were able to obtain a clear vividness effect.

As the Taylor and Thompson (1982) review makes clear, studies relevant to assessing vividness effects differ widely, both in terms of dependent variables (e.g., attitudes and attitude change, attributions, and frequency estimations) and types of vividness manipulations employed (e.g., videotaped vs. audiotaped vs. written communications; pictorially vs. not pictorially illustrated information; concrete vs. abstract information; case history vs. base rate or other statistical information). Because of the heterogeneous nature of the vividness literature, the specific implications of the present analysis for understanding vividness phenomena in general are necessarily limited. Thus, there are several aspects of our analysis that may be important when investigating vividness phenomena in the modality-persuasion literature but largely irrelevant when analyzing other vividness phenomena: (a) our distinction between types of information (communicator cues vs. message content), (b) our contention that communication modality often influences the vividness of one type of information (communicator cues) rather than the other (message content), and (c) our suggestion that other persuasion variables (e.g., involvement—see Footnote 2) need to be considered because of their possible moderating effect on the persuasive impact of vivid and nonvivid information. Yet, despite the diversity of experimental paradigms used in vividness research, these aspects of our analysis of the modality-persuasion literature do suggest some general guidelines for "stalking" vividness effects: (a) experimental settings should be fully analyzed in terms of the kind(s) of information available to subjects

and the theoretical relevance of this information to the judgment under study, (b) vividness manipulations need to be more carefully examined in terms of what information they render more vivid, and (c) other factors in the experimental setting (manipulated or not) may need to be considered because of their possible moderating influence on the judgmental impact of vividly and nonvividly presented information.

CONCLUSION

We have suggested that media effects in persuasion can be fruitfully explored in terms of the message recipient's mode of processing information (Chaiken, 1978, 1980, Note 1): The greater salience of communicator cues in the videotaped and audiotaped modalities favors heuristic processing, whereas the relatively greater salience of message content in the written modality favors systematic processing.

As a result of the greater salience of communicator characteristics in the broadcast media, these media may sometimes have a persuasive advantage over the written medium provided that a communicator has positive attributes. Of course, with a communicator who has negative attributes, the video and audio modalities are at a disadvantage.

In an earlier study (Chaiken & Eagly, 1976), we demonstrated that people's ability to comprehend information must be taken into account in understanding media effects. Because message recipients have more trouble understanding complex material in videotaped and audiotaped modalities, the written modality has a persuasive advantage for inherently difficult material because it facilitates comprehension of complex persuasive argumentation. This superior message comprehension with written messages is one indicator of the greater attention to message content that accompanies systematic processing. Further research following from our framework should reveal that message variables other than comprehensibility also contribute to the persuasive impact of communication modality. For example, because of the greater salience of message content in the written modality, high-quality argumentation should be a greater advantage and low-quality argumentation a greater disadvantage in the written (vs. videotaped or audiotaped) modality.

Given these considerations, only highly contingent and tentative advice might be given to those interested in choosing a maximally persuasive medium for conveying a particular message. Maximum persuasiveness could be achieved in one modality or another depending on factors such as communicator attractiveness and message difficulty (and, perhaps, message quality). Further, the persistence of changed opinions is a critical issue when applications are considered. Although, as we have suggested, the written modality may have an inherent advantage as far as enduring change is concerned, so far we can bring little empirical evidence to bear on this important issue.

REFERENCE NOTE

1. Chaiken, S. *The heuristic/systematic processing distinction in persuasion.* Paper presented at the Symposium on Automatic Processing, Society for Experimental Social Psychology, Nashville, Indiana, October 1982.

REFERENCES

Andreoli, V., & Worchel, S. Effects of media, communicator, and message position on attitude change. *Public Opinion Quarterly*, 1978, *42,* 59–70.

Beighley, K. C. An experimental study of the effect of four speech variables on listener comprehension. *Speech Monographs*, 1952, *19*, 249–258.

Brock, T. C. Communication discrepancy and intent to persuade as determinants of counterargument production. *Journal of Experimental Social Psychology*, 1967, *3*, 296–309.

Calder, B. J., Insko, C. A., & Yandell, B. The relation of cognitive and memorial processes to persuasion in a simulated jury trial. *Journal of Applied Social Psychology*, 1974, *4*, 62–93.

Cantril, H., & Allport, G. W. *The psychology of radio.* New York: Harper Brothers, 1935.

Chaiken, S. *The use of source versus message cues in persuasion: An information processing analysis.* Unpublished doctoral dissertation, University of Massachusetts—Amherst, 1978.

Chaiken, S. Heuristic versus systematic information processing and the use of source versus message cues in persuasion. *Journal of Personality and Social Psychology*, 1980, *39*, 752–766.

Chaiken, S., & Eagly, A. H. Communication modality as a determinant of message persuasiveness and message comprehensibility. *Journal of Personality and Social Psychology*, 1976, *34*, 606–614.

Cook, T. D., & Flay, B. R. The persistence of experimentally induced attitude change. In L. Berkowitz (Ed.), *Advances in experimental social psychology* (Vol. 11). New York: Academic Press, 1978.

Eagly, A. H. Comprehensibility of persuasive arguments as a determinant of opinion change. *Journal of Personality and Social Psychology*, 1974, *29*, 758–773.

Eagly, A. H. Sex differences in influenceability. *Psychological Bulletin*, 1978, *85*, 86–116.

Eagly, A. H., & Warren, R. Intelligence, comprehension, and opinion change. *Journal of Personality*, 1976, *44*, 226–242.

Frandsen, K. D. Effects of threat appeals and media of transmission. *Speech Monographs*, 1963, *30*, 101–104.

Harwood, K. A. An experimental comparison of listening comprehensibility with reading comprehensibility. *Speech Monographs*, 1951, *18*, 123–124.

Haugh, O. M. The relative effectivenss of reading and listening to radio drama as ways of imparting information and shifting attitudes. *Journal of Educational Research*, 1952, *45*, 489–498.

Insko, C. A., Lind, E. A., & LaTour, S. Persuasion, recall, and thoughts. *Representative Research in Social Psychology*, 1976, *7*, 66–78.

Keating, J. P., & Latané, B. Politicians on TV: The image is the message. *Journal of Social Issues*, 1976, *32*, 116–132.

Knower, F. H. Experimental studies of changes in attitudes: I. A study of the effect of oral argument on changes of attitude. *Journal of Social Psychology*, 1935, *6*, 315–347.

Knower, F. H. Experimental studies of changes in attitudes: II. A study of the effect of printed argument on changes in attitude. *Journal of Abnormal and Social Psychology*, 1936, *30*, 522–532.

McArthur, L. Z. Illusory causations and illusory correlations: Two epistemological accounts. *Personality and Social Psychology Bulletin*, 1980, *6*, 507–519.

McArthur, L. Z. What grabs you? The role of attention in impression formation and causal attribution. In E. T. Higgins, C. P. Herman, & M. P. Zanna (Eds.), *Social Cognition: The Ontario Symposium* (Vol. 1). Hillsdale, N.J.: Erlbaum, 1981.

McGinnies, E. A cross-cultural comparison of printed communications versus spoken communications in persuasion. *Journal of Psychology*, 1965, *60*, 1–8.

Miller, N., Maruyama, G., Beaber, R. J., & Valone, K. Speed of speech and persuasion. *Journal of Personality and Social Psychology*, 1976, *34*, 615–624.

Minium, E. W. *Statistical reasoning in psychology and education.* New York: Wiley, 1970.

Myers, J. L. *Fundamentals of experimental design* (3rd ed.). Boston: Allyn & Bacon, 1979.

Nisbett, R. E., & Ross, L. *Human inference: Strategies and shortcomings of social judgment.* Englewood Cliffs, N.J.: Prentice-Hall, 1980.

Norman, R. When what is said is important: A comparison of expert and attractive sources. *Journal of Experimental Social Psychology,* 1976, *12,* 294–300.

Osterhouse, R. A., & Brock, T. C. Distraction increases yielding to propaganda by inhibiting counterarguing. *Journal of Personality and Social Psychology,* 1970, *15,* 344–358.

Petty, R. E., Cacioppo, J. T., & Goldman, R. Personal involvement as a determinant of argument-based persuasion. *Journal of Personality and Social Psychology,* 1981, *41,* 847–855.

Short, J. A., Williams, E., & Christie, B. *The social psychology of telecommunications.* London: Wiley International, 1976.

Snyder, M., & Rothbart, M. Communicator attractiveness and opinion change. *Canadian Journal of Behavioral Science,* 1971, *3,* 377–387.

Tannenbaum, P. H., & Kerrick, J. S. Effect of newscast item leads upon listener interpretation. *Journalism Quarterly,* 1954, *31,* 33–37.

Taylor, S. E., & Fiske, S. T. Salience, attention, and attribution: Top of the head phenomena. In L. Berkowitz (Ed.), *Advances in experimental social psychology* (Vol. 11). New York: Academic Press, 1978.

Taylor, S. E., & Thompson, S. C. Stalking the elusive "vividness" effect. *Psychological Review,* 1982, *89,* 155–181.

Werner, C. Intrusivenss and persuasive impact of three communication media. *Journal of Applied Social Psychology,* 1978, *8,* 145–162.

Werner, C., & Latané, B. Responsiveness and communication medium in dyadic interactions. *Bulletin of the Psychonomic Society,* 1976, *8,* 13–15.

Westover, F. L. A comparison of listening and reading as a means of testing. *Journal of Educational Research,* 1958, *52,* 23–26.

Wilke, W. H. An experimental comparison of the speech, the radio, and the printed page as propaganda devices. *Archives of Psychology,* 1934, *25* (No. 169) 32.

Wilson, C. E. The effect of medium on loss of information. *Journalism Quarterly,* 1974, *51,* 111–115.

Worchel, S., Andreoli, V., & Eason, J. Is the medium the message? A study of the effects of media, communicator, and message characteristics on attitude change. *Journal of Applied Social Psychology,* 1975, *5,* 157–172.

9

The Effects of Involvement on Responses to Argument Quantity and Quality: Central and Peripheral Routes to Persuasion

Richard E. Petty and John T. Cacioppo

Like the Chaiken and Eagly paper, this contemporary paper on attitude change focuses on two basic processes of persuasion. In this case, the "central" route to persuasion, in which the person thinks about the merits of the arguments, is contrasted with the "peripheral" route, in which more extraneous cues (such as the mere number of arguments, or communicator characteristics) are decisive. Petty and Cacioppo hypothesized that personal involvement in the issue produces more central processing, and therefore they selected topics of high versus low personal concern for the students who served as subjects. The main study, rather than the pilot study, deserves most attention here. The main findings are shown in Figures 1 and 2: With high personal involvement, the quality of arguments is the decisive determinant of acceptance of a persuasive communication. With low personal involvement, the main factor is simply the number of arguments given, as if the subjects did not actually process the content of the arguments. As in the previous paper, an effort is also made to obtain direct measures of the quality of processing, using the "thought-listing" technique. These results are shown in Figure 3, and they parallel those obtained for the main dependent variable. This again raises the question of whether or not such measures really provide independent measures of the underlying process, or just provide alternate measures of the dependent variable itself. This research illustrates the current emphasis on social cognition and use of more comprehensive and complex theories that often results in the prediction of interactions.

ABSTRACT. *A pilot study and an experiment were conducted to test the view that the number of arguments in a message could affect agreement with a communication by serving as a simple acceptance cue when personal involvement was low but could affect agreement by enhancing issue-relevant thinking when personal involvement was high. In addition to manipulating the personal relevance of the communication topic in each study, both the number and the quality of the arguments in the message were varied. In the pilot study, when the issue was of low relevance, subjects showed more agreement in* response to a message containing six arguments (3 strong and 3 weak) than to messages containing either three strong or three weak arguments. Under high involvement, however, the six-argument message did not increase agreement over the message containing only three strong arguments. In the full experiment, subjects received either three or nine arguments that were either all cogent or all specious under conditions of either high or low involvement. The manipulation of argument number had a greater impact under low than under high involvement, but the manipulation of argument quality had a greater impact under high than under low involvement. Together, the studies indicated that increasing the number of arguments in a message could affect persuasion *whether or not the actual content of the arguments was scrutinized.*

Persuasion is defined by the presentation of persuasive arguments, and the accumulated research in social psychology has generally supported the view that increasing the number of arguments in a message enhances its persuasive impact (e.g., Eagly & Warren, 1976; Maddux & Rogers, 1980; Norman, 1976). Previous analyses of this effect have suggested that increasing the number of arguments in a message enhances persuasion by giving people more information to think about. More specifically, people are postulated to generate favorable issue-relevant thoughts in response to cogent issue-relevant arguments, and the more issue-relevant arguments presented (at least up to some reasonable limit; see Calder, 1978), the more favorable thoughts that should result and the more persuasion that should occur. For example, Calder, Insko, & Yandell (1974; Experiment 2) varied the number of prosecution and defense arguments in the case materials for a hypothetical trial and found that persuasion generally followed the preponderance of arguments. In addition to attitude measures, these authors included a measure of subjects' idiosyncratic thoughts about the trial (see Brock, 1967) and concluded that "beliefs are derived from thoughts about the communication; and these thoughts themselves are partially a function of the amount of objective information on either side of the case" (Calder et al., 1974, p. 86; see also Chaiken, 1980, and Insko, Lind, & LaTour, 1976, for additional evidence consistent with this view).

Although increasing the number of arguments may enhance persuasion by increasing favorable issue-relevant thoughts in some instances, we have suggested that increasing the number of arguments in a message can induce attitude change even if people are *not* thinking about the arguments at all (Petty, Cacioppo, & Goldman, 1981). If people are unmotivated or are unable to think about the message, and no other salient cues are available, they might invoke the simple but reasonable decision rule, "the more arguments the better," and their attitudes might change in the absence of think-

ing about or scrutinizing the arguments. Accordingly, persuasion may require only that people realize that the message contains either relatively few or relatively many arguments. A major goal of this article is to provide empirical evidence for the view that the number of arguments in a message can affect persuasion either by affecting issue-relevant thinking or by serving as a simple acceptance cue.

CENTRAL AND PERIPHERAL ROUTES TO PERSUASION

In a recent review of the attitude-change literature (Petty & Cacioppo, 1981), we proposed that, even though the many different theories of persuasion have different terminologies, postulates, underlying motives, and particular effects that they specialize in explaining, most approaches to persuasion emphasize one of two distinct routes to attitude change. One, called the *central route*, says that attitude change results from a person's careful consideration of information that reflects what that person feels are the true merits of a particular attitudinal position. According to this view, if under scrutiny the message arguments are found to be cogent and compelling, favorable thoughts will be elicited that will result in attitude change in the direction of the advocacy. If the arguments are found to be weak and specious, they will be counterargued and the message will be resisted—or boomerang (change opposite to that intended) may even occur. To the extent that increasing the number of arguments in a message affects persuasion by enhancing issue-relevant cognitive activity, the central route to persuasion has been followed.

However, people are not always motivated to think about the information to which they are exposed, nor do they always have the ability to do so, yet attitudes may change nonetheless. Attitude changes that occur via the second or *peripheral route* do not occur because the person has diligently considered the pros and cons of the issue; they occur because the person associates the attitude issue or object with positive or negative cues or makes a simple inference about the merits of the advocated position based on various simple cues in the persuasion context. For example, rather than carefully evaluating the issue-relevant arguments, a person may accept an advocacy simply because it is presented during a pleasant lunch or because the message source is an expert. Similarly, a person may reject an advocacy simply because the position presented appears to be too extreme or because the source is unattractive. These cues (e.g., good food, expert and attractive sources, extreme positions) may shape attitudes or allow a person to decide what attitudinal position to adopt without the need for engaging in any extensive thought about the arguments presented. To the extent that a person agrees with a recommendation because of the simple perception that there are a lot of arguments to support it, the peripheral route to persuasion has been followed.

As we noted earlier, previous researchers have made the reasonable suggestion that the number of arguments in a message affects agreement by giving recipients more to think about (central route; see Calder et al., 1974; Chaiken, 1980; Insko et al., 1976) but have not tested the possibility that the number of arguments in a message might serve as a peripheral cue to the validity of the advocacy. Social psychological studies of leadership have strongly supported the view that attitudes and beliefs may be affected by the mere number of things that a person says (e.g., Bavelas, Hastorf, Gross, & Kite, 1965; Stang, 1973). For example, the greater the amount of information presented by a group member, the more likely that person is to be rated or chosen as a leader (e.g., Jaffe & Lucas, 1969; Regula & Julian, 1973; Sorrentino & Boutillier, 1975). It is important that the quantity of information presented by a group member has not been found to affect perceptions of leadership if group members have an alternative and more salient cue on which to base their judgments. For instance, Ginter & Lindskold (1975) varied the quantity of information that a group member (confederate) provided and whether she was introduced as an expert prior to the group interaction. The amount of the confederate's participation affected perceptions of leadership only when she was not described as an

expert. When the expertise of the confederate was made salient, she received most of the leader nominations whether she said a little or a lot.

Similar effects have been observed in the persuasion literature. For example, in two experiments Cook (1969) varied the number of arguments in a message (1 vs. 8 in Experiment 1; 2 vs. 10 in Experiment 2) and the expertise of the message source. Although both experiments used similar topics (cultural truisms), in the first experiment subjects' attitudes were affected more by the expertise than by the number of arguments manipulation, and in the second study the opposite occurred. One possible explanation for this result is that in Experiment 1 the expertise manipulation was more salient than the number-of-arguments manipulation, but in Experiment 2 the reverse was true. In fact, the descriptions of the high- and low-expert sources averaged 87 words in the first study and only 7 words in the second experiment. These results suggest quite reasonably that when two peripheral cues compete, the more salient cue has more impact.

According to the central/peripheral analysis of attitude change, people should follow the central route to persuasion when their motivation and ability to think about the issue-relevant arguments presented are relatively high, but the peripheral route should be followed when either motivation or ability to scrutinize the message arguments is relatively low. Many variables have been shown to affect persuasion by enhancing or reducing the motivation and/or the ability to think about issue-relevant arguments (see Petty & Cacioppo, 1981, 1983, for reviews). Recent research suggests that if people have the ability to think about a message (i.e., the message is not too complex, few distractions are present, etc.), one important motivational moderator of the route to persuasion is the personal relevance of the advocacy. As an issue increases in personal relevance or consequences, it becomes more important and adaptive to form a reasoned and veridical opinion, and people become more motivated to devote the cognitive effort required to evaluate the issue-relevant arguments that are presented. Thus, when a message is high in personal relevance, the quality of the issue-relevant arguments in the message is an important determinant of persuasion (Petty & Cacioppo, 1979b). When personal relevance is low, however, people are less motivated to engage in the considerable cognitive work necessary to evaluate the issue-relevant arguments and they rely more on peripheral cues to evaluate the advocacy. Thus, when a message is low in relevance, variables such as the expertise or the likableness of the message source have a greater impact on attitude change than the nature of the arguments provided (Chaiken, 1980; Petty et al., 1981; Petty, Cacioppo, & Schumann, 1983).

The central/peripheral analysis suggests that manipulating the number of arguments in a message can induce persuasion via either the central or the peripheral route. Specifically, increasing the number of arguments in a message might enhance persuasion by invoking a simple decision rule, "the more the better," when the personal relevance of a message is low, because people are unmotivated to exert the cognitive effort necessary to evaluate the merits of the arguments (peripheral route). However, increasing the number of arguments in a message might enhance persuasion by affecting issue-relevant thinking when the personal relevance of a message is high, because when the advocacy has personal consequences, it is adaptive to exert the effort necessary to evaluate the true merits of the proposal (central route).

PILOT STUDY

To provide an exploratory test of the idea that the number of arguments in a message could affect persuasion by either the central or the peripheral route, 46 undergraduates were asked to read one of three messages that they were led to believe had either high or low personal relevance. All of the messages concerned a faculty proposal to increase student tuition. In the high-involvement conditions, the message advocated that the tuition be increased at the students' own university, whereas in the low-involvement conditions, the message advocated

cated that the tuition be increased at a distant, but comparable, university. The message that subjects read contained either three cogent arguments (e.g., part of the increased revenue could be used to decrease class size at the university, which would facilitate teacher/student interaction), three specious arguments (e.g., part of the increased revenue could be used to improve the blackboards at the university, which would impress campus visitors), or three cogent and three specious arguments (with the cogent arguments presented first). After reading the message, subjects made a slash on a 64-mm line to indicate the extent to which they agreed with the idea of raising tuition.

If the number of arguments in a message served as a peripheral cue to the validity of the message under low involvement, then subjects exposed to the six-argument message should express more agreement with the tuition increase than subjects exposed to either of the messages with three arguments. On the other hand, if subjects evaluated the nature of the arguments under high involvement, then the six-argument message should produce a level of agreement intermediate to the messages containing three strong and three weak arguments. A 2×3 (Involvement $\times$ Message) analysis of variance (ANOVA) on the attitude measure produced a main effect for message type, $F(2, 40) = 11.27, p < .001$, and an Involvement $\times$ Message interaction, $F(2, 40) = 2.72$, $p < .07$, that was consistent with our hypothesis. A Neuman-Keuls analysis of this interaction revealed that under low involvement, three strong arguments did not elicit significantly more agreement than three weak arguments, but six arguments (3 strong plus 3 weak) elicited significantly more agreement than either of the three argument conditions ($ps < .05$). Under high involvement, however, three strong arguments elicited significantly more agreement than three weak arguments ($p < .05$), but the six-argument message did not produce significantly more agreement than did the three strong arguments (although it did produce more agreement than the 3 weak arguments). These results are consistent with the view that under low involvement, people do not evaluate the message arguments, but the number of arguments in a message serves as a peripheral cue as to the worth of the advocacy. Thus, under low involvement, attitudes were affected by the mere number of arguments presented, and quality was unimportant (peripheral route). Under high involvement, however, people were motivated to think about the issue-relevant information presented and thus argument quality was more important than number (central route).

To ensure the reliability of the basic attitudinal effect observed in our pilot study, we conducted a conceptual replication using a different manipulation of involvement and a different attitude issue. In this study, in addition to manipulating the personal relevance of the message, subjects received either three or nine arguments that presented either all cogent or all specious reasons in favor of the advocated position. Also, in addition to the crucial attitude measure, several other measures were obtained. These included questions designed to check on the experimental manipulations and measures of subjects' idiosyncratic thoughts about the message.

Our major hypothesis was conceptually the same as that for the pilot study. Specifically, we hypothesized that under low issue involvement, the number of arguments in the message is a more important determinant of attitudes than is the quality of the arguments. Under low involvement, increasing the number of arguments, whether cogent or specious, should enhance agreement as subjects, who are not motivated to think about the arguments, would employ the simple decision rule, the more the better. On the other hand, under high involvement, we predicted that the quality of the message arguments is a more important determinant of attitudes than is number of arguments. Under high involvement, where subjects are motivated to think about the issue-relevant information, we expected that subjects would think about each new argument presented. If recipients think about each new argument under high involvement—generating favorable thoughts to cogent arguments and unfavorable thoughts to specious ones—then attitudes in response to the cogent and to the specious ar-

guments should be more polarized when nine, rather than only three, arguments are presented.

METHOD

Procedure

One hundred sixty-eight male and female undergraduates at the University of Missouri participated to earn extra credit in an introductory psychology course. The design was a 2 (issue involvement: low or high) × 2 (quality of arguments: weak or strong) × 2 (number of arguments: three or nine) factorial. Subjects were tested in groups of from 6 to 14 in a large classroom that precluded subject interaction. It was possible to conduct all experimental conditions in any one session if enough subjects were present.

On arrival at the appropriate location, subjects received a folder that contained an instruction sheet, an essay, and a questionnaire booklet. The instruction sheet explained that

There are many sources of first impressions—looks, dress, voice, etc. Today we would like for you to look at a sample of what someone else has written and to try to form an impression of that person.

After reading these background comments and a brief description of the author of the passage (see below), all of the subjects were instructed to read the essay contained in the folder. They were also told that as soon as they finished reading the essay, they should respond to the questionnaire booklet and then give it to the experimenter at the front of the room. On completion of the dependent measures, subjects were escorted to another room, where they were thoroughly debriefed, thanked for their participation, and dismissed.

Independent Variables

Issue involvement. In the brief descriptions of the author that accompanied each essay, all of the subjects read that the author of the essay was a faculty member, who was chairperson of the University Committee on Academic Policy. The function of the committee was described as "advising the chancellor on changes in academic policy that should be instituted." In the high-involvement conditions, subjects read that the committee was working on academic changes to be initiated the next year. In the low-involvement conditions, they read that the committee was working on recommendations to take effect in 10 years. Additionally, subjects read:

One of the changes being recommended for (next year/10 years from now) is the imposition of a requirement that seniors take a comprehensive exam in their major area prior to graduation. The exam would be a test of what the student had learned after completing the major, and a certain score would be required if the student was to graduate. The material you will read is the summary section of the report written by the chairperson in which he or she outlines the major reasons why the committee feels the exam policy should begin (next year/in 10 years).

Whereas in the pilot study involvement was manipulated by varying the institution for which the policy change was advocated (the subjects' university or a distant one), the present experiment manipulated involvement by changing the advocated date for implementation at the subjects' own institution. Previous research indicates that this manipulation does not affect attitudes per se (Petty et al., 1981) and is comparable to the involvement manipulation used in the pilot study (see Petty & Cacioppo, 1979a).

Argument quality. For all subjects, the essay began with the statement, "In summary, here are the major reasons why comprehensive exams for seniors should be instituted." Following this statement, one of two different kinds of arguments was presented: strong or weak. Nine separate strong and weak arguments were prepared and pretested (most were elaborations of the strong and the very weak arguments described by Petty, Harkins, & Williams, 1980). In a pretest in which subjects were instructed to think about the arguments, the strong arguments elicited primarily favorable thoughts and

the weak arguments elicited primarily unfavorable thoughts in a postmessage thought listing (see Cacioppo, Harkins, & Petty, 1981, for a description of the thought-listing technique). In addition, pretest ratings of the strong and weak arguments revealed that they did not differ in the extent to which they were "difficult to understand," "hard to follow," or possessed "complex structure." The arguments did, of course, differ in their rated "persuasiveness."

Argument number. Each argument in the message was presented in a distinct, typed paragraph that covered about one third of an 8½ × 11 in. sheet of paper. Subjects were either exposed to all nine of the strong or weak arguments or to three strong or weak arguments randomly selected from the appropriate pool of nine. Specifically, in the three argument conditions, the nine strong and weak arguments were each divided into three unique sets of three arguments, and subjects were exposed to one of these sets. Because subsequent analyses revealed that the particular set of strong or weak arguments to which subjects were exposed failed to affect any of the key dependent measures, we will not discuss this feature of the experimental design further.

Dependent Variables

The first question in the dependent-variable booklet assessed subjects' attitudes toward the senior comprehensive exam proposal. The subjects were informed that because their personal opinions about senior comprehensive exams might bias their ratings of the author, the investigators wanted an indication of their personal feelings on the issue. Subjects were asked to respond to the phrase "Comprehensive Exams for Seniors are" on four 9-point semantic differential scales (good/bad, beneficial/harmful, foolish/wise, and unfavorable/favorable). Because the responses to these scales were highly intercorrelated (average $r = .88$), subjects' scores were summed to form one general index of attitude toward the senior comprehensive exam proposal.

Following the crucial attitude measure, subjects were asked to rate the author of the essay on a variety of dimensions (e.g., shy/outgoing, warm/cold) that were consistent with the cover story.[1] Next, subjects responded to a few questions (described below) that were designed to assess the effectiveness of the experimental manipulations.

Finally, subjects were asked to list five thoughts that occurred to them as they were reading the author's proposal: "Your thoughts may have been about the author, or about the proposal, or neither. Just try to remember the thoughts that crossed your mind while you were reading the material." Five lines were provided for subjects to list their thoughts, one per line. This procedure is somewhat different from the typical methodology employed to assess subjects' idiosyncratic thoughts about a persuasive communication. In the typical assessment of cognitive responses (e.g., Brock, 1967; Cacioppo & Petty, 1979; Eagly, 1974; Greenwald, 1968; Insko et al., 1976; Wood, 1982), subjects are given a brief period of time (e.g., 2–10 min) in which to list their thoughts. The time limit is imposed to maximize the likelihood that subjects list only those thoughts that occurred during message exposure and that they do not have enough time to generate new thoughts (Cacioppo & Petty, 1981). Because previous research with the senior comprehensive exam issue revealed that subjects typically list about four to five thoughts on this topic, it was expected that five spaces would accommodate most subjects without forcing them to generate new responses. The major advantage of the present procedure was that it allowed all experimental groups to be conducted in one session, because subjects were allowed to read their messages (which varied in length) at their own pace and complete the thought listing without being timed. Two trained judges, who were blind to the manipulations and hypotheses, subsequently scored the thoughts listed as either favorable (i.e., a statement expressing a positive reaction to the

comprehensive exam proposal or to the arguments in the message; e.g., "It's about time someone was concerned about a quality education"), unfavorable (i.e., a statement expressing a negative reaction to the arguments or proposal; e.g., "We should do what students want, not parents"), or neither. Interrater agreement was high (average $r = .92$), and disagreements were resolved through discussion.

RESULTS

Manipulation Checks

Three variables were manipulated: argument quality (weak or strong), argument number (3 or 9), and issue involvement (low or high). Evidence for the effectiveness of the argument-quality manipulation comes from the postmessage thought-listing measure. Subjects generated significantly more favorable thoughts in response to the strong ($M = 1.82$) than to the weak ($M = .93$) message arguments, $F(1, 158) = 16.98, p < .0001$, and they generated more unfavorable thoughts in response to the weak ($M = 2.37$) than to the strong ($M = 1.33$) message arguments, $F(1, 158) = 19.61, p < .0001$.[2]

To check subjects' perceptions of the number of arguments contained in the message that they received, they were asked, "About how many arguments did the author put forth in favor of the advocated proposal?" Subjects were free to record any number they wanted, and those exposed to the nine-argument messages claimed that there were significantly more arguments in their messages ($M = 6.60$) than did subjects exposed to the three-argument messages ($M = 3.68$), $F(1, 158) = 87.17, p < .0001$. Thus, subjects had a general idea of how many arguments their messages contained, and this information could therefore serve as a peripheral cue.

---

[1] Only one of these measures was affected significantly by the manipulations. Subjects exposed to the strong arguments rated the author as more intelligent ($M = 8.9$) than subjects exposed to the weak arguments ($M = 8.2$), $F(1, 156) = 7.26, p < .008$.

[2] A preliminary analysis including sex as a factor produced neither main effects nor interactions involving sex on any of the key dependent measures. Thus, this variable was ignored in all subsequent analyses. In the pilot study, sex of subject was not recorded, and, thus, an analysis by sex could not be performed.

Finally, to check the personal-involvement manipulation, subjects were asked to rate the likelihood that comprehensive exams would be instituted at their university before they graduated. On a scale ranging from *not very likely* (1) to *very likely* (11), subjects in the high-involvement conditions rated the likelihood as higher ($M = 6.78$) than did subjects in the low-involvement conditions ($M = 4.38$), $F(1, 158) = 34.16$, $p < .0001$. In addition, a main effect for argument quality, $F(1, 158) = 7.59$, $p < .007$, and an Argument Quality × Involvement interaction, $F(1, 158) = 4.69$, $p < .03$, appeared on this measure. The first effect indicated that subjects exposed to the strong arguments thought that it was more likely that their university would institute the exam requirement before they graduated than did subjects exposed to the weak arguments. The interaction revealed that the effect of argument quality on estimated likelihood was significant only for subjects exposed to the high-involvement message. This finding is consistent with our hypothesis that subjects would scrutinize the message more carefully under high- than under low-involvement conditions.

In sum, it appears that all three independent variables were manipulated successfully. High-involvement subjects perceived that it was more likely that the exam proposal would affect them personally than did low-involvement subjects; subjects receiving the nine-argument messages perceived the messages to contain more arguments than did subjects receiving the three-argument messages; and subjects' thoughts reflected the quality of the arguments in the messages.

Attitudes and Thoughts

All cell means and standard deviations for the attitude and thought data are presented in Table 1. A three-way ANOVA on the index of attitude toward senior comprehensive exams produced three significant effects. First, a main effect for the argument-quality manipulation revealed, not surprisingly, that subjects exposed to the strong arguments ($M = 8.30$) had more favorable attitudes toward the exam proposal than did subjects exposed to the weak

Table 1   Means for Each Experimental Cell on the Attitude and Thoughts Measure

	ARGUMENTS			
	Weak		Strong	
Measure	*3*	*9*	*3*	*9*
Low involvement				
Attitude	4.52	7.71	4.95	8.66
Favorable thoughts	1.14	1.19	1.48	1.57
Unfavorable thoughts	1.62	2.14	1.52	1.33
High involvement				
Attitude	4.10	1.05	8.32	11.30
Favorable thoughts	.75	.65	1.82	2.45
Unfavorable thoughts	3.00	2.70	1.50	.95

Note. Attitude scores represent the sum of ratings on four 9-point semantic differential scales anchored at -4 and $+4$.

arguments ($M = 4.34$), $F(1, 158) = 18.74$, $p < .0001$. More important, however, was the appearance of two significant interactions. First, an Involvement × Number of Arguments interaction, $F(1, 158) = 3.98$, $p < .05$, revealed that the number manipulation had a stronger impact on attitudes under low personal-involvement conditions than under high personal-involvement conditions (see top panel of Figure 1). In fact, a simple effects test of this interaction revealed that increasing the number of arguments produced significantly more agreement under the low-involvement conditions, $F(1, 158) = 9.12$, $p < .01$, but not under the high-involvement conditions ($F < 1$). A complementary Involvement × Quality of Arguments interaction, $F(1, 158) = 13.04$, $p < .0004$, demonstrated that the argument-quality manipulation had a stronger effect under high personal-involvement conditions than under low personal-involvement conditions (see bottom panel of Figure 1). A simple effects test of this interaction revealed that the strong arguments produced significantly more agreement than did the weak arguments under the high-involvement conditions, $F(1, 158) = 32.87$, $p < .0001$, but not under the low-involvement conditions ($F < 1$). In sum, under low involvement, attitudes were affected by number of arguments but not quality, and un-

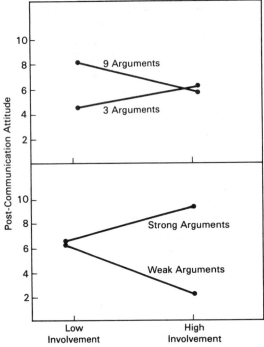

Figure 1.   Top panel: Interactive effect of involvement and number of arguments on postcommunication attitudes. Bottom panel: Interactive effect of involvement and quality of arguments on postcommunication attitudes.

der high involvement, attitudes were affected by quality but not by number.[3]

Although the interactions of both argument number and argument quality with issue involvement provided strong statistical support for our major hypothesis, we further explored

the different effects of the number and quality of arguments manipulations under low- and high-involvement conditions by computing separate Number × Quality anovas for the low- and high-involvement subjects. Under conditions of low involvement, the only effect to emerge was a significant main effect for the number manipulation, $F(1, 79) = 6.89$, $p < .01$. As can be seen in the left panel of Figure 2, under low-involvement conditions, increasing the number of arguments enhanced agreement for both strong and weak arguments. In sharp contrast, in the analysis on high-involvement subjects, two effects emerged. First, as can be seen in the right panel of Figure 2, a main effect for the argument-quality manipulation, $F(1, 79) = 34.57$, $p < .0001$, indicated that subjects showed more agreement to strong than to weak arguments. Second, a significant Number of Arguments × Quality of Arguments interaction, $F(1, 79) = 6.11$, $p < .02$, emerged. This interaction was the result of the joint tendencies for increasing the number of arguments to increase agreement when the arguments were strong, $F(1, 79) = 2.94$, $p <$

[3] In addition, three marginal effects emerged in the analysis. First, a main effect for the number-of-arguments manipulation, $F(1, 158) = 3.52$, $p < .06$, indicated that subjects tended to agree more with the nine- than with the three-argument messages. Second, a Number of Arguments × Quality of Arguments interaction, $F(1, 158) = 3.24$, $p < .07$, revealed that increasing the number of arguments enhanced persuasion only when the arguments were strong. When the arguments were weak, increasing the number of arguments had no effect. The overall lack of an effect of number of arguments on persuasion for weak arguments is consistent with the joint operation of tendencies for increasing the number of weak arguments to enhance agreement under low involvement (where number serves as a cue) but to reduce agreement under high involvement (where subjects think about the arguments). The differential impact of number and quality of arguments on attitudes yielded a marginal three-way interaction, $F(1, 158) = 2.37$, $p < .12$, which is discussed further in the text (see also Figure 2).

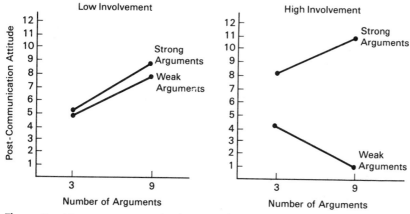

Figure 2. Mean postcommunication attitude in relation to argument quantity and quality for low- and high-involvement recipients.

.10, but to decrease agreement when the arguments were weak, $F(1, 79) = 3.06$, $p < .10$. As a result of these two tendencies, subjects showed greater attitudinal differentiation of the strong from the weak arguments when nine, rather than when three, arguments were presented.

An analysis of subjects' cognitive responses revealed two interaction effects in addition to the main effects already described in the section on manipulation checks. Specifically, an Involvement × Argument Quality interaction appeared on both the number of favorable, $F(1, 158) = 6.11$, $p < .01$, and the number of unfavorable, $F(1, 158) = 6.51$, $p < .01$, thoughts that the subjects listed. The interactions resulted from the subjects' tendencies to generate thoughts that were more consistent with the quality of the arguments when involvement was high rather than when involvement was low. Subjects tended to generate more favorable thoughts to the strong arguments and fewer favorable thoughts to the weak arguments when involvement was high rather than when involvement was low (see left panel of Figure 3) and to generate more unfavorable thoughts to the weak arguments and fewer unfavorable thoughts to the strong arguments when involvement was high rather than when involvement was low (see right panel of Figure 3). These joint tendencies resulted in a pattern where subjects' thoughts significantly differen-

tiated the strong from the weak arguments only when the issue was high in relevance—favorable thoughts, $F(1, 158) = 20.94$, $p < .0001$; unfavorable thoughts, $F(1, 158) = 23.85$, $p < .0001$—and not when the issue was low in relevance ($Fs = 1.36$ and 1.92, respectively).[4]

Discussion

The present research provided initial evidence for the view that increasing the number of arguments in a message can affect attitude change either by enhancing issue-relevant thinking or by serving as a relatively simple acceptance cue. Thus, in the present studies it was observed that if college students were evaluating a relatively low-involvement proposal to raise tuition at a distant university (pilot study) or to institute comprehensive exams at

---

[4] Consistent with these interactions, correlational analyses revealed that although subjects' issue-relevant thoughts were significantly related to attitudes under both low- and high-involvement conditions, the correlation between favorable thoughts and attitudes tended to be higher under high ($r = .56$) than under low involvement ($r = .33$; $Z = 1.83$, $p < .07$). Similarly, the correlation between unfavorable thoughts and attitudes tended to be higher under high ($r = -.52$) than under low involvement ($r = -.38$; $Z = 1.11$, ns). In addition, subjects' perceptions of the number of arguments in the message showed a marginal relationship to attitudes under low involvement ($r = .19$, $p < .09$), but not under high involvement ($r = .02$).

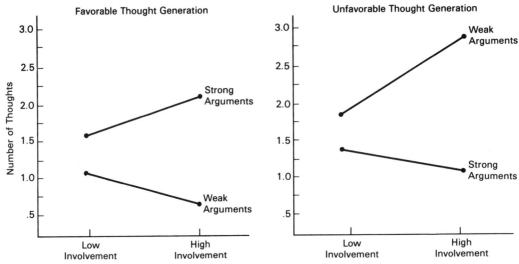

Figure 3. Interactive effect of involvement and quality of arguments on the mean number of favorable and unfavorable thoughts generated.

their own university 10 years in the future, the students found the proposal to be more acceptable the more arguments that were presented in support of it. The quality of the arguments didn't have much impact. On the other hand, when the proposal concerned a relatively immediate increase in tuition or the institution of senior comprehensive exams at their own university, acceptance of the proposal depended more on the quality than on the number of issue-relevant arguments provided.

Previous persuasion studies exploring the effects of increasing the number of arguments have not manipulated quality of arguments, and thus it was not possible to tell if the greater agreement engendered by increasing the number of arguments resulted from increased thinking about the arguments or if the greater agreement resulted from the operation of a simple acceptance cue. The present data suggest that a manipulation of number of arguments can affect attitudes with or without issue-relevant thinking. If the arguments presented are thought about and are strong, then it is likely that the more arguments presented up to some limit (see Calder, 1978), the more favorable cognitions and the more agreement that will result. On the other hand, even if the arguments are not thought about, increas-

ing the number of arguments can still increase agreement because people may employ the simple inference, the more the better, or make the assumption that the more arguments, the more carefully researched the proposal must be. Thus, if a persuasion study manipulates number of arguments but employs only cogent arguments (e.g., Calder et al., 1974; Chaiken, 1980; Eagly & Warren, 1976; Insko et al., 1976; Maddux & Rogers, 1980; Norman, 1976), both types of explanations (issue-relevant thinking and simple inference) make the same prediction: With more arguments, agreement should increase. A manipulation of quality of arguments allows a distinction of these two views because argument quality can affect attitudes only if people think about, scrutinize, and evaluate the information presented. Thus, by manipulating argument quantity and quality in the same study along with the personal relevance of the message, it was possible to determine whether different information-processing strategies were being employed under high and low involvement. The present data strongly indicate that the number of arguments in a message serves as a peripheral cue under low involvement but that the arguments presented are carefully evaluated under high involvement. In addition to issue involvement, other variables that affect a person's motivation and/or ability to scrutinize issue-relevant arguments (e.g., prior knowledge; Cacioppo & Petty, 1980) should also determine the extent to which the mere number of arguments in a message serves as a simple acceptance cue. In general, as motivation or ability to process arguments decreases, the more likely is the number of arguments in a message to affect persuasion by serving as a cue.

Although previous research on peripheral cues has focused on how attributes of the message source (e.g., expertise, attractiveness) can induce persuasion without issue-relevant thinking when people are either relatively unmotivated or unable to think about issue-relevant arguments (Chaiken, 1980; Chaiken & Eagly, 1983; Pallak, Murroni, & Koch, 1983; Petty et al., 1981, 1983), the present research provides an initial indication that features of the persuasive message may also serve as peripheral cues. Thus, in addition to number of arguments, message factors such as the length of the arguments and the complexity of the language employed in the message might also serve as simple cues as to the validity of the message (cf. Wood, Kallgren & Priesler, 1982). Furthermore, in addition to source and message factors, peripheral cues might also be associated with the audience (e.g., the presence of hecklers), the message recipient (e.g., the perception of accelerated heart rate), and the overall persuasion context (e.g., the presence of pleasant surroundings). According to the central/peripheral framework, when motivation or ability to expend cognitive effort are low, cues residing in any of these places may lead people to infer that they like or don't like the advocacy or that it is or is not worth supporting.

In introducing the present study, we note that over the past 30 years of persuasion research, the theories of attitude change that have developed have tended to emphasize either issue-relevant thinking (central route) or some simple cue or inference that is capable of producing attitude change in the absence of issue-relevant thought (peripheral route). The approaches falling under the central route have emphasized factors such as (a) the cogni-

tive justification of attitude-discrepant behavior (Festinger, 1957); (b) the comprehension, learning, and retention of issue-relevant information (e.g., Hovland, Janis, & Kelley, 1953; McGuire, 1969); (c) the nature of a person's idiosyncratic cognitive responses to external communications (e.g., Greenwald, 1968; Petty, Ostrom, & Brock, 1981); and (d) the manner in which a person combines and integrates issue-relevant information into an overall evaluative reaction (e.g., Ajzen & Fishbein, 1980; Anderson, 1981).

In contrast to this focus on the extensive cognitive activity that is central to an evaluation of the merits of a particular attitudinal position, the peripheral approaches have emphasized factors such as whether or not (a) a simple inference can be made based on observing one's own behavior (Bem, 1972), (b) the advocacy falls within one's predetermined latitude of acceptance or rejection (Sherif & Sherif, 1967), (c) some transient situational utility is associated with adopting a particular attitude (Schlenker, 1980), and (d) an advocated position is classically conditioned to basic cues such as food and pain (e.g., Janis, Kaye, & Kirschner, 1965; Zanna, Kiesler, & Pilkonis, 1970) or is associated with secondary cues such as pleasant words or attractive sources (e.g., Kelman, 1961; Staats & Staats, 1958).[5]

The accumulated research on persuasion clearly indicates that neither the central nor the peripheral approaches can account for the diversity of attitude-change results observed (cf., Cialdini, Petty, & Cacioppo, 1981; Eagly & Himmelfarb, 1978). A general framework for understanding attitude change must consider that in some situations people are avid seekers and manipulators of information, whereas at other times people are best described as "cognitive misers" who eschew any difficult information-processing activity (Mc-

---

[5] Our classification of different persuasion theories under either the central or the peripheral route is meant to be suggestive rather than absolute. For example, although self-perception processes may generally induce attitude change via a simple inference, under some circumstances (e.g., high involvement) the observation of one's own behavior might lead to extended issue-relevant thinking (Liebhart, 1979).

Guire, 1969). Given that there are two relatively distinct routes to persuasion, an important question for future research concerns the differential consequences, if any, of the attitude changes induced under each route. We have suggested that there may be two very important consequences of the route to persuasion (Petty & Cacioppo, 1980; 1983).

First, attitude changes induced via the central route may persist longer than changes induced via the peripheral route (Chaiken, 1980; Cialdini, Levy, Herman, Kozlowski, & Petty, 1976). When an attitude change is based on an extensive foundation of issue-relevant beliefs, and these beliefs are rehearsed, the attitude change is likely to persist because the issue-relevant beliefs are likely to remain salient (especially if they are self-generated; see Greenwald, 1968; Slamecka & Graf, 1978). Furthermore, even if a few of the favorable cognitions elicited at the time of message exposure are forgotten, others are likely to remain. On the other hand, attitude changes that result from one prominent cue (e.g., an attractive source) or one simple inference (e.g., if there are so many arguments, it must be good), would appear to be more vulnerable to forgetting. These changes are likely to endure only if the person has been exposed to the persuasive message many times, rendering the cue or inference relatively permanent. Even then, however, such attitude changes would appear to be highly susceptible to counterpropaganda, because the person has so little on which to base a positive or a negative opinion. Thus, the new attitude would be difficult to defend if challenged severely.

A second consequence of the two routes to persuasion is that attitudes formed or changed via the central route may be more predictive of behavior than attitudes formed or changed via the peripheral route (Pallak et al., 1983; Petty et al., 1983). People may have more confidence in attitudes that are based on issue-relevant thinking rather than on peripheral cues, and thus they may be more willing to act on these attitudes. In addition, attitudes based on issue-relevant thinking may be more salient in memory than attitudes based on peripheral

cues, and thus people may be more able to act on them (see Fazio & Zanna, 1981).

Even if future work confirms our speculation about the consequences of the two routes to persuasion, this does not mean that the central route will necessarily be the preferred persuasion strategy. Although the possible benefits of the central route appear prepotent (i.e., greater temporal persistence and more predictive of behavior), a major disadvantage may be the difficulty in inducing persuasion via this route. For persuasion to be induced via the central route, people must have both the ability and the motivation to think about the issue-relevant arguments presented, and the arguments presented must be very convincing and compelling when scrutinized. In laboratory research, it is possible for theory-testing purposes to fabricate cogent evidence and arguments for a given position. In most applied settings (e.g., advertising, psychotherapy, the courtroom), however, there are natural (and legal) constraints on the arguments that can be presented. Thus, for example, in a relatively uninteresting court case where the quality of evidence on each side is about equal, or the evidence is weak, an effective strategy might be to overwhelm the opponent with large amounts of evidence. It is interesting that although social psychologists have addressed how to inoculate people against persuasion via the central route (McGuire, 1964), little research has been conducted on strategies for inoculating people from the invidious use of the peripheral route.

REFERENCES

Ajzen, I., & Fishbein, M. (1980). *Understanding attitudes and predicting social behavior.* Englewood Cliffs, NJ: Prentice-Hall.

Anderson, N. H. (1981). Integration theory applied to cognitive responses and attitudes. In R. E. Petty, T. M. Ostrom, & T. C. Brock (Eds.), *Cognitive responses in persuasion* (pp. 361–397). Hillsdale, NJ: Erlbaum.

Bavelas, A., Hastorf, A. H., Gross, A. E., & Kite, W. R. (1965). Experiments on the alteration of group structure. *Journal of Experimental Social Psychology, 1,* 55–70.

Bem, D. J. (1972). Self-perception theory. In L. Berkowitz (Ed.), *Advances in experimental social psychology* (Vol. 6, pp. 1–62). New York: Academic.

Brock, T. C. (1967). Communication discrepancy and intent to persuade as determinants of counterargument production. *Journal of Experimental Social Psychology, 3,* 269–309.

Cacioppo, J. T., Harkins, S. G., & Petty, R. E. (1981). The nature of attitudes and cognitive responses and their relationships to behavior. In. R. E. Petty, T. M. Ostrom, & T. C. Brock (Eds.), *Cognitive responses in persuasion* (pp. 31–54). Hillsdale, NJ: Erlbaum.

Cacioppo, J. T., & Petty, R. E. (1979). Effects of message repetition and position on cognitive responses, recall, and persuasion. *Journal of Personality and Social Psychology, 37,* 97–109.

Cacioppo, J. T., & Petty, R. E. (1980). Sex differences in influenceability: Toward specifying the underlying processes. *Personality and Social Psychology Bulletin, 6,* 651–656.

Cacioppo, J. T., & Petty, R. E. (1981). Social psychological procedures for cognitive response assessment. In T. Merluzzi, C. Glass, & M. Genest (Eds.), *Cognitive assessment* (pp. 309–342). New York: Guilford.

Calder, B. J. (1978). Cognitive response, imagery, and scripts: What is the cognitive basis of attitude? *Advances in Consumer Research, 5,* 630–634.

Calder, B. J., Insko, C. A., & Yandell, B. (1974). The relation of cognitive and memorial processes to persuasion in a simulated jury trial. *Journal of Applied Social Psychology, 4,* 62–93.

Chaiken, S. (1980). Heuristic versus systematic information processing and the use of source versus message cues in persuasion. *Journal of Personality and Social Psychology, 39,* 752–766.

Chaiken, S., & Eagly, A. H. (1983). Communication modality as a determinant of persuasion: The role of communicator salience. *Journal of Personality and Social Psychology, 45,* 241–256.

Cialdini, R. B., Levy, A., Herman, P., Kozlowski, L., & Petty, R. (1976). Elastic shifts of opinion: Determinants of direction and durability. *Journal of Personality and Social Psychology, 34,* 663–672.

Cialdini, R. B., Petty, R. E., & Cacioppo, J. T. (1981). Attitude and attitude change. *Annual Review of Psychology, 32,* 357–404.

Cook, T. D. (1969). Competence, counterarguing, and attitude change. *Journal of Personality, 37,* 342–358.

Eagly, A. H. (1974). Comprehensibility of persuasive arguments as a determinant of opinion change. *Journal of Personality and Social Psychology, 29,* 758–773.

Eagly, A. H., & Himmelfarb, S. (1978). Attitudes and opinions. *Annual Review of Psychology, 29,* 517–554.

Eagly, A. H., & Warren, R. (1976). Intelligence, comprehension, and opinion change. *Journal of Personality, 44,* 226–242.

Fazio, R. H., & Zanna, M. P. (1981). Direct experience and attitude behavior consistency. In L. Berkowitz (Ed.), *Advances in experimental social psychology* (Vol. 14, pp. 161–202). New York: Academic.

Festinger, L. (1957). *A theory of cognitive dissonance.* Stanford, CA: Stanford University Press.

Ginter, G., & Lindskold, S. (1975). Rate of participation and expertise as factors influencing leader choice. *Journal of Personality and Social Psychology, 32,* 1085–1089.

Greenwald, A. G. (1968). Cognitive learning, cognitive response to persuasion, and attitude change. In A. Greenwald, T. Brock, & T. Ostrom (Eds.), *Psychological foundations of attitudes* (pp. 148–170). New York: Academic.

Hovland, C. I., Janis, I. L., & Kelley, H. H. (1953). *Communication and persuasion: Psychological studies of opinion change.* New Haven, CT: Yale University Press.

Insko, C. A., Lind, E. A., & LaTour, S. (1976). Persuasion, recall, and thoughts. *Representative Research in Social Psychology, 7,* 66–78.

Jaffe, C. L., & Lucas, R. M. (1969). Effects of rates of talking and correctness of decision on leader choice in small groups. *Journal of Social Psychology, 79,* 247–254.

Janis, I. L., Kaye, D., & Kirschner, P. (1965). Facilitating effects of "eating while reading" on responsiveness to persuasive communications. *Journal of Personality and Social Psychology, 1,* 181–186.

Kelman, H. C. (1961). Processes of opinion change. *Public Opinion Quarterly, 25,* 57–78.

Liebhart, E. H. (1979). Information search and attribution: Cognitive processes mediating the effect of false autonomic feedback. *European Journal of Social Psychology, 9,* 19–37.

Maddux, J. E., & Rogers, R. W. (1980). Effects of source expertness, physical attractiveness, and supporting arguments on persuasion. A case of brains over beauty. *Journal of Personality and Social Psychology, 38,* 235–244.

McGuire, W. J. (1964). Inducing resistance to persuasion: Some contemporary approaches. In L. Berkowitz (Ed.), *Advances in Experimental Social Psychology* (Vol. 1, pp. 192–229). New York: Academic.

McGuire, W. J. (1969). The nature of attitudes and attitude change. In G. Lindzey & E. Aronson (Eds.), *The handbook of social psychology* (2nd ed., Vol. 3, pp. 136–314). Reading, MA: Addison-Wesley.

Norman, R. (1976). When what is said is important: A comparison of expert and attractive sources. *Journal of Experimental Social Psychology, 12,* 294–300.

Pallak, S. R., Murroni, E., & Koch, J. (1983). Communicator attractiveness and expertise, emotional versus rational appeals, and persuasion. *Social Cognition*, *2*, 122–141.

Petty, R. E., & Cacioppo, J. T. (1979a). Effects of forewarning of persuasive intent and involvement on cognitive responses and persuasion. *Personality and Social Psychology Bulletin*, *5*, 173–176.

Petty, R. E., & Cacioppo, J. T. (1979b). Issue-involvement can increase or decrease persuasion by enhancing message-relevant cognitive responses. *Journal of Personality and Social Psychology*, *37*, 1915–1926.

Petty, R. E., & Cacioppo, J. T. (1980). Effects of issue involvement on attitudes in an advertising context. In G. Gorn & M. Goldberg (Eds.), *Proceedings of the Division 23 Program* (pp. 75–79). Montreal, Canada: American Psychological Association.

Petty, R. E., & Cacioppo, J. T. (1981). *Attitudes and persuasion: Classic and contemporary approaches.* Dubuque, IA: Wm. C. Brown.

Petty, R. E., & Cacioppo, J. T. (1983). Central and peripheral routes to persuasion: Application to advertising. In L. Percy & A. Woodside (Eds.), *Advertising and consumer psychology* (pp. 3–23). Lexington, MA: D.C. Heath.

Petty, R. E., Cacioppo, J. T., & Goldman, R. (1981). Personal involvement as a determinant of argument-based persuasion. *Journal of Personality and Social Psychology*, *41*, 847–855.

Petty, R. E., Cacioppo, J. T., & Schumann, D. (1983). Central and peripheral routes to advertising effectiveness: The moderating role of involvement. *Journal of Consumer Research*, *10*, 134–148.

Petty, R. E., Harkins, S. G., & Williams, K. D. (1980). The effects of group diffusion of cognitive effort on attitudes: An information processing view. *Journal of Personality and Social Psychology*, *38*, 81–92.

Petty, R. E., Ostrom, T. M., & Brock, T. C. (1981). Historical foundations of the cognitive response approach to attitudes and persuasion. In R. E. Petty, T. M. Ostrom, & T. C. Brock (Eds.), *Cognitive responses in persuasion* (pp. 5–29). Hillsdale, NJ: Erlbaum.

Regula, R. C., & Julian, J. W. (1973). The impact of quality and frequency of task contributions on perceived ability. *Journal of Social Psychology*, *89*, 115–122.

Schlenker, B. R. (1980). *Impression management: The self-concept, social identity, and interpersonal relations.* Monterey, CA: Brooks/Cole.

Sherif, M., & Sherif, C. W. (1967). Attitude as the individual's own categories: The social judgment-involvement approach to attitude and attitude change. In C. W. Sherif & M. Sherif (Eds.), *Attitude, ego-involvement, and change.* New York: Wiley.

Slamecka, N. J., & Graf, P. (1978). The generation effect: Delineation of a phenomenon. *Journal of Experimental Psychology: Human Learning and Memory*, *4*, 592–604.

Sorrentino, R. M., & Boutillier, R. G. (1975). The effect of quantity and quality of verbal interaction on ratings of leadership ability. *Journal of Experimental Social Psychology*, *11*, 403–411.

Staats, A. W., & Staats, C. K. (1958). Attitudes established by classical conditioning. *Journal of Abnormal and Social Psychology*, *57*, 37–40.

Stang, D. J. (1973). Effect of interaction rate on ratings of leadership and liking. *Journal of Personality and Social Psychology*, *27*, 405–408.

Wood, W. (1982). Retrieval of attitude-relevant information from memory: Effects on susceptibility to persuasion and on intrinsic motivation. *Journal of Personality and Social Psychology*, *42*, 798–810.

Wood, W., Kallgren, C., & Priesler, R. (1982). *Access to attitude-relevant information in memory as a determinant of persuasion: The role of message and communicator attributes.* Unpublished manuscript, Texas A & M University.

Zanna, M. P., Kiesler, C. A., & Pilkonis, P. A. (1970). Positive and negative attitudinal affect established by classical conditioning. *Journal of Personality and Social Psychology*, *14*, 321–328.

PART III Interpersonal Attraction and Relationships

10

The Ecological Bases of Friendship

Leon Festinger, Stanley Schachter, and Kurt Back

How do we choose our friends? Research on interpersonal attraction has shown that we tend to select as friends people who share our interests, attitudes, and values. But friendships are also influenced by chance factors outside our control, such as the random assignment of a lab partner in a science class. In this classic study conducted in the late 1940s, Festinger, Schachter, and Back examine how ecological or environmental factors influence the development of friendships. The study took place in two married student apartment complexes, Westgate and Westgate West, where residents were more or less randomly assigned to particular apartments. The researchers cleverly used this naturally occurring experiment to study the impact of geographical proximity on friendship formation. They hypothesized that friendships are encouraged by frequent casual or "passive" contacts that occur as neighbors chat by their mailboxes or see each other on the stairways. These contacts depend in turn on the physical distance between apartments (measured in feet and inches) and the "functional distance" (aspects of the building design such as the location of stairways and doors). The researchers measured friendship by asking each resident to make "sociometric choices," that is, to indicate the three people in the apartment buildings whom they "see most of socially." The results of several analyses showed that proximity was closely linked to friendship. Since residents did not choose their neighbors, we can conclude that close proximity was a cause of the development of these friendships. The closer people lived to each other, the more likely they were to interact and, as a result, to become friends. As you read this report, think about how your own friendships now and in childhood have been influenced by such environmental factors as where your family lived, which schools you attended, and where you sat in class.

From *Social Pressures in Informal Groups* by Leon Festinger, Stanley Schachter, and Kurt Back. Copyright 1950 by Leon Festinger, Stanley Schachter, and Kurt Back. Adapted with permission of Stanford University Press and the authors.

In communities such as Westgate or Westgate West, where people moving into the area have few or no previous contacts in the community, friendships are likely to develop on the basis of the brief and passive contacts made going to and from home or walking about the neighborhood. These brief meetings, if they are frequent enough, may develop into nodding acquaintanceships, then into speaking relationships, and eventually, if psychological factors are right, into friendships. Such casual or involuntary meetings we will call passive contacts.

Passive contacts are determined by the required paths followed in entering or leaving one's home for any purpose. For example, in going from one's door to the stairway one must pass certain apartments; in walking to the butcher shop one must go by certain houses. These specific required paths are determined by the physical structure of the area.

In relating physical structure to the formation of friendships, it is necessary to distinguish between two ecological factors, (1) physical distance, and (2) positional relationships and features of design which we may call functional distance.

1. Physical distance is measured distance and is one of the major determinants of whether or not passive contacts will occur. Obviously there is a high negative relationship between the physical distance separating the homes of two people and the probability that these people will make passive contact. The smaller the physical distance the greater the number of required paths neighbors are likely to share and the greater the probability of passive contacts. For example, in hanging clothes out to dry, or putting out the garbage, or simply sitting on the porch, one is much more likely to meet next-door neighbors than people living four or five houses away.

2. Factors such as the design of a building or the positional relationships among a group of houses are also important determinants of which people will become friends. It is these functional factors of design and position which determine the specific pattern of required paths in an area and consequently determine which people will meet. For example, if there is a stairway at each end of a floor, there is a good chance that people living at opposite ends of the floor will never or rarely meet. Functional distance is measured by the number of passive contacts that position and design encourage.

Both physical distance and functional distance, therefore, will affect the pattern and number of passive contacts. Obviously, they cannot be considered as independent variables, for we can expect a high relationship between the two. In particular cases, however, the distinction becomes clear. For example, two back-to-back houses which are thirty feet apart and have neither back doors nor back yards would be considered functionally farther apart than two back-to-back houses, also thirty feet apart, which do have back doors and yards. Thus we can have varying functional distances while physical distance remains constant.

THE EFFECT OF PHYSICAL DISTANCE ON THE FORMATION OF FRIENDSHIPS

Figure 1 is a schematized representation of the front of a Westgate West building. The porch area provides the only means of entering or leaving the building and is, therefore, the only place within the building in which passive contacts can occur. Each of the doorways is the entrance to a different apartment and the numbers on the doorways will be used to desig-

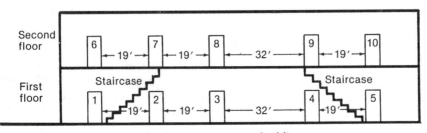

Figure 1. Schematic diagram of a Westgate West building.

nate each apartment position. Each floor consists of five directly adjoining apartments and the two floors are connected by stairways at each end of the porch. With two exceptions the doorways of all adjoining apartments are separated by almost 19 feet. Apartments 3 and 4 and apartments 8 and 9 are separated by 32 feet. The maximum separation on any one floor is the 88 feet between the end apartments.

In order to simplify the presentation of data we have adopted a unit of approximate physical distance to describe the difference between any two apartments in a building. Each unit is the equivalent of the physical distance separating any two neighboring doorways. Thus, in Figure 1, apartments 1 and 2 are one unit of approximate physical distance apart; apartments 1 and 3 are two units apart; apartments 1 and 5 and apartments 6 and 10 are four units apart, and so on. In specifying the distance between apartments on different floors, the letter S is employed as a symbol for the stairways between the first and second floors. Thus, apartments 9 and 1 are separated by two units of physical distance and a stairway and this distance is designated as $2S$; apartments 2 and 7 are separated by 1 unit and a stairway and are $1S$ units apart, and so on. Despite the fact that the stairway on the right-hand side of the building ends midway between apartments 9 and 10, the units are calculated as if this stairway ended right in front of the door of apartment number 9. This procedure has been adopted for simplicity's sake and makes little difference in our results. Where there are two possible routes connecting any apartment on one floor to any apartment on the other floor, the units are always computed for the shorter route.

In order to study the effect of these physical design features on the formation of friendships we may relate such things as physical distance to sociometric choices. These sociometric data were gathered on all residents of Westgate and 166 of the 170 Westgate West residents by asking, "What three people in Westgate or Westgate West do you see most of socially?"

Table 1 presents the data for Westgate West on choices given to people living in the same building and on the same floor as the person who chooses them. The data for all seventeen Westgate West buildings are grouped since all of these buildings are exactly the same.

In column (1) of Table 1 are listed all the approximate physical distances which can separate any two persons living on the same floor. Column (2) presents the total number of choices given to persons living at each distance away from the people who are choosing. These figures, however, are inadequate in this form because there are great differences in the total number of potential choices between people separated by the various distances. There are, for example, many more 1 unit choices than 4 unit choices possible. These figures in column (2) must, consequently, be corrected on the basis of the total number of such possible choices.

Column (3) presents the correction factors for each distance of separation between apartments. The figures in this column represent the total number of choices that could exist in the entire Westgate West project at each separation distance. Thus, at three units distance, there are four possible choices within any one floor; apartments 4 to 1, 5 to 2, 1 to 4, and 2 to 5 on the first floor or, symmetrically,

Table 1 The Relationship Between Sociometric Choice and Physical Distance on One Floor of a Westgate West Building

(1)	(2)	(3)	(4)
Units of Approximate Physical Distance	*Total Number of Choices Given*	*Total Number of Possible Choices*	*Choices Given (2) / Possible Choices (3)*
1	112	8 × 34	.412
2	46	6 × 34	.225
3	22	4 × 34	.162
4	7	2 × 34	.103

apartments 9 to 6, 10 to 7, 6 to 9, and 7 to 10 on the second floor. Since there are seventeen buildings, each with two floors, the number of possible choices at each distance is multiplied by thirty-four. Column (4) presents the corrected sociometric choices at each distance. These figures are arrived at by dividing the figures in column (2) by those in column (3). They state specifically the percentage of possible choices at each distance that were actually made. Thus, 41.2 percent of the 272 possible one unit choices were actually made; 22.5 percent of the 204 possible two unit choices were made.

The data in Table 1 show unequivocally that within the floor of a Westgate West building there is a high relationship between friendships and physical distance. The greatest percentage of possible choices are made to next-door neighbors. These percentages decrease constantly with distance to a minimum of 10.3 percent of all choices that could be exchanged between people four units apart, that is, between those who live at opposite ends of the same floor. It must be remembered that these distances are actually small. Neighboring apartments are about 22 feet apart and apartments at opposite ends of the same floor are only 88 feet apart. Yet these small differences in distance seem to be major determinants of whether or not friendships will form.

These choices given to people living on the same floor represent a very sizeable proportion of the total number of choices given. Forty-four percent of the 426 choices made were given to people living on the same floor as the chooser.

We find a similar relationship of sociometric choice to physical distance in choices given to people living in the same building but on a different floor. Table 2 presents data for between-floor choices. The meaning of each of the columns is the same as in Table 1. The letter S in column (1) is the symbol for stairway.

The data in Table 2 show a high relationship between choices exchanged among people living on different floors of the same barracks and the distance between these people. Again, those people having the smallest physical separation give each other the highest proportion of the total number of possible choices. Thus, 20.6 percent of the 68 possible choices are made at S units, the shortest possible distance between apartments on different floors. These percentages decrease constantly with increasing distance to a low point of 5.9 percent of possible choices between apartments with a separation of 3S or 4S units of approximate physical distance.

Whereas 44 percent of the total number of sociometric choices in Westgate West were made to others on their own floor, only 21 percent of the total choices were made between floors.

The data in columns (4) of Tables 1 and 2 are presented graphically in Figure 2. This figure plots the percentage of the total possible choices made at each approximate physical distance for choices within the same floor and choices between floors. Both curves are monotonically decreasing curves.

Though both curves decrease there are differences between them. The curve for same-floor choices drops sharply from point to point.

Table 2   The Relationship of Sociometric Choices Between Floors of a Westgate West Building to Physical Distance

(1)	(2)	(3)	(4)
Units of Approximate Physical Distance	*Total Number of Choices Given*	*Total Number of Possible Choices*	*Choices Given (2)* / *Possible Choices (3)*
S	14	2 × 34	.206
1S	39	6 × 34	.191
2S	20	8 × 34	.074
3S	14	7 × 34	.059
4S	4	2 × 34	.059

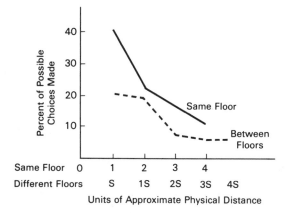

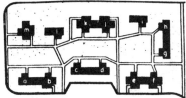

Figure 2. Relationship between physical distance and sociometric choices in Westgate West.

The first two points of the curve for between-floor choices are at about the same level. The curve then drops and the next three points again are all at about the same low level. Both curves are, in part, affected by functional factors but positional relationships have played so strong a part in shaping the between-floor curve that it may well be considered more a curve of functional than of physical distance.

Data on the effects of physical distance on friendship formation are more difficult to obtain for Westgate. Within any one court there are houses next to one another and houses facing one another. Some of the back-to-back houses have back doors while others do not, and so on. Even if one wishes to ignore the possible effects of different functional relationships throughout this community, it would be almost impossible to compute the relationship of physical distance per se to friendship formation because of the extreme difficulty of determining the necessary correction factors for the number of possible choices at various distances.

However, for part of each side of a large Westgate U-shaped court it is possible partially to isolate the effect of physical distance. Figure

3 is a schematic representation of any pair of the six identically designed courts which face one another across the street dividing the project in two. Each of the letters in Figure 3 represents a different house. The houses lettered *b, c, d, e, f,* and those lettered *l, k, j, i, h* are approximately arranged in rows and are somewhat similar in this respect to the five apartments on each floor of a Westgate West building. The end houses *a* and *m* are not included in this grouping because they face onto the street whereas all of the other houses in the row face into the courtyard.

Analysis of the sociometric choices exchanged among the people living in each row of houses follows the same pattern as the analysis of choices among apartments on the same floor of a Westgate West building. Distance between houses is again handled in terms of units of approximate physical distance. Thus, *b* is separated from *c* by one unit, from *d* by two units, and so on. The average measured distance between houses is about 45 feet. Choices are again categorized according to the units of distance separating the house of the person chosen from that of the person choos-

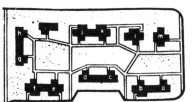

Figure 3. Schematic diagram of the arrangement of the Westgate court.

Table 3   The Relationship of Sociometric Choices Among the Houses in a Row in Westgate Courts to Physical Distance

(1)	(2)	(3)	(4)
Units of Approximate Physical Distance	*Total Number of Choices Given*	*Total Number of Possible Choices*	*Choices Given* (2) / *Possible Choices* (3)
1	26	8 × 12	.271
2	6	6 × 12	.083
3	2	4 × 12	.042
4	0	2 × 12	.000

ing. The data for all twelve rows are pooled and are presented in Table 3. Again, there is the same marked relationship between sociometric choice and physical distance. The greatest proportion of possible choices is made to next-door neighbors. This proportion decreases with increasing distance to the low point of no choices at all to people living four units away.

These data are presented graphically in Figure 4. The curve is similar to the one obtained for choices within one floor of a Westgate West building.

In summary, data for two differently designed housing projects show a strong relationship between sociometric choice and physical distance. In both projects the greatest number of choices were made to people living closest to the person choosing and the choices decreased continuously as distance from the home of the chooser increased. The actual

measured distances involved were quite small, in no case being larger than 180 feet. Yet the effect of even these small distances is so marked that in a Westgate row no choices at all were made between houses with the maximum separation of four units or 180 feet.

THE EFFECT OF PHYSICAL DISTANCE ON CHOICES OUTSIDE OF OWN COURT OR BUILDING

The data presented so far have explored the relationships between sociometric choices and physical distances within a court or building. This same relationship holds for choices outside of the court or building. The greater the physical separation between any two points in these communities, the fewer the friendships. Table 4 presents the data for choices given by Westgaters to people living anywhere in

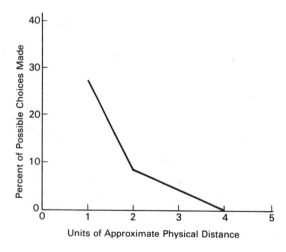

Units of Approximate Physical Distance

Figure 4.   Relationship between physical distance and sociometric choices along each side of the Westgate courts.

Table 4 Sociometric Choices Given by Westgaters to People Living Anywhere in the Two Projects

(1)	(2)	(3)	(4)
			Choices Given (2)
Location of Person Chosen	*Total Number of Choices*	*Total Number of Possibilities*	Possible Choices (3)
Own court	143	1076	.133
Adjacent court	51	2016	.025
Other courts	47	6794	.007
Westgate West	17	17,000	.001

the two projects. Column (1) lists the places of residence of the people chosen. "Own court" refers to a choice made within the court of the chooser; "adjacent court" refers to choices given to people living in immediately neighboring courts. "Other courts" refers to any choice within Westgate which does not fall into the first two categories. "Westgate West" includes all choices given by Westgaters to people in Westgate West. In the order given, these categories approximate a continuum of physical distance. In general, though not in all cases, "own court" choices are physically closer than "adjacent court" choices and so on.

Table 4 makes it obvious that the relationship between physical distance and sociometric choice holds for out-of-court choices as well as in-court choices. Column (4) again shows that the percentage of possible choices made decreases with increasing distance.

The data for Westgate West presents a similar picture. Table 5 shows that for Westgate West, too, there is an inverse relationship between the percentage of possible choices actually made and physical distance.

THE EFFECT OF FUNCTIONAL DISTANCE ON THE FORMATION OF FRIENDSHIPS

Let us now examine the effects of functional distance in Westgate West. Figure 1 shows that each building has a long porch on each floor, with the entrances to each apartment opening out onto the porch. Short stairways (not shown) lead up to each of the lower-floor apartments. Outside stairways at each end of the lower-floor porch connect the two floors, and form the only paths by which upper-floor people can reach their floor.

The left-hand stairway connecting the two floors passes directly in front of the doorway of apartment 1 and close to the door of apartment 7. The connecting stairway on the right passes close by, though not directly in front of, the doorway to apartment 5, and directly between the doorways of the two right-hand apartments, 9 and 10, on the upper floor.

Each of the lower-floor apartments has a small mailbox directly adjoining its doorway. Near the lower-floor apartment 5 is a cluster of five mailboxes which serve all of the upper-floor apartments.

Table 5 Sociometric Choices Given by Westgate West People to People Living Anywhere in the Two Projects

(1)	(2)	(3)	(4)
	Total Number of Choices		Choices Given (2)
Location of Person Chosen	*Made*	*Total Number of Possibilities*	Possible Choices (3)
Own buildings	278	1530	.182
Own quadrangle	49	4000	.012
Other buildings	66	23,200	.003
Westgate	33	17,000	.002

Table 6 The Number of Sociometric Choices the Lower-Floor People Give to and Receive from People Living on the Upper Floors of the Westgate West Buildings

1. Apartment position	1	2	3	4	5
2. Choices given to upper floor	13	5	8	6	11
3. Choices received from upper floor	14	3	12	4	15

These are the details of construction which of themselves will determine the required paths followed in moving in or out of the building. From the nature of these details of design and the required paths they impose on the residents of these buildings, it is possible to make a number of derivations about the relative frequency of passive contacts and, consequently, the sociometric choices exchanged among particular people or groups of people living in each of the buildings. These derivations demand only one assumption—that the people living in these barracks will most frequently use the shortest path between their apartment and their destination.

1. *The people living in the end apartments 1 and 5 on the lower floor should receive from and give to the upper-floor residents more sociometric choices than the people living in any other apartment on the lower floor.*

We can expect this because apartments 1 and 5 are at the foot of the stairways connecting the two floors and are, therefore, the only lower-floor apartments which upper-floor residents must pass in entering or leaving the building. In using the left-hand stairway, upper-floor people must pass directly in front of the doorway of apartment 1. In using the right-hand stairway, upper-floor people pass close to, though not directly in front of, the doorway of apartment 5. In going to their mailboxes upper-floor people do pass the doorway of apartment 5.

Table 6 presents the number of sociometric choices lower-floor people give to and receive from people living on the upper floor. The figures in Row 1 are the apartment numbers as diagrammed in Figure 1. Row 2 presents the number of choices the people in each apartment position on the lower floor give to people on the upper floor of their building, and row

3 presents the number of choices lower-floor people receive from their upstairs neighbors. The figures in Rows 2 and 3 are the combined totals for all seventeen buildings.

We see, then, that the end apartments on the lower floor give far more choices to upper-floor people than do any of the other apartments. The end apartments average 12 choices each to upstairs neighbors, compared to only 6.33 for the three middle apartments. Choices given by apartments 1 and 5 are significantly higher than choices given by 2, 3, and 4 at the 5 percent level of confidence.[1]

Similarly, the end apartments receive more choices from the upper floor than do any of their lower-floor neighbors. They receive an average of 14.5 choices each and the three middle apartments receive only an average of 6.33 choices apiece. Apartments 1 and 5 differ from apartments 2 and 4 at the 5 percent level of significance. They do not, however, differ significantly from middle apartment 3.

Clearly the derivation is upheld. The end apartments on the lower floor both give and receive more upper-floor choices than do any of the other lower-floor apartments. A theoretical difficulty, however, exists in the unusually high number of choices which middle apartment 3 receives from the upper floor. Apartment 3 receives twelve choices, while its immediate neighbors, apartments 2 and 4, receive only three and four choices respectively. Even if, for some reason we know nothing about, upper-floor people should have to pass by apartment 3, they would also have to pass apartments 2 and 4, and passive contacts with

---

[1] Significance of differences, unless otherwise noted, were calculated by means of an analysis of variance. The significance consequently depends upon the consistency of the results among all the separate buildings.

upper-floor people should be about the same for all three apartments. We have not been able to find an unequivocal explanation for the large number of choices of apartment 3 by their upstairs neighbors. One possible explanation is that the people in apartment 3, as will be shown later, receive the greatest number of lower-floor choices, and perhaps could meet more upper-floor people through their many lower-floor friends. However, this possible factor seems hardly sufficient to account for the observed data, and the high number of upper-floor choices received by apartment 3 remains the one puzzling inconsistency in the body of data.

Table 6 helps to explain the peculiar shape noted in the lower curve in Figure 2 which plots the choices exchanged between floors. This curve has about the same high level for distance units S and 1S, then a sudden drop to a low level at which distances 2S, 3S, and 4S all have about the same value. Distance units S and 1S are made up largely of choices exchanged between end apartments 1 and 5 and the upper floor, while distances 2S, 3S and 4S are made up predominantly of choices exchanged between the upper floor and the middle apartments 2, 3, and 4. This explanation of the shape of this curve also suggests that for choices between floors, functional distance is far more important than physical distance.

In line with this explanation, we would expect that the end apartments on the first floor would give and receive a high number of upper-floor choices whereas the middle apartments, 2, 3, and 4, would give and receive a uniformly low number of upper-floor choices. Table 6 shows that this is true for choices given to the upper floor and, with the exception of apartment 3, also true for choices received from the upper floor.

2. *Apartments 1 and 6 should exchange more choices than apartments 2 and 7. Similarly, apartments 5 and 10 should exchange more choices than apartments 4 and 9.*

Apartments 1 and 6 and apartments 2 and 7 are both exactly 53 feet apart. However in using the left-hand stairway, the people in apartment 6 must pass by apartment 1, whereas the people living in 7 will not pass by apartment

2. Therefore we can expect that there will be many more passive contacts between 1 and 6 than between 2 and 7, and there should consequently be more choices between 1 and 6 than between 2 and 7. The data substantiate this derivation. Apartments 1 and 6 exchange eleven choices and apartments 2 and 7 only four choices.

The same considerations should apply for choices between 5 and 10 as compared with 4 and 9. These apartments are within seven feet of being equidistant. Apartments 5 and 10 exchange nine choices while 4 and 9 give each other four choices. The Chi Square test for both sets of differences combined is significant at almost the 1 percent level.

These data give clear evidence that it is possible to have equal physical distances but very different functional distances.

3. *Apartment 7 will choose 6 more than it will choose 8; apartment 9 will choose 10 more than it will choose 8. This will not be true for first-floor apartments in similar positions.*

Apartments 6 and 7 will use predominantly the left-hand stairway. Apartments 9 and 10 will use predominantly the right-hand stairway. Apartment 8, however, which is approximately equidistant from both stairways should sometimes use one end and sometimes the other. Therefore, there should be a greater number of passive contacts between 6 and 7 and between 9 and 10 than between 7 and 8 or 9 and 8. Again the sociometric data bear out the derivation. The choices from apartment 7 to 6 and from apartment 9 to 10 add up to a total of nineteen. They give to apartment 8, however, a total of only ten choices. The Chi Square for this difference is significant at almost the 2 percent level.

We should not expect this result on the first floor since each of the apartments has its own short stairway leading to the outside of the building. Apartment 2 gives to apartment 1, and 4 gives to 5, a total of twenty choices. Apartments 2 and 4 give seventeen choices to apartment 3. This difference is not significant.

4. *The upper-floor choices apartment 1 gives and receives should be concentrated in apartments 6 and 7 and should taper off for apartments 8, 9, and 10. The upper-floor choices apartment 5 gives and*

receives should still be heaviest for apartments 9 and 10 but should decrease more gradually for apartments 8, 7, and 6.

Only apartments 6 and 7 use the left-hand stairway consistently; 8, located between the two stairways, uses it occasionally, and 9 and 10 only rarely if at all. Therefore, apartment 1 will make most contacts with 6 and 7, a few with 8, and almost none at all with 9 and 10. The data in Table 7 support this derivation. Apartment 1 gives ten of its thirteen choices to 6 and 7, two choices to 8, one to 9, and none at all to 10. Of the fourteen choices 1 receives, ten come from apartments 6 and 7, two from 8, and one each from 9 and 10.

Numbers 9 and 10 are the only upstairs apartments that use the right-hand connecting stairway consistently in order to leave the building. Though this stairway does not pass directly in front of number 5, the people using it also use the short stairway out from the lower porch which is used by apartment 5 and are likely, therefore, to make contacts with 5. Apartment 8 will use the right-hand stairway occasionally in leaving the building, and 6 and 7 only rarely. In addition, however, upper-floor people who wish to go to their mailboxes will pass apartment 5. Therefore, apartment 5 will make contacts with all upper-floor persons, but the most frequent contacts will be made with 9 and 10. Again the data support the derivation. Table 7 shows that 9 and 10 receive six of the eleven choices apartment 5 makes, 8 receives three choices, and 7 and 6 one choice apiece. Similarly, apartments 9 and 10 give eight of the fifteen upstairs choices 5 receives, and the remaining seven are received from apartments 6, 7, and 8. As predicted, apartment 1 has a heavier concentration of choices in 6 and 7 than does apartment 5 in 9 and 10. Twenty

of the twenty-seven choices apartment 1 gives and receives are concentrated in apartments 6 and 7, whereas only fourteen of the twenty-six choices made by and to apartment 5 are centered in apartments 9 and 10. For this difference Chi Square is significant at about the 12 percent level.

The data so far presented all support the hypotheses from which the numerous derivations about the effects of physical and functional factors were made. These hypotheses stated simply that in these two communities friendships will depend upon the occurrence of passive contacts and that the pattern and frequency of passive contacts among particular people will depend upon the ecological factors of physical and functional distance. The only finding inconsistent with these hypotheses is the large number of choices which the lower-floor middle apartment receives from upper-floor residents. There are, however, implicit in these hypotheses a series of rather interesting derivations which it has been impossible to check because of the great difficulty of isolating the effects of physical and functional distance.

Let us assume that we have a row of five identically designed houses with equal physical distance between any two adjoining houses. For reference we may label these houses a, b, c, d, and e in order along the row.

It is apparent that of all five house positions, the middle house, c, has the minimum total separation from all other houses in the row. The farther a house is from the middle position, the greater is its total physical separation from all other houses in the row.

Let us assume that within any given time interval the probability of a passive contact occurring between residents of houses which are one unit apart is greater than the probability of a contact occurring between residents of houses 2 units apart and so on. The probability of a passive contact occurring between residents living 4 units apart would be lowest.

The resident of house c will generally have made contact with all others living in the row sooner than any other resident. If enough time is allowed to elapse one might be relatively certain that all residents would have had at

Table 7 Upper-Floor Choices Apartments 1 and 5 Give and Receive

Apartment position	6	7	8	9	10
Choices 1 gives	6	4	2	1	0
Choices 1 receives	5	5	2	1	1
Choices 5 gives	1	1	3	2	4
Choices 5 receives	2	1	4	3	5

least one passive contact with all others in the row, but the resident in house *c* will have had the greatest number of such contacts, the residents of houses *b* and *d* the next largest number, and the residents of houses *a* and *e* would have had the least number. Therefore, we can expect that if a sociometric test were administered *c* would receive the greatest number of choices, *b* and *d* somewhat fewer choices, and *a* and *e* fewest choices of all. Thus, if we plotted a curve of number of choices against house position, we would expect a symmetrical curve monotonically decreasing with distance from the central position. Further, we would expect that as more and more contacts are made among all people living in this row, with the passage of time the curve would tend to flatten out.

To check these derivations specifically against the data available for Westgate and Westgate West is impossible, because in all cases both physical and functional distance have influenced the assignment of sociometric choices. A specific case may illustrate the difficulties involved. The lower floors of the Westgate West buildings resemble the theoretical arrangement of houses suggested above. There are five apartments arranged in a row with roughly equal physical separations between all apartments. Functionally, however, the two end apartments are very different from the middle apartments, for they are at the foot of the stairways connecting the two floors and therefore make many passive contacts with upstairs people. This increased number of between-floor contacts affects the relation the people in the end apartments have with others on their own floor. Table 8 presents the data on the number of choices given to each apartment position by people living on the lower floor. Indeed, there is a peak at the middle apartment. The number of choices received by apartment 3 is greater at the 5 percent level

of significance than the number received by the other lower-floor apartments. Contrary to expectations, apartment 1 receives more choices than 2, and 5 receives more choices than 4.

In analyzing the data specifically for choices exchanged between particular apartment positions, we learn that apartment 4 gives 5 a total of nine choices whereas 5 gives 4 only four choices. Similarly, 2 gives eleven choices to apartment 1 and receives nine choices from 1. Thus, the major part of the differences between 5 and 4, and 1 and 2, is made up of unreciprocated choices from 4 and 2 to 5 and 1. The fact that many of these choices go unreciprocated is explained by the functional relationships between the end apartments 1 and 5, and the upper floor. Since these end apartments make so many passive contacts with the upper-floor residents, many of their choices will inevitably go to upper-floor people (see Table 6). Since the sociometric question limited the number of choices to three, it necessarily follows that many of the lower-floor choices to the end apartments must go unreciprocated.

THE ECOLOGICAL BASIS FOR FORMATION OF GROUPS

The data presented have been stated largely in terms of specific friendships between people living in particular house positions. We have shown that, in these two communities, friendships will be determined in large part by physical and functional distance. In terms of these ecological considerations we can further expect that a large proportion of all sociometric choices will be exchanged among people living within the same court or building. We know that in a Westgate court the houses are close to one another and with a few exceptions face into the same area. In general, the people living

Table 8 Number of Sociometric Choices Given to Each Lower-Floor Apartment Position by People Living on the Lower Floor

Apartment position	1	2	3	4	5
Number of sociometric choices	22	19	28	11	17

in each court are both physically and functionally closer to one another than to anyone else living in Westgate. This is obviously also true for the people living in each Westgate West building. The data corroborate the expectation. Of the 426 choices made by Westgate West people, 278 or 65.3 percent were given to people living in the same building as the choosers. Similarly for Westgate, 143 or 55.5 percent of the 258 choices made were given to people living in the same court as the choosers. Further, 85.5 percent of all people in Westgate West chose at least one person living in the same building and 80 percent of Westgaters chose at least one person in their court. If the end houses facing the street, which positionally at least are not members of the court, are excluded from this count, the figure for Westgate rises to 87.4 percent. Thus, a large share of all friendships in both of these communities was among people living in the same court or building.

If one accepts the definition of a group as a number of interacting and sociometrically connected people, it follows that these ecological factors determine not only specific friendships but the composition of groups within these communities as well. Each court and building is populated by people who have most of their friends in the same living unit. Thus the people in each court or building will work together, play together, and, in general, see

more of each other than of any other individuals living in the projects.

SUMMARY

The hypothesis has been advanced that friendships and group membership will be determined in these communities by passive contacts between neighbors. The pattern and number of such contacts among particular people will depend upon physical and functional distance. Data have been presented which reveal a striking relationship between these ecological factors and sociometric choice.

Obviously, there are other methods of making friends. The men of the project undoubtedly meet one another in class and school activities. People probably meet at parties, and so on. However, the relationships between ecological and sociometric structures is so very marked that there can be little doubt that in these communities passive contacts are a major determinant of friendship and group formation.

It should be remembered that Westgate and Westgate West represent homogeneous communities. Whether these ecological factors would be as effective in more heterogeneous communities is, of course, a question for further empirical study. It seems likely that in such communities ecological factors will play some part, though a less important one, in determining sociometric structure.

11

"Playing Hard to Get": Understanding an Elusive Phenomenon

Elaine (Walster) Hatfield, G. William Walster, Jane Piliavin,
and Lynn Schmidt

Why are we strongly attracted to one person and "turned off" by another? What are the origins of romantic interest? In the early 1970s, social psychologists began to focus attention on these questions. In this paper, Elaine Hatfield and her colleagues describe several experiments designed to test whether men are more attracted to women who "play hard to get" or to women who appear to be less selective. The researchers' innovative methods included setting up a "computer matching service" for college students and conducting a field experiment in which a prostitute randomly assigned her male clients to one of two selectivity conditions. Ultimately, the researchers concluded that men are more strongly attracted to a prospective partner who is easy for *them* to get, but who is highly selective about her reactions to *other* men. In reading about this research from the early 1970s, consider two issues. First, in the past, men were almost always the initiators in dating relationships. As a result, the researchers did not ask whether or not women prefer men who are hard to get. Do you think changing sex roles have altered these patterns today? Would women also prefer to date men who play hard to get? Second, consider the ethics of this research. Do you think that the benefits of the deception involved (which was considered appropriate at the time) outweighed possible harm to the subjects?

ABSTRACT. *According to folklore, the woman who is hard to get is a more desirable catch than the woman who is too eager for an alliance. Five experiments were conducted to demonstrate that individuals value hard-to-get dates more than easy-to-get ones. All five experiments failed. In Experiment VI, we finally gained an understanding of this elusive phenomenon. We proposed that two components contribute to a woman's desirability: (a) how hard the woman is for the subject to get and (b) how hard she is for other men to get. We predicted that the selectively hard-to-get woman (i.e., a woman who is easy for the subject to get but hard for all other men to get) would be preferred to either a uniformly hard-to-get woman, a uniformly easy-to-get woman, or a woman about which the subject had no information. This hypothesis received strong support. The reason for the popularity of the selective woman was evident. Men ascribe to her all of the assets of uniformly hard-to-get and the uniformly easy-to-get woman and none of their liabilities.*

According to folklore, the woman who is hard to get is a more desirable catch than is the woman who is overly eager for alliance. Socrates, Ovid, Terence, the *Kama Sutra*, and Dear Abby all agree that the person whose affection is easily won is unlikely to inspire passion in another. Ovid (1963), for example, argued:

Reprinted from the *Journal of Personality and Social Psychology*, 1973, 26, pp. 113–121. Copyright 1973 by the American Psychological Association. Reprinted by permission of publisher and authors.

Fool, if you feel no need to guard your girl for her own sake, see that you guard her for mine, so I may want her the more. Easy things nobody wants, but what is forbidden is tempting. . . . Anyone who can love the wife of an indolent cuckold, I should suppose, would steal buckets of sand from the shore [pp. 65–66].

When we first began our investigation, we accepted cultural lore. We assumed that men would prefer a hard-to-get woman. Thus, we began our research by interviewing college men as to why they preferred hard-to-get women. Predictably, the men responded to experimenter demands. They explained that they preferred hard-to-get women because the elusive woman is almost inevitably a valuable woman. They pointed out that a woman can only afford to be "choosy" if she is popular—and a woman is popular for some reason. When a woman is hard to get, it is usually a tip-off that she is especially pretty, has a good personality, is sexy, etc. Men also were intrigued by the challenge that the elusive woman offered. One can spend a great deal of time fantasizing about what it would be like to date such a woman. Since the hard-to-get woman's desirability is well recognized, a man can gain prestige if he is seen with her.

An easy-to-get woman, on the other hand, spells trouble. She is probably desperate for a date. She is probably the kind of woman who will make too many demands on a person; she might want to get serious right away. Even worse, she might have a "disease."

In brief, nearly all interviewees agreed with our hypothesis that a hard-to-get woman is a valuable woman, and they could supply abundant justification for their prejudice. A few isolated men refused to cooperate. These dissenters noted that an elusive woman is not always more desirable than an available woman. Sometimes the hard-to-get woman is not only hard to get—she is *impossible* to get, because she is misanthropic and cold. Sometimes a woman is easy to get because she is a friendly, outgoing woman who boosts one's ego and insures that dates are "no hassle." We ignored the testimony of these deviant types.

We then conducted five experiments designed to demonstrate that an individual values a hard-to-get date more highly than an easy-to-get date. All five experiments failed.

Theoretical Rationale

Let us first review the theoretical rationale underlying these experiments.

In Walster, Walster, and Berscheid (1971) we argued that if playing hard to get does increase one's desirability, several psychological theories could account for this phenomenon:

1. Dissonance theory predicts that if one must expend great energy to attain a goal, he is unusually appreciative of the goal (see Aronson & Mills, 1959; Gerard & Mathewson, 1966; Zimbardo, 1965). The hard-to-get date requires a suitor to expend more effort in her pursuit than he would normally expend. One way for the suitor to justify such unusual effort is by aggrandizing her.

2. According to learning history, an elusive person should have two distinct advantages: (a) Frustration may increase drive—by waiting until the suitor has achieved a high sexual drive state, heightening his drive level by introducing momentary frustration, and then finally rewarding him, the hard-to-get woman can maximize the impact of the sexual reward she provides (see Kimball, 1961, for evidence that frustration does energize behavior and does increase the impact of appropriate rewards). (b) Elusiveness and value may be associated—individuals may have discovered through frequent experience that there is more competition for socially desirable dates than for undesirable partners. Thus, being "hard to get" comes to be associated with "value." As a consequence, the conditioned stimulus (CS) of being hard to get generates a fractional antedating goal response and a fractional goal response which leads to the conditioned response of liking.

3. In an extension of Schachterian theory, Walster (1971) argued that two components are necessary before an individual can experience passionate love: (a) He must be physiologically aroused; and (b) the setting must make it appropriate for him to conclude that his aroused feelings are due to love. On both counts, the person who plays hard to get might be expected to generate unusual passion. Frustration should increase the suitor's physiological arousal, and the association of "elusiveness"

with "value" should increase the probability that the suitor will label his reaction to the other as "love."

From the preceding discussion, it is evident that several conceptually distinct variables may account for the hard-to-get phenomenon. In spite of the fact that we can suggest a plethora of reasons as to why playing hard-to-get strategy might be an effective strategy, all five studies failed to provide any support for the contention that an elusive woman is a desirable woman. Two experiments failed to demonstrate that outside observers perceive a hard-to-get individual as especially "valuable." Three experiments failed to demonstrate that a suitor perceives a hard-to-get date as especially valuable.

Walster, Walster, and Berscheid (1971) conducted two experiments to test the hypothesis that teenagers would deduce that a hard-to-get boy or girl was more socially desirable than was a teenager whose affection could be easily obtained. In these experiments high school juniors and seniors were told that we were interested in finding out what kind of first impression various teenagers made on others. They were shown pictures and biographies of a couple. They were told how romantically interested the stimulus person (a boy or girl) was in his partner after they had met only four times. The stimulus person was to have liked the partner "extremely much," to have provided no information to us, or to like her "not particularly much." The teenagers were then asked how socially desirable both teenagers seemed (i.e., how likable, how physically attractive, etc., both teenagers seemed). Walster, Walster, and Berscheid, of course, predicted that the more romantic interest the stimulus person expressed in a slight acquaintance, the less socially desirable that stimulus person would appear to an outside observer. The results were diametrically opposed to those predicted. The more romantic interest the stimulus person expressed in an acquaintance, the *more* socially desirable teenagers judged him to be. Restraint does not appear to buy respect. Instead, it appears that "All the world *does* love a lover."

Lyons, Walster, and Walster (1971) con-

ducted a field study and a laboratory experiment in an attempt to demonstrate that men prefer a date who plays hard to get. Both experiments were conducted in the context of a computer matching service. Experiment III was a field experiment. Women who signed up for the computer matching program were contacted and hired as experimenters. They were then given precise instructions as to how to respond when their computer match called them for a date. Half of the time they were told to pause and think for 3 seconds before accepting the date. (These women were labeled "hard to get.") Half of the time they were told to accept the date immediately. (These women were labeled "easy to get.") The data indicated that elusiveness had no impact on the man's liking for his computer date.

Experiment IV was a laboratory experiment. In this experiment, Lyons et al. hypothesized that the knowledge that a woman is elusive gives one indirect evidence that she is socially desirable. Such indirect evidence should have the biggest impact when a man has no way of acquiring *direct* evidence about a coed's value or when he has little confidence in his own ability to assess value. When direct evidence is available, and the man possesses supreme confidence in his ability to make correct judgments, information about a woman's elusiveness should have little impact on a man's reaction to her. Lyons et al. thus predicted that when men lacked direct evidence as to a woman's desirability, a man's self-esteem and the woman's elusiveness should interact in determining his respect and liking for her. Lyons et al. measured males' self-esteem via Rosenberg's (1965) measure of self-esteem, Rosenfeld's (1964) measure of fear or rejection, and Berger's (1952) measure of self-acceptance.

The dating counselor then told subjects that the computer had assigned them a date. They were asked to telephone her from the office phone, invite her out, and then report their first impression of her. Presumably the pair would then go out on a date, and eventually give us further information about how successful our computer matching techniques had been. Actually, all men were assigned a confederate as a date. Half of the time the woman played hard to get. When the man asked her out she replied:

Mmm [slight pause] No, I've got a date then. It seems like I signed up for that Date Match thing a long time ago and I've met more people since then—I'm really pretty busy all this week.

She paused again. If the subject suggested another time, the confederate hesitated only slightly, then accepted. If he did not suggest another time, the confederate would take the initiative of suggesting: "How about some time next week—or just meeting for coffee in the Union some afternoon?" And again, she accepted the next invitation. Half of the time, in the easy-to-get condition, the confederate eagerly accepted the man's offer of a date.

Lyons et al. predicted that since men in this blind date setting lacked direct evidence as to a woman's desirability, low-self-esteem men should be more receptive to the hard-to-get woman than were high-self-esteem men. Although Lyons et al.'s manipulation checks indicate that their manipulations were successful and their self-esteem measure was reliable, their hypothesis was not confirmed. Elusiveness had no impact on liking, regardless of subject's self-esteem level.

Did we give up our hypothesis? Heavens no. After all, it had only been disconfirmed four times.

By Experiment V, we had decided that perhaps the hard-to-get hypothesis must be tested in a sexual setting. After all, the first theorist who advised a woman to play hard to get was Socrates; his pupil was Theodota, a prostitute. He advised:

They will appreciate your favors most highly if you wait till they ask for them. The sweetest meats, you see, if served before they are wanted seem sour, and to those who had enough they are positively nauseating; but even poor fare is very welcome when offered to a hungry man. [Theodota inquired] And how can I make them hungry for my fare? [Socrates' reply] Why, in the first place, you must not offer it to them when they have had enough—but prompt them by behaving as a model of Propriety, by a show of reluctance to yield, and by holding back until they are as keen as can be; and then the same gifts are much

more to the recipient than when they're offered before they are desired [see Xenophon, 1923, p. 48].

Walster, Walster, and Lambert (1971) thus proposed that a prostitute who states that she is selective in her choice of customers will be held in higher regard than will be the prostitute who admits that she is completely unselective in her choice of partners.

In this experiment, a prostitute served as the experimenter. When the customer arrived, she mixed a drink for him; then she delivered the experimental manipulation. Half of the time, in the hard-to-get condition, she stated, "Just because I see you this time it doesn't mean that you can have my phone number or see me again. I'm going to start school soon, so I won't have much time, so I'll only be able to see the people that I like the best." Half of the time, in the easy-to-get condition, she did not communicate this information. From this point on, the prostitute and the customer interacted in conventional ways.

The client's liking for the prostitute was determined in two ways: First, the prostitute estimated how much the client had seemed to like her. (i.e., How much did he seem to like you? Did he make arrangements to return? How much did he pay you?) Second, the experimenter recorded how many times within the next 30 days the client arranged to have subsequent sexual relations with her.

Once again we failed to confirm the hard-to-get hypothesis. If anything, those clients who were told that the prostitute did not take just anyone were *less* likely to call back and liked the prostitute less than did other clients.

At this point, we ruefully decided that we had been on the wrong track. We decided that perhaps all those practitioners who advise women to play hard to get are wrong. Or perhaps it is only under very special circumstances that it will benefit one to play hard to get.

Thus, we began again. We reinterviewed students—this time with an open mind. This time we asked men to tell us about the advantages *and* disadvantages of hard-to-get *and* easy-to-get women. This time replies were more informative. According to reports, choosing between a hard-to-get woman and an easy-to-get woman was like choosing between Scylla and Charybdis—each woman was uniquely desirable and uniquely frightening.

Although the elusive woman was likely to be a popular prestige date, she presented certain problems. Since she was not particularly enthusiastic about you, she might stand you up or humiliate you in front of your friends. She was likely to be unfriendly, cold, and to possess inflexible standards.

The easy-to-get woman was certain to boost one's ego and to make a date a relaxing, enjoyable experience, but. . . . Unfortunately, dating an easy woman was a risky business. Such a woman might be easy to get, but hard to get rid of. She might "get serious." Perhaps she would be so oversexed or overaffectionate in public that she would embarrass you. Your buddies might snicker when they saw you together. After all, they would know perfectly well why you were dating *her*.

The interlocking assets and difficulties envisioned when they attempted to decide which was better—a hard-to-get or an easy-to-get woman—gave us a clue as to why our previous experiments had not worked out. The assets and liabilities of the elusive and the easy dates had evidently generally balanced out. On the average, then, both types of women tended to be equally well liked. When a slight difference in liking did appear, it favored the easy-to-get woman.

It finally impinged on us that there are *two* components that are important determinants of how much a man likes a woman: (*a*) How hard or easy she is for him to get; (*b*) how hard or easy she is for *other men* to get. So long as we were examining the desirability of women who were hard or easy for everyone to get, things balanced out. The minute we examined other possible configurations, it becomes evident that there is one type of woman who can transcend the limitations of the uniformly hard-to-get or the uniformly easy-to-get woman. If a woman has a reputation for being hard to get, but for some reason she is easy for the subject to get, she should be maximally appealing. Dating such a woman should insure one of great prestige; she is, after all,

hard to get. Yet, since she is exceedingly available to the subject, the dating situation should be a relaxed, rewarding experience. Such a *selectively* hard-to-get woman possesses the assets of both the easy-to-get and the hard-to-get women, while avoiding all of their liabilities.

Thus, in Experiment VI, we hypothesized that a selectively hard-to-get woman (i.e., a woman who is easy for the subject to get but very hard for any other man to get) will be especially liked by her date. Women who are hard for everyone—including the subject—to get, or who are easy for everyone to get—or control women, about whom the subject had no information—will be liked a lesser amount.

METHOD

Subjects were 71 male summer students at the University of Wisconsin. They were recruited for a dating research project. This project was ostensibly designed to determine whether computer matching techniques are in fact more effective than is random matching. All participants were invited to come into the dating center in order to choose a date from a set of five potential dates.

When the subject arrived at the computer match office, he was handed folders containing background information on five women. Some of these women had supposedly been "randomly" matched with him; others had been "computer matched" with him. (He was not told which women were which.)

In reality, all five folders contained information about fictitious women. The first item in the folder was a "background questionnaire" on which the woman had presumably described herself. This questionnaire was similar to one the subject had completed when signing up for the match program. We attempted to make the five women's descriptions different enough to be believable, yet similar enough to minimize variance. Therefore, the way the five women described themselves was systematically varied. They claimed to be 18 or 19 years old; freshmen or sophomores; from a Wisconsin city, ranging in size from over 500,000 to under 50,000; 5 feet 2 inches to 5 feet 4 inches tall;

Protestant, Catholic, Jewish, or had no preference; graduated in the upper 10%–50% of their high school class; and Caucasians who did not object to being matched with a person of another race. The women claimed to vary on a political spectrum from "left of center" through "moderate" to "near right of center"; to place little or no importance on politics and religion; and to like recent popular movies. Each woman listed four or five activities she liked to do on a first date (i.e., go to a movie, talk in a quiet place, etc.).

In addition to the background questionnaire, three of the five folders contained five "date selection forms." The experimenter explained that some of the women had already been able to come in, examine the background information of their matches, and indicate their first impression of them. Two of the subject's matches had not yet come in. Three of the women had already come in and evaluated the subject along with her four other matches. These women would have five date selection forms in their folders. The subject was shown the forms, which consisted of a scale ranging from "definitely do *not* want to date" (−10) to "definitely want to date" (+10). A check appeared on each scale. Presumably the check indicated how much the woman had liked a given date. (At this point, the subject was told his identification dating number. Since all dates were identified by numbers on the forms, this identification number enabled him to ascertain how each date had evaluated both him and her four other matches.)

The date selection forms allowed us to manipulate the elusiveness of the woman. One woman appeared to be uniformly hard to get. She indicated that though she was willing to date any of the men assigned to her, she was not enthusiastic about any of them. She rated all five of her date choices from +1 to +2, including the subject (who was rated 1.75).

One woman appeared to be uniformly easy to get. She indicated that she was enthusiastic about dating all five of the men assigned to her. She rated her desire to date all five of her date choices +7 to +9. This included the subject, who was rated 8.

One woman appeared to be easy for the subject to get but hard for anyone else to get (i.e., the selectively hard-to-get woman). She indicated minimal enthusiasm for four of her date choices, rating them from +2 to +3, and extreme enthusiasm (+8) for the subject.

Two women had no date selection forms in their folders (i.e., no information women).

Naturally, each woman appears in each of the five conditions.

The experimenter asked the man to consider the folders, complete a "first impression questionnaire" for each woman, and then decide which *one* of the women he wished to date. (The subject's rating of the dates constitute our verbal measure of liking; his choice in a date constitutes our behavioral measure of liking.)

The experimenter explained that she was conducting a study of first impressions in conjuction with the dating research project. The study, she continued, was designed to learn more about how good people are at forming first impressions of others on the basis of rather limited information. She explained that filling out the forms would probably make it easier for the man to decide which one of the five women he wished to date.

The first impression questionnaire consisted of three sections:

1. *Liking for various dates.* Two questions assessed subject's liking for each woman: "If you went out with this girl, how well do you think you would get along?"—with possible responses ranging from "get along extremely well" (5) to "not get along at all" (1)—and "What was your overall impression of the girl?"—with possible responses ranging from "extremely favorable" (7) to "extremely unfavorable" (1). Scores on these two questions were summed to form an index of expressed liking. This index enables us to compare subject's liking for each of the women.

2. *Assets and liabilities ascribed to various dates.* We predicted that subjects would prefer the selective woman, because they would expect her to possess the good qualities of both the uniformly hard-to-get and the uniformly easy-to-get woman, while avoiding the bad qualities of both her rivals. Thus, the second section was designed to determine the extent to which

subjects imputed good and bad qualities to the various dates.

This section was comprised of 10 pairs of polar opposites. Subjects were asked to rate how friendly–unfriendly, cold–warm, attractive–unattractive, easygoing–rigid, exciting–boring, shy–outgoing, funloving–dull, popular–unpopular, aggressive–passive, selective–nonselective each woman was. Ratings were made on a 7-point scale. The more desirable the trait ascribed to a woman, the higher the score she was given.

3. *Liabilities attributed to easy-to-get women.* The third scale was designed to assess the extent to which subjects attributed selected negative attributes to each woman. The third scale consisted of six statements:

She would more than likely do something to embarrass me in public.
She probably would demand too much attention and affection from me.
She seems like the type who would be too dependent on me.
She might turn out to be too sexually promiscuous.
She probably would make me feel uneasy when I'm with her in a group.
She seems like the type who doesn't distinguish between the boys she dates. I probably would be "just another date."

Subjects were asked whether they anticipated any of the above difficulties in their relationship with each woman. They indicated their misgivings on a scale ranging from "certainly true of her" (1) to "certainly not true of her" (7).

The experimenter suggested that the subject carefully examine both the background questionnaire and the date selection forms of all potential dates in order to decide whom he wanted to date. Then she left the subject. (The

experimenter was, of course, unaware of what date was in what folder.)

The experimenter did not return until the subject had completed the first impression questionnaires. Then she asked him which woman he had decided to date.

After his choice had been made, the experimenter questioned him as to what factors influenced his choice. Frequently men who chose the selectively easy-to-get woman said that "She chose me, and that made me feel really good" or "She seemed more selective than the others." The uniformly easy-to-get woman was often rejected by subjects who complained "She must be awfully hard up for a date—she really would take anyone." The uniformly hard-to-get woman was once described as a "challenge," but more often rejected as being "snotty" or "too picky."

At the end of the session, the experimenter debriefed the subject and then gave him the names of five actual dates who had been matched with him.

RESULTS

We predicted that the selectively hard-to-get woman (easy for me to get but hard for everyone else to get) would be liked more than women who were uniformly hard to get, uniformly easy to get, or neutral (the no information women). We had no prediction as to whether or not her three rivals would differ in attractiveness. The results strongly support our hypothesis.

Dating Choices

When we examine the men's choices in dates, we see that the selective woman is far more popular than any of her rivals. (See Table 1.) We conducted a chi-square test to determine

Table 1 Men's Choices in a Date

Item	Selectively Hard to Get	Uniformly Hard to Get	Uniformly Easy to Get	No Information for No. 1	No Information for No. 2
Number of men choosing to date each woman	42	6	5	11	7

whether or not men's choices in dates were randomly distributed. They were not ($\chi^2 = 69.5$, $df = 4$, $p < .001$). Nearly all subjects preferred to date the selective woman. When we compare the frequency with which her four rivals (combined) are chosen, we see that the selective woman does get far more than her share of dates ($\chi^2 = 68.03$, $df = 1$, $p < .001$).

We also conducted an analysis to determine whether or not the women who are uniformly hard to get, uniformly easy to get, or whose popularity is unknown, differed in popularity. We see that they did not ($\chi^2 = 2.86$, $df = 3$).

Liking for the Various Dates

Two questions tapped the men's romantic liking for the various dates: (a) "If you went out with this woman, how well do you think you'd get along?" and (b) "What was your overall impression of the woman?" Scores on these two indexes were summed to form an index of liking. Possible scores ranged from 2 to 12.

A contrast was then set up to test our hypothesis that the selective woman will be preferred to her rivals. The contrast that tests this hypothesis is of the form $\Gamma_1 = 4\mu$ (selectively hard to get) $- 1\mu$ (uniformly hard to get) $- 2\mu$ (neutral). We tested the hypothesis $\Gamma_1 = 0$ against the alternative hypothesis $\Gamma_1 \neq 0$. An explanation of this basically simple procedure may be found in Hays (1963). If our hypothesis is true, the preceding contrast should be large. If our hypothesis is false, the resulting contrast should not differ significantly from 0. The data again provide strong support for the hypothesis that the selective woman is better liked than her rivals ($F = 23.92$, $df = 1/70$, $p < .001$).

Additional Data Snooping

We also conducted a second set of contrasts to determine whether the rivals (i.e., the uniformly hard-to-get woman, the uniformly easy-to-get woman, and the control woman) were differentially liked. Using the procedure presented by Morrison (1967) in Chapter 4, the data indicate that the rivals are differentially liked ($F = 4.43$, $df = 2/69$). As Table 2 indicates, the uniformly hard-to-get woman seems to be liked slightly less than the easy-to-get or control women.

In any attempt to explore data, one must account for the fact that observing the data permits the researcher to capitalize on chance. Thus, one must use simultaneous testing methods so as not to spuriously inflate the probability of attaining statistical significance. In the present situation, we are interested in comparing the mean of a number of dependent measures, namely the liking for the different women in the dating situation. To perform post hoc multiple comparisons in this situation, one can use a transformation of Hotelling's t^2 statistic which is distributed as F. The procedure is directly analogous to Scheffé's multiple-comparison procedure for independent groups, except where one compares means of a number of dependent measures.

To make it abundantly clear that the main result is that the discriminating woman is better liked than each of the other rivals, we performed an additional post hoc analysis, pitting each of the rivals separately against the discriminating woman. In these analyses, we see that the selective woman is better liked than the woman who is uniformly easy to get ($F = 3.99$, $df = 3/68$), than the woman who is uniformly hard to get ($F = 9.47$, $df = 3/68$), and finally, than the control women ($F = 4.93$, $df = 3/68$).

Thus, it is clear that although there are slight differences in the way rivals are liked, these differences are small, relative to the overwhelming attractiveness of the selective woman.

Assets and Liabilities Attributed to Dates

We can now attempt to ascertain *why* the selective woman is more popular than her rivals. Earlier, we argued that the selectively hard-to-get woman should occupy a unique position; she should be assumed to possess all of the virtues of her rivals, but none of their flaws.

The virtues and flaws that the subject ascribed to each woman were tapped by the polar–opposite scale. Subjects evaluated each woman on 10 characteristics.

We expected that subjects would associate two assets with a uniformly hard-to-get woman: Such a woman should be perceived to be both "selective" and "popular." Unfortunately, such a woman should also be assumed to possess three liabilities—she should be perceived to be "unfriendly," "cold," and "rigid." Subjects should ascribe exactly the opposite virtues and liabilities to the easy-to-get woman: Such a woman should possess the assets of "friendliness," "warmth," and "flexibility," and the liabilities of "unpopularity" and "lack of selectivity." The selective woman was expected to possess only assets: She should be perceived to be as "selective" and "popular" as the uniformly elusive woman, and as "friendly," "warm," and "easy-going" as the uniformly easy woman. A contrast was set up to test this specific hypothesis. (Once again, see Hays for the procedure.) This contrast indicates that our hypothesis is confirmed ($F = 62.43$, $df = 1/70$). The selective woman is rated most like the uniformly hard-to-get woman on the first two positive characteristics; most like the uniformly easy-to-get woman on the last three characteristics.

For the reader's interest, the subjects' ratings of all five women's assets and liabilities are presented in Table 2.

Comparing the Selective and the Easy Women

Scale 3 was designed to assess whether or not subjects anticipated fewer problems when they envisioned dating the selective woman than when they envisioned dating the uniformly easy-to-get woman. On the basis of pretest interviews, we compiled a list of many of the concerns men had about easy women (e.g., "She would more than likely do something to embarrass me in public.")

We, of course, predicted that subjects would experience more problems when contemplating dating the uniformly easy woman than when contemplating dating a woman who was easy for *them* to get, but hard for anyone else to get (i.e., the selective woman).

Men were asked to say whether or not they envisioned each of the difficulties were they to date each of the women. Possible replies varied from 1 (certainly true of her) to 7 (certainly not true of her). The subjects' evaluations of each woman were summed to form an index of anticipated difficulties. Possible scores ranged from 6 to 42.

A contrast was set up to determine whether the selective woman engendered less concern than the uniformly easy-to-get woman. The data indicate that she does ($F = 17.50$, $df =$

Table 2 Men's Reactions to Various Dates

| Item | Type of Date | | | |
	Selectively Hard to Get	*Uniformly Hard to Get*	*Uniformly Easy to Get*	*No Information*
Men's liking for dates	9.41[a]	7.90	8.53	8.58
Evaluation of women's assets and liabilities				
Selective[b]	5.23	4.39	2.85	4.30
Popular[b]	4.83	4.58	4.65	4.83
Friendly[c]	5.58	5.07	5.52	5.37
Warm[c]	5.15	4.51	4.99	4.79
Easy-going[c]	4.83	4.42	4.82	4.61
Problems expected in dating	5.23[d]	4.86	4.77	4.99

[a] The higher the number, the more liking the man is expressing for the date.

[b] Traits we expected to be ascribed to the selectively hard-to-get and the uniformly hard-to-get dates.

[c] Traits we expected to be ascribed to the selectively hard-to-get and the uniformly easy-to-get dates.

[d] The higher the number the *fewer* the problems the subject anticipates in dating.

1/70). If the reader is interested in comparing concern engendered by each woman, these data are available in Table 2.

The data provide clear support for our hypotheses: The selective woman is strongly preferred to any of her rivals. The reason for her popularity is evident. Men ascribe to her all of the assets of the uniformly hard-to-get and the uniformly easy-to-get women, and none of their liabilities.

Thus, after five futile attempts to understand the "hard-to-get" phenomenon, it appears that we have finally gained an understanding of this process. It appears that a woman can intensify her desirability if she acquires a reputation for being hard-to-get and then, by her behavior, makes it clear to a selected romantic partner that she is attracted to him.

In retrospect, especially in view of the strongly supportive data, the logic underlying our predictions sounds compelling. In fact, after examining our data, a colleague who had helped design the five ill-fated experiments noted that, "That is exactly what I would have predicted" (given his economic view of man). Unfortunately, we are all better at postdiction than prediction.

REFERENCES

Aronson, E., & Mills, J. The effect of severity of initiation on liking for a group. *Journal of Abnormal and Social Psychology*, 1959, *67*, 31–36.

Berger, E. M. The relation between expressed acceptance of self and expressed acceptance of others. *Journal of Abnormal and Social Psychology*, 1952, *47*, 778–782.

Gerard, H. B., & Mathewson, G. C. The effects of severity of initiation and liking for a group: A replication. *Journal of Experimental Social Psychology*, 1966, *2*, 278–287.

Hays, W. L. *Statistics for psychologists*. New York: Holt, Rinehart, 1963.

Kimball, G. A. *Hilgard and Marquis' conditioning and learning*. New York: Appleton-Century-Crofts, 1961.

Lyons, J., Walster, E., & Walster, G. W. Playing hard-to-get: An elusive phenomenon. University of Wisconsin, Madison: Author, 1971. (Mimeo)

Morrison, D. F. *Multivariate statistical methods*. New York: McGraw-Hill, 1967.

Ovid. *The art of love*. Bloomington: University of Indiana Press, 1963.

Rosenberg, M. *Society and the adolescent self image*. Princeton, N.J.: Princeton University Press, 1965.

Rosenfeld, H. M. Social choice conceived as a level of aspiration. *Journal of Abnormal and Social Psychology*, 1964, *68*, 491–499.

Walster, E. Passionate love. In B. I. Murstein (Ed.), *Theories of attraction and love*. New York: Springer, 1971.

Walster, E., Walster, G. W., & Berscheid, E. The efficacy of playing hard-to-get. *Journal of Experimental Education*, 1971, *39*, 73–77.

Walster, E., Walster, G. W., & Lambert, P. Playing hard-to-get: A field study. University of Wisconsin, Madison: Author, 1971.

Xenophon, *Memorabilia*. London: Heinemann, 1923.

Zimbardo, P. G. The effect of effort and improvisation on self-persuasion produced by role-playing. *Journal of Experimental Social Psychology*, 1965, *1*, 103–120.

12

Breakups Before Marriage: The End of 103 Affairs

Charles T. Hill, Zick Rubin, and Letitia Anne Peplau

In the mid-1970s, social-psychological research on close relationships began to shift away from a focus on experimental studies of initial attraction among strangers toward questionnaire studies of the dynamics of long-term relationships. Representative of this new emphasis is a longitudinal study of college dating couples conducted by Hill, Rubin, and Peplau. In this paper, the researchers use data obtained over a two-year period to identify factors that lead some dating couples to end their relationships and other couples to stay together. The researchers found that breakups were more likely when couples were initially low in love for each other, when one person was more "involved" in the relationship than the partner, and when partners were dissimilar in such characteristics as intelligence and physical attractiveness. The results also suggested that boyfriends and girlfriends may differ somewhat in how they experience romantic breakups. Finally, one unexpected finding was that the timing of breakups among college couples was affected by the academic calendar—breakups peaked during June, September, and winter vacation. Here, as in the paper by Festinger, Schachter, and Back (selection 10), we see how environmental factors can influence social relationships.

ABSTRACT. *Factors that predicted breakups before marriage, investigated as part of a two-year study of dating relationships among college students, included unequal involvement in the relationship (as suggested by exchange theory) and discrepant age, educational aspirations, intelligence, and physical attractiveness (as suggested by filtering models). The timing of breakups was highly related to the school calendar, pointing to the importance of external factors in structuring breakups. The desire to break up was seldom mutual; women were more likely than men to perceive problems in premarital relationships and somewhat more likely to be the ones to precipitate the breakups. Findings are discussed in terms of their relevance for the process of mate selection and their implications for marital breakup. ("The best divorce is the one you get before you get married.")*

From *Divorce and Separation: Contexts, Causes, and Consequences*, edited by George Levinger and Oliver C. Moles. Copyright © 1979 by The Society for the Psychological Study of Social Issues. Reprinted by permission of Basic Books, Inc.

For all the concern with the high incidence of divorce in contemporary America, marital separation accounts for only a small proportion of the breakups of intimate male-female relationships among American couples. For every recorded instance of the ending of a marriage, there are many instances, typically unrecorded, of the ending of a relationship among partners who were dating or "going together." Such breakups before marriage are of fundamental importance to an understanding of marital separation for two major reasons.

First and foremost, breakups before marriage play a central role in the larger system of mate selection. In an ideal mate selection system, all breakups of intimate male-female relationships might take place before marriage. Boyfriends and girlfriends who are not well-suited for each other would discover this in the course of dating and would eventually break up. In practice, however, the system does not achieve this ideal. Many couples who subsequently prove to be poorly suited for marrying each other do not discover this until after they are married. In many other instances, couples may be aware of serious strains in their relationship but nevertheless find themselves unable or unwilling to break up before marriage. Many future sources of marital strain may be totally unpredictable at the time that a couple decides to get married; individuals' needs and values may change over the course of time in ways that could not have been anticipated initially. Nevertheless, it is possible that the selection system could be made to operate more efficiently than it currently does. Although the psychic cost of a premarital breakup is often substantial, by breaking up before marriage couples might spare themselves the much greater costs of breaking up afterward.

Second, breakup before marriage may provide a revealing comparison against which to view marital breakup. Many of the psychological bonds of unmarried couples resemble those of married couples. Thus the requirements and difficulties of "uncoupling" in the two cases may show similarities (see Davis, 1973). On the other hand, breakup before marriage takes place in a very different social context from that of divorce. The ending of a dating relationship is relatively unaffected by factors that play central roles in divorces—for example, changes in residence, economic arrangements, child custody, legal battles, and stigmatization by kin and community. Thus the examination of breakups before marriage may be helpful in untangling the complex of psychological and social factors that influence divorce and its aftermath.

Breakups before marriage have remained largely unexplored by social scientists. Although there has been a great deal of research and speculation about mate selection (Rubin, 1973), this work has rather thoroughly ignored the process of breaking up. One major investigation of breaking up before marriage is the study of broken engagements conducted in the 1930s and 1940s by Burgess and Wallin (1953) as part of their larger study of engagement and marriage.

In this paper, we report on breakups before marriage among a large sample of dating couples in the 1970s. Our data are primarily descriptive: How were those couples who broke up over a two-year period different from those who stayed together? What were the reasons for the breakups, as perceived by the former partners themselves? What were the central features of the breaking-up process: its precipitating factors, its timing, and its aftermath? We pay special attention to the two-sidedness of breaking up: the frequent differences in the two partners' perceptions of what is taking place and why, the pervasive role differentiation of breaker-upper and broken-up-with, and the possibility that there are important differences between men's and women's characteristic orientations toward breaking up before marriage.

THE RESEARCH CONTEXT

In the spring of 1972, for a longitudinal study of dating relationships (Rubin, Peplau, & Hill, 1981), we sent a letter to a random sample of 5000 sophomores and juniors, 2500 men and 2500 women, at four colleges in the Boston area. The colleges, chosen with a view toward diversity, included a large private university (2000 letters) and a small private college, a Catholic university, and a state college for commuter students (1000 letters per school). Each student · was sent a two-page questionnaire which asked if he or she would be interested in participating in a study of "college students and their opposite-sex relationships." A total of 2520 students (57% of the women and 44% of the men) returned this questionnaire. Of these, 62% of the women and 54% of the men indicated that they were currently "going with" someone. Those who said that they and their partner might be interested in participating in a study were invited to attend a questionnaire session—with their boyfriend or girlfriend— either at their own school or at Harvard.

The 202 couples who responded to our invitation, plus an additional 29 couples who were recruited by advertising at one of the four schools, constitute our sample (Hill, Rubin, Peplau & Willard, 1979). At the time of the initial questionnaire, almost all participants (95%) were—or had been—college students. The modal couple consisted of a sophomore woman dating a junior man. About half of the participants' fathers had graduated from college and about one-fourth of the fathers held graduate degrees. About 44% of the respondents were Catholic, 26% were Protestant, and 25% were Jewish, reflecting the religious composition of colleges in the Boston area. Virtually all of the participants (97%) were white; about 25% lived at home with their parents, another 35% lived in apartments or houses by themselves or with roommates, and 38% lived in college dormitories. Almost all of the participants—97% of the women and 96% of the men—thought that they would eventually get married, although not necessarily to their current dating partner.

At the beginning of the study, the couples had been dating for a median period of about eight months—a third for 5 months or less, a third between 5 and 10 months, and a third for longer than that. In three-fourths of the couples both persons were dating their partner exclusively, but only 10% of the couples were engaged and relatively few had concrete plans for marriage. Four-fifths of the couples had had sexual intercourse, and one-fifth were living together "all or most of the time." Sixty percent were seeing one another every day.

Data Collection

In addition to the initial questionnaire, a follow-up questionnaire was administered in person or by mail six months, one year, and two years after the initial session. At all points response rates were good. For example, in the one-year follow-up, two thirds of the initial participants attended questionnaire sessions and another 14% returned short questionnaires in the mail. Four-fifths of the original participants returned the two-year mail questionnaire. To categorize a relationship as intact or broken after two years, we have reports from at least one member of all but 10 of the 231 couples. In all cases, boyfriends and girlfriends were asked to fill out the questionnaires individually. They were assured that their responses would be kept in strict confidence, and would never be revealed to their partners. They were each paid $1.50 for the initial one-hour ques-

tionnaire session and $3.00 for a somewhat longer session one year later. To supplement these data, a smaller number of individuals and couples were interviewed intensively. Of particular relevance to this paper is a series of interviews conducted in the fall of 1972 with 18 people whose relationships ended after they began their participation in the study.

WHICH COUPLES BROKE UP?

By the end of the two-year study period, 103 couples (45% of the total sample) had broken up. (Of the remaining couples, 65 were dating, 9 were engaged, 43 were married, 10 had an unknown status, and one partner had died.) The length of time that breakup couples had been dating before ending their relationship ranged from 1 month to 5 years; the median was 16 months. On the basis of data obtained in the initial questionnaire, could these breakups have been predicted in advance?

Measures of Intimacy

Burgess and Wallin (1953) list "slight emotional attachment" as a major factor associated with the endings of premarital relationships. Our data indicate that in general those couples who were less intimate or less attached to one another when the study began were more likely to break up (Table 1). On the initial questionnaire, compared to couples who stayed together, couples who were subsequently to break up reported that they felt less close and saw less likelihood of marrying each other; they were less likely to be "in love" or dating exclusively, and tended to have been dating for a shorter period of time. The data also indicate, however, that many relationships which were quite "intimate" in 1972 did not survive beyond 1974. For example, over half of the partners in breakup couples felt that they were both in love at the time of the initial questionnaire. Whereas some of the couples who were to break up apparently never developed much intimacy in the first place, others had a high degree of intimacy that they were unable or unwilling to sustain.

Table 1   Initial Intimacy Ratings by Status Two Years Later

	Women's Reports		Men's Reports	
	Together	*Breakup*	*Together*	*Breakup*
Mean Ratings				
Self-report of closeness (9-pt. scale)	7.9	7.3**	8.0	7.2**
Estimate of marriage probability (as percentage)	65.4	46.4**	63.1	42.7**
Love scale (max = 100)	81.2	70.2**	77.8	71.5**
Liking scale (max = 100)	78.5	74.0*	73.2	69.6
Number of months dated	13.1	9.9*	12.7	9.9*
Percentages				
Couple is "in love"	80.0	55.3**	81.2	58.0**
Dating exclusively	92.3	68.0**	92.2	77.5**
Seeing partner daily	67.5	52.0	60.7	53.4
Had sexual intercourse	79.6	78.6	80.6	78.6
Living together	24.8	20.4	23.1	20.4

Note: N = 117 together, 103 breakup for both men and women. Significance by *t* tests or chi-square for together-breakup differences.
*p < .05.
**p < .01.

The various measures of intimacy listed in Table 1 tend to be correlated with one another, and therefore are not independent predictors; however, some measures predicted survival (or breakup) better than others. The partners' "love" was a better predictor of the couple's survival than their "liking" for one another, as measured by scales previously developed by Rubin (1970, 1973). This distinction is in accord with the conceptual meaning of the two scales, with love including elements of attachment and intimacy, while liking refers to favorable evaluations that do not necessarily reflect such intimacy. In addition, the women's love for their boyfriends tended to be a better predictor of dating status (point-biserial r = .32) than the men's love for their girlfriends (r = .18). Thus the woman's feelings toward her dating partner may have a more powerful effect on a relationship and/or provide a more sensitive barometer of its viability than do the man's.

Finally, two important measures of couple intimacy were totally unrelated to breaking up: having had sexual intercourse or having lived together. These behaviors apparently reflect a couple's social values at least as much as the depth of their attachment to one another. Having sex or living together may bring a couple closer, but they may also give rise to additional problems such as coordinating sexual desires or agreeing on the division of household tasks.

Relative Degree of Involvement

In addition to "slight emotional attachment," Burgess and Wallin (1953) list "unequal attachment" as a factor underlying breakups. The hypothesis that equal involvement facilitates the development of a relationship was spelled out by Blau:

Commitments must stay abreast for a love relationship to develop into a lasting mutual attachment. . . . Only when two lovers' affection for and commitment to one another expand at roughly the same pace do they tend mutually to reinforce their love. (1964, p. 84)

Our data provide strong support for Blau's hypothesis. Of the couples in which both members reported that they were equally involved in the relationship in 1972, only 23% broke up; in contrast, 54% of those couples in which at least one member reported that they were unequally involved subsequently broke up. It should be noted, however, that there was a significant association between reporting high intimacy on a variety of measures (e.g., those in Table 1) and reporting equal involvement.

Similarity and Matching

Probably the best documented finding in the research literature on interpersonal attraction and mate selection is the "birds-of-a-feather principle"—people tend to be most attracted to one another if they are similar or equally matched on a variety of social, physical, and intellectual characteristics and attitudes (Rubin, 1973). Evidence for such matching was found among the couples in our study. The significant correlations in the left-hand column of Table 2 make it clear that the partners were matched to some degree on a wide variety of characteristics, especially in the domain of social attitudes and values.

Although there is less empirical support for it, some researchers have put forth "sequential filtering" models of mate selection which propose that social and psychological similarities or dissimilarities are recognized and responded to in particular sequences. For example, Kerckhoff and Davis (1962) and Murstein (1971) propose that filtering (i.e., the elimination of mismatches) takes place first with respect to social background, physical, and other external or stimulus factors, and later with respect to important attitudes and values (Udry, 1971).

The intracouple correlations of the breakup and together groups in our sample reveal that couples were more likely to stay together if they were relatively well-matched with respect to age, educational plans, intelligence (measured by self-reported SAT scores), and physical attractiveness (measured by judges' ratings of individual color photographs). On the other hand, there was no suggestion of filtering during the period of study on such other presumably important characteristics as social class (indexed by father's education), religion, sex-role

Table 2 Couple Similarity by Status Two Years Later

Correlation of Partners'	All Couples (N = 231)	Together Couples (N = 117)	Breakup Couples (N = 103)
Characteristics			
Age	.19**	.38**	.13
Highest degree planned	.28**	.31**	.17
SAT, math	.22**	.31**	.11
SAT, verbal	.24**	.33**	.15
Physical attractiveness	.24**	.32**	.16
Father's educational level	.11	.12	.12
Height	.21**	.22*	.22*
Religion (% same)	51%**	51%**	52%**
Attitudes			
Sex-role traditionalism (10-item scale)	.47**	.50**	.41**
Favorability toward women's liberation	.38**	.36**	.43**
Approval of sex among "acquaintances"	.25**	.27**	.21*
Romanticism (6-item scale)	.20*	.21*	.15
Self-report of religiosity	.37**	.39**	.37**
Number of children wanted	.51**	.43**	.57**

Note: Total N for SAT scores = 187, for physical attractiveness = 174. Physical attractiveness based on ratings of color photographs by 4 judges. Religion categorized as Catholic, Protestant, or Jewish; random pairing would have yielded 41% same religion.

Probability of difference between Together and Breakup correlations (one-tailed) for age is $p < .05$, for SAT math and SAT verbal is $0.5 < p < .10$, for highest degree planned and for physical attractiveness is $.10 < p < .15$.

Significance levels indicated in the table are for chance probabilities.

*$p < .05$.

**$p < .01$.

traditionalism, religiosity, or desired family size. It may be surmised that any filtering on such factors had already taken place before the time of our initial questionnaire.

Methodological problems, most notably involving the effects of varying ranges of scores on the correlations that may be obtained within subgroups, dictate caution in interpreting Table 2. But it may at least be speculated that if there is any general sequence of filters in mate selection, it is different from the ones usually proposed. Whereas models like those of Kerckhoff and Davis (1962) and Murstein (1971) propose that couples are first filtered on social characteristics and stimulus factors, and later on attitudes and values, our data suggest a more complex pattern. It appears that social and stimulus factors (including age, education, intelligence, and physical attractiveness) may continue to be important even after attitudinal and value filtering have occurred. Thus our data lend support to the operation of social and psychological filters in mate selection, but lead us to question the value of simple fixed-sequence theories of filtering (Levinger, Senn & Jorgensen, 1970; Rubin & Levinger, 1974).

THE PROCESS OF BREAKING UP

Brief synopses of two breakups, taken from among the sample we interviewed, may help to illustrate the process of breaking up. Neither of these cases is presented as typical, but the two illustrate several features that are characteristic of the aggregate findings.

Kathy and Joe had been going together during the school year when she was a sophomore and he was a junior. Both of them agree that Kathy was the one who wanted to break up. She felt they were too tied down to one another, that Joe was too dependent and demanded her exclusive attention—even in groups of friends he would draw her aside. As early as the spring Joe came to feel that Kathy was no longer as much in love as he, but it took him a long time to reconcile himself to the notion that things were ending. They gradually saw each other less and less over the summer months, until finally she began to date someone else. The first time that the two

were together after the start of the next school year Kathy was in a bad mood, but wouldn't talk to Joe about it. The following morning Joe told Kathy, "I guess things are over with." Later when they were able to talk further, he found out that she was already dating someone else. Kathy's reaction to the breakup was mainly a feeling of release—both from Joe and from the guilt she felt when she was secretly dating someone else. But Joe had deep regrets about the relationship. For at least some months afterward he regretted that they didn't give the relationship one more chance—he thought they might have been able to make it work. He said that he learned something from the relationship, but hoped he hadn't become jaded by it. "If I fall in love again," he said, "it might be with the reservation that I'm going to keep awake this time. I don't know if you can keep an innocent attitude toward relationships and keep watch at the same time, but I hope so." Meanwhile, however, he had not begun to make any new social contacts, and instead seemed focused on working through the old relationship, and, since Kathy and he sometimes see each other at school, in learning to be comfortable in her presence.

David and Ruth had gone together off-and-on for several years. David was less involved in the relationship than Ruth was, but it is clear that Ruth was the one who precipitated the final breakup. According to Ruth, David was spending more and more time with his own group of friends, and this bothered her. She recalled one night in particular when "they were showing *The Last Picture Show* in one of the dorms, and we went to see it. I was sitting next to him, but it was as if he wasn't really there. He was running around talking to all these people and I was following him around and I felt like his kid sister. So I knew I wasn't going to put up with that much longer." When she talked to him about this and other problems, he said "I'm sorry"— but did not change. Shortly thereafter Ruth wanted to see a movie in Cambridge and asked David if he would go with her. He replied, "No, there's something going on in the dorm!" This was the last straw for Ruth, and she told him she would not go out with him anymore. David started to cry, as if the relationship had really meant something to him—but at that point it was too late. At the time we talked to her, Ruth had not found another boyfriend, but she said she had no regrets about the relationship or about its ending. "It's probably the most worthwhile thing that's ever happened to me in my 21 years, so I don't regret having the experience at all. But after being in the supportive role, *I* want a little support now. That's the main thing I look for." She added that "I don't think I ever felt romantic [about David]—I felt practical. I had the feeling that I'd better make the most of it because it won't last that long."

The Timing of Breakups

If dating relationships were unaffected by their social context, it seems likely that they could end at most any time of the year. But the relationships of the couples in our sample were most likely to break up at key turning points of the school year—in the months of May-June, September, and December-January rather than at other times. This tendency, found for the 103 breakups, is illustrated most dramatically in reports of the ending of all respondents' previous relationships, for which there were more than 400 cases (Figure 1).

This pattern of breakups suggests that factors external to a relationship (leaving for vacations, arriving at school, graduation, etc.) may interact with internal factors (such as conflicting values or goals) to cause relationships to end at particular times. For example, changes in living arrangements and schedules at the beginning or end of a semester may make it easier to meet new dating partners (e.g., in a new class) or make it more difficult to maintain previous ties (e.g., when schedules conflict or

one moves away). Such changes may raise issues concerning the future of a relationship: Should we get an apartment together? Should we spend our vacation apart? Should I accept a job out of state? Should we get together after vacation? If one has already been considering terminating a relationship, such changes may make it easier to call the relationship off. For example, it is probably easier to say, "While we're apart we ought to date others" than it is to say, "I've grown tired of you and would rather not date you any more." If one is able to attribute the impending breakup to external circumstances, one may be able to avoid some of the ambivalence, embarrassment, and guilt that may be associated with calling a relationship off.

The structuring of breakups by the calendar year was also related to another aspect of the breakup process. In the majority of breakups, like the case of Kathy and Joe, the ending was desired more by the partner who was *less* involved in the relationship (in this instance, Kathy). In a significant minority of cases, however, the breakup was desired more by the *more* involved partner (like Ruth), who finally decides that the costs of remaining in the relationship are higher than he or she can bear. We found a strong tendency for the breakups desired by the less-involved partner to take place near the end or beginning of the school year or during the intervening summer months— 71.1% April-September vs. 28.9% October-

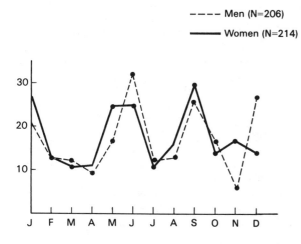

---- Men (N=206)

—— Women (N=214)

Figure 1. Months of the year in which respondents' previous relationships ended. "Previous relationship" refers to the relationship each participant had with the person dated most intensively during the two years before dating the current partner (Hill, 1974).

March. The breakups desired by the more-involved partner, in contrast, were relatively more likely to take place during the school year—59.1% October-March vs. 40.9% April-September ($\chi^2 = 5.68$, $p < .02$). The summer months are, of course, times when college student couples are most likely to be separated because of external factors—for example, returning to homes or jobs in different areas. It seems plausible that less-involved partners would be likely to let their remaining interest in the relationship wane during such periods of separation. Summer separations may also provide a good excuse for the less-involved partner to say good-bye. For the more-involved partner, on the other hand, the period of separation may, if anything, intensify interest in the relationship—"Absence extinguishes small passions and increases great ones" (La Rochefoucauld, quoted in Heider, 1958). The more-involved partner may be most likely to end the relationship in response to continuing pain and frustration. As in the case of Ruth, the final break may be precipitated by some "last straw" that occurs while the two partners are still together.

The Two Sides of Breaking Up

The central principle that *there are two sides to every breakup* has both substantive and methodological implications. Very few breakups are truly mutual, with both parties deciding at more or less the same time that they would like to discontinue the relationship. In the present study, 85% of the women and 87% of the men reported that one person wanted to end the relationship at least somewhat more than the other. Thus in the large majority of cases there are two distinct roles: "breaker-upper" (to be more literary about it, the rejecting lover) and "broken-up-with" (the rejected lover). Identifying these roles is crucial to understanding anything else about a breakup—its underlying reasons, the termination process itself, or its aftermath.

The impact of this role differentiation emerged particularly clearly in self-reports of the emotional aftermath of breaking up (reports available on one-year follow-up for 31 women, 36 men). Both women and men felt considerably less depressed, less lonely, freer, happier, but more guilty when they were the breaker-uppers than when they were the broken-up-with (for most differences, $p < .01$). For example, whereas Kathy reacted to her breakup with relief, Joe felt deep regret. Indeed, there was a general tendency for the two partners' reactions to a breakup to be inversely related. The freer one partner reported feeling after the breakup, the less free the other partner reported feeling ($r = -.57$, $p < .05$; $N = 15$ cases with both reports). Similar inverse correlations—but of lesser magnitude—characterized the former partners' self-reports of depression, loneliness, and happiness.

A second sense in which there are two sides to every breakup is in the perceptions of the participants; the experience of breaking up is different for each of the two parties involved. For example, although members of couples agreed almost completely on the month in which their relationship finally ended ($r = .98$, $N = 77$), there was only slight agreement on the more subjective question of how gradually or abruptly the ending came about ($r = .24$, $N = 77$). When the former partners were asked to provide their attributions of the causes of the breakup, there was moderate to high agreement on the contribution of nondyadic factors but little or no agreement on factors characterizing the dyad (Table 3).

One systematic way in which partners' reports disagree concerns who wanted to break up. Although there is a high correlation between men's and women's reports of who wanted the relationship to end ($r = .85$, $N = 76$), there was a systematic self-bias in the reports. There seems to be a general tendency for respondents to say that they themselves, rather than their partners, were the ones who wanted to break up—51.3% "I," 35.5% "partner," 13.0% mutual in the women's reports; 46.1% "I," 39.5% "partner," 15.0% mutual in the men's reports ($N = 76$). Apparently it is easier to accept and cope with a breakup if one views it as a desired outcome (as precipitated by oneself or as mutual) than as an outcome imposed against one's will. A similar self-bias appeared in ratings of factors contributing to the breakup—both men and women cited

Table 3 Factors Contributing to the Ending of a Relationship (Percentage Reporting)

	Women's Reports	Men's Reports	Partner Correlation
Dyadic Factors			
Becoming bored with the relationship	76.7	76.7	.23*
Differences in interests	72.8	61.1	.04
Differences in backgrounds	44.2	46.8	.05
Differences in intelligence	19.5	10.4	.17
Conflicting sexual attitudes	48.1	42.9	.33**
Conflicting marriage ideas	43.4	28.9	.25*
Nondyadic Factors			
Woman's desire to be independent	73.7	50.0	.57**
Man's desire to be independent	46.8	61.1	.55**
Woman's interest in someone else	40.3	31.2	.56**
Man's interest in someone else	18.2	28.6	.60**
Living too far apart	28.2	41.0	.57**
Pressure from woman's parents	18.2	13.0	.33**
Pressure from man's parents	10.4	9.1	.58**

Note: Data for those couples for which both man's and woman's reports were available ($N = 77$). Factors labelled "man's" and "woman's" above were labelled as "my" or "partner's" in the questionnaires. Percentages are those citing factor as "a contributing factor" or as "one of the most important factors." Correlations are based on 3-point scales.

* $p < .05$

** $p < .01$

"my" desire to be independent as more important than "partner's" desire to be independent.

For some purposes, therefore, it is difficult to speak confidently about *the* breakup, as if it refers to a single, objective set of events. Instead it seems necessary to attend separately to "his breakup" and to "her breakup," in each instance looking at the matter from the respective partner's point of view—see Bernard's (1972) discussion of "his marriage" and "her marriage." This distinction seems particularly necessary since our data suggest that there may be some systematic differences between men and women in their orientations toward breaking up.

SEX DIFFERENCES IN BREAKING UP

Rubin, Peplau, and Hill (1981) suggest that in respect to dating or premarital relationships in middle-class America today: (a) men tend to fall in love more readily than women, and (b) women tend to fall out of love more readily

than men. Evidence for the first proposition is reviewed elsewhere (Rubin, Peplau, & Hill, 1981). To cite just one datum from the present study, on the initial questionnaire respondents were asked to indicate how important each of a variety of goals was to them as a reason for entering the relationship. Prevailing stereotypes about romantic women to the contrary, men rated the "desire to fall in love" as a significantly more important reason for entering the relationship than did women (4.1 vs. 3.6 on a 9-point scale, $p = .03$). We will review here some of the evidence relating to the second proposition.

Perceived Problems

When participants who had broken up were presented a list of common problems and asked to indicate which had contributed to the breakup (Table 3), women rated more problems as important than did men ($p < .003$). In particular, more women than men cited "differences in interests," "differences in intelligence," "conflicting ideas about marriage," "my desire to be independent," and "my interest in someone else." Men were only more likely to cite "living too far apart." Although these reports are retrospective and clearly susceptible to distortion, they suggest that women tended to be more sensitive than men to problem areas in their relationship, and that women were more likely than men to compare the relationship to alternatives, whether potential or actual. These tendencies seem consistent with the hypothesis.

Who Precipitates the Breakup?

If women indeed tend to fall out of love more readily than men, we would expect them to be more likely to play the role of breaker-upper and men to play the role of broken-up-with. Combining men's and women's reports of who wanted to break up and classifying a breakup as nonmutual if either partner described it so, we estimate that the woman was more interested in breaking up in 51% of the couples, the man in 42%, and the breakup was clearly mutual in 7%. The participants' reports (200-plus cases for each sex) of breakups in previous opposite-sex relationships (Hill, 1974) suggested a similar preponderance of female-initiated breakups. In an earlier study, Rubin (1969) found that 17 of 25 nonmutual breakups among dating couples at the University of Michigan had been initiated by women.

One possible explanation for this datum is that women might have been less involved in these relationships than the men. But that was not the case. Once the relationships had proceeded beyond their early stages, the women were by all indications at least as involved as the men. Combining the two partners' reports before the time of the breakup, women were categorized as the more involved partner in 45% of all couples and men as more involved in 36%; in 19% they were classified as equally involved.

As Blau (1964) has suggested, however, a relationship in which there is unequal involvement will not always be ended by the less involved party: "Whereas rewards experienced in the relationship may lead to its continuation for a while, the weak interest of the less committed or the frustrations of the more committed probably will sooner or later prompt one or

the other to terminate it" (p. 84). Our data suggest that Blau's postulated patterns describe a substantial number of breakups precipitated by women. Relationships were often ended by women when they were the less involved partner (67.6% of the 34 cases)—like Kathy in the first of the cases presented—and wanted to move on to better alternatives. Relationships were also likely to be ended by women when they were the more involved partner (37.2% of the 43 cases)—like Ruth in the second case—and finally abandoned the relationship when they realized that their commitment was not reciprocated. When breakups were precipitated by men, only the first of the two patterns was common. Relationships were frequently ended by men when they were the less involved partner (60.5% of the 43 cases), but rarely when they were the more involved (20.6% of the 34 cases). These data seem quite consistent with our generalization: Whereas many highly involved women sooner or later find it necessary and possible to terminate the relationship, men seem to find that more difficult.

Staying Friends

If men find it more difficult than women to renounce their love, we might also expect relations between former partners to be more strained after the woman has rejected the man than vice versa. Whereas a rejected woman may be able to redefine her relationship with her former boyfriend from "love" to "friendship"— which, as Davis (1973) notes, is often a euphemism for "acquaintance"—a rejected man may find it more difficult to accomplish such a redefinition. In such cases, staying friends is likely to be impossible. The data support this expectation. A couple was much more likely to stay friends when the man had been the one who precipitated the breakup (70%), or when the breakup was mutual (71%), than when the woman precipitated it (46%) ($\chi^2 = 5.83$, $p < .06$).

Emotional Aftermath

Our generalization would also suggest that breaking up would be a more traumatic experience for men than for women. Unfortunately, the data available to test this proposition are limited to the 15 couples in which we obtained reports of emotional reactions from both partners on the one-year follow-up. These data suggest that men were hit harder than women by the breakup. Men tended more than women to report that in the wake of the breakup they felt depressed, lonely, less happy, less free, and less guilty. Goethals (1973) presents a clinical discussion of sex differences in reactions to breaking up that seems consistent with these data. In our interviews, we were struck by a particular reaction that appeared among several of the men but not among the women. Some men found it extremely difficult to reconcile themselves to the fact that they were no longer loved and that the relationship was over (Jim, in the first of the cases reported above, is illustrative). Women who are rejected may also react with considerable grief and despair, but they seem less likely to retain the hope that their rejectors "really love them after all."

Two Interpretations

The evidence provides converging support for the notion that women tend to fall out of love more readily than men, just as men may tend to fall in love more readily than women (Rubin, Peplau, & Hill, 1981). Needless to say, these generalizations are offered as actuarial propositions; they take on importance to the extent that they are informative about aspects of the socialization of the two sexes for close relationships in contemporary America. Two aspects of sex-roles may help account for these tendencies.

Simple economics. Contrary to prevailing stereotypes about romantic and sentimental women, women may be more practical than men about mate selection for simple economic reasons. In most marriages, the wife's status, income, and life chances are far more dependent upon her husband's than vice versa. For this reason, parents in almost all societies have been more concerned with finding appropriate mates for their daughters than for their sons. In "free choice" systems of mate selection like our own, the woman must be especially discriminating. She cannot allow herself to fall in love

too quickly, nor can she afford to stay in love too long with the wrong person (Goode, 1959). Men, on the other hand, can afford the luxury of being romantic. The fact that a woman's years of marriageability tend to be more limited than a man's also contributes to her greater need to be selective. Waller (1938) put the matter most bluntly when he wrote:

There is this difference between the man and the woman in the pattern of bourgeois family life: a man, when he marries, chooses a companion and perhaps a helpmate, but a woman chooses a companion and at the same time a standard of living. It is necessary for a woman to be mercenary. (p. 243)

Interpersonal sensitivity. Women are traditionally the social-emotional specialists in most societies, including our own, while men are the traditional task specialists (Parsons & Bales, 1955). The emphasis upon social-emotional matters in women's socialization may lead women to be more sensitive than men to the quality of their interpersonal relationships, both in the present and projecting into the future. One possible reflection of women's greater interpersonal sensitivity is the finding, replicated in the present study, that women distinguish more sharply than men between "liking" and "loving" components of interpersonal sentiments (Rubin, 1970). Because of greater interpersonal sensitivity and discrimination, it may also be more important for women than for men that the quality of a relationship remain high. Thus women's criteria for falling in love—and for staying in love—may be higher than men's, and they may reevaluate their relationships more carefully.

BREAKUPS BEFORE AND AFTER MARRIAGE

We have suggested that breakups before marriage are relevant to an understanding of marital breakup in two different ways. First, breakups before marriage provide an interesting comparison against which to view marital disruption. Second, breakups before marriage can serve to prevent marriages that would otherwise be likely to end in divorce. We will briefly consider our results from each of these two perspectives.

Comparisons with Marital Breakups

There are profound differences between the process of breaking up before marriage and the process of breaking up afterward. Some of the breakups of couples in this study took place quite casually—boyfriends and girlfriends went home at the end of the school year and simply never got back together again. Marriages seldom end so casually. Our interview data also made it clear that the experience of breaking up before marriage is generally less stressful than the experience of marital disruption (cf. Weiss, 1976). Such differences reflect fundamental differences between the social-psychological contexts of premarital breakups and divorce. Breakups before marriage take place in the context of a dating system in which coupling, uncoupling, and recoupling are approved and accepted elements. In this context it may be relatively easy for a person who has ended an old relationship to replace it with a new one. Marital disruption, on the other hand, remains a counter-normative phenomenon which is often stigmatized by kin and community. A marriage is typically ended only with considerable effort and stress, and the process of getting back into circulation and replacing a lost partner is likely to be much more difficult for both parties.

Comparing breakups before and after marriage allows us to focus also on commonalities—features that may be intrinsic to the process of ending close relationships (Davis, 1973). One such similarity may be the two-sidedness of breaking up; although there are exceptions, it is probably rare for any sort of breakup to be entirely mutual. As a relationship weakens or deteriorates, the balance of attraction of the two partners is likely to become increasingly unequal. We have found that whereas equal involvement tends to be associated with the growth of a relationship, unequal involvement is associated with its decay. In this asymmetrical context, one party is likely to be the breaker-upper, the other the broken-up-with. In addition, the finding that former partners often

have very different perceptions of their breakup is probably true in the case of marital breakup as well. Given the fundamental asymmetries that characterize a weakening relationship, it may be inevitable for each party to see events differently, from his or her point of view. This difference in perspective leads to the recommendation that students of marital separation make every effort to obtain reports from both partners. Although this leads to complications in the interpretation of data, they are complications that seem to be an intrinsic part of the phenomenon being studied.

Another similarity between premarital breakup and divorce may be the possibility of sex differences in orientations towards breaking up. Just as we found that women cited more reasons for their breakups than did men, Levinger (1966) found that women cited more marital complaints than men in interviews of applicants for divorce. It is possible, however, that different processes underlie these findings since the kinds of problems cited were not the same. Just as we found some evidence that more women than men wanted to end their dating relationships, Goode (1956) found that women were more likely than men to first suggest getting a divorce. Although Goode hypothesized that the men were really the ones more interested in ending the marriage and that they drove their wives to seek a divorce, since he only obtained reports from the women, it was not possible to check that hypothesis.

Breakups as Preventors of Divorce

Breakups before marriage are highly relevant to divorce; as someone's grandfather used to say, "The best divorce is the one you get before you get married." A good deal of filtering takes place in the mate-selection process—although, as we have noted, the process is probably more complicated than that suggested by fixed-sequence filter theories. A central question for students of divorce, however, is what prevents still further filtering of the sort that would prevent marriages that result in divorce.

For some (e.g., DeRougemont, 1949), "romantic love" is seen as the culprit, blinding lovers to all practical considerations. But although a large proportion of the couples in our sample felt that they were "in love" (Table 1), many nevertheless managed to seek out partners who were similar to themselves with respect to such factors as age, education, intelligence, and, especially, social attitudes and values (Table 2). Moreover, many of the couples who were "in love" subsequently decided to break up. The central obstacle is not, in our view, the overwhelming power of romantic love.

Two obstacles which seem to have greater importance are the difficulty one may have in terminating a relationship without access to appropriate facilitating factors (e.g., external excuses) and the difficulty some people—especially men—have in withdrawing from a relationship in which their commitment is not reciprocated. External factors, such as separations that are orchestrated by the school calendar (Figure 1), seemed to be helpful in facilitating breakups, both because they encouraged comparisons between the relationship and alternatives and because they helped to provide easier verbal formulas for breaking up. As Albert and Kessler (1973) have remarked, special rituals and formulas are often necessary to facilitate the ending of brief encounters between friends or acquaintances in such a way as to keep intact the esteem of both parties. The availability of such formulas—for example, the ability to say, "I'll see you in the fall" (even when the nature of the relationship may shift in the interim) rather than "I don't want to see you any more"—seems even more necessary to facilitate the ending of close relationships.

This dependence on facilitating circumstances suggests that it may be useful for couples to consider and to create their own occasions for redefining and discussing their relationships. One way in which a couple may be able to do this is by participating in a study such as the present one—which, we have discovered, had the effect of doubling as "couples counseling" (Rubin & Mitchell, 1976). Taking part in the study had the effects of clarifying participants' definitions of their relationships and of facilitating disclosure of feelings, issues, and concerns. Other attempts to facilitate such self-examination and confrontation, whether through college courses, counseling programs, or the mass media, are of potentially great value.

An unwillingness to disengage oneself from a relationship in which one has invested heavily is probably a general human tendency. As Becker (1960) has noted, the investing of time and energy and the foregoing of alternative relationships commit one to remain in a relationship even if it turns out to be a painful one. Our comparison of men's and women's orientations toward loving and leaving suggests that this unwillingness to withdraw may be especially characteristic of men. More generally, the fact that one partner (regardless of sex) typically carries most of the burdens of breaking up makes the process especially difficult. The roles of breaker-upper and broken-up-with are probably common to all sorts of breakup, but this may not be an inevitable differentiation. Ideally, the two partners would be able to discuss and "have out" their differences, and to decide mutually to break up at some point before marriage if they anticipate several strains or irreconcilable differences. How this ideal might be achieved is, of course, a difficult challenge. It is hoped, however, that continued research into the phenomenon of breaking up before marriage—and the dissemination of this research to young couples—may help to provide the sort of enlightenment that will ease the process for all.

REFERENCES

Albert, S., & Kessler, S. *A theory for the ending of social encounters.* Unpublished manuscript, City University of New York, 1973.

Becker, H. Notes on the concept of commitment. *American Journal of Sociology,* 1960, *66,* 32–40.

Bernard, J., *The future of marriage.* New York: World Book Co., 1972.

Blau, P. M. *Exchange and power in social life.* New York: Wiley, 1964.

Burgess, E., & Wallin, P. *Engagement and marriage.* Philadelphia: Lippincott, 1953.

Davis, M. S. *Intimate relations.* New York: Free Press, 1973.

DeRougemont, D. The crisis of the modern couple. In R. N. Anshen (Ed.), *The family: Its function and destiny.* New York: Harper & Row, 1949.

Goethals, G. W. Symbiosis and the life cycle. *British Journal of Medical Psychology*, 1973, *46*, 91–96.

Goode, W. J. *After divorce*. Glencoe, Ill.: Free Press, 1956.

Goode, W. J. The theoretical importance of love. *American Sociological Review*, 1959, *24*, 38–47.

Heider, F. *The psychology of interpersonal relations*. New York: Wiley, 1958.

Hill, C. T. *The ending of successive opposite-sex relationships*. Unpublished doctoral dissertation, Harvard University, 1974.

Hill, C. T., Rubin, Z., Peplau, L. A., & Willard, S. G. The volunteer couple: Sex differences, couple commitment and participation in research on interpersonal relationships. *Social Psychology Quarterly*, 1979, *42*, 415–420.

Kerckhoff, A. C., & Davis, K. E. Value consensus and need complementarity in mate selection. *American Sociological Review*, 1962, *27*, 295–303.

Levinger, G. Sources of marital dissatisfaction among applicants for divorce. *American Journal of Orthopsychiatry*, 1966, *36*, 803–807.

Levinger, G., Senn, D. J., & Jorgensen, B. W. Progress toward permanence in courtship: A test of the Kerckhoff-Davis hypothesis. *Sociometry*, 1970, *33*, 427–443.

Murstein, B. I. A theory of marital choice and its applicability to marriage adjustment. In B. I. Murstein (Ed.), *Theories of attraction and love*. New York: Springer, 1971.

Parsons, T., & Bales, R. F. *Family, socialization, and interaction processes*. Glencoe, Ill.: Free Press, 1955.

Rubin, Z. The social psychology of romantic love (Doctoral dissertation, University of Michigan, 1969). (University microfilms No. 70–4179)

Rubin, Z. Measurement of romantic love. *Journal of Personality and Social Psychology*, 1970, *16*, 265–273.

Rubin, Z. *Liking and loving: An invitation to social psychology*. New York: Holt, Rinehart, & Winston, 1973.

Rubin, Z., & Levinger, G. Theory and data badly mated: A critique of Murstein's SVR and Lewis's PDF models of mate selection. *Journal of Marriage and the Family*, 1974, *36*, 226–230.

Rubin, Z., & Mitchell, C. Couples research as couples counseling: Some unintended effects of studying close relationships. *American Psychologist*, 1976, *31*, 17–25.

Rubin, Z., Peplau, L. A., & Hill, C. T. Loving and leaving: Sex differences in romantic attachments. *Sex Roles*, 1981, 7(8), 821–835.

Udry, J. *The social context of marriage* (2nd ed.) New York: Lippincott, 1971.

Waller, W. *The family: A dynamic interpretation*. New York: Dryden, 1938.

Weiss, R. S. The emotional impact of marital separation. *Journal of Social Issues*, 1976, *32*(1).

13

Commitment in Close Relationships: The Investment Model

CARYL E. RUSBULT

Statistics suggest that close to half of all new American marriages may ultimately end in divorce. Why do some close relationships break up while others endure "for better or for worse"? What are the sources of commitment in dating and marriage? In this recent paper, Caryl Rusbult extends ideas from social exchange theory to understand commitment in close relationships. She begins by distinguishing between two related concepts: our satisfaction with a relationship and our degree of commitment (defined as the tendency to maintain a relationship and to feel psychologically attached to it). Rusbult proposes that commitment depends on three factors: (1) the satisfactions we derive from the relationship; (2) the quality of alternative relationships available to us; and (3) the investments we have made in the relationship, such as time, energy, or self-disclosures. Commitment should be high when we are happy in a relationship, have no desirable alternatives, and have invested a great deal in the current relationship. Rusbult has tested these ideas in an impressive series of studies using diverse methods. She has asked some subjects to consider how they might behave in hypothetical commitment situations, and asked others to describe their own personal relationships. She has collected both cross-sectional and longitudinal data, and her studies have considered not only heterosexual relationships but also the relationships of lesbians and gay men. Taken together, these results provide strong support for the investment model of commitment.

Why do people stick with their partners in close relationships? What is the "glue" that holds relationships together? Merely understanding the factors that encourage us to like or love another person does not fully explain why some relationships persist through hard times and conflict "until death does us part," while other promising relationships fall apart. Two examples help illustrate the inadequacy of the concept of attraction—liking, loving, satisfaction—in accounting for the stability of relationships:

John and Mary have an unhappy marriage. They have had a pretty miserable marriage for the past

10 years—they fight constantly, they have no intimate connection at all, and there is little love lost between them—but neither has ever seriously considered divorce. They have been married for 20 years, own a home in the suburbs, and have four children, three of whom are still living with them. They are in their mid-40s, and all of their friends and acquaintances are *very* married"; they simply do not know any single people any more.

Dennis and Lisa have had a delightful relationship for the past six months—both of them love new wave bars, old movies, and pasta, and they always have a great time together. But though they thoroughly enjoy one another's company, neither has ever really talked to the other about the things

This paper was written in 1987 specifically for this second edition.

147

that are most inportant in their lives. And throughout their involvement both have regularly dated other people—after all, they are around attractive single people every day at work. When Lisa meets David, an extraordinarily attractive man who sweeps her off her feet, she drops Dennis like a hot potato.

John and Mary are not very satisfied, yet their relationship persists: Dennis and Lisa are a happy and contented couple, yet their relationship neither grows nor endures. Experience with relationships tells us that satisfaction and commitment are not one and the same: Sometimes people feel committed to maintaining relationships even though they are no longer satisfied with their partners or relationships. Thus, an unhappy marriage may persist for decades "for the sake of the children"; witness John and Mary. Conversely, individuals sometimes end relationships even though they feel relatively strong attraction to their partners; witness Dennis and Lisa. As Johnson (1982) notes, "people stay in relationships for two major reasons: because they want to, and because they have to" (pp. 52–53). In other words, some people stay in relationships because they are satisfied with their relationships; other people, however, stay because they become entrapped. What we need is a general theory of close relationships that can explain not only the development of attraction and satisfaction, but also the development of commitment to maintain relationships. The investment model attempts to achieve these goals.

THE INVESTMENT MODEL

The investment model (Rusbult, 1980a, 1983) is a simple extension of concepts developed within the exchange tradition in social psychology, particularly interdependence theory (Kelley & Thibaut, 1978; Thibaut & Kelley, 1959). Following interdependence theory, the investment model distinguishes between *satisfaction*—positivity of feelings or attraction to one's partner and relationship—and *commitment*—the tendency to maintain a relationship and to feel psychologically attached to it. The definition of commitment includes two elements: behav-

ioral intent and psychological attachment (cf. Johnson, 1973, 1982; Rosenblatt, 1977). Commitment is thus a psychological state that directly affects the individual's decision to continue or end a relationship—the individual feels connected to the relationship and intends to stick with it. It is because of differences in commitment that Mary—who is horribly dissatisfied—continues her relationship, whereas Lisa—who really has a great time with Dennis—ends hers.

Satisfaction with Relationships

Following interdependence theory, the investment model asserts that a person should feel satisfied with a relationship to the extent that the relationship provides high rewards and low costs, and exceeds the person's generalized expectations, or comparison level. If an individual shares many common interests with a romantic partner (i.e., derives high rewards) with whom he or she seldom argues (i.e., incurs few costs), and has never really expected much from relationships (i.e., has a low comparison level), then satisfaction with the relationship should be strong.

It is interesting to note that people in relationships with objectively equivalent reward-cost levels will be differentially satisfied to the degree that they have different comparison levels; a person with lower expectations should feel more satisfied than a person with greater expectations. For example, let us assume that both Sue and Linda are involved with men who are moderately smart, fun, and witty. However, the two women have different comparison levels because they have had different sorts of experiences in the past: Sue has had a number of really terrific close relationships, and she tends to expect a lot of her partners in general. In contrast, Linda has never really had a decent relationship in her life—and she's seen one after another marriage end horribly, including that of her parents—so she just does not count on much. Linda should be tremendously satisfied with her relationship, because it so far exceeds what she has come to expect. Though Sue's relationship is just as good objectively, she will feel less satisfied because she expects so much. Persons with lower expectations are likely to experience greater satisfaction in relationships.

Commitment to Maintain Relationships

Obviously, commitment to maintain a relationship should be greater to the degree that the relationship is a satisfying one for the individual. People tend to stick with relationships that are going well. But satisfaction is not the sole determinant of commitment: Happy partners do not necessarily stay together; unhappy partners do not necessarily break up. One of the most important goals of our work has been to identify other crucial determinants of commitment.

Following interdependence theory, the investment model proposes that individuals who have only poor alternatives should be more committed to their relationships than people with many attractive alternatives. The perceived quality of alternatives, like satisfaction with current relationships, is influenced by the anticipated rewards and costs of the alternative. However, in the case of alternatives, the object of evaluation is a specific alternative relationship, solitude, dating around, or spending time with friends or relatives—whatever is the best available alternative. For example, if a teenager really does not mind spending time alone, believes that there are others she could date, and/or does not have a strong need for romance, she should feel lower commitment to a current relationship—she does not *have* to stick with it if she does not want to do so.

Another means of becoming committed to a relationship is by investing numerous or sizable resources in that involvement. Investments can be either intrinsic or extrinsic. Intrinsic investments are those resources that are put directly into the relationship, such as time, emotional energy, or self-disclosures. Extrinsic investment occurs when extraneous resources—things that really have little to do with the relationship itself—become inextricably connected to the relationship (e.g., mutual friends, shared memories or material possessions, activities/persons/objects uniquely associated with the relationship). Investments of both

sorts increase commitment by increasing the costs of ending the relationship, because leaving would require abandoning all that has been invested in that relationship over time. Thus, joint home ownership, children, exerting great effort for one's partner, or even being tennis partners may serve as investments that strengthen commitment to relationships. The present use of the investment concept is similar to constructs advanced by other authors—Becker's (1960) notion of "side bets," Levinger's (1979) discussion of "barrier forces"—or issues related to entrapment and investments as presented by Rubin (Rubin & Brockner, 1975), Blau (1964), Staw (1976), or Teger (1980).

The key ideas of the investment model can be summarized in several propositions: First, *satisfaction* in a relationship depends on rewards, costs, and the person's comparison level. Second, *commitment* in a relationship depends on satisfaction, alternatives, and investments. And third, whether a person *stays in or leaves* a relationship depends most directly on the person's level of commitment. Because satisfaction and commitment are not necessarily strongly correlated—strong commitment may be produced by poor alternatives or large investments—it is possible to be dissatisfied with a relationship and yet remain committed to it and stay involved in it. For example, a women who suffers regular physical or emotional abuse in her marriage and is thus dissatisfied may remain committed to the marriage because her alternatives are poor (e.g., she has no job, little education) and/or because she has invested heavily in the relationship (e.g., she and her spouse have several children, she has invested several decades of time and effort in her marriage). Alternatively, an individual might leave a relatively satisfying involvement because of the availability of a highly attractive alternative coupled with low investments in the current relationship.

Before moving on, we should note the beneficial aspects of large investments and poor alternatives. On the one hand, high investments and poor alternatives can serve to trap an individual in an unhappy relationship. On the other hand, high investments and poor alternatives can serve to produce peace and stability in a happy relationship. To burn one's bridges by cutting off available alternatives and to throw in one's lot in life with another by investing heavily in that relationship is not necessarily to trap oneself hopelessly in a hellish relationship. If partners continue to love one another, if they continue to feel satisfied with their relationship, those burned bridges and invested resources can be thought of as insurance: These may be the ballast that hold the relationship together during tougher times. An important task, thus, is to know when a relationship is worth taking the risk—when is it good enough to risk investing resources in it, when is it good enough to risk cutting off alternatives?

The next section of this paper describes research conducted to date to test predictions of the investment model. This research examines the impact of rewards and costs on satisfaction, the impact of a three-factor model (satisfaction, investments, and alternatives) on commitment, and the impact of a *four-factor model* (rewards, costs, investments, and alternatives) on commitment. The research reported also explores the process by which satisfaction and commitment develop, as well as the relationship between investment model variables and individual decisions to stay with or to end their relationships.

TESTING THE INVESTMENT MODEL

The predictive power of the investment model was initially tested by carrying out two complementary studies of dating relationships (Rusbult, 1980a). Study 1 used a role-playing methodology. Research participants were asked to read essays describing hypothetical relationships, to put themselves in the position of the major character of the essay, and to indicate how they would react in such a situation. Twelve versions of the essay orthogonally manipulated costs (low or high), alternatives (low or high), and investments (low, medium, or high). (We did not manipulate relationship rewards in this study.)

Relationship cost was manipulated through variations in the difficulty of maintaining the relationship: In the high cost condition, one partner had moved 1000 miles away and was able to see the other infrequently, whereas in the low cost condition the partner had moved only sixty miles away, enabling several visits every week. Alternative quality was manipulated by varying the attractiveness of an alternative partner interested in dating the main character. The alternative date was either exceptionally appealing in terms of intelligence, personality, physical attractiveness, and wit (high alternative quality) or mediocre on each of these dimensions (low alternative quality). A third manipulation varied both intrinsic and extrinsic investment size, and therefore had three levels: In the low investments condition, the main character had dated the partner for only one month prior to his or her move, and in the medium investments condition, the main character had dated the partner for one year prior to his or her move. A comparison of these two conditions tests the effects of the intrinsic investment in the relationship of time. In the high investments condition, the main character had dated the partner for one year prior to the partner's move, and also had an extrinsic investment connected to the relationship—the main character was employed by his or her partner's father. Thus, a comparison of the medium and high investment conditions tests the effects of an extrinsic investment in the relationship.

After reading and familiarizing themselves with one of the twelve essays, participants completed a questionnaire indicating how satisfied they would be and how committed they would feel to maintaining the relationship if they were in the position of the main character of the essay. Analysis of variance was utilized to determine the degree to which each manipulation influenced reported satisfaction and commitment. Consistent with predictions, the manipulation of relationship costs significantly affected reported satisfaction: The mean satisfaction score was 9.01 for the low cost condition and 8.29 for the high cost condition. Also, as predicted, average commitment differed significantly as a function of alternative quality: Commitment was 16.46 for those with attractive alternatives and 18.67 for those with less attractive alternatives. Both intrinsic and extrinsic investments significantly influenced commitment to maintain relationships: Mean commitment was 16.61 for the low investments condition, 17.50 for the medium investments condition, and 18.58 for the high investments condition. However, commitment was not significantly influenced by relationship costs, though the means were in the predicted direction: Average commitment was 17.19 for the high cost condition and 17.93 for the low cost condition. Thus, this study provided good, though not perfect, support for model predictions.

This study was complemented by Study 2, a cross-sectional survey of ongoing dating relationships. Study 1 really just explored participants' guesses about how they might behave in hypothetical situations. Study 2 explored the investment model in actual, ongoing dating relationships. Participants in this project completed questionnaires that measured all variables in the investment model—relationship rewards (e.g., physical attractiveness, complementary needs, intelligence, sense of humor), relationship costs (e.g., embarrassing behaviors, failure to live up to agreements, lack of faithfulness), alternative attractiveness (e.g., beginning a relationship with another person, spending time alone), investment size (e.g., mutual friends, shared memories, shared material possessions), satisfaction (e.g., attraction to relationship, closeness of relationship to ideal), and commitment (e.g., probability of ending relationship, attachment to relationship).

Correlational analyses revealed excellent support for investment model predictions: Satisfaction was best predicted by a combination of the rewards and costs associated with the relationship. Together, these two factors accounted for 46 percent of the variation in reported satisfaction. One set of analyses showed that, as predicted, commitment was strongly linked to satisfaction, investment size, and alternative quality. Remember that according to the theory, satisfaction is itself determined by rewards and costs. We were interested in determining whether both rewards and costs are equally important components of satisfaction when it comes to influencing commitment. To answer this question, we carried out another analysis in which we substituted separate measures of rewards and costs for satisfaction, and used these two factors along with investments and alternatives to predict commitment. Two interesting findings emerged. First, this less direct test of our prediction was not as good at explaining commitment. The model accounted for 37 percent of the variation in commitment, compared to 61 percent accounted for by the earlier model including satisfaction. More interestingly, however, was the second finding that rewards and costs were not equally important factors in affecting commitment. Although rewards strongly influenced commitment, costs only weakly influenced it. This general pattern also emerges in studies described later: Costs seem to be a less important factor in commitment than rewards; it is not so much that pain in a relationship makes us less satisfied as it is that pleasure in a relationship makes us more satisfied. The romantic ideal that one accepts a mate "for better or worse" may prevent us from feeling less committed to others as the costs of doing so increase. However, recent research found that cost value—along with other investment model variables—*did* predict commitment in friendships and business associations, where the romantic ideal does not apply (Farrell & Rusbult, 1981; Rusbult, 1980b).

TESTS OF THE GENERALIZABILITY OF THE INVESTMENT MODEL

The studies just reported provided good support for investment model predictions (Rusbult, 1980a). However, the generalizability of those findings is limited in at least one important respect: Both studies examined the predictive power of the model in college-age dating relationships. University students differ from the larger population in a number of significant respects—they are, in general, younger, of higher socio-economic status, better educated, and involved in relationships of briefer duration. If the investment model is to serve as a general theory of close relationships, we must demonstrate that it can predict satisfaction and commitment in a wide range of involvements. To assess the model in more long-standing relationships, and in a more heterogeneous population, we conducted a mailed survey of ongoing, adult romantic involvements in a moderate-sized midwestern city (Rusbult, Johnson, & Morrow, 1986). The questionnaire was similar to that used in Study 2, described earlier.

Correlational analyses tested the investment model and, again, showed very good support for our predictions. Together, rewards and costs accounted for 30 percent of the variability in satisfaction. Satisfaction, investments, and alternatives accounted for 48 percent of the variance in commitment. The four-factor model including rewards, costs, investments, and alternatives accounted for less variance in commitment—38 percent. As before, although rewards, investments, and alternatives were significant components of this model, relationship costs did not significantly affect commitment. Furthermore, these findings held across a wide range of demographically defined subgroups—for women and men, married and single persons, younger and older persons, persons with greater and lesser education and income—and for briefer and more enduring relationships.

Thus, the relationships among model variables predicted by the investment model appear to be applicable to the larger population. These findings represent an important step toward establishing the validity of the investment model. Unfortunately, the generalizability of this research is still limited in one very important respect: We explored only heterosexual involvements. Therefore, one further test of the generalizability of the model was carried out, this time using matched samples of individuals in lesbian, gay male, and heterosexual relationships (Duffy & Rusbult, 1986). Once again, the questionnaire was similar to those employed in previous research (Rusbult, 1980a; Rusbult et al., 1986), modified where appropriate for these populations.

Generally, lesbians, gay men, and heterosexual women and men described their relationships in quite similar ways. All groups reported relatively high rewards and low costs, moderately poor alternatives, moderately high invest-

ments, and very strong satisfaction and commitment. Even when we explored differences in *specific* rewards, costs, investments, and alternatives (e.g., need complementarity, conflicts, sexual faithfulness, self-disclosure, appeal of casual dating), we found that gender distinguished between individuals more powerfully and consistently than did sexual orientation. That is, being male or female itself seems to have much more to do with experiences in close relationships than does whether one prefers same-sex or different-sex partners. For example, women—both lesbians and heterosexuals—invest more in their relationships and feel more committed to their relationships than do men—gay or straight.

In addition, once again analyses strongly supported the investment model. Satisfaction was significantly predicted by a combination of reward and costs values for the sample as a whole (accounting for 49 percent of the variance) and for each subgroup (accounting for 52 to 88 percent of the variance). Rewards predicted satisfaction for everyone, but high costs were significantly predictive of lower satisfaction only for women, both lesbians and heterosexuals. Commitment was effectively predicted by satisfaction, investments, and alternatives for the sample as a whole (67 percent of the variance) and for each subgroup 62 to 88 percent of the variance). That is, strong commitment was linked to high satisfaction, large investments, and poor quality alternatives for the sample as a whole and for each subgroup. Finally, the four-factor model of commitment—from rewards, costs, alternatives, and investments—effectively predicted commitment for the sample as a whole (59 percent of the variance) and for each subgroup (59 to 88 percent of the variance). Rewards, investments, and alternatives related to commitment as predicted for all groups. However, costs were significantly predictive of lower commitment only for women—lesbians and heterosexuals.

Why do the costs of relationships have no effect on men's satisfaction with or commitment to their relationships? It may be that because males tend to believe more strongly in the romantic ideal (Hatkoff & Lasswell, 1979; Rubin, Peplau, & Hill, 1981), satisfaction and commitment are unrelated to perceived costs. That is, belief in the romantic ideal that one accepts a partner "for better or worse" (i.e., given high rewards *or* costs) may protect men's reported satisfaction and commitment from the influence of increases in the costs of involvement. This finding remains to be explored in future research.

A LONGITUDINAL TEST OF THE INVESTMENT MODEL

The work reported so far has been essentially "static" in nature. That is, our work evaluated the investment model at a single point in time. The model was originally advanced to explain the development and deterioration of satisfaction and commitment over time. Thus, an important test of the model would be to explore the "ebb and flow" of satisfaction and commitment over the course of a relationship. For example, to what extent do fluctuations in commitment directly mediate decisions to leave a relationship? A longitudinal study of dating relationships was conducted to examine these issues (Rusbult, 1983).

Respondents in this project were 34 male and female undergraduates who had recently begun new dating relationships. The study began near the start of the academic year, and respondents' participation ended when their relationships broke up or the study itself ended seven months later, at the end of the academic year. Respondents received questionnaires through the mail every 17 days, and returned completed questionnaires within a few days of their receipt. The project consisted of a total of 13 questionnaires. Respondents received a nominal payment of $2.50 for each questionnaire they completed.

Correlational analyses were conducted to explore the dynamics by which satisfaction and commitment grow or deteriorate over time. Participants were divided into three groups: *Stayers* were those who remained in their relationships throughout the duration of the study, the *abandoned* were those whose partners ended their relationships, and *leavers* were those who themselves ended their relationships. Compared to leavers, stayers' rewards increased

more over time, costs increased less, satisfaction increased more, alternative quality declined more (leavers' reported alternative quality increased), investment size increased more (leavers actually reported a sort of divestiture, whereby investments were withdrawn from the relationship), and commitment increased more (leavers' commitment declined over time). The abandoned group was somewhere between these two groups in terms of rewards, costs, and satisfaction. But even though their satisfaction did not increase much over time, their alternatives continued to decline in quality and they continued to invest as much in their relationships as did stayers. This pattern of results might be termed "entrapment"—abandoned respondents were not completely satisfied with their relationships, but felt strongly committed because they had invested much in their relationships and because their alternatives were not very appealing.

Furthermore, *changes* in each investment model variable effectively accounted for changes in individuals' satisfaction and commitment. For example, it is not just the fact of having invested highly that makes one feel committed; more importantly, it is the fact of investing more and more over time that produces commitment: Midway into a relationship John may have invested at only moderate levels. But if he began by investing almost nothing, the drastic increase in willingness to invest should be accompanied by greatly increased commitment. Indeed, changes over time in levels of satisfaction, alternatives, and investments accounted for 78 percent of the variability in commitment. However, once again, the impact of costs on commitment to relationships was quite weak.

Other tests examined whether changes over time in commitment directly mediate decisions to remain in or to end relationships. All of the investment model variables—rewards, costs, satisfaction, alternatives, and commitment—were significantly related to stay/leave decisions. However, such decisions were most directly and powerfully predicted by changes over time in commitment. This finding provides excellent support for the validity of the commitment construct: Changes over time in commitment are indeed most central in determining whether or not a relationship will persist.

Finally, we looked at general patterns of relationship development over time. It was gratifying to find that, on average, rewards, satisfaction, investments, and commitment all increased substantially over time. It was surprising, however, to find that over time participants reported that the quality of their alternatives declined substantially. Whether this decline is actual (i.e., potential partners do not approach the individual because of knowledge of his or her involvement with another) or merely perceived (i.e., over time, individuals come to derogate available alternatives as a means of maintaining strong commitment) could not be determined based on the data from this project. Another surprising finding was that over time in relationships, costs increased significantly. It may be that at the beginning of a relationship, individuals try hard to display their best selves, and their partners are generous in overlooking any faults or problems that do become apparent. However, at later stages of involvement persons may relax and allow their true, flawed selves to emerge, and their partners may adopt a more realistic and unbiased view of the relationship. This possibility remains to be explored in future research.

DEROGATION OF ALTERNATIVES AS A MEANS OF MAINTAINING COMMITMENT

In our longitudinal study, participants' perceptions of the attractiveness of alternative involvements declined substantially over time. Furthermore, this change in the way people viewed their alternatives occurred only for people who maintained their relationships; among persons who ended their relationships, attractiveness of alternatives actually increased over time. These findings suggest that changes in an individual's evaluation of alternative partners may play an important role in maintaining commitment to current partners. By what process do such changes come about?

First, it could be that alternatives really do become worse over time. Alternative partners

may be reluctant to approach a committed individual because of awareness that he or she is involved with another. As Kelley (1983) notes, "Other persons who might have been available as partners now take themselves out of the running and look elsewhere for associations" (p. 305). A second explanation argues for changes in individuals' perceptions of available alternatives. If alternative partners merely *look* less appealing to the committed individual, the relationship is protected. For example, if a highly attractive alternative were to approach me for a date, my strong commitment to my current partner and my desire to maintain our relationship might lead me to derogate the newcomer in some way so as to reduce his threat to my existing relationship. I might tell myself that he probably has a terrible sense of humor or would ultimately hurt me and make me unhappy. By so doing, I can protect my current relationship from strong external threat.

We designed an experiment to test this second notion—that in relation to less committed persons, more highly committed individuals derogate potential alternative partners, especially attractive ones (Johnson & Rusbult, 1987). We told participants that we were interested in assessing student interest in a computer dating service. Each participant was asked to evaluate a potential date, an "early applicant for the service." In evaluating this person, participants had a photograph of the potential date and a faked application form that provided sketchy information about that person. Participants indicated the degree to which they were interested in actually dating that person, and rated this person on a number of dimensions (e.g., likely pleasantness of personality, probable sense of humor). They also completed questionnaires designed to measure their commitment to their current dating relationships.

Do highly committed persons derogate potential alternatives? When we divided our participants into low and high commitment groups, we found that highly committed persons reported lesser anticipated satisfaction with the alternative, and were less interested in dating the alternative. Why do we do this;

by what theoretical process does this effect come about? Three theoretical accounts were examined: First, dissonance theory would explain that when personally evaluating an exceptionally attractive alternative, dissonance is aroused (Festinger, 1957). Dissonance can be reduced by putting down the alternative and enhancing the attractiveness of the current partner—by "spreading the attractiveness of the options." Second, self-perception theory would explain that when we observe ourselves continuing with our current partners even though we are being pursued by exceptionally attractive alternatives, we infer that we must be very strongly attracted to our current partners and/or that the alternative is critically flawed in some irredeemable fashion. And third, interdependence theory might explain that the individual's current relationship serves as a standard against which to evaluate all other relationships. Because many highly committed persons may also be very satisfied, it may simply be that the alternative just looks less appealing in comparison to their terrific current partners. The experiment included several experimental manipulations to attempt to determine which of these accounts is most viable, and some support was obtained for the comparison level and dissonance theory explanations. The self-perception explanation received little support in the present work.

Thus, when we are very committed to our partners we tend to reject and disparage available alternatives, especially exceedingly attractive ones. Such rejection or disparagement of alternative partners is an effective way to guarantee a more stable close relationship. These findings contribute to our understanding of the means by which individuals evaluate alternative partners, and suggest that two types of process may help us reject alternatives and maintain our close relationships.

THE IMPACT OF SOCIAL NORMS ON COMMITMENT

Johnson (1987) extended the investment model by studying the impact of social norms on individuals' feelings of commitment to their relationships. Social norms are rules of behav-

ior—communicated openly or implicitly by family, friends, religion, and society at large—that specify not only how an individual should or should not behave in a given situation, but also the social costs for failing to comply with the norm. The costs of violating a norm vary from a disapproving look from a friend to excommunication from one's church. Johnson reasoned that commitment should be greater to the extent that social norms stress the importance of maintaining the relationship and the individual is motivated to comply with those norms.

To assess the contribution of social norms to the prediction of commitment, Johnson replicated the two initial tests of the investment model reported earlier (Rusbult, 1980a)—the role-playing study and the survey study. Both studies demonstrated that social norms, along with the other investment model variables, are an important element of individuals' commitment to their relationships. He also found that social norms become increasingly important as the relationship becomes increasingly intimate. That is, social norms "matter" more in more longstanding, established relationships. These findings suggest that norms regarding the maintenance of close relationships may play an important role in holding relationships together.

RESEARCH ON COMMITMENT IN OTHER DOMAINS

The body of research reported here provides excellent support for investment model predictions. Thus, it seems quite clear that the theory is a powerful model for predicting the development of commitment in at least one domain: close relationships. Is the model equally powerful in accounting for commitment in other forms of social relationship? We carried out a survey of college students' friendships (Rusbult, 1980b), measuring rewards, costs, alternatives, investments, and commitment. As expected, the variables that predicted satisfaction and commitment in romantic relationships also predicted satisfaction and commitment in friendships.

We also conducted research on organizational behavior—work designed to determine whether the investment model could account for employees' job satisfaction, job commitment, and turnover decisions. In three separate studies—a laboratory experiment, a cross-sectional survey, and a longitudinal study—investment model predictions were once again strongly supported (Farrell & Rusbult, 1981; Rusbult & Farrell, 1983). Thus, the investment model accounts for the development of commitment and stability in a wide range of social relationships.

CONCLUSIONS

People stick with their relationships for a variety of reasons. Sometimes people feel strongly committed to their partners and relationships because they are involved in wonderfully satisfying relationships. In such relationships, individuals may actively drive away appealing alternatives and throw numerous investments into the relationship in an attempt to produce unshakeable stability. But strong commitment is often the result of factors that have nothing to do with the quality of a relationship. Sometimes people become committed to dissatisfying relationships because they have put so much into them, and sometimes people become committed to relatively unappealing partners because they have no other options. The research we have conducted provides consistent support for investment model predictions, and demonstrates that this model is generalizable to a wide range of social relationship. Because of its foundation in interpersonal interdependence theory, one of the few *general* theories of social behavior, the model shows promise in accounting for a wide range of social exchange phenomena.

REFERENCES

Becker, H. S. (1960). Notes on the concept of commitment. *American Journal of Sociology, 66,* 32–40.

Blau, P. M. (1964). *Exchange and power in social life.* New York: Wiley.

Duffy, S. M., & Rusbult, C. E. (1986). Satisfaction and commitment in homosexual and heterosexual relationships. *Journal of Homosexuality, 12,* 1–23.

Farrell, D., & Rusbult, C. E. (1981). Exchange variables as predictors of job satisfaction, job commitment, and turnover: The impact of rewards, costs, alternatives, and investments. *Organizational Behavior and Human Performance, 27,* 78–95.

Festinger, L. (1957). *A theory of cognitive dissonance.* Evanston, Ill.: Row, Peterson.

Hatkoff, T. S., & Lasswell, T. E. (1979). Male-female similarities and differences in conceptualizing love. In M. Cook & G. Wilson (Eds.), *Love and attraction* (pp. 221–227). New York: Pergamon.

Johnson, D. J. (1987). *Commitment in close relationships: A function of investment model variables and social norms.* Unpublished manuscript, Illinois State University.

Johnson, D. J., & Rusbult, C. E. (1987). *Rejection and disparagement of alternative partners as a means of maintaining close relationships.* Unpublished manuscript, Illinois State University.

Johnson, M. P. (1973). Commitment: A conceptual and empirical application. *Sociological Quarterly, 14,* 395–406.

Johnson, M. P. (1982). Social and cognitive features of the dissolution of commitment to relationships. In S. Duck (Ed.), *Personal relationships 4: Dissolving personal relationships* (pp. 51–73). Academic Press: London.

Kelley, H. H. (1983). Love and commitment. In H. H. Kelley, E. Berscheid, A. Christensen, J. H. Harvey, T. L. Huston, G. Levinger, E. McClintock, L. A. Peplau, & D. P. Peterson, *Close relationships* (pp. 265–314). New York: W. H. Freeman.

Kelley, H. H., & Thibaut, J. W. (1978). *Interpersonal relations: A theory of interdependence.* New York: Wiley.

Levinger, G. A. (1979). A social exchange view on the dissolution of pair relationships. In R. L. Burgess & T. L. Huston (Eds.), *Social exchange in developing relationships* (pp. 169–193). New York: Academic Press.

Rosenblatt, P. C. (1977). Needed research on commitment in marriage. In G. Levinger & H. L. Raush (Eds.), *Close relationships: Perspectives on the meaning of intimacy* (pp. 73–86). Amherst: University of Massachusetts Press.

Rubin, J. Z., & Brockner, J. (1975). Factors affecting entrapment in waiting situations: The Rosencrantz and Guildenstern effect. *Journal of Personality and Social Psychology, 31,* 1054–1063.

Rubin, Z., Peplau, L. A., & Hill, C. T. (1981). Loving and leaving: Sex differences in romantic attachments. *Sex Roles, 7,* 821–835.

Rusbult, C. E. (1980a). Commitment and satisfaction to romantic associations: A test of the investment model. *Journal of Experimental Social Psychology, 16,* 172–186.

Rusbult, C. E. (1980b). Satisfaction and commitment in friendships. *Representative Research in Social Psychology, 11*, 96–105.

Rusbult, C. E. (1983). A longitudinal test of the investment model: The development (and deterioration) of satisfaction and commitment in heterosexual involvements. *Journal of Personality and Social Psychology, 45*, 101–117.

Rusbult, C. E., & Farrell, D. (1983). A longitudinal test of the investment model: The impact on job satisfaction, job commitment, and turnover of variations in rewards, costs, alternatives, and investments. *Journal of Applied Psychology, 68*, 429–438.

Rusbult, C. E., Johnson, D. J., & Morrow, G. D. (1986). Predicting satisfaction and commitment in adult romantic involvements: An assessment of the generalizability of the investment model. *Social Psychology Quarterly, 49*, 81–89.

Staw, B. M. (1976). Knee-deep in the big muddy: A study of escalating commitment to a chosen course of action. *Organizational Behavior and Human Performance, 16*, 27–44.

Teger, A. I. (1980). *Too much invested to quit.* New York: Pergamon.

Thibaut, J. W., & Kelley, H. H. (1959). *The social psychology of groups.* New York: Wiley.

14

Imitation of Film-Mediated Aggressive Models

Albert Bandura, Dorothea Ross, and Sheila A. Ross

The primary goal of this study was to provide a laboratory example of the real-life process by which children imitate aggressive adults. It was especially intended to demonstrate that children imitate aggressive adults who only appear on film, to illustrate the process by which the authors assumed media violence produces aggressive children. The study also was intended to analyze the process by which imitation occurs, by testing the effects of sex of the model and sex of the child. It is an example of observational research, since all the measures are collected by observers who code the children's behavior. This study has become a classic mainly because it has been taken as providing a laboratory demonstration of an important real-life event: children's learning to commit aggressive acts by imitating the aggression committed by adults. One might question whether or not the children in this study are really engaging in aggression in the normal sense, or are merely engaging in play with a new toy. If so, the study would presumably still have value in demonstrating how readily children imitate, but it might not be such a classic demonstration of copying antisocial, intentionally hurtful, and destructive aggression.

ABSTRACT. *In a test of the hypothesis that exposure of children to film-mediated aggressive models would increase the probability of Ss' aggression to subsequent frustration, 1 group of experimental Ss observed real-life aggressive models, a 2nd observed these same models portraying aggression on film, while a 3rd group viewed a film depicting an aggressive cartoon character. Following the exposure treatment, Ss were mildly frustrated and tested for the amount of imitative and nonimitative aggression in a different experimental setting. The overall results provide evidence for both the facilitating and the modeling influence* *of film-mediated aggressive stimulation. In addition, the findings reveal that the effects of such exposure are to some extent a function of the sex of the model, sex of the child, and the reality cues of the model.*

Most of the research on the possible effects of film-mediated stimulation upon subsequent aggressive behavior has focused primarily on the drive reducing function of fantasy. While the experimental evidence for the catharsis or drive reduction theory is equivocal (Albert, 1957; Berkowitz, 1962; Emery, 1959; Feshbach, 1955, 1958; Kenny, 1952; Lövaas, 1961; Siegel, 1956), the modeling influence of pictorial stimuli has received little research attention.

Reprinted from *Journal of Abnormal and Social Psychology*, 1963, 66, pp. 3–11. Copyright 1963 by the American Psychological Association. Reprinted by permission of publisher and authors.

A recent incident (San Francisco Chronicle, 1961) in which a boy was seriously knifed during a re-enactment of a switchblade knife fight the boys had seen the previous evening on a televised rerun of the James Dean movie, *Rebel Without a Cause*, is a dramatic illustration of the possible imitative influence of film stimulation. Indeed, anecdotal data suggest that portrayal of aggression through pictorial media may be more influential in shaping the form aggression will take when a person is instigated on later occasions, than in altering the level of instigation to aggression.

In an earlier experiment (Bandura & Huston, 1961), it was shown that children readily imitated aggressive behavior exhibited by a model in the presence of the model. A succeeding investigation (Bandura, Ross, & Ross, 1961), demonstrated that children exposed to aggressive models generalized aggressive responses to a new setting in which the model was absent. The present study sought to determine the extent to which film-mediated aggressive models may serve as an important source of imitative behavior.

Aggressive models can be ordered on a reality-fictional stimulus dimension with real-life models located at the reality end of the continuum, nonhuman cartoon characters at the fictional end, and films portraying human models occupying an intermediate position. It was predicted, on the basis of saliency and similarity of cues, that the more remote the model was from reality, the weaker would be the tendency for subjects to imitate the behavior of the model.

Of the various interpretations of imitative learning, the sensory feedback theory of imitation recently proposed by Mowrer (1960) is elaborated in greatest detail. According to this theory, if certain responses have been repeatedly positively reinforced, proprioceptive stimuli associated with these responses acquire secondary reinforcing properties and thus the individual is predisposed to perform the behavior for the positive feedback. Similarly, if responses have been negatively reinforced, response correlated stimuli acquire the capacity to arouse anxiety which, in turn, inhibit the occurrence of the negatively valenced behavior. On the basis of these considerations, it was predicted subjects who manifest high aggression anxiety would perform significantly less imitative and nonimitative aggression than subjects who display little anxiety over aggression. Since aggression is generally considered female inappropriate behavior, and therefore likely to be negatively reinforced in girls (Sears, Maccoby, & Levin, 1957), it was also predicted that male subjects would be more imitative of aggression than females.

To the extent that observation of adults displaying aggression conveys a certain degree of permissiveness for aggressive behavior, it may be assumed that such exposure not only facilitates the learning of new aggressive responses but also weakens competing inhibitory responses in subjects and thereby increases the probability of occurrence of previously learned patterns of aggression. It was predicted, therefore, that subjects who observed aggressive models would display significantly more aggression when subsequently frustrated than subjects who were equally frustrated but who had no prior exposure to models exhibiting aggression.

METHOD

Subjects

The subjects were 48 boys and 48 girls enrolled in the Stanford University Nursery School. They ranged in age from 35 to 69 months, with a mean age of 52 months.

Two adults, a male and a female, served in the role of models both in the real-life and the human film-aggression condition, and one female experimenter conducted the study for all 96 children.

General Procedure

Subjects were divided into three experimental groups and one control group of 24 subjects each. One group of experimental subjects observed real-life aggressive models, a second group observed these same models portraying aggression on film, while a third group viewed a film depicting an aggressive cartoon character. The experimental groups were further sub-divided into male and female subjects so that half the subjects in the two conditions involving human models were exposed to same-sex models, while the remaining subjects viewed models of the opposite sex.

Following the exposure experience, subjects were tested for the amount of imitative and nonimitative aggression in a different experimental setting in the absence of the models.

The control group subjects had no exposure to the aggressive models and were tested only in the generalization situation.

Subjects in the experimental and control groups were matched individually on the basis of ratings of their aggressive behavior in social interactions in the nursery school. The experimenter and a nursery school teacher rated the subjects on four five-point rating scales which measured the extent to which subjects displayed physical aggression, verbal aggression, aggression toward inanimate objects, and aggression inhibition. The latter scale, which dealt with the subjects' tendency to inhibit aggressive reactions in the face of high instigation, provided the measure of aggression anxiety. Seventy-one percent of the subjects were rated independently by both judges so as to permit an assessment of interrater agreement. The reliability of the composite aggression score, estimated by means of the Pearson product-moment correlation, was .80.

Data for subjects in the real-life aggression condition and in the control group were collected as part of a previous experiment (Bandura et al., 1961). Since the procedure is described in detail in the earlier report, only a brief description of it will be presented here.

Experimental Conditions

Subjects in the Real-Life Aggressive condition were brought individually by the experimenter to the experimental room and the model, who was in the hallway outside the room, was invited by the experimenter to come and join in the game. The subject was then escorted to one corner of the room and seated at a small table which contained potato prints, multicolor picture stickers, and colored paper.

After demonstrating how the subject could design pictures with the materials provided, the experimenter escorted the model to the opposite corner of the room which contained a small table and chair, a tinker toy set, a mallet, and a 5-foot inflated Bobo doll. The experimenter explained that this was the model's play area and after the model was seated, the experimenter left the experimental room.

The model began the session by assembling the tinker toys but after approximately a minute had elapsed, the model turned to the Bobo doll and spent the remainder of the period aggressing toward it with highly novel responses which are unlikely to be performed by children independently of the observation of the model's behavior. Thus, in addition to punching the Bobo doll, the model exhibited the following distinctive aggressive acts which were to be scored as imitative responses:

The model sat on the Bobo doll and punched it repeatedly in the nose.

The model then raised the Bobo doll and pommeled it on the head with a mallet.

Following the mallet aggression, the model tossed the doll up in the air aggressively and kicked it about the room. This sequence of physically aggressive acts was repeated approximately three times, interspersed with verbally aggressive responses such as, "Sock him in the nose . . . ," "Hit him down . . . ," "Throw him in the air . . . ," "Kick him . . . ," and "Pow."

Subjects in the Human Film-Aggression condition were brought by the experimenter to the semi-darkened experimental room, introduced to the picture materials, and informed that while the subjects worked on potato prints, a movie would be shown on a screen, positioned approximately 6 feet from the subject's table. The movie projector was located in a distant corner of the room and was screened from the subject's view by large wooden panels.

The color movie and a tape recording of the sound track was begun by a male projectionist as soon as the experimenter left the experimental room and was shown for a duration of 10 minutes. The models in the film presentations were the same adult males and females who participated in the Real-Life condition of the experiment. Similarly, the aggressive behavior they portrayed in the film was identical with their real-life performances.

For subjects in the Cartoon Film-Aggression condition, after seating the subject at the table with the picture construction material, the experimenter walked over to a television console approximately 3 feet in front of the subject's table, remarked, "I guess I'll turn on the color TV," and ostensibly tuned in a cartoon program. The experimenter then left the experimental room. The cartoon was shown on a glass lens screen in the television set by means of a rear projection arrangement screened from the subject's view by large panels.

The sequence of aggressive acts in the cartoon was performed by the female model costumed as a black cat similar to the many cartoon cats. In order to heighten the level of irreality of the cartoon, the floor area was covered with artificial grass and the walls forming the backdrop were adorned with brightly colored trees, birds, and butterflies creating a fantasyland setting. The cartoon began with a close-up of a stage on which the curtains were slowly drawn revealing a picture of a cartoon cat along with the title, *Herman the Cat*. The remainder of the film showed the cat pommeling the Bobo doll on the head with a mallet, sitting on the doll and punching it in the nose, tossing the doll in the air, and kicking it about the room in a manner identical with the performance in the other experimental conditions except that the cat's movements were characteristically feline. To induce further a cartoon set, the program was introduced and concluded with appropriate cartoon music, and the cat's verbal aggression was repeated in a high-pitched, animated voice.

In both film conditions, at the conclusion of the movie the experimenter entered the room and then escorted the subject to the test room.

Aggression Instigation

In order to differentiate clearly the exposure and test situations subjects were tested for the amount of imitative learning in a different experimental room which was set off from the main nursery school building.

The degree to which a child has learned aggressive patterns of behavior through imitation becomes most evident when the child is instigated to aggression on later occasions. Thus, for example, the effects of viewing the movie, *Rebel Without a Cause*, were not evident until the boys were instigated to aggression the following day, at which time they re-enacted the televised switchblade knife fight in considerable detail. For this reason, the children in the experiment, both those in the control group and those who were exposed to the aggressive models, were mildly frustrated before they were brought to the test room.

Following the exposure experience, the experimenter brought the subject to an anteroom which contained a varied array of highly attractive toys. The experimenter explained that the toys were for the subject to play with, but, as soon as the subject became sufficiently involved with the play material, the experimenter remarked that these were her very best toys, that she did not let just anyone play with them, and that she had decided to reserve these toys for some other children. However, the subject could play with any of the toys in the next room. The experimenter and the subject then entered the adjoining experimental room.

It was necessary for the experimenter to remain in the room during the experimental session; otherwise, a number of the children would either refuse to remain alone or would leave before the termination of the session. In order to minimize any influence her presence might have on the subject's behavior, the experimenter remained as inconspicuous as possible by busying herself with paper work at a desk in the far corner of the room and avoiding any interaction with the child.

Test for Delayed Imitation

The experimental room contained a variety of toys, some of which could be used in imitative or nonimitative aggression, and others which tended to elicit predominantly nonagressive forms of behavior. The aggressive toys included a 3-foot Bobo doll, a mallet and peg board, two dart guns, and a tether ball with a face painted on it which hung from the ceiling. The nonaggressive toys, on the other hand, included a tea set, crayons and coloring paper, a ball, two dolls, three bears, cars and trucks, and plastic farm animals.

In order to eliminate any variation in behavior due to mere placement of the toys in the room, the play material was arranged in a fixed order for each of the sessions.

The subject spent 20 minutes in the experimental room during which time his behavior was rated in terms of predetermined response categories by judges who observed the session through a one-way mirror in an adjoining observation room. The 20-minute session was divided in 5-second intervals by means of an electric interval timer, thus yielding a total number of 240 response units for each subject.

The male model scored the experimental sessions for all subjects. In order to provide an estimate of interjudge agreement, the performances of 40% of the subjects were scored independently by a second observer. The responses scored involved highly specific concrete classes of behavior, and yielded high interscorer reliabilities, the product-moment coefficients being in the .90s.

Response Measures

The following response measures were obtained:

Imitative aggression. This category included acts of striking the Bobo doll with the mallet, sitting on the doll and punching it in the nose, kicking the doll, tossing it in the air, and the verbally aggressive responses, "Sock him," "Hit him down," "Kick him," "Throw him in the air," and "Pow."

Partially imitative responses. A number of subjects imitated the essential components of the model's behavior but did not perform the complete act, or they directed the imitative aggressive response to some object other than the Bobo doll. Two responses of this type were scored and were interpreted as partially imitative behavior:

Mallet aggression. The subject strikes objects other than the Bobo doll aggressively with the mallet.

Sits on Bobo doll. The subject lays the Bobo doll on its side and sits on it, but does not aggress toward it.

Nonimitative aggression. This category included acts of punching, slapping, or pushing the doll, physically aggressive acts directed toward objects other than the Bobo doll, and any hostile remarks except for those in the verbal imitation category; for example, "Shoot the Bobo," "Cut him," "Stupid ball," "Knock over people," "Horses fighting, biting."

Aggressive gun play. The subject shoots darts or aims the guns and fires imaginary shots at objects in the room.

Ratings were also made of the number of behavior units in which subjects played nonaggressively or sat quietly and did not play with any of the material at all.

RESULTS

The mean imitative and nonimitative aggression scores for subjects in the various experimental and control groups are presented in Table 1.

Since the distributions of scores departed from normality and the assumption of homogeneity of variance could not be made for most of the measures, the Freidman two-way analysis of variance by ranks was employed for testing the significance of the obtained differences.

Total Aggression

The mean total aggression scores for subjects in the real-life, human film, cartoon film, and the control groups are 83, 92, 99, and 54, respectively. The results of the analysis of variance performed on these scores reveal that the main effect of treatment conditions is significant ($\chi_r^2 = 9.06$, $p < .05$), confirming the prediction that exposure of subjects to aggressive models increases the probability that subjects will respond aggressively when instigated on later occasions. Further analyses of pairs of scores by means of the Wilcoxon matched-pairs signed-ranks test show that subjects who viewed the real-life models and the film-mediated models do not differ from each other in total aggressiveness but all three experimental

Table 1   Mean Aggression Scores for Subgroups of Experimental and Control Subjects

| | EXPERIMENTAL GROUPS | | | | | |
| | Real-Life Aggressive | | Human Film-Aggressive | | Cartoon Film-Aggressive | Control Group |
Response Category	Female Model	Male Model	Female Model	Male Model		
Total aggression						
Girls	65.8	57.3	87.0	79.5	80.9	36.4
Boys	76.8	131.8	114.5	85.0	117.2	72.2
Imitative aggression						
Girls	19.2	9.2	10.0	8.0	7.8	1.8
Boys	18.4	38.4	34.3	13.3	16.2	3.9
Mallet aggression						
Girls	17.2	18.7	49.2	19.5	36.8	13.1
Boys	15.5	28.8	20.5	16.3	12.5	13.5
Sits on Bobo doll[a]						
Girls	10.4	5.6	10.3	4.5	15.3	3.3
Boys	1.3	0.7	7.7	0.0	5.6	0.6
Nonimitative aggression						
Girls	27.6	24.9	24.0	34.3	27.5	17.8
Boys	35.5	48.6	46.8	31.8	71.8	40.4
Aggressive gun play						
Girls	1.8	4.5	3.8	17.6	8.8	3.7
Boys	7.3	15.9	12.8	23.7	16.6	14.3

[a] This response category was not included in the total aggression score.

groups expressed significantly more aggressive behavior than the control subjects (Table 2).

Imitative Aggressive Responses

The Freidman analysis reveals that exposure of subjects to aggressive models is also a highly effective method for shaping subjects' aggressive responses ($\chi_r^2 = 23.88, p < .001$). Comparisons of treatment conditions by the Wilcoxon test reveal that subjects who observed the real-life models and the film-mediated models, relative to subjects in the control group, performed considerably more imitative physical and verbal aggression (Table 2).

Indeed, some of the subjects became virtually "carbon copies" of their models in aggressive behavior.

Table 2   Significance of the Differences between Experimental and Control Groups in the Expression of Aggression

| | | | Comparison of Treatment Conditions[a] | | | | | |
Response Category	χ^2	p	Live vs. Film p	Live vs. Cartoon p	Film vs. Cartoon p	Live vs. Control p	Film vs. Control p	Cartoon vs. Control p
Total aggression	9.06	<.05	ns	ns	ns	<.01	<.01	<.005
Imitative aggression	23.88	<.001	ns	<.05	ns	<.001	<001	<.005
Partial imitation								
Mallet aggression	7.36	.10 > p > .05						
Sits on Bobo doll	8.05	<.05	ns	ns	ns	ns	<.05	<.005
Nonimitative aggression	7.28	.10 > p > .05						
Aggressive gun play	8.06	<.05	<.01[b]	ns	ns	ns	<.05	ns

[a] The probability values are based on the Wilcoxon test.

[b] This probability value is based on a two-tailed test of significance.

The prediction that imitation is positively related to the reality cues of the model was only partially supported. While subjects who observed the real-life aggressive models exhibited significantly more imitative aggression than subjects who viewed the cartoon model, no significant differences were found between the live and film, and the film and cartoon conditions, nor did the three experimental groups differ significantly in total aggression or in the performances of partially imitative behavior (Table 2). Indeed, the available data suggest that, of the three experimental conditions, exposure to humans on film portraying aggression was the most influential in eliciting and shaping aggressive behavior. Subjects in this condition, in relation to the control subjects, exhibited more total aggression, more imitative aggression, more partially imitative behavior, such as sitting on the Bobo doll and mallet aggression, and they engaged in significantly more aggressive gun play. In addition, they performed significantly more aggressive gun play than did subjects who were exposed to the real-life aggressive models (Table 2).

Influence of Sex of Model and Sex of Child

In order to determine the influence of sex of model and sex of child on the expression of imitative and nonimitative aggression, the data from the experimental groups were combined and the significance of the differences between groups was assessed by t tests for uncorrelated means. In statistical comparisons involving relatively skewed distributions of scores the Mann-Whitney U test was employed.

Sex of subjects had a highly significant effect on both the learning and the performance of aggression. Boys, in relation to girls, exhibited significantly more total aggression ($t = 2.69$, $p < .01$), more imitative aggression ($t = 2.82$, $p < .005$), more aggressive gun play ($z = 3.38$, $p < .001$), and more nonimitative aggressive behavior ($t = 2.98$, $p < .005$). Girls, on the other hand, were more inclined than boys to sit on the Bobo doll but refrained from punching it ($z = 3.47$, $p < .001$).

The analyses also disclosed some influences of the sex of the model. Subjects exposed to the male model, as compared to the female model, expressed significantly more aggressive gun play ($z = 2.83$, $p < .005$). The most marked differences in aggressive gun play ($U = 9.5$, $p < .001$), however, were found between girls exposed to the female model ($M = 2.9$) and males who observed the male model ($M = 19.8$). Although the overall model difference in partially imitative behavior, Sits on Bobo, was not significant, Sex $\times$ Model subgroup comparisons yielded some interesting results. Boys who observed the aggressive female model, for example, were more likely to sit on the Bobo doll without punching it than boys who viewed the male model ($U = 33$, $p < .05$). Girls reproduced the nonaggressive component of the male model's aggressive pattern of behavior (i.e., sat on the doll without punching it) with considerably higher frequency than did boys who observed the same model ($U = 21.5$, $p < .02$). The highest incidence of partially imitative responses was yielded by the group of girls who viewed the aggressive female model ($M = 10.4$), and the lowest values by the boys who were exposed to the male model ($M = 0.3$). This difference was significant beyond the .05 significance level. These findings, along with the sex of child and sex of model differences reported in the preceding sections, provide further support for the view that the influence of models in promoting social learning is determined, in part, by the sex appropriateness of the model's behavior (Bandura et al., 1961).

Aggressive Predisposition and Imitation

Since the correlations between ratings of aggression and the measures of imitative and total aggressive behavior, calculated separately for boys and girls in each of the experimental conditions, did not differ significantly, the data were combined. The correlational analyses performed on these pooled data failed to yield any significant relationships between ratings of aggression anxiety, frequency of aggressive behavior, and the experimental aggression measures. In fact, the array means suggested nonlinear regressions although the departures from linearity were not of sufficient magnitude to be statistically significant.

DISCUSSION

The results of the present study provide strong evidence that exposure to filmed aggression heightens aggressive reactions in children. Subjects who viewed the aggressive human and cartoon models on film exhibited nearly twice as much aggression than did subjects in the control group who were not exposed to the aggressive film content.

In the experimental design typically employed for testing the possible cathartic functions of vicarious aggression, subjects are first frustrated, then provided with an opportunity to view an aggressive film following which their overt or fantasy aggression is measured. While this procedure yields some information on the immediate influence of film-mediated aggression, the full effects of such exposure may not be revealed until subjects are instigated to aggression on a later occasion. Thus, the present study, and one recently reported by Lövaas (1961), both utilizing a design in which subjects first observed filmed aggression and then were frustrated, clearly reveal that observation of models portraying aggression on film substantially increases rather than decreases the probability of aggressive reactions to subsequent frustrations.

Filmed aggression, not only facilitated the expression of aggression, but also effectively shaped the form of the subjects' aggressive behavior. The finding that children modeled their behavior to some extent after the film characters suggests that pictorial mass media, particularly television, may serve as an important source of social behavior. In fact, a possible generalization of responses originally learned in the television situation to the experimental film may account for the significantly greater amount of aggressive gun play displayed by subjects in the film condition as compared to subjects in the real-life and control groups. It is unfortunate that the qualitative features of the gun behavior were not scored since subjects in the film condition, unlike those in the other two groups, developed interesting elaborations in gun play (for example, stalking the imaginary opponent, quick drawing, and rapid firing), characteristic of the Western gun fighter.

The view that the social learning of aggression through exposure to aggressive film content is confined to deviant children (Schramm, Lyle, & Parker, 1961), finds little support in our data. The children who participated in the experiment are by no means a deviant sample, nevertheless, 88% of the subjects in the Real-Life and in the Human Film condition, and 79% of the subjects in the Cartoon Film condition, exhibited varying degrees of imitative aggression. In assessing the possible influence of televised stimulation on viewers' behavior, however, it is important to distinguish between learning and overt performance. Although the results of the present experiment demonstrate that the vast majority of children *learn* patterns of social behavior through pictorial stimulation, nevertheless, informal observation suggests that children do not, as a rule, *perform* indiscriminately the behavior of televised characters, even those they regard as highly attractive models. The replies of parents whose children participated in the present study to an open-end questionnaire item concerning their handling of imitative behavior suggest that this may be in part a function of negative reinforcement, as most parents were quick to discourage their children's overt imitation of television characters by prohibiting certain programs or by labeling the imitative behavior in a disapproving manner. From our knowledge of the effects of punishment on behavior, the responses in question would be expected to retain their original strength and could reappear on later occasions in the presence of appropriate eliciting stimuli, particularly if instigation is high, the instruments for aggression are available, and the threat of noxious consequences is reduced.

The absence of any relationships between ratings of the children's predisposition to aggression and their aggressive behavior in the experimental setting may simply reflect the inadequacy of the predictor measures. It may be pointed out, however, that the reliability of the ratings was relatively high. While this does not assure validity of the measures, it does at least indicate there was consistency in the raters' estimates of the children's aggressive tendencies.

A second, and perhaps more probable, explanation is that proprioceptive feedback[*] alone is not sufficient to account for response inhibition or facilitation. For example, the proprioceptive cues arising from hitting responses directed toward parents and toward peers may differ little, if any; nevertheless, tendencies to aggress toward parents are apt to be strongly inhibited while peer aggression may be readily expressed (Bandura, 1960; Bandura & Walters, 1959). In most social interaction sequences, proprioceptive cues make up only a small part of the total stimulus complex and, therefore, it is necessary to take into consideration additional stimulus components, for the most part external, which probably serve as important discriminative cues for the expression of aggression. Consequently, prediction of the occurrence or inhibition of specific classes of responses would be expected to depend upon the presence of a certain pattern of proprioceptive or introceptive stimulation together with relevant discriminative external stimuli.

According to this line of reasoning, failure to obtain the expected positive relationships between the measures of aggression may be due primarily to the fact that permissiveness for aggression, conveyed by situational cues in the form of aggressive film content and play material, was sufficient to override the influence of internal stimuli generated by the commission of aggressive responses. If, in fact, the behavior of young children, as compared to that of adults, is less likely to be under internal stimulus control, one might expect environmental cues to play a relatively important role in eliciting or inhibiting aggressive behavior.

A question may be raised as to whether the aggressive acts studied in the present experiment constituted "genuine" aggressive responses. Aggression is typically defined as behavior, the goal or intent of which is injury to a person, or destruction of an object (Bandura & Walters, 1959; Dollard, Doob, Miller, Mowrer, & Sears, 1939; Sears, Maccoby, & Levin, 1957). Since intentionality is not a prop-

erty of behavior but primarily an inference concerning antecedent events, the categorization of an act as "aggressive" involves a consideration of both stimulus and mediating or terminal response events.

According to a social learning theory of aggression recently proposed by Bandura and Walters (in press), most of the responses utilized to hurt or to injure others (for example, striking, kicking, and other responses of high magnitude), are probably learned for prosocial purposes under nonfrustration conditions. Since frustration generally elicits responses of high magnitude, the latter classes of responses, once acquired, may be called out in social interactions for the purpose of injuring others. On the basis of this theory it would be predicted that the aggressive responses acquired imitatively, while not necessarily mediating aggressive goals in the experimental situation, would be utilized to serve such purposes in other social settings with higher frequency by children in the experimental conditions than by children in the control group.

The present study involved primarily vicarious or empathic learning (Mowrer, 1960) in that subjects acquired a relatively complex repertoire of aggressive responses by the mere sight of a model's behavior. It has been generally assumed that the necessary conditions for the occurrence of such learning is that the model perform certain responses followed by positive reinforcement to the model (Hill, 1960; Mowrer, 1960). According to this theory, to the extent that the observer experiences the model's reinforcement vicariously, the observer will be prone to reproduce the model's behavior. While there is some evidence from experiments involving both human (Lewis & Duncan, 1958; McBrearty, Marston, & Kanfer, 1961; Sechrest, 1961) and animal subjects (Darby & Riopelle, 1959; Warden, Fjeld, & Koch, 1940), that vicarious reinforcement may in fact increase the probability of the behavior in question, it is apparent from the results of the experiment reported in this paper that a good deal of human imitative learning can occur without any reinforcers delivered either to the model or to the observer. In order to test systematically the influence of vicarious

---

[*] Awareness of one's muscular movement and tension [Ed.].

reinforcement on imitation, however, a study is planned in which the degree of imitative learning will be compared in situations in which the model's behavior is paired with reinforcement with those in which the model's responses go unrewarded.

REFERENCES

Albert, R. S. The role of mass media and the effect of aggressive film content upon children's aggressive responses and identification choices. *Genet. psychol. Monogr.*, 1957, *55*, 221–285.

Bandura, A. Relationship of family patterns to child behavior disorders. Progress Report, 1960, Stanford University, Project No. M-1734, United States Public Health Service.

Bandura, A., & Huston, Aletha C. Identification as a process of incidental learning. *J. abnorm. soc. Psychol.*, 1961, *63*, 311–318.

Bandura, A., Ross, Dorothea, & Ross, Sheila A. Transmission of aggression through imitation of aggressive models. *J. abnorm. soc. Psychol.*, 1961, *63*, 575–582.

Bandura, A., & Walters, R. H. *Adolescent aggression.* New York: Ronald, 1959.

Bandura, A., & Walters, R. H. *The social learning of deviant behavior: A behavioristic approach to socialization.* New York: Holt, Rinehart, & Winston, in press.

Berkowitz, L. *Aggression: A social psychological analysis.* New York: McGraw-Hill, 1962.

Darby, C. L., & Riopelle, A. J. Observational learning in the Rhesus monkey. *J. comp. physiol. Psychol.*, 1959, *52*, 94–98.

Dollard, J., Doob, L. W., Miller, N. E., Mowrer, O. H., & Sears, R. R. *Frustration and aggression.* New Haven: Yale Univer. Press, 1939.

Emery, F. E. Psychological effects of the Western film: A study in television viewing: II. The experimental study. *Hum. Relat.*, 1959, *12*, 215–232.

Feshbach, S. The drive-reducing function of fantasy behavior. *J. abnorm. soc. Psychol.*, 1955, *50*, 3–11.

Feshbach, S. The stimulating versus cathartic effects of a vicarious aggressive activity. Paper read at the Eastern Psychological Association, 1958.

Hill, W. F. Learning theory and the acquisition of values. *Psychol. Rev.*, 1960, *67*, 317–331.

Kenny, D. T. An experimental test of the catharsis theory of aggression. Unpublished doctoral dissertation, University of Washington, 1952.

Lewis, D. J., & Duncan, C. P. Vicarious experience and partial reinforcement. *J. abnorm. soc. Psychol.*, 1958, *57*, 321–326.

Lövaas, O. J. Effect of exposure to symbolic aggression on aggressive behavior. *Child Develpm.*, 1961, *32*, 37–44.

McBrearty, J. F., Marston, A. R., & Kanfer, F. H. Conditioning a verbal operant in a group setting: Direct vs. vicarious reinforcement. *Amer. Psychologist*, 1961, *16*, 425. (Abstract)

Mowrer, O. H. *Learning theory and the symbolic processes.* New York: Wiley, 1960.

San Francisco Chronicle. "James Dean" knifing in South City. *San Francisco Chron.*, March 1, 1961, 6.

Schramm, W., Lyle, J., & Parker, E. B. *Television in the lives of our children.* Stanford: Stanford Univer. Press, 1961.

Sears, R. R., Maccoby, Eleanor E., & Levin, H. *Patterns of child rearing.* Evanston: Row, Peterson, 1957.

Sechrest, L. Vicarious reinforcement of responses. *Amer. Psychologist*, 1961, *16*, 356. (Abstract)

Siegel, Alberta E. Film-mediated fantasy aggression and strength of aggressive drive. *Child Develpm.*, 1956, *27*, 365–378.

Warden, C. J., Fjeld, H. A., & Koch, A. M. Imitative behavior in cebus and Rhesus monkeys. *J. genet. Psychol.*, 1940, *56*, 311–322.

15

Television and Violent Behavior: Ten Years of Scientific Progress

NATIONAL INSTITUTE OF MENTAL HEALTH

The potential influence of television and film violence on real-life antisocial aggression is an important policy issue as well as one of inherent socio-psychological interest. It has inspired a great deal of basic and applied research, and has been the subject of several government commissions. In 1972 the U.S. Surgeon General (see reference 4) published a report that cautiously suggested that media violence may cause aggressive behavior. Ten years later, a new government report came to a fairly strong conclusion about the negative effects of media violence. This excerpt illustrates several common features of government commission reports in general. Reports are usually influenced by political considerations as well as scholarly ones. In this case, the commission was committed to the view that television and movies contribute to antisocial violence in our society. Most of the evidence they review consists of correlations between television viewing and aggressive behavior. Such correlational data often have a variety of plausible interpretations. For example, it may be that watching TV violence increases a child's aggressiveness. Or it may be that particularly aggressive children are more attracted to violent television shows, explaining the correlation in a manner that exonerates the media. Do you think the conclusions are justified, given the evidence they review? Do you think the evidence is strong enough to justify government action to reduce media violence?

Public interest and concern have long focused on the issue of violence on television. Attention to that issue began in the 1950s and has remained there ever since. Although the field of television and human behavior has gone far beyond the study of violence, many researchers are still committed to finding an answer to the question about the effects of televised violence on the viewer.

One reason for this continued commitment is that, despite all the research that has been done both for the report of the Surgeon General's advisory committee and since then, the conclusions are not completely unequivocal. While much of the research shows a causal relationship between televised violence and aggressive behavior, proponents of the "no effects" position, while in diminished number, continue to argue their case.

VIOLENCE IN TELEVISION CONTENT

The first congressional hearing on television programming took place in 1952, when the House Committee on Interstate and Foreign Commerce investigated television entertainment to ascertain if it was excessively violent and sexually provocative and if it had pernicious effects. Over the next 12 years, the Senate Committee on the Judiciary held many more hearings; because data were so scarce and

Reprinted from *Television and Behavior: Ten Years of Scientific Progress and Implications for the Eighties*, Volume I: Summary Report. U.S. Department of Health and Human Services Publication No. (ADM) 82–1195, printed 1982.

sparse, the hearings were lengthy, acrimonious, and widely publicized. Television as a cause of delinquent behavior became the focus of inquiry. The Congressmen were critical of the industry, and the broadcasters were defensive.

During the period from 1952 to 1967, analyses of programs found a great deal of violence on them. One analysis in 1954 reported an average of 11 threats or acts of violence per hour. (1) Later analysis confirmed that violence on television was increasing and that it was increasing more rapidly on programs with large numbers of children in the audience. (2)

Two governmental commissions looked into the problem of television violence in the late 1960s. One was the National Commission on the Causes and Prevention of Violence, which issued a report in 1969 summarizing available information about the prevalence of violence on television and the evidence for its effects; data from laboratory experiments, it concluded, demonstrated that viewing violent programs increases the likelihood of a viewer to behave violently. (3) The other commission was the Surgeon General's Scientific Advisory Committee on Television and Social Behavior. In 1972, the committee issued a report stating that the convergence of evidence from both laboratory and field studies suggested that viewing violent television programs contributes to aggressive behavior. (4)

Content analyses in 1967, 1968, and 1969 showed that the frequency of violent acts remained about the same as in previous years except for a decrease in fatalities; cartoons were more violent than prime time programs; the networks differed somewhat in the amount of violence they broadcast; two-thirds of the leading characters were violent; retribution by violence was common; and most of the male roles were violent. (5)

These years of intensive scrutiny not only saw the beginnings of an annual content analysis of television programs, but they also were the time when many other studies of television violence and other kinds of research were started. In addition, the events of the period led to a series of arguments and controversies that are not yet resolved.

The two major governmental inquiries made the problem of television violence more visible to both scientists and the public. They also increased acceptance of the notion that violence on television leads to aggressive behavior by viewers. The most important aftermath of the two commission reports was the controversy among scientists, on the one hand, and the unexpected apathy on the part of the public, on the other. (6)

Much of the controversy among the scientists revolved around the cautious conclusions of the Surgeon General's Committee. (7) This caution seemed to lead to different interpretations of the research results, with some readers—including newspaper writers and television critics—reporting that television had no effect on aggressive behavior and others that it did have an effect. In general, behavioral scientists felt that the committee had been too cautious and conservative. Some people blamed the tentative and somewhat ambiguous phraseology of the report on the makeup of the committee; the television industry had been asked to name members to the committee, and the industry had veto power over those who were being considered for appointment. The other scientific controversy has centered on the usefulness, legitimacy, and pertinence of monitoring television violence.

During this period, the public was not much interested in television violence for reasons not discernible, although a few citizens' groups, such as Action for Children's Television, were beginning to gather strength.

The year 1975 brought several new developments. Congress again became concerned with violence on television and also with obscenity and sexual provocativeness and prevailed upon the Federal Communications Commission (FCC) to do something. The FCC Commissioners worked with the networks to establish the "family viewing hours" in the early evening. This arrangement was challenged in the courts by writers and producers who argued that it violated the First Amendment and infringed on their right of trade. The judge ruled in their favor, but the networks continued the family hour on an informal basis.

During this time also, a number of citizen

groups raised protests against various broadcasting practices. The American Medical Association adopted a resolution asking broadcasters to reduce the amount of violence because it was a threat to the social health of the country; the National Parent-Teachers Association held public forums throughout the country and began monitoring television content; and the National Citizens Committee for Broadcasting linked advertisers with violent content. (8)

A subcommittee of the House Committee on Interstate and Foreign Commerce held several hearings in cities throughout the country. Their report, published in 1977, indcated dissatisfaction with the situation, but it did not place blame on the broadcasters nor ask for any action. (9)

Information on trends in violence depends, of course, on the definitions of violence and on the analytic procedures used. Nonetheless, all analyses agree that the evening hours after 9 P.M. contain more violence than other hours on television. (10) Beginning with the 1975–76 season, however, there was some increase in the early evening hours and some decrease in the later hours, although the later hours remained the most violent. There was a slight overall increase in violence between 1976 and 1977 and the slight decrease between 1977 and 1978. In 1979, it was about the same as in 1978. Over the past 10 years, there also has been more violence on children's weekend programs than on prime time television.

It appears, then, that the violence on television that began back in the 1950s has continued. There have been a few changes and fluctuations, but, in general, television, despite the concerns of Congressmen and citizens' groups, remains a violent form of entertainment.

EFFECTS OF TELEVISED VIOLENCE

The discussion about the effects of televised violence needs to be evaluated not only in the light of existing evidence but also in terms of how that evidence is to be assessed. Most of the researchers look at the totality of evidence and conclude, as did the Surgeon General's advisory committee, that the convergence of findings supports the conclusion of a causal relationship between televised violence and later aggressive behavior. The evidence now is drawn from a large body of literature. Adherents to this convergence approach agree that the conclusions reached in the Surgeon General's program have been significantly strengthened by more recent research. Not only has the evidence been augmented, but the processes by which the aggressive behavior is produced have been further examined.

In the past 10 years, several important field studies have found that televised violence results in aggressive behavior. Here are some examples:

A study funded by the Columbia Broadcasting System reported that teenage boys in London, according to their own accounts of their activities, were more likely to engage in "serious violence" after exposed to television violence. (11)

Two independent studies by the same investigators followed 3- and 4-year-old children over a year's time and correlated their television viewing at home with the various types of behavior they showed during free-play periods at daycare centers. (12) In each study there were consistent associations between heavy television viewing of violent programs and unwarranted aggressive behavior in their free play. It was concluded that, for these preschool children, watching violence on television was a cause of heightened aggressiveness.

In a 5-year study of 732 children, several kinds of aggression—conflict with parents, fighting, and delinquency—were all positively correlated with the total amount of television viewing, not just viewing of violent programs. (13)

Two additional studies were able to compare aggressiveness in children before and after their communities had television. (14) In one study there was a significant increase in both verbal and physical aggression following the introduction of television. In the other study, after the introduction of television, aggressiveness increased in those children who looked at it a great deal.

Another long-term study currently has been collecting extensive data on children in several countries. (*15*) Results are available for grade-school children in the United States, Finland, and Poland. In all three countries, a positive relationship was found between television violence and aggression in both boys and girls. In previous studies by these investigators, the relationship was found only for boys. The sheer amount of television viewing, regardless of the kind of program, was the best predictor of aggression.

Two other field studies reported similar results with different groups of children. One on teenagers found that those who perceived a program as violent or who thought that violence is an acceptable way to achieve a goal were more violent than the others. (*16*) The other study reported that the positive correlations between violence and aggression in English school children were just about the same as in American school children. (*17*)

In contrast, in a large scale study sponsored by the National Broadcasting Company a group of researchers reached a different conclusion. (*18*) In this technically sophisticated panel study, data were collected on several hundred elementary school boys and girls and teenage high school boys. For the elementary school children, measurements of aggression were taken six times during a 3-year period, and for the high school boys the measurements were taken five times. The elementary school children gave "peer nominations" of aggression, and the teenagers gave "self reports." Both the elementary school children and the teenagers reported on which television programs they watched, and, for purposes of the analyses, the investigators picked those programs that could be classified as violent. The results showed that for the measures of violence on television and aggressive behavior taken at the same time, there were small but positive correlations. This is consistent with other cross-sectional survey results. But, when the measurements taken at different times were compared, no relationship was found. These investigators wanted to learn whether the short-term effects of television would accumulate over time and produce stable patterns of aggressive behavior in the real world. They found: the study did not provide evidence that

television violence was causally implicated in the development of aggressive behavior patterns in children and adolescents over the time periods studied.

But according to many researchers, the evidence accumulated in the 1970s seems overwhelming that televised violence and aggression are positively correlated in children. The issue now is what processes produce the relation. Four such processes have been suggested; observational learning, attitude changes, physiological arousal, and justification processes.

Observational Learning

Proponents of the observational learning theory hold that children learn to behave aggressively from the violence they see on television in the same way they learn cognitive and social skills from watching their parents, siblings, peers, teachers, and others. (*19*) Laboratory studies have demonstrated many times that children imitate aggressive behavior immediately after they have seen it on film or television, but there are still questions about the role of observational learning in field studies. What do the data show? A longitudinal study published in 1977 gave the first substantial evidence that observational learning is the most plausible explanation for the positive relation between televised violence and aggressive behaviors. (*20*) Several other observational and field studies agree with these results. (*21*) Although these studies can be criticized on methodological grounds—and, indeed, the "clean" outcomes of laboratory experiments are rarely found in field studies—they nevertheless are important supports for the learning of behaviors from the observations of models.

Researchers have also analyzed specific issues related to observational learning. (*22*) In the first place, if children see someone rewarded for doing certain things, more likely they also will perform these acts. Thus, if children see a television character rewarded for aggressive behavior, they will probably imitate that behavior. If the actor is punished, the children are less apt to imitate the aggressive behavior. These vicarious reinforcements—either reward or punishment—can influence the behavior's occurrence. The persistence of the behavior, however, seems to be related to the children's own reinforcement, in other words, if the children themselves are rewarded or punished.

Observational learning may be related to age. (23) Some investigators say that, by the time children reach their teens, behavior may no longer be affected significantly by observational learning. Young children, however, who do not see the relation between the aggression and the motives for it, may be more prone to imitate the aggressive behavior. Children start to imitate what they see on television when they are very young, some as early as 2-years-old.

Identification with the actor or actress whose behavior is being imitated is also thought to be important, but the evidence is not clear-cut. (24) For example, it has been shown that both boys and girls are more likely to imitate male than female characters, and the males are the more aggressive. Girls who are aggressive may, it is true, identify more with the men characters. When children were asked to try to think in the same way as an aggressive character, they become more aggressive. (25) It appears that there are no simple relations between observational learning and identification.

Another approach had been to tie the observational learning to specific cues on the programs, even apparently irrelevant cues. (26) A tragic case from real life is the incident of a gang who burned a woman to death after a similar event occurred on a television show. In both the show and the real incident, the person was carrying a red gasoline can.

If these ideas about observational learning are analyzed in cognitive-processing terms, it can be hypothesized that children encode what they see and hear and then store it in their memories. To be encoded, the behavior must be salient or noticeable, and, to be retrieved in future behavior, it must be rehearsed with the same cues as those in the first observation present. If a child rehearses aggressive acts by daydreaming about them or uses them in make-believe play, the probability is increased that these acts will occur. There is some evidence that aggressive fantasies are related to aggressive acts. (27)

These hypotheses are relevant to another theory, namely, disinhibition. In disinhibition theory, it is assumed that children and others are inhibited by training and experience from being aggressive. But if they see a lot of violence on television, they lose their inhibitions—they are disinhibited. This is an interesting idea, but some theorists say that cognitive-processing theory does not need to call upon disinhibition functions to explain observational learning, even though disinhibition probably occurs. Rather, if children see a great deal of aggressive behavior on television, they will store and retrieve that behavior for future action.

Attitude Change

Watching television influences people's attitudes. The more television children watch, the more accepting they are of aggressive behavior. (28) It has been shown that persons who often watch television tend to be more suspicious and distrustful of others, and they also think there is more violence in the world than do those who do not watch much television. (29)

Attitudes in psychological theory are "attributions, rules, and explanations" that people gradually learn from observations of behavior. Therefore, it can be assumed that, if someone watches a lot of television, attitudes will be built up on the basis of what is seen, and the attitudes will, in turn, have an effect on behavior. A clever experiment showed how the television movie *Roots* changed attitudes and subsequent behavior. (30) Unruly behavior of white and black high school students was recorded before, during, and after the show was broadcast. During the week that *Roots* was shown, the black students were more unruly, as measured by after-school detentions. This change was interpreted to mean that the black students had a change in attitudes toward obedience after watching *Roots*.

Looking at violent scenes for even a very brief time makes young children more willing to accept aggressive behavior of other children. This acceptance of aggression makes it likely that the children will themselves be more aggressive. (31)

Other studies have shown that children's attitudes are changed if adults discuss the program. (*32*) In an experimental study, one group of children who regularly watched violent programs were shown excerpts from violent shows and then took part in sessions about the unreality of television violence and wrote essays about it. (*33*) The other group who also watched many violent programs were shown nonviolent excerpts, followed by a discussion of the content. The group who saw the violent television and then took part in the sessions on unreality were much less aggressive than the other group.

Arousal Processes

Processes involving physiological arousal are thought to have three possible consequences. One is desensitization. For example boys who regularly looked at violent programs showed less physiological arousal when they looked at new violent programs. (*34*) Another possibility is that merely the increase of general arousal level will boost aggressiveness. (*35*) A third alternative suggests that people seek an optimal level of arousal; aggressive behavior is arousing, and the persons who are desensitized may act aggressively to raise their levels of arousal. (*36*) Then, once the desired level is reached, aggression will continue, because the behavior most likely to be continued is the behavior readily retrievable from memory. All these theories need more empirical verification.

Justification Processes

In the justification theory, it is assumed that people who are already aggressive like to look at violent television programs because they can then justify their own behavior, even if only to themselves. (*37*) They can believe that they are acting like a favorite television hero. In this theory, watching televised violence is a result, rather than a cause, of aggressive behavior. So little research has been done on this theory that it cannot be evaluated.

Catharsis Theory

Contrary to these four theories is the catharsis theory, which predicts that aggression will be reduced after watching violence on televi-sion. Supposedly through catharsis, the need or desire to be aggressive is dissipated by looking at violence on television. Since practically all the evidence points to an increase in aggressive behavior, rather than a decrease, the theory is contradicted by the data.

In general, it appears that observational learning and attitude changes are the most likely explanations of television's effects on aggressive behavior.

METHODOLOGICAL ISSUES IN RESEARCH ON VIOLENCE AND AGGRESSION

Another aspect of the entire question about violence and aggression must be examined: What is meant by "violence" on television? Objective and reliable measures of violence are necessary before inferences can be made about its relationship to aggressive behavior. How these measures have been made and what has been revealed are to be found in an examination of the content analyses of televised violence. Such measurements have themselves been the source of considerable controversy.

Violence is assessed primarily by use of two procedures: content analysis and ratings. In a content analysis, the first step is to design the recording instrument. The trained coders observe the television programs and code them in accordance with predetermined criteria, with the aim of measuring violence as precisely and consistently as possible.

In the rating procedures, the raters are given lists of television programs and asked to rate them in terms of violence. The raters may be television critics, television researchers, or "ordinary people"; children have sometimes been used as raters. Sometimes definitions of violence are given to the raters, but many investigators believe that definitions are not necessary.

The longest and most extensive content analysis of television programs is the Cultural Indicators Project at the University of Pennsylvania's Annenberg School of Communications. (*38*) The project consists of two parts: One part is the "message system analysis," which is an annual content analysis of 1 week of prime time and weekend daytime dramatic programs. The second part is "cultivation analysis," which is a means of determining conceptions of social reality that television viewing may cultivate in various groups of viewers.

Definitions of Violence

Violence seems to be something everybody feels they can recognize when they see it, yet it is difficult to define unambiguously. Many different definitions are now in use, and there is much disagreement about them.

The Cultural Indicators Project defines violence as:

the overt expression of physical force (with or without a weapon, against self or other) compelling action against one's will on pain of being hurt or killed, or actually hurting or killing. (*39*)

The Columbia Broadcasting System's monitoring project defines violence as:

the use of physical force against persons or animals, or the articulated, explicit threat of physical force to compel particular behavior on the part of that person. (*40*)

The Parent-Teachers Association is concerned with gratuitous violence, which they define as:

violence to maintain interest, violence not necessary for plot development, glorified violence. (*41*)

Other definitions are:

physical acts or the threat of physical acts by humans designed to inflict physical injury to persons or damage to property.

acts involving the use of force, threats of force, or intent of force against others. (*42*)

how much fighting, shouting, yelling, or killing there is in a show. (*43*)

Most of the definitions involve physical force, including hurting or killing. Some definitions include psychological violence and violence against property; others do not. Some include comic violence, accidents, and acts of nature, such as floods and earthquakes. The rationale for including "acts of nature" is, according to those who include them, that they are analyzing entertainment and dramatic programs in which the writers and producers have deliberately put in violent "natural" events. Obviously, the reported amount of violence in a program will depend on the definition.

Unitization of Violence

Another problem is found in deciding how to isolate specific acts of violence. In other words, if one wishes to count the number of violent actions, it is necessary to know when a violent action starts and stops.

The Cultural Indicators Project states a violent action is a scene confined to the same participants. Any change in the characters is a new action.

The CBS monitoring project defines a single violent action as:

One sustained dramatically continuous event involving violence, with essentially the same group of participants and with no major interruption in continuity. (*44*)

As with the definitions of violence, the different unitizations produce different results. For example, CBS finds less violence in programs than does the Cultural Indicators Project.

An Index of Violence

The Cultural Indicators Project has developed an Index of Violence that combines several violence-related measures into a single score. (*45*) The Index is composed of three sets of data: the prevalence, rate, and role of violence. "Prevalence" is the percentage of programs in a particular sample containing any violence at all. "Rate" is the frequency of violent action. "Role" is the portrayal of characters as "violents" (committing violence) or as victims (subjected to violence). These three measures are combined into a formula that yields the Index of Violence. There has been controversy about this Index, but its users maintain that although it is arbitrary—as is true of all indices—it is useful to illustrate trends and to facilitate comparisons.

CONCLUSION

In conclusion, the interesting characteristics of violence on television are its overall stability and regularity, despite fluctuations by networks, genre, and time. The percentage of programs containing violence has remained about the same since 1967, although the number of violent acts per program has increased. Children's shows are violent in a cyclical way, up one year and down the next.

The amount of violence on television, according to some researchers, will almost certainly remain about the same as it has been, and they do not call for its total elimination. The concern is more with the kinds of violence, who commits violence, and who is victimized, because these portrayals may be critical mechanisms of social control.

The cultivation analysis aspects of the Cultural Indicators Project has a basic thesis that the more time viewers spend watching television, the more they will conceive the world to be similar to television portrayals. Thus, as stated in the discussion of attitude change, people who view a great deal of television—and who consequently see a great deal of violence—are more likely to view the world as a mean and scary place. These heavy viewers also exhibit more fear, mistrust, and apprehension than do light viewers. Because there are more victims than there are aggressors, this finding may ultimately be of more significance than the direct relationship between televised violence and aggression.

REFERENCES

(1) Remmers, H. H. *Four years of New York television*: 1951–1954. Urbana: National Association of Educational Broadcasters. June 1954.

(2) Greenberg, B. S. The content and context of violence in the mass media. In R. K. Baker and S. J. Ball (Eds.), *Violence and the media: A staff report to the National Commission on the Causes and Prevention of Violence*. Washington: U.S. Government Printing Office, 1969.

Head, S. W. Content analysis of television drama programs. *Quarterly of Film, Radio and Television*, 1954, *9*, 175–194.

Larsen, O. N., Gray, L. N., and Fortis, J. G. Goals and goal-achievement in television content: Models for anomie? *Sociological Inquiry*, 1963, *33*, 180–196.

Smythe, D. W. Reality as presented by television. *Public Opinion Quarterly*, 1954, *18*, 143–156.

(3) Baker, R. K., and Ball, S. J. (Eds.) *Violence and the media: A staff report to the National Commission on the Causes and Prevention of Violence*. Washington: U.S. Government Printing Office, 1963.

(4) Surgeon General's Scientific Advisory Committee on Television and Social Behavior. *Television and growing up: The impact of televised violence*. Report to the Surgeon General, United States Public Health Service. Washington: U.S. Government Printing Office, 1972.

(5) Gerbner, G. Violence in television drama: Trends and symbolic functions. In G. A. Comstock and E. A. Rubinstein (Eds.), *Television and social behavior* (Vol. 1). *Media content and control*. Washington: U.S. Government Printing Office, 1972.

(6) Boffey, P. M., and Walsh, J. Study of TV violence: Seven top researchers blackballed from panel. *Science*, 1970, *168*, 949–952.

Cater, D., and Strickland, S. *TV violence and the child: The evolution and fate of the Surgeon General's report*. New York: Russell Sage Foundation, 1975.

(7) Paisley, M. B. *Social policy research and the realities of the system: Violence done to TV research*. Stanford, Calif.: Institute for Communication Research, Stanford University, March 1972.

(8) Slaby, R. G., Quarforth, G. R., and McConnachie, G. A. Television violence and its sponsors. *Journal of Communication*, 1976, *26* (1), 88–96.

(9) United States Congress. House Committee on Interstate and Foreign Commerce. Hearings before the subcommittee on communications. *Sex and violence on TV*. 94th Congress, 2nd session, 1976. Washington: U.S. Government Printing Office, 1976.

United States Congress. House Committee on Interstate and Foreign Commerce. Report of the subcommittee on communications. *Violence on television*. 95th Congress, 1st session, 1977. Washington: U.S. Government Printing Office, 1977.

(10) Columbia Broadcasting System. *Network primetime tabulations for 1975–76 season*. Unpublished manuscript. CBS, New York, April 1976. Columbia Broadcasting System. Network primetime violence tabulations for 1978–79 season. New York: CBS, 1980.

Gerbner, G., Gross, L. Eleey, M. F., Jackson-Beeck, M., Jeffries-Fox, S., and Signorielli, N. *Violence profile no. 8. Trends in network television drama and viewer conceptions of social reality, 1967–1976*. Philadelphia: Annenberg School of Communications, University of Pennsylvania, 1977.

Gerbner, G., Gross, L., Signorielli, N., Morgan,

M., and Jackson-Beeck, M. *Violence profile no. 10; Trends in network television drama and viewer conceptions of social reality.* Philadelphia: Annenberg School of Communications, University of Pennsylvania, 1979.

Gerbner, G., Gross, L., Morgan, M., and Signorielli, N. The "mainstreaming" of America: Violence profile no. 11. *Journal of Communication*, 1980, *30* (3), 10–29.

(*11*) Belson, W. *Television violence and the adolescent boy.* London: Saxon House, 1978.

(*12*) Singer, J. L., and Singer, D. G. Television, imagination and aggression: A study of preschoolers play. Hillsdale, N.J.: Erlbaum, 1980.

(*13*) McCarthy, E. D., Langner, T. S., Gersten, J. C., Eisenberg, J. G., and Orzeck, L. Violence and behavior disorders. *Journal of Communication*, 1975, *25* (4), 71–85.

(*14*) Williams, T. M. *Differential impact of TV on children: A natural experiment in communities with and without TV.* Paper presented at the meeting of the International Society for Research on Aggression, Washington, 1978.

Granszberg, G., and Steinberg, J. *Television and the Canadian Indian.* Technical report, Department of Anthropology, University of Winnipeg, 1980.

(*15*) Eron, L. D., and Huesmann, L. R. Adolescent aggression and television. *Annals of the New York Academy of Sciences*, 1980, *347*, 319–331.

Eron, L. D. and Huesmann, L. R. *Integrating field and laboratory investigations of televised violence and aggression.* Paper presented at the meeting of the American Psychological Association, Montreal, 1980.

Huesmann, L. R., Eron, L. D., Klein, R., Briece, P., Fischer, P. *Mitigating the imitation of aggressive behavior.* Technical report, Department of Psychology, University of Illinois, 1981.

(*16*) Hartnagel, T. F., Teevan, J. J., Jr., and McIntyre, J. J. Television violence and violent behavior. *Social Forces*, 1975, *54*, 341–351.

(*17*) Greenberg, B. S. British children and televised violence. *Public Opinion Quarterly*, 1975, *38*, 531–547.

(*18*) Milavsky, J. R., Kessler, R., Stipp, H., and Rubens, W. S. *Television and aggression: Results of a panel study.* In preparation, 1981.

(*19*) Bandura, A. *Social learning theory.* Englewood Cliffs, N.J.; Prentice-Hall, 1977.

(*20*) Lefkowitz, M. M., Eron, L. D., Walder, L. O., and Huesmann, L. R. *Growing up to be violent: A longitudinal study of the development of aggression.* New York: Pergamon Press, 1977.

(*21*) Friedrich-Cofer, L. K., Huston-Stein, A., Kipnis, D., Susman, E. J., and Clevitt, A. S. Environmental enhancement of prosocial television content: Effects on interpersonal behavior, imaginative play, and self-regulation in a natural setting. *Developmental Psychology*, 1979, *15*, 637–646.

Leyens, J. P., Parke, R. D., Camino, L., and Berkowitz, L. Effects of movie violence on aggression in a field setting as a function of group dominance and cohesion. *Journal of Personality and Social Psychology*, 1975, *32*, 346–360.

Huesmann, L. R., Eron, L. D., Lefkowitz, M. M., and Walder, L. O. *Causal analyses of longitudinal data: An application to the study of television violence and aggression.* Technical report. Department of Psychology, University of Illinois at Chicago Circle, 1979.

Parke, R. D., Berkowitz, L., Leyens, J. P., West, S., and Sebastian, R. J. Some effects of violent and nonviolent movies on the behavior of juvenile delinquents. In L. Berkowitz (Ed.), *Advances in experimental social psychology* (Vol. 10). New York: Academic Press, 1977.

Singer, J. L., and Singer, D. G. 1980. Op. cit.

(*22*) Bandura A. Influence of models' reinforcement contingencies on the acquisition of imitative responses. *Journal of Personality and Social Psychology*, 1965, *1*, 589–595.

(*23*) Collins, W. A., Berndt, T. J., and Hess, V. L. Observational learning of motives and consequences for television aggression: A developmental study. *Child Development*, 1974, *45*, 799–802.

Eron, L. D., Huesmann, L. R., Lefkowitz, M. M., and Walder, L. O. Does television violence cause aggression? *American Psychologist*, 1972, *27*, 253–263.

Hearold, S. L. *Meta-analysis of the effects of television on social behavior.* Unpublished doctoral dissertation, University of Colorado, 1979.

McCall, R. B., Parke, R. D., and Kavanaugh, R. D. Imitation of live and televised models by children one to three years of age. *Monographs of the Society for Research in Child Development*, 1977, *42.* (5). 94. p.

Newcomb, A. F., and Collins, W. A. Children's comprehension of family role portrayals in televised dramas: Effects of socioeconomic status, ethnicity, and age. *Developmental Psychology*, 1979, *15*, 417–423.

(*24*) Bandura, A., Ross, D., and Ross, S. A. Imitation of film-mediated aggressive models. *Journal of Abnormal and Social Psychology*, 1963, *66*, 3–11.

Bandura, A., Ross, D., and Ross, S. A. Vicarious reinforcement and imitative learning. *Journal of Abnormal and Social Psychology*, 1963, *67*, 601–607.

Huesmann, L. R., Fischer, P. F., Eron, L. D., Mermelstein, R., Kaplan-Shain, E., and Morikawa, S. *Children's sex-role preference, sex of television model, and imitation of aggressive behaviors.* Paper presented at the meeting of the International Society for Research on Aggression, Washington, D.C., 1978.

(*25*) Turner, C. W., and Berkowitz, L. Identification with film aggressor (covert role taking) and reactions to film violence. *Journal of Personality and Social Psychology*, 1972, *21*, 256–264.

(26) Berkowitz, L. Some determinants of impulsive aggression: The role of mediated associations with reinforcements for aggression. *Psychological Review*, 1974, *81*, 165–176.

Turner, C. W., and Fenn, M. R. *Effects of white noise and memory cues on verbal aggression.* Paper presented at the meeting of the International Society for Research on Aggression, Washington, D.C. 1978.

(27) Rosenfeld, E., Maloney, S., Huesmann, L. R., Eron, L. D., Fischer, P. F., Musonis, V., and Washington, A. *The effect of fantasy behaviors and fantasy-reality discrimination upon observational learning of aggression.* Paper presented at the meeting of the International Society for Research on Aggression, Washington, D.C., 1978.

(28) Dominick, J. R., and Greenberg, B. S. Attitudes toward violence: The interaction of television exposure, family attitudes, and social class. In G. A. Comstock and E. A. Rubinstein (Eds.), *Television and social behavior.* (Vol. 3). *Television and adolescent aggressiveness.* Washington: U.S. Government Printing Office, 1972.

(29) Gerbner, G., and Gross, L. *Violence profile no. 6: Trends in network television drama and viewer conceptions of social reality: 1967–1973.* Unpublished manuscript. Annenberg School of Communications, University of Pennsylvania, 1974.

(30) Ryback, D., and Connel, R. H. Differential racial patterns of school discipline during the broadcasting of "Roots." *Psychological Reports*, 1976, *42*, 514.

(31) Drabman, R. S., and Thomas, M. H. Does media violence increase children's toleration of real-life aggression? *Developmental Psychology*, 1974, *10*, 418–421.

Thomas, M. H., and Drabman, R. S. Toleration of real life aggression as a function of exposure to televised violence and age of subject. *Merrill-Palmer Quarterly*, 1975, *21*, 227–232.

(32) Friedrich-Cofer, L. K., Huston-Stein, A., Kipnis, D., Susman, E. J., and Clevitt, A. S., 1979. Op. cit. Singer, J. L., and Singer, D. G., 1980. Op. cit.

(33) Eron, L. D., and Huesmann, L. R., 1980. Op. cit. Huesmann, L. R., Eron, L. D., Klein, R., Briece, P., Fisher, P., 1981. Op. cit.

(34) Zillman, D. Excitation transfer on communication-mediated aggressive behavior. *Journal of Experimental Social Psychology*, 1971, *7*, 419–434.

(36) Tannenbaum, P. H. Entertainment as vicarious emotional experience. In P. H. Tannenbaum (Ed.), *The entertainment functions of television.* Hillsdale, N.J.: Erlbaum, 1980.

(37) Kaplan, R. M., and Singer, R. D. Television violence and viewer aggression: A reexamination of the evidence. *Journal of Social Issues*, 1976, *32*, 35–70.

(38) Gerbner, G. Cultural Indicators: The third voice. In G. Gerbner, L. P. Gross, and W. H. Melody (Eds.), *Communications technology and social policy.* New York: Wiley, 1973.

Gerbner, G., Gross, L., Jackson-Beeck, M., Jeffries-Fox, S., and Signorielli, N. Cultural Indicators: Violence profile no. 9. *Journal of Communication*, 1978, *28* (3), 176–207.

Gerbner, G., Gross, L., Morgan, M., and Signorielli, N., 1980. Op. cit.

Gerbner, G., Gross, L., Morgan, M., and Signorielli, N. *Violence profile no. 11: Trends in network television drama and viewer conceptions of social reality, 1967–1979.* Technical report, Annenberg School of Communications, University of Pennsylvania, 1980.

(39) Gerbner, G., Gross, L., Jackson-Beeck, M., Jeffries-Fox, S., and Signorielli, N., 1978. Op. cit.

(40) Columbia Broadcasting System, Inc., Office of Social Research. *Network prime-time violence tabulations for 1976–77 season and instructions to coders, 1976–77.*

(41) *Individual Monitor Form*, National PTA Action Center, 700 N. Rush St., Chicago, Ill. 60611.

(42) Clark, D. G., and Blankenburg, W. B. Trends in violent content in selected mass media. In G. A. Comstock and E. A. Rubinstein (Eds.) *Television and social behavior* (Vol. 1). *Media content and control.* Washington: U.S. Government Printing Office, 1972.

(43) Greenberg, B. S., and Gordon, T. F. Critics' and public perception of violence in television programs. *Journal of Broadcasting*, 1970–71, *15*, 24–43.

Abel, J. D., and Beninson. M. E. Perceptions of TV program violence by children and mothers. *Journal of Broadcasting*, 1976, *20*, 355–363.

(44) Columbia Broadcasting System, Inc., Office of Social Research, 1976–77. Op. cit.

(45) See references by Gerbner and by Gerbner et al. listed above.

16

Bystander Intervention in Emergencies: Diffusion of Responsibility

John M. Darley and Bibb Latané

On March 13, 1964, the public was shocked by the brutal murder of Kitty Genovese, a young woman stabbed to death on a street in New York City while 38 people in nearby apartments ignored her cries for help. The fact that not one person came to her aid or telephoned the police was a troubling reminder that people do not always help strangers in distress. This incident spurred social psychological research on helping behavior and bystander intervention in emergencies. In this pioneering experiment, Darley and Latané staged a fake emergency in the laboratory to test the impact of the number of bystanders on helping behavior. Are people more likely to help someone in distress if they are the only bystander, or if there are several people present? Darley and Latané found that individual subjects were more likely to help if they believed they were the sole bystander; they were less likely to help if they thought that others also knew about the emergency. The researchers do not interpret these results as signs of apathy: Most subjects seemed genuinely concerned about the person in distress. Rather, Darley and Latané propose that subjects experienced conflict—wanting to help but also fearing that they might be seen by others as overreacting. Further, since the experiment was arranged so that subjects could not directly observe how other subjects were reacting, some subjects may have assumed that someone else had already reported the incident to the experimenter. This study is important because it provided an early model for studying bystander intervention in the laboratory and because it proposed a social-psychological process—the diffusion of responsibility—as a crucial factor in helping. Subsequent research has confirmed the importance of perceived responsibility for helping others in distress.

ABSTRACT. *Ss overheard an epileptic seizure. They believed either that they alone heard the emergency, or that 1 or 4 unseen others were also present. As predicted the presence of other bystanders reduced the individual's feelings of personal responsibility and lowered his speed of reporting (p < .01). In groups of size 3, males reported no faster than females, and females reported no slower when the 1 other bystander was a male rather than a female. In general, personality and background measures were not* predictive of helping. Bystander inaction in real-life emergencies is often explained by "apathy," "alienation," and "anomie." This experiment suggests that the explanation may lie more in the bystander's response to other observers than in his indifference to the victim.

Reprinted from the *Journal of Personality and Social Psychology*, 1968, 8, pp. 377–383. Copyright 1968 by the American Psychological Association. Reprinted by permission of publisher and authors.

Several years ago, a young woman was stabbed to death in the middle of a street in a residential section of New York City. Although such murders are not entirely routine, the incident received little public attention until several weeks later when the New York Times

179

disclosed another side to the case: at least 38 witnesses had observed the attack—and none had even attempted to intervene. Although the attacker took more than half an hour to kill Kitty Genovese, not one of the 38 people who watched from the safety of their own apartments came out to assist her. Not one even lifted the telephone to call the police (Rosenthal, 1964).

Preachers, professors, and news commentators sought the reasons for such apparently conscienceless and inhumane lack of intervention. Their conclusions ranged from "moral decay," to "dehumanization produced by the urban environment," to "alienation," "anomie," and "existential despair." An analysis of the situation, however, suggests that factors other than apathy and indifference were involved.

A person witnessing an emergency situation, particularly such a frightening and dangerous one as a stabbing, is in conflict. There are obvious humanitarian norms about helping the victim, but there are also rational and irrational fears about what might happen to a person who does intervene (Milgram & Hollander, 1964). "I didn't want to get involved," is a familiar comment, and behind it lies fears of physical harm, public embarrassment, involvement with police procedures, lost work days and jobs, and other unknown dangers.

In certain circumstances, the norms favoring intervention may be weakened, leading bystanders to resolve the conflict in the direction of nonintervention. One of these circumstances may be the presence of other onlookers. For example, in the case above, each observer, by seeing lights and figures in other apartment house windows, knew that others were also watching. However, there was no way to tell how the other observers were reacting. These two facts provide several reasons why any individual may have delayed or failed to help. The responsibility for helping was diffused among the observers; there was also diffusion of any potential blame for not taking action; and finally, it was possible that somebody, unperceived, had already initiated helping action.

When only one bystander is present in an emergency, if help is to come, it must come from him. Although he may choose to ignore it (out of concern for his personal safety, or desires "not to get involved"), any pressure to intervene focuses uniquely on him. When there are several observers present, however, the pressures to intervene do not focus on any one of the observers; instead the responsibility for intervention is shared among all the onlookers and is not unique to any one. As a result, no one helps.

A second possibility is that potential blame may be diffused. However much we may wish to think that an individual's moral behavior is divorced from considerations of personal punishment or reward, there is both theory and evidence to the contrary (Aronfreed, 1964; Miller & Dollard, 1941, Whiting & Child, 1953). It is perfectly reasonable to assume that, under circumstances of group responsibility for a punishable act, the punishment or blame that accrues to any one individual is often slight or nonexistent.

Finally, if others are known to be present, but their behavior cannot be closely observed, any one bystander can assume that one of the other observers is already taking action to end the emergency. Therefore, his own intervention would be only redundant—perhaps harmfully or confusingly so. Thus, given the presence of other onlookers whose behavior cannot be observed, any given bystander can rationalize his own inaction by convincing himself that "somebody else must be doing something."

These considerations lead to the hypothesis that the more bystanders to an emergency, the less likely, or the more slowly, any one bystander will intervene to provide aid. To test this proposition it would be necessary to create a situation in which a realistic "emergency" could plausibly occur. Each subject should also be blocked from communicating with others to prevent his getting information about their behavior during the emergency. Finally, the experimental situation should allow for the assessment of the speed and frequency of the subjects' reaction to the emergency. The experiment reported below attempted to fulfill these conditions.

PROCEDURE

Overview

A college student arrived in the laboratory and was ushered into an individual room from which a communication system would enable him to talk to the other participants. It was explained to him that he was to take part in a discussion about personal problems associated with college life and that the discussion would be held over the intercom system, rather than face-to-face, in order to avoid embarrassment by preserving the anonymity of the subjects. During the course of the discussion, one of the other subjects underwent what appeared to be a very serious nervous seizure similar to epilepsy. During the fit it was impossible for the subject to talk to the other discussants or to find out what, if anything, they were doing about the emergency. The dependent variable was the speed with which the subjects reported the emergency to the experimenter. The major independent variable was the number of people the subject thought to be in the discussion group.

Subjects

Fifty-nine female and thirteen male students in introductory psychology courses at New York University were contacted to take part in an unspecified experiment as part of a class requirement.

Method

Upon arriving for the experiment, the subject found himself in a long corridor with doors opening off it to several small rooms. An experimental assistant met him, took him to one of the rooms, and seated him at a table. After filling out a background information form, the subject was given a pair of headphones with an attached microphone and was told to listen for instructions.

Over the intercom, the experimenter explained that he was interested in learning about the kinds of personal problems faced by normal college students in a high pressure, urban environment. He said that to avoid possible embarrassment about discussing personal problems with strangers several precautions had been taken. First, subjects would remain anonymous, which was why they had been placed in individual rooms rather than face-to-face. (The actual reason for this was to allow tape recorder simulation of the other subjects and the emergency.) Second, since the discussion might be inhibited by the presence of outside listeners, the experimenter would not listen to the initial discussion, but would get the subject's reactions later, by questionnaire. (The real purpose of this was to remove the obviously responsible experimenter from the scene of the emergency.)

The subjects were told that since the experimenter was not present, it was necessary to impose some organization. Each person would talk in turn, presenting his problems to the group. Next, each person in turn would comment on what the others had said, and finally, there would be a free discussion. A mechanical switching device would regulate this discussion sequence and each subject's microphone would be on for about 2 minutes. While any microphone was on, all other microphones would be off. Only one subject, therefore, could be heard over the network at any given time. The subjects were thus led to realize when they later heard the seizure that only the victim's microphone was on and that there was no way of determining what any of the other witnesses were doing, nor of discussing the event and its possible solution with the others. When these instructions had been given, the discussion began.

In the discussion, the future victim spoke first, saying that he found it difficult to get adjusted to New York City and to his studies. Very hesitantly, and with obvious embarrassment, he mentioned that he was prone to seizures, particularly when studying hard or taking exams. The other people, including the real subject, took their turns and discussed similar problems (minus, of course, the proneness to seizures). The naive subject talked last in the series, after the last prerecorded voice was played.[1]

When it was again the victim's turn to talk, he made a few relatively calm comments, and then, growing increasingly louder and incoherent, he continued:

I-er-um-I think I-I need-er-if-if could-er-er-somebody er-er-er-er-er-er-er give me a little-er-give me a little help here because-er-I-er-I'm-er-er-h-h-having a-a-a real problem-er-right now and I-er-if somebody could help me out it would-it would-er-er s-s-sure be-sure be good . . .because-er-there-er-er-a cause I-er-I-uh-I've got a-a one of the-er-sei-----er-er-things coming on and-and-and I could really-er-use some help so if somebody would-er-give me a little h-help-uh-er-er-er-er-er c-could somebody-er-er-help-er-uh-uh-uh (choking sounds). . . . I'm gonna die-er-er-I'm . . . gonna die-er-help-er-er-seizure-er-[chokes, then quiet].

The experimenter began timing the speed of the real subject's response at the beginning of the victim's speech. Informed judges listening to the tape have estimated that the victim's increasingly louder and more disconnected ramblings clearly represented a breakdown about 70 seconds after the signal for the victim's second speech. The victim's speech was abruptly cut off 125 seconds after this signal, which could be interpreted by the subject as indicating that the time allotted for that speaker had elapsed and the switching circuits had switched away from him. Times reported in the results are measured from the start of the fit.

Group size variable. The major independent variable of the study was the number of other people that the subject believed also heard the fit. By the assistant's comments before the experiment, and also by the number of voices heard to speak in the first round of the group discussion, the subject was led to believe that the discussion group was one of three sizes: either a two-person group (consisting of a person who

---

[1] To test whether the order in which the subjects spoke in the first discussion round significantly affected the subjects' speed of report, the order in which the subjects spoke was varied (in the six-person group). This had no significant or noticeable effect on the speed of the subjects' reports.

would later have a fit and the real subject), a three-person group (consisting of the victim, the real subject, and one confederate voice), or a six-person group (consisting of the victim, the real subject, and four confederate voices). All the confederates' voices were tape-recorded.

Variations in group composition. Varying the kind as well as the number of bystanders present at an emergency should also vary the amount of responsibility felt by any single bystander. To test this, several variations of the three-person group were run. In one three-person condition, the taped bystander voice was that of a female, in another a male, and in the third a male who said that he was a premedical student who occasionally worked in the emergency wards at Bellevue hospital.

In the above conditions, the subjects were female college students. In a final condition males drawn from the same introductory psychology subject pool were tested in a three-person female-bystander condition.

Time to help. The major dependent variable was the time elapsed from the start of the victim's fit until the subject left her experimental cubicle. When the subject left her room, she saw the experimental assistant seated at the end of the hall, and invariably went to the assistant. If 6 minutes elapsed without the subject having emerged from her room, the experiment was terminated.

As soon as the subject reported the emergency, or after 6 minutes had elapsed, the experimental assistant disclosed the true nature of the experiment, and dealt with any emotions aroused in the subject. Finally the subject filled out a questionnaire concerning her thoughts and feelings during the emergency, and completed scales of Machiavellianism, anomie, and authoritarianism (Christie, 1964), a social desirability scale (Crowne & Marlowe, 1964), a social responsibility scale (Daniels & Berkowitz, 1964), and reported vital statistics and socioeconomic data.

RESULTS

Plausibility of Manipulation

Judging by the subjects' nervousness when they reported the fit to the experimenter, by

Table 1 Effects of Group Size on Likelihood and Speed of Response

Group Size	N	% Responding by End of It	Time in Sec.	Speed Score
2 (S & victim)	13	85	52	.87
3 (S, victim, & 1 other)	26	62	93	.72
6 (S, victim, & 4 others)	13	31	166	.51

Note.—p value of differences: $\chi^2 = 7.91$, $p < .02$; $F = 8.09$, $p < .01$, for speed scores.

their surprise when they discovered that the fit was simulated, and by comments they made during the fit (when they thought their microphones were off), one can conclude that almost all of the subjects perceived the fit as real. There were two exceptions in different experimental conditions, and the data for these subjects were dropped from the analysis.

Effect of Group Size on Helping

The number of bystanders that the subject perceived to be present had a major effect on the likelihood with which she would report the emergency (Table 1). Eighty-five percent of the subjects who thought they alone knew of the victim's plight reported the seizure before the victim was cut off, only 31% of those who thought four other bystanders were present did so.

Every one of the subjects in the two-person groups, but only 62% of the subjects in the six-person groups, ever reported the emergency. The cumulative distributions of response times for groups of different perceived size (Figure 1) indicates that, by any point in time, more subjects from the two-person groups had responded than from the three-person groups, and more from the three-person groups than from the six-person groups.

Ninety-five percent of all the subjects who ever responded did so within the first half of the time available to them. No subject who had not reported within 3 minutes after the fit ever did so. The shape of these distributions suggest that had the experiment been allowed to run for a considerably longer time, few additional subjects would have responded.

Speed of Response

To achieve a more detailed analysis of the results, each subject's time score was transformed into a "speed" score by taking the reciprocal of the response time in seconds and multiplying by 100. The effect of this transformation was to deemphasize differences between longer time scores, thus reducing the contribution to the results of the arbitrary 6-minute limit on scores. A high speed score indicates a fast response.

An analysis of variance indicates that the effect of group size is highly significant ($p < .01$). Duncan multiple-range tests indicate that all but the two- and three-person groups differ significantly from one another ($p < .05$).

Victim's Likelihood of Being Helped

An individual subject is less likely to respond if he thinks that others are present. But what

Figure 1. Cumulative distributions of helping responses.

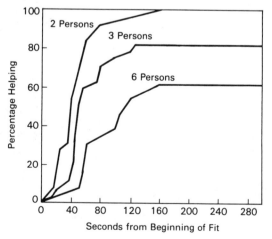

Table 2 Effects of Group Composition on Likelihood and Speed of Response[a]

Group Composition	N	% Responding by End of It	Time in Sec.	Speed Score
Female S, male other	13	62	94	74
Female S, female other	13	62	92	71
Female S, male medic other	5	100	60	77
Male S, female other	13	69	110	68

[a] Three-person group, male victim.

of the victim? Is the inhibition of the response of each individual strong enough to counteract the fact that with five onlookers there are five times as many people available to help? From the data of this experiment, it is possible mathematically to create hypothetical groups with one, two, or five observers.[2] The calculations indicate that the victim is about equally likely to get help from one bystander as from two. The victim is considerably more likely to have gotten help from one or two observers than from five during the first minute of the fit. For instance, by 45 seconds after the start of the fit, the victim's chances of having been helped by the single bystanders were about 50%, compared to none in the five observer condition. After the first minute, the likelihood of getting help from at least one person is high in all three conditions.

Effect of Group Composition on Helping the Victim

Several variations of the three-person group were run. In one pair of variations, the female subject thought the other bystander was either male or female; in another, she thought the other bystander was a premedical student who worked in an emergency ward at Bellevue hospital. As Table 2 shows, the variations in sex and medical competence of the other bystander had no important or detectable affect on speed of response. Subjects responded equally frequently and fast whether the other bystander was female, male, or medically experienced.

---

[2] The formula for the probability that at least one person will help by a given time is $1 - (1 - P)^n$ where n is the number of observers and P is the probability of a single individual (who thinks he is one of n observers) helping by that time.

Sex of the Subject and Speed of Response

Coping with emergencies is often thought to be the duty of males, especially when females are present, but there was no evidence that this was the case in this study. Male subjects responded to the emergency with almost exactly the same speed as did females (Table 2).

Reasons for Intervention or Nonintervention

After the debriefing at the end of the experiment each subject was given a 15-item checklist and asked to check those thoughts which had "crossed your mind when you heard Subject 1 calling for help." Whatever the condition, each subject checked very few thoughts, and there were no significant differences in number or kind of thoughts in the different experimental groups. The only thoughts checked by more than a few subjects were "I didn't know what to do" (18 out of 65 subjects), "I thought it must be some sort of fake" (20 out of 65), and "I didn't know exactly what was happening" (26 out of 65).

It is possible that subjects were ashamed to report socially undesirable rationalizations, or, since the subjects checked the list *after* the true nature of the experiment had been explained to them, their memories might have been blurred. It is our impression, however, that most subjects checked few reasons because they had few coherent thoughts during the fit.

We asked all subjects whether the presence or absence of other bystanders had entered their minds during the time that they were hearing the fit. Subjects in the three- and six-person groups reported that they were aware that other people were present, but they felt that this made no difference to their own behavior.

Individual Difference Correlates of Speed of Report

The correlations between speed of report and various individual differences on the personality and background measures were obtained by normalizing the distribution of report speeds within each experimental condition and pooling these scores across all conditions (n = 62–65). Personality measures showed no important or significant correlations with speed of reporting the emergency. In fact, only one of the 16 individual difference measures, the size of the community in which the subject grew up, correlated ($r = -.26$, $p < .05$) with the speed of helping.

DISCUSSION

Subjects, whether or not they intervened, believed the fit to be genuine and serious. "My God, he's having a fit," many subjects said to themselves (and were overheard via their microphones) at the onset of the fit. Others gasped or simply said "Oh." Several of the male subjects swore. One subject said to herself, "It's just my kind of luck, something has to happen to me!" Several subjects spoke aloud of their confusion about what course of action to take, "Oh God, what should I do?"

When those subjects who intervened stepped out of their rooms, they found the experimental assistant down the hall. With some uncertainty, but without panic, they reported the situation. "Hey, I think Number 1 is very sick. He's having a fit or something." After ostensibly checking on the situation, the experimenter returned to report that "everything is under control." The subjects accepted these assurances with obvious relief.

Subjects who failed to report the emergency showed few signs of the apathy and indifference thought to characterize "unresponsive bystanders." When the experimenter entered her room to terminate the situation, the subject often asked if the victim was "all right." "Is he being taken care of?" "He's all right isn't

he?" Many of these subjects showed physical signs of nervousness; they often had trembling hands and sweating palms. If anything, they seemed more emotionally aroused than did the subjects who reported the emergency.

Why, then, didn't they respond? It is our impression that nonintervening subjects had not decided *not* to respond. Rather they were still in a state of indecision and conflict concerning whether to respond or not. The emotional behavior of these nonresponding subjects was a sign of their continuing conflict, a conflict that other subjects resolved by responding.

The fit created a conflict situation of the avoidance-avoidance type. On the one hand, subjects worried about the guilt and shame they would feel if they did not help the person in distress. On the other hand, they were concerned not to make fools of themselves by overreacting, not to ruin the ongoing experiment by leaving their intercom, and not to destroy the anonymous nature of the situation which the experimenter had earlier stressed as important. For subjects in the two-person condition, the obvious distress of the victim and his need for help were so important that their conflict was easily resolved. For the subjects who knew there were other bystanders present, the cost of not helping was reduced and the conflict they were in more acute. Caught between the two negative alternatives of letting the victim continue to suffer or the costs of rushing in to help, the nonresponding bystanders vacillated between them rather than choosing not to respond. This distinction may be academic for the victim, since he got no help in either case, but it is an extremely important one for arriving at an understanding of the causes of bystanders' failures to help.

Although the subjects experienced stress and conflict during the experiment, their general reactions to it were highly positive. On a questionnaire administered after the experimenter had discussed the nature and purpose of the experiment, every single subject found the experiment either "interesting" or "very interesting" and was willing to participate in similar experiments in the future. All subjects felt they understood what the experiment was about and indicated that they thought the deceptions were necessary and justified. All but one felt they were better informed about the nature of psychological research in general.

Male subjects reported the emergency no faster than did females. These results (or lack of them) seem to conflict with the Berkowitz, Klanderman, and Harris (1964) finding that males tend to assume more responsibility and take more initiative than females in giving help to dependent others. Also, females reacted equally fast when the other bystander was another female, a male, or even a person practiced in dealing with medical emergencies. The ineffectiveness of these manipulations of group composition cannot be explained by general insensitivity of the speed measure, since the group-size variable had a marked effect on report speed.

It might be helpful in understanding this lack of difference to distinguish two general classes of intervention in emergency situations: direct and reportorial. Direct intervention (breaking up a fight, extinguishing a fire, swimming out to save a drowner) often requires skill, knowledge, or physical power. It may involve danger. American cultural norms and Berkowitz's results seem to suggest that males are more responsible than females for this kind of direct intervention.

A second way of dealing with an emergency is to report it to someone qualified to handle it, such as the police. For this kind of intervention, there seem to be no norms requiring male action. In the present study, subjects clearly intended to report the emergency rather than take direct action. For such indirect intervention, sex or medical competence does not appear to affect one's qualifications or responsibilities. Anybody, male or female, medically trained or not, can find the experimenter.

In this study, no subject was able to tell how the other subjects reacted to the fit. (Indeed, there were no other subjects actually present.) The effects of group size on speed of helping, therefore, are due simply to the perceived presence of others rather than to the influence of their actions. This means that the experimental situation is unlike emergencies, such as a fire, in which bystanders interact with each other. It is, however, similar to emergencies, such as

the Genovese murder, in which spectators knew others were also watching but were prevented by walls between them from communication that might have counteracted the diffusion of responsibility.

The present results create serious difficulties for one class of commonly given explanations for the failure of bystanders to intervene in actual emergencies, those involving apathy or indifference. These explanations generally assert that people who fail to intervene are somehow different in kind from the rest of us, that they are "alienated by industrialization," "dehumanized by urbanization," "depersonalized by living in the cold society," or "psychopaths." These explanations serve a dual function for people who adopt them. First, they explain (if only in a nominal way) the puzzling and frightening problem of why people watch others die. Second, they give individuals reason to deny that they too might fail to help in a similar situation.

The results of this experiment seem to indicate that such personality variables may not be as important as these explanations suggest. Alienation, Machiavellianism, acceptance of social responsibility, need for approval, and authoritarianism are often cited in these explanations. Yet they did not predict the speed or likelihood of help. In sharp contrast, the perceived number of bystanders did. The explanation of bystander "apathy" may lie more in the bystander's response to other observers than in presumed personality deficiencies of "apathetic" individuals. Although this realization may force us to face the guilt-provoking possibility that we too might fail to intervene, it also suggests that individuals are not, of necessity, "nonintervenes" because of their personalities. If people understand the situational forces that can make them hesitate to intervene, they may better overcome them.

REFERENCES

Aronfreed, J. The origin of self-criticism. *Psychological Review*, 1964, *71*, 193–219.
Berkowitz, L., Klanderman, S., & Harris, R. Effects of experimenter awareness and sex of subject on reac-

tions to dependency relationships. *Sociometry*, 1964, 27, 327–329.

Christie, R. The prevalence of machiavellian orientations. Paper presented at the meeting of the American Psychological Association, Los Angeles, 1964.

Crowne, D., & Marlowe, D. *The approval motive.* New York: Wiley, 1964.

Daniels, L., & Berkowitz, L. Liking and response to dependency relationships. *Human Relations*, 1963,

16, 141–148.

Milgram, S., & Hollander, P. Murder they heard. *Nation*, 1964, *198*, 602–604.

Miller, N., & Dollard, J. *Social learning and imitation.* New Haven: Yale University Press, 1941.

Rosenthal, A. M. *Thirty-eight witnesses.* New York: McGraw-Hill, 1964.

Whiting, J. W. M., & Child, I. *Child training and personality.* New Haven: Yale University Press, 1953.

17

Counterfactual Thinking and Victim Compensation: A Test of Norm Theory

Dale T. Miller and Cathy McFarland

Recent research on helping behavior has shown that our emotional reaction to a victim affects our willingness to offer assistance. Situations that increase sympathy and positive feelings for a victim encourage helping. In this study, Miller and McFarland draw on new work from social cognition to show how irrelevant aspects of a situation can lead us to react to victims in seemingly nonlogical ("counterfactual") ways. Specifically, they propose that we feel greater sympathy toward a victim whose plight occurs in an unusual way that differs from the norm; we feel less sympathy for someone injured as part of a regular routine. The researchers show, for example, that subjects will offer less monetary compensation to a victim who is shot in front of a store that he regularly uses than to a victim shot in front of a store that he seldom uses and went to for a "change of pace." Although the victims suffer identical injuries in both cases, subjects appear to perceive the harmful event as worse if it results from a behavior that is out of the ordinary. This study represents a beginning effort to apply new ideas from social cognition research to the important real-world issue of helping those in need.

ABSTRACT. *Norm theory (Kahneman & Miller, 1986) identifies factors that determine the ease with which alternatives to reality can be imagined or constructed. One assumption of norm theory is that the greater the availability of imagined alternatives to an event, the stronger will be the affective reaction elicited by the event. The present two experiments* explore this assumption in the context of observers' reactions to victims. It was predicted that negative outcomes that strongly evoked positive alternatives would elicit more sympathy from observers than negative outcomes that weakly evoked positive alternatives. The ease of counterfactual thought was manipulated in the first experiment by the spatial distance between the negative outcome and a positive alternative, and in the second experiment by the habitualness of the actions that precipitated the victimization. Consistent with norm theory, subjects recommended more compensation for victims of fates for which a positive

Reprinted from *Personality and Social Psychology Bulletin*, 1986, 12(4), pp. 513–519. Copyright 1987 by the Society for Personality and Social Psychology, Inc. Reprinted by permission of Sage Publications, Inc. and the authors.

alternative was highly available. Implications of the results for various types of reactions to victims are discussed.

Consider two victims: a soldier who is killed on the last day of a war, a victim of a plane crash who switched to the fatal flight only minutes before take-off. If your reactions are similar to ours, the fates of these victims seem more "poignant" or "tragic" than those of the following two victims: a soldier who is killed six months before the end of a war and a victim of a plane crash who was booked on the fatal flight for three months. The outcome is clearly the same in these two sets of events, so why do they produce different reactions?

An explanation of this difference was proposed recently by Kahneman and Miller (1986). These authors contend that the affective impact of an event is influenced by its normality, which they define as the ease with which an alternative event can be imagined. The more strongly events evoke alternative outcomes, the more *abnormal* the events are, and the stronger is the emotional reaction that they elicit.

The normality of an outcome differs importantly from its probability. Judgments of probability are precomputed, whereas judgments of normality are postcomputed and reflect not what was expected but what the event itself evokes. In the airplane crash scenario, for example, it is not precomputed probability estimates that differentiate the two versions: the probability of being killed in a plane crash is unaffected by whether or not one switches flights. What differentiates the two versions is the postcomputed availability of a more positive alternative (Turnbull, 1981).

Kahneman and Miller (1986) proposed a number of principles that determine the abnormality of events as well as the affective reaction they elicit. One principle focuses on the distance (temporal or spatial) between the outcome and an imagined alternative outcome: the shorter the distance, the more abnormal the outcome. In the example of the soldier's death, it is easier to imagine the passage of 24 hours than 6 months and thus a death occurring 24 hours before the end of a war is more abnormal than one occurring 6 months before

the end. A second principle is that outcomes that follow unusual actions are easier to undo mentally or imagine otherwise, than outcomes that follow routine actions. This principle is illustrated in the example involving the plane crash victims. Because it is unusual to switch flights, a death that follows this action is abnormal, and will evoke a stronger reaction than the identical outcome preceded by a more typical sequence.

The present two experiments explore the relevance of norm theory for an understanding of observers' reactions to victims of negative events. The rationale guiding these experiments is that the more abnormal a victim's fate, the more sympathy the victim will elicit from observers. Each experiment presented subjects with descriptions of negative fates and elicited their recommendations for victim compensation. The experiments differed in the means by which abnormality was manipulated.

EXPERIMENT 1

Kahneman and Miller (1986) proposed that it is easier to imagine alternatives to abnormal or unusual actions than to normal or routine actions. They further argued that consequences that follow from abnormal actions are themselves more abnormal than consequences that follow from normal actions. Kahneman and Tversky (1982) tested this hypothesis by asking subjects to predict the degree of regret that victims of two different car crashes would experience. In one case the victim had taken his usual route to work and in the other case he had taken an atypical route. Subjects were virtually unanimous in their anticipation that the latter (abnormal) victim would experience more regret. The present experiment attempted to extend Kahneman and Tversky's (1982) findings to the domain of sympathy. Specifically, it was predicted that negative outcomes that follow abnormal actions would generate more sympathy in observers than ones that follow normal actions.

METHOD

Subjects and Procedure

Subjects were 164 volunteers recruited from an introductory psychology class. The study was described as being concerned with the factors that influence recommendations for victim compensation. Ostensibly, the goal of the experiment was to establish the amount of monetary payment that the public considers reasonable for various types of victims. Subjects were instructed to read a brief description of a victim who had recently applied for compensation and then decide upon monetary payment.

Subjects were provided with one of three descriptions that differed only in the abnormality of the outcome depicted. In all three conditions, the male victim was described as having lost the use of his right arm as a result of a gunshot wound. He had been shot when he walked in on a robbery occurring in a convenience store in his neighborhood. Further, they read that there were two convenience stores located near the victim's home, one of which he frequented more regularly than the other. In the normal outcome condition (n = 58), subjects read that on the night he was shot, the victim had gone to the store he most commonly frequented. We included two abnormal outcome conditions. In the first ($n = 48$), subjects read that on the night he was shot the victim had gone to the store that he rarely frequented for a "change of pace." In the second abnormal outcome condition ($n = 57$), subjects learned that the victim had gone to the store he rarely frequented because his usual store was temporarily closed for renovations. We employed two abnormal versions to assess whether the origins of the abnormal action (self-produced versus other-produced) would affect the sympathy evoked by the victim.

After reading the description, all subjects indicated on an 11-point scale how much money they believed the victim should receive in compensation for his loss (from zero dollars, 0, to one million dollars, 10). They were informed that the typical award was $500,000 (5).

RESULTS

A preliminary analysis revealed no significant difference between the two abnormal conditions ($t < 1$); thus, these conditions were collapsed for the subsequent analysis.

It was hypothesized that subjects would assign greater compensation to an individual whose victimization was preceded by abnormal actions than to one whose victimization was preceded by normal actions. This prediction was confirmed. Subjects assigned the victim who was shot at a store he rarely visited significantly more compensation, $M = 5.37$, than the victim who was shot at his regular store, $M = 4.52$, $t(162) = 2.17$, $p < .03$.

DISCUSSION

The results of Experiment 1 supported the hypothesis that victims whose negative fates follow abnormal actions receive more sympathy than victims whose negative fates follow normal actions. The negative fates in the two cases were identical, as were the prior probabilities of the two actions leading to the outcome in question. According to norm theory, the fate elicited stronger reactions when it stemmed from abnormal actions than when it stemmed from normal actions because it is easier for observers to imagine the event not happening in the former than in the latter instance. The fact that it almost did not happen appears to have made the fate worse and the sympathy for the victim greater.[1] A similar mechanism would appear to generate the strong reaction to the fate of the victim of the

---

[1] A possible alternative explanation of this finding deserves comment. Subjects may have believed that the victim in the normal condition was deserving of less compensation because he should have foreseen potential dangers. This account suggests that the condition difference occurred because the description in the normal condition suppressed sympathy rather than because the description in the abnormal condition facilitated sympathy. To rule this possibility out decisively it would be necessary to show that the observed effect occurred even when it was made explicit that the victim had no reason to expect that the commonly frequented store was any more dangerous than the less preferred store. This feature was not included in the present experiment, although it does not seem highly plausible that subjects believed that the victim would customarily frequent a store he knew to be more dangerous, especially when there was a readily available alternative store. In any event, the design of Experiment 2 avoided this interpretational problem.

plane crash who switched flights at the last minute. It is so easy to imagine this individual not switching, and thus not being on the fatal flight, that his or her death seems especially tragic.

EXPERIMENT 2

This experiment tested the hypothesis that the less distance that needs to be covered in order for a negative fate to be avoided, the more abnormal the fate will be and the more sympathy the victim will receive. Kahneman and Tversky (1982) also tested a variant of this principle in their investigation of emotional scripts. Subjects were presented with a description of two individuals (Mr. C. and Mr. D) who had missed their respective planes because the limousine they had shared from a downtown hotel had been delayed in traffic. Both men arrived at the airport expecting their plane to have departed 30 minutes earlier, but Mr. D discovered that his plane had been delayed and had departed only 5 minutes earlier. Subjects were asked to indicate whom they thought would be more upset. The virtually unanimous response was that Mr. D would be more upset. Here, then, is a case in which two fates that differed from one another neither in surprise (both parties expected to miss their flight) nor in consequence (both parties did miss their flight) elicited differential predictions of frustration. From the perspective of norm theory, this occurred because it is easier to imagine how 5 minutes might have been saved than 30 minutes. Mr. D, in effect, came closer to avoiding his fate than did Mr. C. The present experiment tested the hypothesis that the closer a victim is to a more positive alternative, the more sympathy the victim will generate in observers.

METHOD

Subjects and Procedure

Subjects were 25 volunteers recruited from an upper level psychology class. The rationale presented to subjects was identical to that in

Experiment 1. Subjects read one of two descriptions that varied in terms of the abnormality of the outcome. In both conditions, subjects read about a man who died when the small plane on which he was a passenger crashed in a remote northern area. Having received only minor injuries, the man had attempted to walk to safety. In the normal outcome condition ($n = 13$), he was described as having died from exposure 75 miles from the nearest town. In the abnormal outcome condition ($n = 12$), he was described as having died $\frac{1}{4}$ mile from the nearest town. After reading the description, subjects were asked to assign compensation to the victim's family (a wife and two children) using the same scale as that employed in Experiment 1.

RESULTS AND DISCUSSION

Again, we hypothesized that subjects in the abnormal outcome condition would recommend greater compensation than subjects in the normal outcome condition. This hypothesis was confirmed. The victim who died $\frac{1}{4}$ mile from safety was assigned significantly greater compensation, $M = 7.0$, than the victim who died 75 miles from safety, $M = 5.38$, $t(23) = 2.48$, $p < .02$.

The results supported the hypothesis that the closer a negative event is to not happening, the stronger is the reaction provoked by the event. This principle presumably also accounts for the poignancy of the death of a soldier on the last day of a war. Because the war was almost over, the death was almost avoided and hence was particularly tragic.

GENERAL DISCUSSION

According to norm theory (Kahneman & Miller, 1986), the more strongly outcomes evoke alternatives, the stronger will be any emotional reaction elicited by them. In support of their theory Kahneman and Miller described subjects' responses to questions about the degree of regret that various types of victims might be expected to experience. Consistent with their predictions, the more easily undone or imagined otherwise an event was, the more regret subjects expected it to generate.

The present studies extended the empirical scope of norm theory in a number of respects. Previous tests of the theory (Kahneman & Tversky, 1982) have focused exclusively on subjects' predictions about how recipients of differentially abnormal fates would react. Moreover, subjects' intuitions were probed in within-subject designs that presented subjects with two contrasting fates. The present studies, on the other hand, employed between-subject designs and elicited subjects' personal reactions to the victim, not their predictions of the victim's reaction. Finally, the present studies employed a socially relevant dependent measure: recommendations for victim compensation. The current results supported the guiding hypothesis that the sympathy generated by the victim of a negative event increases as the abnormality of the event increases. Abnormal fates elicited higher recommendations for compensation than normal ones, although they were objectively neither more severe nor more probable.

The present results suggest that norm theory may have considerable relevance for our understanding of reactions to victims. As a final illustration of norm theory's application to this domain, consider an incident that occurred some years ago in France. The incident was a bomb attack on a synagogue during which a number of people were injured. France's Prime Minister, Raymond Barre, publicly denounced the attack and expressed his sympathy for both the Jews who were inside the synagogue and the innocent passersby. Barre's differentiation of the victims into Jews and innocent passersby provoked considerable controversy because many interpreted it as implying that Barre did not consider the Jews to be as innocent as the passersby.

Certainly, the term "innocent" has a strong moral connotation, but should we assume that Barre's remarks reflect anti-Semitism? Not necessarily. According to norm theory, his failure to apply the term "innocent" to the Jews inside

the synagogue may simply reflect the fact that their fate is less abnormal than that of the passersby. It is easier mentally to remove the passersby from the immediate vicinity of the synagogue than the Jews. This analysis might also account for the special public sympathy that injured tourists received when a bomb went off in London's Harrods department store some years ago. Tourists and passersby are not entailed by the department store and synagogue scripts (Abelson, 1981), respectively, and as such their presence in these contexts is abnormal. The foregoing example suggests that one reason that the abnormality of a victim's fate affects the sympathy that he or she receives is because it affects the perceived innocence of the victim. Judgments of guilt or innocence may follow from, as well as influence, affective reactions to the suffering of others. Thus, not only may victims perceived to be innocent provoke strong affective reactions, but victims whose abnormality provokes strong affective reactions may be viewed as innocent.

In pursuing the implications of norm theory in the victim domain it is important to realize that it is not a theory of justice—it is a theory of emotional amplitude (Abelson, 1983). Norm theory makes predictions about the factors that influence the intensity of people's reactions to events, not their direction. In the present study, greater abnormality was associated with greater sympathy, but future research may find that in other situations greater abnormality is associated with greater blame or derogation. Further tests of the hypothesis might profitably include measures of blame, responsibility, and victim evaluation. More direct assessments of counterfactual thinking should also be included in future research.

REFERENCES

Abelson, R. P. (1981). The psychological status of the script concept. *American Psychologist, 36,* 715–729.

Abelson, R. P. (1983). Whatever became of consistency theory? *Personality and Social Psychology Bulletin, 9,* 37–54.

Kahneman, D., & Miller, D. T. (1986). Norm theory: Comparing reality to its alternatives. *Psychological Review, 93*, 136–153.

Kahneman, D., & Tversky, A. (1982). The simulation heuristic. In D. Kahneman, P. Slovic, & A. Tversky (Eds.), *Judgment under uncertainty: Heuristics and biases* (pp. 201–208). New York: Cambridge University Press.

Turnbull, W. (1981). Naive conceptions of free will and the deterministic paradox. *Canadian Journal of Behavioural Science, 13*, 1–13.

18

Opinions and Social Pressure

SOLOMON E. ASCH

Conformity can be defined as the voluntary performance of an act because others also do it. The teenager who dresses in the latest trendy fashions is conforming to social pressures; so is her father who wears the same conservative business suits as his corporate associates. People often have mixed attitudes about conformity— we want to be "rugged individualists" but fear being seen as a "deviate"; we recognize the virtues of being a "team player" but resist being called a "conformist." Social psychologists have long been interested in situational forces that lead to conformity. In a classic study conducted in the 1950s, Solomon Asch used laboratory experiments to study conformity. His method was simple. Subjects were asked to make judgments about the length of lines printed on cards—to indicate which of three comparison lines was the same length as a standard line. The task was easy and when subjects worked alone, they seldom made errors. But how would subjects react when confronted with a group who gave wrong answers? Would they go along with the majority or remain true to their own perceptions? Asch's findings— that a substantial proportion of individuals gave obviously wrong answers in order to go along with the group—provided evidence of the strength of social influence. But his research also provides hints of factors that make it easier for people to resist group pressures, such as the presence of another dissenter. Based on your own experiences, why do you think people sometimes yield to group pressure?

That social influences shape every person's practices, judgments and beliefs is a truism to which anyone will readily assent. A child masters his "native" dialect down to the finest nuances; a member of a tribe of cannibals accepts cannibalism as altogether fitting and proper. All the social sciences take their departure from the observation of the profound ef-

fects that groups exert on their members. For psychologists, group pressure upon the minds of individuals raises a host of questions they would like to investigate in detail.

How, and to what extent, do social forces constrain people's opinions and attitudes? This question is especially pertinent in our day. The same epoch that has witnessed the unprecedented technical extension of communication has also brought into existence the deliberate manipulation of opinion and the "engineering of consent." There are many good reasons why, as citizens and as scientists, we should be concerned with studying the ways in which human beings form their opinions and the role that social conditions play.

Studies of these questions began with the interest in hypnosis aroused by the French physician Jean Martin Charcot (a teacher of Sigmund Freud) toward the end of the 19th century. Charcot believed that only hysterical patients could be fully hypnotized, but this view was soon challenged by two other physicians, Hyppolyte Bernheim and A. A. Liébault, who demonstrated that they could put most people under the hypnotic spell. Bernheim proposed that hypnosis was but an extreme form of a normal psychological process which became known as "suggestibility." It was shown that monotonous reiteration of instructions could induce in normal persons in the waking state involuntary bodily changes such as swaying or rigidity of the arms, and sensations such as warmth and odor.

It was not long before social thinkers seized upon these discoveries as a basis for explaining numerous social phenomena, from the spread of opinion to the formation of crowds and the following of leaders. The sociologist Gabriel Tarde summed it all up in the aphorism: "Social man is a somnambulist."

When the new discipline of social psychology was born at the beginning of this century, its first experiments were essentially adaptations of the suggestion demonstration. The technique generally followed a simple plan. The subjects, usually college students, were asked to give their opinions or preferences concerning various matters; some time later they were again asked to state their choices, but now they were also informed of the opinions held by authorities or large groups of their peers on the same matters. (Often the alleged consensus was fictitious.) Most of these studies had substantially the same result: confronted with opinions contrary to their own, many subjects apparently shifted their judgments in the direction of the views of the majorities or the experts. The late psychologist Edward L. Thorndike reported that he had succeeded in modifying the esthetic preferences of adults

by this procedure. Other psychologists reported that people's evaluations of the merit of a literary passage could be raised or lowered by ascribing the passage to different authors. Apparently the sheer weight of numbers or authority sufficed to change opinions, even when no arguments for the opinions themselves were provided.

Now the very ease of success in these experiments arouses suspicion. Did the subjects actually change their opinions, or were the experimental victories scored only on paper? On grounds of common sense, one must question whether opinions are generally as watery as these studies indicate. There is some reason to wonder whether it was not the investigators who, in their enthusiasm for a theory, were suggestible, and whether the ostensibly gullible subjects were not providing answers which they thought good subjects were expected to give.

The investigations were guided by certain underlying assumptions, which today are common currency and account for much that is thought and said about the operations of propaganda and public opinion. The assumptions are that people submit uncritically and painlessly to external manipulation by suggestion or prestige, and that any given idea or value can be "sold" or "unsold" without reference to its merits. We should be skeptical, however, of the supposition that the power of social pressure necessarily implies uncritical submission to it: independence and the capacity to rise above group passion are also open to human beings. Further, one may question on psychological grounds whether it is possible as a rule to change a person's judgment of a situation or an object without first changing his knowledge or assumptions about it.

In what follows I shall describe some experiments in an investigation of the effects of group pressure which was carried out recently with the help of a number of my associates. The tests not only demonstrate the operations of group pressure upon individuals but also illustrate a new kind of attack on the problem and some of the more subtle questions that it raises.

A group of seven to nine young men, all college students, are assembled in a classroom for a "psychological experiment" in visual judgment. The experimenter informs them that they will be comparing the lengths of lines. He shows two large white cards. On one is a single vertical black line—the standard whose length is to be matched. On the other card are three vertical lines of various lengths. The subjects are to choose the one that is of the same length as the line on the other card. One of the three actually is of the same length; the other two are substantially different, the difference ranging from three quarters of an inch to an inch and three quarters. (See Figure 1.)

The experiment opens uneventfully. The subjects announce their answers in the order in which they have been seated in the room, and on the first round every person chooses the same matching line. Then a second set of cards is exposed; again the group is unanimous. The members appear ready to endure politely another boring experiment. On the third trial there is an unexpected disturbance. One person near the end of the group disagrees with all the others in his selection of the matching line. He looks surprised, indeed incredulous, about the disagreement. On the following trial he disagrees again, while the others remain unanimous in their choice. The dissenter becomes more and more worried and hesitant as the disagreement continues in succeeding trials; he may pause before announcing his answer and speak in a low voice, or he may smile in an embarrassed way.

What the dissenter does not know is that all the other members of the group were in-

structed by the experimenter beforehand to give incorrect answers in unanimity at certain points. The single individual who is not a party to this prearrangement is the focal subject of our experiment. He is placed in a position in which, while he is actually giving the correct answers, he finds himself unexpectedly in a minority of one, opposed by a unanimous and arbitrary majority with respect to a clear and simple fact. Upon him we have brought to bear two opposed forces: the evidence of his senses and the unanimous opinion of a group of his peers. Also, he must declare his judgments in public, before a majority which has also stated its position publicly.

The instructed majority occasionally reports correctly in order to reduce the possibility that the naive subject will suspect collusion against him. (In only a few cases did the subject actually show suspicion; when this happened, the experiment was stopped and the results were not counted.) There are 18 trials in each series, and on 12 of these the majority responds erroneously.

How do people respond to group pressure in this situation? I shall report first the statistical results of a series in which a total of 123 subjects from three institutions of higher learning (not including my own, Swarthmore College) were placed in the minority situation described above.

Two alternatives were open to the subject: he could act independently, repudiating the majority, or he could go along with the majority, repudiating the evidence of his senses. Of the 123 put to the test, a considerable percentage yielded to the majority. Whereas in ordinary circumstances individuals matching the lines will make mistakes less than 1 percent of the time, under group pressure the minority subjects swung to acceptance of the misleading majority's wrong judgments in 36.8 percent of the selections. (See Figure 2.)

Of course individuals differed in response. At one extreme, about one quarter of the subjects were completely independent and never agreed with the erroneous judgments of the majority. At the other extreme, some individuals went with the majority nearly all the time. The performances of individuals in this experi-

Figure 1. Subjects were shown two cards. One bore a standard line. The other bore three lines, one of which was the same length as the standard. The subjects were asked to choose the line of the same length as the standard.

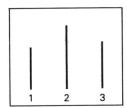

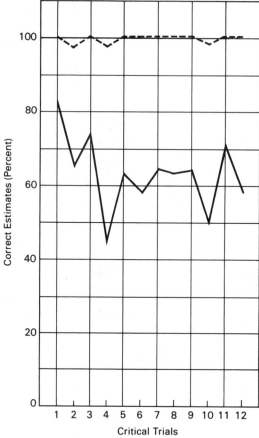

Figure 2. The accuracy of 123 subjects, each of whom compared lines in the presence of six to eight opponents, is plotted in the solid curve. The accuracy of judgments by subjects not under group pressure is indicated by the dotted line at top.

ment tend to be highly consistent. Those who strike out on the path of independence do not, as a rule, succumb to the majority even over an extended series of trials, while those who choose the path of compliance are unable to free themselves as the ordeal is prolonged.

The reasons for the startling individual differences have not yet been investigated in detail. At this point we can only report some tentative generalizations from talks with the subjects, each of whom was interviewed at the end of the experiment. Among the independent individuals were many who held fast because of staunch confidence in their own judgment. The most significant fact about them was not absence of responsiveness to the majority but a capacity to recover from doubt and to reestablish their equilibrium. Others who acted independently came to believe that the majority was correct in its answers, but they continued their dissent on the simple ground that it was their obligation to call the play as they saw it.

Among the extremely yielding persons we found a group who quickly reached the conclusion: "I am wrong, they are right." Others yielded in order "not to spoil your results." Many of the individuals who went along suspected that the majority were "sheep" following the first responder, or that the majority were victims of an optical illusion; nevertheless, these suspicions failed to free them at the moment of decision. More disquieting were the reactions of subjects who construed their difference from the majority as a sign of some general deficiency in themselves, which at all costs they must hide. On this basis they desperately tried to merge with the majority, not realizing the longer-range consequences to themselves. All the yielding subjects underestimated the frequency with which they conformed.

Which aspect of the influence of a majority is more important—the size of the majority or its unanimity? The experiment was modified to examine this question. In one series the size of the opposition was varied from one to 15 persons. The results showed a clear trend. (See Figure 3.) When a subject was confronted with only a single individual who contradicted his answers, he was swayed little: he continued to answer independently and correctly in nearly all trials. When the opposition was increased to two, the pressure became substantial: minority subjects now accepted the wrong answer 13.6 percent of the time. Under the pressure of a majority of three, the subjects' errors jumped to 31.8 percent. But further increases in the size of the majority apparently did not increase the weight of the pressure substantially. Clearly the size of the opposition is important only up to a point.

Disturbance of the majority's unanimity had a striking effect. In this experiment the subject was given the support of a truthful partner—

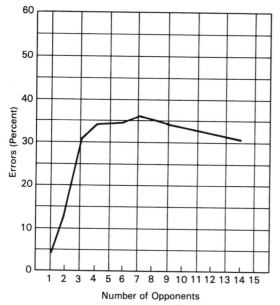

Figure 3. The size of the majority which opposed them had an effect on the subjects. With a single opponent the subject erred only 3.6 percent of the time; with two opponents he erred 13.6 percent of the time.

either another individual who did not know of the prearranged agreement among the rest of the group, or a person who was instructed to give correct answers throughout.

The presence of a supporting partner depleted the majority of much of its power. Its pressure on the dissenting individual was reduced to one fourth: that is, subjects answered incorrectly only one fourth as often as under the pressure of a unanimous majority. (See Figure 4.) The weakest persons did not yield as readily. Most interesting were the reactions to the partner. Generally the feeling toward him was one of warmth and closeness; he was credited with inspiring confidence. However, the subjects repudiated the suggestion that the partner decided them to be independent.

Was the partner's effect a consequence of his dissent, or was it related to his accuracy? We now introduced into the experimental group a person who was instructed to dissent from the majority but also to disagree with the subject. In some experiments the majority

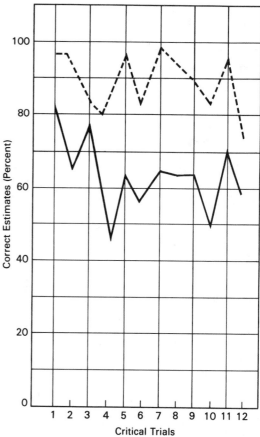

Figure 4. Two subjects supporting each other against a majority made fewer errors (dotted line at top) than one subject did against a majority (solid line at bottom).

was always to choose the worst of the comparison lines and the instructed dissenter to pick the line that was closer to the length of the standard one; in others the majority was consistently intermediate and the dissenter most in error. In this manner we were able to study the relative influence of "compromising" and "extremist" dissenters.

Again the results are clear. When a moderate dissenter is present, the effect of the majority on the subject decreases by approximately one third, and extremes of yielding disappear. Moreover, most of the errors the subjects do make are moderate, rather than flagrant. In short, the dissenter largely controls the choice of errors. To this extent the subjects broke away from the majority even while bending to it.

On the other hand, when the dissenter always chose the line that was more flagrantly different from the standard, the results were of quite a different kind. The extremist dissenter produced a remarkable freeing of the subjects; their errors dropped to only 9 percent. Furthermore, all the errors were of the moderate variety. We were able to conclude that dissent *per se* increased independence and moderated the errors that occurred, and that the direction of dissent exerted consistent effects.

In all the foregoing experiments each subject was observed only in a single setting. We now turned to studying the effects upon a given individual of a change in the situation to which he was exposed. The first experiment examined the consequences of losing or gaining a partner. The instructed partner began by answering correctly on the first six trials. With his support the subject usually resisted pressure from the majority: 18 of 27 subjects were completely independent. But after six trials the partner joined the majority. As soon as he did so, there was an abrupt rise in the subjects' errors. Their submission to the majority was just about as frequent as when the minority subject was opposed by a unanimous majority throughout.

It was surprising to find that the experience of having had a partner and of having braved the majority opposition with him had failed to strengthen the individuals' independence. Questioning at the conclusion of the experiment suggested that we had overlooked an important circumstance; namely, the strong specific effect of "desertion" by the partner to the other side. We therefore changed the conditions so that the partner would simply leave the group at the proper point. (To allay suspicion it was announced in advance that he had an appointment with the dean.) In this form of the experiment, the partner's effect outlasted his presence. The errors increased after his departure, but less markedly than after a partner switched to the majority.

In a variant of this procedure the trials began with the majority unanimously giving correct answers. Then they gradually broke away until on the sixth trial the naive subject was alone and the group unanimously against him. As long as the subject had anyone on his side, he was almost invariably independent, but as soon as he found himself alone, the tendency to conform to the majority rose abruptly.

As might be expected, an individual's resistance to group pressure in these experiments depends to a considerable degree on how wrong the majority is. We varied the discrepancy between the standard line and the other lines systematically, with the hope of reaching a point where the error of the majority would be so glaring that every subject would repudiate it and choose independently. In this we regretfully did not succeed. Even when the difference between the lines was seven inches, there were still some who yielded to the error of the majority.

The study provides clear answers to a few relatively simple questions, and it raises many others that await investigation. We would like to know the degree of consistency of persons in situations which differ in content and structure. If consistency of independence or conformity in behavior is shown to be a fact, how is it functionally related to qualities of character and personality? In what ways is independence related to sociological or cultural conditions? Are leaders more independent than other people, or are they adept at following their followers? These and many other questions may perhaps be answerable by investigations of the type described here.

Life in society requires consensus as an indispensable condition. But consensus, to be productive, requires that each individual contribute independently out of his experience and insight. When consensus comes under the dominance of conformity, the social process is polluted and the individual at the same time surrenders the powers on which his functioning as a feeling and thinking being depends. That we have found the tendency to conformity in our society so strong that reasonably intelligent and well-meaning young people are willing to call white black is a matter of concern. It raises questions about our ways of education and about the values that guide our conduct.

Yet anyone inclined to draw too pessimistic conclusions from this report would do well to remind himself that the capacities for indepen-

dence are not to be underestimated. He may also draw some consolation from a further observation: those who participated in this challenging experiment agreed nearly without exception that independence was preferable to conformity.

19

Behavioral Study of Obedience

STANLEY MILGRAM

Modern society depends on the willingness of people to follow the orders of legitimate authorities. Imagine the social chaos that would result if airline pilots refused to follow the directives of air traffic controllers, if citizens refused to follow orders from police officers and firefighters, if students en masse resisted the directions of their teachers, and if children invariably disobeyed their parents. But what are the limits of obedience to authority? When should people disobey authority and instead follow the dictates of their personal conscience and moral values? In a famous series of laboratory studies, Stanley Milgram provided a dramatic demonstration of just how difficult it can be for people to resist the requests of an authority figure, even when the subjects are asked to hurt another person. In this classic paper, Milgram describes in detail the method and results of his first obedience study. As you read Milgram's surprising results, think about the possible implications of this research for everyday life. Notice also that this study involves an elaborate deception in which naive subjects are led to believe that they are causing severe pain to a helpless victim. Some researchers have challenged the ethics of Milgram's research, arguing that it was inappropriate and possibly harmful to deceive subjects and to put them in such a stressful situation. Selections 27 and 28 take a closer look at this ethical debate.

ABSTRACT. This article describes a procedure for the study of destructive obedience in the laboratory. It consists of ordering a naive S to administer increasingly more severe punishment to a victim in the context of a learning experiment. Punishment is administered by means of a shock generator with 30 graded switches ranging from Slight Shock to Danger: Severe Shock. The victim is a confederate of the E.

The primary dependent variable is the maximum shock the S is willing to administer before he refuses to continue further. 26 Ss obeyed the experimental commands fully, and administered the highest shock on the generator. 14 Ss broke off the experiment at some point after the victim protested and refused to provide further answers. The procedure created extreme levels of nervous tension in some Ss. Profuse sweating, trembling, and stuttering were typical expressions of this emotional disturbance. One unexpected sign of tension—yet to be explained—was the regular occurrence of nervous laughter, which in

Reprinted from the *Journal of Abnormal and Social Psychology,* 1963, 67, pp. 371–378. Copyright 1963 by the American Psychological Association. Reprinted by permission of publisher and author.

some Ss developed into uncontrollable seizures. The variety of interesting behavioral dynamics observed in the experiment, the reality of the situation for the S, and the possibility of parametric variation within the framework of the procedure, point to the fruitfulness of further study.

Obedience is as basic an element in the structure of social life as one can point to. Some system of authority is a requirement of all communal living, and it is only the man dwelling in isolation who is not forced to respond, through defiance or submission, to the commands of others. Obedience, as a determinant of behavior, is of particular relevance to our time. It has been reliably established that from 1933–45 millions of innocent persons were systematically slaughtered on command. Gas chambers were built, death camps were guarded, daily quotas of corpses were produced with the same efficiency as the manufacture of appliances. These inhumane policies may have originated in the mind of a single person, but they could only be carried out on a massive scale if a very large number of persons obeyed orders.

Obedience is the psychological mechanism that links individual action to political purpose. It is the dispositional cement that binds men to systems of authority. Facts of recent history and observation in daily life suggest that for many persons obedience may be a deeply ingrained behavior tendency, indeed, a prepotent impulse overriding training in ethics, sympathy, and moral conduct. C. P. Snow (1961) points to its importance when he writes:

When you think of the long and gloomy history of man, you will find more hideous crimes have been committed in the name of obedience than have ever been committed in the name of rebellion. If you doubt that, read William Shirer's "Rise and Fall of the Third Reich." The German Officer Corps were brought up in the most rigorous code of obedience . . . in the name of obedience they were party to, and assisted in, the most wicked large scale actions in the history of the world [p. 24].

While the particular form of obedience dealt with in the present study has its antecedents in these episodes, it must not be thought all obedience entails acts of aggression against others. Obedience serves numerous productive functions. Indeed, the very life of society is predicated on its existence. Obedience may be ennobling and educative and refer to acts of charity and kindness, as well as to destruction.

General Procedure

A procedure was devised which seems useful as a tool for studying obedience (Milgram, 1961). It consists of ordering a naive subject to administer electric shock to a victim. A simulated shock generator is used, with 30 clearly marked voltage levels that range from 15 to 450 volts. The instrument bears verbal designations that range from Slight Shock to Danger: Severe Shock. The responses of the victim, who is a trained confederate of the experimenter, are standardized. The orders to administer shocks are given to the naive subject in the context of a "learning experiment" ostensibly set up to study the effects of punishment on memory. As the experiment proceeds the naive subject is commanded to administer increasingly more intense shocks to the victim, even to the point of reaching the level marked Danger: Severe Shock. Internal resistances become stronger, and at a certain point the subject refuses to go on with the experiment. Behavior prior to this rupture is considered "obedience," in that the subject complies with the commands of the experimenter. The point of rupture is the act of disobedience. A quantitative value is assigned to the subject's performance based on the maximum intensity shock he is willing to administer before he refuses to participate further. Thus for any particular subject and for any particular experimental condition the degree of obedience may be specified with a numerical value. The crux of the study is to systematically vary the factors believed to alter the degree of obedience to the experimental commands.

The technique allows important variables to be manipulated at several points in the experiment. One may vary aspects of the source of command, content and form of command, instrumentalities for its execution, target object, general social setting, etc. The problem, therefore, is not one of designing increasingly more numerous experimental conditions, but of selecting those that best illuminate the *process* of obedience from the sociopsychological standpoint.

Related Studies

The inquiry bears an important relation to philosophic analyses of obedience and authority (Arendt, 1958; Friedrich, 1958; Weber, 1947), an early experimental study of obedience by Frank (1944), studies in "authoritarianism" (Adorno, Frenkel-Brunswik, Levinson, & Sanford, 1950; Rokeach, 1961), and a recent series of analytic and empirical studies in social power (Cartwright, 1959). It owes much to the long concern with *suggestion* in social psychology, both in its normal forms (e.g., Binet, 1900) and in its clinical manifestations (Charcot, 1881). But it derives, in the first instance, from direct observation of a social fact; the individual who is commanded by a legitimate authority ordinarily obeys. Obedience comes easily and often. It is a ubiquitous and indispensable feature of social life.

METHOD

Subjects

The subjects were 40 males between the ages of 20 and 50, drawn from New Haven and the surrounding communities. Subjects were obtained by a newspaper advertisement and direct mail solicitation. Those who responded to the appeal believed they were to participate in a study of memory and learning at Yale University. A wide range of occupations is represented in the sample. Typical subjects were postal clerks, high school teachers, salesmen, engineers, and laborers. Subjects ranged in educational level from one who had not finished elementary school, to those who had doctorate and other professional degrees. They were paid $4.50 for their participation in the experiment. However, subjects were told that payment was simply for coming to the laboratory, and that the money was theirs no matter what happened

Table 1 Distribution of Age and Occupational Types in the Experiment

Occupations	20–29 Years *n*	30–39 Years *n*	40–50 Years *n*	*Percentage of Total (Occupations)*
Workers, skilled and unskilled	4	5	6	37.5
Sales, business, and white-collar	3	6	7	40.0
Professional	1	5	3	22.5
Percentage of total (Age)	20	40	40	

Note.—Total *N* = 40.

after they arrived. Table 1 shows the proportion of age and occupational types assigned to the experimental condition.

Personnel and Locale

The experiment was conducted on the grounds of Yale University in the elegant interaction laboratory. (This detail is relevant to the perceived legitimacy of the experiment. In further variations, the experiment was dissociated from the university, with consequences for performance.) The role of experimenter was played by a 31-year-old high school teacher of biology. His manner was impassive, and his appearance somewhat stern throughout the experiment. He was dressed in a gray technician's coat. The victim was played by a 47-year-old accountant, trained for the role; he was of Irish-American stock, whom most observers found mild-mannered and likable.

Procedure

One naive subject and one victim (an accomplice) performed in each experiment. A pretext had to be devised that would justify the administration of electric shock by the naive subject. This was effectively accomplished by the cover story. After a general introduction on the presumed relation between punishment and learning, subjects were told:

But actually, we know *very little* about the effect of punishment on learning, because almost no truly scientific studies have been made of it in human beings.

For instance, we don't know how *much* punishment is best for learning—and we don't know how much difference it makes as to who is giving the punishment, whether an adult learns best from a younger or an older person than himself—or many things of that sort.

So in this study we are bringing together a number of adults of different occupations and ages. And we're asking some of them to be teachers and some of them to be learners.

We want to find out just what effect different people have on each other as teachers and learners, and also what effect *punishment* will have on learning in this situation.

Therefore, I'm going to ask one of you to be the teacher here tonight and the other one to be the learner.

Does either of you have a preference?

Subjects then drew slips of paper from a hat to determine who would be the teacher and who would be the learner in the experiment. The drawing was rigged so that the naive subject was always the teacher and the accomplice always the learner. (Both slips contained the word "Teacher.") Immediately after the drawing, the teacher and learner were taken to an adjacent room and the learner was strapped into an "electric chair" apparatus.

The experimenter explained that the straps were to prevent excessive movement while the learner was being shocked. The effect was to make it impossible for him to escape from the situation. An electrode was attached to the learner's wrist, and electrode paste was applied "to avoid blisters and burns." Subjects were told that the electrode was attached to the shock generator in the adjoining room.

In order to improve credibility the experimenter declared, in response to a question by the learner: "Although the shocks can be extremely painful, they cause no permanent tissue damage."

Learning task. The lesson administered by the subject was a paired-associate learning task. The subject read a series of word pairs to the learner, and then read the first word of the pair along with four terms. The learner was to indicate which of the four terms had originally been paired with the first word. He com-

municated his answer by pressing one of four switches in front of him, which in turn lit up one of four numbered quadrants in an answer-box located atop the shock generator.

Shock generator. The instrument panel consists of 30 lever switches set in a horizontal line. Each switch is clearly labeled with a voltage designation that ranges from 15 to 450 volts. There is a 15-volt increment from one switch to the next going from left to right. In addition, the following verbal designations are clearly indicated for groups of four switches going from left to right: Slight Shock, Moderate Shock, Strong Shock, Very Strong Shock, Intense Shock, Extreme Intensity Shock, Danger: Severe Shock. (Two switches after this last designation are simply marked XXX.)

Upon depressing a switch: a pilot light corresponding to each switch is illuminated in bright red; an electric buzzing is heard; an electric blue light, labeled "voltage energizer," flashes; the dial on the voltage meter swings to the right; various relay clicks are sounded.

The upper left-hand corner of the generator is labeled Shock Generator, Type ZLB, Dyson Instrument Company, Waltham, Mass. Output 15 Volts–450 Volts.

Details of the instrument were carefully handled to insure an appearance of authenticity. The panel was engraved by precision industrial engravers, and all components were of high quality. No subject in the experiment suspected that the instrument was merely a simulated shock generator.

Sample shock. Each naive subject is given a sample shock on the shock generator, prior to beginning his run as teacher. This shock is always 45 volts, and is applied by pressing the third switch of the generator. The shock is applied to the wrist of the naive subject, and has its source in a 45-volt battery wired into the generator. This further convinces the subject of the authenticity of the generator.

Shock instructions. The subject is told to administer a shock to the learner each time he gives a wrong response. Moreover—and this is the key command—the subject is instructed to "move one level higher on the shock generator each time the learner flashes a wrong answer." He is also instructed to announce the voltage level before administering a shock. This serves to continually remind subjects of the increasing intensity of shocks administered to the learner.

Preliminary and regular run. Pretests revealed that the procedure of reading words and administering shocks requires some practice before it can be handled smoothly. Therefore, immediately preceding the regular run, the teacher is given a preliminary series of 10 words to read to the learner. There are 3 neutral words in the practice series (i.e., words that the learner answers correctly), so that shocks are administered for 7 of the words, with the maximum shock at 105 volts (moderate shock). Almost all subjects master the procedure by the time the preliminary run is over.

Subjects are then presented with a second list, and are told that the procedure is the same as for the first list; the experimenter adds, however:

When you get to the bottom of the list, repeat it over again, and continue giving shocks, until the learner has learned all the pairs correctly.

The experimenter instructs the subject to

start from 15 volts and increase the shock level one step each time the learner gives a wrong answer.

Feedback from the victim. In all conditions the learner gives a predetermined set of responses to the word pair test, based on a schedule of approximately three wrong answers to one correct answer. In the present experimental condition no vocal response or other sign of protest is heard from the learner until Shock Level 300 is reached. When the 300-volt shock is administered, the learner pounds on the wall of the room in which he is bound to the electric chair. The pounding can be heard by the subject. From this point on, the learner's answers no longer appear on the four-way panel.

At this juncture, subjects ordinarily turn to the experimenter for guidance. The experimenter instructs the subject to treat the absence of a response as a wrong answer, and to shock the subject according to the usual schedule.

He advises the subjects to allow 5–10 seconds before considering no response as a wrong answer, and to increase the shock level one step each time the learner fails to respond correctly. The learner's pounding is repeated after the 315-volt shock is administered; afterwards he is not heard from, nor do his answers reappear on the four-way signal box.

Experimenter feedback. At various points in the experiment the subject may turn to the experimenter for advice on whether he should continue to administer shocks. Or he may indicate that he does not wish to go on. It was important to standardize the experimenter's responses to these inquiries and reactions.

If the subject indicated his unwillingness to go on, the experimenter responded with a sequence of "prods," using as many as necessary to bring the subject into line.

Prod 1: Please continue. *or* Please go on.
Prod 2: The experiment requires that you continue.
Prod 3: It is absolutely essential that you continue.
Prod 4: You have no other choice, you *must* go on.

The prods were always made in sequence: Only if Prod 1 had been unsuccessful, could Prod 2 be used. If the subject refused to obey the experimenter after Prod 4, the experiment was terminated. The experimenter's tone of voice was at all times firm, but not impolite. The sequence was begun anew on each occasion that the subject balked or showed reluctance to follow orders.

Special prods. If the subject asked if the learner was liable to suffer permanent physical injury, the experimenter said:

Although the shocks may be painful, there is no permanent tissue damage, so please go on. [Followed by Prods 2, 3, and 4 if necessary.]

If the subject said that the learner did not want to go on, the experimenter replied:

Whether the learner likes it or not, you must go on until he has learned all the word pairs correctly. So please go on. [Followed by Prods 2, 3, and 4 if necessary.]

Dependent Measures

The primary dependent measure for any subject is the maximum shock he administers before he refuses to go any further. In principle this may vary from 0 (for a subject who refuses to administer even the first shock) to 30 (for a subject who administers the highest shock on the generator). A subject who breaks off the experiment at any point prior to administering the thirtieth shock level is termed a *defiant* subject. One who complies with experimental commands fully, and proceeds to administer all shock levels commanded, is termed an *obedient* subject.

Further records. With few exceptions, experimental sessions were recorded on magnetic tape. Occasional photographs were taken through one-way mirrors. Notes were kept on any unusual behavior occurring during the course of the experiments. On occasion, additional observers were directed to write objective descriptions of the subjects' behavior. The latency and duration of shocks were measured by accurate timing devices.

Interview and dehoax. Following the experiment, subjects were interviewed; open-ended questions, projective measures, and attitude scales were employed. After the interview, procedures were undertaken to assure that the subject would leave the laboratory in a state of well being. A friendly reconciliation was arranged between the subject and the victim, and an effort was made to reduce any tensions that arose as a result of the experiment.

RESULTS

Preliminary Notions

Before giving an account of the experimental results, it is instructive to consider how persons predict others will perform when commanded to administer powerful shocks to another person. Fourteen Yale seniors, all psychology majors, were provided with a detailed description of the experimental situation. They were asked to reflect carefully on it, and to predict the behavior of 100 hypothetical subjects. More specifically, they were instructed to plot the distribution of obedience of "100 Americans of diverse occupations, and ranging in age from 20 to 50 years," who were placed in the experimental situation.

There was considerable agreement among the respondents on the expected behavior of hypothetical subjects. All respondents predicted that only an insignificant minority would go through to the end of the shock series. (The estimates ranged from 0 to 3%; i.e., the most "pessimistic" member of the class predicted that of 100 persons, 3 would continue through to the most potent shock available on the shock generator—450 volts.) The class mean was 1.2%. The question was also posed informally to colleagues of the author, and the most general feeling was that few if any subjects would go beyond the designation Very Strong Shock.

Result of Experiment 1

Subjects accept situation. With few exceptions subjects were convinced of the reality of the experimental situation, that they were administering shocks to another person, and the most potent shocks were extremely painful. In the post-experimental interview subjects were asked: "How painful to the learner were the last few shocks that you administered to him?" Subjects were instructed to indicate their answers on a printed 14-point scale ranging from "Not at all painful" to "Extremely painful." The modal response was 14 (Extremely painful) with the mean at 13.42.

Signs of extreme tension. Many subjects showed signs of nervousness in the experimental situation, and especially upon administering the more powerful shocks. In a large number of cases the degree of tension reached extremes that are rarely seen in sociopsychological laboratory studies. Subjects were observed to sweat, tremble, stutter, bite their lips, groan, and dig their fingernails into their flesh. These were characteristic rather than exceptional responses to the experiment.

One sign of tension was the regular occurrence of nervous laughing fits. Fourteen of the 40 subjects showed definite signs of nervous laughter and smiling. The laughter seemed entirely out of place, even bizarre. Full-blown, uncontrollable seizures were observed for 3 subjects. On one occasion we observed a seizure so violently convulsive that it was necessary to call a halt to the experiment. The subject, a 46-year-old encyclopedia salesman, was seriously embarrassed by his untoward and uncontrollable behavior. In the post-experimental interviews subjects took pains to point out that they were not sadistic types, and that the laughter did not mean they enjoyed shocking the victim.

Distribution of scores. It had been conjectured that persons would not, in general, agree to administer shocks beyond the level designated as Very Strong Shock. The distribution of maximum shocks for this experiment is shown in Table 2. The obtained distribution of scores deviates radically from the prediction.

Upon command of the experimenter, each of the 40 subjects went beyond the expected breakoff point. No subject stopped prior to administering Shock Level 20. (At this level—300 volts—the victim kicks on the wall and no longer provides answers to the teacher's multiple-choice questions.)

Of the 40 subjects, 5 refused to obey the experimental commands beyond the 300-volt level. Four more subjects administered one further shock, and then refused to go on. Two broke off at the 330-volt level, and 1 each at 345, 360, and 375 volts. Thus a total of 14 subjects defied the experimenter. It is instructive to reprint their remarks at the point of defiance, as transcribed from the tape recordings:

[0124] I think he's trying to communicate, he's knocking. . . . Well it's not fair to shock the guy . . . these are terrific volts. I don't think this is very humane. . . . Oh, I can't go on with this; no, this isn't right. It's a hell of an experiment. The guy is suffering in there. No, I don't want to go on. This is crazy. [Subject refused to administer more shocks.]

[0123] He's banging in there. I'm gonna chicken out. I'd like to continue, but I can't do that to a man. . . . I'm sorry I can't do that to a man. I'll hurt his heart. You take your check. . . . No really, I couldn't do it.

These subjects were frequently in a highly agitated and even angered state. Sometimes,

Table 2 Distribution of Breakoff Points

Verbal Designation and Voltage Indication	Number of Subjects for Whom This Was Maximum Shock
Slight Shock	
15	0
30	0
45	0
60	0
Moderate Shock	
75	0
90	0
105	0
120	0
Strong Shock	
135	0
150	0
165	0
180	0
Very Strong Shock	
195	0
210	0
225	0
240	0
Intense Shock	
255	0
270	0
285	0
300	5
Extreme Intensity Shock	
315	4
330	2
345	1
360	1
Danger: Severe Shock	
375	1
390	0
405	0
420	0
XXX	
435	0
450	26

verbal protest was at a minimum, and the subject simply got up from his chair in front of the shock generator, and indicated that he wished to leave the laboratory.

Of the 40 subjects, 26 obeyed the orders of the experimenter to the end, proceeding to punish the victim until they reached the most potent shock available on the shock generator. At that point, the experimenter called a halt to the session. (The maximum shock is labeled 450 volts, and is two steps beyond the designation: Danger: Severe Shock.) Although obedient subjects continued to administer shocks, they often did so under extreme stress. Some expressed reluctance to administer shocks beyond the 300-volt level, and displayed fears similar to those who defied the experimenter; yet they obeyed.

After the maximum shocks had been delivered, and the experimenter called a halt to the proceedings, many obedient subjects heaved sighs of relief, mopped their brows, rubbed their fingers over their eyes, or nervously fumbled cigarettes. Some shook their heads, apparently in regret. Some subjects had remained calm throughout the experiment, and displayed only minimal signs of tension from beginning to end.

DISCUSSION

The experiment yielded two findings that were surprising. The first finding concerns the sheer strength of obedient tendencies manifested in this situation. Subjects have learned from childhood that it is a fundamental breach of moral conduct to hurt another person against his will. Yet, 26 subjects abandon this tenet in following the instructions of an authority who has no special powers to enforce his commands. To disobey would bring no material loss to the subject; no punishment would ensue. It is clear from the remarks and outward behavior of many participants that in punishing the victim they are often acting against their own values. Subjects often expressed deep disapproval of shocking a man in the face of his objections, and others denounced it as stupid and senseless. Yet the majority complied with the experimental commands. This outcome was surprising from two perspectives: first, from the standpoint of predictions made in the questionnaire described earlier. (Here, however, it is possible that the remoteness of the respondents from the actual situation, and the difficulty of conveying to them the concrete details of the ex-

periment, could account for the serious underestimation of obedience.)

But the results were also unexpected to persons who observed the experiment in progress, through one-way mirrors. Observers often uttered expressions of disbelief upon seeing a subject administer more powerful shocks to the victim. These persons had a full acquaintance with the details of the situation, and yet systematically underestimated the amount of obedience that subjects would display.

The second unanticipated effect was the extraordinary tension generated by the procedures. One might suppose that a subject would simply break off or continue as his conscience dictated. Yet, this is very far from what happened. There were striking reactions of tension and emotional strain. One observer related:

I observed a mature and initially poised businessman enter the laboratory smiling and confident. Within 20 minutes he was reduced to a twitching, stuttering wreck, who was rapidly approaching a point of nervous collapse. He constantly pulled on his earlobe, and twisted his hands. At one point he pushed his fist into his forehead and muttered: "Oh God, let's stop it." And yet he continued to respond to every word of the experimenter, and obeyed to the end.

Any understanding of the phenomenon of obedience must rest on an analysis of the particular conditions in which it occurs. The following features of the experiment go some distance in explaining the high amount of obedience observed in the situation.

1. The experiment is sponsored by and takes place on the grounds of an institution of unimpeachable reputation, Yale University. It may be reasonably presumed that the personnel are competent and reputable. The importance of this background authority is now being studied by conducting a series of experiments outside of New Haven, and without any visible ties to the university.

2. The experiment is, on the face of it, designed to attain a worthy purpose—advancement of knowledge about learning and memory. Obedience occurs not as an end in itself, but as an instrumental element in a situation

that the subject construes as significant, and meaningful. He may not be able to see its full significance, but he may properly assume that the experimenter does.

3. The subject perceives that the victim has voluntarily submitted to the authority system of the experimenter. He is not (at first) an unwilling captive impressed for involuntary service. He has taken the trouble to come to the laboratory presumably to aid the experimental research. That he later becomes an involuntary subject does not alter the fact that, initially, he consented to participate without qualification. Thus he has in some degree incurred an obligation toward the experimenter.

4. The subject, too, has entered the experiment voluntarily, and perceives himself under obligation to aid the experimenter. He has made a commitment, and to disrupt the experiment is a repudiation of this initial promise of aid.

5. Certain features of the procedure strengthen the subject's sense of obligation to the experimenter. For one, he has been paid for coming to the laboratory. In part this is canceled out by the experimenter's statement that:

Of course, as in all experiments, the money is yours simply for coming to the laboratory. From this point on, no matter what happens, the money is yours.[1]

6. From the subject's standpoint, the fact that he is the teacher and the other man the learner is purely a chance consequence (it is determined by drawing lots) and he, the subject, ran the same risk as the other man in being assigned the role of learner. Since the assignment of positions in the experiment was achieved by fair means, the learner is deprived of any basis of complaint on this count. (A similar situation obtains in Army units, in which—in the absence of volunteers—a particularly dangerous mission may be assigned by

drawing lots, and the unlucky soldier is expected to bear his misfortune with sportsmanship.)

7. There is, at best, ambiguity with regard to the prerogatives of a psychologist and the corresponding rights of his subject. There is a vagueness of expectation concerning what a psychologist may require of his subject, and when he is overstepping acceptable limits. Moreover, the experiment occurs in a closed setting, and thus provides no opportunity for the subject to remove these ambiguities by discussion with others. There are few standards that seem directly applicable to the situation, which is a novel one for most subjects.

8. The subjects are assured that the shocks administered to the subject are "painful but not dangerous." Thus they assume that the discomfort caused the victim is momentary, while the scientific gains resulting from the experiment are enduring.

9. Through Shock Level 20 the victim continues to provide answers on the signal box. The subject may construe this as a sign that the victim is still willing to "play the game." It is only after Shock Level 20 that the victim repudiates the rules completely, refusing to answer further.

These features help to explain the high amount of obedience obtained in this experiment. Many of the arguments raised need not remain matters of speculation, but can be reduced to testable propositions to be confirmed or disproved by further experiments.

The following features of the experiment concern the nature of the conflict which the subject faces.

10. The subject is placed in a position in which he must respond to the competing demands of two persons: the experimenter and the victim. The conflict must be resolved by meeting the demands of one or the other; satisfaction of the victim and the experimenter are mutually exclusive. Moreover, the resolution must take the form of a highly visible action, that of continuing to shock the victim or breaking off the experiment. Thus the subject is forced into a public conflict that does not permit any completely satisfactory solution.

11. While the demands of the experimenter

---

[1] Forty-three subjects, undergraduates at Yale University, were run in the experiment without payment. The results are very similar to those obtained with paid subjects.

carry the weight of scientific authority, the demands of the victim spring from his personal experience of pain and suffering. The two claims need not be regarded as equally pressing and legitimate. The experimenter seeks an abstract scientific datum; the victim cries out for relief from physical suffering caused by the subject's actions.

12. The experiment gives the subject little time for reflection. The conflict comes on rapidly. It is only minutes after the subject has been seated before the shock generator that the victim begins his protests. Moreover, the subject perceives that he has gone through but two-thirds of the shock levels at the time the subject's first protests are heard. Thus he understands that the conflict will have a persistent aspect to it, and may well become more intense as increasingly more powerful shocks are required. The rapidity with which the conflict descends on the subject, and his realization that it is predictably recurrent may well be sources of tension to him.

13. At a more general level, the conflict stems from the opposition of two deeply ingrained behavior dispositions: first, the disposition not to harm other people, and second, the tendency to obey those whom we perceive to be legitimate authorities.

REFERENCES

Adorno, T., Frenkel-Brunswik, Else, Levinson, D. J., & Sanford, R. N. *The authoritarian personality.* New York: Harper, 1950.

Arendt, H. What was authority? In C. J. Friedrich (Ed.), *Authority.* Cambridge: Harvard University Press, 1958. Pp. 81–112.

Binet, A. *La suggestibilité.* Paris: Schleicher, 1900.

Buss, A. H. *The psychology of aggression.* New York: Wiley, 1961.

Cartwright, S. (Ed.) *Studies in social power.* Ann Arbor: University of Michigan Institute for Social Research, 1959.

Charcot, J. M. *Oeuvres complètes.* Paris: Bureaux du Progrès Médical, 1881.

Frank, J. D. Experimental studies of personal pressure and resistance. *Journal of General Psychology,* 1944, *30,* 23–64.

Friedrich, C. J. (Ed.) *Authority.* Cambridge: Harvard University Press, 1958.

Milgram, S. *Dynamics of obedience.* Washington: National Science Foundation, 25 January 1961. (Mimeo)

Milgram, S. Some conditions of obedience and disobedience to authority. *Human Relations,* 1964, in press.

Rokeach, M. Authority, authoritarianism, and conformity. In I. A. Berg & B. M. Bass (Eds.), *Conformity and deviation.* New York: Harper, 1961. Pp. 230–257.

Snow, C. P. Either-or. *Progressive,* 1961(Feb.), *24.*

Weber, M. *The theory of social and economic organization.* Oxford: Oxford University Press, 1947.

20

Experiments in Group Conflict

Muzafer Sherif

The news provides frequent evidence of group conflicts: warring nations, striking workers, opposing religious factions, rival teenage gangs, child custody battles, and many others. Are there common social-psychological processes that help us to understand the origins of intergroup conflict and perhaps point to solutions? In the late 1940s, Muzafer Sherif proposed that intergroup tension and hostility arise when groups are put in a situation of direct competition where a win for one group means a loss for the other. Therefore, intergroup conflict can be reduced by changing the conditions of interdependence between groups, so that they must work cooperatively to achieve shared goals. To demonstrate these principles, Sherif designed an ingenious naturalistic field experiment. For three summers, Sherif and his colleagues ran a summer camp for boys. Although the children didn't know it, they were randomly assigned to groups, and then systematically exposed to different types of intergroup contact (isolation, competition, or cooperation), all as part of typical camp activities. The results of Sherif's work demonstrated the importance of competition and cooperation in intergroup relations. In the 40 years since this classic research was undertaken, numerous studies have confirmed this basic finding and have further specified the precise conditions of contact between groups that are most likely to produce harmony. What might be the implications of this research for reducing interracial conflict in inner city schools or for negotiating child custody arrangements following a divorce?

Conflict between groups—whether between boys' gangs, social classes, "races" or nations—has no simple cause, nor is mankind yet in sight of a cure. It is often rooted deep in personal, social, economic, religious and historical forces. Nevertheless it is possible to identify certain general factors which have a crucial influence on the attitude of any group toward others. Social scientists have long sought to bring these factors to light by studying what might be called the "natural history" of groups and group relations. Intergroup conflict and harmony is not a subject that lends itself easily to laboratory experiments. But in recent years there has been a beginning of attempts to investigate the problem under controlled yet lifelike conditions, and I shall report here the results of a program of experimental studies of groups which I started in 1948. Among the persons working with me were Marvin B. Sussman, Robert Huntington, O. J. Harvey, B. Jack White, William R. Hood and Carolyn W. Sherif. The experiments were conducted in 1949, 1953 and 1954; this article gives a composite of the findings.

We wanted to conduct our study with groups of the informal type, where group organization and attitudes would evolve naturally and spontaneously, without formal direction or external pressures. For this purpose we conceived that an isolated summer camp would make a good experimental setting, and that decision led us

From "Experiments in Group Conflict" by Muzafer Sherif. *Scientific American*, 1956, *195*(5), pp. 54–58. Copyright © 1956 by Scientific American, Inc. All rights reserved.

to choose as subjects boys about 11 or 12 years old, who would find camping natural and fascinating. Since our aim was to study the development of group relations among these boys under carefully controlled conditions, with as little interference as possible from personal neuroses, background influences or prior experiences, we selected normal boys of homogeneous background who did not know one another before they came to the camp.

They were picked by a long and thorough procedure. We interviewed each boy's family, teachers and school officials, studied his school and medical records, obtained his scores on personality tests and observed him in his classes and at play with his schoolmates. With all this information we were able to assure ourselves that the boys chosen were of like kind and background: all were healthy, socially well-adjusted, somewhat above average in intelligence and from stable, white, Protestant, middleclass homes.

None of the boys was aware that he was part of an experiment on group relations. The investigators appeared as a regular camp staff—camp directors, counselors and so on. The boys met one another for the first time in buses that took them to the camp, and so far as they knew it was a normal summer of camping. To keep the situation as lifelike as possible, we conducted all our experiments within the framework of regular camp activities and games. We set up projects which were so interesting and attractive that the boys plunged into them enthusiastically without suspecting that they might be test situations. Unobtrusively we made records of their behavior, even using "candid" cameras and microphones when feasible.

We began by observing how the boys became a coherent group. The first of our camps was conducted in the hills of northern Connecticut in the summer of 1949. When the boys arrived, they were all housed at first in one large bunkhouse. As was to be expected, they quickly formed particular friendships and chose buddies. We had deliberately put all the boys together in this expectation, because we wanted to see what would happen later after the boys were separated into different groups. Our object was to reduce the factor of personal attraction in the formation of groups. In a few days we divided the boys into two groups and put them in different cabins. Before doing so, we asked each boy informally who his best friends were, and then took pains to place the "best friends" in different groups so far as possible. (The pain of separation was assuaged by allowing each group to go at once on a hike and camp-out.)

As everyone knows, a group of strangers brought together in some common activity soon acquires an informal and spontaneous kind of organization. It comes to look upon some members as leaders, divides up duties, adopts unwritten norms of behavior, develops an *esprit de corps*. Our boys followed this pattern as they shared a series of experiences. In each group the boys pooled their efforts, organized duties and divided up tasks in work and play. Different individuals assumed different responsibilities. One boy excelled in cooking. Another led in athletics. Others, though not outstanding in any one skill, could be counted on to pitch in and do their level best in anything the group attempted. One or two seemed to disrupt activities, to start teasing at the wrong moment or offer useless suggestions. A few boys consistently had good suggestions and showed ability to coordinate the efforts of others in carrying them through. Within a few days one person had proved himself more resourceful and skillful than the rest. Thus, rather quickly, a leader and lieutenants emerged. Some boys sifted toward the bottom of the heap, while others jockeyed for higher positions.

We watched these developments closely and rated the boys' relative positions in the group, not only on the basis of our own observations but also by informal sounding of the boys' opinions as to who got things started, who got things done, who could be counted on to support group activities.

As the group became an organization, the boys coined nicknames. The big, blond, hardy leader of one group was dubbed "Baby Face" by his admiring followers. A boy with a rather long head became "Lemon Head." Each group developed its own jargon, special jokes, secrets and special ways of performing tasks. One group, after killing a snake near a place where it had gone to swim, named the place "Moccasin Creek" and thereafter preferred this swimming hole to any other, though there were better ones nearby.

Wayward members who failed to do things "right" or who did not contribute their bit to the common effort found themselves receiving the "silent treatment," ridicule or even threats. Each group selected symbols and a name, and they had these put on their caps and T-shirts. The 1954 camp was conducted in Oklahoma, near a famous hideaway of Jesse James called Robber's Cave. The two groups of boys at this camp named themselves the Rattlers and the Eagles.

Our conclusions on every phase of the study were based on a variety of observations, rather than on any single method. For example, we devised a game to test the boys' evaluations of one another. Before an important baseball game, we set up a target board for the boys to throw at, on the pretense of making practice for the game more interesting. There were no marks on the front of the board for the boys to judge objectively how close the ball came to a bull's-eye, but, unknown to them, the board was wired to flashing lights behind so that an observer could see exactly where the ball hit. We found that the boys consistently overestimated the performances by the most highly regarded members of their group and underestimated the scores of those of low social standing.

The attitudes of group members were even more dramatically illustrated during a cookout in the woods. The staff supplied the boys with unprepared food and let them cook it themselves. One boy promptly started to build a fire, asking for help in getting wood. Another attacked the raw hamburger to make patties. Others prepared a place to put buns, relishes and the like. Two mixed soft drinks from flavoring and sugar. One boy who stood around without helping was told by the others to "get to it." Shortly the fire was blazing and the cook had hamburgers sizzling. Two boys distributed them as rapidly as they became edible. Soon

it was time for the watermelon. A low-ranking member of the group took a knife and started toward the melon. Some of the boys protested. The most highly regarded boy in the group took over the knife, saying, "You guys who yell the loudest get yours last."

When the two groups in the camp had developed group organization and spirit, we proceeded to the experimental studies of intergroup relations. The groups had had no previous encounters; indeed, in the 1954 camp at Robber's Cave the two groups came in separate buses and were kept apart while each acquired a group feeling.

Our working hypothesis was that when two groups have conflicting aims—*i.e.*, when one can achieve its ends only at the expense of the other—their members will become hostile to each other even though the groups are composed of normal well-adjusted individuals. There is a corollary to this assumption which we shall consider later. To produce friction between the groups of boys we arranged a tournament of games: baseball, touch football, a tug-of-war, a treasure hunt and so on. The tournament started in a spirit of good sportsmanship. But as it progressed good feeling soon evaporated. The members of each group began to call their rivals "stinkers," "sneaks" and "cheaters." They refused to have anything more to do with individuals in the opposing group. The boys in the 1949 camp turned against buddies whom they had chosen as "best friends" when they first arrived at the camp. A large proportion of the boys in each group gave negative ratings to all the boys in the other. The rival groups made threatening posters and planned raids, collecting secret hoards of green apples for ammunition. In the Robber's Cave camp the Eagles, after a defeat in a tournament game, burned a banner left behind by the Rattlers; the next morning the Rattlers seized the Eagles' flag when they arrived on the athletic field. From that time on name-calling, scuffles and raids were the rule of the day.

Within each group, of course, solidarity increased. These were changes: one group deposed its leader because he could not "take it" in the contests with the adversary; another group overnight made something of a hero of a big boy who had previously been regarded as a bully. But morale and cooperativeness within the group became stronger. It is noteworthy that this heightening of cooperativeness and generally democratic behavior did not carry over to the group's relations with other groups.

We now turned to the other side of the problem: How can two groups in conflict be brought into harmony? We first undertook to test the theory that pleasant social contacts between members of conflicting groups will reduce friction between them. In the 1954 camp we brought the hostile Rattlers and Eagles together for social events: going to the movies, eating in the same dining room and so on. But far from reducing conflict, these situations only served as opportunities for the rival groups to berate and attack each other. In the dining-hall line they shoved each other aside, and the group that lost the contest for the head of the line shouted "Ladies first!" at the winner. They threw paper, food and vile names at each other at the tables. An Eagle bumped by a Rattler was admonished by his fellow Eagles to brush "the dirt" off his clothes.

We then returned to the corollary of our assumption about the creation of conflict. Just as competition generates friction, working in a common endeavor should promote harmony. It seemed to us, considering group relations in the everyday world, that where harmony between groups is established, the most decisive factor is the existence of "superordinate" goals which have a compelling appeal for both but which neither could achieve without the other. To test this hypothesis experimentally, we created a series of urgent, and natural, situations which challenged our boys.

One was a breakdown in the water supply. Water came to our camp in pipes from a tank about a mile away. We arranged to interrupt it and then called the boys together to inform them of the crisis. Both groups promptly volunteered to search the water line for the trouble. They worked together harmoniously, and be-

fore the end of the afternoon they had located and corrected the difficulty.

A similar opportunity offered itself when the boys requested a movie. We told them that the camp could not afford to rent one. The two groups then got together, figured out how much each group would have to contribute, chose the film by a vote and enjoyed the showing together.

One day the two groups went on an outing at a lake some distance away. A large truck was to go to town for food. But when everyone was hungry and ready to eat, it developed that the truck would not start (we had taken care of that). The boys got a rope—the same rope they had used in their acrimonious tug-of-war—and all pulled together to start the truck.

These joint efforts did not immediately dispel hostility. At first the groups returned to the old bickering and name-calling as soon as the job in hand was finished. But gradually the series of cooperative acts reduced friction and conflict. The members of the two groups began to feel more friendly to each other. For example, a Rattler whom the Eagles disliked for his sharp tongue and skill in defeating them became a "good egg." The boys stopped shoving in the meal line. They no longer called each other names, and sat together at the table. New friendships developed between individuals in the two groups.

In the end the groups were actively seeking opportunities to mingle, to entertain and "treat" each other. They decided to hold a joint campfire. They took turns presenting skits and songs. Members of both groups requested that they go home together on the same bus, rather than on the separate buses in which they had come. On the way the bus stopped for refreshments. One group still had five dollars which they had won as a prize in a contest. They decided to spend this sum on refreshments. On their own initiative they invited their former rivals to be their guests for malted milks.

Our interviews with the boys confirmed this change. From choosing their "best friends" almost exclusively in their own group, many of them shifted to listing boys in the other group as best friends. They were glad to have a second chance to rate boys in the other group, some of them remarking that they had changed their minds since the first rating made after the tournament. Indeed they had. The new ratings were largely favorable.

Efforts to reduce friction and prejudice between groups in our society have usually followed rather different methods. Much attention has been given to bringing members of hostile groups together socially, to communicating accurate and favorable information about one group to the other, and to bringing the leaders of groups together to enlist their influence. But as everyone knows, such measures sometimes reduce intergroup tensions and sometimes do not. Social contacts, as our experiments demonstrated, may only serve as occasions for intensifying conflict. Favorable information about a disliked group may be ignored or reinterpreted to fit stereotyped notions about the group. Leaders cannot act without regard for the prevailing temper in their own groups.

What our limited experiments have shown is that the possibilities for achieving harmony are greatly enhanced when groups are brought together to work toward common ends. Then favorable information about a disliked group is seen in a new light, and leaders are in a position to take bolder steps toward cooperation. In short, hostility gives way when groups pull together to achieve overriding goals which are real and compelling to all concerned.

21

Identifiability as a Deterrent to Social Loafing: Two Cheering Experiments

KIPLING WILLIAMS, STEPHEN HARKINS, AND BIBB LATANÉ

At a major sports event, the roar of the crowd can be deafening, as loyal fans cheer their team toward victory. The question is, does an individual cheer as loudly when part of a group as he or she does when alone? The answer from socio-psychological research may surprise you. In one study, for example, college students were asked to make as much noise as they could by shouting. When students shouted in groups of six, each individual shouted only 74 percent as intensely as when shouting alone. This phenomenon—that people sometimes exert less effort when working in groups compared to working alone—has been called "social loafing." In this paper, Williams, Harkins, and Latané attempt to explain "social loafing" by investigating the importance of identifiability. They argue that in groups, the work of each individual is usually unidentifiable and so motivation to work hard is diminished. In contrast, when people work alone, their effort is usually readily apparent and so motivation is higher. In two experiments using cheering as the measure of effort, the researchers separate the effects of group size and identifiability. Results support the importance of identifiability, by showing that social loafing can be eliminated in groups, and that people whose work is not identifiable tend to loaf even when alone. What lessons might group leaders learn from this research about how to get group members to perform at their best?

ABSTRACT. *Two experiments tested the extent to which the identifiability of one's individual output moderates social loafing—the reduction of individual efforts due to the social presence of others. In the first stage of Experiment 1, participants were asked to produce noise either alone, in groups of two and six, or in pseudogroups where the individuals actually shouted alone but believed that one or five other people were shouting with them. As in previous research, people exerted less effort when they thought that they were shouting in groups than when they shouted alone. In the second stage, the same people were led to believe that their outputs would be identifiable even when they cheered in groups. This manipu-lation eliminated social loafing. Experiment 2 demonstrated that when individual outputs are al-ways identifiable (even in groups), people consistently exert high levels of effort, and if their outputs are never identifiable (even when alone), they consistently exert low levels of effort across all group sizes. In concert, these studies suggest that identifiability is an important mediator of social loafing.*

In Western civilization it is commonly believed that being identified as the source of one's accomplishments and errors has an important effect on performance. Painters would be less motivated to create masterpieces if they could not sign their work in order to gain their deserved recognition. Actors are often as concerned about their billings as their roles. Athletes perform with one eye on their teams'

Reprinted from the *Journal of Personality and Social Psychology*, 1981, *40*, pp. 303–311. Copyright 1981 by the American Psychological Association. Reprinted by permission of publisher and authors.

standing and another on their individual statistics. Even in the People's Republic of China, where collective accomplishments enjoy ideological primacy, assembly line workers are asked to sign their work, presumably to improve the quantity and quality of the product. As a final example, we suspect that researchers might be less motivated to conduct experiments and write them up if they were not able to display their names somewhere on the published work.

In short, people seem to be more likely to do a task well if their work is identifiable to other people, especially if the other people are in some way important sources of reinforcement. Conversely, when people's outputs are unidentifiable, they seem to feel less motivated to perform well, either because they are unable to reap their proper rewards or because they can "get away" with taking it easy without incurring criticism or blame.

We feel that this process of reduced effort due to unidentifiability will help to explain a relatively old phenomenon that has recently been receiving renewed attention—a phenomenon we call "social loafing." Social loafing refers to the reduction of individual effort exerted when people work in groups compared to when they work alone.

In the first of a recent series of experiments on social loafing, Latané, Williams, and Harkins (1979) asked college students to generate noise, either alone or in concert. Sometimes clapping, sometimes shouting, participants managed to produce only twice as much noise in groups of four and 2.4 times as much in groups of six as when alone. In a second experiment designed to analyze the causes of this shortfall of collective effort, Latané et al. asked participants to shout either alone, in actual groups of two and six, or in pseudogroups in which each individual actually shouted alone, but believed she or he was shouting with one or five other persons. The existence of social loafing is demonstrated by the fact that when performers believed that one other person was yelling, they shouted 82% as intensely as when alone but when they believed that five others were yelling, they shouted only 74% as intensely. From these and other data, Latané et

al. concluded that about half of the decrement in group performance on this task was due to social loafing, with the rest being attributable to inefficiencies of group coordination and sound cancellation (Steiner, 1972). Harkins, Latané, and Williams (1980) replicated these results with a between-subjects as well as a within-subjects design.

Similar results have been obtained by Ingham, Levinger, Graves, and Peckham (1974) who, replicating an early study by Ringelmann (reported by Dashiell, 1935, and Moede, 1927), found that participants in a tug-of-war pulled less hard on the rope if they believed that other people are pulling with them, and by Kerr and Brunn (in press) who found that participants pumped a rubber sphymograph bulb less hard when they believed that three other people were pumping with them.

Common to each of these demonstrations of social loafing is that there was but a single instrument for measuring group productivity. In the case of rope pulling, one strain gauge measured the total amount of pressure exerted; for bulb pumping, one spirometer measured the total airflow produced; and in sound production tasks, one sound-level meter measured the total amount of noise. Thus, for each type of task there was only one reading for a solitary performance and only one reading for a group performance. In Davis' (1969) terminology, these tasks are information-reducing in contrast to information-conserving tasks that preserve individual performances.

Because of this feature, individual efforts were identifiable only when participants worked alone. When in groups, individual outputs were lost in the crowd, submerged in the total, separately unrecoverable by the experimenters. This lack of identifiability in groups may have led people to feel less motivation to do well, less need to work hard. This could be due to expectations that they could not be blamed for poor performances nor receive credit for good performances (e.g., Maslach, 1974). Thus, decreases in individual performance when working in groups compared to working alone may result from the fact that individual performances are less identifiable when working in groups than when alone.

The present set of experiments attempts to demonstrate that identifiability is a crucial factor in accounting for the decrement in individual performance in groups. If this is the case, making individual outputs identifiable even when performing in groups should eliminate the decrement. Experiment 1 was designed to test this prediction.

EXPERIMENT 1

Groups of six college males were asked to shout as loudly as they could for a series of 5-sec trials, sometimes shouting alone, and at other times shouting in pairs or sixes. They were unable to see or hear themselves, the other members of their group, or the experimenters. In Stage 1, participants believed that their outputs would be identifiable to the experimenters when they shouted alone, but not when they shouted in groups, since only the group total was accessible. In Stage 2 all persons were given microphones and told that their individual outputs would be identifiable to the experimenters even when they shouted in groups.

In fact, we were able to measure individual outputs alone and in pseudogroups throughout both stages. This was necessary because analysis of total group output results in additional sources of collective inefficiency such as coordination loss and sound cancellation, where maximum outputs are not simultaneously exerted or effective.

Method

Eight groups of six male undergraduate volunteers, a group at a time, heard the following instructions:

In our experiment today we are interested in the effects of sensory feedback on the production of sound in social groups. We will ask you to produce sounds by shouting in groups of one, two, or six, and we will record the sound output on the sound-level meter that you can see up here in front. Although this is not a competition and you will not learn your scores until the end of the experiment, we would like you to make your sounds as loud as possible. Since we are interested in sensory feedback, we will ask you to wear blindfolds and earphones and, as you will see, will arrange it so that you will not be able to hear yourself as you shout.

We realize it may seem strange to you to shout as loud as you can, especially since other people are around. Remember that the room is soundproofed and that people outside the room will not be able to hear you. In addition, because you will be wearing blindfolds and headsets, the other subjects will not be able to hear you or see you. Please, therefore, feel free to let loose and really shout. As I said, we are interested in how loud you can shout and there is no reason not to do your best. Here's your chance to really give it a try. Do you have any questions?

Stage 1. Once participants had donned their headsets and blindfolds, they went through a series of 25 trials on which one to six people shouted. Each trial was preceded by the announcement of the identification letters of participants who were to perform. Their yells were coordinated by a tape-recorded voice counting backwards from 3, followed by a ring of a bell. Thirteen of the trials consisted of each person shouting four times in a group of six, once in a group of two, and once by himself. Interspersed with these trials were twelve trials, two for each participant, in which one person's headset was switched to a separate track on the stereophonic instruction tape. On these trials, everyone was told that only that person should shout, but the person himself was led to believe either that one other person would shout with him or that all six would shout. Thus, each person had eight chances to yell (each shouted by himself) in actual groups of two and six and in pseudogroups of two and six. Trials were arranged such that everyone had approximately equal rest periods between the trials on which he performed and so that pseudogroup trials were evenly distributed to eliminate possible confounds with practice and fatigue. After the first series of 25 trials people were invited to remove their blindfolds and headsets and to take a breather.

Stage 2. Participants were then told:

Up to this point we haven't monitored your individual outputs when you have shouted in groups but have looked only at the group total. So when you yelled in groups of two or six we could not tell how loudly each of you yelled. Now, however, we are going to put individual microphones on each of you. In this way we will be able to tell exactly how loudly you are yelling alone or in groups of two and six and can determine each person's contribution to the group output. Remember that this is not a competition and you will not know your scores until afterwards, but we want you to shout as loudly as you can.

Everyone was given an individual lavaliere microphone to hang around his neck. One experimenter went into the adjoining control room where, visible through the one-way window, he spent about 5 minutes carefully calibrating for each person in turn a bank of compressor amplifiers. Each participant was asked to shout at exactly 75 dB (C) while, with a great many hand signals and other messages, the experimenters adjusted the compressor amplifiers appropriately. After the completion of calibration, participants were cautioned about moving their microphones and they donned their headsets and blindfolds once again in preparation for the second series of 25 trials.

Although it is possible that with the appropriate microphones and associated circuitry we might actually have been able to monitor individual performance levels, our equipment did not in fact allow us to do this. This failing is not serious, however, since the logic of the experiment demanded only that participants *believe* that they were being individually monitored.

Sound production was measured by a General Radio Model 1565B sound-level meter set to the slow time constant and C scale and located 4 m in front of and equidistant from each participant. The dB readings, which are logarithmically scaled, were converted to dynes/cm^2, the physical unit of measurement for sound. Dynes/cm^2 are ratio scaled, allowing us to make inferences about their relative magnitudes. Data were analyzed in a 2 (Stage) $\times$ 3 (Group Size) analysis of variance (ANOVA) in which both variables were within-subjects factors. The unit of analysis was the group and each score was based on the average output per person.

Results

We believe participants took the task seriously and devoted a good deal of effort to doing well on it. When shouting alone, they averaged 9.50 dynes/cm^2 (94 dB). This sound level is very close to that obtained in previous experiments in this series (Latané et al., 1979) and, from a distance of 4 m, is comparable to the noise in a subway station when a train comes through.

Stage 1. Although people were able to produce more total sound pressure when they shouted in groups, groups did not produce as much sound as would be expected by merely summing the solitary performances, with actual pairs shouting at only 59% and sixes at only 31% of their potential. In Stage 1 of Figure 1, the area below the line connecting the solid circles represents the amount of noise produced per person in pairs and in sixes. This can be compared to the line at the top representing the sum of the individual potentials. Not all of the apparent reduction in sound output can be attributed to social loafing, however. The decreased per person sound pressure produced by actual groups reflects a decrement due to coordination loss and sound cancellation as well. Therefore we must examine individual performances in pseudogroups in order to determine how much of the reduction in group output is due to social loafing.

People made 69% as much noise when they shouted in pseudopairs and 63% when they shouted in pseudosixes as when alone, $F(1, 7) = 55.8$, $p < .0001$. This difference between individuals shouting alone and when they believed they were shouting in groups indicates that people do exert less effort in groups than when performing alone, and represents what we have called social loafing. The stipled area bounded on the top by the hypothetically efficient group and on the bottom by the line connecting the hollow circles in Stage 1 of Figure 1 shows how much of the total group inefficiency is caused by social loafing.

Stage 2. People responded conscientiously to the calibration task. They worked hard to maintain a 75 dB tone so that the experimen-

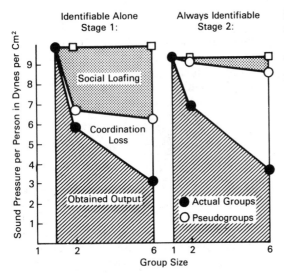

Figure 1. Sound pressure as a function of size of group and identifiability: Experiment 1.

ters could adjust their equipment and gave no indications of suspicion; in fact, participants seemed quite impressed with our technical facilities.

The addition of microphones did not affect the amount of effort exerted when people performed alone. Participants produced 9.86 dynes/cm^2 in Stage 1 and 9.22 dynes/cm^2 in Stage 2 (*ns*). We can conclude that people felt equally identifiable when shouting alone, with or without the microphones, and made a lot of noise.

Wearing microphones did affect performance in pseudogroups. When shouting in pseudopairs, individuals produced 98% (9.06 dynes/cm^2) of their solitary efforts and in pseudosixes 92% (8.48 dynes/cm^2). Neither of these levels differ significantly from the rate for solitary subjects, but they do differ from the comparable pseudogroup performances in Stage 1, $F(1, 7) = 37.8$, $p < .0005$. It is apparent that the addition of microphones virtually eliminated social loafing in groups (Figure 1, Stage 2).

Questionnaire data. At the end of the experiment, participants were asked to estimate, in terms of the percentage of how loudly they could shout if their lives literally depended on it, how loudly they had shouted alone, in pairs, and with five other people. Participants reported that they shouted louder with microphones than without, 79% versus 76%, $F(1, 40) = 13.9$, $p < .01$, and that this held true even when performing alone, a claim not supported by actual performances. Further support for the suggestion that people's reports of their behavior and their actual behavior do not always agree comes from the fact that participants incorrectly reported that group size had no effect on their behavior. As shown in Table 1, they reported that without microphones they always shouted at 76% of their capacities. Asked directly to compare how loud they and the others were when alone and in groups, participants again saw no differences due to group size.

Thus, in response to two different sets of questions, participants were unable or unwilling to acknowledge the fact that group size influenced their efforts or the efforts of the other participants. If participants simply did not want to admit that they were not shouting as loudly as possible throughout the experiment, they should not have confessed to shouting less than 80% of their capacity. Therefore, the data seem to indicate that people are unaware of the influence the group has on either their own or others' outputs, and that whatever the reason they did not shout as loudly in groups, it was not due to a conscious decision.

Discussion

It appears that making individual outputs identifiable when people perform in groups discourages social loafing. When people wear microphones they perform about as well in groups as they do when performing alone. This suggests that without individual microphones

Table 1   Estimated Shouting Intensity

Condition	Unidentifiable	Identifiable
Alone	76%	91%
Pairs	76%	78%
Sixes	76%	78%

Note. Subjects in the *identifiable* conditions wore microphones; those in the *unidentifiable* conditions did not.

people felt identifiable only when they were alone and not when they were in groups. Since their solitary performances were identifiable, they either wanted to or felt they had to exert as much effort as possible to comply with the experimenter's request. In contrast, group performances allowed people to slacken their efforts, since their outputs could not be assessed by anyone.

Experiment 1 supports the inference that identifiability deters people from loafing, since making peoples' outputs always identifiable even when in groups leads them to perform at a consistently high level across all group sizes. If identifiability is the mediator, then convincing people that their outputs are *never* identifiable, even when they perform alone, should cause them to perform at a consistently low level across all group sizes. Experiment 2 will test this hypothesis.

EXPERIMENT 2

Experiment 2 employed a between-subjects design in which some participants were always identifiable, some were never identifiable and some were identifiable only when shouting alone. We predicted that when they were always identifiable, people would shout at a high level, comparable to when they were alone, irrespective of group size. Those who were never identifiable should perform at a low level of effort, comparable to that obtained in group conditions, irrespective of group size. Group size effects should be obtained only for those people who were identifiable only when alone, as in our typical individual–group comparisons.

In Experiment 1, since the same people performed in both Stage 2 and in Stage 1, it is possible that they were more used to the task, more tired of shouting, less embarrassed, or their throats may have been hurting more. However, we think it is unlikely that practice or fatigue had any simple effects on the overall level of noise production since: (a) people tried no harder in the solitary condition in Stage 2 than in Stage 1, and (b) previous research on sound production tasks has shown no signs of such effects over three replications of the

basic 25 trial sequences (Latané et al., 1979). It is possible, although we think implausible, that the group size effects depended on the fact that participants experienced both conditions of identifiability. Since the experimenters knew from Stage 1 how loudly people could shout, participants may have felt obligated to maintain that level in Stage 2. In Experiment 2 identifiability was a between- rather than a within-subjects factor, eliminating the possibility of such interpretations.

Method

One hundred eight undergraduate males were tested in groups of four. The groups were randomly assigned to one of three instructional sets with nine groups of four people in each. As in the previous study participants were told that we were interested in the effects of the reduction of sensory feedback on the production of sound in social groups and were shown the sound measuring system, which now consisted of a microphone (or individual lavaliere microphones in the *always identifiable* condition), and a "24 channel FM tape recorder interfaced with a Data General Nova 1200 Laboratory Computer."

In the *identifiable only when alone* condition, intended to replicate the basic social loafing effect, participants were told:

Your outputs or the outputs of your group will be recorded so that when we are through with the experiment they can be analyzed by the computer to determine how much noise you make when shouting alone and how much noise your group makes. This means that we will not be able to tell how much noise each of you makes individually when you are shouting in groups, but only the total amount produced by the group. However, we will, of course, be able to tell how much noise you make alone. We are interested in how much noise you or your group can make, and we would like you to make as much noise as you can.

In the *always identifiable* condition, intended to replicate Stage 2 of Experiment 1, participants were told:

Your output when you shout alone and when others shout at the same time will be recorded so that when we are through with the experiment it can be analyzed by the computer to determine how much noise you make when you shout alone and when you shout in groups. This means we will be able to tell how much noise each of you makes individually even when you are shouting in groups. We will also, of course, be able to tell how much noise you make alone. We are interested in how much noise you can make when you are alone and when others are shouting with you, and we would like you to make as much noise as you can.

Finally, in the *never identifiable* condition, participants were informed:

All of your outputs when you shout alone or in groups will be recorded so that when we are through with the experiment they can be analyzed by the computer to determine the total amount of noise produced when the four of you shout alone or in groups. This means that we will not be able to tell how much noise you make individually, even when you shout alone. We will also, of course, not be able to tell how much noise each of you makes in groups. We are interested in the total amount of noise produced by the four of you when you shout alone or in groups and we would like you to make as much noise as you can.

All participants then went through two blocks of 24 trials within each of which everyone shouted twice alone, twice in actual pairs, twice in actual foursomes, and once each in pseudopairs and pseudofoursomes. The single and pseudogroup shouts were transformed into dynes/cm^2, averaged within group size and analyzed in a $3 \times 3 \times 2$ ANOVA with identifiability instructions as a between-groups factor, and group size (1, 2, 4) and trial block as within-groups factors.

Results

As in previous research in this series, in the identifiable only when alone condition, people exerted less effort in groups than when alone, $F(1, 48) = 16.4, p < .01$, although the amount of loafing was not as great as in Experiment 1. In pseudopairs, people produced 81% (7.29 dynes/cm^2) of their solitary performances (8.97 dynes/cm^2), compared to 69% for pseudopairs in Experiment 1.

Replicating State 2 in Experiment 1 in the always identifiable condition, people produced virtually the same amount of sound pressure alone as when they were in groups and this level of sound pressure was as high as in the solitary condition of the identifiable when alone condition. People produced 8.81 dynes/cm^2 alone, and 8.79 and 8.75 in pseudopairs and pseudofours (99% of their solitary performances), resulting in no significant differences due to group size, $p < .50$.

In the never identifiable condition, group size again had no effect on peoples' performances. Shouting at the same level as in the pseudogroup trials of the identifiable only when alone condition, people produced 7.52 dynes/cm^2 when alone, 7.51 in pseudopairs, and 7.27 in pseudofours, $p > .50$. This was significantly less noise than people produced in the always identifiable condition, $F(1, 48) = 17.5, p < .01$.

These results, presented in Figure 2, are in the expected pattern. The overall analysis supports this pattern with a significant Instruction X Group Size interaction, $F(4, 48) = 5.25, p < .01$. There were no effects or interactions for trial block, indicating that practice, fatigue or boredom did not affect overall performance or the tendency toward social loafing.

Questionnaire data. Participants estimated that both they and the other participants shouted at 82% of capacity and that neither set of judgments was affected by group size. Participants did report feeling more responsible to the experimenter when shouting alone than in groups, $F(2, 210) = 9.70, p < .01$. It appears that people are willing to admit that group size has some effect on them, but not that lessened responsibility justifies lessened effort.

DISCUSSION

Each experiment has replicated past research on social loafing showing that people work less hard in groups compared to when they work alone. Both Experiments 1 and 2 showed that

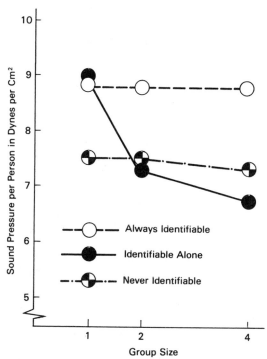

Figure 2. Sound pressure as a function of size of pseudogroup and identifiability: Experiment 2.

making peoples' outputs identifiable even when they perform in groups eliminates social loafing. Experiment 2 also demonstrated that making their outputs unidentifiable even when they perform alone causes them to loaf even without the participation of others. The results of both experiments suggest that identifiability of individual efforts is indeed a critical factor in social loafing—but why?

Identifiability could be important because it enables one's performance to be evaluated by other people. When performing, participants may have felt themselves subject to evaluation by the experimenter. They may have experienced "evaluation apprehension," an "anxiety-toned concern" (Rosenberg, 1969) that would motivate them to satisfy the experimenters' explicitly stated desire that they always shout as loudly as they could. Evaluation apprehension may have been especially high when performing alone or while wearing individual microphones when performances would

be highly identifiable. Evaluation apprehension may have been lower when performing in groups or when individual scores were to be summed and performances would be unidentifiable.

Cottrell's (1972) version of social facilitation theory posits that an evaluative other increases a person's arousal level, which in turn increases the likelihood or strength of a dominant response. It is interesting that this theory generally leads to the prediction that the presence of coactors will lead people to perform harder on well-learned tasks. In the present set of experiments the same explanation would seem to predict the opposite effect. That is, the presence of coactors should reduce a performer's level of identifiability and hence his level of evaluation and apprehension, leading him to experience less arousal and to work less hard than when working alone. This line of thought will necessitate a revision of the usual summary of social facilitation effects. There are cases in which one should predict that people will perform worse on a well-learned task when in groups than when working alone. A key difference between the standard social facilitation paradigm and the present one is that evaluation apprehension increases when coactors or audience members can evaluate an actor's performance in the social facilitation paradigm, whereas in the present paradigm coactors reduce each individual's potential for being evaluated (cf. Jackson & Latané, 1981).

More generally, we believe that identifiability is important because it assures the contingency between effort and outcome. When individual performances are unidentifiable, there can be no causal relation between response and outcome. Whether earning credit for a good performance or avoiding blame for a poor one, identifiability assures the person that this contingency can be operative. Although it is unclear what outcomes people expected to earn in the present studies, it is clear that they were motivated by them.

Seligman's (1975) theory of learned helplessness has drawn attention to the issue of effort–outcome contingencies. He claims that people and animals exposed to situations in which there is no relationship between their responses and their outcomes, whether positive or negative, learn to experience a feeling of helplessness. Helplessness can lead to anything from a loss of motivation to severe depression and death. It seems unlikely that the decreased contingencies between effort and outcome involved when people engage in collective action would have such catastrophic consequences, but they could lead people to slacken their efforts.

In the present studies, identifiability consisted of the participant's knowledge that his outputs could be linked to him by the experimenter. The concept, however, is obviously similar to other states, such as anonymity, deindividuation, and diffusion of responsibility, all of which should be enhanced by performing in groups.

Identifiable to whom? Participants in Experiment 1 were led to believe that after the session was over each person would be able to see his own and everyone else's scores. Being able to examine one's own scores as well as to compare them with those of the other group members may have heightened the competitive nature of the task and motivated people to perform well on these trials for which their scores were recoverable. However, in Experiment 2 participants were told that they would not get to see their scores even after the experiment was over and that only the experimenters would see how loudly they had shouted. Clearly social comparison and competitiveness are not necessary components of identifiability.

The experimenters in the first study stayed in the room with the participants and could directly observe their performance and evaluate it both subjectively and objectively. In Experiment 2, they were in different rooms and could only determine their objective dB meter reading. Whether identifiability involves subjective versus objective evaluation of output does not seem to be critical to the elimination of social loafing.

It appears that monitoring people's performance is sufficient to prevent social loafing. It is probably true that both the evaluation and the evaluator(s) must be regarded as important by the performer for social loafing to be effectively deterred.

Identifiability and the passage of time. Does identifiability lose its impact on the person if his or her output becomes identifiable only at a later time? It seems reasonable that the sooner one's output becomes identifiable, the more motivating it is. Performance in Stage 2 and in the alone conditions of Experiment 1 were identifiable immediately. Performances in the comparable conditions of Experiment 2 were to be collected in the computer and only looked at after the experiment was over. This decrease in differential identifiability may have accounted for the decrease in social loafing found in Experiment 2.

Are there degrees of identifiability? It may be that identifiability either exists or does not exist for a given individual at any given time, or people may experience varying degrees of identifiability, feeling somewhat identifiable, very identifiable, and so on. If the latter possibility is true, identifiability should be inversely proportional to the number of people performing together and we should detect differences in loafing among groups of differing size as well as between solitary and group conditions. In the present studies, although there was a tendency for people to loaf less in pairs than in the larger groups (69% vs. 63% effort in Experiment 1, 81% vs. 74% in Experiment 2), these differences did not reach conventional levels of significance. In line with predictions from social impact theory (Latané, in press), sound pressure in the conditions where social loafing was expected (Stage 1 of Experiment 1 and the identifiability only when alone conditions of Experiment 2) was well described by inverse power functions with exponents of about $-.2$, accounting for 84% of the variance in means.

Cultural determinants of social loafing. Many societies, including traditional Oriental cultures and socialist political systems, emphasize group goals over personal achievement and collective action over individual effort. It is possible that such emphases would foster social loafing, because individual efforts would not receive the appropriate amount of credit or blame. On the other hand, it is possible that people successfully socialized into primary concern for the group would not loaf, since individual identifiability may not be important for them. Cross-national and cross-cultural research investigating these possibilities would help to determine whether social loafing is limited to modern Western urban cultures and the extent to which social loafing is modifiable by personal values, religious orientation, or political ideology.

Two Real-World Cases of Social Loafing

We conclude this article with a brief description of two real world cases of social loafing that, although not particularly serious or relevant to the central issues of our time, help to demonstrate the pervasiveness of the phenomenon and to illustrate the importance of identifiability.

Pickle packing. Turner (1978) described the problems facing production line workers in a pickle factory. A key job is stuffing dill pickle halves into jars. Only dill halves of a certain length can be used. Those that are too long will not fit and those that are too short will float and dance inside and look cheap and crummy. The dill halves and the jars are carried on separate high speed conveyor belts past the contingent of pickle stuffers. If the stuffers don't stuff quickly enough the jars pile up at the workers' stations while they look for pickles of the appropriate length, so stuffers have a great temptation to stuff whatever pickles come readily to hand. The individual outputs of the stuffers are unidentifiable, since all jars go into a common hopper before they reach the quality control section. Responsibility for the output cannot be focused on any one worker. This combination of factors leads to poor performance and improper packing. The present research suggests making individual production identifiable and raises the question, "How many pickles could a pickle packer pack if pickle packers were only paid for properly packed pickles?"

Football linemen. Certain members of athletic teams enjoy less recognition than others. Football linemen, for instance, receive relatively little in the way of fan attention or media coverage. Unsung heroes, they work in obscurity while their efforts seem to go unnoticed by all but their running backs and a few linemen on the other team. Our present research might suggest that this lack of identifiability would lead these players not to exert themselves as strenuously as their more visible teammates. However, successful coaches work hard to counteract this tendency. For example, at Ohio State University under the coaching regime of Woody Hayes (policies continued under Earle Bruce), movies of each play and player were taken from isolated cameras and viewed by the entire coaching staff and players after each game. The staff screened and graded each play and computed the average percentage of perfection of each individual, a score known to teammates and helping to determine whether a player would start the next game. Also, weekly press luncheons were called to announce "lineman of the week" honors and the award of "buckeye" decals to adorn players' helmets, signifying their 110% effort on the field to teammates and crowd. Although it is not possible to test the effectiveness of these tactics directly, Ohio State has long been famous for the holes its linemen tear in opposing defenses.

Summary. Identifiability seems to be an important, albeit complex, psychological variable and appears to have great implications for human motivation and performance. Our findings suggest that identifiability may serve as an effective deterrent to social loafing. We believe that the results, like the methods, of our two experiments are cheering, since we regard social loafing as a social disease that threatens effective collective endeavor.

REFERENCES

Cottrell, N. Social facilitation. In C. McClintock (Ed.), *Experimental social psychology*. New York: Holt, Rinehart, & Winston, 1972.

Davis, J. H. *Group performance*. Reading, Mass.: Addison-Wesley, 1969.

Dashiell, J. F. Experimental studies of the influence of social situations on the behavior of individual human adults. In C. Murchison (Ed.), *A handbook of social psychology*. Worcester, Mass.: Clark University Press, 1935.

Ingham, A. G., Levinger, G., Graves, J., & Peckham, V.

The Ringelmann effect: Studies of group size and group performance. *Journal of Experimental Social Psychology*, 1974, *10*, 371–384.

Harkins, S., Latané, B., & Williams, K. Social Loafing: Allocating effort or taking it easy? *Journal of Experimental Social Psychology*, 1980, *16*, 457–465.

Jackson, J. M., & Latané, B. All alone in front of all those people: Stage fright as a function of the strength and number of coperformers and audience. *Journal of Personality and Social Psychology*, 1981, *40*, 73–85.

Kerr, N., & Bruun, S. The Ringelmann effect revisited: Alternative explanations to the social loafing effect. *Personality and Social Psychology Bulletin*, in press.

Latané, B. The psychology of social impact. *American Psychologist*, in press.

Latané, B., Williams, K., & Harkins, S. Many hands make light the work: The causes and consequences of social loafing. *Journal of Personality and Social Psychology*, 1979, *37*, 822–832.

Maslach, C. Social and personal bases of individuation. *Journal of Personality and Social Psychology*, 1974, *29*, 411–425.

Moede, W. Die Richtlinien der Leistungs-Psychologie. *Industrielle Psychotechnik*, 1927, *4*, 193–207.

Rosenberg, M. J. The conditions and consequences of evaluation apprehension. In R. Rosenthal, & R. L. Rosnow, (Eds.), *Artifact in behavioral research*. New York: Academic Press, 1969.

Seligman, M. E. P. *Helplessness*. San Francisco: Freeman, 1975.

Steiner, I. D. *Group process and productivity*. New York: Academic Press, 1972.

Turner, S. The life and times of a pickle packer. *Boston Sunday Globe*, New England section, January 8, 1978, pp. 10–22.

22

Experimenting on Social Issues: The Case of School Desegregation

STUART W. COOK

In this paper, Cook analyzes the conditions under which desegregation in real life will have beneficial effects. The paper is a good example of applied social psychology, since it takes some well-established principles about the effects of cooperative interdependence and applies them to a specific problem: school desegregation. Cook believes that it is necessary to apply experimental rather than correlational techniques, for reasons that he specifies clearly at the beginning. But he draws independent variables from those that are at work in real-life situations in the schools: task interdependence, cooperation, task success, stereotype-disconfirming behavior on the part of minorities, and the like. So he attempts in his research to simulate the real-life situation—i.e., to produce "mundane realism." It also should be noted that Cook begins with contact theory, for many years the major socio-psychological theory of prejudice reduction. But he adopts a fairly complex and sophisticated version of it, specifying a number of conditions that are necessary if interracial contact is to have beneficial effects. He notes that these vital conditions have only rarely been present when schools have actually been desegregated. Given this analysis, what do you see as the prospects for future efforts to desegregate schools?

ABSTRACT. *This article presents and illustrates the argument for an experimental approach to the study of problems to which social science evidence and theory can make a practical contribution. First, following exploratory research to identify potentially weighty influences on the social behavior under consideration, quasi-experiments are conducted to gain further confidence that these influences are of significance. The next step is to recreate the social behavior under laboratory control and study its determinants experimentally. A final step is to study separately the most significant variables in true experiments. These may be conducted in both laboratory and field settings. The process is illustrated with studies of variables involved in involuntary cross-racial contact as they affect race relations and attitude change. The relevance to constructive contributions to the process of school desegregation is discussed.*

Reprinted from the *American Psychologist*, 1985, 40, pp. 452–460. Copyright 1985 by the American Psychological Association. Reprinted by permission of publisher and author.

In this article I discuss my research on the effect of personal contact on attitudes and relationships with persons from disliked groups. Such work is often referred to as research on the contact hypothesis.

I first became interested in the contact hypothesis in the late 1940s, immediately following World War II. Concern for reducing racial and religious prejudice was high at the time. In the immediate background was the Jewish holocaust. In addition to serving as a direct shock, the Jewish tragedy had the indirect effect of raising the level of consciousness regarding racial discrimination in the United States. Two things attracted me personally to the contact approach to prejudice—in contrast, for example, with major alternative approaches such as persuasive communication or education. One consideration was the political climate of the times, which made government-enforced desegregation seem possible. I realized that if this were to happen, more knowledge about involuntary racial contact would be needed from behavioral scientists. The second consideration was my personal history. I grew up in the rural South and had many opportunities to observe and experience a type of interracial contact that left prejudice untouched.

What we had to go on in the late 1940s were some questionnaire studies and several wartime racial desegregation studies. They seemed to show that, if contact was to be effective in changing attitudes, it had to be equal-status contact. They also suggested that contact involving cooperation in the achievement of a joint goal had more favorable outcomes than contact without such cooperation.

QUASI-EXPERIMENTS

At the time, I was research director for the Commission on Community Interrelations, the research division of the American Jewish Congress. Together with colleagues such as John Harding and Morton Deutsch, I initiated additional field studies. They took the form of quasi-experiments in which persons with equal-status contact in desegregated recreation, desegregated businesses, or desegregated public

housing were compared with those from segregated settings. Among the more informative of these field studies were two large-scale studies of desegregated housing. The first was carried out by Morton Deutsch and Mary Collins. Two years later, after we had established the Research Center for Human Relations at New York University, Daniel Wilner, Rosabelle Walkley, and I did a second study of the same type. The Deutsch and Collins research is described in a book entitled *Interracial Housing: A Psychological Evaluation of a Social Experiment* (Deutsch & Collins, 1951). The book describing the Wilner, Walkley, and Cook study is entitled *Human Relations in Interracial Housing* (Wilner, Walkley, & Cook, 1955).

These studies gave strong support to the contact hypothesis. Deutsch and Collins found that desegregated white tenants had more favorable racial attitudes than did segregated ones. Wilner et al. (1955) supplemented this with the finding that within desegregated housing, the closer white tenants lived to blacks, the more favorable their attitudes. Although it was not possible to say with certainty why this was the case, the interpretation we favored was that it was due to two intervening factors. The first was that the closer white tenants lived to black tenants, the more cooperative and intimate were their contacts. In turn, more cooperative and intimate contacts were associated with more favorable attitudes. The second was that tenants of one race who lived closer to those of the other race had more opportunity to observe cross-racial interaction and were more likely to infer from such interaction that peer group norms favored interracial equality. The strength of perceived peer group norms was, in turn, related to attitude strength.

However, the field studies raised a persistent question of interpretation due to the possibility of subject selection bias. Almost all studies were carried out in situations where whites and blacks were already in contact at the time of the investigation. Consequently, when attitudinal differences were found between groups of subjects who differed in the amount and nature of interracial contact, there was always the possibility that these differences resulted from selective entry of favorable subjects into the contact experience or from selective withdrawal of unfavorable subjects.

I think many investigators presented convincing evidence that biased selection was not a likely explanation of their results. Nevertheless, I decided in the early 1960s that uncertainty about the contact hypothesis could be further reduced by testing it under conditions approximating those of laboratory control.

The contact hypothesis, as I use it, predicts that a favorable change in attitude and interpersonal attraction will result when there is personal contact with members of a disliked group, provided that five conditions hold:

1. The first condition is that the status of the participants from the two social groups must be equal in the situation in which the contact occurs.

2. The second is that attributes of the disliked group that become apparent during the contact must be such as to disconfirm the prevailing stereotyped beliefs about this group.

3. The third is that the contact situation must encourage, or perhaps require, a mutually interdependent relationship, that is, cooperation in the achievement of a joint goal.

4. The fourth is that the contact situation must have high acquaintance potential, that is, it must promote association of a sort that will reveal enough detail about members of the disliked group to encourage seeing them as individuals rather than as persons with stereotyped group characteristics.

5. The fifth condition is that the social norms of the contact situation must favor the concept of group equality and equalitarian intergroup association.

In the rest of the article I describe three somewhat different groups of studies. After I describe the laboratory studies of the contact hypothesis I discuss field experiments focused on the cooperative interdependence aspect of intergroup contact. I conclude with some additional laboratory experiments that ask questions about what makes cooperative intergroup contact more effective. In other words, what variables enhance or diminish the level of respect and liking resulting from such contact?

LABORATORY STUDY
OF THE CONTACT HYPOTHESIS

The initial laboratory study was done in collaboration with Lawrence Wrightsman (Cook, 1969, 1971). The intent of the study was to construct an experimental environment that would expose persons to intergroup contact under the conditions specified in the contact hypothesis. The experimental environment was a part-time job. Each research participant was employed for 20 days, 2 hours per day. Employees were told that the purpose of the job was to help try out a training exercise being developed for use elsewhere.

The training exercise was a type of management task. The task was to operate an imaginary railroad system with the help of two co-workers. To make a profit with the system was a challenge. It was composed of several railroad lines, 10 cities, and 500 freight cars of six different types. Successful operation involved learning how to maintain an appropriate distribution of these cars so that they were located where needed when shipping orders were placed with the railroad. When the team received requests to ship merchandise of specified types from one city to another, it made decisions regarding the route to follow and the types of cars to use. These decisions were telephoned to the experimenter working in another room.

The management of the railroad was subdivided into three jobs. One of the jobs was filled by the subject. Another was filled by a black co-worker. The third was filled by a white co-worker. The two co-workers were experimental confederates.

The management task, as used, lasted for 40 half-hour periods we called "work days." Two such half-hour periods, separated by a 30-minute break, made up an experimental session.

In initiating the experiment a financial incentive was introduced. This was the team's opportunity to make additional "bonus" money by excelling the performance of prior teams. After answering questions (some of which were asked purposely by the confederates), the experimenter presented the first day's shipping requests and retired to another room. Communication with the team thereafter was by telephone.

Next came the 30-minute break. During this time the team members conversed and consumed a free lunch. These conversations were a key part of the experiment. They were guided by the trained confederates and had two functions. The first was to allow the black co-worker to introduce individualizing personal information; the second was to give the white co-worker opportunities to voice equalitarian views regarding race relations. Both the content and the timing of the conversations were carefully programmed.

At intervals of 3 to 4 calendar days, a team learned how its profits compared with those of earlier teams, whose performance it had to surpass to earn a bonus. Although its fortunes varied from report to report, it was prearranged that the team finally won out and earned the hoped-for extra money.

In constructing the experimental environment the primary objective, of course, was to incorporate the elements of the contact hypothesis. This was accomplished as follows:

1. First, equality of status in the contact situation was achieved through the assignment of white and black participants to task roles of equivalent responsibility.

2. Second, contact with stereotype-disconfirming blacks was ensured through the experimenter's selection of black confederates who had educational backgrounds equivalent to those of the research subjects.

3. Third, a cooperative relationship was encouraged by the choice of a task that required interdependence in its execution and provided a reward (a financial bonus) for group success.

4. Fourth, the contact situation was given a high acquaintance potential by arranging for lunch break conversations during which the black confederates brought out individualizing information about themselves.

5. Fifth, social norms favoring equalitarian race relations and racial equality were established during the course of the lunch break conversations. Ten of these half-hour conversations were guided by the confederates into

topics that gave the white co-worker opportunities to express support for desegregation, nondiscriminatory employment and educational policies, cross-racial social contact, and so on.

The subjects were white Anglo students from the border South who responded to an advertisement sponsored by a fictitious out-of-town testing institute. The ad was posted at two fundamentalist colleges. This did not include the college where the study was conducted. The ad offered to pay volunteers to participate in test development. Three steps were taken to keep the testing situation from being associated with the research. First, the relevant attitude measures were dispersed throughout an extensive battery of personality, interest, and opinion measures administered in two sittings over a period of 10 to 12 hours. Second, these measures were administered at a location in the city different from that at which the experiment was conducted. Third, the testing took place in groups of 10 to 15.

From each of these small pools of potential participants, the most prejudiced pair was selected. One was assigned to the experimental group and the other to the control group. The experimental subjects discovered that they were to have black co-workers only after they had been trained separately for the railroad management task and were owed money that they could not collect until their entire period of employment was over.

Four weeks after their job had begun, the subjects rated each of their two co-workers on various aspects of competence, character, and personality. This provided the needed data to study the development of the subjects' liking and respect for their black co-workers. These ratings were made after the subjects had said a last goodbye to their teammates following the final work session. They believed, of course, that they, in turn, were being rated by their exteammates.

Several months later the experimental and control subjects were retested—again in a setting removed from that of the experiment. This was accomplished by having the fictitious testing institute contact the subjects and again offer to pay for participating in its extensive test battery. As before, the tests were taken in groups of 10 to 15 with other students who responded to the testing institute's posted advertisement.

Two studies were carried out. The initial study utilized 23 experimental subjects, plus an equal number of controls. Because each subject participated for approximately one month, it was possible to study a maximum of 9 subjects per academic year. Hence, the study covered a total elapsed time of 2.5 years. After a lapse of 3 years, a replication of the initial study was conducted. The replication involved 19 experimental subjects plus 19 controls, and lasted somewhat over 2 years.

Results

To answer the main question in the experiment, attitude change in the experimental subjects was compared to that in the controls. Recall that the pretests were administered several weeks in advance of participation in the experiment and the posttests from 2 to 3 months after participation. The attitude measures used were of three types: One measured the level of intimacy of relationships into which another racial group would be accepted. A second measured attitudes toward desegregation. A third measured behavioral or action tendencies toward blacks when confronted with potential interracial contact under various circumstances. Also, a composite attitude score was computed with equal weight given to the three separate measures. To do this I took advantage of the fact that I had accumulated in each of the two experiments a pool of more than 200 potential participants who had completed the test battery. The distribution of scores for these individuals provided a convenient means of converting raw scores on each of the attitude measures to standard scores. These standard scores were combined to form the composite score.

Three methods were used to assess attitude change. The first compared pretest-posttest difference scores for subjects and controls. By this method the experimental group changed significantly more than the control group in both the initial experiment and the replication experiment.

The second method was to treat the posttest scores by analysis of covariance, using the pretest scores as a covariate. By this method the experimental group changed significantly more than the control group in the replication experiment but not in the initial experiment, although in the latter the adjusted scores also favored the experimental group.

The third method was to compare the experimental and control groups in terms of the number of subjects who showed a large attitude change. A *large change* was defined empirically. It was based on the composite attitude change score expressed in standard score terms. It happened that in both experiments a certain number of experimental subjects and controls exceeded a change score of .8 of a standard score—a very substantial change. There was a natural break between these individuals and the remainder, who changed less or not at all. Defining the latter as small change or no change, we set up a 2 × 2 chi square for larger change versus smaller or no change by experimental and control groups. The chi square for the combined experiments was significant at the .01 level, indicating that more experimental than control subjects had shown the so-called large attitude change toward blacks. In percentage terms, 40% of the experimental subjects in the two experiments versus 12% of the controls fell into the large change category.

None of these analyses portrays the nature of the attitude changes that took place. The only way to understand these changes is to look at the responses that made up the scores. The following statements were taken from a typical subject in the large change category. (Remember that all subjects were initially highly prejudiced.) On the pretest this particular subject rejected blacks in social relationships such as attending an interracial party, having blacks as dinner guests, attending a church supper to which a black youth group had been invited, and using a swimming pool also used by blacks. On the posttest all of these relationships were accepted. Although on the pretest the subject objected to voting for a black person for Congress and rejected the idea of taking a job interview from a black personnel director, on the posttest these views were reversed. Also, on the pretest the subject rejected beliefs about racial equality and opposed desegregation but accepted both concepts on the posttest.

In describing the behavior of the subjects during the experiment, two things are of special interest. One is that a casual observer would not have suspected the degree of prejudice that characterized the subjects. In the work setting created for the experiment, their behavior was polite and correct. The second is that the subjects' postexperimental ratings of their black co-workers were uniformly very favorable.

COOPERATIVE INTERGROUP CONTACT IN A DESEGREGATED SCHOOL SETTING

Now that I had gained some additional confidence in the contact hypothesis from these studies, I decided to focus on one of its components. The one I chose was cooperative interdependence in achieving a joint goal. Although I conducted two true experiments in field settings on this variable, I will describe only one of them. The experiment I will describe was carried out together with Russell Weigel and Patricia Wiser in newly desegregated junior and senior high schools (Weigel, Wiser, & Cook, 1975). Cooperative interdependence was arranged by organizing students into racially mixed learning teams. Although each team was heterogeneous in terms of the past academic performance of its members, all teams were comparable in terms of average performance. Teachers modified their assignments to require teams to turn in team reports. On each such assignment, the quality of the team's work was judged, and the teacher announced the names of teams that did best. Special privileges were awarded these teams.

We took the idea of cooperating interracial teams into two Denver schools that were just initiating desegregation by busing—one junior high and one senior high. We found 10 English literature teachers who were willing to teach one of their class sections by a new method and another by the traditional procedure. Permission was obtained from the school district to assign students to these 20 English literature

sections in advance of the opening of the fall term. Neither the students nor their parents knew that this had happened. This made it possible for us to balance the interracial composition of the pairs of class sections without creating the atmosphere of an experiment. One of each teacher's pair of sections was randomly assigned to the team-learning condition. Students in that section were divided into five-person teams made up of one black, one Hispanic, and three white Anglo students. A research associate who had been a teacher helped the teachers devise curriculum units that adapted the regular content of the course to group assignments—for example, the analysis of a play with each group member handling a part of an oral report to the class. She also helped them identify various practical ways of rewarding teams that did the best work. As anticipated, the students developed team spirit and started helping one another complete their assignments and prepare for tests. One effect of this was that considerable cross-ethnic and interracial helping took place. Laggards in a group were urged by their teammates to complete their part of the team's assigned task. In behavioral analysis terms, the contingencies of reward had been changed from individual achievement to team achievement, and the behavior changed accordingly.

We had attempted to set up our experimental classrooms in conformity with the contact hypothesis. Students in those classrooms were to experience interracial and cross-ethnic contact under conditions, first, of equal situational status; second, of school authority norms that would support interracial association; third, of cooperative interdependence in learning teams; and fourth, of working relationships that would provide individualizing acquaintanceship. The fifth condition, that of stereotype disconfirmation, could not be controlled. We know that in many metropolitan areas minority students from previously segregated schools enter desegregated schools with measurable achievement handicaps. Hence, we had no way of knowing how the minority students in our study would relate to the stereotype of low academic ability.

However, there was a potential confound in the study. Whenever something new is introduced, as was the case with student learning teams, it may work only because of its novelty and the special effort that goes along with being part of something special. We did what we could to counter this by stressing to the teachers the fact that certain things could be done better under the traditional classroom organization. In particular, we noted that one of education's highest values, that of individualizing instruction, was easier to implement under classroom procedures oriented to individual children than it would be when instruction was oriented to groups. We do not know the effect of these efforts, of course. We did find in interviewing teachers that they recalled having no expectations of more favorable racial or ethnic relationships under one method of instruction than under the other.

Results

In analyzing the data, we compared the students taught by team learning and by traditional methods on four classes of variables. These were cross-ethnic and interracial conflict, ratings of classmates of each ethnic group on a number of desirable attributes, choice of friends from each ethnic group, and attitudes toward other ethnic groups. The attitude interviews were conducted in the students' homes by persons who introduced themselves as being from an opinion polling organization. Care was taken to ensure that the interviewers made no reference to schools while conducting the interviews. Moreover, on the within-school measures, such as the classmate ratings, race or ethnic group was never mentioned. Identification of target persons was made by name only.

The first result was a large and significant difference in the amount of interracial and cross-ethnic conflict; it was lower among the students taught in learning teams than among those taught traditionally.

The second result had to do with perceived attributes of classmates from other ethnic groups. In order to make it easier for students to give frank assessments of one another, classmates were dispersed in an auditorium. The test administration and monitoring were done by persons not associated with the school. When ratings of own-ethnic-group classmates were compared with ratings of other-ethnic-group classmates, we found the following: White Anglo students in the learning team classes rated their Hispanic classmates as favorably as they did their Anglo classmates. In contrast, Anglo students in the traditional classrooms rated their Hispanic classmates less favorably than their Anglo classmates. The difference between the difference scores in the two types of classrooms was statistically significant ($p < .001$). However, we did not find a similar effect for the white Anglo students' ratings of their black classmates. The Anglo students in the two types of classrooms behaved similarly, that is, in both cases they rated their Anglo classmates higher than their black classmates.

To determine friendship patterns under the two teaching procedures we had students choose 10 schoolmates from their entire school grade (7th or 10th) with whom to share each of two activities, one task-oriented and one social in nature. The percentage of cross-ethnic choices made by white Anglo students for Hispanic schoolmates was significantly higher in the classes taught in learning teams than in the classes taught by traditional methods ($p < .04$). The percentage of choices by white Anglos of black schoolmates, in contrast, was equivalent in the two types of classrooms. No differences were found in generalized intergroup attitudes between students in experimental and traditional classrooms.

Several investigators became interested in cooperative interdependence in desegregated schools at about the same time our study was done. At the present time there have been 13 experiments comparing cross-racial or cross-ethnic relationships in classrooms with ethnically mixed learning teams and those without. In 11 of these 13, the interdependent classrooms have surpassed the equally desegregated traditional classrooms on some measure of cross-racial climate, liking, and friendship choices. However, none have found generalized attitude change.

EXPERIMENTS ON THE DETERMINANTS OF RESPECT AND LIKING IN COOPERATING INTERRACIAL LABORATORY GROUPS

Following the two field experiments on cooperative interdependence in interracial contact, a second question seemed relevant. If cooperative interdependence increases the probability of favorable outcomes in nonvoluntary intergroup contact, as it seems to, are there factors that magnify or diminish this increase? For example, if a cooperating interracial group is successful in what it undertakes, will respect and liking be higher among the group members than if it fails? Or, to take another example, will the reaction of a less competent team member to being helped by a groupmate be such as to lower attraction for the helper, particularly if the helper comes from a disliked ethnic group?

In the last few years I have conducted eight experiments that focused on such questions (Cook, 1984a). My colleagues in this work have been Fletcher Blanchard, Jeryl Mumpower, Michael Pelfrey, and Russell Weigel. The setting for the experiments was the railroad management task I described earlier. The three-person management team conducted its business, in this case, in a single 2-hour session. One team member was the research subject. The other two were confederates, one of whom was black and one white. Subjects were young white males from the Southeastern portion of the United States. Such individuals were chosen because of their reputation for racial prejudice in opinion polls. The typical study used a three-variable factorial design. To illustrate, one experiment involved these variables: first, success versus failure of the group in its task; second, the experience of being helped—or not being helped—by a teammate; and third, the race of the helper. The fact that a number of variables were included in each experiment means that we have several replications of the effect of each.

Results

Two of the variables were attributes of teammates: One of these was the level of competence on the team task. The competence

variable was manipulated through the behavior of the confederates. At prescribed points throughout the experiment the confederate in the less competent role made serious and costly errors in the performance of his duties. The errors, which were obvious to the subject, resulted in fines against the group and in significant losses in profits.

We found that more competent teammates were liked and respected significantly more than less competent ones. The effect was large—roughly equivalent to the standard deviation of the sample. The difference in reaction to more competent versus less competent black teammates, and in reaction to more versus less competent white teammates, was approximately the same. Incidentally, we compared the reactions of subjects to teammates filling parallel positions on their respective teams. It might be easy to get the incorrect idea that the comparisons were being made between a given subject's own two teammates.

The second of the teammate attributes was race. We have 10 tests of its effect. In 7 of the 10 we found no effect. In the other 3 there was a significant but small preference for white teammates. What this says is that within cooperating interracial groups the development of respect and liking for teammates of other ethnic groups is approximately equivalent to that for teammates from the individual's own ethnic group.

A third variable in the series of experiments was the outcome of the group's assigned task. In natural settings, task-oriented groups may succeed in achieving their goals, or they may fail to do so. In our experiments we controlled success and failure through the experimenter's reports. Successful groups were told they had surpassed the performance of comparison groups and were given a financial reward. In fact, however, their objective performance was identical with that of groups who supposedly "failed." Group success, like teammate competence, has a large and consistent positive effect on respect and liking for teammates. Of special interest was the fact that the effect was observed primarily in reactions to confederates in the role of the less competent teammate.

Several variables examined in the series of

experiments concerned aspects of the individual's own role as a team member. One of these was the level of participation in the group's operational decisions. This was controlled by the behavior of the two trained confederates. Throughout the course of the task, major changes in the way the group operated its business were needed in order to increase the group's efficiency. In the low-participation condition, the insights underlying these changes seemed to the subject to be "discovered" in discussions between the two confederates and were then implemented by the confederate who was the "executive officer" of the team. The subject neither participated in the discussions leading to the discovery nor exercised any say in the decision to implement it. By contrast, in the high-participation condition, the confederates guided discussions in such a way that the subject contributed to the discovery of the principles of efficient operation.

The question of whether the level of participation in deciding group procedures consistently influences respect and liking for teammates remains to be settled. In one study it had a significant effect; in another it did not. The two studies in question differed in the strength of the success-failure manipulation. When success was accompanied by a meaningful financial reward, there was no participation effect. When it was not, participation did increase respect and liking for teammates.

The second of the individual role variables, that of helping a teammate, derives its interest, in part, from the repeated observation that members of interdependent groups are very likely to help one another. This arouses concern that the experience of helping teammates who have difficulty will highlight their lesser competence and further lessen attraction for them. Such concern has special significance in recently desegregated schools in which minority members of cooperating interracial groups may be the least well prepared academically.

What we found is that the fact that a teammate must be helped does indeed enhance the perception of lower competence and decreases respect and liking for the helped person. Personally rendering the help, however, neither magnifies nor diminishes this effect. We must

remember to understand these findings in their team context. Helping a teammate has a function—namely, it enhances the team's chances for success. And, as just noted, success is one of the major contributors to heightened respect and liking for teammates of lower competence.

A final experiment focused on the experience of being the recipient of help rather than the helper. Previous research on the recipient of help in dyadic relationships, as well as at the level of international aid, has called attention to the possibility that persons receiving help may show a decrement in liking for their helpers. One of the circumstances under which this is likely to occur is when the helped person is unable to reciprocate the assistance received. Such reciprocation is difficult to arrange when team members are unequal in abilities needed for the group task. When such differences exist, most help will be given by more accomplished teammates and received by less accomplished ones.

The research subject in our recipient of help experiment was put in the position of needing help by assigning him an overload of duties. Being unfamiliar with the duties of teammates, the subject was unaware that this had happened. Consequently, when subjects found themselves delaying the team's progress, they experienced considerable embarrassment and discomfort. In one of the three experimental treatments the subject received no help despite the fact that one teammate/confederate regularly finished his duties early and was available to help; in this treatment condition team members had been instructed to do only their own work. In a second experimental treatment, the teammate who finished early voluntarily helped the subject by doing part of his work. In a third treatment, the same confederate helped, but under instructions to do so by the experimenter. These instructions were delivered in the subject's presence.

We found a significant relationship between the helping condition variable and respect and liking for the helper ($p < .03$). However, in apparent contrast to previous research, respect and liking under the voluntary helping condition was high whereas respect and liking in the absence of helping was low ($p < .05$). (Attraction for the helper when he was instructed to help by the experimenter was intermediate.) There was no interaction between the helping variable and race of helper, and within-race means indicated that both whites and blacks contributed to the main effect. One implication of this, of course, is that within the context of an interdependent group, a prejudiced white person who has received help from a black teammate will have greater respect and liking for that teammate than would be the case had the black teammate not helped. A recent review of research on the recipient of aid in dyadic relationships concluded that threat to self-esteem is the most likely antecedent of negative affect toward the donor. From our results we may infer that, even when the donor is a peer from a low-status group, unreciprocated help may be received without loss of self-esteem if this happens in the context of a cooperating group with a common goal.

CONCLUSIONS

In order to summarize where I think matters stand, considerable oversimplification is necessary. Intergroup contact under the conditions specified in the contact hypothesis will induce friendly interracial behavior and promote cross-racial respect and liking between those individuals who are present in the desegregated social setting. These outcomes will be magnified when cooperative interdependence is present and diminished when it is not.

Under circumstances that are not yet clear, these situational effects will be accompanied by generalized racial attitude change. One such circumstance may be that in which individuals experience cooperative equal status contact over a longer period of time than is typical of experimental interventions. Another may be the presence of some factor that facilitates generalization from experiences with individuals to the ethnic group from which they come. It has long been supposed that negative attitudes survive intergroup contact experiences because of the tendency to perceive liked individuals as exceptions to their ethnic group. This would imply the need to introduce some

element into the cooperative experience to serve as a sort of "cognitive booster" for generalization from affective changes toward individuals to attitudes toward their ethnic groups. Among the studies I described, such an element was present only in the initial experiments on the overall contact hypothesis. The element in question was the guided conversations between the prejudiced research subject and a peer group confederate. The starting point in these conversations was shared disapproval of discriminatory treatment of a minority individual who had become a friend in the course of the experiment. When the peer group confederate voiced opposition to policies that permitted the discriminatory treatment in question, the research subject was able to relate this to the experience of his or her new minority group friend. Once this had happened, the subject often joined in condemning the discriminatory policy or practice. It was as though the positive affect developed for black friends had generalized to disapproval of discriminatory behaviors toward them. Although a direct application of this procedure to other settings is not possible, it should be feasible to develop analogous approaches.

Teachers and other supervisory personnel who are contemplating the use of cooperating interracial groups in desegregated settings should be alert to the effect upon teammate respect and liking of several factors. One of these is the positive effect of group success. A second, though less well established, is the positive effect of participating in decisions regarding group operating procedures. A negative effect is associated with a team member's difficulty in doing his or her share of the team task. However, other effects associated with helping teammates and being helped by them are such that full utilization of the group's potential for assisting one another should be encouraged.

RELATION TO SOCIAL ISSUES

How does all of this relate to the study of social issues? In very general terms the answer is by way of the potential guidance it offers to the social management of desegregation. Such guidance is badly needed. This is particularly true in the business world, in the armed services, and in public education.

To date, the relation to education has attracted the most attention. Thirty years ago behavioral scientists were drawn into a major policy decision. The occasion was the 1954 Supreme Court decision that led to school desegregation, and the issue was government-enforced segregation. At the time, 17 states and the District of Columbia either required or explicitly permitted segregated schools.

The historical record indicates that the Supreme Court justices knew that segregated schools had the support of a large majority of the population. They were worried about whether the country would accept a decision to desegregate. Because of this, the lawyers who were handling the litigation suspected that the justices might be more confident in reaching an unpopular decision if they had supporting evidence from scientists.

I helped two other social psychologists, Kenneth Clark and Isidor Chein, prepare a statement for submission to the Court. The statement reviewed available evidence regarding the negative educational and emotional consequences of government-enforced segregation. It was submitted to the Court over the signature of 32 psychologists, sociologists, anthropologists, and psychiatrists. Students of the Court's procedures have argued that the decision incorporated points made by the social scientists, noting for example that the justices referred to a number of studies that the social scientists had cited.

Unfortunately, the content of the Social Science Statement has been unintentionally misrepresented. This occurred most recently in the August 1983 issue of the *American Psychologist* (Gerard, 1983). Partly because the statement is of some historical interest to psychologists, I have reviewed it in the August 1984 issue of the *American Psychologist* (Cook, 1984b). The aspect of the Social Science Statement that is of relevance here is its discussion of the conditions under which desegregation might produce friendlier race relations and more favorable racial attitudes. I think it is particularly important to note these because they have rarely characterized school desegregation as it has been carried out. Note the similarity of the following conditions to those suggested in the contact hypothesis: (a) equivalence of activities and opportunities among all students regardless of racial background, (b) firm and consistent endorsement of desegregation by those in authority, (c) the absence of competition among students from the different racial groups, and (d) interracial contacts among students of the type that permit learning about one another as individuals. In addition, the statement included the point that simultaneous desegregation should occur in all comparable units of a school system.

There have been many reviews of the impact of school desegregation on children. All share the view that only a small fraction of its constructive potential has been realized—not only for race relations but also for academic achievement. My own assessment is given in the previously mentioned *American Psychologist* article (Cook, 1984b). In concluding that article I raised the following question: If, in fact, school desegregation has not lived up to its constructive potential, do we social scientists share any part of the responsibility? My answer—an unpopular one—is that we do. Please understand that I know my answer overlooks the typical constraints of time and money that so often are the determining factors of what we study. Disregarding this reality for the moment, my argument is that social scientists have generally responded to the challenge of desegregation in a reactive rather than an innovative fashion. Their role has been to evaluate the outcome of desegregation experiences just as these have occurred. They have not, by contrast, proposed and studied alternative methods by which school desegregation might be carried out.

The consequences of this reactive orientation have been unfortunate for the following reasons. The circumstances under which schools desegregate vary in many important ways including, for example, the general quality of race relations in the community, the norms of the parents and school administrators regarding interethnic association, and the degree to which teachers have been trained to anticipate and prevent cross-racial misunderstandings. It was probably inevitable, therefore, that outcomes would appear favorable in some cases and unfavorable in others. The confused picture that emerged from research documenting these outcomes offered little guidance for educational policy and programs.

By contrast, an innovative orientation to school desegregation, as opposed to a purely reactive one, would have asked whether a given teaching method, a particular social arrangement in the classroom, or some other factor might yield more positive outcomes. In other words, an innovative approach would initiate and study the effects of alternative strategies for implementing integration in the schools.

Fortunately, within the last 7 or 8 years things have taken a turn for the better. For example, I know of at least four research groups that are studying the use of cooperating interracial teams in desegregated schools. By one estimate, 1,500 schools have tried this approach to classroom learning. I should note, by the way, that classrooms using learning teams not only improve ethnic relations, but they also regularly excell traditional classrooms in academic achievement and in self-esteem of minority group children. I take some satisfaction in the fact that the research I have described has sometimes been credited with strengthening the scientific basis for these developments.

For those who would like greater detail on factors that facilitate constructive outcomes of desegregation, I recommend a book entitled *Groups in Contact: The Psychology of Desegregation* (Miller & Brewer, 1984).

To conclude, I hope I have conveyed my optimism that experimenting on social issues is potentially useful. For me it has also been theoretically stimulating, because it has directed attention to weighty variables and otherwise unnoticed questions. I realize, of course, that what can be learned about significant societal questions from experiments is only part of what we need to know. Such knowledge can only supplement and be interpreted in the context of knowledge gained from other sources and by other methods. Nevertheless, my hope is that, in our commitment to relate psychology to the public interest, we do not overlook the potential of experimenting on social issues.

REFERENCES

Cook, S. W. (1969). Motives in a conceptual analysis of attitude-related behavior. In W. J. Arnold & D. Levine (Eds.), *Nebraska Symposium on Motivation* (pp. 179–235). Lincoln: University of Nebraska Press.

Cook, S. W. (1971). *The effect of unintended interracial contact upon racial interaction and attitude change* (Final report, Project No. 5–1320). Washington, DC: U.S. Department of Health, Education and Welfare, Office of Education.

Cook, S. W. (1984a). Cooperative interaction in multiethnic contexts. In N. Miller & M. Brewer (Eds.), *Groups in contact: The psychology of desegregation* (pp. 155–185). New York: Academic Press.

Cook, S. W. (1984b). The 1954 social science statement and school desegregation: A reply to Gerard. *American Psychologist, 39,* 819–832.

Deutsch, M., & Collins, M. E. (1951). *Interracial housing: A psychological evaluation of a social experiment.* Minneapolis: University of Minnesota Press.

Gerard, H. B. (1983). School desegregation: The social science role. *American Psychologist, 38,* 869–877.

Miller, N., & Brewer, M. (1984). *Groups in contact: The psychology of desegregation.* New York: Academic Press.

Weigel, R. H., Wiser, P. L., & Cook, S. W. (1975). The impact of cooperative learning experiments on cross-ethnic relations and attitudes. *Journal of Social Issues, 31,* 219–244.

Wilner, D. M., Walkley, R. O., & Cook, S. W. (1955). *Human relations in interracial housing.* Minneapolis: University of Minnesota Press.

23

Baby X Revisited

Laura S. Sidorowicz and G. Sparks Lunney

Stereotypes are beliefs about the typical characteristics of members of a group or social category. Most of us have stereotypes about the sexes. We tend to believe, for instance, that men are more aggressive, competitive, and adventurous, whereas women are more dependent, quiet, and gentle. In this laboratory experiment, Sidorowicz and Lunney show how gender stereotypes can shape social behavior. They asked college students to give one of three toys to an infant. Some students were told that the infant was a boy, and others were told that it was a girl. Those who thought they were playing with a "boy" usually offered the infant a football; those who thought they were playing with a "girl" offered a doll. Presumably, the college students thought some toys are more appropriate for boys than for girls, even for infants. Most toy manufacturers also seem to believe that boys and girls have quite different interests. By treating children in such a sex-typed way from early infancy on, adults can actually create differences in the toy preferences of male and female children. Can you think of other ways in which adults may subtly teach boys and girls distinctive, sex-typed behaviors?

ABSTRACT. The present study is a replication of a study reported by Seavy, Katz, and Zalk (1975) in which subjects interacted with a 3-month-old female infant who was either introduced as a boy, a girl, or without any specific gender information. In the present study infants of both genders were used as stimuli, and 60 college undergraduates served as subjects. The results of the present study are similar to the findings of the original investigators. The gender labels provided to the subject resulted in highly sex-stereotyped behavior concerning toy choice.

From the moment of gender assignment at birth, the social world interacts differentially with the developing individual, depending on her or his gender. This has been documented in numerous empirical studies. For example, several studies have shown that parents give boys of preschool and elementary school age much more freedom to roam in the physical environment without special permission or adult accompanment than is the case for girls of the same age (Landy, 1965; Nerlove, Munroe, & Munroe, 1971; Saegert & Hart, 1977). Rheingold and Cook (1975), in examining the rooms of children from age 1 month to 6 years, found boys had more categories of toys. Both Rheingold and Cook, and Rosenfeld (1975) found that boys were given toys which elicit more competence behavior than toys given girls. Several studies (Bronson, 1971; Gesell, 1942; Goldberg & Lewis, 1969; Jacklin, Maccoby, & Dick, 1973; Liebert, McCall, & Hanratty, 1971; Montemayer, 1976; Stein, Pohly, & Mueller, 1971) show that after being presented with "gender appropriate" toys, children spend more time playing with them, develop competence in their use, and gradually perform better, in general, at tasks and play labeled as gender appropriate.

From *Sex Roles*, 1980, 6(1), pp. 67–73. Copyright 1980 by Plenum Publishing Corporation. Reprinted by permission of the publisher and authors.

Researchers have consistently found that parents stimulate and respond more to gross motor behavior in infant sons than in infant daughters (Lewis, 1972; Moss, 1967; Tasch, 1952; Yarrow, Rubenstein & Pederson, 1971). Empirical research has also shown that girls are treated as if they were more fragile, both by mothers (Minton, Kagan, & Levine, 1971) and fathers (Pederson & Robson, 1969). Several studies (e.g., Fling & Manosevitz, 1972; Lansky, 1967) show that parents are extremely upset by any sign that their boys are "sissies," while girls are encouraged to be neat and obedient and to be "feminine" in both behavior and dress.

Boys are consistently more likely to be punished by spanking and other forms of physical punishment (Maccoby & Jacklin, 1974), while girls generally receive soft-voiced verbal reprimands (Servin, O'Leary, Kent, & Tonick, 1973). Rubin, Provenzano, & Luria (1974) found that parents describe their newborn infant's physical attributes and personality in sex-stereotyped ways within 24 hours of the child's birth. Williams, Bennett, and Best (1975) found that kindergarten children show knowledge of sex-role stereotypes both verbally and behaviorally.

Indeed, even among the general public, there is little disagreement with the suggestion that boys and girls are typically treated differently. A far more controversial question, however, is, Ought they to be? The answer to this question is generally grounded in one of two conflicting assumptions about the essential differences or lack of differences between males and females.

Those who argue that the nature of the developing individual's socialization ought not be dependent on her or his gender usually suggest that except for differential reproductive functions, persons of either gender are essentially similar and that the observable gender-linked differences in attitudes and behavior are the result of differential socialization (e.g., Gagnon & Simon, 1973; Laws & Schwartz, 1977; Lunney, 1978).

Those who urge that society continued differential socialization of males and females typ-

ically argue that males and females have distinctly different underlying personalities which are necessary, adaptive, and logically follow from their differing functions in reproductive behavior. Differential socialization, then, is seen as logical and necessary in order to produce in the individual attitudes and behaviors which reflect her or his biological reproductive role within society. This position assumes that males and females are essentially quite different, independent of socialization. For example, Goldberg (1973) states; "the stereotype that sees the male as more logical than the female is unquestionably correct in its observation and probably correct in its assumption that the qualities observed conform to innate sexual limitations analogous to those relevant to physical strength" (p. 204). Nash (1979) also presents this position clearly; stating that "parents have different behaviors *elicited* from them by boys and by girls and these differential responses tend further to augment sex-appropriate behavior" (p. 197).

One study which addresses this issue was conducted by Seavey, Katz, and Zalk (1975). In this study the behavior of adults was investigated while they interacted with a 3-month-old female infant. The infant was introduced either as a boy, a girl, or without any gender information. A football, doll, and teething ring (gender neutral) were available for use during the interaction. Subjects generally made sex-stereotyped choices, especially when the infant was introduced as a female. Overall, the authors of the original study note, "The most salient finding of the present investigation is that adults interact differently with the same infant as a function of the gender label used or its absence" (p. 108).

One shortfall of the original study, however, was the use of only one infant and consequently only one gender as stimulus. It could be hypothesized that while a systematic effect could be obtained by varying the gender label of a female infant, this would not hold true for a male infant. The present study is essentially a replication of the toy choice paradigm used in the original study, using infants of both genders.

METHOD

Subjects

Subjects were 60 undergraduate students at Hunter College of the City University of New York. Thirty-five (58%) female, and 25 (42%) male, subjects were approached in the cafeteria and at other locations on campus and asked to participate in a study concerning "young infants' responses to strangers." Subjects ranged in age from 17 to 45 years, with the mean age being 26, and most (over 80%) being in their 20s. The racial composition of the sample included Whites, Blacks, Hispanics, and Orientals, but was approximately 50% White.

Procedure

Subjects were brought into the main laboratory room and were instructed to interact with a young infant, who was placed in one corner of the room on a blanket. Subjects were told that the study concerned the responses of infants to strangers and were encouraged to talk with, play with, touch, and pick up the infant. Subjects were then escorted to the area of the room where the infant was located. In this area, but out of reach of the infant, was located a small toy football, a doll, and teething ring (gender neutral).

The entire interaction of each subject with the infant was monitored via a closed-circuit TV camera and recorded on videotape for subsequent analysis. Interactions between subjects and infants ranged from somewhat over 1 minute to nearly 4 minutes, with a mean of 2 minutes and 37 seconds.[1] The session was terminated shortly after the subject had chosen a toy and started to interact with the infant using the toy selected.

The stimulus infants were all similarly dressed in undershirts and diapers so that no gender cues would be provided by their clothing. Two male infants and one female infant

were used, ranging from 3 to 11 months in age, with a mean age of 6.6 months. Twenty-two trials were conducted with the female infant, and 38 trials were conducted with the male infants.[2]

Subjects were randomly assigned to one of three conditions: male label, female label, or neutral (no gender information provided). Those in the male and female conditions were told that they would be interacting with a ____-month-old baby boy named Johnny or a ____-month-old baby girl named Jenny. Those in the neutral condition were told that they would be interacting with a ____-month-old baby. Subjects were provided with the correct age of the particular infant. As in the 1975 study, if a subject in the neutral condition asked the infant's gender, he or she was told by the experimenter: "I'm really not sure which infant we are using today."

At the conclusion of the play session, the subject was taken to another area, debriefed, and told the purpose of the experiment. Those in the gender-neutral condition were also asked to indicate which sex they thought the baby was and then informed of the stimulus infant's actual gender.

RESULTS

As can be seen in Table 1, the gender labels provided to the subject resulted in highly sex-stereotyped behavior concerning toy choice during the interaction. A five-way analysis of variance was carried out for Assigned Gender × Real Gender × Subject's Sex × Subject's Race × Subject's Age. Only assigned gender had a significant effect on toy choice, $F(2, 59) = 5.423$, $p = .016$. There were no significant higher order interactions.

In the present study toy choice was highly influenced by gender label. When the infant was designated as male, 50% of male subjects and 80% of female subjects chose the football. The effect for choice of the football in the male

---

[1] The variation is the result of a very few shy subjects and, on occasion, the crying or falling asleep of a stimulus infant.

[2] This was the result of differential availability of the stimulus infants.

Table 1 Toy Choice, by Condition and Subject's Sex (to Nearest Whole Percent)

Gender label	Football	Doll	Teething Ring
Male			
Male subjects	50	20	30
Female subjects	80	20	0
All subjects	65	20	15
Female			
Male subjects	0	89	11
Female subjects	28	73	0
All subjects	15	80	05
Neutral			
Male subjects	33	50	17
Female subjects	21	36	43
All subjects	25	40	35

gender label conditions was more pronounced in the present study than in the 1975 study. This may be due to the use of undergraduate subjects rather than graduate students. The original study used graduate students, who may have been more sophisticated or more experienced with infants and may have reasoned that a soft Raggedy Ann doll was a more appropriate toy for a young infant, regardless of gender, than was a plastic football. Another possible explanation is the older mean age of the stimulus infants in the present study.

When the infant was given the gender label of female, the effect was similar to the 1975 study; that is, this condition elicited the most consistent sex-stereotyped responses: Altogether, 72.7% of the female subjects and 88.8% of the male subjects chose the doll when the infant was identified as female. No male chose the football when the infant was identified as a female.

In the original study males chose the teething ring in the gender-neutral condition, while females most frequently chose either the doll or the teething ring. In the present study, the reverse was found to be true. The reason for this reversal is unclear; it may also be related to the use of an undergraduate rather than a graduate student sample.

One finding which was clearly similar to those of the original investigators was that sub-

jects in the gender-neutral condition invariably asked or tried to guess the infant's gender. When debriefed and asked to guess the infant's actual gender, subjects in this condition showed attributional patterns similar to subjects in the original study. For example, "She is friendly and female infants smile more" (male infant, male subject); "[She is a girl] because girls are more satisfied and accepting" (male infant, female subject); and "He doesn't like strangers" (female infant, female subject).

DISCUSSION

As was the case in the 1975 study, the present replication found that adults interacted in systematically different and sex-stereotyped ways with the same infant depending on the gender label provided. Perhaps the most significant finding of the present study is that this was true for both male and female stimulus infants; that is, the actual gender of the infant did not result in differential responses from subjects. Nor was the subject's sex, age, or race a significant factor.

The present study supports the original findings, and our conclusions are the same as those of the original investigators—that gender-linked variations in infants' behavior, if present at all, appear far less important in determining adults' expectancies and behaviors in interaction than does the providing of a gender label.

REFERENCES

Bronson, W. *Exploratory behavior of 15-month-old infants in a novel situation*. Paper presented at the meeting for the Society for Research in Child Development, Minneapolis, 1971.

Fling, S., & Manosevitz, M. Sex typing in nursery school children's play interests. *Developmental Psychology*, 1972, 7, 146–152.

Gagnon, J., & Simon, W. *Sexual conduct*. Chicago: Aldine, 1973.

Gesell, A., & Ilg. L. *Infant and child in the culture of today*. New York: Harper & Row, 1942.

Goldberg, S. *The inevitability of patriarchy*. New York: William Morrow and Co., 1973.

Goldberg, S., & Lewis, R. Play behavior in the year-old infant: Early sex differences. *Child Development*, 1969, *40*, 21–31.

Jacklin, C., Maccoby, E. E., & Dick, A. Barrier behavior and toy preference: Sex differences (and their absence) in the year-old child. *Child Development*, 1973, *44*, 196–200.

Landy, D. *Tropical childhood*. New York: Harper & Row, 1965.

Laws, J., & Schwartz, P. *Sexual scripts*. Hinsdale, Ill.: Dryden Press, 1977.

Lewis, M. State as an infant-environmental interaction: An analysis of mother-infant behavior as a function of sex. *Merrill-Palmer Quarterly*, 1972, *18*, 95–211.

Liebert, R., & Hanratty, M. Effects of sex-typed information on children's toy preference. *Journal of Genetic Psychology*, 1971, *119*, 113–136.

Lunney, G. S., *The social construction of sexual intercourse*. Unpublished doctoral dissertation, City University of New York, 1978.

Maccoby, E. E., & Jacklin, C. N. *The psychology of sex differences*. Stanford: Stanford University Press, 1974.

Margolin, G., & Patterson, G. Differential consequences provided by mothers and fathers for their sons and daughters. *Developmental Psychology*, 1975, *11*, 537–538.

Minton, C., Kagan, J., & Levine, J. Maternal control and obedience in the two-year-old child. *Child Development*, 1971, *42*, 1873–1894.

Montemayor, R. Children's performance in a game and their attraction to it as a function of sex-typed labels. *Child Development*, 1974, *45*, 152–156.

Moss, H. Sex, age and state as determinants of mother-infant interaction. *Merrill-Palmer Quarterly*, 1967, *13*, 19–36.

Nash, J. *Developmental psychology: A psychological approach*. Englewood Cliffs, N.J.: Prentice-Hall, 1970.

Nerlove, S., Munroe, R., & Munroe, R. Effect of environmental experience on spatial ability: A replication. *Journal of Social Psychology*, 1971, *84*, 3–10.

Pederson, F., & Robson, K. Father participation in infancy. *American Journal of Psychiatry*, 1969, *39*, 466–472.

Rheingold, H., & Cook, K. The contents of boys' and girls' rooms as an index of parent behavior. *Child Development*, 1975, *46*, 459–463.

Rubin, T., Provenzano, F., & Luria, Z. The eye of the beholder: Parents' view on sex of newborns. *American Journal of Orthopsychiatry*, 1974, *44*, 512–519.

Saegert, S., & Hart, R. The development of environmental competence in girls and boys. In P. Burnet (Ed.), *Women in society*. Chicago: Maaroufa Press, 1976.

Seavey, C., Katz, P., & Zalk, S. Baby X: The effect of gender labels on adult responses to infants. *Sex Roles*, 1975, *1*, 103–109.

Serbin, L., O'Leary, K., Kent, R., & Tonick, I. A comparison of teacher response to the preacademic and problem behavior of boys and girls. *Child Development*, 1973, *44*, 796–804.

Stein, A., Pohly, R., & Mueller, E. The influence of masculine, feminine, and neutral tasks on children's achievement behavior: Expectancies of success and attainment value. *Child Development*, 1971, *42*, 195–207.

Tasch, R. The role of the father in the family. *Journal of Experimental Education*, 1952, *20*, 319–361.

Williams J., Bennett, S., & Best, D. Awareness and expression of sex stereotypes in young children. *Developmental Psychology*, 1975, *11*, 635–642.

Yarrow, L., Rubenstein, J., & Pederson, F. *Dimensions of early stimulation: Differential effects on infant development*. Paper presented at the meeting of the Society for Research in Child Development, 1971.

24

Reducing the Stress of High-Density Living:
An Architectural Intervention

ANDREW BAUM AND GLENN E. DAVIS

Research is beginning to document what students have long suspected, that the architectural design of dormitories can make an important psychological difference in the experience of college living. In this innovative study, Baum and Davis compare the impact of living on a long dormitory corridor with 40 students to living on smaller corridors with 20 students. The researchers found that even though the actual dorm rooms were all quite similar, the overall size of the living group made a significant difference. Compared to students in the smaller units, students who had been randomly assigned to the larger living environment felt less successful in making friends, were more likely to complain of unwanted social contacts on their floor, and generally felt more crowded. Three aspects of this study are especially noteworthy. First, the researchers designed a naturalistic experiment in which students were randomly assigned to specific living environments. Second, the research was longitudinal. This proved to be important, since some of the effects of larger living units did not emerge until students had lived in the dorms for several weeks. Third, the researchers used a rich variety of measures, including observations of behavior in the dorms, self-report questionnaires, and behavior in laboratory sessions. What other features of architectural design such as suites versus corridors, or low-rise versus high-rise buildings might make a difference in the experience of dormitory living?

ABSTRACT. *The present study assesses the effects of an architectural intervention on residential crowding stress and poststressor effects. Residents of long-corridor, short-corridor, and long-corridor-intervention dormitory floors were surveyed and social behavior and space use patterns were systematically observed over a 3-month period. As predicted, although students living in the three environments were initially comparable, residents of the long-corridor floor (40 residents sharing space) reported more crowding and residential social problems over time, whereas short-corridor residents (20 residents sharing space) and modified long-corridor residents (20 residents sharing space) reported fewer of these prob-* *lems. The results are interpreted in terms of a model of crowding in which architectural features of interior spaces are associated with space use patterns that facilitate or inhibit informal group development and regulation of the frequency of interaction and the amount of privacy. These conditions, in turn, are related to stress and stresslike symptoms.*

The psychological study of crowding has been spurred, in part, by disagreement over the effects of exposure to high-density living situations. Early laboratory research failed to confirm expectations that crowding was uniformly aversive (e.g., Freedman, 1975), indicating instead that crowding was a complex process mediated by a number of variables. More recent research in both laboratory and field settings has shown that crowding (the percep-

Reprinted from the *Journal of Personality and Social Psychology,* 1980, *38,* 471–481. Copyright 1980 by the American Psychological Association. Reprinted by permission of publisher and authors.

tion of unwanted high density) is associated with increased blood pressure, arousal, discomfort, and symptom reporting (Aiello, Epstein, & Karlin, 1975; D'Atri, 1975; McCain, Cox, & Paulus, 1976). Crowding has also been associated with alienation, withdrawal, helplessness, and death (McCarthy & Saegert, 1979; Paulus, McCain, & Cox, 1978). The preponderance of research now indicates that crowding is aversive under many conditions (cf. Sundstrom, 1978).

Researchers have now turned their attention to the development of strategies to prevent crowding stress or minimize its debilitating effects. As would be expected, much of this work has focused on variables that mediate crowding. Since high density is difficult to change directly, interventions have been studied by examining variables that make density more or less aversive. A number of models of crowding that focus on these mediating variables have emphasized the ways in which they affect personal control (Baron & Rodin, 1978; Baum & Valins, 1979; Cohen & Sherrod, 1978; Stokols, 1978). These models suggest interventions that can reduce the aversiveness of crowding.

We had two goals for the present research. First, we were concerned with testing the efficacy of an architectural intervention as a stress reducer in high-density residences. Attempts to reduce crowding stress have typically sought to "treat" people already exposed to high density by providing skills or information that would reduce stress without changing underlying conditions. Thus, clinical interventions have been directed towards helping subjects restructure the situation, distract themselves from it, or relax more effectively (e.g., Karlin, Katz, Epstein, & Woolfolk, 1979), and nonclinical strategies have attempted to provide alternative attributions for arousal (e.g., Worchel, 1978; Aiello, Note 1) or preparatory information that would reduce discomfort and improve coping (e.g., Langer & Saegert, 1977; Fisher & Baum, Note 2). Studies have also reported that when people are provided with actual or perceived control over the situation, the discomfort of crowding and the psychological costs associated with its stress are reduced

(Rodin, Solomon, & Metcalf, 1978; Sherrod, 1974).

Our intervention strategy followed from another approach directed toward preventing the experience of crowding rather than reducing stress once it is experienced. These attempts have sought to alter underlying conditions of high density either by providing subjects with the anticipation of experimenter control over group interactions or by separating subjects by placing barriers between them (e.g., Baum & Koman, 1976; Nicosia, Hyman, Karlin, Epstein, & Aiello, in press; Stokols, Smith, & Proster, 1975; Schopler & Walton, Note 3). However, these efforts have typically been short-term, temporary interventions, primarily in laboratory settings. The present research was concerned with architectural intervention in naturalistic settings and the long-term effects of intervention both in the residential setting that was changed and in the laboratory, where the psychological costs of residential crowding have been found to persist (Baum & Valins, 1977).

Since this intervention was derived from earlier findings that group formation and regulatory control of social interaction were primary mediators of crowding stress in high-density residential settings (Baum & Valins, 1977), our second intent was to further examine the usefulness of our conceptualization of density and crowding.

Architectural Design and Crowding

Our research has indicated that some interior design variables mediate the effects of high density by affecting the degree to which groups form or that individuals are able to control their social experience (Baum & Valins, 1977). Architectural manipulations that arbitrarily controlled group size by arrangement of rooms and sleeping quarters were found to be associated with inhibition of residential group development and with regulatory control over social contact. These problems were in turn associated with negative affect, withdrawal, behavior symptomatic of learned helplessness, and crowding—the subjective correlate of social density.

Interior designs with relatively large clusters of residents (32–40) around shared spaces resulted in more frequent and less predictable use of the central hallway (connecting bedrooms, lounges, and bathrooms). These long-corridor designs also increased the number of different people likely to use shared space. Residents of these dormitories reported more frequent unwanted interaction and were less able to predict or determine the nature and frequency of social contact than were residents of suite or short-corridor dormitories that clustered residents in smaller numbers (6–20).

These control problems both contributed to and were exacerbated by inhibited group formation in the long-corridor dormitories. The nonbedroom areas in this design were shared by many people, and it was particularly difficult for residents to regulate contact in these places. As a result, small groups were less likely to form than in the short-corridor/suite dormitories where space was differentiated and routinely used by a smaller number of people. The general failure of residents to form groups in long-corridor housing made individual control over social experience even more difficult. When groups did form in these settings or when expectations for control were still fairly high, crowding, withdrawal, and helplessness behaviors were not observed. As time passed, however, residents who were without group-derived control in these dormitories felt crowded, avoided social contact with neighbors and strangers, and appeared to be less motivated in nonsocial laboratory situations (Baum, Aiello, & Calesnick, 1978; Baum, Harpin, & Valins, 1975).

Simply stated, control over social experience appears to be an important aspect of response to high density; when such control is threatened or reduced, crowding and associated costs are more likely to occur. Group formation in these settings is an influential component of this control; the structures provided by a group reinforce individual members' ability to regulate interaction. Thus, the designs of the different dormitories determine residential group size, which in turn influences group development and regulatory control. Our intervention was designed to modify the group size associated with the long-corridor dormitory, increasing both the likelihood of small group formation and the ease of regulating contact with neighbors. The intervention should provide a test of our conceptualizations as well as reveal the usefulness of architectural interventions in high density settings, particularly when contrasted with studies of a similar theoretical nature conducted in analogous laboratory settings.

The field studies were conducted in some of the dormitories of a small residential liberal arts college. The architectural modifications had been completed during the summer preceding our investigation. Three settings were employed: a standard long corridor (LC), a short corridor (SC), and a long corridor altered by our architectural interventions (LCI). At the same time, housing officials allowed random assignment of residents to the long- and short-corridor dormitories.

Our approach to studying the intervention followed from our earlier work. We have viewed exposure to the different dormitory conditions as a manipulation, the strength of which is the length of time residents are exposed to them. Survey data have been used as a check on this manipulation: Subjects have been asked to indicate how crowded and controllable their dormitory floors were and to rate the development of small groups on the floor. Observational data have been used to describe the effects of exposure to residential conditions on behavior in the dormitory environment. Indices of willingness to interact (e.g., numbers of bedroom doors left open) as well as instances of interaction in the hallway have been obtained. The laboratory phase of research is seen as an assessment of the persistence and generalizability of the effects of exposure to different residential conditions. Measures of willingness to interact with an unknown other (e.g., interindividual distance, facial regard) have been obtained, and when subjects have been asked to work on a task that requires persistence in order to perform well, motivational deficits have been observed.

All of these measures have yielded reliable

differences between dormitory settings and were therefore used to assess the effectiveness of an intervention that modified the physical characteristics of a residence hall. Thus, survey, observational, and laboratory findings were expected to reflect more positive social experience and less withdrawal and helplessness among residents of the long-corridor-intervention floor than on the intact long-corridor floor. It was predicted that residents of the altered floor would resemble short-corridor residents in experiences reported and in behaviors observed and that both of these groups would diverge increasingly from the unaltered long-corridor floor as the semester progressed.

METHOD

Intervention

The long corridor of the second floor was selected as the site of the intervention. Since residents of all three floors of this dormitory responded comparably on our premeasures, the third floor was used as an unaltered comparison floor (see Figure 1). Residents of a short-corridor floor in a different but comparable dormitory were also sampled. Thus, three levels of the residential variables (a long corridor housing students in a group of 40, an altered long-corridor-intervention floor housing students in two groups of 20, and a short corridor housing students in three groups of 20) were considered, allowing comparison of the altered floor with both large and small residential group conditions previously observed in our research.

The intervention chosen represented a simple design modification (see Figure 1, Intervention floor). The second floor of the long-corridor dormitory was bisected by a three-room lounge area enclosed by unlocked doors. By converting three central bedrooms (two single, one double-occupancy rooms) to lounge space, the number of residents on this floor was reduced from 43 to 39. More importantly, the number of people sharing bathroom and hallway space was reduced; instead of a single

BR = Bedroom
B = Bathroom
L = Lounge

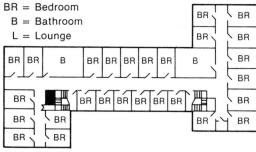

Long-corridor floor

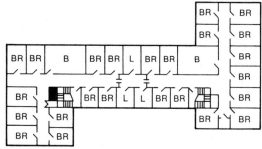

Intervention floor

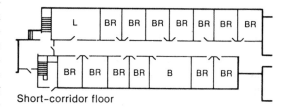

Short-corridor floor

Figure 1. Floor plans of the dormitory floors.

group of more than 40 residents, the floor now housed two groups of about 20.

Subjects

The dormitories were used primarily for freshmen, and the floors chosen housed only women. Subjects were first-year-student residents of the long- and short-corridor dormitories. Eighty-six residents completed questionnaires during orientation, but attrition over the course of the semester (approximately 20%)

resulted in only 67 residents completing all three in usable form.[1]

Fifty-four subjects (18 in each group) were randomly selected from these residential groups for participation in the laboratory phase of the study.

Survey Procedures

During the evening of the first day of orientation, and again after 5 and 12 weeks of dormitory residence, subjects were asked to complete questionnaires assessing their feelings about college and dormitory life. Questionnaires were administered in the subjects' bedrooms.

The questionnaires varied in format over the three administration periods, but all assessed subjects' feelings about the college, dormitory life, other students, and how they spent their time. Of primary interest were questions asking students to rate (on 5- and 7-point scales) how crowded, hectic, and predictable they found dormitory life on their floor, success at and expectations for maintaining control over social experience in the residential setting, and perceptions of group formation and control of space in the dormitory.

Observational Procedures

Observation of resident behavior in the dormitory environments was conducted on week nights (10:00 to 11:00 p.m.) between the 3rd and 14th weeks of residence by a college-age male observer who was trained to 90% agreement with the first author. The observer was unaware of the experimental hypotheses. Each floor was observed three times a week each week except for the 7th, 8th, and 13th weeks (these periods corresponded to exam periods, an open week, and Thanksgiving recess, during which most students were not on campus). The

observer moved through the three dormitory settings in a changing but predetermined order, noting the location and nature of social and nonsocial behaviors. The number of bedroom doors open during the observation period was also recorded. Upon entering a dormitory floor, the observer spent 5 minutes at one end of the floor, slowly worked his way toward the other end, and spent an additional 5 minutes observing from this position. Observations were made covertly, and none of the residents were able to identify the observer when asked at the end of the semester.

Experimental Procedures

Laboratory assessment of resident behavior was conducted between the 5th and 11th weeks of dormitory residence. Each subject arrived at the laboratory alone, expecting to participate in a study of "impression formation." After greeting the subject, the experimenter repeated the purpose of the experiment, adding that the sessions were running late and that it would be a few minutes before everything was ready. The subject was then asked to wait in an adjoining room until the experiment was ready to begin. When she was shown into this waiting room, she encountered a same-sex confederate sitting in the first of five chairs lined up against one wall of the room. Subjects were told that the confederate was another subject waiting for the same experiment. Confederates remained responsive during the waiting session, but did not initiate eye contact or conversation.

Once the subject had selected a seat, the experimenter began observation from behind a one-way mirror across from the row of chairs. Seat position was noted, and a continuous record of facial regard (number of seconds spent looking at the face or eyes of the confederate) was kept. At the end of 5 minutes, the experimenter ended the observation period and entered the waiting room with a single-page assessment questionnaire. It asked the subject to indicate how much sleep she had had the night before, when she had last eaten, how comfortable she felt at that moment, how much control she felt she would have over the

---

[1] It was not possible to survey all residents during orientation. Some did not arrive on campus until later in the week, and six refused to complete the questionnaires. Attrition of subjects over the course of the semester was largely accounted for by illness or by scheduling problems; four students refused to complete subsequent questionnaires, two students moved to different dormitories, and eight were ill during the weeks that questionnaires were administered.

session, and how she felt about the room in which she was waiting. This questionnaire required a few minutes for completion. Following that, the confederate and subject were shown into different rooms; the confederate helped ready materials for the next session while the subject was presented with an experimental task.

The subject was presented with a list of 12 difficult (but solvable) anagrams.[2] Each anagram was printed on an index card, and the 12 cards were spread out in front of the subject. Instructions informed the subject that no writing was allowed; all work on the anagrams had to be done "in your head." She was told that she would be allowed 20 sec to solve each anagram, but that she could come back and request additional trials on any that were missed after attempting all 12 on the list. As with initial presentations, repeat trials lasted 20 sec. It was explained that the subject could attempt any item as often as she wished.

Following completion of this task (either after the subject had solved all of the anagrams or after she indicated that she did not wish to continue), she was debriefed and thanked for her participation.

RESULTS

The questionnaire data provided evidence of continued stress and control-related problems among residents of the unaltered long-corridor floor and indicated that the intervention reduced these problems on the altered long-corridor floor. As predicted, long-corridor residents reported more crowding and control-related problems and less small group development than did either of the other two groups. After one day of residence (during orientation), long- and short-corridor residents gave similar reports on a number of dimensions, but several weeks later, long-corridor residents' reports diverged from those of the short-corridor or the long-corridor-intervention residents. These differences will be examined variable by variable.

Some of the variables were assessed on all three questionnaires (orientation, 5th week, and 12th week administrations), and some were assessed on only the two latter questionnaires.[3] Multivariate analyses of variance were performed on related data, and multivariate effects for each group of variables are presented first, followed by univariate effects for component variables. Reported mean contrasts were done using procedures suggested by Tukey (e.g., Myers, 1966).

Control

During orientation, residents of all three environments reported comparable feelings of control in the dormitory, but during the 5th and 12th weeks of residence, long-corridor residents reported less perceived control than did the other students, $F(18, 106) = 6.183$, $p < .001$. Long-corridor residents reported increasing difficulties in regulating social contact in the dormitory and perceived dormitory life to be more hectic and less controllable than did residents of the other environments, $F(4, 126) = 21.520$, $p < .001$; $F(4, 126) = 3.800$, $p < .01$; and $F(4, 128) = 9.740$, $p < .001$ (see Table 1). Long-corridor residents were also more likely to attribute problems to the large number of people with whom they lived, $F(4, 126) = 6.380$, $p < .01$.

Long-corridor residents also expressed less confidence in their ability to control experience in both dormitory and nondormitory settings. $F(8, 120) = 9.961$, $p < .001$. Univariate analyses indicated that long-corridor residents showed stronger disagreement with the statement, "In your dormitory it is worthwhile to try to structure your interaction with others" than did residents of intervention or short-corridor floors,

---

[2] Items for this task were 5-to-8-letter anagrams constructed for the study. They were pretested for difficulty by administering them to 60 juniors and seniors at the same college. Mean number of anagrams solved by this group was 3.8.

[3] Because some of the questions that we asked were meaningless to a student who had just arrived on campus for orientation, they were not included on the first questionnaire. Thus, questions pertaining to group development were asked only after 5 and 12 weeks of residence.

Table 1   Mean Ratings of Perceived Control and Difficulty Regulating Social Contact Over Time

Dormitory Design	Perceived Control			Difficulty Regulating Experience		
	Orientation	5th Week of Residence	10th Week of Residence	Orientation	5th Week of Residence	10th Week of Residence
Long corridor	3.42	2.70	2.40	1.82	3.27	3.77
Long-corridor intervention	3.59	3.73	3.56	2.12	2.07	1.96
Short corridor	3.33	3.37	3.84	2.22	2.33	2.06

Note. Ratings are on 5-point scales where higher values represent more of the dimension being measured.

$F(2, 61) = 37.82, p < .001$ (see Table 2). They more strongly agreed with the statement, "It is often not worth the effort to try to change the way things are" than did residents of intervention and short-corridor floors, $F(2, 61) = 44.05, p < .001$ (see Table 2).

Group Formation

Long-corridor residents reported that small groups were less likely to form on their floor than did residents of the other floors, $F(12, 112) = 7.683, p < .001$. Univariate analyses indicated that long-corridor residents felt less successful in making friends or forming small groups on their floor than did residents of the intervention and short corridor floors, $F(2, 61) = 8.13, p < .001$, and $F(2, 61) = 30.13, p < .001$.

Additional data indicated that although residents of all three environments reported knowing comparable numbers of neighbors during orientation, long-corridor residents reported knowing fewer as friends after 5 and 12 weeks of residence, $F(4, 120) = 2.812, p < .05$.

Crowding

There were no differences across residential groups for perceived crowding in the dormitory during orientation, but during the 5th and 12th weeks of residence, long-corridor residents felt more crowded in the dormitory ($M = 5.0; M = 4.7$) than did residents of the intervention floor ($M = 2.7; M = 2.9$) or the short-corridor building ($M = 2.6; M = 2.9$), $F(2, 63) = 36.648, p < .001$.

Observational Findings

Behaviors observed in the long-corridor setting were comparable to those observed in other settings during the first 5 weeks of residence, but were more suggestive of withdrawal during the last 7 weeks of the semester than were those in the other environments. Although as many people were observed in the long-corridor setting as in the short-corridor and intervention settings, less social activity (two or more people interacting) was observed in the long-corridor environment, $F(2, 60) = 8.503, p < .001$. These differences did not

Table 2   Mean Disagreement With Statements Reflecting Motivation to Achieve Control

Dormitory Design	Not Worth Effort to Change		Worthwhile Structuring Interaction	
	5th Week of Residence	10th Week of Residence	5th Week of Residence	10th Week of Residence
Long corridor	3.00	2.36	3.41	3.68
Long-corridor intervention	4.15	3.96	2.27	2.12
Short corridor	4.06	4.39	2.61	2.11

Note. Ratings are on 5-point scales where higher values represent greater disagreement with the statement.

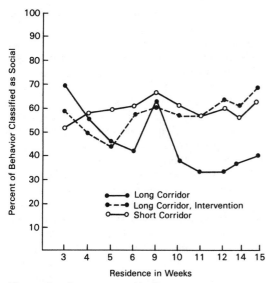

Figure 2. Percentage of hallway activity on dormitory floors rated as social.

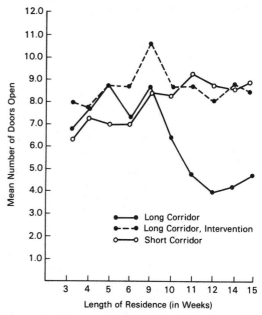

Figure 3. Mean number of doors open during 15-minute observation periods.

emerge immediately (see Figure 2); an interaction between residential group and length of residence indicated that clear differences were not found until the 10th week of residence, $F(18, 75) = 2.033$, $p < .05$. Mean contrasts indicated that there were no differences among the three residential groups during the 3rd through 9th weeks, but that the number of social behaviors observed on the long-corridor floor was significantly less than that observed on other floors during the 10th through 15th weeks ($p < .05$).

Previous research has indicated that open bedroom doors on the dormitory floor are a signal that the occupants are willing to interact with neighbors. Counts of open doors in the present research indicated that long-corridor residents were less likely to leave their doors open than were short-corridor or long-corridor-intervention residents, $F(2, 60) = 19.193$, $p < .001$.

This was qualified by an interaction with length of residence (see Figure 3), $F(18, 60) = 2.251$, $p < .01$. The number of doors open on the floor slowly increased for all residential settings during the first 8 weeks of the semester; following that, the number of open

doors on the long-corridor floor decreased over time, and significant differences emerged between it and the other two settings ($p < .05$).

Laboratory Findings

Differences between residents of the long-corridor, short-corridor, and long-corridor-intervention floors were also evident in the laboratory. Three residents of each residential group were observed in the laboratory during the 5th through 11th weeks of dormitory residence (excepting the 9th), and their behavior in the laboratory was consistent with previous findings that long-corridor residents persist in avoiding contact by assuming more withdrawn postures than the others, $F(12, 94) = 3.666$, $p < .001$. Also consistent with previous research, no effects of length of residence were found. Long-corridor residents sat farther away from the confederate, $F(2, 52) = 9.196$, $p < .01$; looked at her less often, $F(2, 52) = 4.620$, $p < .01$; and felt more uncomfortable following the 5-minute waiting period, $F(2, 52) = 19.843$, $p < .001$, than did residents of the other floors (see Table 3).

Table 3 Mean Responses to the Confederate in the Laboratory

Dormitory Design	Seats Away From Confederate	Facial Regard for Confederate (in sec)	Discomfort After Waiting
Long corridor	2.6$_a$	18.2$_a$	4.3$_a$
Long-corridor intervention	1.9$_b$	50.3$_b$	2.8$_b$
Short corridor	2.0$_b$	52.0$_b$	2.7$_b$

Note. Discomfort was assessed on a 7-point scale where higher values represented greater discomfort. Numbers with different subscripts are significantly different from one another ($p < .05$).

Long-corridor residents expected to have less control ($M = 2.4$) over the session once it started than did either of the other groups ($M_{SC} = 3.9$; $M_{LCI} = 3.6$), $F(2, 52) = 7.180$, $p < .01$. No other differences among residential groups were found for behavior or mood in the waiting situation.

Although there were no differences among residential groups on number of anagrams correctly solved, long-corridor residents attempted fewer anagram trials ($M = 15.8$) than did residents of short-corridor or long-corridor-intervention settings ($M_{SC} = 20.6$; $M_{LCI} = 21.8$), $F(2, 52) = 6.986$, $p < .01$. In order to control for the possibility that these findings were related to success on the anagram task, an analysis of covariance was performed. This analysis, using number of anagrams correctly solved as a covariate, indicated that success did not influence persistence on the task.

DISCUSSION

Bisection of the long-corridor floor resulted in more positive interaction on the dormitory floor, more local group development, more confidence among residents in their ability to control events in the dormitory, and less withdrawal in both residential and nonresidential settings compared with the unaltered long-corridor floor.[4] The altered floor was characterized by local social patterns more similar to those observed in short-corridor settings than to those characterizing the long-corridor floor. Residents of the short-corridor and intervention floors actively developed and used shared spaces for social purposes, were able to more effectively regulate social contact with neighbors, and experienced less crowding stress than did long-corridor residents.

These findings are of interest for a number of theoretical and practical reasons. First, they provide confirmation of the conceptualizations that we have developed to explain our findings over the past 7 years. Second, they offer some evidence of a sequential pattern of crowding stress based on loss of control and the expectations of regaining it (e.g., Baum et al., 1978; Wortman & Brehm, 1975). Third, the usefulness of architectural intervention in high-density residential settings is highlighted, suggesting that behavioral data can be used in design of residential environments.

Our explanation for dormitory-based differences in crowding and sociability has revolved around architecturally determined residential group size, group development, and control. The accuracy of these explanations may be gauged, in part, by the degree to which intervention to reduce group size affected social behavior. By reducing residential group size from more than 40 to about 20 residents sharing common areas, the symptoms of stress, withdrawal, and helplessness observed on the unaltered floor were prevented. Residents of the bisected floor did not complain of frequent

---

[4] It is unlikely that the observed effects were due merely to residents' awareness of our studies or to the simple effects of change. Residents of all three dormitory settings were told that their residences were being studied as part of a campus-wide environmental investigation, and refurbishing had been conducted on all settings during the summer. Although substantive changes had been made in only one setting, residents were under the impression that improvements had been made in all of them. It is also unlikely that the extra lounge space provided by the intervention was responsible for our findings. Observations indicated that these lounge rooms were rarely used, and they were not fully furnished until the second semester.

unwanted contact or difficulty in controlling interaction, but residents of the unaltered floor did. Group development was more extensive on the intervention floor, and withdrawal and reduced persistence on challenging tasks did not generalize to the laboratory as it did among long-corridor residents. By modifying group size, local group formation was facilitated and most of the control-relevant problems associated with crowding were mitigated. Residents of a floor previously associated with crowding stress described it as a positive, uncrowded, and controllable environment.

Most studies of residential crowding or architectural determinants of behavior have of necessity been retrospective and correlational in nature. Few, if any, have considered randomly assigned residents, have been able to trace the development of social networks, or have been able to draw causal relationships between design variables and behavioral outcomes. Further, the opportunity to actually manipulate and study the nature of architectural interventions has been rare. In fact, one of the primary criticisms of our past research has been the belief that it is impossible to separate our effects from background variables inherent in the buildings we have studied or the people living in them.

The present study considered randomly assigned residents in a prospective study of an intervention that we planned and manipulated. The results, because they are based on a controlled study of randomly assigned subjects, argue against alternative explanations based on background or personality variables. The data also suggest that features of the dormitory building other than those related to group size are not related to our findings. Dormitories characterized by suite or short-corridor designs were newer, had more pleasant views, and were located across campus from long-corridor housing. It is therefore conceivable that factors other than social density influenced our findings (see, for example, Baron & Mandel, 1978). The present research, however, indicates that these factors were not influential. Since the long-corridor and intervention floors were located in the same building and shared the same

view, potential effects of different buildings could not be a factor in the differences observed between floors.

It is important to note that crowding and withdrawal emerged gradually over the course of the semester. Previous research (Baum et al., 1978) has indicated that the process by which these phenomena characterize long-corridor environments is sequential. The present research also indicates that some of the effects of the different architectural designs are linked to length of residence. Differences between the unaltered long corridor and the other residential groups in their self-reports of crowding, social control, and friendship formation emerged after 5 weeks. Differences in observable social activity on the dormitory floor, however, did not emerge consistently until the 10th week. These findings suggest that problems related to regulation of contact with neighbors inhibited group development in the long-corridor environment and that the relative absence of small groups reduced individual control over shared spaces in the dormitory. As these problems intensified over time, residents of long-corridor housing became more withdrawn and began to exhibit symptoms of helplessness.

Closer examination of the observational data reveals an unexpected increase in long-corridor residents' sociability during the 9th week. This sudden increase, which was followed by a decrease in social interaction, may be interpreted in terms of the open-week period (used by most students as a vacation) preceding the 9th week. Upon returning from vacation, long-corridor residents were more socially active, and this may have reflected an attempt to reinvolve themselves in dormitory life. However, since interacting in shared spaces and leaving their doors open exposed them to stressful conditions and again threatened social regulatory control, they responded by withdrawing. Since the decline in long-corridor residents' sociability is greater from Week 9 to Week 10 than for any other 2-week interval, reexposure after "time out" from crowding stress appears to be more psychologically potent than 2 weeks of constant exposure. Reexposure may have reactivated coping mechanisms that were already partially learned.

Finally, the results suggest that architectural interventions that reduce the size of residential groupings can prevent crowding stress. Even though residents of all three settings responded similarly on their arrival on campus, the responses and behaviors of intervention-floor residents were more comparable to those of short-corridor residents after 5 and 12 weeks, and those of residents of the unaltered long-corridor environment consistently differed. By modifying the physical environment, social dynamics may be altered for the benefit of inhabitants. Direct architectural intervention prevented crowding stress and poststressor effects. In the long run, a preventive strategy of the kind taken in the present research may be more beneficial to residents of high-density settings than treatment programs instituted after the problem has been identified.[5]

Despite the nature of the present data, the architectural intervention employed in this study should not be routinely extrapolated to other settings. Studies of processes in one setting may not be good predictors of outcomes in other settings. Based on similar multilevel analyses of the interface between architectural and social systems in other settings, physical interventions specifically tailored to a setting may be designed and implemented. However, the direct applicability of interventions used in college dormitory environments to noncollege populations in other, larger scale environments must be seriously questioned. Although we must caution against assumptions regarding the generalizibility of our own particular inter-

vention, we believe that the theory on which it was based should generalize to similar settings. We are presently planning an analysis of urban neighborhoods, and the variables underlying crowding stress appear to be remarkably similar to those discussed here (Baum, Davis, & Aiello, 1978). However, alteration of existing neighborhood designs is impractical. Thus, the important practical implications of this research are for the design decisions made during the planning stage of residential environments. Better environments may be designed if planning can be based on research that delineates how physical environments accommodate the needs and preferences that mediate residential experience and behavior.

REFERENCE NOTES

1. Aiello, J. *Just how funny can crowding be: Humor as a distractor under high-density conditions.* Paper presented at the meeting of the Eastern Psychological Association, March 1978.
2. Fisher, J., & Baum, A. *Situation-related information as a mediator of responses to crowding.* Unpublished manuscript, Trinity College, 1977.
3. Schopler, J., & Walton, M. *The effects of expected structure, expected enjoyment, and participants internality–externality upon feelings of being crowded.* Unpublished manuscript, University of North Carolina, 1974.

REFERENCES

Aiello, J., Epstein, Y., & Karlin, R. Effects of crowding on electrodermal activity. *Sociological Symposium*, 1975, *14*, 43–57.

Baron, R., & Mandel, D. Toward an ecological model of density effects in dormitory settings. In A. Baum & Y. Epstein (Eds.), *Human response to crowding.* Hillsdale, N.J.: Erlbaum, 1978.

Baron, R., & Rodin, J. Perceived control and crowding stress: Processes mediating the impact of spatial and social density. In A. Baum & Y. Epstein (Eds.), *Human response to crowding.* Hillsdale, N.J.: Erlbaum, 1978.

Baum, A., Aiello, J. R., & Calesnick, L. Crowding and personal control: Social density and the development of learned helplessness. *Journal of Personality and Social Psychology*, 1978, *36*, 1000–1011.

Baum, A., Davis, G., & Aiello, J. R. Crowding and neighborhood mediation of urban density. *Journal of Population*, 1978, *1*, 266–279.

---

[5] It is likely that the same kinds of benefits observed in this research might have been accomplished by simply reducing the occupancy of each room from two to one. This would have effected the same change in group size on the dormitory floor, and was, in fact, considered as an option by the college housing office. However, such a strategy would have been costly, sacrificing 20 residential spots at a cost of about $20,000. Our approach to the problem was effective and cost the college only $4,000 in lost revenues. Therefore, the cost effectiveness of the intervention was reasonably good. Experimentally, the alternative would have been unfortunate, since social density would have been confounded with room occupancy.

Baum, A., Harpin, R. E., & Valins, S. The role of group phenomena in the experience of crowding. *Environment and Behavior*, 1975, 7, 185–197.

Baum, A., & Koman, S. Differential response to anticipated crowding: Psychological effects of social and spatial density. *Journal of Personality and Social Psychology*, 1976, *34*, 526–536.

Baum, A., & Valins, S. *Architecture and social behavior*. Hillsdale, N.J.: Erlbaum, 1977.

Baum, A., & Valins, S. Architectural mediation of residential density and control: Crowding and the regulation of social contact. In L. Berkowitz (Ed.), *Advances in experimental social psychology* (Vol. 12). New York: Academic Press, 1979.

Cohen, S., & Sherrod, D. When density matters: Environmental control as a determinant of crowding effects in laboratory and residential settings. *Journal of Population*, 1978, *1*, 189–202.

D'Atri, D. Psychophysiological responses to crowding. *Environment and Behavior*, 1975, 7, 237–252.

Freedman, J. *Crowding and behavior*. San Francisco: Freeman, 1975.

Karlin, R., Katz, S., Epstein, Y., & Woolfolk, R. The use of therapeutic interventions to reduce crowding related arousal: A preliminary investigation. *Environmental Psychology & Nonverbal Behavior*, 1979, *3*, 219–227.

Langer, E., & Saegert, S. Crowding and cognitive control. *Journal of Personality and Behavior*, 1977, *8*, 283–290.

McCain, G., Cox, V., & Paulus, P. The relationship between illness complaints and degree of crowding in a prison environment. *Environment and Behavior*, 1976, *8*, 283–290.

McCarthy, D., & Saegert, A. Residential density, social overload, and social withdrawal. In J. Aiello & A.

Baum, *Residential crowding and design*. New York: Plenum Press, 1979.

Myers, J. E. *Fundamentals of experimental design*. Boston: Allyn & Bacon, 1966.

Nicosia, G., Hyman, D., Karlin, R., Epstein, Y., & Aiello, J. Effects of bodily contact on reactions to crowding. *Journal of Applied Social Psychology*, 1979, in press.

Paulus, P., McCain, G., & Cox, V. Death rates, psychiatric commitments, blood pressure, and perceived crowding as a function of institutional crowding. *Environment, Psychology and Nonverbal Behavior*, 1978, *36*, 998–999.

Rodin, J., Solomon, S., & Metcalf, J. Role of control in mediating perceptions of density. *Journal of Personality and Social Psychology*, 1978, *36*, 998–999.

Sherrod, D. Crowding, perceived control, and behavioral effects. *Journal of Applied Social Psychology*, 1974, *4*, 171–186.

Stokols, D. A typology of crowding experiments. In A. Baum & Y. Epstein (Eds.), *Human response to crowding*. Hillsdale, N.J.: Erlbaum, 1978.

Stokols, D., Smith, T. E., & Proster, J. Partitioning and perceived crowding in a public place. *American Behavioral Scientist*, 1975, *18*, 792–814.

Sundstrom, E. Crowding as sequential process: Review of research on the effects of population density on humans. In A. Baum & Y. Epstein (Eds.), *Human response to crowding*. Hillsdale, N.J.: Erlbaum, 1978.

Worchel, S. Reducing crowding without increasing space: Some applications of an attributional theory of crowding. *Journal of Population*, 1978, *1*, 216–230.

Wortman, C., & Brehm, J. Responses to uncontrollable outcomes: An integration of reactance and the learned helplessness model. In L. Berkowitz (Ed.), *Advances in experimental social psychology* (Vol. 8). New York: Academic Press, 1975.

25

Adjustment to Threatening Events:
A Theory of Cognitive Adaptation

Shelley E. Taylor

Chronic diseases such as cancer, heart disease, and diabetes are now the major health threats that face industrialized nations. Yet until relatively recently, psychologists had not investigated the impact of these often traumatizing experiences. In this article, Shelley Taylor presents one viewpoint of how people adjust to threatening events, in this case a diagnosis of breast cancer. Taylor suggests that the adjustment process involves an attempt to find meaning in the experience, efforts to regain a sense of mastery over the events and over one's life more generally, and an effort to restore self-esteem. In offering this prospective, Taylor maintains that when confronted with threatening events, people draw upon illusions that help them to maintain positive views of themselves and their situations even in the face of present and future threat. Taylor noted that, as a consequence, these women were not devastated by their experience, but rather actually seemed to benefit in some ways from this potentially destructive event. Thus, while a chronic disease often creates frustrating and complex physical, social, and psychological adjustments, paradoxically it can also confer nobility and heroism on its victims, as they struggle to integrate the complexities of the disorder into their lives.

ABSTRACT: A theory of cognitive adaptation to threatening events is proposed. It is argued that the adjustment process centers around three themes: A search for meaning in the experience, an attempt to regain mastery over the event in particular and over one's life more generally, and an effort to restore self-esteem through self-enhancing evaluations. These themes are discussed with reference to cancer patients' coping efforts. It is maintained that successful adjustment depends, in a large part, on the ability to sustain and modify illusions that buffer not only against present threats but also against possible future setbacks.

One of the most impressive qualities of the human psyche is its ability to withstand severe personal tragedy successfully. Despite serious setbacks such as personal illness or the death of a family member, the majority of people facing such blows achieve a quality of life or level of happiness equivalent to or even exceeding their prior level of satisfaction.[1] Not everyone readjusts, of course (Silver & Wortman, 1980), but most do, and furthermore they do so substantially on their own. That is, typically people do not seek professional help in dealing with personal problems. They use their social networks and individual resources, and their apparent cure rate, if self-reports of satisfaction are to be trusted, is impressive even by profes-

Reprinted from the *American Psychologist*, 1983, *38*, pp. 1161–1173. Copyright 1983 by the American Psychological Association, Inc. Reprinted by permission of publisher and author.

---

[1] See Turk (1979); Visotsky, Hamburg, Goss, and Lebovits (1961); Tavormina, Kastner, Slater, and Watt (1976); Andreasen and Norris (1972); Weisman (1979); Follick and Turk (Note 1); Katz (1963); Myers, Friedman, and Weiner (1970); see also Silver and Wortman (1980); Leon, Butcher, Kleinman, Goldberg, and Almagor (1981).

sional standards (Gurin, Veroff, & Feld, 1960; Wills, 1982).

These self-curing abilities are a formidable resource, and our recent work with cancer patients, cardiac patients, rape victims, and other individuals facing life-threatening events has explored them. The consequence of these investigations is a theory of cognitive adaptation. I will argue that when an individual has experienced a personally threatening event, the readjustment process focuses around three themes: a search for meaning in the experience, an attempt to regain mastery over the event in particular and over one's life more generally, and an effort to enhance one's self-esteem— to feel good about oneself again despite the personal setback.

Specifically, meaning is an effort to understand the event: why it happened and what impact it has had. The search for meaning attempts to answer the question, What is the significance of the event? Meaning is exemplified by, but not exclusively determined by, the results of an attributional search that answers the question, What caused the event to happen? Meaning is also reflected in the answer to the question, What does my life mean now? The theme of mastery centers around gaining control over the event and one's life. It is exemplified by, but not exclusively served by, beliefs about personal control. Efforts at mastery center on the questions, How can I keep this or a similar event from happening again? and What can I do to manage it now? The third theme is self-enhancement. Victimizing events often reduce self-esteem (e.g., Briar, 1966; Pearlin & Schooler, 1978; Ryan, 1971) even when the individual had no responsibility for bringing the event about. Many intrapsychic efforts at recovery accordingly involve finding ways to feel good about oneself again. The theme of self-enhancement is not addressed by one particular cognition (it is served by many), but in our own work, social comparisons have been a chief vehicle by which self-enhancement occurred.

Before turning to an analysis of these three themes, an important quality that they share merits mention. I will maintain that the individual's efforts to successfully resolve these three themes rest fundamentally upon the ability to form and maintain a set of illusions. By illusions, I do not mean that the beliefs are necessarily opposite to known facts. Rather, their maintenance requires looking at the known facts in a particular light, because a different slant would yield a less positive picture, or the beliefs have yet to yield any factual basis of support. The viewpoint that successful recovery from tragedy rests on illusion may seem overly cynical, but I hope to convince the reader that it is not.

The following analysis draws heavily on the responses of 78 women with breast cancer and many of their family members whom Rosemary Lichtman, Joanne Wood, and I have intensively interviewed during the past two years (Taylor, Lichtman, & Wood, Note 2). Some of these women have good prognoses, others do not. Some have achieved a high quality of life following their illness (although it may have taken them several years to do so), others have not. But virtually all of them have shown some attempt to resolve the three issues of meaning, mastery, and self-enhancement.

In the remainder of the article I will first describe the processes that contribute to cognitive adaptation, namely those that center around these three themes. Next, I will address the issue of illusion and maintain that, far from impeding adjustment, illusion may be critical to mental health. Then, I will focus on the very important question: What happens if the illusions upon which one's satisfaction is based are disconfirmed? I will suggest that disconfirmation of one's beliefs, such as a belief in personal control, may not be as psychologically problematic as currently popular models of the disconfirmation process would lead us to believe. Using principles of cognitive adaptation, I will offer an alternative model of the disconfirmation process.

THE SEARCH FOR MEANING

The search for meaning involves the need to understand why a crisis occurred and what its impact has been. One of the ways in which meaning is addressed is through causal attributions. Attribution theory (Heider, 1958; Kelley, 1967) maintains that following a threatening or dramatic event, people will make attributions so as to understand, predict, and control their environment (Wong & Weiner, 1981). By understanding the cause of an event, one may also begin to understand the significance of the event and what it symbolizes about one's life. In the case of cancer, of course, no one knows the true cause or causes. There are a number of known causes, such as heredity, diet, or specific carcinogens, but a search for the cause of cancer on the part of a patient would seem to be a fruitless endeavor.

Nonetheless, cancer patients do try to understand why they developed cancer. Ninety-five percent of our respondents offered some explanation for why their cancer occurred. In an effort to have some comparison group against which to judge this rate, we also asked the spouses of these patients whether they had any theory about the cause of their partner's cancer. One would also expect spouses' rates of making attributions to be inflated, relative to an uninvolved person, since they, like the patients, have been strongly affected by the cancer experience. Nonetheless, their rate of making causal attributions was significantly less (63%), suggesting that the need for an explanation was more insistent among the patients themselves.

Does any particular form of the attributional explanation meet the search for meaning better than others? This question can be partially addressed by looking at the specific content of the cancer patients' explanations and then relating those explanations to overall psychological adjustment.[2] The largest number (41%) attributed their cancer either to general stress

or to a particular type of stress. When a particular stressor was mentioned, it was often either an ongoing problematic marriage or a recent divorce. Thirty-two percent of the sample attributed their cancer to some particular carcinogen, including ingested substances such as birth control pills, DES, or primarin (which is an estrogen replenisher prescribed for menopausal women) or to environmental carcinogens such as having lived near a chemical dump, a nuclear testing site, or a copper mine. Twenty-six percent of the women attributed their cancer to hereditary factors. Another 17% attributed it to diet (usually to a diet high in protein and fat and low in vegetables), and 10% blamed some blow to the breast such as an automobile accident, a fall, or in one case, being hit in the breast by a frisbee. (The numbers exceed 100% because a number of people had multiple theories.) It is noteworthy that with the exception of heredity, all of these causes are either past, rather than ongoing events, or they are events over which one currently has some control, such as stress or diet. This fact anticipates a point to be made shortly—that meaning and mastery may often be intertwined.

When one relates these specific attributions to overall psychological adjustment to the cancer, no single attribution stands out as more functional than any other. All are uncorrelated with adjustment. It would be premature to conclude from this information that these attributional explanations are functionally interchangeable. However, the high frequency of making attributions, coupled with the fact that no specific attribution produces better adjustment, suggests that causal meaning itself is the goal of the attributional search rather than the specific form through which it is realized.

The search for meaning involves not only understanding why the event occurred, but what its implications for one's life are now. Slightly over half of our respondents reported that the cancer experience had caused them to reappraise their lives. Here is one example from a 61-year-old woman:

You can take a picture of what someone has done, but when you frame it, it becomes significant. I

[2] Psychological adjustment is operationalized in this study as a factor score. The high-loading items are: The physician's rating of the patient on a standardized measure of adjustment termed the Global Adjustment to Illness Scale (GAIS; Derogatis, 1975); the interviewer's independent rating on that same scale; the patient's self-rated adjustment on a 5-point scale; patient self-reports of various psychological symptoms, such as anxiety and depression; the patient's score on the Profile of Mood States (McNair & Lorr, 1964); and the Campbell, Converse, and Rodgers (1976) Index of Well-Being.

feel as if I were for the first time really conscious. My life is framed in a certain amount of time. I always knew it. But I can see it, and it's made better by the knowledge.

For many, the meaning derived from the cancer experience brought a new attitude toward life:

I have much more enjoyment of each day, each moment. I am not so worried about what is or isn't or what I wish I had. All those things you get entangled with don't seem to be part of my life right now.

For others, the meaning gained from the experience was self-knowledge or self-change:

The ability to understand myself more fully is one of the greatest changes I have experienced. I have faced what I went through. It's a bit like holding up a mirror to one's face when one can't turn around. I think that is a very essential thing.

I was very happy to find out I am a very strong person. I have no time for game-playing any more. I want to get on with life. And I have become more introspective and also let others fend for their own responsibilities. And now almost five years later, I have become a very different person.

Typically, individuals have reordered their priorities, giving low priority to such mundane concerns as housework, petty quarrels, and involvement in other people's problems and high priority to relationships with spouse, children, and friends, personal projects, or just plain enjoyment of life (Lichtman, Note 3):

You take a long look at your life and realize that many things that you thought were important before are totally insignificant. That's probably been the major change in my life. What you do is put things into perspective. You find out that things like relationships are really the most important things you have—the people you know and your family—everything else is just way down the line. It's very strange that it takes something so serious to make you realize that.

Not everyone can construe positive meaning from the experience.

I thought I was a well-cared-for, middle-class woman who chose her doctors carefully and who was doing everything right. I was rather pleased with myself. I had thought I could handle pretty much what came my way. And I was completely shattered. My confidence in myself was completely undermined.

However, when positive meaning can be construed from the cancer experience, it produces significantly better psychological adjustment. The cancer threat, then, is perceived by many to have been the catalytic agent for restructuring their lives along more meaningful lines with an overall beneficial effect.

To summarize, the attempt to find meaning in the cancer experience takes at least two forms: a causal analysis that provides an answer to the question of why it happened and a rethinking of one's attitudes and priorities to restructure one's life along more satisfying lines, changes that are prompted by and attributed to the cancer.

GAINING A SENSE OF MASTERY

A sudden threatening event like cancer can easily undermine one's sense of control over one's body and one's life generally (e.g., Leventhal, 1975). Accordingly, a second theme of the adjustment process is gaining a feeling of control over the threatening event so as to manage it or keep it from occurring again. This theme of mastery is exemplified by beliefs about personal control.

Many cancer patients seem to solve the issue of mastery by believing that they personally can keep the cancer from coming back. Two thirds of the patients we interviewed believed they had at least some control over the course of or recurrence of their cancer, and 37% believed they had a lot of control. Some of the remaining one third believed that although they personally had no control over the cancer, it could be controlled by the doctor or by continued treatments. Hence, belief in direct control of the cancer is quite strong. Again, using the significant others as a comparison population, belief in both the patient's ability to control the cancer and the physician's ability to control the cancer are less strong, suggesting that mastery needs are greater among patients. Significantly, both the belief that one can control one's own cancer and the belief that the physician or treatments can control it are strongly associated with overall positive adjustment, and both together are even better.

Many of the patients' efforts at control were mental. One of the most common manifestations was a belief that a positive attitude would keep the cancer from coming back:

I believe that if you're a positive person, your attitude has a lot to do with it. I definitely feel I will never get it again.

My mental attitude, I think, is the biggest control over it I have. I want to feel there is something I can do, that there is some way I can control it.

I think that if you feel you are in control of it, you can control it up to a point. I absolutely refuse to have any more cancer.

A substantial number attempted to control their cancer by using specific techniques of psychological control. These techniques included meditation, imaging, self-hypnosis, positive thinking, or a combination of factors. Many had read the Simonton and Simonton (1975) work suggesting that people can control their own cancers using these kinds of methods, and they saw no harm in trying them on their own; a number had great faith in them.

Causal attributions can also contribute to a sense of mastery if the perceived initial cause is believed to be no longer in effect. Apropos of this point, for many patients the perception of a discontinuity between the time before their cancer and their present life is very important. They need to be able to say that "things are different now." For some, this perceived temporal discontinuity was tied to a relationship. One woman, for example, characterized her first husband as a "boorish rapist" and believed that this destructive relationship had produced the cancer; her new involvement with her "wonderful" second husband, she felt, would keep her cancer-free. Another woman, who attributed her cancer to a poor immune system, believed that the cancer had structurally altered

her body—she called it "realigning the cells." As a consequence, she felt she would no longer be vulnerable to cancer. This expression of a discontinuity between precancer and postcancer time—the sense that things are different now—is echoed many times and seems to be important to producing a sense of mastery by maintaining, in part, that the initial cause is no longer in effect.

Although many patients have regained a sense of mastery by thinking about their cancer differently, others adopt direct behavioral efforts to keep the cancer from coming back. In a number of cases, patients made changes in their lives that both enabled them to reduce the likelihood of recurrence (they believed) and gave them something to control now. For some, these were dietary changes; a full 49% of our sample had changed their diet since the cancer bout, usually in the direction of adding fresh fruit and vegetables and cutting down on red meats and fats. For others, eliminating the medications they had taken like birth control pills or estrogen replenishers fulfilled the same function. The relationship of these changes to the need for mastery was verbalized by some patients:

[Where the cancer came from] was an important question to me at first. The doctor's answer was that it was a multifaceted illness. I looked over the known causes of cancer, like viruses, radiation, genetic mutation, environmental carcinogens, and the one I focused on very strongly was diet. I know now why I focused on it. It was the only one that was simple enough for me to understand and change. You eat something that's bad for you, you get sick.

A sense of mastery can be fulfilled by other than direct efforts to control the cancer. Assuming control over aspects of one's cancer care can meet the same need. One such effort at control is acquiring information about cancer, so one can participate in or be knowledgeable about one's care. As one woman put it:

I felt that I had lost control of my body somehow, and the way for me to get back some control was to find out as much as I could. It really became almost an obsession.

One spouse described his wife:

She got books, she got pamphlets, she studied, she talked to cancer patients, she found out everything that was happening to her, and she fought it. She went to war with it. She calls it taking in her covered wagons and surrounding it.

Attempting to control the side effects of one's treatments represents another effort at mastery. For example, 92% of the patients who received chemotherapy did something to control its side effects. For slightly under half, this involved simply medications or sleep, but the remaining half used a combination of mental efforts at control. These included imaging, self-hypnosis, distraction, and meditation. Similar efforts were made to control the less debilitating but still unpleasant side effects of radiation therapy. For example, one woman who was undergoing radiation therapy would imagine that there was a protective shield keeping her body from being burned by the radiation. Another woman imaged her chemotherapy as powerful cannons which blasted away pieces of the dragon, cancer. One 61-year-old woman simply focused her attention on healing with the instruction to her body, "Body, cut this shit out."

A sense of mastery, then, can be achieved by believing that one can control the cancer by taking active steps that are perceived as directly controlling the cancer or by assuming control over related aspects of one's cancer, such as treatment. This belief in mastery and its relationship to adjustment ties in with a large body of literature indicating that manipulated feelings of control enhance coping with short-term aversive events (Averill, 1973; see Thompson, 1981, for a recent review). The cancer patients' experiences suggest that self-generated feelings of control over a chronic condition can achieve the same beneficial effects.

THE PROCESS OF SELF-ENHANCEMENT

The third theme identified in our patients' adjustment process was an effort to enhance the self and restore self-esteem. Researchers ex-ploring a range of threatening events from the death of one's child (Chodoff, Friedman, & Hamburg, 1964) to going on welfare (Briar, 1966) have documented the toll such events can take on self-regard. Even when the events can be legitimately attributed to external forces beyond the individual's control, there is often a precipitous drop in self-esteem. After experiencing such a drop, however, many individuals then initiate cognitive efforts to pull themselves back out of their low self-regard.

In some cases, esteem-enhancing cognitions are quite direct. During our interviews, we asked our respondents to describe any changes that had occurred in their lives since the cancer incident. To digress momentarily, I think people are always curious about how others change their lives when they have had a life-threatening experience. Popular images would have patients changing jobs, changing spouses, moving, or squandering all their money on a series of self-indulgent adventures. In fact, these major changes are fairly rare, and when they do occur, they are associated with unsuccessful overall adjustment. Frequently, a couple will have one "binge" such as taking a cruise or buying a Cadillac, but otherwise there are typically few overt dramatic changes. After people reported the changes they had experienced in their lives since cancer, we asked them to indicate whether those changes were positive or negative. Only 17% reported *any* negative changes in their lives. Fifty-three percent reported only positive changes; the remainder reported no changes. We also asked our patients to rate their emotional adjustment before any signs of cancer, at various points during the cancer bout, and at the time of the interview. Not only did patients see themselves as generally well adjusted at the time of the interview and as better adjusted than they were during the cancer bout, they also saw themselves as better adjusted than before they had any signs of cancer! When you consider that these women usually had had disfiguring surgery, had often had painful follow-up care, and had been seriously frightened and lived under the shadow of possible recurrence, this is a remarkable ability to construe personal benefit from potential tragedy.

Some of the most intriguing illusions that contribute to self-enhancement are generated by social comparisons (Festinger, 1954; Latané, 1966; Suls & Miller, 1977). Drawing on some provocative suggestions by Wortman and Dunkel-Schetter (1979) concerning cancer patients' needs for social comparison, we hypothesized that if we could identify the women's objects of comparison we could predict who would perceive themselves as coping well or badly. The media highlight people who are models of good adjustment to crises. With respect to breast cancer, women such as Betty Ford, Shirley Temple Black, or Marvella Bayh come to mind. We reasoned that such models might demoralize normal women by making them feel they were not doing well by comparison (Taylor & Levin, 1976). In contrast, comparisons with average women who might be experiencing a number of more negative reactions to cancer should yield more favorable self-evaluations. An alternative prediction derived from Festinger's (1954) social comparison theory (Wheeler, 1966) is that people will compare themselves with someone doing slightly better than they are—in other words, make upward comparisons in order to learn how to cope more effectively.

What we found conformed neither to our analysis nor to the upward comparison prediction (Wood, Taylor, & Lichtman, Note 4). Instead, virtually all the women we interviewed thought they were doing as well as or somewhat better than other women coping with the same crisis. Only two said they were doing somewhat worse. If we had an unusually well-adjusted sample, of course, these perceptions could be veridical, but we know from other information that this was not true.[3] These results suggest that these women are making downward comparisons, comparing themselves with women who were as fortunate or less fortunate than they. These results tie in with a more general body of literature recently brought together

by Wills (1981) indicating that when faced with threat, individuals will usually make self-enhancing comparisons in an apparent effort to bolster self-esteem. Downward comparisons, then, would seem to be a fairly robust method of self-protection against threat.

In some cases, these downward comparisons were drawn explicitly. For example, one woman took great glee from the fact that her Reach to Recovery volunteer (the woman sent in by the American Cancer Society to serve as a model of good adjustment) seemed to be more poorly adjusted than she was. Despite some direct comparisons, however, many of the social comparisons seem to be made against hypothetical women:

Some of these women just seemed to be devastated. And with really less problems than I encountered, you know, smaller tumors.

You read about a few who handle it well, but it still seems like the majority really feel sorry for themselves. And I really don't think they cope with it that well. I don't understand it, because it doesn't bother me at all.

I think I did extremely well under the circumstances. I know that there are just some women who aren't strong enough, who fall apart and become psychologically disturbed and what have you. It's a big adjustment for them.

It seems, then, that the need to come out of the comparison process appearing better off drives the process itself; the process does not determine the outcome. If a comparison person who makes one appear well adjusted is not available from personal experience, such a person may be manufactured.

Choice of comparison target is not the only way that social comparison processes can operate to enhance self-esteem. One must also consider the dimensions selected for evaluation. Conceivably, one could select a dimension that would make one appear more advantaged than others or one could select a dimension for evaluation that would put one at a disadvantage. To illustrate what our patients did, let me offer a few of their statements. The following is a comparison made by a woman whose cancer was treated with a lumpectomy (removal of

_____
[3] Comparison of participants in the study with nonparticipants from the same practice on a large number of disease-related and adjustment-related variables revealed to no significant differences between the two (Taylor, Lichtman, & Wood, Note 2).

the lump itself) rather than a mastectomy (which involves the removal of the entire breast):

I had a comparatively small amount of surgery. How awful it must be for women who have had a mastectomy. I just can't imagine, it would seem it would be so difficult.

These are the remarks of a woman who had a mastectomy:

It was not tragic. It's worked out okay. Now if the thing had spread all over, I would have had a whole different story for you.

An older woman:

The people I really feel sorry for are these young gals. To lose a breast when you're so young must be awful. I'm 73; what do I need a breast for?

A young woman:

If I hadn't been married, I think this thing would have really gotten to me. I can't imagine dating or whatever knowing you have this thing and not knowing how to tell the man about it.

The point, of course, is that everyone is better off than someone as long as one picks the right dimension. In our study, several women with lumpectomies compared themselves favorably to women with mastectomies; no woman with a mastectomy ever evaluated herself against a woman with a lumpectomy. Older women considered themselves better off than younger women; no younger woman expressed the wish that she had been older. Married women pitied the single woman; no single woman pointed out that it would have been easier if she'd been married. The women who were the worst off consoled themselves with the fact that they were not dying or were not in pain. The amount of self-enhancement in these dimensional comparisons is striking. Not only choice of comparison target, then, but also choice of comparison dimension is important for restoring self-enhancement in the face of threat. The issue of dimension selection in

social comparisons is one that has been almost entirely ignored in the social comparison literature. This would seem to be an important oversight, particularly for research that examines social comparisons made under threat (Taylor, Wood, & Lichtman, in press).

The fact that social comparison processes can be used to enhance oneself is important, because it meshes social psychological processes with clinically significant outcomes. However, these social comparisons appear to serve important functions other than just self-enhancement. Several researchers (e.g., Fazio, 1979; Singer, 1966) have made a distinction between social comparisons that are made to validate one's self-impression versus social comparisons that are drawn to construct self-impressions. The results just described can be construed as efforts to validate a favorable self-image. However, one can also see evidence of constructive social comparisons among the respondents. Specifically, some of the comparisons involved instances in which women selected as comparison objects other women who were worse off physically (such as women with nodal involvement, women with metastatic cancer, or women with double mastectomies) but who were coping very well. Such comparisons are self-enhancing, but they are also instructive and motivating. That is, the fact that women worse off are coping well seems to inspire the person drawing the comparison to try to do as well and to pattern her own behavior after the comparison person. These comparisons are particularly important because self-enhancement, and indeed cognitive illusion generally, is often written off as defensive and dysfunctional. Instead, these illusions may have multiple functions. In addition to self-enhancement, they can instill motivation and provide information, as these downward comparisons apparently did for some of our respondents (see Brickman & Bulman, 1977). I will discuss this point more fully in a later portion of the article.

What, then, can be learned from the analysis of cancer patients' comparative processes? These women made downward comparisons instead of upward ones, and appear to have selected their comparison persons to enhance their self-esteem, rather than letting their self-esteem be determined by who was available for comparison. If other appropriate persons were not readily available for comparison, they manufactured a norm that other women were worse off than they were. The dimensions singled out for comparison were ones on which they appeared better, rather than worse, off. Physically disadvantaged but successful copers also were selected as models. One, then, has the best of both worlds: The comparisons enable one to feel better about oneself, but one does not lose the advantage of having a successful model on which to pattern one's efforts at adjustment.

IMPLICATIONS OF COGNITIVE ADAPTATION FOR COGNITIVE PROCESSING

Given these themes that constitute the tasks of cognitive adaptation to threatening events, it is now useful to examine the form of these cognitive adaptations more generally and discuss their implications for cognitive processing. The themes of meaning, mastery, and self-enhancement could be observed in nearly every patient as a consequence of the threat she was experiencing, and yet the form through which the theme was expressed differed from patient to patient. For example, although the specific attributions made by our cancer patients were varied, virtually every patient had a theory about her cancer. Likewise, although cognitions about what one could control varied from patient to patient, an effort at control was present for most. Although the specific form of social comparisons varied, their self-enhancing quality was highly robust. These findings imply that the specific form of the cognitions patients hold about their illness may matter less than the functions those cognitions serve.

Indeed, cognitions are both the easiest and the hardest thing to study empirically. They are easy because there are so many of them, and they are hard because it is so difficult to know which ones are important and when. The meaning of specific cognitions can vary substantially from situation to situation. To take an empirical example, consider the specific cog-

nition of self-blame for a negative outcome. Self-blame may serve some needs under some circumstances and other needs under others. In Bulman and Wortman's (1977) research on quadriplegics and paraplegics, self-blame was associated with good coping outcomes, perhaps because it signified a restored sense of mastery. In our cancer work (Taylor, Lichtman, & Wood, Note 2), self-blame was uncorrelated with adjustment; for some, self-blame may have produced guilt and self-recrimination (cf. Abrams & Finesinger, 1953), whereas for others it was associated with mastery. In recent research Buf Meyer and I conducted on rape victims (Meyer & Taylor, Note 5), self-blame was associated with poor coping, because it may well have led people to question their sense of mastery. Note, then, the robustness of the mastery need, but the different ways that the specific cognition of self-blame related to it. Thus, a particular cognition may mean one thing under one set of circumstances and something completely different under others.

Moreover, specific cognitions (such as attributions, beliefs about control, or social comparisons) are in some cases functionally equivalent or at least functionally overlapping. The need for self-enhancement can conceivably be served by believing one has control or by making downward comparisons. Likewise, the need to find meaning in the experience can be served by finding an explanation for the event or by laying out a plan for controlling things in the future. Not only do specific cognitions functionally overlap, but individual cognitions may serve several needs simultaneously. For example, a causal explanation can simultaneously provide meaning for an experience and increase one's sense of mastery. Rothbaum, Weisz, and Snyder (1982) have argued that attempts to find meaning in an aversive experience actually represent an effort at interpretive control, a secondary form of control that involves flowing with the experience rather than trying to change it.

Perhaps the best example of meeting dual needs through a single cognition is the downward social comparisons our cancer patients made. By selecting someone worse off physically but who was coping very well, these women both came off looking advantaged and also provided themselves with a model of how to cope, thus contributing to their mastery needs. To summarize, specific cognitions may mean different things under different circumstances, they may be functionally overlapping rather than functionally distinct, and they may satisfy several functions simultaneously.

This portrait of cognitions is very different from that typically provided by psychological research on social cognitions. These usually laboratory-based efforts often portray specific cognitions as if they were highly robust rather than fluid and ephemeral (cf. Wortman & Dintzer, 1978). Cognitions are often discussed as if they had a fixed meaning across situations rather than multiple and changing meanings. The functions specific cognitions serve, such as those identified in the present study, are almost entirely ignored in laboratory investigations. The present results argue, at the very least, for expanding the study of cognitions to include field situations of high involvement; such situations may more properly capture the function–cognition interface that is necessary for interpreting the specific form through which a cognitive theme is expressed. There are other implications as well. As will be seen shortly, the preceding points regarding the form of specific cognitions assume increasing importance in the context of the disconfirmation of cognitions. Before that issue is discussed, however, an important attribute of cognitive adaptations to threatening events merits extended comment, and that is their illusion-based nature.

ILLUSION AS ESSENTIAL TO NORMAL COGNITIVE FUNCTIONING

The cognitions upon which meaning, mastery, and self-enhancement depend are in a large part founded on illusions. Causes for cancer are manufactured despite the fact that the true causes of cancer remain substantially unknown. Belief in control over one's cancer persists despite little evidence that such faith is well placed. Self-enhancing social comparisons are drawn, and when no disadvantaged person exists against whom one can compare oneself, she is made up. I have argued that these illusions are beneficial in bringing about psychological adaptation. However, in the past, mental health researchers and clinicians have assumed that positive mental functioning depends upon being in touch with reality (e.g., Erikson, 1950; Haan, 1977; Jahoda, 1958; Maslow, 1954; Menninger, 1963; Vaillant, 1977; see Lazarus, 1983, for a discussion of this point). Indeed, one goal of therapy has been considered to be the stripping away of illusions so that a more accurate view of the world and one's problems can emerge. As Lazarus (1983) put it: "to be sophisticated [meant] accepting accurate reality testing as the hallmark of mental health. . . . Everyone knew that self-deception was tantamount to mental disorder" (p. 1).

However, the idea that normal mental functioning depends upon illusion is gaining increasing support. In his new look at denial, Lazarus (1983) points out that denial is no longer denounced as the primitive, ultimately unsuccessful defense it once was; rather, clinicians and health psychologists are now recognizing its value in protecting people against crises, both in the initial stages of threat and intermittently when people must come to terms with information that is difficult to accept, such as the diagnosis of a terminal illness.

Greenwald's (1980) recent analysis of the totalitarian ego points out how the maintenance of the self-concept depends upon the revision of one's personal history. One remembers oneself as more successful and more often correct than one really is. Attribution research reveals that good outcomes are attributed to oneself much more than are bad outcomes (e.g., Bradley, 1978; Miller & Ross, 1975; Snyder, Stephan, & Rosenfield, 1978). Optimism pervades our thinking (Tiger, 1979). People believe that the present is better than the past and that the future will be even better (Brickman, Coates, & Janoff-Bulman, 1978; Free & Cantril, 1968; Weinstein, 1980). People expect to succeed and improve in the future. All these views of oneself and the world become even more extreme under ego-involving conditions (see Greenwald, 1980).

Perhaps the clearest evidence for the benefits of illusions comes from the study of depressive cognitions. Independent work by several investigators has shown that relative to depressives, normals show several characteristics. Normals inflate others' views of them (Lewinsohn, Mischel, Chaplin, & Barton, 1980). They are more prone to an illusion of control—that is, the perception that they can control objectively uncontrollable outcomes (Alloy & Abramson, in press; Alloy, Abramson, & Viscusi, 1981; Golin, Terrell, & Johnson, 1977; Golin, Terrell, Weitz, & Drost, 1979). Nondepressives underestimate the amount of negative feedback they have received (DeMonbreun & Craighead, 1977; Nelson & Craighead, 1977). Nondepressives overestimate the predictability of and control they have over positive outcomes and underestimate the predictability of undesired outcomes (Alloy & Abramson, 1979, 1980; Alloy et al., 1981). They reward themselves more than their objective performance warrants (Rozensky, Rehm, Pry, & Roth, 1977), and they tend to attribute their successes to internal stable causes and their failures to external, unstable, specific ones (Abramson & Alloy, 1981). Finally, on an issue quite similar to the cancer experience, Silver and Wortman (1980) found that often unrealistic beliefs among quadriplegics and paraplegics about the relationship between their own efforts and likelihood of improving led to better emotional functioning and better coping.

Illusion clearly pervades normal cognitive functioning, and the researchers who have investigated this area have suggested several reasons why. Such illusions may have evolutionary significance: As Greenwald (1980) notes, they contribute to maintaining the self as a highly organized information processing system, and they produce behavioral persistence. Behavioral persistence may also be the adaptive significance of the illusion of control and other exaggerated perceptions of contingency (Lewinsohn et al., 1980) in that high expectations of control should enhance efforts at control. Self-enhancement biases likewise are functional: Positive self-perceptions can make one behave more favorably toward both the self and others, such as by increasing helping behavior (Isen, Shalker, Clark, & Karp, 1978; Rosenhan, Underwood, & Boore, 1974). Self-reinforcement, which normals appear to do to excess, increases rate of responding at a task (see Rozensky et al., 1977). The so-called "warm glow" produced by these illusion-based perceptions, then, may have implications for a wide variety of adaptive self-regulatory mechanisms (Lewinsohn et al., 1980). In our own work, it is clear that the sense of meaning, mastery, and self-enhancement, and the specific cognitions through which they are achieved, enable people to make sense of the cancer, to take controlling efforts to attempt to forestall a recurrence, to assert control in aspects of their lives where control is possible, and to change perceptions of themselves and their lives in ways that are self-enhancing and psychologically beneficial. The effective individual in the face of threat, then, seems to be one who permits the development of illusions, nurtures those illusions, and is ultimately restored by those illusions.

THE DISCONFIRMATION OF THE COGNITIVE MANAGEMENT OF THREAT

There is one potential problem in arguing for the adaptive significance of illusion, which is that beliefs that rest on illusion are vulnerable to disconfirmation. The belief that one can control one's cancer can, for example, be abruptly disconfirmed by a recurrence. The belief that one's cancer came from a particular cause, such as an auto accident, can be quickly disconfirmed by a physician or a knowledgeable acquaintance. If people's adjustment to threat depends on the maintenance of illusions, what happens when these illusions are challenged or destroyed?

This has been an extremely important issue in social cognition, especially in work on psychological control (e.g., Wortman & Brehm, 1975). Whereas considerable research highlights the benefits of control (Thompson, 1981), there is growing suspicion that when efforts at control are exerted in an environment where no control exists, controlling efforts will lead to poorer rather than more successful adjustment (e.g., Seligman, 1975; Wortman & Brehm, 1975). A sense of mastery may be fine so long as nothing happens to undermine it. This suspicion about the potential adverse effects of control is sustained by two models of the disconfirmation process furnished by psychological theory. The first is reactance (Brehm, 1966; Brehm & Brehm, 1981), which maintains that threats to freedom or loss of it produce arousal, hostility, and direct or indirect efforts to restore those freedoms. The second, more widely researched, model is learned helplessness (Abramson, Seligman, & Teasdale, 1978; Seligman, 1975), which maintains that after repeated unsuccessful efforts at control, the individual will give up responding. Motivational, cognitive, and emotional deficits may then arise that will interfere with learning in a new environment. Central to these models is the belief that when lack of control exists in reality, those who attempted to exercise it will be worse off behaviorally, emotionally, cognitively, and motivationally than those who do not.

Both reactance theory and learned helplessness theory, however, suffer from the problems of laboratory-based investigations of social cognition described earlier. Both greatly simplify the environments within which loss of control is introduced, creating several difficulties in interpreting both the meaning of loss of control and the cognitive and behavioral responses to loss of control. For example, potential controlling efforts are often limited to a restricted set of responses, such as a bar press or a verbalized choice. In the world in which loss of control is usually experienced, however, a range of response options is often available to an individual. Accordingly, the potential responses to loss of control are far greater than the range made available in typical studies of learned helplessness or reactance. It is therefore hard to know how to interpret persistence or giving up when those are the only possible responses available. A greater conceptual problem of both theories is that they focus attention on the controlling response itself and the fact that it has been blocked, rather than on the goal or function that the response was designed to

serve. In life, however, controlling responses are not made in a vacuum; they are made in response to some goal that achieves some value or function. From the standpoint of cognitive adaptation theory, the specific response (and its blocking) has no fixed meaning independent of the goals or functions it serves. The specific form matters little or not at all. Knowing the value or function of the goal can enable one to look for its expression elsewhere, if expression through some specific form is blocked.

Accordingly, let me propose a third model of the disconfirmation process that more fully captures the fluidity of cognitive adaptations. This model owes its genesis, in part, to some observations on mundane plans. Barbara and Frederick Hayes-Roth, two cognitive psychologists, have studied mundane plans extensively (Hayes-Roth, 1981; Hayes-Roth & Hayes-Roth, 1979), and they report one highly robust and quite curious finding. It is that people grossly overestimate how much they can accomplish in a given period of time and continue to do so in the face of repeated negative feedback. Anyone who makes a daily "to-do" list must be aware of the following phenomenon. Each morning, one makes an extensive list of what one plans to do for the day. One then does perhaps 40% of the items, starts another 40%, and leaves 20% completely untouched. One then shifts the uncompleted items over to the next day or, if the day was particularly unproductive, crosses out the name of the day at the top of the list—for example, Monday—and changes it to the next day! What is interesting is that this process goes on day after day with no disruption to one's functioning, little if any emotional upset, and more to the point, no modification in behavior. Disconfirmation of our expectations of getting things done is a fact of life about which we are apparently unperturbed.

I believe this model of cheerful ineptitude, which associates have variously dubbed "learned haplessness" or "proactance," similarly characterizes the disconfirmation of illusions in the adjustment to threat. The model is appropriately derived from behavior in complex environments. It conceives of specific cognitions, like control or attributions, not as individual responses to be observed in isolation, but rather outlines general themes that are themselves made up of a number of potential specific cognitive responses. It conceptualizes disconfirmation not as the violation of a single expectation, but as a temporary frustration. According to the model, disconfirmation of a single effort at control or a single attribution would be little more frustrating than would finding a particular store closed when one was running one's errands.

An additional important feature of the planning literature that makes it an appropriate source for a model of the disconfirmation process is its emphasis on the plan–goal relationship. Specific plans (which here function as analogues to specific cognitions) have no meaning independent of the goals or values they serve. Accordingly, when a particular plan is thwarted, some alternative plan is substituted that accomplishes the same goal or achieves the same value. It is only when the goal or value itself is blocked, as by the blockage of *all* possible tactics or plans, that one may see goal frustration rather than response substitution as the consequence of loss of control. Even then, goal substitution or value substitution may occur (see Schank & Abelson, 1977; Wilensky, 1981).[4]

Applying the model to the cancer experience leads to specific predictions. If one's belief about the cause of one's cancer is disconfirmed, one finds another potential cause to satisfy one's search for meaning. If one felt that one could control one's cancer and a recurrence occurred, then one would shift to control something else that *was* controllable, such as one's responses to chemotherapy. Before I create an incorrect impression, let me hasten to add that I do not mean that people face setbacks with aplomb. One does not, for example, react calmly to a recurrence of cancer. What I mean is that people who believed they understood the cause of their cancer, believed they could control it, or believed they were handling it

well, and who then discover their beliefs are untrue, are not worse off for having thought so. In fact, they may be better off.

This possibility first suggested itself in our examination of causal attributions among the seriously ill. Having been wedded to laboratory models of the attribution process, we believed that the specific attribution an individual made for his or her cancer would predict adjustment. It was therefore somewhat unnerving that when we asked people what they thought caused their cancer, a large number of them listed several possibilities. More to the point, they encompassed the entire range of dimensions thought to be theoretically important in understanding the consequences of causal attributions. Furthermore, some of the theories people had originally advanced for their cancer had been disconfirmed by a physician or other knowledgeable individual with no apparent emotional costs. For example, one woman who had been in an auto accident just prior to the detection of her tumor wanted to file suit against the other driver for causing her cancer. Her doctor and lawyer, of course, quickly disabused her of this notion. She promptly came up with another explanation. She is one illustration of the general point: People often hold multiple or serial theories about their cancer that would seem to have vastly different psychological consequences, but which apparently do not. Moreover, having one or more theories disconfirmed does not seem to be particularly bothersome.

The issue of disconfirmation is most important in the area of psychological control, and at present, our own investigations do not provide a large data base on the effects of failure of control. One example, however, is particularly illustrative of the point I want to make. One of the women I interviewed told me that after detection of her breast tumor, she had believed she could prevent future recurrences by controlling her diet. She had, among other things, consumed huge quantities of Vitamin A through the singularly unappetizing medium of mashed asparagus. A year and a half later, she developed a second malignancy. This, of course, is precisely the situation all control

---

[4] The author apologizes to these planning investigators for vastly oversimplifying their models.

researchers are interested in: a dramatic disconfirmation of efforts to control. I asked her how she felt when that happened. She shrugged and said she guessed she'd been wrong. She then decided to quit her dull job and use her remaining time to write short stories—something she had always wanted to do. Having lost control in one area of her life, she turned to another area, her work life, that *was* controllable.

This example is raised not as proof, but as an instance of what was observed several times. Disconfirmation of efforts at control did not produce the emotional upset or inactivity that one might predict from reactance or learned helplessness theory. Rather, there are many things that can potentially be controlled, and if one's need to control a situation is great, one will control what one can and give up attempting to control what one cannot (cf. Rothbaum et al., 1982).

Cognitive adaptation theory, then, is proposed as an alternative model of the disconfirmation process, not because it has been proven to be better—it has not yet—but because it offers a very different view of the human organism than do currently available models. It views people as adaptable, self-protective, and functional in the face of setbacks.

CONCLUSION

I have offered a theory of cognitive adaptation to threatening events. The theory maintains that when individuals experience personal tragedies or setbacks, they respond with cognitively adaptive efforts that may enable them to return to or exceed their previous level of psychological functioning. The themes around which such adaptations occur include a search for meaning, an effort to gain mastery, and an attempt to enhance the self. Meaning is addressed by such cognitive processes as finding a causal explanation for the experience and restructuring the meaning of one's life around the setback. Mastery involves efforts to gain control over the threatening event in particular and over one's life more generally

by believing that one has control and by exerting behavioral control over threat-related events. Self-enhancement occurs by construing personal benefit from the experience, by comparing oneself with others who are less fortunate, and by focusing on aspects of one's own situation that make one appear to be well off.

I have maintained that these cognitive restructurings are in large part based on illusions, that is, beliefs that have no factual basis or that require looking at known facts in a particular way. Illusion has, in the past, been treated with mild contempt. In the psychological community, illusion is often equated with defensiveness, relegated to being primarily of clinical interest, and is seen as ignorant, static, and as ineffective for learning and action. Even in literature in which the need for illusion is a common theme, the self-deluded characters are often portrayed as naive or pathetic (see Lazarus, 1983). Consider as examples *Don Quixote* (Cervantes, 1605, 1615/1956), *The Iceman Cometh* (O'Neill, 1946), or *Who's Afraid of Virginia Woolf?* (Albee, 1964). In contrast, I maintain that illusions can have a dynamic force. They can simultaneously protect and prompt constructive thought and action. As the literature on depression and on the self makes clear, normal cognitive processing and behavior may depend on a substantial degree of illusion, whereas the ability to see things clearly can be associated with depression and inactivity. Thus, far from impeding adjustment, illusion may be essential for adequate coping.

Perhaps the most important implication of cognitive adaptation theory is its metatheoretical stance regarding the nature of cognitions themselves. Specific cognitions are viewed not as robust elements that maintain a cross-situational meaning, but as strategic changing elements that serve general value-laden themes. Specific cognitions may change their meanings from situation to situation, they may be functionally overlapping rather than functionally distinct, and they may serve several functions simultaneously. Viewed from this perspective, the disconfirmation of a specific cognition, such as a belief in personal control over a recurrence of cancer, may not be as psychologically problematic as previous models of the disconfirmation process (reactance, learned helplessness) have suggested. Rather, given the flexibility of the relationship between cognitions and themes, the individual may find an alternative response that serves the same function and thus continue to adapt as well as or better than the individual who makes no adaptive effort at all.

As a theoretical and empirical venture, cognitive adaptation theory is still in its infancy. It suggests a general strategy for studying adaptation to threatening events by focusing on multiple cognitively adaptive efforts simultaneously, rather than upon the adaptive value of particular cognitions in isolation. It also takes a stand against laboratory-based examinations of reactions to threat that fail to acknowledge the relation of particular cognitions to overriding goals or values. More specifically, the theory points to some directions for beginning research. Systematically documenting the themes of meaning, mastery, and self-enhancement in adjustment to threatening events other than cancer is an important empirical step. In this context, it is encouraging to note that evidence for each of the three themes—meaning (Chodoff et al., 1964; Frankl, 1963; Mechanic, 1977; Visotsky et al., 1961; Weisman & Worden, 1975), mastery (Bulman & Wortman, 1977; Janoff-Bulman, 1979; Rothbaum et al., 1982), and self-enhancement (Pearlin & Schooler, 1978; Wills, 1981)—has already been reported by investigators exploring misfortunes as varied as economic difficulty, marital problems, rape, and physical illness other than cancer. A second beginning line of research stems from the different predictions that cognitive adaptation theory generates for reactions to disconfirmation of cognitions, as compared with reactance or learned helplessness theory. The theory suggests, for example, that in field settings where people have multiple response options at their disposal, they will turn their frustrated efforts at control, understanding, or self-enhancement to tasks on which they are more likely to be successful. Our current empirical work focuses on this very question: What happens when people's efforts to exert control in a threatening environment are unsuccessful?

My biologist acquaintances frequently note that the more they know about the human body, the more, not less, miraculous it seems. The recuperative powers of the mind merit similar awe. The process of cognitive adaptation to threat, though often time-consuming and not always successful, nonetheless restores many people to their prior level of functioning and inspires others to find new meaning in their lives. For this reason, cognitive adaptation occupies a special place in the roster of human capabilities.

REFERENCE NOTES

1. Follick, M. J., & Turk, D. C. *Problem specification by ostomy patients.* Paper presented at the meeting of the Association for Advancement of Behavior Therapy, Chicago, November 1978.
2. Taylor, S. E., Lichtman, R. R., & Wood, J. V. *Adjustment to breast cancer: Physical, socio-demographic, and psychological predictors.* Manuscript submitted for publication, 1982.
3. Lichtman, R. R. *Close relationships after breast cancer.* Unpublished doctoral dissertation, 1982.
4. Wood, J. V., Taylor, S. E., & Lichtman, R. R. *Social comparison processes in adjustment to cancer.* Manuscript submitted for publication, 1982.
5. Meyer, B., & Taylor, S. E. *Adjustment to rape.* Manuscript submitted for publication, 1982.

REFERENCES

Abrams, R. D., & Finesinger, J. E. Guilt reactions in patients with cancer. *Cancer*, 1953, *6*, 474–482.

Abramson, L. Y., & Alloy, L. B. Depression, nondepression, and cognitive illusions: Reply to Schwartz. *Journal of Experimental Psychology: General*, 1981, *110*, 436–447.

Abramson, L. Y., Seligman, M. E. P., & Teasdale, J. Learned helplessness in humans: Critique and reformulation. *Journal of Abnormal Psychology*, 1978, *87*, 49–74.

Albee, E. *Who's Afraid of Virginia Woolf?* New York: Atheneum, 1964.

Alloy, L. B., & Abramson, L. Y. Judgment of contingency in depressed and nondepressed students: Sadder but wiser? *Journal of Experimental Psychology: General*, 1979, *108*, 441–485.

Alloy, L. B., & Abramson, L. Y. The cognitive component of human helplessness and depression: A critical analysis. In J. Garber & M. E. P. Seligman (Eds.), *Human helplessness: Theory and application.* New York: Academic Press, 1980.

Alloy, L. B., & Abramson, L. Y. Learned helplessness, depression, and the illusion of control. *Journal of Personality and Social Psychology*, in press.

Alloy, L. B., Abramson, L. Y., & Viscusi, D. Induced mood and the illusion of control. *Journal of Personality and Social Psychology*, 1981, *41*, 1129–1140.

Andreasen, N. I. C., & Norris, A. S. Long-term adjustment and adaptation mechanisms in severely burned adults. *Journal of Nervous and Mental Disease*, 1972, *154*, 352–362.

Averill, J. R. Personal control over aversive stimuli and its relationship to stress. *Psychological Bulletin*, 1973, *80*, 286–303.

Bradley, G. W. Self-serving biases in the attribution process: A reexamination of the fact or fiction question. *Journal of Personality and Social Psychology*, 1978, *36*, 56–71.

Brehm, J. W. *Response to loss of freedom: A theory of psychological reactance.* New York: Academic Press, 1966.

Brehm, S. S., & Brehm, J. W. *Psychological reactance: A theory of freedom and control.* New York: Academic Press, 1981.

Briar, S. Welfare from below: Recipient's views of the public welfare system. *California Law Review*, 1966, *54*, 370–385.

Brickman, P., & Bulman, R. J. Pleasure and pain in social comparison. In J. M. Suls & R. L. Miller (Eds.), *Social comparison processes: Theoretical and empirical perspectives.* Washington, D.C.: Hemisphere, 1977.

Brickman, P., Coates, D., & Janoff-Bulman, R. Lottery winners and accident victims: Is happiness relative? *Journal of Personality and Social Psychology*, 1978, *36*, 917–927.

Bulman, R. J., & Wortman, C. B. Attributions of blame and coping in the "real world": Severe accident victims react to their lot. *Journal of Personality and Social Psychology*, 1977, *35*, 351–363.

Campbell, A., Converse, P. E., & Rodgers, W. L. *The quality of American life: Perceptions, evaluations, and satisfactions.* New York: Russell Sage Foundation, 1976.

Cervantes, S. M. de. *The adventures of Don Quixote* (J. M. Cohen, trans.). Baltimore, Md.: Penguin Books, 1956. (Original publications in Spanish: Part I, 1605; Part II, 1615.)

Chodoff, P., Friedman, P. B., & Hamburg, D. A. Stress, defenses and coping behavior: Observations in parents of children with malignant disease. *American Journal of Psychiatry*, 1964, *120*, 743–749.

DeMonbreun, B. G., & Craighead, W. E. Distortion of perception and recall of positive and neutral feedback in depression. *Cognitive Therapy and Research*, 1977, *1*, 311–329.

Derogatis, L. R. *The global adjustment to illness scale (GAIS).* Baltimore, Md.: Clinical Psychometric Research, 1975.

Erikson, E. H. *Childhood and society:* New York: Norton, 1950.

Fazio, R. H. Motives for social comparison: The construction-validation distinction. *Journal of Personality and Social Psychology*, 1979, *37*, 1683–1698.

Festinger, L. A theory of social comparison processes. *Human Relations*, 1954, 7, 117–140.

Frankl, V. E. *Man's search for meaning.* New York: Washington Square Press, 1963.

Free, L. A., & Cantril, H. *The political beliefs of Americans: A study of public opinion.* New York: Clarion, 1968.

Golin, S., Terrell, F., & Johnson, B. Depression and the illusion of control. *Journal of Abnormal Psychology*, 1977, *86*, 440–442.

Golin, S., Terrell, F., Weitz, J., & Drost, P. L. The illusion of control among depressed patients. *Journal of Abnormal Psychology*, 1979, *88*, 454–457.

Greenwald, A. G. The totalitarian ego: Fabrication and revision of personal history. *American Psychologist*, 1980, *35*, 603–618.

Gurin, G., Veroff, J., & Feld, S. *Americans view their mental health.* New York: Basic Books, 1960.

Haan, N. *Coping and defending.* New York: Academic Press, 1977.

Hayes-Roth, B. A cognitive science approach to improving planning. In *Proceedings of the third annual conference of the Cognitive Science Society.* Berkeley, Calif.: Cognitive Science Society, August 19–21, 1981.

Hayes-Roth, B., & Hayes-Roth, F. A cognitive model of planning. *Cognitive Science*, 1979, *3*, 275–310.

Heider, F. *The psychology of interpersonal relations.* New York: Wiley, 1958.

Isen, A. M., Shalker, T. E., Clark, M., & Karp, L. Affect, accessibility of material in memory, and behavior: A cognitive loop? *Journal of Personality and Social Psychology*, 1978, *36*, 1–12.

Jahoda, M. *Current conceptions of positive mental health.* New York: Basic Books, 1958.

Janoff-Bulman, R. Characterological versus behavioral self-blame: Inquiries into depression and rape. *Journal of Personality and Social Psychology*, 1979, *37*, 1798–1809.

Katz, A. H. Social adaptation in chronic illness: A study of hemophilia. *American Journal of Public Health*, 1963, *53*, 1666–1675.

Kelley, H. H. Attribution theory in social psychology. In D. Levine (Ed.), *Nebraska Symposium on Motivation*

(Vol. 15). Lincoln: University of Nebraska Press, 1967.

Latané, B. Studies in social comparison: Introduction and overview. *Journal of Experimental Social Psychology*, 1966, *Supplement 1*, 1–5

Lazarus, R. S. The costs and benefits of denial. In S. Breznitz (Ed.), *Denial of stress.* New York: International Universities Press, 1983.

Leon, G. R., Butcher, J. N., Kleinman, M., Goldberg, A., & Almagor, M. Survivors of the Holocaust and their children: Current status and adjustment. *Journal of Personality and Social Psychology*, 1981, *41*, 503–516.

Leventhal, H. The consequences of depersonalization during illness and treatment. In J. Howard & A. Strauss (Eds.), *Humanizing health care.* New York: Wiley, 1975.

Lewinsohn, P. M., Mischel, W., Chaplin, W., & Barton, R. Social competence and depression: The role of illusory self-perceptions. *Journal of Abnormal Psychology*, 1980, *89*, 203–212.

Maslow, A. H. *Motivation and personality.* New York: Harper & Row, 1954.

McNair, D. M., & Lorr, M. An analysis of mood in neurotics. *Journal of Abnormal Psychology*, 1964, *69*, 620–627.

Mechanic, D. Illness behavior, social adaptation, and the management of illness. *Journal of Nervous and Mental Disease*, 1977, *165*, 79–87.

Menninger, K. *The vital balance.* New York: Viking, 1963.

Miller, D. T., & Ross, M. Self-serving biases in the attribution of causality: Fact or fiction? *Psychological Bulletin*, 1975, *82*, 213–225.

Myers, B. A., Friedman, S. B., & Weiner, I. B. Coping with a chronic disability: Psychosocial observations of girls with scoliosis. *American Journal of Diseases of Children*, 1970, *120*, 175–181.

Nelson, R. E., & Craighead, W. E. Selective recall of positive and negative feedback, self-control behaviors, and depression. *Journal of Abnormal Psychology*, 1977, *86*, 379–388.

O'Neill, E. *The iceman cometh.* New York: Random House, 1946.

Pearlin, L. I., & Schooler, C. The structure of coping. *Journal of Health and Social Behavior*, 1978, *19*, 2–21.

Rosenhan, D., Underwood, B., & Boore, B. Affect moderates self-gratification and altruism. *Journal of Personality and Social Psychology*, 1974, *30*, 546–552.

Rothbaum, F., Weisz, J. R., & Snyder, S. S. Changing the world and changing the self: A two-process model of perceived control. *Journal of Personality and Social Psychology*, 1982, *42*, 5–37.

Rozensky, R. H., Rehm, L. P., Pry, G., & Roth, D. De-

pression and self-reinforcement behavior in hospitalized patients. *Journal of Behavioral Therapy and Experimental Psychiatry*, 1977, *8*, 31–34.

Ryan, W. *Blaming the victim.* New York: Vintage Books, 1971.

Schank, R. C., & Abelson, R. P. *Scripts, plans, goals, and understanding: An inquiry into human knowledge structures.* Hillsdale, N.J.: Erlbaum, 1977.

Seligman, M. E. P. *Helplessness: On depression, development, and death.* San Francisco: Freeman, 1975.

Silver, R. L., & Wortman, C. B. Coping with undesirable life events. In J. Garber & M. E. P. Seligman (Eds.), *Human helplessness: Theory and applications.* New York: Academic Press, 1980.

Simonton, O. C., & Simonton, S. Belief systems and management of the emotional aspects of malignancy. *Journal of Transpersonal Psychology*, 1975, *7*, 29–48.

Singer, J. E. Social comparison: Progress and issues. *Journal of Experimental Social Psychology*, 1966, *Supplement 1*, 103–110.

Snyder, M. L., Stephan, W. G., & Rosenfield, C. Attributional egotism. In J. H. Harvey, W. J. Ickes, & R. F. Kidd (Eds.), *New directions in attribution research* (Vol. 2). Hillsdale, N. J.: Erlbaum, 1978.

Suls, J. M., & Miller, R. L. M. *Social comparison processes: Theoretical and empirical perspectives.* New York: Wiley, 1977.

Tavormina, J. B., Kastner, L. S. Slater, P. M., & Watt, S. L. Chronically ill children: A psychologically and emotionally deviant population? *Journal of Abnormal Child Psychology*, 1976, *4*, 99–110.

Taylor, S. E., & Levin, S. *The psychological impact of breast cancer: Theory and practice.* San Francisco: West Coast Cancer Foundation, 1976.

Taylor, S. E., Wood, J. V., & Lichtman, R. R. It could be worse: Selective evaluation as a response to victimization. *Journal of Social Issues*, in press.

Thompson, S. C. Will it hurt less if I can control it? A complex answer to a simple question. *Psychological Bulletin*, 1981, *90*, 89–101.

Tiger, L. *Optimism: The biology of hope.* New York: Simon & Schuster, 1979.

Turk, D. C. Factors influencing the adaptive process with chronic illness: Implications for intervention. In I. G. Sarason & C. D. Spielberger (Eds.), *Stress and anxiety* (Vol. 6). Washington, D.C.: Hemisphere, 1979.

Vaillant, G. *Adaptation to life.* Boston: Little, Brown, 1977.

Visotsky, H. M., Hamburg, D. A., Goss, M. E., & Lebovits, B. Z. Coping behavior under extreme stress. *Archives of General Psychiatry*, 1961, *5*, 423–448.

Weinstein, N. D. Unrealistic optimism about future life

events. *Journal of Personality and Social Psychology*, 1980, *39*, 806–820.

Weisman, A. D. *Coping with cancer*. New York: McGraw-Hill, 1979.

Weisman, A. D., & Worden, J. W. Psychological analysis of cancer deaths. *Omega*, 1975, *6*, 61–75.

Wheeler, L. Motivation as a determinant of upward comparison. *Journal of Experimental Social Psychology*, 1966, *Supplement 1*, 27–31.

Wilensky, R. A model for planning in everyday situations. In *Proceedings of the third annual conference of the Cognitive Science Society*. Berkeley, Calif.: Cognitive Science Society, August 19–21, 1981.

Wills, T. A. Downward comparison principles in social psychology. *Psychological Bulletin*, 1981, *90*, 245–271.

Wills, T. A. Social comparison and help-seeking. In B. M. DePaulo, A. Nadler, & J. D. Fisher (Eds.), *New directions in helping: Vol. 2. Help-seeking*. New York: Academic Press, 1982.

Wong, P. T. P., & Weiner, B. When people ask "why" questions, and the heuristics of attributional search. *Journal of Personality and Social Psychology*, 1981, *40*, 650–663.

Wortman, C. B., & Brehm, J. W. Responses to uncontrollable outcomes: An integration of reactance theory and the learned helplessness model. In L. Berkowitz (Ed.), *Advances in experimental social psychology* (Vol. 8). New York: Academic Press, 1975.

Wortman, C. B., & Dintzer, L. Is an attributional analysis of the learned helplessness phenomenon viable? A critique of the Abramson–Seligman–Teasdale reformulation. *Journal of Abnormal Psychology*, 1978, *87*, 75–90.

Wortman, C. B., & Dunkel-Schetter, C. Interpersonal relationships and cancer: A theoretical analysis. *Journal of Social Issues*, 1979, *35*, 120–155.

26

The Evening News and Presidential Evaluations

Shanto Iyengar, Donald R. Kinder, Mark D. Peters, and Jon A. Krosnick

This paper comes from a long tradition of research showing that political mass communications apparently have minimal success in changing public attitudes. Recently, research attention has shifted away from attitude change to agenda-setting as an important effect of the political media: If the media do not tell us what to think, do they at least tell us what to think about? Experiment 2 is particularly noteworthy because it attempts to achieve mundane realism by using ordinary citizens (rather than college students) as subjects, and by exposing them to excerpts from genuine network news broadcasts, rather than experimentally concocted communications. The key findings are shown in Tables 1 and 3. They show that evaluations of President Carter's performance as president are dependent upon the respondent's evaluation of his performance in the particular policy area emphasized in the news broadcast just viewed. But Tables 2 and 4 show that the news broadcasts did not influence the favorability of these evaluations. So, the news influenced the *criteria* by which Carter was judged, without influencing the favorability of those judgments. In other words, the media affected the agenda, but not the attitudes.

ABSTRACT. Two experiments show that by drawing attention to certain national problems while ignoring others, television news programs help define the standards by which presidents are evaluated. As predicted, this effect is greater for evaluations of the president's general performance than for judgments of his competence and integrity, and it is more pronounced among novices than among experts.

Our evaluations of others are deeply influenced by circumstance. Information that circumstance makes accessible often dominates our evaluations, whereas equally pertinent but less accessible information is set aside. In Salancik's (1974) study of teaching evaluations, for example, students were induced to consider either intrinsic or extrinsic reasons for their class participation. Among students primed with intrinsic reasons, course evaluations and grades were virtually independent; among students primed with extrinsic reasons, evaluations and grades were almost perfectly correlated. Salancik's manipulation made one set of standards rather than another accessible and thereby radically altered the information that students relied on in reaching overall evaluations. More generally, as a number of experiments demonstrate, momentarily accessible information may often pervade social judgments. (For excellent reviews consult Higgins & King, 1981, and Wyer & Hartwick, 1980.)

The research reported here is intended to deepen our understanding of the accessibility effect by identifying those general considerations that mitigate or enhance it. In particular, we examine the degree to which the effect depends on the relevance of the triggering stimulus configuration to the judgment at hand and the way in which manipulations of accessibility interact with prior knowledge, here called *expertise*.

Reprinted from the *Journal of Personality and Social Psychology*, 1984, 46, pp. 778–787. Copyright 1984 by the American Psychological Association. Reprinted by permission of publisher and authors.

Our investigation takes place within the domain of political cognition. Specifically, we focus on the judgments that Americans make regarding the performance and character of their president. Thus our work complements conventional research on social judgment, which ordinarily entails informationally impoverished judgments about hypothetical persons. Presidents are, of course, hardly hypothetical. They are both notorious and complex, judged according to the policies they promote, the party they represent, the achievements and failures they preside over, the personal qualities they exhibit, the feelings they invoke, and more (Kinder & Sears, in press). Like most naturally occurring social judgments, however, evaluations of the president should depend in part on what information happens to be momentarily accessible.

One powerful provider of information pertinent to judgments of the president is television news. Americans depend heavily on that source for their information about politics in general and about the president in particular (Comstock, Chaffee, Katzman, McCombs, & Roberts, 1978; Graber, 1980). In previous experimental work (Iyengar, Peters, & Kinder, 1982), we have demonstrated that the public's beliefs about which national problems are important and which are not are greatly influenced by television news.

Here we take up a further and more subtle question: whether television news programs, by calling attention to some aspects of presidential performance while ignoring others, might also determine the standards by which presidents are judged. We suggest that the criteria involved in presidential evaluations may be determined largely by the stories that television news programs choose to cover. Coverage of a particular problem provides new information that is accessible by its recency. Coverage may also provoke viewers to recollect what they already know about the problem. Consequently, both newly acquired and previously acquired information may be made highly available and therefore perhaps particularly influential.[1]

Accessibility does not guarantee influence, however. The impact of accessible information may be great or negligible depending on the relevance of the accessible information to the judgment at hand. The information used in judging a person's intelligence may be largely and safely ignored when judging the same person's honesty (cf. Hamilton & Fallot, 1974). The general point is that information influencing one kind of summary evaluation may be innocuous for another. Increasing the accessibility of some information will not alter all judgments, only those to which the information is relevant, and only to that degree.[2]

In studying presidential evaluations, it is useful to distinguish among three types of judgments: evaluations of the president's general performance, competence, and integrity. Average Americans make such distinctions when they evaluate presidents and presidential hopefuls (Kinder & Abelson, 1981; Kinder, Abelson, & Fiske, 1979; Markus, 1982; Miller & Shanks, 1982); so should we. General performance, competence, and integrity represent correlated but distinct dimensions of presidential evaluation.

Information made accessible by television news coverage that is deemed highly relevant for one of these judgments may be regarded as largely irrelevant for another. Because our experiments manipulated coverage of national problems, we expected to see the greatest impact on the standards that viewers use in judging the president's overall performance. Judgments of overall performance, after all, are presumably just some weighted average of how well the president is doing on unemployment, foreign affairs, energy, and other pressing national problems. Inducing viewers to concentrate on one of these problems should therefore substantially influence the relative importance

knowledge stored in memory may also influence how new and ambiguous information is interpreted (Higgins, Rholes, & Jones, 1977; Srull & Wyer, 1979).

[2] We do not mean to make too fine a point here, for it is easy enough to demonstrate the intrusion of logically irrelevant factors in social and political judgment (Kinder & Abelson, 1981; Nisbett & Ross, 1980; Nisbett & Wilson, 1977; Markus, 1982).

[1] Here we concentrate on the consequences of accessibility for evaluation. Enhancing the accessibility of

they assign to it in judging how well the president is performing overall.

The standards used in judging competence should also be influenced, but not as much, because Americans no doubt recognize that performance on any particular problem reflects the president's competence imperfectly. Performance is always determined in part by forces beyond even the most competent president's control. In the case of energy, for example, many other agents and forces come into play: the international economy, the Organization of Petroleum Exporting Countries (OPEC), Congress, oil companies, and more. In our nomenclature, variations in television news coverage are more relevant for viewers' judgments of the president's overall performance than for judgments of his competence.

Finally, how well the president is dealing with problems like unemployment or rising prices—the focus of our experimental manipulations—has little to do with the president's personal integrity, a point with which most citizens would no doubt agree. Consequently, judgments of the president's integrity should be little influenced by variations in television coverage of national problems.

The influence of accessible information may depend not only on its relevance but also on the characteristics of the audience. Some people may be more vulnerable to manipulations of accessibility than others. This seems highly plausible, yet research on social judgment has tended to slight individual differences of any kind, focusing instead on knowledge that is assumed to be consensual and strategies that are assumed to be universal. Work on problem solving has explored individual differences, however, and differences in expertise in particular. From this research we know that compared with novices, experts not only know more, their knowledge is better organized. As this is true for chess (Chase & Simon, 1973), algebra (Hinsley, Hayes, & Simon, 1977), physics (Larkin, McDermott, Simon, & Simon, 1980), and even dinosaurs (Chi & Koeske, 1983), so should it be true for public affairs. Although some Americans possess an enormous array of facts and theories about the nation's defense, others know hardly anything

at all. This difference reflects variations in problem expertise (Fiske & Kinder, 1981).

The significance of extreme natural variation in problem expertise is that experts and novices may react differently to manipulations of accessibility, and for a number of reasons. First, because their knowledge is denser and better organized, experts possess a greater and more flexible ability to deal with new information. Novices have their minds full just coming to terms with the meaning of what is being said; in a sense they are swept away. Experts are free to examine information more deeply and perhaps more critically (Fiske, Kinder, & Larter, 1983). Second, experts possess so much cognitive support for their ideas about the importance of the particular problem that they may be impossible to budge. Third, drawing attention to the problem may only remind experts of what they already know. Manipulations of accessibility are redundant for experts but not for novices.

This line of argument is consistent with our earlier experimental results, which indicated that television news programs influenced experts less than novices in the importance each assigned to national problems (Iyengar et al., 1982). Here we want to see whether experts are also less vulnerable than novices to the influence of television news in their judgments of the president.

To observe the effects of accessibility, relevance, and expertise on presidential evaluations, we conducted two experiments. In each, subjects viewed television news programs in which the amount of attention given to various national problems was manipulated. Consistent with the accessibility hypothesis, we expected that the more attention a problem received (i.e., the more a problem domain was primed), the more viewers would inject information about that problem into their summary evaluations of the president. In keeping with the relevance hypothesis, we expected the effect to be stronger on evaluations of the president's general performance, intermediate on judgments of the president's competence, and smaller still on judgments of the president's integrity. Consistent with our argument regarding expertise, we expected the accessibility effect to be pronounced among novices and sharply diminished among experts (tested in Experiment 2 only).

EXPERIMENT 1

Participants in Experiment 1 viewed a collection of network news stories. Depending on condition, they saw either no stories, a few stories, or many stories on the subject of energy. After the presentation, participants judged the importance of various national problems, rated presidential performance, indicated their opinions on political issues, and reported their reactions to the news stories.

METHOD

Subjects. Seventy-three Yale University undergraduates who were enrolled in an introductory psychology class completed the experiment in April and May of 1981 as part of the course requirement. Roughly 25 students were randomly assigned to each of three experimental conditions defined by level of exposure to stories about energy (none, intermediate, and high).

Materials. The various collections were assembled from videotape recordings of 1979 and 1980 network evening newscasts, selected from the Vanderbilt Television News Archive. Each ran approximately 40 min. The high-exposure condition presentation included six stories about energy, totaling 16 min; the intermediate-exposure condition presentation included three, totaling 8.5 min; and the no-exposure presentation of course made no reference to energy problems at all. In the high- and intermediate-exposure conditions, the energy stories were distributed evenly throughout the collection. All three presentations were filled out by stories bearing on a variety of other contemporary problems: United States–Soviet relations, civil rights, environmental deterioration, weaknesses in defense, and economic difficulties. No condition included more than a single story on any of these other problems.

After viewing the videotape, participants completed a questionnaire that covered a wide range of political topics. Central to our hypotheses are (a) judgments of President Carter's performance in each of eight specific areas, including "implementing a national energy policy" (ranging from very good to very poor); (b) judgments of President Carter's general performance as president (ranging from very good to very poor); and (c) judgments of how well each of six trait adjectives described President Carter (ranging from extremely well to not well at all). Three of the traits—knowledgeable, smart, and weak—reflect judgments of President Carter's competence; the remaining three—dishonest, power-hungry, and unstable—reflect judgments of Carter's integrity (Kinder & Abelson, 1981; Kinder et al., 1979). Replies to the first set were averaged to form a competence index (with ratings of weak reflected); replies to the second set were averaged to form an integrity index. All judgments—problem-specific performance, general performance, competence, and integrity—ranged in principle (low to high) from one to four. As expected, the three represent correlated but distinct components of presidential evaluation: The Pearson correlation between general performance ratings and competence ratings among all subjects was .53; between general performance and integrity ratings, .27; and between competence and integrity ratings, .33.

Procedure. As many as three students were permitted to sign up for any single experimental session, which was then randomly assigned to experimental condition. When students arrived, they were seated in front of a television monitor and told that the purpose of the study was to investigate selective perception: the way individuals' political values influence their evaluation of television news. To test for selective perception, the students were told, they would view a half hour's worth of "typical" news stories taken from the Vanderbilt Television News Archive. They were informed that following the news presentation they would complete two questionnaires, one assessing their political opinions and the other soliciting their reactions to the news stories. The videotape was then played and, following that, the questionnaires administered. Post-experimental discussions confirmed the plausibility of our cover story. Not a single student expressed any skepticism about what the experiment was really about.

RESULTS

If the accessibility hypothesis is correct, then students who saw stories about energy should have attached greater importance than control subjects did to energy performance in evaluating President Carter. An appropriate test of the hypothesis is provided by regression analysis. We computed regression coefficients indexing the effect of energy performance ratings on judgments of overall performance, competence, and integrity and then compared coefficients between groups of subjects assigned to different conditions. In line with the accessibility hypothesis, we expected the coefficients to be greater among subjects who saw news about energy than among those who did not. Because we could detect no difference whatsoever associated with the moderate- versus high-exposure conditions (neither here nor in Experiment 2), our analysis combines the two. We relied on unstandardized rather than standardized regression coefficients (or correlation coefficients), because comparisons based on the latter can be misleading should the variances of the measures differ across conditions (Duncan, 1975).

Table 1 displays the appropriate unstandardized regression coefficients, computed separately within control and experimental

Table 1 Impact of Energy Performance Ratings on Overall Ratings: Experiment 1

| | CONDITION | | | |
| | No Coverage ($n = 21$) | | Some Coverage ($n = 73$) | |
Category	Coefficient	SE	Coefficient	SE
General performance	0.10	0.14	0.27	0.09
Competence	0.15	0.20	0.19	0.11
Integrity	0.00	0.09	0.06	0.08

Note. "Coefficients" are unstandardized regression coefficients. SE refers to the standard error of the performance rating indicated.

groups, for general performance, competence, and integrity. Consistent with the accessibility hypothesis, the coefficients are larger in all three instances among experimental subjects. And consistent with the relevance hypothesis, the experimental–control difference is most pronounced for judgments of the president's general performance. Indeed, the impact of ratings of Carter's energy performance on ratings of his general performance was nearly three times as great among experimental subjects than among control subjects (.10 vs. .27). Although in the correct direction the differences were far weaker in ratings of Carter's competence (.15 vs. .19) and integrity (.00 vs. .06).

To test the statistical significance of these differences—and hence to test formally the accessibility and relevance hypotheses—we made use of multiple regression analysis. Three regression equations were estimated, one for evaluations of President Carter's general performance, one for ratings of his competence, and one for ratings of his integrity. In each case, overall evaluation (general performance, competence, or integrity) was regressed upon ratings of Carter's management of energy and an interaction term that captured the treatment effect, as specified in Equation 1.1, as follows: Summary evaluation = $b_0 + b_1$ (energy performance) + b_2 (Energy Performance × Treatment) + u, where Treatment = 1 for treatment subjects and 0 for control subjects. The accessibility hypothesis is tested by b_2. It estimates the increment in the influence of energy performance ratings on overall evaluations that results from exposure to energy news. A statistically significant and positively signed b_2 means that students exposed to stories about energy increased the weight they granted to Carter's energy performance in their summary evaluations of the President.

The results from this formal test were as expected. Consistent with the accessibility hypothesis, energy performance ratings were more influential in evaluations of Carter's general performance among students exposed to stories about energy than among those exposed to no stories about energy ($b_2 = .07, p < .05$). Elsewhere, however, accessibility effects were negligible (for competence ratings, $b_2 = 0.00$, ns; for integrity ratings, $b_2 = -0.02$, ns). This pattern of diminishing effects is of course consistent with the logic of the relevance hypothesis. We expected a gradient of effects, though, not a cliff.

Although consistent with the accessibility hypothesis, the one positive result can be understood in another way. Perhaps our experimental manipulations influenced viewers to alter their judgments of Carter's performance on energy, which then had predictable consequences for their evaluations of his general performance. This influence interpretation implies that there should be systematic differences in ratings of Carter between subjects who saw energy stories and those who did not, but there were none. As indicated in Table 2, control subjects rated President Carter's general performance a shade more favorable (2.54 vs. 2.67), $F(1, 67) = 0.88$, $p = .35$; were slightly less impressed with his competence (2.46 vs. 2.36), $F(1, 66) = 0.39$, $p = .53$, and his integrity (3.33 vs. 3.31), $F(1, 69) = 0.04$, $p = .83$; and were somewhat more critical of his performance on energy (3.71 vs. 3.28), $F(1, 65) = 3.43$, $p = .07$. These results mean that experimental manipulation of coverage did not systematically alter students' evaluations of President Carter. Consequently, to the degree we find effects, they appear to be due not to influence but to accessibility.

In sum, the results of Experiment 1 are checkered: strong support for accessibility and more dramatic support for relevance than we had anticipated. To explore these findings further, to examine their external validity, and to see how they might interact with viewers' expertise, we conducted Experiment 2. There we tested our hypotheses with three national problems rather than just one and recruited New Haven, Connecticut, residents rather than Yale undergraduates as subjects.

EXPERIMENT 2

Experiment 2 was run during September and October of 1981 and followed a 2×3 factorial design. As in Experiment 1, two levels of exposure were investigated, this time for each of three problems: energy, defense, and inflation. Participants assigned to either of the two exposure conditions for a particular problem (e.g., defense) saw no stories about the other two problems (energy, inflation). This arrangement enabled us to test for accessibility effects associated with some exposure to a problem versus no exposure, as in Experiment 1. One hundred forty participants served in Experiment 2, with approximately 24 randomly assigned to each condition. Except as noted below, the Experiment 2 procedure was identical to that of Experiment 1.

METHOD

Subjects. Participants were recruited from the New Haven community via a classified advertisement in the local newspaper. The advertisement promised $5 for watching one half hour of television and completing a questionnaire. Individuals who responded to the advertisement were scheduled for an experimental session at their convenience. Sessions were then randomly assigned to treatments. As we hoped, this procedure recruited a diverse pool of participants, roughly representative of the New Haven population. Participants were evenly divided between men and women, predominantly white, and drawn primarily from blue-collar and clerical occupations.

Materials. As in Experiment 1, high-exposure conditions included 6 stories bearing on the target problem; intermediate-exposure conditions contained 3. (See Appendix for details.)

Table 2 Ratings of President Carter: Experiment 1

| | CONDITION | | | |
| | No Coverage (n = 21) | | Some Coverage (n = 73) | |
Category	M	SD	M	SD
General performance	2.54	0.39	2.67	0.53
Competence	2.46	0.55	2.36	0.63
Integrity	3.33	0.29	3.31	0.45
Energy performance	3.71	0.77	3.28	0.83

Note. None of the experimental-control comparisons surpasses statistical significance.

Table 3   Impact of Problem Performance Ratings on Overall Ratings: Experiment 2

	Energy		Defense		Inflation	
Category	No Coverage (n = 92)	Some Coverage (n = 48)	No Coverage (n = 94)	Some Coverage (n = 46)	No Coverage (n = 94)	Some Coverage (n = 46)
General performance						
Coefficient	0.43	0.51	0.37	0.52	0.65	0.71
Standard error	0.07	0.10	0.10	0.12	0.11	0.08
Competence						
Coefficient	0.17	0.13	0.17	0.33	0.28	0.28
Standard error	0.06	0.08	0.07	0.07	0.08	0.08
Integrity						
Coefficient	0.14	0.19	0.17	0.03	0.24	0.15
Standard error	0.06	0.08	0.07	0.12	0.09	0.08

The total number of stories was held to 12 across all conditions. Following the television presentation, participants evaluated President Carter's performance in specific areas, including implementing a national energy policy, holding inflation in check, and maintaining a strong national defense. They also rated Carter's general performance, his competence, and his integrity. As in Experiment 1, these judgments were correlated but distinct. The Pearson correlation between general performance and competence was .49; between general performance and integrity, .38; and between competence and integrity, .35. Finally, participants also completed a nine-item battery intended to tap political expertise. The nine items were distributed equally among the three target problems. In the case of energy, for example, participants were asked to identify three members of OPEC, name the country from which the United States imports the greatest quantity of crude oil, and describe any policy decision made by the Reagan Administration bearing on energy.[3]

RESULTS

Did experimental manipulations of coverage increase the impact of subjects' ratings of Carter's performance in specific areas on their im-

pressions of his general ability, as the accessibility hypothesis prescribes? Preliminary answers are given in Table 3, which reports the appropriate unstandardized coefficients indexing the importance of specific problem ratings for overall general judgments. As in Experiment 1, the coefficients are generally larger among subjects receiving coverage of the particular problem than among those who received no coverage. And as in Experiment 1, the results are clearest for general performance ratings and seem to disappear, if not reverse, for judgments of the president's integrity, in keeping with the relevance hypothesis.

For a precise test of our hypotheses, we turned again to multiple regression analysis. The procedure that was required to estimate accessibility effects is slightly more complicated here than in Experiment 1, because Experiment 2 involves three problems, not just one. Consequently, we need to estimate the impact of any one specific performance rating controlling on the effects of the other two. Equation 2.1, which tests the accessibility and relevance hypotheses, therefore contains six predictors: Summary evaluation = $b_0 + b_1$ (energy performance) + b_2 (Energy Performance × Treatment$_1$) + b_3 (defense performance) + b_4 (Defense Performance × Treatment$_2$) + b_5 (inflation performance) + b_6 (Inflation performance × Treatment$_3$) + u, where Treatment$_1$ = 1 for subjects exposed to energy stories and 0 otherwise; Treatment$_2$ = 1 for subjects exposed to defense stories and 0 otherwise; and

---

[3] Answers to none of the nine knowledge items could be picked up from the experimental news presentations.

Treatment$_3$ = 1 for subjects exposed to inflation stories and 0 otherwise.

The results from the equation indicate strong support for the accessibility hypothesis. In the first place, the impact of enhanced coverage on general job performance evaluations was sizable. For energy, defense, and inflation alike, exposure to stories about the problem substantially strengthened the relationship between specific problem performance ratings and evaluations of general performance. To take the case of energy, which is of intermediate magnitude, the strengthening amounts to a near doubling of the baseline relationship. That is, for viewers who saw no stories about energy, the impact of energy performance ratings on general performance evaluations is 0.186 (b_1); among those who saw energy stories, the impact rose to 0.323 ($b_1 + b_2$; $p < .05$). For defense, the corresponding comparison is 0.035 versus 0.118 ($p < .20$), and for inflation, 0.251 versus 0.393 ($p < .05$). Such effects constitute strong support for the accessibility hypothesis.

By comparison, ratings of the president's competence were much less influenced by manipulations of accessibility. For each of the three problems, the pertinent coefficient was positively signed, as predicted, but none quite reached statistical significance ($ps = .19, .20, .24$, respectively). The effects of accessibility diminished still further when it came to judg-

ment of the president's integrity. In fact, each of the three coefficients indexing the impact of accessibility was negatively signed, contrary to prediction, though none significantly so ($ps > .25$ in all three instances).

This pattern of diminishing accessibility effects conforms nicely to the relevance hypothesis. The consequences of accessibility are most pronounced in evaluations of President Carter's general performance; they appear modestly in evaluations of Carter's competence and are altogether invisible in judgments of his integrity.

Once again, these results could be due to social influence. Yet once again, they seem not to be. Table 4 presents President Carter's average ratings across conditions. Even more emphatically than in Experiment 1, there were no differences. In some instances experimental subjects rated Carter more favorably; in other instances, they rated him less favorably. In no instance was the difference statistically significant. Presenting information about a problem did not lead viewers to alter their judgments regarding President Carter's performance; instead, greater coverage of a problem increased the significance of that problem for viewers' overall judgment.

This brings us finally to expertise. We expected that those viewers who already knew a good bit about a particular problem would be influenced less by television news programs

Table 4 Ratings of President Carter: Experiment 2

	Energy		Defense		Inflation	
Category	No Coverage (n = 92)	Some Coverage (n = 48)	No Coverage (n = 94)	Some Coverage (n = 47)	No Coverage (n = 94)	Some Coverage (n = 46)
General performance						
Mean	3.14	2.96	3.10	3.04	3.00	3.24
Standard deviation	0.96	1.06	1.01	0.97	1.01	0.95
Competence						
Mean	2.50	2.42	2.44	2.54	2.48	2.46
Standard deviation	0.63	0.67	0.66	0.61	0.64	0.66
Integrity						
Mean	3.26	3.28	3.32	3.15	3.22	3.36
Standard deviation	0.69	0.72	0.65	0.79	0.75	0.57
Energy performance						
Mean	3.24	3.02	3.16	3.38	3.72	3.71
Standard deviation	1.16	1.26	1.02	1.05	0.84	1.08

Table 5   Estimated Coverage
Effect on General Job
Performance by Level
of Expertise

Issue	Novices	Experts
Energy	0.19	0.06
Inflation	0.16	0.05
Defense	0.15	0.10

Note. Table entries are unstandardized regression coefficients, estimated by Equation 2.2.

than would those viewers who knew little. To test this expectation, we estimated Equation 2.2: Summary evaluation = b_0 + b_1 (energy performance) + b_2 (Energy Performance × Treatment$_1$) + b_3 (Energy Performance × Treatment$_1$ × Energy Expertise) + b_4 (defense performance) + b_5 (Defense Performance × Treatment$_2$) + b_6 (Defense Performance × Treatment × Defense Expertise) + b_7 (inflation performance) + b_8 (Inflation Performance × Treatment$_3$) + b_9 (Inflation Performance × Treatment$_3$ × Inflation Expertise) + u, where the expertise variables are scored from 0 (all answers wrong) to 3 (all answers correct), and all other variables are as defined in Equation 2.1.[4]

The coefficients of interest here are b_3, b_6, and b_9. We expected them to be negatively signed, meaning that exposure to stories about, say, energy problems would influence presidential judgments less among those who knew a lot about energy than among those who knew little.

The estimated coefficients support this hypothesis well: Eight of the nine coefficients took the predicted negative sign, and the only exception differed trivially from zero (b = 0.022, p = .56). Moreover, five of the eight properly signed coefficients at least approached statistical significance (p < .15).

The results regarding expertise for evalua-

tions of Mr. Carter's general performance are summarized in Table 5. Table 5 presents the estimated impact of treatment, taken from Equation 2.2, for those most knowledgeable about a particular problem (score of 3) and for those who are most ignorant (score of 0). Table 5 makes clear the importance of expertise. As expected, the effects of television news coverage on the standards that are applied to presidential evaluations were much more pronounced among the uninformed; experts were influenced much less.

DISCUSSION

By providing glimpses of some national problems while neglecting others, television news broadcasts help define the evaluative standards that viewers apply to presidents. In our experiments, evaluations of President Carter by people exposed to news about inflation were influenced especially by judgments of how well Carter was managing the economy, evaluations of President Carter by those shown stories about the country's energy problems were influenced especially by judgments of Carter's performance on energy, and evaluations by those exposed to stories about the nation's defense were influenced especially by judgments of his performance on defense. These results constitute strong support for the accessibility hypothesis.

At least two mechanisms may underlie such effects. First, it may be that watching a story about, say, the nation's defense automatically evokes the knowledge that viewers have accumulated in the past on that subject. As a result, such information is more easily accessible and comes to mind more quickly when the viewer is asked to evaluate presidential performance. This account portrays citizens as highly susceptible to the vagaries of circumstance and largely unaware of their own swaying back and forth. Alternatively, viewers may be quite aware of shifts in their evaluational standards. We know that increased exposure to stories about a national problem enhances the importance that people attach to that problem (Iyengar et al., 1982). As a result, they may consciously decide

---

[4] Because the main effects associated with treatment and expertise approached conventional levels of statistical significance, these terms were also included in Equation 2.2.

to accord more weight to that problem in presidential evaluations. Thus, the process may occur within consciousness or outside of it; our results are noncommittal on this point.

Our experiments do, however, specify some boundaries of the accessibility effect. It is not as if television news can unilaterally and completely define the way the public thinks about the president. Real constraints are operating here. In the first place, accessible information will be more or less influential depending on its perceived relevance to the judgment at hand. Manipulations of the impact of accessibility were most pronounced for evaluations of President Carter's general performance, intermediate for appraisals of his competence, and absent for appraisals of his integrity. Effects such as these, falling regularly along a gradient defined by relevance, should be the rule in studies of accessibility.

The particular shape taken by the gradient here is most likely a product of our particular experimental manipulations, however. The presentations we assembled concentrated on three substantive problems facing Mr. Carter: United States' dependence on foreign oil, rising prices, and deterioration in the nation's defense. When such problems are made accessible, as by television news programs, it is only natural that viewers consider Carter's performance in dealing with such problems as more relevant to his competence than to his integrity. Had we instead compiled a collection of news stories bearing on "moral" performance—the Bert Lance affair, Hamilton Jordon's escapades, brother Billy's wheeling and dealing—then integrity and competence might well have exchanged positions on the effects gradient.

Accessible information will be more or less influential depending also on the viewer's expertise. Experts are relatively immune to manipulations of accessibility by television news programs, perhaps because they have already worked out for themselves the national significance of the problem and how heavily the president figures into it. Their standards are well established and already highly accessible. In contrast, novices, whose standards are not nearly so entrenched, are influenced much more by television news stories. These results

serve as a general reminder that the criteria people apply in reaching social judgments have both internal and external origins; they reflect both predisposition and circumstance.

Finally, we should say a word about the political implications of our results. A president's power in Washington depends partly on how favorably he is evaluated by the nation. A popular president tends to have things his way with Congress, the bureaucracy, the private sector, and the executive branch itself (Neustadt, 1960; Rivers & Rose, 1981). As a consequence, understanding the part played by accessibility in presidential evaluations tells us something about the exercise of tangible political power. One implication of our results is that a president's program may be advantaged or completely undone by what happens to come flickering across the nation's television screens.

REFERENCES

Chase, W. G., & Simon, H. A. (1973). The mind's eye in chess. In W. G. Chase (Ed.), *Visual information processing* (pp. 215–281). New York: Academic Press.

Chi, M. T. H., & Koeske, R. (1983). Network representation of a child's dinosaur knowledge. *Developmental Psychology, 19*, 29–39.

Comstock, G., Chaffee, S., Katzman, N., McCombs, M., & Roberts, D. (1978). *Television and human behavior.* New York: Columbia University Press.

Duncan, O. D. (1975). *Introduction to structural equation models.* New York: Academic Press.

Fiske, S. T., & Kinder, D. R. (1981). Involvement, expertise, and schema use: Evidence from political cognition. In N. Cantor & J. Kihlstrom (Eds.), *Personality, cognition, and social interaction* (pp. 171–190). Hillsdale, NJ: Erlbaum.

Fiske, S. T., Kinder, D. R., & Larter, W. M. (1983). The novice and the expert: Knowledge-based strategies in political cognition. *Journal of Experimental Social Psychology, 19*, 381–400.

Graber, D. (1980). *Mass media and American politics.* Washington, DC: Congressional Quarterly Press.

Hamilton, D. L., & Fallot, R. D. (1974). Information salience as a weighting factor in impression formation. *Journal of Personality and Social Psychology, 30*, 444–448.

Higgins, E. T., & King, G. (1981). Accessibility of social constructs: Information-processing consequences of individual and contextual variability. In N. Cantor & J. Kihlstrom (Eds.), *Personality, cognition, and social interaction* (pp. 69–121). Hillsdale, NJ: Erlbaum.

Higgins, E. T., Rholes, W. S., & Jones, C. R. (1977). Category accessibility and impression formation. *Journal of Experimental Social Psychology, 13,* 141–154.

Hinsley, D. A., Hayes, J. R., & Simon, H. A. (1977). From words to equations: Meaning and representation in algebra word problems. In M. A. Just & P. S. Carpenter (Eds.), *Cognitive processes in comprehension,* pp. 89–106. Hillsdale, NJ: Erlbaum.

Iyengar, S., Peters, M. D., & Kinder, D. R. (1982). Experimental demonstrations of the not-so-minimal political consequences of mass media. *American Political Science Review, 76,* 848–858.

Kinder, D. R., & Abelson, R. P. (1981, September). *Appraising presidential candidates: Personality and affect in the 1980 campaign.* Paper delivered at the 1981 Annual Meeting of the American Political Science Association, New York City.

Kinder, D. R., Abelson, R. P., & Fiske, S. T. (1979). *Developmental research on candidate instrumentation: Results and recommendations.* Report available from Center for Political Studies, ISR, University of Michigan, Ann Arbor, Michigan 48106.

Kinder, D. R., & Sears, D. O. (in press). Public opinion and political action. In G. Lindzey and E. Aronson (Eds.), *Handbook of social psychology* (3rd ed.). Reading, MA: Addison-Wesley.

Larkin, J. H., McDermott, J., Simon, D. P., & Simon, H. A. (1980). Models of competence in solving physics problems. *Science, 208,* 1335–1342.

Markus, G. B. (1982). Political attitudes during an election year: A report on the 1980 NES Panel Study. *American Political Science Review, 76,* 538–560.

Miller, W. E., & Shanks, J. M. (1982). Policy directions and presidential leadership: Alternative interpretations of the 1980 presidential election. *British Journal of Political Science, 12,* 299–356.

Neustadt, R. E. (1960). *Presidential power.* New York: Wiley.

Nisbett, R. E., & Ross, L. (1980). *Human inference: Strategies and shortcomings of social judgment.* Englewood Cliffs, NJ: Prentice-Hall.

Nisbett, R. E., & Wilson, T. D. (1977). Telling more than we can know: Verbal reports on mental processes. *Psychological Review, 84,* 231–259.

Rivers, D., & Rose, N. (1981, April). *Passing the president's program.* Paper delivered at the Annual Meeting of the Mid-West Political Science Association, Chicago.

Salancik, G. R. (1974). Inferences of one's attitude from behavior recalled under linguistically manipulated cognitive sets. *Journal of Experimental Social Psychology, 10,* 415–427.

Srull, T. K., & Wyer, R. S. (1979). The role of category accessibility in the interpretation of information about persons: Some determinants and implications. *Journal of Personality and Social Psychology, 37,* 1160–1172.

Wyer, R. S., & Hartwick, J. (1980). The role of information retrieval and conditional inference processes in belief formation and change. In L. Berkowitz (Ed.), *Advances in Experimental Social Psychology* (Vol. 13, pp. 241–284). New York: Academic Press.

27

Some Thoughts on the Ethics of Research:
After Reading Milgram's "Behavioral Study of Obedience"

DIANA BAUMRIND

The obedience studies of Stanley Milgram (see selection 19) sparked an unprece-dented debate about the ethics of research. In this paper first published in 1964, Diana Baumrind criticizes Milgram for exposing his subjects to psychological distress, embarrassment, and loss of dignity. She suggests that Milgram did not take seriously enough the reactions that subjects had to his study, and she questions whether the debriefing following the experiment was successful in restoring the psychological well-being of subjects. Baumrind suggests that the study may have had long-term effects on subjects, causing them to lose self-esteem or to lose trust in authorities. Finally, she also expresses concern that this research may tarnish the public image of psychology as a profession. In the next article, we present Milgram's reply.

Twenty-five years later, it is safe to say that professional psychology has weathered this storm, and has learned a good deal in the process. Today, psychologists are much more aware of the potential risks of psychological research. In addition, the U.S. Government has established strict guidelines for the protection of human re-search subjects, some of which are presented in selection 29. An important part of current procedures is for research projects to be evaluated in advance, by a panel of experts, so that an individual researcher can no longer decide alone that a study is ethically sound. It is doubtful that the Milgram study would gain approval today. Baumrind would likely see this as a success, but other psychologists would argue that we gained such important information from the Milgram studies that they were ethically justifiable. Read Milgram's reply, and then decide for yourself.

Certain problems in psychological research require the experimenter to balance his career and scientific interests against the interests of his prospective subjects. When such occasions arise the experimenter's stated objective fre-quently is to do the best possible job with the least possible harm to his subjects. The experi-menter seldom perceives in more positive terms an indebtedness to the subject for his services, perhaps because the detachment

Reprinted from the *American Psychologist*, 1964, *19*(6), pp. 421–423. Copyright 1964 by the American Psychological Association. Reprinted by permission of publisher and author.

which his functions require prevents appreciation of the subject as an individual.

Yet a debt does exist, even when the subject's reason for volunteering includes course credit or monetary gain. Often a subject participates unwillingly in order to satisfy a course requirement. These requirements are of questionable merit ethically, and do not alter the experimenter's responsibility to the subject.

Most experimental conditions do not cause the subjects pain or indignity, and are sufficiently interesting or challenging to present no problem of an ethical nature to the experimenter. But where the experimental conditions expose the subject to loss of dignity, or offer him nothing of value, then the experimenter is obliged to consider the reasons why the subject volunteered and to reward him accordingly.

The subject's public motives for volunteering include having an enjoyable or stimulating experience, acquiring knowledge, doing the experimenter a favor which may some day be reciprocated, and making a contribution to science. These motives can be taken into account rather easily by the experimenter who is willing to spend a few minutes with the subject afterwards to thank him for his participation, answer his questions, reassure him that he did well, and chat with him a bit. Most volunteers also have less manifest, but equally legitimate, motives. A subject may be seeking an opportunity to have contact with, be noticed by, and perhaps confide in a person with psychological training. The dependent attitude of most subjects toward the experimenter is an artifact of the experimental situation as well as an expression of some subjects' personal need systems at the time they volunteer.

The dependent, obedient attitude assumed by most subjects in the experimental setting is appropriate to that situation. The "game" is defined by the experimenter and he makes the rules. By volunteering, the subject agrees implicitly to assume a posture of trust and obedience. While the experimental conditions leave him exposed, the subject has the right to assume that his security and self-esteem will be protected.

There are other professional situations in which one member—the patient or client—expects help and protection from the other—the physician or psychologist. But the interpersonal relationship between experimenter and subject additionally has unique features which are likely to provoke initial anxiety in the subject. The laboratory is unfamiliar as a setting and the rules of behavior ambiguous compared to a clinician's office. Because of the anxiety and passivity generated by the setting, the subject is more prone to behave in an obedient, suggestible manner in the laboratory than elsewhere. Therefore, the laboratory is not the place to study degree of obedience or suggestibility, as a function of a particular experimental condition, since the base line for these phenomena as found in the laboratory is probably much higher than in most other settings. Thus experiments in which the relationship to the experimenter as an authority is used as an independent condition are imperfectly designed for the same reason that they are prone to injure the subjects involved. They disregard the special quality of trust and obedience with which the subject appropriately regards the experimenter.

Other phenomena which present ethical decisions, unlike those mentioned above, *can* be reproduced successfully in the laboratory. Failure experience, conformity to peer judgment, and isolation are among such phenomena. In these cases we can expect the experimenter to take whatever measures are necessary to prevent the subject from leaving the laboratory more humiliated, insecure, alienated, or hostile than when he arrived. To guarantee that an especially sensitive subject leaves a stressful experimental experience in the proper state sometimes requires special clinical training. But usually an attitude of compassion, respect, gratitude, and common sense will suffice, and no amount of clinical training will substitute. The subject has the right to expect that the psychologist with whom he is interacting has some concern for his welfare, and the personal attributes and professional skill to express his good will effectively.

Unfortunately, the subject is not always treated with the respect he deserves. It has become more commonplace in sociopsychological laboratory studies to manipulate, embarrass, and discomfort subjects. At times the insult to the subject's sensibilities extends to the journal reader when the results are reported. Milgram's (1963) study is a case in point. The following is Milgram's abstract of his experiment:

This article describes a procedure for the study of destructive obedience in the laboratory. It consists of ordering a naive *S* to administer increasingly more severe punishment to a victim in the context of a learning experiment. Punishment is administered by means of a shock generator with 30 graded switches ranging from Slight Shock to Danger: Severe Shock. The victim is a confederate of *E*. The primary dependent variable is the maximum shock the *S* is willing to administer before he refuses to continue further. 26 *Ss* obeyed the experimental commands fully, and administered the highest shock on the generator. 14 *Ss* broke off the experiment at some point after the victim protested and refused to provide further answers. The procedure created extreme levels of nervous tension in some *Ss*. Profuse sweating, trembling, and stuttering were typical expressions of this emotional disturbance. One unexpected sign of tension—yet to be explained— was the regular occurrence of nervous laughter, which in some *Ss* developed into uncontrollable seizures. The variety of interesting behavioral dynamics observed in the experiment, the reality of the situation for the *S*, and the possibility of parametric variation within the framework of the procedure, point to the fruitfulness of further study [p. 371].

The detached, objective manner in which Milgram reports the emotional disturbance suffered by his subject contrasts sharply with his graphic account of that disturbance. Following are two other quotes describing the effects on his subjects of the experimental conditions:

I observed a mature and initially poised businessman enter the laboratory smiling and confident. Within 20 minutes he was reduced to a twitching, stuttering wreck, who was rapidly approaching a point of nervous collapse. He constantly pulled on his earlobe, and twisted his hands. At one point he pushed his fist into his forehead and muttered: "Oh God, let's stop it." And yet he continued to respond to every word

of the experimenter, and obeyed to the end [p. 377].

In a large number of cases the degree of tension reached extremes that are rarely seen in sociopsychological laboratory studies. Subjects were observed to sweat, tremble, stutter, bite their lips, groan, and dig their fingernails into their flesh. These were characteristic rather than exceptional responses to the experiment.

One sign of tension was the regular occurrence of nervous laughing fits. Fourteen of the 40 subjects showed definite signs of nervous laughter and smiling. The laughter seemed entirely out of place, even bizarre. Full-blown, uncontrollable seizures were observed for 3 subjects. On one occasion we observed a seizure so violently convulsive that it was necessary to call a halt to the experiment . . . [p. 375].

Milgram does state that,

After the interview, procedures were undertaken to assure that the subject would leave the laboratory in a state of well being. A friendly reconciliation was arranged between the subject and the victim, and an effort was made to reduce any tensions that arose as a result of the experiment [p. 374].

It would be interesting to know what sort of procedures could dissipate the type of emotional disturbance just described. In view of the effects on subjects, traumatic to a degree which Milgram himself considers nearly unprecedented in sociopsychological experiments, his casual assurance that these tensions were dissipated before the subject left the laboratory is unconvincing.

What could be the rational basis for such a posture of indifference? Perhaps Milgram supplies the answer himself when he partially explains the subject's destructive obedience as follows, "Thus they assume that the discomfort caused the victim is momentary, while the scientific gains resulting from the experiment are enduring [p. 378]." Indeed such a rationale might suffice to justify the means used to achieve his end if that end were of inestimable value to humanity or were not itself transformed by the means by which it was attained.

The behavioral psychologist is not in as good a position to objectify his faith in the significance of his work as medical colleagues at points of breakthrough. His experimental situations are not sufficiently accurate models of real-life experience; his sampling techniques are seldom of a scope which would justify the meaning with which he would like to endow his results; and these results are hard to reproduce by colleagues with opposing theoretical views. Unlike the Sabin vaccine, for example, the concrete benefit to humanity of his particular piece of work, no matter how competently handled, cannot justify the risk that real harm will be done to the subject. I am not speaking of physical discomfort, inconvenience, or experimental deception per se, but of permanent harm, however slight. I do regard the emotional disturbance described by Milgram as potentially harmful because it could easily effect an alteration in the subject's self-image or ability to trust adult authorities in the future. It is potentially harmful to a subject to commit, in the course of an experiment, acts which he himself considers unworthy, particularly when he has been entrapped into committing such acts by an individual he has reason to trust. The subject's personal responsibility for his actions is not erased because the experimenter reveals to him the means which he used to stimulate these actions. The subject realizes that he would have hurt the victim if the current were on. The realization that he also made a fool of himself by accepting the experimental set results in additional loss of self-esteem. Moreover, the subject finds it difficult to express his anger outwardly after the experimenter in a self-acceptant but friendly manner reveals the hoax.

A fairly intense corrective interpersonal experience is indicated wherein the subject admits and accepts his responsibility for his own actions, and at the same time gives vent to his hurt and anger at being fooled. Perhaps an experience as distressing as the one described by Milgram can be integrated by the subject, provided that careful thought is given to the matter. The propriety of such experimentation is still in question even if such a reparational experience were forthcoming. Without it I would expect a naive, sensitive subject to remain deeply hurt and anxious for some time, and a sophisticated, cynical subject to become even more alienated and distrustful.

In addition the experimental procedure used by Milgram does not appear suited to the objectives of the study because it does not take into account the special quality of the set which the subject has in the experimental situation. Milgram is concerned with a very important problem, namely, the social consequences of destructive obedience. He says,

Gas chambers were built, death camps were guarded, daily quotas of corpses were produced with the same efficiency as the manufacture of appliances. These inhumane policies may have originated in the mind of a single person, but they could only be carried out on a massive scale if a very large number of persons obeyed orders [p. 371].

But the parallel between authority-subordinate relationships in Hitler's Germany and in Milgram's laboratory is unclear. In the former situation the SS man or member of the German Officer Corps, when obeying orders to slaughter, had no reason to think of his superior officer as benignly disposed towards himself or their victims. The victims were perceived as subhuman and not worthy of consideration. The subordinate officer was an agent in a great cause. He did not need to feel guilt or conflict because within his frame of reference he was acting rightly.

It is obvious from Milgram's own descriptions that most of his subjects were concerned about their victims and did trust the experimenter, and that their distressful conflict was generated in part by the consequences of these two disparate but appropriate attitudes. Their distress may have resulted from shock at what the experimenter was doing to them as well as from what they thought they were doing to their victims. In any case there is not a convincing parallel between the phenomena studied by Milgram and destructive obedience as that concept would apply to the subordinate-authority relationship demonstrated in Hitler Germany. If the experiments were conducted "outside of New Haven and without any visible ties to the university," I would still question their validity on similar although not identical grounds. In addition, I would question the representativeness of a sample of subjects who would voluntarily participate within a noninstitutional setting.

In summary, the experimental objectives of the psychologist are seldom incompatible with the subject's ongoing state of well being, provided that the experimenter is willing to take the subject's motives and interests into consideration when planning his methods and correctives. Section 4b in *Ethical Standards of Psychologists* (APA, undated) reads in part:

Only when a problem is significant and can be investigated in no other way, is the psychologist justified in exposing human subjects to emotional stress or other possible harm. In conducting such research, the psychologist must seriously consider the possibility of harmful aftereffects, and should be prepared to remove them as soon as permitted by the design of the experiment. Where the danger of serious aftereffects exists, research should be conducted only when the subjects or their responsible agents are fully informed of this possibility and volunteer nevertheless [p. 12].

From the subject's point of view procedures which involve loss of dignity, self-esteem, and trust in rational authority are probably most harmful in the long run and require the most thoughtfully planned reparations, if engaged in at all. The public image of psychology as a profession is highly related to our own actions, and some of these actions are changeworthy. It is important that as research psychologists we protect our ethical sensibilities rather than adapt our personal standards to include as appropriate the kind of indignities to which Milgram's subjects were exposed. I would not like to see experiments such as Milgram's proceed unless the subjects were fully informed of the dangers of serious aftereffects and his correctives were clearly shown to be effective in restoring their state of well being.

REFERENCES

American Psychological Association. Ethical Standards of Psychologists: A summary of ethical principles. Washington, D.C.: APA, undated.

Milgram, S. Behavioral study of obedience. *Journal of Abnormal Social Psychology*, 1963, *67*, 371–378.

28

Issues in the Study of Obedience:
A Reply to Baumrind

Stanley Milgram

In this paper, Stanley Milgram responds to the criticisms of his work by Diana Baumrind. Current ethical guidelines for human research ask investigators to weigh the risks to subjects against the benefits to be derived from their research. Milgram addresses both issues. First, he emphasizes that the study was not ultimately harmful to subjects. He describes in some detail the way in which subjects were debriefed after the study (the "dehoax" as Milgram calls it)—to explain and justify the deception, and to restore their sense of well-being. Milgram reports the results of a one-year followup which found no evidence of long-term harm. He also indicates that most subjects expressed positive feelings about the research. Second, Milgram emphasizes the value of his research. He explains that the extreme tension experienced by subjects was unexpected, something that neither he nor his colleagues anticipated, He and others were greatly surprised by the levels of obedience observed in the lab, making this finding about human behavior all the more significant. Milgram also notes that his study has "ecological validity." Since the relationship between research subject and experimenter is inherently one of subordinate and authority figure, it provides a realistic and meaningful context in which to study legitimate obedience. After reading both sides of this debate, what do you conclude about the value and ethics of the obedience studies?

Obedience serves numerous productive functions in society. It may be ennobling and educative and entail acts of charity and kindness. Yet the problem of destructive obedience, because it is the most disturbing expression of obedience in our time, and because it is the most perplexing, merits intensive study.

In its most general terms, the problem of destructive obedience may be defined thus: If X tells Y to hurt Z, under what conditions will Y carry out the command of X, and under what conditions will he refuse? In the concrete setting of a laboratory, the question may assume this form: If an experimenter tells a sub-

ject to act against another person, under what conditions will the subject go along with the instruction, and under what conditions will he refuse to obey?

A simple procedure was devised for studying obedience (Milgram, 1963). A person comes to the laboratory, and in the context of a learning experiment, he is told to give increasingly severe electric shocks to another person. (The other person is an actor, who does not really receive any shocks.) The experimenter tells the subject to continue stepping up the shock level, even to the point of reaching the level marked "Danger: Severe Shock." The purpose of the experiment is to see how far the naive subject will proceed before he refuses to comply with the experimenter's instructions. Behavior prior to this rupture is considered "obedience" in

Reprinted from the *American Psychologist*, 1964, *19*, pp. 848–852. Copyright 1964 by the American Psychological Association. Reprinted by permission of the publisher and author.

that the subject does what the experimenter tells him to do. The point of rupture is the act of disobedience. Once the basic procedure is established, it becomes possible to vary conditions of the experiment, to learn under what circumstances obedience to authority is most probable, and under what conditions defiance is brought to the fore (Milgram, in press).

The results of the experiment (Milgram, 1963) showed, first, that it is more difficult for many people to defy the experimenter's authority than was generally supposed. A substantial number of subjects go through to the end of the shock board. The second finding is that the situation often places a person in considerable conflict. In the course of the experiment, subjects fidget, sweat, and sometimes break out into nervous fits of laughter. On the one hand, subjects want to aid the experimenter; and on the other hand, they do not want to shock the learner. The conflict is expressed in nervous reactions.

In a recent issue of *American Psychologist,* Diana Baumrind (1964) raised a number of questions concerning the obedience report. Baumrind expressed concern for the welfare of subjects who served in the experiment, and wondered whether adequate measures were taken to protect the participants. She also questioned the adequacy of the experimental design.

Patently, "Behavioral Study of Obedience" did not contain all the information needed for an assessment of the experiment. But it is clearly indicated in the references and footnotes (pp. 373, 378) that this was only one of a series of reports on the experimental program, and Baumrind's article was deficient in information that could have been obtained easily. I thank the editor for allotting space in this journal to review this information, to amplify it, and to discuss some of the issues touched on by Baumrind.

At the outset, Baumrind confuses the unanticipated outcome of an experiment with its basic procedure. She writes, for example, as if the production of stress in our subjects was an intended and deliberate effect of the experimental manipulation. There are many laboratory procedures specifically designed to create stress (Lazarus, 1964), but the obedience paradigm was not one of them. The extreme tension induced in some subjects was unexpected. Before conducting the experiment, the procedures were discussed with many colleagues, and none anticipated the reactions that subsequently took place. Foreknowledge of results can never be the invariable accompaniment of an experimental probe. Understanding grows because we examine situations in which the end is unknown. An investigator unwilling to accept this degree of risk must give up the idea of scientific inquiry.

Moreover, there was every reason to expect, prior to actual experimentation, that subjects would refuse to follow the experimenter's instructions beyond the point where the victim protested; many colleagues and psychiatrists were questioned on this point, and they virtually all felt this would be the case. Indeed, to initiate an experiment in which the critical measure hangs on disobedience, one must start with a belief in certain spontaneous resources in men that enable them to overcome pressure from authority.

It is true that after a reasonable number of subjects had been exposed to the procedures, it became evident that some would go to the end of the shock board, and some would experience stress. That point, it seems to me, is the first legitimate juncture at which one could even start to wonder whether or not to abandon the study. But momentary excitement is not the same as harm. As the experiment progressed there was no indication of injurious effects in the subjects; and as the subjects themselves strongly endorsed the experiment, the judgment I made was to continue the investigation.

Is not Baumrind's criticism based as much on the unanticipated findings as on the method? The findings were that some subjects performed in what appeared to be a shockingly immoral way. If, instead, every one of the subjects had broken off at "slight shock," or at the first sign of the learner's discomfort, the results would have been pleasant, and reassuring, and who would protest?

PROCEDURES AND BENEFITS

A most important aspect of the procedure occurred at the end of the experimental session. A careful post-experimental treatment was administered to all subjects. The exact content of the dehoax varied from condition to condition and with increasing experience on our part. At the very least all subjects were told that the victim had not received dangerous electric shocks. Each subject had a friendly reconciliation with the unharmed victim, and an extended discussion with the experimenter. The experiment was explained to the defiant subjects in a way that supported their decision to disobey the experimenter. Obedient subjects were assured of the fact that their behavior was entirely normal and that their feelings of conflict or tension were shared by other participants. Subjects were told that they would receive a comprehensive report at the conclusion of the experimental series. In some instances, additional detailed and lengthy discussions of the experiments were also carried out with individual subjects.

When the experimental series was complete, subjects received a written report which presented details of the experimental procedure and results. Again their own part in the experi-

ments was treated in a dignified way and their behavior in the experiment respected. All subjects received a follow-up questionnaire regarding their participation in the research, which again allowed expression of thoughts and feelings about their behavior.

The replies to the questionnaire confirmed my impression that participants felt positively toward the experiment. In its quantitative aspect (see Table 1), 84% of the subjects stated they were glad to have been in the experiment; 15% indicated neutral feelings, and 1.3% indicated negative feelings. To be sure, such findings are to be interpreted cautiously, but they cannot be disregarded.

Further, four-fifths of the subjects felt that more experiments of this sort should be carried out, and 74% indicated that they had learned something of personal importance as a result of being in the study. The results of the interviews, questionnaire responses, and actual transcripts of the debriefing procedures will be presented more fully in a forthcoming monograph.

The debriefing and assessment procedures were carried out as a matter of course, and were not stimulated by any observation of special risk in the experimental procedure. In my judgment, at no point were subjects exposed

Table 1 Excerpt from Questionnaire Used in a Follow-Up Study of the Obedience Research

Now That I Have Read the Report, and All Things Considered . . .	Defiant	Obedient	All
1. I am very glad to have been in the experiment	40.0%	47.8%	43.5%
2. I am glad to have been in the experiment	43.8%	35.7%	40.2%
3. I am neither sorry nor glad to have been in the experiment	15.3%	14.8%	15.1%
4. I am sorry to have been in the experiment	0.8%	0.7%	0.8%
5. I am very sorry to have been in the experiment	0.0%	1.0%	0.5%

Note—Ninety-two percent of the subjects returned the questionnaire. The characteristics of the nonrespondents were checked against the respondents. They differed from the respondents only with regard to age; younger people were overrepresented in the nonresponding group.

to danger and at no point did they run the risk of injurious effects resulting from participation. If it had been otherwise, the experiment would have been terminated at once.

Baumrind states that, after he has performed in the experiment, the subject cannot justify his behavior and must bear the full brunt of his actions. By and large it does not work this way. The same mechanisms that allow the subject to perform the act, to obey rather than to defy the experimenter, transcend the moment of performance and continue to justify his behavior for him. The same viewpoint the subject takes while performing the actions is the viewpoint from which he later sees his behavior, that is, the perspective of "carrying out the task assigned by the person in authority."

Because the idea of shocking the victim is repugnant, there is a tendency among those who hear of the design to say "people will not do it." When the results are made known, this attitude is expressed as "if they do it they will not be able to live with themselves afterward." These two forms of denying the experimental findings are equally inappropriate misreadings of the facts of human social behavior. Many subjects do, indeed, obey to the end, and there is no indication of injurious effects.

The absence of injury is a minimal condition of experimentation; there can be, however, an important positive side to participation. Baumrind suggests that subjects derived no benefit from being in the obedience study, but this is false. By their statements and actions, subjects indicated that they had learned a good deal, and many felt gratified to have taken part in scientific research they considered to be of significance. A year after his participation one subject wrote:

This experiment has strengthened my belief that man should avoid harm to his fellow man even at the risk of violating authority.

Another stated:

To me, the experiment pointed up . . . the extent to which each individual should have or discover firm ground on which to base his decisions, no matter how trivial they appear to be. I think people should think more deeply about themselves

and their relation to their world and to other people. If this experiment serves to jar people out of complacency, it will have served its end.

These statements are illustrative of a broad array of appreciative and insightful comments by those who participated.

The 5-page report sent to each subject on the completion of the experimental series was specifically designed to enhance the value of his experience. It layed out the broad conception of the experimental program as well as the logic of its design. It described the results of a dozen of the experiments, discussed the causes of tension, and attempted to indicate the possible significance of the experiment. Subjects responded enthusiastically; many indicated a desire to be in further experimental research. This report was sent to all subjects several years ago. The care with which it was prepared does not support Baumrind's assertion that the experimenter was indifferent to the value subjects derived from their participation.

Baumrind's fear is that participants will be alienated from psychological experiments because of the intensity of experience associated with laboratory procedures. My own observation is that subjects more commonly respond with distaste to the "empty" laboratory hour, in which cardboard procedures are employed, and the only possible feeling upon emerging from the laboratory is that one has wasted time in a patently trivial and useless exercise.

The subjects in the obedience experiment, on the whole, felt quite differently about their participation. They viewed the experience as an opportunity to learn something of importance about themselves, and more generally, about the conditions of human action.

A year after the experimental program was completed, I initiated an additional follow-up study. In this connection an impartial medical examiner, experienced in outpatient treatment, interviewed 40 experimental subjects. The examining psychiatrist focused on those subjects he felt would be most likely to have suffered consequences from participation. His aim was to identify possible injurious effects resulting from the experiment. He concluded that, although extreme stress had been experienced by several subjects,

> none was found by this interviewer to show signs of having been harmed by his experience. . . . Each subject seemed to handle his task [in the experiment] in a manner consistent with well-established patterns of behavior. No evidence was found of any traumatic reactions.

Such evidence ought to be weighed before judging the experiment.

OTHER ISSUES

Baumrind's discussion is not limited to the treatment of subjects, but diffuses to a generalized rejection of the work.

Baumrind feels that obedience cannot be meaningfully studied in a laboratory setting: The reason she offers is that "The dependent, obedient attitude assumed by most subjects in the experimental setting is appropriate to that situation [p. 421]." Here, Baumrind has cited the very best reason for examining obedience in this setting, namely that it possesses "ecological validity." Here is one social context in which compliance occurs regularly. Military and job situations are also particularly meaningful settings for the study of obedience precisely because obedience is natural and appropriate to these contexts. I reject Baumrind's argument that the observed obedience does not count because it occurred where it is appropriate. That is precisely why it *does* count. A soldier's obedience is no less meaningful because it occurs in a pertinent military context. A subject's obedience is no less problematical because it occurs within a social institution called the psychological experiment.

Baumrind writes: "The game is defined by the experimenter and he makes the rules [p. 421]." It is true that for disobedience to occur the framework of the experiment must be shattered. That, indeed, is the point of the design. That is why obedience and disobedience are genuine issues for the subject. *He must really assert himself as a person against a legitimate authority.*

Further, Baumrind wants us to believe that outside the laboratory we could not find a comparably high expression of obedience. Yet, the fact that ordinary citizens are recruited to military service and, on command, perform far harsher acts against people is beyond dispute. Few of them know or are concerned with the complex policy issues underlying martial action; fewer still become conscientious objectors. Good soldiers do as they are told, and on both sides of the battle line. However, a debate on whether a higher level of obedience is represented by (a) killing men in the service of one's country, or (b) merely shocking them in the service of Yale science, is largely unprofitable. The real question is: What are the forces underlying obedient action?

Another question raised by Baumrind concerns the degree of parallel between obedience in the laboratory and in Nazi Germany. Obviously, there are enormous differences: Consider the disparity in time scale. The laboratory experiment takes an hour; the Nazi calamity unfolded in the space of a decade. There is a great deal that needs to be said on this issue, and only a few points can be touched on here.

1. In arguing this matter, Baumrind mistakes the background metaphor for the precise subject matter of investigation. The German event was cited to point up a serious problem in the human situation: the potentially destructive effect of obedience. But the best way to tackle the problem of obedience, from a scientific standpoint, is in no way restricted by "what happened exactly" in Germany. What happened exactly can *never* be duplicated in the laboratory or anywhere else. The real task is to learn more about the general problem of destructive obedience using a workable approach. Hopefully, such inquiry will stimulate insights and yield general propositions that can be applied to a wide variety of situations.

2. One may ask in a general way: How does a man behave when he is told by a legitimate authority to act against a third individual? In trying to find an answer to this question, the laboratory situation is one useful starting point—and for the very reason stated by Baumrind—namely, the experimenter does constitute a genuine authority for the subject. The

fact that trust and dependence on the experimenter are maintained, despite the extraordinary harshness he displays toward the victim, is itself a remarkable phenomenon.

3. In the laboratory, through a set of rather simple manipulations, ordinary persons no longer perceived themselves as a responsible part of the causal chain leading to action against a person. The means through which responsibility is cast off, and individuals become thoughtless agents of action, is of general import. Other processes were revealed that indicate that the experiments will help us to understand why men obey. That understanding will come, of course, by examining the full account of experimental work and not alone the brief report in which the procedure and demonstrational results were exposed.

At root, Baumrind senses that it is not proper to test obedience in this situation, because she construes it as one in which there is no reasonable alternative to obedience. In adopting this view, she has lost sight of this fact: A substantial proportion of subjects do disobey. By their example, disobedience is shown to be a genuine possibility, one that is in no sense ruled out by the general structure of the experimental situation.

Baumrind is uncomfortable with the high level of obedience obtained in the first experiment. In the condition she focused on, 65% of the subjects obeyed to the end. However, her sentiment does not take into account that within the general framework of the psychological experiment obedience varied enormously from one condition to the next. In some variations, 90% of the subjects *dis*obeyed. It seems to be *not* only the fact of an experiment, but the particular structure of elements within the experimental situation that accounts for rates of obedience and disobedience. And these elements were varied systematically in the program of research.

A concern with human dignity is based on a respect for a man's potential to act morally. Baumrind feels that the experimenter *made* the subject shock the victim. This conception is alien to my view. The experimenter tells the subject to do something. But between the command and the outcome there is a paramount

force, the acting person who may obey or disobey. I started with the belief that every person who came to the laboratory was free to accept or to reject the dictates of authority. This view sustains a conception of human dignity insofar as it sees in each man a capacity for *choosing* his own behavior. And as it turned out, many subjects did, indeed, choose to reject the experimenter's commands, providing a powerful affirmation of human ideals.

Baumrind also criticizes the experiment on the grounds that "it could easily effect an alteration in the subject's . . . ability to trust adult authorities in the future [p. 422]." But I do not think she can have it both ways. On the one hand, she argues the experimental situation is so special that it has no generality; on the other hand, she states it has such generalizing potential that it will cause subjects to distrust all authority. But the experimenter is not just any authority: He is an authority who tells the subject to act harshly and inhumanely against another man. I would consider it of the highest value if participation in the experiment could, indeed, inculcate a skepticism of this kind of authority. Here, perhaps, a difference in philosophy emerges most clearly. Baumrind sees the subject as a passive creature, completely controlled by the experimenter. I started from a different viewpoint. A person who comes to the laboratory is an active, choosing adult, capable of accepting or rejecting the prescriptions for action addressed to him. Baumrind sees the effect of the experiment as undermining the subject's trust of authority. I see it as a potentially valuable experience insofar as it makes people aware of the problem of indiscriminate submission to authority.

CONCLUSION

My feeling is that viewed in the total context of values served by the experiment, approximately the right course was followed. In review, the facts are these: (*a*) At the outset, there was the problem of studying obedience by means of a simple experimental procedure. The results could not be foreseen before the experiment was carried out. (*b*) Although the experiment generated momentary stress in some subjects, this stress dissipated quickly and was not injurious. (*c*) Dehoax and follow-up procedures were carried out to insure the subjects' well-being. (*d*) These procedures were assessed through questionnaire and psychiatric studies and were found to be effective. (*e*) Additional steps were taken to enhance the value of the laboratory experience for participants, for example, submitting to each subject a careful report on the experimental program. (*f*) The subjects themselves strongly endorse the experiment, and indicate satisfaction at having participated.

If there is a moral to be learned from the obedience study, it is that every man must be responsible for his own actions. This author accepts full responsibility for the design and execution of the study. Some people may feel it should not have been done. I disagree and accept the burden of their judgment.

Baumrind's judgment, someone has said, not only represents a personal conviction, but also reflects a cleavage in American psychology between those whose primary concern is with *helping* people and those who are interested mainly in *learning* about people. I see little value

in perpetuating divisive forces in psychology when there is so much to learn from every side. A schism may exist, but it does not correspond to the true ideals of the discipline. The psychologist intent on healing knows that his power to help rests on knowledge; he is aware that a scientific grasp of all aspects of life is essential for his work, and is in itself a worthy human aspiration. At the same time, the laboratory psychologist senses his work will lead to human betterment, not only because enlightenment is more dignified than ignorance, but because new knowledge is pregnant with humane consequences.

REFERENCES

Baumrind, D. Some thoughts on ethics of research: After reading Milgram's "Behavioral study of obedience." *American Psychologist*, 1964, *19*, 421–423.

Lazarus, R. A laboratory approach to the dynamics of psychological stress. *American Psychologist*, 1964, *19*, 400–411.

Milgram, S. Behavioral study of obedience. *Journal of Abnormal and Social Psychology*, 1963, *67*, 371–378.

Milgram, S. Some conditions of obedience and disobedience to authority. *Human Relations*, in press.

29

Federal Regulations for the Protection of Human Research Subjects

U.S. Department of Health and Human Services

Federal regulations about the use of human subjects in research were first put into place in the 1970s. Today, these regulations have been adopted by virtually every university in the country engaging in research. We include these excerpts for several reasons. Most important, these regulations were generated because there had been some serious abuses of human subjects by researchers, and it was rightly felt that not all researchers could be fully trusted to treat subjects in an ethical manner. To be sure, most of the abuses occurred in medical, not social-psychological, research. But when government becomes involved in such matters, political as well as scientific considerations are important. The usual effect is a politically negotiated mixture of tight regulation with loose oversight. So, for example, you might note (in section 101) that a number of research areas are simply exempt from regulation. Those decisions were partly influenced by political considerations: where the strongest lobbying occurred. A major decision, which prevented major conflicts between government and scientists, was to allow each research organization or university to have its own review committee (IRB), so that decisions about individual projects are made by peers at the researcher's institution rather than in Washington or by political appointees (§107). This also meant that the most difficult and sensitive judgments, of minimal risk and risk-benefit assessments, were made locally and by peers (§ 111). Finally, other areas, particularly rules about informed consent (§§ 116, 117) were spelled out in exacting detail. Why do you think some areas were regulated so much more closely than others?

§46.101 To what do these regulations apply?

(a) Except as provided in paragraph (b) of this section, this subpart applies to all research involving human subjects conducted by the Department of Health and Human Services or funded in whole or in part by a Department grant, contract, cooperative agreement or fellowship.

(1) This includes research conducted by Department employees, except each Principal Operating Component head may adopt such nonsubstantive, procedural modifications as may be appropriate from an administrative standpoint.

(2) It also includes research conducted or funded by the Department of Health and Human Services outside the United States, but in appropriate circumstances, the Secretary may, under paragraph (e) of this section waive the applicability of some or all of the requirements of these regulations for research of this type.

(b) Research activities in which the only involvement of human subjects will be in one or more of the following categories are exempt from these regulations unless the research is covered by other subparts of this part:

Excerpted from the Code of Federal Regulations pertaining to the Protection of Human Subjects, issued by the U.S. Department of Health and Human Services, March 8, 1983.

(1) Research conducted in established or commonly accepted educational settings, involving normal educational practices, such as (i) research on regular and special education instructional strategies, or (ii) research on the effectiveness of or the comparison among instructional techniques, curricula, or classroom management methods.

(2) Research involving the use of educational tests (cognitive, diagnostic, aptitude, achievement), if information taken from these sources is recorded in such a manner that subjects cannot be identified, directly or through identifiers linked to the subjects.

(3) Research involving survey or interview procedures, except where all of the following conditions exist: (i) responses are recorded in such a manner that the human subject can be identified, directly or through identifiers linked to the subjects, (ii) the subject's responses, if they became known outside the research, could reasonably place the subject at risk of criminal or civil liability or be damaging to the subject's financial standing or employability, and (iii) the research deals with sensitive aspects of the subject's own behavior, such as illegal conduct, drug use, sexual behavior, or use of alcohol. All research involving survey or interview procedures is exempt, without exception, when the respondents are elected or appointed public officials or candidates for public office.

(4) Research involving the observation (including observation by participants) of public behavior, except where all of the following conditons exist: (i) observations are recorded in such a manner that the human subjects can be identified, directly or through identifiers linked to the subjects, (ii) the observations recorded about the individual, if they became known outside the research, could reasonably place the subject at risk of criminal or civil liability or be damaging to the subject's financial standing or employability, and (iii) the research deals with sensitive aspects of the subject's own behavior such as illegal conduct, drug use, sexual behavior, or use of alcohol.

(5) Research involving the collection or study of existing data, documents, records, pathological specimens, or diagnostic speci-

mens, if these sources are publicly available or if the information is recorded by the investigator in such a manner that subjects cannot be identified, directly or through identifiers linked to the subjects.

(6) Unless specifically required by statute (and except to the extent specified in paragraph (i)), research and demonstration projects which are conducted by or subject to the approval of the Department of Health and Human Services, and which are designed to study, evaluate, or otherwise examine: (i) programs under the Social Security Act, or other public benefit or service programs; (ii) procedures for obtaining benefits or services under those programs; (iii) possible changes in or alternatives to those programs or procedures; or (iv) possible changes in methods or levels of payment for benefits or services under those programs.

(c) The Secretary has final authority to determine whether a particular activity is covered by these regulations.

(d) The Secretary may require that specific research activities or classes of research activities conducted or funded by the Department, but not otherwise covered by these regulations, comply with some or all of these regulations.

(e) The Secretary may also waive applicability of these regulations to specific research activities or classes of research activities, otherwise covered by these regulations. Notices of these actions will be published in the *Federal Register* as they occur.

(f) No individual may receive Department funding for research covered by these regulations unless the individual is affiliated with or sponsored by an institution which assumes responsibility for the research under an assurance satisfying the requirements of this part, or the individual makes other arrangements with the Department.

(g) Compliance with these regulations will in no way render inapplicable pertinent federal, state, or local laws or regulations.

(h) Each subpart of these regulations contains a separate section describing to what the subpart applies. Research which is covered by more than one subpart shall comply with all applicable subparts.

(i) If, following review of proposed research

activities that are exempt from these regulations under paragraph (b)(6), the Secretary determines that a research or demonstration project presents a danger to the physical, mental, or emotional well-being of a participant or subject of the research or demonstration project, then federal funds may not be expended for such a project without the written, informed consent of each participant or subject.

§46.102 Definitions.

(a) "Secretary" means the Secretary of Health and Human Services and any other officer or employee of the Department of Health and Human Services to whom authority has been delegated.

(b) "Department" or "HHS" means the Department of Health and Human Services.

(c) "Institution" means any public or private entity or agency (including federal, state, and other agencies).

(d) "Legally authorized representative" means an individual or judicial or other body authorized under applicable law to consent on behalf of a prospective subject to the subject's participation in the procedure(s) involved in the research.

(e) "Research" means a systematic investigation designed to develop or contribute to generalizable knowledge. Activities which meet this definition constitute "research" for purposes of these regulations, whether or not they are supported or funded under a program which is considered research for other purposes. For example, some "demonstration" and "service" programs may include research activities.

(f) "Human subject" means a living individual about whom an investigator (whether professional or student) conducting research obtains (1) data through intervention or interaction with the individual, or (2) identifiable private information. "Intervention" includes both physical procedures by which data are gathered (for example, venipuncture) and manipulations of the subject or the subject's environment that are performed for research purposes. "Interaction" includes communication or interpersonal contact between investigator and subject. "Private information" includes information about behavior that occurs in a context in which an individual can reasonably expect that no observation or recording is taking place, and information which has been provided for specific purposes by an individual and which the individual can reasonably expect will not be made public (for example, a medical record). Private information must be individually identifiable (i.e., the identity of the subject is or may readily be ascertained by the investigator or associated with the information) in order for obtaining the information to constitute research involving human subjects.

(g) "Minimal risk" means that the risks of harm anticipated in the proposed research are not greater, considering probability and magnitude, than those ordinarily encountered in daily life or during the performance of routine physical or psychological examinations or tests.

(h) "Certification" means the official notification by the institution to the Department in accordance with the requirements of this part that a research project or activity involving human subjects has been reviewed and approved by the Institutional Review Board (IRB) in accordance with the approved assurance on file at HHS. (Certification is required when the research is funded by the Department and not otherwise exempt in accordance with §46.101(b).)

§46.107 IRB membership.

(a) Each IRB shall have at least five members, with varying backgrounds to promote complete and adequate review of research activities commonly conducted by the institution. The IRB shall be sufficiently qualified through the experience and expertise of its members, and the diversity of the members' backgrounds including consideration of the racial and cultural backgrounds of members and sensitivity to such issues as community attitudes, to promote respect for its advice and counsel in safeguarding the rights and welfare of human subjects. In addition to possessing the professional competence necessary to review specific research activities, the IRB shall be able to ascertain the acceptability of proposed research in terms of institutional commitments and regulations, applicable law, and standards of professional conduct and practice. The IRB shall therefore include persons knowledgeable in these areas. If an IRB regularly reviews research that involves a vulnerable category of subjects, including but not limited to subjects covered by other subparts of this part, the IRB shall include one or more individuals who are primarily concerned with the welfare of these subjects.

(b) No IRB may consist entirely of men or entirely of women, or entirely of members of one profession.

(c) Each IRB shall include at least one member whose primary concerns are in nonscientific areas; for example: lawyers, ethicists, members of the clergy.

(d) Each IRB shall include at least one member who is not otherwise affiliated with the institution and who is not part of the immediate family of a person who is affiliated with the institution.

(e) No IRB may have a member participating in the IRB's initial or continuing review of any project in which the member has a conflicting interest, except to provide information requested by the IRB.

(f) An IRB may, in its discretion, invite individuals with competence in special areas to assist in the review of complex issues which require expertise beyond or in addition to that available on the IRB. These individuals may not vote with the IRB.

§46.111 Criteria for IRB approval of research.

(a) In order to approve research covered by these regulations the IRB shall determine that all of the following requirements are satisfied:

(1) Risks to subjects are minimized: (i) By using procedures which are consistent with sound research design and which do not unnecessarily expose subjects to risk, and (ii) whenever appropriate, by using procedures already being performed on the subjects for diagnostic or treatment purposes.

(2) Risks to subjects are reasonable in relation to anticipated benefits, if any, to subjects, and the importance of the knowledge that may reasonably be expected to result. In evaluating

risks and benefits, the IRB should consider only those risks and benefits that may result from the research (as distinguished from risks and benefits of therapies subjects would receive even if not participating in the research). The IRB should not consider possible long-range effects of applying knowledge gained in the research (for example, the possible effects of the research on public policy) as among those research risks that fall within the purview of its responsibility.

(3) Selection of subjects is equitable. In making this assessment the IRB should take into account the purposes of the research and the setting in which the research will be conducted.

(4) Informed consent will be sought from each prospective subject or the subject's legally authorized representative, in accordance with, and to the extent required by §46.116.

(5) Informed consent will be appropriately documented, in accordance with, and to the extent required by §46.117.

(6) Where appropriate, the research plan makes adequate provision for monitoring the data collected to insure the safety of subjects.

(7) Where appropriate, there are adequate provisions to protect the privacy of subjects and to maintain the confidentiality of data.

(b) Where some or all of the subjects are likely to be vulnerable to coercion or undue influence, such as persons with acute or severe physical or mental illness, or persons who are economically or educationally disadvantaged, appropriate additional safeguards have been included in the study to protect the rights and welfare of these subjects.

§46.116 General requirements for informed consent.

Except as provided elsewhere in this or other subparts, no investigator may involve a human being as a subject in research covered by these regulations unless the investigator has obtained the legally effective informed consent of the subject or the subject's legally authorized representative. An investigator shall seek such consent only under circumstances that provide the prospective subject or the representative sufficient opportunity to consider whether or not to participate and that minimize the possibility of coercion or undue influence. The information that is given to the subject or the representative shall be in language understandable to the subject or the representative. No informed consent, whether oral or written, may include any exculpatory language through which the subject or the representative is made to waive or appear to waive any of the subject's legal rights, or releases or appears to release the investigator, the sponsor, the institution or its agents from liability for negligence.

(a) Basic elements of informed consent. Except as provided in paragraph (c) or (d) of this section, in seeking informed consent the following information shall be provided to each subject:

(1) A statement that the study involves research, an explanation of the purposes of the research and the expected duration of the subject's participation, a description of the procedures to be followed, and identification of any procedures which are experimental;

(2) A description of any reasonably foreseeable risks or discomforts to the subject;

(3) A description of any benefits to the subject or to others which may reasonably be expected from the research;

(4) A disclosure of appropriate alternative procedures or courses of treatment, if any, that might be advantageous to the subject;

(5) A statement describing the extent, if any, to which confidentiality of records identifying the subject will be maintained;

(6) For research involving more than minimal risk, an explanation as to whether any compensation and an explanation as to whether any medical treatments are available if injury occurs and, if so, what they consist of, or where further information may be obtained;

(7) An explanation of whom to contact for answers to pertinent questions about the research and research subjects' rights, and whom to contact in the event of a research-related injury to the subject; and

(8) A statement that participation is voluntary, refusal to participate will involve no penalty or loss of benefits to which the subject is otherwise entitled, and the subject may discontinue participation at any time without penalty

or loss of benefits to which the subject is otherwise entitled.

(b) Additional elements of informed consent. When appropriate, one or more of the following elements of information shall also be provided to each subject:

(1) A statement that the particular treatment or procedure may involve risks to the subject (or to the embryo or fetus, if the subject is or may become pregnant) which are currently unforeseeable;

(2) Anticipated circumstances under which the subject's participation may be terminated by the investigator without regard to the subject's consent;

(3) Any additional costs to the subject that may result from participation in the research;

(4) The consequences of a subject's decision to withdraw from the research and procedures for orderly termination of participation by the subject;

(5) A statement that significant new findings developed during the course of the research which may relate to the subject's willingness to continue participation will be provided to the subject; and

(6) The approximate number of subjects involved in the study.

(c) An IRB may approve a consent procedure which does not include, or which alters, some or all of the elements of informed consent set forth above, or waive the requirement to obtain informed consent provided the IRB finds and documents that:

(1) The research or demonstration project is to be conducted by or subject to the approval of state or local government officials and is designed to study, evaluate, or otherwise examine: (i) programs under the Social Security Act, or other public benefit or service programs; (ii) procedures for obtaining benefits or services under those programs; (iii) possible changes in or alternatives to those programs or procedures; or (iv) possible changes in methods or levels of payment for benefits or services under those programs; and

(2) The research could not practicably be carried out without the waiver or alteration.

(d) An IRB may approve a consent procedure which does not include, or which alters, some or all of the elements of informed consent set forth above, or waive the requirements to obtain informed consent provided the IRB finds and documents that:

(1) The research involves no more than minimal risk to the subjects;

(2) The waiver or alteration will not adversely affect the rights and welfare of the subjects;

(3) The research could not practicably be carried out without the waiver or alteration; and

(4) Whenever appropriate, the subjects will be provided with additional pertinent information after participation.

(e) The informed consent requirements in these regulations are not intended to preempt any applicable federal, state, or local laws which require additional information to be disclosed in order for informed consent to be legally effective.

(f) Nothing in these regulations is intended to limit the authority of a physician to provide emergency medical care, to the extent the physician is permitted to do so under applicable federal, state, or local law.

§46.117 Documentation of informed consent.

(a) Except as provided in paragraph (c) of this section, informed consent shall be documented by the use of a written consent form approved by the IRB and signed by the subject or the subject's legally authorized representative. A copy shall be given to the person signing the form.

(b) Except as provided in paragraph (c) of this section, the consent form may be either of the following:

(1) A written consent document that embodies the elements of informed consent required by §46.116. This form may be read to the subject or the subject's legally authorized representative, but in any event, the investigator shall give either the subject or the representative adequate opportunity to read it before it is signed; or

(2) A "short form" written consent document stating that the elements of informed consent required by §46.116 have been presented orally to the subject or the subject's legally authorized representative. When this method is used, there shall be a witness to the oral presentation. Also, the IRB shall approve a written summary of what is to be said to the subject or the representative. Only the short form itself is to be signed by the subject or the representative. However, the witness shall sign both the short form and a copy of the summary, and the person actually obtaining consent shall sign a copy of the summary. A copy of the summary shall be given to the subject or the representative, in addition to a copy of the "short form."

(c) An IRB may waive the requirement for the investigator to obtain a signed consent form for some or all subjects if it finds either:

(1) That the only record linking the subject and the research would be the consent document and the principal risk would be potential harm resulting from a breach of confidentiality. Each subject will be asked whether the subject wants documentation linking the subject with the research, and the subject's wishes will govern; or

(2) That the research presents no more than minimal risk of harm to subjects and involves no procedures for which written consent is normally required outside the research context.

In cases where the documentation requirement is waived, the IRB may require the investigator to provide subjects with a written statement regarding the research.

30

The Yin and Yang of Progress in Social Psychology: Seven Koan

WILLIAM J. McGUIRE

In 1972, William McGuire, a senior social psychologist at Yale University, was invited to give a lecture at an international meeting of psychologists in Tokyo, Japan. He used this opportunity to comment on an emerging "crisis" of confidence in social psychology. In the 1960s, most research by social psychologists had used as a model or paradigm the strategy of designing laboratory experiments to test hypotheses derived from general theories. In the 1970s, however, critics began to question the value of highly contrived laboratory studies that greatly oversimplified the complexity of social life and ignored the social problems of the day. In this paper, McGuire provides a detailed and thoughtful analysis of the limitations of lab experiments in social psychology. He then examines the trend toward field experiments, and argues that this approach fails to overcome the inadequacies of lab experiments. Ultimately, he suggests that social psychology needs to create a new paradigm or model for research. Although McGuire is uncertain of what this paradigm will be, he presents seven issues relevant to developing a new research perspective. McGuire offers these commentaries in the form of seven Japanese "koan," a Zen term for thought-provoking questions or ideas worthy of serious meditation. Some of McGuire's proposals have been put into practice in the most recent articles in this volume. In particular, advances in computers and statistics have enabled social psychologists to investigate more complex conceptual models that take into account interactions among many variables.

ABSTRACT. We describe the current dissatisfactions with the paradigm that has recently guided experimental social psychology—testing of theory-derived hypotheses by means of laboratory manipulational experiments. The emerging variant of doing field experiments does not meet the criticisms. It is argued that an adequate new paradigm will be a more radical departure involving, on the creative side, deriving hypotheses from a systems theory of social and cognitive structures that takes into account multiple and bidirectional causality among social variables. On the critical side, its hypotheses testing will be done in multivariate correlational designs with naturally fluctuating variables. Some steps toward this new paradigm are described in the form of seven koan.

THE PARADIGM RECENTLY GUIDING EXPERIMENTAL SOCIAL PSYCHOLOGY

In the late 1960s, social psychology appeared to be in a golden age. It was a prestigious and productive area in which droves of bright young people, a sufficiency of middle-aged colonels, and a few grand old men were pursuing their research with a confidence and energy that is found in those who know where they

Reprinted from the Journal of Social and Personality Psychology, 1973, 26, pp. 446–456. Copyright 1973 by the American Psychological Association. Reprinted by permission of publisher and author.

are going. Any moments of doubt we experienced involved anxiety as to whether we were doing our thing well, rather than uncertainty as to whether it needed to be done at all.

The image of these golden boys (and a few, but all too few, golden girls) of social psychology, glowing with confidence and chutzpah, blissfully unaware of the strident attacks which were soon to strike confusion into the field, brings to mind a beautiful Japanese haiku poem of Buson which I translate as follows

> On a temple bell
> Settled, asleep,
> A butterfly.

We social psychology researchers know all too well that the peaceful temple bell on which we were then displaying ourselves has now rudely rung. The vibrations which could be vaguely sensed a few years ago have gathered force. Now the temple bell has tolled and tolled again, rudely disturbing the stream of experimental social psychological research and shaking the confidence of many of us who work in the area.

The first half of this paper is devoted to describing the three successive waves of this current history. First, I shall describe the experimental social psychology paradigm that has recently guided our prolific research. Second, I shall discuss why this recent paradigm is being attacked and what, superficially at least, appears to be emerging in its place. Third, I shall say why I feel the seemingly emerging new paradigm is as inadequate as the one we would replace. Then, in the second half of this paper I shall offer, in the form of seven koan, my prescriptions for a new paradigm, more radically different from the recent one, but more in tune with the times and the march of history than is the variant that is supposedly emerging.

The Old Paradigm

What was the experimental social psychology paradigm which until recently had been unquestioningly accepted by the great majority of us but which now is being so vigorously attacked? Like any adequate paradigm it had two aspects, a creative and a critical component (McGuire, 1969, pp. 22–25). By the creative aspect, I mean the part of our scientific thinking that involves hypothesis generation, and by the critical aspect, I mean the hypothesis-testing part of our work.

The creative aspect of the recent paradigm inclined us to derive our hypotheses from current theoretical formulations. Typically, these theoretical formulations were borrowed from other areas of psychology (such as the study of psychopathology or of learning and memory), though without the level of refinement and quantification which those theories had reached in their fields or origin.

The critical, hypothesis-testing aspect of the recent paradigm called for manipulational experiments carried out in the laboratory. The experimental social psychologist attempted to simulate in the laboratory the gist of the situation to which he hoped to generalize, and he measured the dependent variable after deliberately manipulating the independent variable while trying to hold constant all other factors likely to affect the social behavior under study. In brief, the recent paradigm called for selecting our hypotheses for their relevance to broad theoretical formulations and testing them by laboratory manipulational experiments. McGuire (1965) presented an emphatic assertion of this recent paradigm in its heyday.

Assaults on the Old Paradigm

During the past several years both the creative and the critical aspects of this experimental social psychology paradigm have come under increasing attack. The creative aspect of formulating hypotheses for their relevance to theory has been denounced as out of phase with the needs of our time. It has been argued that hypotheses should be formulated for their relevance to social problems rather than for their relevance to theoretical issues. Such urgings come from people inside and outside social psychology, reflecting both the increasing social concern of researchers themselves and the demands of an articulate public for greater payoff from expensive scientific research. While many of us still insist with Lewin that

"There is nothing so practical as a good theory," the extent to which the pendulum has swung from the theoretically relevant toward the socially relevant pole is shown in the recent upsurge of publications on socially important topics of ad hoc interest, such as bystander intervention, the use of local space, the mass media and violence, the determinants of love, responses to victimization, nonverbal communication, etc.

At least as strong and successful an assault has been launched on the critical aspect of the recent paradigm, namely, the notion that hypotheses should be tested by manipulational laboratory experiments. It has been urged that laboratory experiments are full of artifacts (such as experimenter bias, demand character, evaluation apprehension, etc.) which make their results very hard to interpret. Ethical questions also have been raised against the laboratory social experiments on the grounds that they expose the participants to an unacceptable amount of deception, coercion, and stress.

In place of the laboratory manipulational experiment, there has been a definite trend toward experiments conducted in field settings and toward correlational analysis of data from naturalistic situations. A variety of recent methodological advances has made alternative hypothesis-testing procedures more attractive.

The attacks on the old paradigm of theory-derived hypotheses tested in laboratory manipulational experiments have certainly shaken confidence in that approach. At the same time, there is some suggestion of an emerging new paradigm which has as its creative aspect the derivation of new hypotheses for their ad hoc interest and social relevance. And in its critical aspect, this new paradigm involves testing these hypotheses by field experiments and, where necessary, by the correlational analysis of naturalistic data. McGuire (1967, 1969) described in more detail the worries about the recent paradigm and the nature of the purportedly emerging one. Higbee and Wells (1972) and Fried, Gumpper, and Allen (1973) suggested that reports by McGuire, by Sears and Abeles (1969), etc., of the demise of the recent paradigm may be exaggerated, but perhaps they

have underestimated the time that must intervene before a change of vogue by the leaders shows up in mass analysis of the methods used in published research.

MORE BASIC QUESTIONS REGARDING BOTH THE RECENT AND EMERGING PARADIGMS

My own position on the relative merits of the recent paradigm and this supposedly emerging new paradigm is a complex and developing one which I have detailed in print (McGuire, 1965, 1967, 1969) so the reader will be spared here a recital of my Byzantine opinions on this issue. Instead, I am raising the more fundamental issue of whether or not both the recent and the seemingly emerging paradigms which I have just described fail to come to grips with the deeper questions which lie behind our present unease. It seems to me that any truly new paradigm that ultimately arises from the present unrest is going to be more radically different from the recent one than is the supposedly emerging paradigm I have just depicted. It will represent a more fundamental departure on both the creative and the critical sides.

Inadequacies on the Creative Side

The switch from theory relevance to social relevance as the criterion in the creative, hypothesis-generating aspect of our work seems to me to constitute only a superficial cosmetic change that masks rather than corrects the basic problem. Socially relevant hypotheses, no less than theoretically relevant hypotheses, tend to be based on a simple linear process model, a sequential chain of cause and effect which is inadequate to simulate the true complexities of the individual's cognitive system or of the social system which we are typically trying to describe. Such simple a-affects-b hypotheses fail to catch the complexities of parallel processing, bidirectional causality, and reverberating feedback that characterize both cognitive and social organizations. The simple sequential model had its uses, but these have been largely exploited in past progress, and we must now deal with the complexities of systems in order to continue the progress on a new level.

The real inadequacy of the theory-derived hypotheses of the recent paradigm is not, as those now advocating socially relevant hypotheses insist, that it focused on the wrong variables (those that were theory rather than problem relevant). Rather, the basic shortcoming of the theory-relevant and the socially relevant hypotheses alike is that they fail to come to grips with the complexities with which the variables are organized in the individual and social systems.

Inadequacies of the Critical Aspect of the Recent Paradigm

The critical, hypothesis-testing aspect of the purportedly emerging paradigm also has the defect of being but a minor variant of the recent experimental social psychology paradigm rather than the fundamental departure which is called for. Let me first describe some of the deep epistemological uneasiness some of us have been expressing about the manipulational laboratory experiment that was the hypothesis-testing procedure of the recent paradigm. The crux of this objection is that we social psychologists have tended to use the manipulational laboratory experiment not to test our hypotheses but to demonstrate their obvious truth. We tend to start off with an hypothesis that is so clearly true (given the implicit and explicit assumptions) and which we have no intention of rejecting however the experiment comes out. Such a stance is quite appropriate, since the hypothesis by its meaningfulness and plausibility to reasonable people is tautologically true in the assumed context. As Blake said, "Everything possible to be believ'd is an image of truth."

The area of interpersonal attraction will serve to illustrate my point. The researcher might start off with a *really* obvious proposition, such as "The more someone perceives another person as having attitudes similar to his own, the more he tends to like that other person." Or a somewhat more flashy researcher, a little hungrier for novelty, might hypothesize the opposite. That is, he could look for certain circumstances in which the generally true, obvious hypothesis would obviously be reversed. He might hypothesize exceptional circumstances where attitudinal similarity would be anxiety arousing and a source of hostility; for example, if one loves one's wife, then one might actually dislike some other man to the extent that one perceives that other as also loving one's wife. Or another exceptional reversal might be that some people may think so poorly of themselves that they think less well of another person to the extent that the other person is like themselves. If the negative relationship is not found, we are likely to conclude that the person did not have a sufficiently low self-image, not that the hypothesis is wrong. Both the original obvious hypothesis and the obvious reversed hypothesis are reasonable and valid in the sense that if all our premises obtained, then our conclusion would pretty much have to follow.

Experiments on such hypotheses naturally turn out to be more like demonstrations than tests. If the experiment does not come out "right," then the researcher does not say that the hypothesis is wrong but rather that something was wrong with the experiment, and he corrects and revises it, perhaps by using more appropriate subjects, by strengthening the independent variable manipulation, by blocking off extraneous response possibilities, or by setting up a more appropriate context, etc. Sometimes he may have such continuous bad luck that he finally gives up the demonstration because the phenomenon proves to be so elusive as to be beyond his ability to demonstrate. The more persistent of us typically manage at last to get control of the experimental situation so that we can reliably demonstrate the hypothesized relationship. But note that what the experiment tests is not whether the hypothesis is true but rather whether the experimenter is a sufficiently ingenious stage manager to produce in the laboratory conditions which demonstrate that an obviously true hypothesis is correct. In our graduate programs in social psychology, we try to train people who are good enough stage managers so that they can create in the laboratory simulations of realities in which the obvious correctness of our hypothesis can be demonstrated.

It is this kind of epistemological worry about manipulational laboratory experiments that a half-dozen years back caused a number of observers (e.g., McGuire, 1967) to urge social psychology to search for interrelations among naturally varying factors in the world outside the laboratory. Out of these urgings has come the critical aspect of the apparently emerging paradigm which I have described above, calling for research in the field rather than in the laboratory.

Inadequacies of the Critical Aspects of the Purportedly Emerging New Field-Experiment Paradigm

Recently, I have come to recognize that this flight from the laboratory manipulational experiment to the field study, which I myself helped to instigate, is a tactical evasion which fails to meet the basic problem. We would grant that in the field we put the question to nature in a world we never made, where the context factors cannot be so confounded by our stage management proclivities as they were in the laboratory. But in this natural world research, the basic problem remains that we are not really testing our hypotheses. Rather, just as in the laboratory experiment we were testing our stage-managing abilities, in the field study we are testing our ability as "finders," if I may use a term from real estate and merchandising. When our field test of the hypothesis does not come out correctly, we are probably going to assume not that the hypothesis is wrong but that we unwisely chose an inappropriate natural setting in which to test it, and so we shall try again to test it in some other setting in which the conditions are more relevant to the hypothesis. Increasing our own and our graduate students' critical skill will involve making us not better hypothesis testers or better stage managers but rather better finders of situations in which our hypotheses can be demonstrated as tautologically true. Though I shall not pursue the point here, other objections to the laboratory experiment, including ethical and methodological considerations, that have been used (McGuire, 1969) to argue for more field research could similarly be turned against experiments conducted in the natural environment.

What I am arguing here is that changing from a theory-relevant to a socially relevant criterion for variable selection does not constitute a real answer to the basic problem with the creative aspect of our recent social psychology paradigm. And again, the switch from laboratory to field manipulation does not meet the basic objection to the critical aspect of the old paradigm. Neither the recent paradigm nor the supposedly emerging one really supplies the answer to our present needs. The discontent is a quite healthy one, and we should indeed be dissatisfied with the recent paradigm of testing theory-derived hypotheses by means of laboratory manipulational experiments. But our healthy discontent should carry us to a more fundamentally new outlook than is provided by this supposedly emerging variant paradigm of testing socially relevant hypotheses by experiments in natural settings.

SOURCES OF THE NEW SOCIAL PSYCHOLOGY

The Ultimate Shape of the New Paradigm

What I have written in the previous section suggests my general vision of what the more radically different new paradigm for social psychology will look like. On the creative side, it will involve theoretical models of the cognitive and social systems in their true multivariate complexity, involving a great deal of parallel processing, bidirectional relationships, and feedback circuits. Since such complex theoretical formulations will be far more in accord with actual individual and social reality than our present a-affects-b linear models, it follows that theory-derived hypotheses will be similar to hypotheses selected for their relevance to social issues. Correspondingly, the critical aspect of this new paradigm involves hypothesis testing by multivariate time series designs that recognize the obsolescence of our current simplistic a-affects-b sequential designs with their distinctions between dependent and independent variables.

But I feel somewhat uncomfortable here in trying to describe in detail what the next, radi-

cally different paradigm will look like. It will
be hammered out by theoretically and empirically skilled researchers in a hundred eyeball-
to-eyeball confrontations of thought with data,
all the while obscured by a thousand mediocre
and irrelevant studies which will constitute the
background noise in which the true signal will
be detected only gradually. Trying to predict
precisely what new paradigm will emerge is
almost as foolish as trying to control it.

But there is a subsidiary task with which I
feel more comfortable and to which I shall devote the rest of this paper. I have come to
feel that some specific tactical changes should
be made in our creative and critical work in
social psychology so as to enhance the momen-
tum and the ultimate sweep of this wave of
the future, whatever form it may take. I shall
here recommend a few of these needed innova-
tions and correctives, presenting them as koans
and commentaries thereon, to mask my own
uncertainties.

Koan 1: The Sound of One Hand Clapping . . . and the Wrong Hand

One drastic change that is called for in our
teaching of research methodology is that we
should emphasize the creative, hypothesis-
formation stage relative to the critical, hypothesis-testing stage of research. It is my guess that
at least 90% of the time in our current courses
on methodology is devoted to presenting ways
of testing hypotheses and that little time is
spent on the prior and more important process
of how one creates these hypotheses in the
first place. Both the creation and testing of
hypotheses are important parts of the scientific
method, but the creative phase is the more
important of the two. If our hypotheses are
trivial, it is hardly worth amassing a great methodological arsenal to test them; to paraphrase
Maslow, what is not worth doing, is not worth
doing well. Surely, we all recognize that the
creation of hypotheses is an essential part of
the scientific process. The neglect of the creative phase in our methodology courses probably comes neither from a failure to recognize
its importance nor a belief that it is trivially
simple. Rather, the neglect is probably due to
the suspicion that so complex a creative process

as hypothesis formation is something that cannot be taught.

I admit that creative hypothesis formation
cannot be reduced to teachable rules, and that
there are individual differences among us in
ultimate capacity for creative hypothesis generation. Still, it seems to me that we have to give
increased time in our own thinking and teaching about methodology to the hypothesis-
generating phase of research, even at the expense of reducing the time spent discussing
hypothesis testing. In my own methodology
courses, I make a point of stressing the importance of the hypothesis-generating phase of
our work by describing and illustrating at least
a dozen or so different approaches to hypothesis formation which have been used in psychological research, some of which I can briefly
describe here, including case study, paradoxical incident, analogy, hypothetico-deductive
method, functional analysis, rules of thumb,
conflicting results, accounting for exceptions,
and straightening out complex relationships.

For example, there is the intensive case
study, such as Piaget's of his children's cognitive
development or Freud's mulling over and over
of the Dora or the Wolf Man case or his own
dreams or memory difficulties. Often the case
is hardly an exceptional one—for example,
Dora strikes me as a rather mild and uninteresting case of hysteria—so that it almost seems
as if any case studied intensively might serve
as a Rorschach card to provoke interesting hypotheses. Perhaps an even surer method of
arriving at an interesting hypothesis is to try
to account for a paradoxical incident. For example, in a study of rumors circulating in
Bihar, India, after a devastating earthquake,
Prasad found that the rumors tended to predict
further catastrophes. It seemed paradoxical
that the victims of the disaster did not seek
some gratification in fantasy, when reality was
so harsh, by generating rumors that would be
gratifying rather than further disturbing. I believe that attempting to explain this paradox
played a more than trivial role in Festinger's
formulation of dissonance theory and Schachter's development of a cognitive theory of emotion.

A third creative method for generating hypothesis is the use of analogy, as in my own work on deriving hypotheses about techniques for inducing resistance to persuasion, where I formulated hypotheses by analogy with the biological process of inoculating the person in advance with a weakened form of the threatening material, an idea suggested in earlier work by Janis and Lumsdaine. A fourth creative procedure is the hypothetico-deductive method, where one puts together a number of commonsensical principles and derives from their conjunction some interesting predictions, as in the Hull and Hovland mathematico-deductive theory of rote learning, or the work by Simon and his colleagues on logical reasoning. The possibility of computer simulation has made this hypothesis-generating procedure increasingly possible and popular.

A fifth way of deriving hypotheses might be called the functional or adaptive approach, as when Hull generated the principles on which we would have to operate if we were to be able to learn from experience to repeat successful actions, and yet eventually be able to learn an alternative shorter path to a goal even though we have already mastered a longer path which does successfully lead us to that goal. A sixth approach involves analyzing the practitioner's rule of thumb. Here when one observes that practitioners or craftsmen generally follow some procedural rule of thumb, we assume that it probably works, and one tries to think of theoretical implications of its effectiveness. One does not have to be a Maoist to admit that the basic researcher can learn something by talking to a practitioner. For example, one's programmed simulation of chess playing is improved by accepting the good player's heuristic of keeping control of the center of the board. Or one's attitude change theorization can be helped by noting the politician's and advertiser's rule that when dealing with public opinion, it is better to ignore your opposition than to refute it. These examples also serve to remind us that the practitioner's rule of thumb is as suggestive by its failures as by its successes.

A seventh technique for provoking new hypotheses is trying to account for conflicting results. For example, in learning and attitude change situations, there are opposite laws of primacy and of recency, each of which sometimes seems valid; or in information integration, sometimes an additive or sometimes an averaging model seems more appropriate. The work by Anderson trying to reconcile these seeming conflicts shows how provocative a technique this can be in generating new theories. An eighth creative method is accounting for exceptions to general findings, as when Hovland tried to account for delayed action effect in opinion change. That is, while usually the persuasive effect of communications dissipates with time, Hovland found that occasionally the impact actually intensifies over time, which provoked him to formulate a variety of interesting hypotheses about delayed action effects. A ninth creative technique for hypothesis formation involves reducing observed complex relationships to simpler component relationships. For example, the somewhat untidy line that illustrates the functional relationship between visual acuity and light intensity can be reduced to a prettier set of rectilinear functions by hypothesizing separate rod and cone processes, a logarithmic transformation, a Blondel-Rey-type threshold phenomenon to account for deviations at very low intensities, etc.

But our purpose here is not to design a methodology course, so it would be inappropriate to prolong this list. Let me say once again, to summarize our first koan, that we have listened too long to the sound of one hand clapping, and the less interesting hand at that, in confining our methodology discussion almost exclusively to hypothesis testing. It is now time to clap more loudly using the other hand as well by stressing the importance of hypothesis generation as part of psychological methodology.

Koan 2: In This Nettle Chaos, We Discern This Pattern, Truth

I stress here the basic point that our cognitive systems and social systems are complex and that the currently conventional simple linear process models have outlived their heuristic usefulness as descriptions of these complex systems. In our actual cognitive and social systems, effects are the outcome of multiple causes which are often in complex interactions; moreover, it is the rule rather than the exception that the effects act back on the causal variables. Hence, students of cognitive and social processes must be encouraged to think big, or rather to think complexly, with conceptual models that involve parallel processing, nets of causally interrelated factors, feedback loops, bidirectional causation, etc.

If we and our students are to begin thinking in terms of these more complex models, then explicit encouragement is necessary since the published literature on social and cognitive processes is dominated by the simple linear models, and our students must be warned against imprinting on them. But our encouragement, while necessary, will not be sufficient to provoke our students into the more complex theorizing. We shall all shy away from the mental strain of keeping in mind so many variables, so completely interrelated. Moreover, such complex theories allow so many degrees of freedom as to threaten the dictum that in order to be scientifically interesting, a theory must be testable, that is, disprovable. These complex theories, with their free-floating parameters, seem to be adjustable to any outcome.

Hence, we have to give our students skill and confidence and be role models to encourage them to use complex formulations. To this end we have to give greater play to techniques like computer simulation, parameter estimation, multivariate time series designs, path analysis, etc. (as discussed further in Koan 5 below), in our graduate training programs.

Koan 3: Observe. But Observe People, Not Data

In our father's house there are many rooms. In the total structure of the intelligentsia, there is a place for the philosopher of mind and the social philosopher, as well as for the scientific psychologist. But the scientific psychologist can offer something beside and beyond these armchair thinkers in that we not only generate delusional systems, but we go further and test our delusional systems against objective data as well as for their subjective plausibility. Between the philosopher of mind and the scientific psychologist, there is the difference of putting the question to nature. Even when our theory seems plausible and so ingenious that it deserves to be true, we are conditioned to consider that we may be wrong.

But I feel that in our determination to maintain this difference we have gone too far. In our determination to confront reality and put our theory to the test of nature, we have plunged through reality, like Alice through the mirror, into a never-never land in which we contemplate not life but data. All too often the scientific psychologist is observing not mind or behavior but summed data and computer printout. He is thus a self-incarcerated prisoner in a platonic cave, where he has placed himself with his back to the outside world, watching its shadows on the walls. There may be a time to watch shadows but not to the exclusion of the real thing.

Perhaps Piaget should be held up as a role model here, as an inspiring example of how a creative mind can be guided in theorizing by direct confrontation with empirical reality. Piaget's close observation of how the developing human mind grapples with carefully devised problems was much more conducive to his interesting theorizing than would have been either the armchair philosopher's test of subjective plausibility or the scientific entrepreneur's massive project in which assistants bring him computer printout, inches thick.

The young student typically enters graduate study wanting to do just what we are proposing, that is, to engage in a direct confrontation with reality. All too often, it is our graduate programs which distract him with shadows. Either by falling into the hands of the humanists, he is diverted into subjectivism and twice-removed scholarly studies of what other subjectivists have said; or, if he falls under the influence of scientific psychologists, he becomes preoccupied with twice-removed sanitized data in the form of computer printout. I am urging that we restructure our graduate programs somewhat to keep the novice's eye on the real rather than distracting and obscuring his view behind a wall of data.

Koan 4: To See the Future in the Present, Find the Present in the Past

One idea whose time has come in social psychology is the accumulation of social data archives. Leaders of both the social science and the political establishments have recognized that we need a quality-of-life index (based perhaps on trace data, social records, self-reports obtained through survey research, etc.). Such social archives will also include data on factors which might affect subjective happiness, and analyses will be done to tease out the complex interrelations among these important variables. The need for such archives is adequately recognized; the interest and advocacy may even have outrun the talent, energy, and funds needed to assemble them.

In this growing interest in social data archives, one essential feature has been neglected, namely, the importance of obtaining time series data on the variables. While it will be useful to have contemporaneous data on a wide variety of social, economic, and psychological variables, the full exploitation of these data becomes possible only when we have recorded them at several sucessive points in time. Likewise, while a nationwide survey of subjective feelings and attitudes is quite useful for its demographic breakdowns at one point in time, the value of such a social survey becomes magnified many times when we have it repeated at successive points in history. It is only when we have the time series provided by a reconstructed or preplanned longitudinal study that we can apply the powerful methodology of time series analyses which allow us to reduce the complexity of the data and identify causality.

Hence, my fourth koan emphasizes the usefulness of collecting and using social data archives but adds that we should collect data on these variables not only at a single contemporaneous point in time, but also that we should set up a time series by reconstructing measures of the variables from the recent and distant past and prospectively by repeated surveys into the future.

Koan 5: The New Methodology Where Correlation Can Indicate Causation

If we agree that the simple linear sequence model has outlived its usefulness for guiding our theorizing about cognitive and social systems, then we must also grant that the laboratory manipulational experiment should not be the standard method for testing psychological hypotheses. But most graduate programs and most of the published studies (Higbee & Wells, 1972) focus disproportionately on descriptive and inferential statistics appropriate mainly to the linear models from the recent paradigm. The methods taught and used are characterized by obsolescent procedures, such as rigorous distinction between dependent and independent variables, two-variable or few-variable designs, an assumption of continuous variables, the setting of equal numbers and equal intervals, etc.

It seems to me that we should revise the methodology curriculum of our graduate programs and our research practice so as to make us better able to cope with the dirty data of the real world, where the intervals cannot be preset equally, where the subjects cannot be assigned randomly and in the same number, and where continuous measures and normal distributions typically cannot be obtained. In previous writings in recent years, I have called attention to advances in these directions which I mention here (McGuire, 1967, 1969), and Campbell (1969) has been in the forefront in devising, assembling, and using such procedures.

Our graduate programs should call the student's attention to new sources of social data, such as archives conveniently storing information from public opinion surveys, and to nonreactive measures of the unobtrusive trace type discussed by Webb and his colleagues.

Our students should also be acquainted with the newer analytic methods that make more possible the reduction of the complex natural field to a manageable number of underlying variables whose interrelations can be determined. To this end, we and our students must have the opportunity to master new techniques for scaling qualitative data, new methods of multivariate analysis, such as those devised by Shepard and others, and the use of time series causal analyses like the cross-lag panel design. More training is also needed in computer simulation and techniques of parameter estimation.

Mastery of these techniques will not be easy. Because we older researchers have already mastered difficult techniques which have served us well, we naturally look upon this retooling task with something less than enthusiasm. We have worked hard and endured much; how much more can be asked of us? But however we answer that question regarding our obligation to master these techniques ourselves, we owe it to our students to make the newer techniques available to those who wish it, rather than requiring all students to preoccupy themselves with the old techniques which have served us so well in reaching the point from which our students must now proceed.

Koan 6: The Riches of Poverty

The industrial countries, where the great bulk of psychological research is conducted, have in the past couple of years suffered economic growing pains which, if they have not quite reduced the amount of funds available for scientific research, at least have reduced the rate at which these funds have been growing. In the United States, at least, the last couple of years have been ones of worry about leveling scientific budgets. It is my feeling that the worry exceeds the actuality. In the United States' situation, psychology has in fact suffered very little as compared with our sister sciences. As an irrepressible optimist I am of the opinion that not only will this privileged position of psychology continue but also that the budgetary retrenchment in the other fields of science is only a temporary one and that, in the long run, the social investment in scientific research will resume a healthy, if not exuberant, rate of growth. I recognize that this optimism on my part will do little to cheer scientists whose own research programs have been hard hit by the financial cuts. To my prediction that in the long run social investment in science will grow again after this temporary recession, they

might point out (like Keynes) that in the long run we shall all be dead.

I persist in my Dr. Pangloss optimism that things are going to turn out well and even engage in gallows humor by saying that what psychological research has needed is a good depression. I do feel that during the recent period of affluence when we in the United States could obtain government funds for psychological research simply by asking, we did develop some fat, some bad habits, and some distorted priorities which should now be corrected. While we could have made these corrections without enforced poverty, at least we can make a virtue of necessity by using this time of budgetary retrenchment to cut out some of the waste and distraction so that we shall emerge from this period of retrenchment stronger than we entered it.

The days of easy research money sometimes induced frenzies of expensive and exhausting activity. We hired many people to help us, often having to dip into less creative populations, and to keep them employed the easiest thing to do was to have them continue doing pretty much what we had already done, resulting in a stereotyping of research and a repetitious output. It tended to result in the collection of more data of the same type and subjecting it to the same kinds of analyses as in the past. It also motivated us to churn out one little study after another, to the neglect of the more solitary and reflective intellectual activity of integrating all the isolated findings into more meaningful big pictures.

Affluence has also produced the complex research project which has removed us from reality into the realm of data as I discussed in Koan 3. The affluent senior researcher often carried out his work through graduate assistants and research associates, who, in turn, often have the actual obsevations done by parapsychological technicians or hourly help, and the data they collect go to cardpunchers who feed them into computers, whose output goes back to the research associate, who might call the more meaningful outcome to the attention of the senior researcher, who is too busy meeting the payrolls to control the form of the printout or look diligently through it when it arrives. A cutback in research funds might in some cases divert these assistants into more productive and satisfying work while freeing the creative senior researcher from wasting his efforts on meeting the payroll rather than observing the phenomena.

I am urging here, then, that if the budgetary cutbacks continue instead of running ever faster on the Big-Science treadmill, we make the best of the bad bargain by changing our research organization, our mode of working, and our priorities. I would suggest that rather than fighting for a bigger slice of the diminishing financial pie, we redirect our efforts somewhat. We should rediscover the gratification of personally observing the phenomena ourselves and experiencing the relief of not having to administer our research empire. Also, I think we should spend a greater portion of our time trying to interpret and integrate the empirical relationships that have been turned up by the recent deluge of studies, rather than simply adding new, undigested relationships to the existing pile.

Koan 7: The Opposite of a Great Truth Is Also True

What I have been prescribing above is not a simple, coherent list. A number of my urgings would pull the field in opposite directions. For example, Koan 1 urges that our methodology courses place more emphasis on the creative hypothesis-forming aspect of research even at the cost of less attention to the critical, hypothesis-testing aspect, but then in Koan 5, I urged that we, or at least our students, master a whole new pattern of hypothesis-testing procedures. Again, Koan 3 urges that we observe concrete phenomena rather than abstract data, but Koan 4 favors assembling social data archives that would reduce concrete historical events to abstract numbers. My prescriptions admittedly ride off in opposite directions, but let us remember that "consistency is the hobgoblin of little minds."

That my attempt to discuss ways in which our current psychological research enterprise

could be improved has led me in opposite directions does not terribly disconcert me. I remember that Bohr has written, "There are trivial truths and great truths. The opposite of a trivial truth is plainly false. The opposite of a great truth is also true." The same paradox has appealed to thinkers of East and West alike since Sikh sacred writings advise that if any two passages in that scripture contradict one another, then both are true. The urging at the same time of seemingly opposed courses is not necessarily false. It should be recognized that I have been giving mini-directives which are only a few parts of the total system which our psychological research and research training should involve. Indeed, I have specified only a few components of such a total research program. Any adequate synthesis of a total program must be expected to contain theses and antitheses.

I have asserted that social psychology is currently passing through a period of more than usual uneasiness, an uneasiness which is felt even more by researchers inside the field than by outside observers. I have tried to analyze and describe the sources of this uneasiness as it is felt at various levels of depth. I have also described a few of the undercurrents which I believe will, or at any rate should, be part of the wave of the future which will eventuate in a new paradigm which will lead us to further successes, after it replaces the recent paradigm which has served us well but shows signs of obsolescence.

A time of troubles like the present one is a worrisome period in which to work, but it is also an exciting period. It is a time of contention when everything is questioned, when it sometimes seems that "the best lack all conviction, while the worst are full of passionate intensity." It may seem that this is the day of the assassin, but remember that "it is he devours death, mocks mutability, has heart to make an end, keeps nature new." These are the times when the "rough beast, its hour come round at last, slouches toward Bethlehem to be born." Ours is a dangerous period, when the stakes have been raised, when nothing seems certain but everything seems possible.

I began this talk by describing the proud

and placid social psychology of a half-dozen years back, just before the bell tolled, as suggesting Buson's beautiful sleeping butterfly. I close by drawing upon his disciple, the angry young man Shiki, for a related but dynamically different image of the new social psychology which is struggling to be born. Shiki wrote a variant on Buson's haiku as follows:

On a temple bell,
Waiting, glittering,
A firefly.

REFERENCES

Campbell, D. T. Reforms as experiments. *American Psychologist*, 1969, *24*, 409–429.

Fried, S. B., Gumpper, D. C., & Allen, J. C. Ten years of social psychology: Is there a growing commitment to field research? *American Psychologist*, 1973, *28*, 155–156.

Higbee, K. L., & Wells, M. G. Some research trends in social psychology during the 1960s. *American Psychologist*, 1972, *27*, 963–966.

McGuire, W. J. Learning theory and social psychology. In O. Klineberg & R. Christie (Eds.), *Perspectives in social psychology*. New York: Holt, Rinehart & Winston, 1965.

McGuire, W. J. Some impending reorientations in social psychology. *Journal of Experimental Social Psychology*, 1967, *3*, 124–139.

McGuire, W. J. Theory-oriented research in natural settings: The best of both worlds for social psychology, In M. Sherif & C. Sherif (Eds.), *Interdisciplinary relationships in the social sciences*. Chicago: Aldine, 1969.

Sears, D. O., & Abeles, R. P. Attitudes and opinions. *Annual Review of Psychology*, 1969, *20*, 253–288.

31

College Sophomores in the Laboratory: Influences of a Narrow Data Base on Psychology's View of Human Nature

This paper begins by presenting archival data on the typical research practices of social psychologists; they mostly use college student subjects in laboratory experiments. Prior critiques have observed that college students are not representative of the general population and that the laboratory is an artificial place, but have not specified the consequences of these distinctive features of social psychological research. This paper takes the critique one step further, and suggests some specific ways in which social psychology's description of human nature might be biased because of our particular database. The paper concludes that college students in the laboratory are appropriate for some purposes and not for others, and argues for methodological pluralism. You might especially note the descriptions given of students and of the laboratory; how plausible do these descriptions seem to you? Note also the account of how such characteristics might have influenced the research conclusions of social psychologists. Is a persuasive case made that these research characteristics bias the view of human nature that emerges from social psychological research? When would college students in the laboratory be a reliable data base? What criteria would you use in making that decision?

ABSTRACT. For the 2 decades prior to 1960, published research in social psychology was based on a wide variety of subjects and research sites. Content analyses show that since then such research has overwhelmingly been based on college students tested in academic laboratories on academiclike tasks. How might this heavy dependence on one narrow data base have biased the main substantive conclusions of sociopsychological research in this era? Research on the full life span suggests that, compared with older adults, college students are likely to have less-crystallized attitudes, less-formulated senses of self, stronger cognitive skills, stronger tendencies to comply with authority, and more unstable peer group relationships. The laboratory setting is likely to exaggerate all these differences. These peculiarities of social psychology's predominant data base may have contributed to central elements of its portrait of human nature. According to this view people (a) are quite compliant and their behavior is easily socially influenced, (b) readily change their attitudes and (c) behave inconsistently with them, and (d) do not rest their self-perceptions on introspection. The narrow data base may also contribute to this portrait of human nature's (e) strong emphasis on cognitive processes and to its lack of emphasis on (f) personality dispositions, (g) material self-interest, (h) emotionally based irrationalities, (i) group norms, and (j) stage-specific phenomena. The analysis implies the need both for more careful examination of sociopsychological propositions for systematic biases introduced by dependence on this narrow data base and for increased reliance on adults tested in their natural habitats with materials drawn from ordinary life.

Reprinted from the *Journal of Personality and Social Psychology*, 1986, *51*, pp. 515–530. Copyright 1986 by the American Psychological Association. Reprinted by permission of publisher and author.

Every science has its own methodological idiosyncracies. Pharmacological research relies heavily on the white rat, research on new birth control techniques is most commonly conducted on non-American women, astronomers use telescopes, and psychoanalysts depend on the self-reports of affluent self-confessed neurotics. Ordinarily, such researchers trust that they have a reasonably good grasp of the biases introduced by their own particular methodological proclivities and that they can correct their conclusions for whatever biases are present. But conclusions can be so corrected only if the direction and magnitude of bias can be estimated on the basis of reliable empirical evidence. Such systematic evidence may not always exist, or it may be hard to find, or it may not even be sought. The danger then is that biases resulting from overreliance on a particular data base may be ignored, and the conclusions of the science may themselves be flawed.

This article suggests that social psychology has risked such biases because of its heavy dependence during the past 25 years on a very narrow data base: college student subjects tested in the academic laboratory with academiclike materials. My concern is that overdependence on this one narrow data base may have unwittingly led us to a portrait of human nature that describes rather accurately the behavior of American college students in an academic context but distorts human social behavior more generally.

This article begins by documenting the growth of social psychology's heavy reliance on this narrow data base. It then proceeds to describe the biases this reliance may have introduced into the central substantive conclusions of the field. These biases could in theory be assessed in two ways. One way is through systematic replication of empirical findings using other populations and situations. In practice, however, these data do not now exist, so this is not a practical approach. The second way involves estimating these biases both from the known differences between our data base and the general population in everyday life, and from the known effects of those differences. That will be my approach, using as examples research on several of the most important top-

ics in the subfields of attitudes and social cognition. This part of the argument is frankly speculative. As a result it should not stimulate wholesale abandonment of our familiar, captive, and largely friendly data base. I would hope, however, that it might generate some serious thought about how this narrow data base has affected our major substantive conclusions. I doubt that they are flat out wrong. But taken together as a cumulative body of knowledge presented by the field of social psychology, they may give quite a distorted portrait of human nature.

A NARROW METHODOLOGICAL BASE

The first great burst of empirical research in social psychology, which occurred in the years surrounding World War II, used a wide variety of subject populations and research sites. Cantril (1940) and Lazarsfeld, Berelson, and Gaudet (1948), for example, investigated radio listeners and voters. Hovland, Lumsdaine, and Sheffield (1949), Merton and Kitt (1950), Shils and Janowitz (1948), and Stouffer, Suchman, De Vinney, Star, and Williams (1949) studied soldiers in training and combat, whereas Lewin (1947) and Cartwright (1949) looked at the civilian end of the war effort, and Bettelheim and Janowitz (1950) at returning veterans. Deutsch and Collins (1951) and Festinger, Schachter, and Back (1950) investigated residents of housing projects, and Coch and French (1948) studied industrial workers in factories. Adorno, Frenkel-Brunswik, Levinson, and Sanford (1950) investigated authoritarianism in a wide range of subjects that included merchant marine officers, veterans, as well as members of unions, the PTA, and the League of Women Voters. Even Leon Festinger, in some ways the godfather of laboratory-based experimental social psychology, based his best-known book, *A Theory of Cognitive Dissonance* (1957), on data bases ranging from the analysis of rumors in India and the participant-observation of a millenial group to carefully crafted laboratory experiments on college students. The conventional methodological wisdom of the era was that the researcher must travel back and forth between field and laboratory (and their differing indigenous populations) in order to bracket properly any sociopsychological phenomenon.

The subsequent generation of social psychologists created the experimental revolution. They were much more thoroughly committed to the laboratory experiment and, inevitably, as thoroughly committed to the use of undergraduate college students (the well-known "college sophomore") as research subjects. By the 1960s, this conjunction of college student subject, laboratory site, and experimental method, usually mixed with some deception, had become the dominant methodology in social psychology, as documented in several systematic content analyses of journal articles (Christie, 1965; Fried, Gumpper, & Allen, 1973; Higbee & Wells, 1972).

Like all revolutions, this one immediately came under attack. There was concern about such internal biases as demand characteristics, experimenter bias, and evaluation apprehension. Others demanded more "relevant" and applied research that would more directly address "real world" problems. Both critiques encouraged broader methodological practice. But the 1970s also witnessed the rapid development of research modeled on work in cognitive psychology that used brief, emotionally neutral laboratory experiments on college students. Paper-and-pencil role-playing studies became especially common.

The net effects of these conflicting developments are best assessed with a systematic inventory of actual methodological practice. Hence we coded, for subject population and research site, articles published during 1980 in the three mainstream outlets for sociopsychological research, *Journal of Personality and Social Psychology* (*JPSP*), *Personality and Social Psychology Bulletin* (*PSPB*), and the *Journal of Experimental Social Psychology* (*JESP*). Subject populations were coded into four categories: (a) recruited directly from a North American undergraduate psychology class; (b) other North American undergraduates; (c) other students (mainly primary and secondary school students or college students in other westernized societies); or (d) adults. The site of the research was coded as

either (a) laboratory or (b) natural habitat. The latter was interpreted quite liberally to include either a physical site in the individual's ordinary life (such as college gymnasiums and dormitories, beaches, military barracks, a voter's living room, or airport waiting rooms) or even self-report questionnaires concerning the individual's daily life and activities (e.g., personality, political and social attitudes, or ongoing interpersonal relationships) no matter where they were administered.[1]

American college undergraduates were overwhelmingly the subject population of choice. In 1980, 75% of the articles in these journals relied solely on undergraduate subjects, almost all from the United States. Most (53%) stated that they used students recruited directly from undergraduate psychology classes, but this is probably an underestimate because many studies relying on undergraduates do not further specify their origin. All totaled, 82% used students of one kind or another. By far the majority (71%) were based on laboratory research. Considering these two dimensions jointly, 85% of the articles used undergraduates and/or a laboratory site; only 15% used adults in their natural habitats or dealt with content concerned with adults' normal lives. All of this is displayed in Table 1.

To provide more current data, all of the issues of these journals were again coded in 1985 (except for the personality section of *JPSP*, because of some dispute over its editorial policies). Table 2 shows that use of undergraduates in the laboratory had diminished only marginally; 83% of the articles coded used students, 74% American undergraduates, 78% the laboratory, and 67% undergraduates in the lab; the latter overwhelmingly remained the data

---

[1] Articles relying on more than one study were given a summary rating on the basis of the majority of their studies. In general, ambiguous decisions were biased in the direction of underestimating the use of college students in the laboratory. A reliability check was made by having a second coder (the author) code three issues of *JPSP*. Both coders agreed on subject population and research site in 97% and 88% of the cases, respectively, with no particular pattern to the disagreements. Since reliability was acceptably high, the first coder's judgments were used in all cases.

Table 1 Subject Population and Research Site in Social Psychologists' 1980 Journal Articles

Code Category	JPSP							JPSP Authors' Other Articles		
	% Atts. & Soc. Cog.	% Interp. Rels. & Grp. Proc.	% Pers. Proc. & Indiv. Diffs.	Total %	% PSPB	% JESP	Total %	% in JPSP, PSPB, or JESP	% In Other Journals	Total %
Subject population										
American undergraduates	85	78	51	70	81	81	75	84	66	72
Psychology classes	56	56	39	52	53	57	53	50	43	46
Other	29	22	12	18	28	24	21	34	23	26
Other students	8	3	19	12	0	8	7	8	12	11
Adults	8	19	30	18	19	11	18	8	22	17
Research site										
Laboratory	88	69	44	64	75	95	71	97	78	85
Natural habitat	12	31	56	36	25	5	29	3	22	15
Combined										
Undergraduates/lab	83	64	32	58	73	78	64	84	59	68
Adults/natural habitat	8	14	28	17	16	3	15	3	11	9
Number of articles										
Total	53	36	59	198	93	42	333	75	162	237
Empirical and codeable	52	36	57	191	73	37	301	62	116	178

Note. JPSP = *Journal of Personality and Social Psychology.* The three sections of *JPSP* are Attitudes and Social Cognition, Interpersonal Relations and Group Processes, and Personality and Individual Differences. *PSPB* = *Personality and Social Psychology Bulletin.* *JESP* = *Journal of Experimental Social Psychology.* The base for all percentages includes only articles shown in the last row (empirical, codeable, and available in the library). Columns 4 and 5–7 include all such 1980 journal articles; columns 1–3 include all such journal articles for April through December 1980, the first 9 months of the tripartite division of the journal; and columns 8–10 are based on all such articles obtained from entries given in the 1980 *Psychological Abstracts.* Some articles could not be located (8%), others could not be coded (3%), and still others were nonempirical articles (15%). The percentages presented exclude all these from the base.

Table 2 Subject Population and Research Site in Social Psychologists' 1985 Journal Articles

	JPSP				
	% Atts. & Soc. Cog.	% Interp. Rels. & Grp. Proc.	% PSPB	% JESP	Total %
Subject population					
American undergraduates	81	58	79	82	74
Psychology classes	55	40	61	53	51
Other	26	19	18	29	23
Other students	8	9	6	12	8
Adults	11	32	16	6	17
Research site					
Laboratory	75	66	84	91	78
Natural habitat	25	34	16	9	22
Combined					
Undergraduates/lab	70	55	71	76	67
Adults/natural habitat	8	26	11	3	13
Number of articles					
Total	58	54	40	35	187
Empirical and codeable	53	33	38	34	178

Note. JPSP = Journal of Personality and Social Psychology. The two sections of *JPSP* are Attitudes and Social Cognition and Interpersonal Relations and Group Processes. *PSPB = Personality and Social Psychology Bulletin. JESP = Journal of Experimental and Social Psychology.* The base for all percentages includes only articles shown in the last row.

base of choice. The one substantial change occurred in the Interpersonal Relations section of *JPSP*, which showed an increase in studies of adults in their natural habitats, from 14% to 26%. But even there, the majority (55%) still used undergraduates in the laboratory.[2]

The later discussion of the implications of this pattern will emphasize the areas of attitudes and social cognition, because they are the areas with which I am most familiar. Table 1 shows that articles in the Attitudes and Social Cognition section of *JPSP* relied as much if not more on college students in the lab than did the others. Similarly, Findley and Cooper (1981) reported that the attitude change chapters of social psychology texts were about at the median in use of college students. So research on attitudes and social cognition is as likely as any other area of social psychology to be vulnerable to whatever problems these methodological practices introduce.

A Flight From Mainstream Journals?

This reliance on laboratory studies of college students might, however, only describe these mainstream journals and not social psychologists' general research practice. Perhaps the editorial policies of these particular journals are dominated by a conformist in-group wedded to this "traditional" mode of research. Or, these journals are known to be the most selective, and so they might tend to reject the somewhat "softer" research that is done in real-world settings on less captive (and less compliant) subject populations. Or perhaps researchers wishing to communicate with colleagues who also conduct nonmainstream research might reach them more directly through more specialized journals; for example, it may be easier to reach public opinion researchers through

---

[2] If the study, rather than the article, is used as the unit of analysis, the codeable *N* for Table 2 rises from 178 to 268, and the results only become stronger: 84% (rather than 83%) used students; 76% (rather than 74%) American undergraduates, 80% (rather than 78%) the lab, and 69% (rather than 67%) both; only 10% (rather than 13%) used adults in their natural habitats.

Public Opinion Quarterly than through *JPSP*. It is possible therefore that social psychologists' research published elsewhere actually uses a broader range of methodologies than is apparent from inspecting these three journals.

To check this, we canvassed articles written by social psychologists that had been published in other journals. We drew a representative sample of social psychologists who had published in *JPSP*, consisting of the one individual listed in each 1980 *JPSP* article as the person to be contacted for reprints (on the grounds that he or she would be the one most likely to have a research career). We then coded the methodological characteristics of all the articles these social psychologists had published elsewhere in a comparable time frame—specifically, all articles listed for each such 1980 *JPSP* "reprint author" in the 1980 *Psychological Abstracts*.

At first glance, these other articles seem to display social psychologists at work in quite a different manner, because *JPSP* authors also publish in a spectacular variety of other journals. In the 1980 *Psychological Abstracts*, they generated no fewer than 237 other entries that appeared in no fewer than 128 different journals. These ranged from such fraternal outlets as the *European Journal of Social Psychology* to distant relatives, arguably even of the same species, such as *Behavior and Neural Biology* or the *Journal of Altered States of Consciousness*. This variety alone might suggest that, once away from the staid scrutiny or narrow conformity pressures of their peers, social psychologists may be using strange and wonderfully different kinds of data bases.

In fact, however, even in their research published in these more distant outlets, social psychologists mainly used college student subjects in laboratory settings. The last column of Table 1 shows that 72% of these other articles used North American undergraduates as subjects, a figure slightly higher than the 70% that held in the original sample of the same authors' articles in *JPSP* (column 4). Use of both college student subjects and the laboratory setting was more common in these social psychologists' other articles (68%) than in their original *JPSP*

articles (58%). Viewed from the opposite perspective, only 9% of their other articles used adults in their natural habitat, whereas 17% of their *JPSP* articles had.

This continuity of methodological practice could simply reflect the fact that many of these other articles themselves had appeared in mainstream outlets. Indeed half of these other articles had appeared in the basic social-personality journals (mostly in *JPSP*, *JESP*, and *PSPB*, with the rest scattered through 11 other journals of similar focus). Another 21% appeared in basic psychological journals outside of the social-personality area (in experimental psychology, psychobiology, and developmental). Only 11% appeared in applied social psychology journals (on health, the environment, public opinion, women's issues, and politics), and 17% in other applied psychology journals (including educational and clinical psychology). But the other articles published outside of the basic social psychology journals also relied primarily on undergraduate subjects in the laboratory (78%); only 11% investigated adults in their natural habitat (Table 1, column 9).

In short, wherever they publish, social psychologists seem to publish laboratory research on college students. A dispositional, rather than a situational, attribution seems most appropriate for social psychologists' methodological proclivities.[3]

Historical Trends

Content analyses show that articles published in mainstream social psychology journals during the immediate postwar years relied heavily on adults. But the proportion of articles published in the *Journal of Abnormal and Social Psychology* that relied on college student subjects more than doubled from 1949 to 1959 (Christie, 1965). And it has held steady ever since. American college students have been the

---

[3] These data do not rule out the possibility that a wholly different set of social psychologists publishes research using more representative subject populations and more realistic settings outside of the mainstream journals. Hence these data should be understood as describing the behavior of social psychologists who publish at least some of the time in the mainstream journals.

primary subject population for at least 70% of the articles in *JPSP* in every sounding done since the early 1960s, without much variation: 73% in 1962–1964, 70% in 1966–1967, 76% in 1969, 77% in 1970–1972, 72% in 1979, 70% in 1980, and 70% in 1985 (see Higbee, Lott, & Graves, 1976; Higbee, Millard, & Folkman, 1982; Higbee & Wells, 1972; Schultz, 1969; Smart, 1966; and Tables 1 and 2). In *JESP*, 80% of the articles in 1969, 81% in 1980, and 82% in 1985 relied on American college students (see Higbee et al., 1976; and Tables 1 and 2).

Also, there has not been any drop in the use of the other aspects of this now traditional methodology in social psychology. About three fourths of the articles in *JPSP* were using the laboratory by the late 1960s (Fried et al., 1973). As Tables 1 and 2 show, this remains true today: Of mainstream journal articles in 1980, 71% used the lab; also, 85% of *JPSP* authors' other articles and even 78% of their articles published in nonmainstream journals were laboratory-based. In 1985, 78% of the articles coded were laboratory-based. Potter (1981) reported the same constancy in laboratory use in British journal articles.

Prestigious Research

These data only describe the subjects used in representative samples of social psychological research articles, not those used in the research generally regarded as most central to our accumulated knowledge. It could be that much of the research that really has a lasting impact is more likely to have been conducted on adults and/or in more realistic settings.

One index of prestigious research is that cited in social psychology textbooks. Findley and Cooper (1981) coded the articles cited in nine widely used textbooks in social psychology for reliance on college students; the median, across content areas, was 73%, very close to the field as a whole at the time (75% of the 1980 articles in mainstream journals and 72% of the other articles used college students, as shown in Table 1).

A second index of prestige is appearance in books of readings. In social psychology, the reader market was dominated from World War II through the early 1960s by the Society for the Psychological Study of Social Issues (SPSSI) series, originally titled *Readings in Social Psychology*. Subsequently the market, such as it was, was dispersed among other books. The articles reprinted in the pre-1960 readers used adult subjects considerably more often than they did college students, as shown in Table 3. After 1960, however, college student subjects took over, both in readers with a social problems focus (e.g., Brigham & Wrightsman, 1982) and those focusing more on basic research (Aronson, 1981; Freedman et al., 1971).

This transition around 1960 to college student subjects is aptly illustrated within the SPSSI reader series itself. In 1965, in lieu of a fourth edition of a general reader, two volumes were issued. *Basic Studies in Social Psychology* was intended to emphasize the "classics" (Proshansky & Seidenberg, 1965) and consisted almost exclusively of articles published prior to 1958 (the median year was actually 1952). *Current Studies in Social Psychology* was intended to represent current research (Steiner & Fishbein, 1965) and consisted exclusively of post-1958 articles (the median publication year was actually 1962). As shown in Table 3, adult subjects predominated in the pre-1958 *Basic Studies*, whereas college students were by far the dominant subject population in the post-1958 *Current Studies*.

A third way to index the most prestigeful research in the field is to select that done by the most frequent contributors to mainstream journals. And those who publish most regularly in the mainstream journals turn out also to be the most likely to use college students in the lab. The other articles of *JPSP* authors that appear in mainstream social psychology journals relied heavily on undergraduate subjects (84%), were almost exclusively based on laboratory studies (97%), and so almost never considered adults in their natural habitats (3%). This is shown in column 8 of Table 1. Prestige in our field therefore seems to be linked closely to the use of college student subjects in laboratory settings.

Table 3 Subject Populations in Selected Books of Readings in Social Psychology

Editors and Pub. Date	Title	Subjects			No. of Codeable Articles
		% College Students	% Other Preadults	% Adults	
	Pre-1960 research				
Swanson, Newcomb, & Hartley (1952)	*Readings in Social Psychology* (2nd ed.)	28	23	49	61
Proshansky & Seidenberg (1965)	*Basic Studies in Social Psychology*	35	18	47	60
	Post-1960 research				
Steiner & Fishbein (1965)	*Current Studies in Social Psychology*	64	12	24	42
Freedman, Carlsmith, & Sears (1971)	*Readings in Social Psychology*	69	13	18	39
Wrightsman & Brigham (1973)	*Contemporary Issues in Social Psychology* (2nd ed.)	57	24	19	21
Brigham & Wrightsman (1977)	*Contemporary Issues in Social Psychology* (3rd ed.)	73	0	27	15
Aronson (1981)	*Readings About the Social Animal* (3rd ed.)	55	16	29	31
Brigham & Wrightsman (1982)	*Contemporary Issues in Social Psychology* (4th ed.)	59	6	35	17

Summary

In short, (a) social psychologists during the late 1940s and 1950s commonly conducted research on adults in their natural habitats, but (b) since the early 1960s the great majority of social psychological studies have relied exclusively on college students tested in the laboratory, (c) at a level that has held quite steady over the past 25 years. Indeed, (d) in the current era, the most prestigious research, as indicated by textbook citations, by inclusion in books of readings, or by having been conducted by the most prolific publishers in the most mainstream journals is, if anything, the most likely to be based on laboratory research with college students. This reliance on undergraduates in the lab (e) seems not to be a product of journal policy or peer review, because it emerges wherever social psychologists publish.

WHAT DIFFERENCE DOES IT MAKE?

That sociopsychological research overwhelmingly uses one rather narrow subject population and artificial laboratory settings does not necessarily mean its results are invalid. Much biomedical research does the same, and few would question the cumulative value of that work. There should be little reason for concern unless it can be shown that such choices threaten the validity of the research.

The Consensus: Little or None

The consensus of the field certainly appears to be that such a heavy reliance on college student subjects does not have major negative consequences. It has typically been assumed that the phenomena under investigation by social psychologists are so ubiquitous and universal that it does not matter much what subjects are used; one might as well use those cheapest and easiest to obtain. As a result, social psychologists have, by and large, ignored the question of subject population and thus have not discussed its possible consequences. Without going into detail, a careful perusal of the most widely used textbooks in the field, the major

books and handbook chapters on methodology, the major handbook and review chapters on attitudes and social cognition, the most recent texts on attitude change or social cognition, and even the several articles in the 1970s expressing concern about a crisis in social psychology reveals that subject selection is generally not mentioned at all. Only a few mention it even in passing, and none express any particular concern about it.

A few critical articles have been published recording the particular characteristics of sociopsychological methodology, most of them cited above in the discussion of historical trends. In general, however, they have not attempted to specify the consequences of these patterns. And in any case they seem to me to have had little impact so far, either upon researchers' practices or on researchers' attitudes toward their practices.

The Potential Hazards of a Narrow Data Base

What kinds of mischief might this narrow data base do? Presumably the principal goal of research in social psychology is to establish a body of causal propositions of the general form $y = a + bx$. Problems could arise when a narrow data base disturbs functional relationships and misrepresents them in some way. But some possibilities seem more threatening than others. Conceivably, the nature of the relationship may be wrongly described, in that either the sign or the shape of the b term may be wrong. However, I doubt that either of these is a major problem in social psychology. Incentives for discovering incorrect signs are quite lavish and usually motivate a great deal of research when they are suspected, as happened following the classic Festinger and Carlsmith (1959) study of forced compliance. And our propositions are usually too crude to invoke subtly shaped relationships.

More likely is that the strength of the relationship may be wrongly described. A test conducted under artificial circumstances is best at telling us whether or not x can cause y under favorable circumstances. Having established that it can, the criterion of success shifts to the validity of the proposition in everyday life:

Is x in general a major cause of y in everyday life? And here, as Converse (1970) has pointed out, the absence of research on the general population in natural situations can leave the experimental social psychologist ignorant of the actuarial mainstream, unaware of what the critical sources of variation are, or are not, in "natural" social processes.

The strength of the relationship can be misestimated in at least three different ways. First, the size of b may be incorrectly estimated from the artificial data base: x may, in everyday life, not influence y much, and/or other variables may influence it more strongly. It would be a serious matter if some seemingly strong functional relationships were in fact limited only to college students in the laboratory or had very small (even if statistically significant) effects elsewhere. A vast amount of research and textbook space might be devoted to variables (or processes) that are simply not very important in general. Conversely, some relationships might hold with ordinary adults in everyday life but not to any visible degree among college students in the laboratory. Our research would fail to detect them, and some key aspects of human nature might thereby be omitted from theories in social psychology.

Second, the range of the x values used in our research may not map well onto their range in ordinary life. This seems to me a particular hazard. The x values in an artificial data base are likely to be set at some ecologically unrepresentative level. For example, laboratory research on media violence usually presents much higher and more concentrated doses of filmed violence than do the everyday mass media; for example, showing only an intensely violent segment of a prize fight as opposed to the occasional violent episode of a typical 1-hr TV show.

Finally, the effort to get pure laboratory conditions is likely to result in testing a narrow and/or atypical sample of possibly interacting conditions. For example, in most aggression experiments, the reigning authority either approves or actually encourages aggression (e.g., with the Buss shock machine), certainly an atypical condition for antisocial aggression in everyday life. Moreover, they do not even enter the range of the threatened punishments for antisocial aggression that in fact control much of its variance in everyday life.[4]

Assessment of Risk

How can one assess the threat to the validity of research findings posed by heavy reliance on this one narrow data base? Two strategies seem evident. Most obviously, one could repeat tests of various cause-and-effect propositions on subject populations of various ages and social locations and in a representative sample of everyday situations. This is the *ecological validity* strategy advocated by Bronfenbrenner (1977) and Brunswik (1955). If some propositions prove to hold for college students in the laboratory but not for ordinary people in everyday life (or vice versa) there would be reason for concern. Although systematic comparisons across subject populations and research sites would provide the most certain evidence of external validity, they have not, to my knowledge, been attempted in any area of social psychology.[5]

---

[4] Berkowitz and Donnerstein (1982), and many others, argued that experimental, rather than mundane, realism is sufficient to test causal hypotheses. This seems less obvious to me than it does to them. Although usually intended to test causal hypotheses, experiments are frequently interpreted as making population estimates (e.g., the important studies by Asch, Bem, Milgram, and those on cognitive heuristics, attributional biases, and attitude-behavior inconsistency). Testing functional relationships may also require more ecological validity than is usually assumed, for the reasons given in the text above. And even experimental realism is rarely assessed in much detail beyond, at most, a relatively narrowly focused manipulation check.

[5] Some have replicated studies with nonstudent populations and/or in sites other than academic laboratories, of course. But the effects of subject characteristic and site variables have not been assessed systematically. For example, Crutchfield (1955) did use some adult subjects in his laboratory studies of conformity, though he made no explicit age comparisons. Similarly, Milgram (1974) took great pains to replicate his findings on obedience to authority with nonstudent subjects of varying age and social class and in a nonuniversity setting. I hope it will not seem churlish to point out that, nevertheless, the effects of age and class were not assessed; that the nonuniversity context did produce a significant reduction in obedience (though it remained at very high levels); and that Milgram felt the laboratory context was

Hence a more realistic (and less expensive) strategy would be to extrapolate from existing information. This would require several steps: identifying the ways in which college students in the laboratory differ from the general population in everyday life, estimating the effects of those factors on the basis of other research, and then making some informed guesses about how this biased data base might affect the resulting substantive generalizations. This was essentially Hovland's (1959) strategy in accounting for the differences between survey and experimental studies of attitude change. This second strategy appears to me to be the only feasible one at the present time, given the very limited amount of evidence available on ordinary people in ordinary life. Presumably if it gives cause for concern, it should be followed by more precisely focused replications using a broader range of subject populations, research sites, and research materials.

How Is the College Student in the Laboratory Unusual?

How might American undergraduates, enrolled in introductory psychology classes and tested in academic laboratories on academiclike tasks, differ systematically from the general population in everyday life in ways that might lead us to mistaken conclusions about human nature in general?

Most obviously, undergraduates usually come from a very narrow age range and are concentrated at the upper levels of educational background. Those who work extensively with survey data on the general population are accustomed to finding that age and education are the two most powerful demographic factors influencing attitudes and attitudinal processes. This alone leads us to suspect that those at the tails of those distributions will be a shaky foundation upon which to generalize to the population as a whole. But it is possible to be more specific.

Introductory psychology tends to be one of the first classes taken by college freshmen: It is usually an easy, popular course that satisfies breadth requirements and has no prerequisites. Hence the students tend to be 17 to 19 years old and thus concentrated in a narrow band of late adolescence. Persons in this particular life stage tend to have a number of quite unique characteristics, as described in the standard texts on adolescence (see Atwater, 1983; Conger, 1977; and Douvan & Adelson, 1966; see also Rubenstein, 1983). At an intrapsychic level, they tend to have (a) a less than fully formulated sense of self, manifested variously in mercurial self-esteem, identity confusion and diffusion, inadequate integration of past, present, and future selves, feelings of insecurity, and depression. One important consequence is that (b) their social and political attitudes tend to be considerably less crystallized at this stage than later in life. They also tend to be (c) substantially more egocentric than older adults. They differ from adults in their interpersonal relationships, as well, having (d) a stronger need for peer approval, manifested in dependency, conformity, and overidentification with peers. However, this need tends to be mixed with (e) highly unstable peer relationships and especially highly unstable peer *group* relationships.

But college students also differ systematically from other late adolescents in general: (f) They have been carefully preselected for having unusually adept cognitive skills, and (g) they have also been selected for compliance to authority; few can successfully navigate 13 years of primary and secondary schooling and obtain good grades and positive letters of recommendation while fighting authority at every turn. (h) College students would also seem likely to have more unstable peer (and peer group) relationships than other later adolescents because of their greater geographical and social mobility and later entry into the work force and family life.[6]

---

crucial in producing the phenomenon. The critical question here is one Milgram speculated extensively about: how common are such settings in ordinary people's natural habitats?

---

[6] The fact that these college students almost all are from the American middle class or other westernized middle-classes and educational systems no doubt has other ramifications, but thorough consideration of such

The use of college students as a subject population cannot be disentangled completely from the equally widespread reliance on the laboratory setting and the academiclike task. Laboratory studies in social psychology would seem likely to induce (i) a considerably more cognitive set than the other sites of ordinary life. They are usually conducted as part of a course requirement in an academic setting, such as a laboratory or classroom, and usually use paper-and-pencil materials that resemble academic tests. They would also seem likely to induce (j) a set to comply with authority, for some of the same reasons: the academic setting, the course requirement, the testlike materials, with an older authority—the experimenter—giving authoritative instructions and controlling the awarding of credit. Finally, most laboratory situations deliberately (k) sever students from whatever close peer (and peer group) relationships they have, in order to minimize contamination of individuals' responses.

The critical question is whether or not these unusual characteristics of college students tested in the laboratory are likely to produce misleading or mistaken substantive conclusions about social behavior. Unfortunately, one cannot extrapolate very well from research in experimental social psychology, because it provides very little direct evidence on these variables. For example, the excellent review of attitude change research by Petty and Cacioppo (1981) refers to age and intelligence only once each, and not at all to educational level or to Hovland's (1959) compelling paper on research site.

On the other hand, we may be able to make such informed guesses if we turn to evidence gathered within other disciplines that have researched persons from the full life span and from a wider variety of ecological locations. Using such sources of evidence and focusing especially on attitudes and social cognition, the remainder of this article attempts to identify major features of our account of human nature which may be misleading as a result of our narrow data base.

---

cultural factors would take this article too far afield (see Miller, 1984, for a recent foray into that territory).

WEAK SELF-DEFINITION

There is much current research on the self. One of its major themes is that people have a rather wobbly definition or sense of the self. For example, the central observation of the social comparison literature (Festinger, 1954) is that people arrive at perceptions of their own attitudes and abilities not through introspection but by comparing themselves with others. The extensive literature on the self-perception of attitudes (Bem, 1972), preferences (Nisbett & Wilson, 1977), and emotions (Schachter & Singer, 1962) also argues that people have relatively impoverished introspective access to their own subjective states. In commonsense language, people do not know their own minds. In a related vein, research on objective self-awareness (Duval & Wicklund, 1972) asserts that self-esteem is highly fragile. It can be significantly lowered by minimal levels of self-reflection, which, it is argued, confronts the individual with the discrepancy between internal standards and reality.

The consensus among developmental psychologists is that adolescents do not have as firm a sense of self, or self-definition, as do older adults. As Erikson (1963) and many others have noted, they frequently do not have a clearly crystallized identity. They are quite uncertain about many of their values, preferences, abilities, and emotions, and for good reason. Many of these dispositions are still developing, many are quite volatile as yet, and the stability that may ultimately come to internal dispositions simply has not yet had time or experience to develop.

It is possible that people of all ages are in fact rather uncertain about their own true attitudes, emotions, and abilities. But research in the areas of social comparison, self-perception, and objective self-awareness has relied almost exclusively on college student subjects. The reliance for empirical data on a subpopulation that is particularly uncertain about its own dispositions could quite naturally, but possibly misleadingly, lead to a view of the whole species as equally uncertain about its own internal states.

UNCRYSTALLIZED ATTITUDES

One important consequence of this wobbly sense of self is that late adolescents and young adults tend to have less-crystallized social and political attitudes than do older people. This has been demonstrated with at least four different methodologies (see Glenn, 1980; Sears, 1983). Panel studies have consistently shown that older adults have more stable social and political attitudes than do late adolescents or young adults (Jennings & Niemi, 1981; also see Jennings & Markus, 1984). Second, young people change attitudes more than older persons in response to political events. In Mueller's (1973) terms, "the public swerves to follow" sudden switches in official foreign policy (such as that concerning the Korean and Vietnam Wars), and the young swerve most (also see Sears, 1969, pp. 351–353). The racial conflicts of the 1960s and the Vietnam War influenced basic party preferences more for young adults than for their parents (Markus, 1979). Similarly, the young were the first to jump on the bandwagons of such right wing extremists as Adolf Hitler and George Wallace (see Lipset & Raab, 1978; Loewenberg, 1971), as well as on those of the radical leftist movements that swept the campuses in the late 1960s and early 1970s. Third, cohort analyses have generally shown younger cohorts to be more responsive to strong long-term period pressures, such as those of the late 1960s and 1970s toward more distrust of government and weaker party identification (Glenn, 1980) and those of the early 1980s toward Reagan and the Republican party (Shanks & Miller, 1985). Converse's (1976) cohort analyses also showed party identification to strengthen with age, especially in "steady state" eras with only weak period effects. Fourth, Kirkpatrick (1976) has shown that older cohorts in the late 1950s and 1960s had more consistent attitudes on social welfare issues than did younger ones, and consistency increased within cohorts as they aged.

In short, four quite different lines of research have shown late adolescents and young adults to have more unstable, changeable, weak, and inconsistent attitudes than older adults. This lesser crystallization of their attitudes may be partially responsible for three important conclusions that social psychologists have generally drawn about human nature primarily on the basis of their research on college students in the laboratory.

Easily Influenced

One core conclusion of modern social psychology is that people are easily influenced. Almost every textbook has chapters on attitudes and attitude change. Almost always the message is that judgments and attitudes are readily changed and that social psychology provides an extensive roster of successful change techniques. Similarly, most textbooks have chapters on conformity and compliance, which are illustrated by the well-known studies by Asch, Milgram, and many others, that document the many ways in which psychologists have shown behavior to be easily controlled through social influence. At this very general level, social psychologists stand somewhat apart from social scientists in some other disciplines who have often found human preferences and behavior to be quite refractory. According to these individuals, mass communications frequently are found to have minimal effects, racial prejudice resists the most painstaking interventions, expensive desegregation programs and other educational reforms do not substantially improve minority children's performance, neuroses fail to succumb to elaborate psychological therapies, and alcohol and other drug dependencies are resistant to all but the most draconian treatment.

The conclusion of relatively easy influence may stem from the unusual data base from which it emerges. Attitude change research generally involves exposing captive college student subjects, with their relatively uncrystallized attitudes, to authoritative communications in an academic atmosphere. Moreover, college students are probably unusually compliant to authority, inasmuch as they are sufficiently well socialized (or conformist) to have successfully followed the arcane directions of dozens, if not hundreds, of teachers, school administrators, parents, and test-givers over the prior 2 decades of their lives.[7] Use of such subjects and research sites, perhaps not surprisingly, thus produces data indicating that attitudes are easily changed and that the independent variables of the laboratory experience are powerful levers on that influence.[8]

Similarly, studies of conformity and obedience conducted with college students in the laboratory may give the false impression that behavior is also generally easily influenced. But their subject population is predisposed to be more compliant, and their atmosphere more authoritative, than is usually true for the general population in its many natural habitats. Distortions here might be of even more consequence inasmuch as the conformity studies of Asch, Milgram, Zimbardo, and others have been among the most widely publicized of all sociopsychological findings.[9]

Attitude-Behavior Inconsistency

Another widely accepted contention is that attitudes only weakly control behavior. However, much evidence indicates that attitude-behavior consistency is substantially enhanced when attitudinal preferences are strong or nonconflicted (Kelley & Mirer, 1974; Norman, 1975), when the attitude is based on relatively more information (Davidson, Yantis, Norwood, & Montano, 1985) or direct experience with the attitude object (Fazio & Zanna, 1981), or when the subject has a vested interest in the issue (Sivacek & Crano, 1982).

Focusing research attention on students,

whose attitudinal dispositions, among other things, are not yet at full strength because they are still developing and are based in relatively poor information and little direct experience, is bound therefore to underestimate the general level of consistency between attitudes and behavior. Moreover, for the reasons given earlier, the environmental press may be stronger in an academic laboratory situation than in most natural habitats, further diminishing the role of such predispositions as attitudes. This is not to argue that attitudes and behavior are invariably highly consistent. But the conventional wisdom has been, I think, that attitudes and behavior are generally not consistent, which is probably overdrawn because of unrepresentative subject populations and research settings (among others, see Schuman & Johnson, 1976).

Self-Perception

Self-perception research has suggested that people frequently arrive at judgments about their own attitudes on the basis of external cues (the situation and their overt behavior), rather than on the basis of introspective access to their true internal attitudes. Sometimes this conclusion has been tempered by suggesting that this process may occur primarily when internal cues are weak (e.g., Bem, 1972). This qualification has, however, received much less attention than assertions that the self-perception process is quite general. As anyone who has lectured on this material knows, the strong form of the assertion is usually received as quite startlingly fresh and original, probably because it so completely violates our own subjective experience of acting on the basis of our introspection.

There is now substantial evidence, however, that these self-perception effects may occur only when the subject has very weak prior attitudes. Chaiken and Baldwin (1981) found that significant self-perception effects occurred only among subjects with poorly defined prior attitudes; Wood (1982) found the same among those who had engaged in relatively few prior

[7] A most useful earlier review of research on "the subject role" in psychological experiments, by Weber and Cook (1972), similarly singles out the *faithful subject* and *apprehensive subject* roles as threats to the validity of laboratory experiments. Their discussion touches on subject selection biases only in passing.

[8] Hovland (1959) earlier noted a number of features of laboratory situations that made attitude change much easier to accomplish there than in the field. The present article should be viewed as following in the same vein, developing certain implications of his argument in greater detail, and adding the fcous on subject selection in particular.

[9] Replications by Crutchfield (1955) and Milgram (1974) put some boundaries on this point. See Footnote 5.

relevant behaviors; and Taylor (1975) found the same when the behavior had no important consequences. According to this research, then, the self-perception phenomenon may occur mainly when people have relatively uncrystallized prior attitudes on the issue in question. Its ubiquity in everyday life may not be as great as it might seem from social psychological experiments, then. These are conducted almost exclusively on students who have generally rather uncrystallized attitudes. They also ordinarily use attitude objects that elicit only mild preferences, presenting alternatives that are novel, artificial, or quite similar.

Drawing subjects from such a narrow age range also prevents our investigating the determinants of life stage differences in attitude crystallization. For example, informational mass, information-processing skills and social support all are likely to vary systematically with life stage (see Sears, 1981, 1983), but assessing their effects would require sampling quite different life stages.

UNINTEGRATED ATTITUDES

If late adolescents' attitudes tend to be relatively uncrystallized and if they have a less than fully formulated self in other respects as well, it is also likely that these attitudes will not be as integrated into other aspects of their personalities as they will prove to be later in life. Early postwar research on anti-Semitism, racial prejudice, and attitude change, heavily influenced by psychoanalytic theory, often viewed these as firmly rooted in chronic personality predispositions (Adorno et al., 1950; Allport, 1954; Sarnoff, 1960). Data for the most extensive work, on authoritarianism and anti-Semitism, came from adults who were given depth interviews in the psychoanalytic mode, both in treatment itself (Ackerman & Jahoda, 1950) and in extended research interviews (Adorno et al., 1950; Bettelheim & Janowitz, 1950; also see Lane, 1962; Smith, Bruner, & White, 1956). The psychodynamic insights thus generated led to the development of questionnaire measures of personality, which were initially ad-

ministered to college students, because they were, as Adorno et al. (1950, pp. 21–22) explicitly acknowledged, the most available, cooperative, and easily retested of possible subjects. However, their research soon moved on to a wide variety of adult subject populations, including veterans, union members, professional women, and so on.

This research received several damaging critiques. Some criticized even this modest pilot use of college student subjects as part of a broader uneasiness about unexamined confounds of educational level with the supposed measures of personality and ethnocentrism (Hyman & Sheatsley, 1954). However, complaints that the research had neglected response sets and authoritarianism of the left demanded more controlled research. This, not surprisingly, led to a virtual avalanche of research on college students, which soon evolved into rather arid and esoteric methodological debates and, as Kirscht and Dillehay pointed out in their excellent review, simply exacerbated the sampling inadequacies of the original work: "that problem is still with us. Its crux is the use of college students for research samples . . . the results are no closer to proper generalization than ten years ago" (1967, pp. 31–32).

The same psychodynamic reasoning led also to intervention programs. Brief insight-therapy experiences were administered, mainly to student subjects to break down ego-defensive support for their prejudice (e.g., Katz, Sarnoff, & McClintock, 1956). These studies generated rather mixed findings, along with more complaints about lack of rigor (see Kiesler, Collins, & Miller, 1969).

Today personality predispositions are no longer portrayed as central determinants of social and political attitudes, either in social psychology or in neighboring disciplines (see Kinder & Sears, 1985; McGuire, 1985). There are clearly several reasons for this. Whatever the merits of other considerations, it seems to me that both research and intervention on personality determinants of attitudes were doomed to failure once the move to students in the laboratory took place. Most late adolescents focus on the world of public affairs only in passing if at all. Their personalities, like their attitudes and other aspects of their selves, have not yet fully crystallized. And if passionately held social attitudes are to become imbedded in the individual's deepest personality needs, it seems most unlikely that that time-consuming and complex psychological task will ordinarily have been completed by the age of 18 or 19. Special cultural and historical circumstances may speed it up, as in Berkeley in the 1960s or in Beirut in the 1980s. But most American college sophomores, in most eras, are far from Berkeley and Beirut.

Are we content with an account of the origins of political and social attitudes that omits the role of personality dynamics? If we believe that they do play a role, is it likely that we could discover it with research on American college students in a laboratory setting?

THE ABSENCE OF SELF-INTEREST

Some potentially powerful determinants of attitudes are nearly absent in late adolescence. Limiting research to that life stage risks omitting those processes from our accounts of human nature. For example, material self-interest has been a dominant factor in many social scientists' theories of attitude formation and change, from Smith, Bentham, and Marx to today's public choice crowd. But it is even touched on by only the most comprehensively taxonomic social psychologists (see Katz, 1960) and almost never researched. Why not? Both the mean and variability of the independent variable, material self-interest, are generally very low in a college student population. Very few social and political issues bear directly on college students' lives, with the occasional exceptions of military issues or the costs and funding of higher education (e.g., Sears, Steck, Lau, & Gahart, 1983). A process that usually cannot be studied with college students probably will not prove very central to social psychologists' theories of human nature. Among adults, self-interest may not have the universal importance some claim, but it is crucial at certain important

junctures (e.g., Sears & Allen, 1984; Sears & Citrin, 1985).

GROUP NORMS AND SOCIAL SUPPORT

Much early empirical research in social psychology demonstrated the great power of group norms over the individual's judgments and attitudes. Sherif's early work on social norms (1936), Newcomb's Bennington study (1943), Kurt Lewin's discussion of group decision (1947), Shils and Janowitz' (1948) research on military morale, Festinger's (1950) and associates' work on small group influence, Berelson, Lazarsfeld, and McPhee (1954) and Converse and Campbell's (1960) treatments of voting behavior, and Kelley's fine work (e.g., 1955) on the role of group loyalties in influence by mass communications, all underlined the powerful effects of primary group loyalties in everything from novel laboratory tasks to the most important political decisions.

Certainly groups remain powerful determinants of sociopolitical attitudes, as witnessed by passionate ethnic and religious rivalries in Northern Ireland and throughout the Mideast, the response of the Afghans to Russian domination and the resistance of Afrikaners to black demands, and black bloc voting in the United States. But social psychologists' accounts of attitude change today generally ignore the role of groups in attitudinal processes and, indeed, rarely even cite the important early studies just mentioned (for examples, see the excellent reviews by Petty and Cacioppo, 1981; McGuire, 1985). Even the numerous accounts of extensive direct interpersonal influence among college students alluded to earlier, such as laboratory studies of conformity, tend to describe influence by unaffiliated strangers rather than by fellow members of ongoing groups. The image of the human being is of a social isolated, atomized individual—an odd portrayal by a "social" psychology.

One reason may be that groups are peculiarly unimportant to an individual undergraduate filling out a questionnaire in an artificial laboratory situation. Partly, life stage plays a role here. Adolescents' dependency on their peer groups is well known, but their group affiliations are in fact notoriously unstable and changeable and provide very little of the long-term social support and anchorage for their judgments and attitudes that they do for more mature individuals. Disruptive changes in primary groups are more common in late adolescence and early adulthood than at any other stage of life, owing to high rates of geographical mobility, entering and/or changing work environments, status mobility, higher education, beginning a marriage or other intimate relationships, and military service (Brown, 1981; Carlsson & Karlsson, 1970). Moreover, since attitude similarity is a powerful determinant of interpersonal attraction (Byrne, 1971), people prove to be increasingly able, as they get older, to assemble attitudinally supportive family, work, and friendship groups (Newcomb, Koenig, Flacks, & Warwick, 1967; Berelson et al., 1954). Thus groups should, with age, become increasingly important sources of social support and resistance to change.

College students may be even less thoroughly tied to stable primary groups than are other late adolescents because they are more likely to have become detached from the groups of their earlier life, and they have not yet become fully embedded in the group relationships of their adulthood, such as in marriage, the workplace, neighborhood, or in recreational, fraternal, and solidarity groups. Further, the laboratory setting usually deliberately severs college students from their close friends and other group ties in order to avoid any contamination as a result of influence by them. They are usually tested individually, or at least individuated (by being given individual questionnaires in a mass testing situation), and on artificial tasks that are irrelevant to peer-group norms, again to minimize group-based resistance.

In short, group norms are very powerful influences on individuals' attitudes but probably considerably more for mature adults in their natural habitats than for college students in the laboratory. Moreover, the nature of that impact most likely also varies systematically across the life span, probably increasingly supporting resistance to change with age. So laboratory research on college students is bound to underemphasize the role of the group, in terms of both influence and social support, and overemphasize the role of purely individual factors.

STAGE-SPECIFIC ATTITUDES

Reliance on this data base may also lead to problems concerning dispositions or processes that vary substantially with life stage. For instance, life-stage or life-cycle theories of attitudes suggest that people tend to adopt certain specific attitudes at specific life stages and to reject them at other stages. The aged are thought to be especially attracted to conservatism because of their material and cognitive stake in maintaining the status quo. The middle-aged are thought to be especially self-interested, because they have hard-earned "stakes" to protect. And late adolescents are thought to be especially attracted to political radicalism, because it serves their stage-specific needs for autonomy and/or rebellion against parents and parent-surrogates, their youthful idealism, or their lack of economic responsibilities (see Glenn, 1980; Sears, 1975).

These stage-specific theories of attitudes simply cannot be assessed in a student population because of its narrow age range. Hence such life-stage theories are rarely mentioned in the standard sociopsychological treatments of attitudes, even though they are fairly common in other social sciences. To be sure, many cohort analyses have found that age differences in attitudes are more likely to be caused by generational than stage-specific factors (see Glenn, 1980; Sears, 1975). Nevertheless, these are potentially important determinants of attitude formation and change and cannot be investigated in a college student population.

COGNITIVE PROCESSES AND RATIONALITY

The oldest and most recurrent debates about attitudes and decision making revolve around the normative question: How good are they?

This in turn usually breaks down into two separate questions, about the rationality of attitudes and decisions and about the relative roles of cognitive, as opposed to affective, processes. Both provoke endless definitional controversies. At a commonsensical level, though, there is probably general agreement that rationality is marked by scanning all available relevant information in an unbiased manner and combining it according to some logical decision rule. Similarly, most would probably agree that emphasizing cognitive processes leads us to focus on perception, memory, and thinking, whereas emphasizing affective processes leads us to focus on emotion, motivation (or need or drive), value, and preference.

Changing Theoretical Emphases

In my view (and certainly to oversimplify), theory and research in social psychology have shifted from a rather strong emphasis on affectively based irrationality in the immediate postwar years to today's emphasis on cognitive processes, though in both rational and irrational forms. In the social psychology of the 1940s and 1950s, attitudes were blindly learned in childhood from parents and schoolmates (Hyman, 1959; Proshansky, 1966) or were driven by powerful psychodynamic forces (Adorno et al., 1950), and they could be changed by such emotions as fear, aggression, and sexual arousal (Hovland, Janis, & Kelley, 1953; Sarnoff, 1960).

During the 1960s, as psychoanalytic and conditioning theories were losing favor, theories based on "rational" processing became more popular, but it still had a strong affective emphasis. Congruity theory (Osgood & Tannenbaum, 1955), Abelson and Rosenberg's (1958) "psycho-logic," Anderson's integration theory (1971), and linear decision-making models (Slovic, Fischoff, & Lichtenstein, 1977) all described the decision-maker as combining a broad and unbiased sample of informational inputs into a decision (or attitude) using a simple and straightforward decision rule, usually a linear model. At the same time, they all described the inputs as coded in evaluative terms and did not invoke configural combinatorial principles or intervening perceptual or cognitive variables. In these senses they depicted rational decision making on the basis of affective, rather than cognitive, processes.

Today social psychology generally portrays people as dominated by cognitive processes. In some cases they process rationally as well. In the pure form of Kelley's covariance model of attribution (1967), the individual thoroughly scans available information and uses a statistical algorithm to arrive at a logical attribution. Cognitive response theory (Petty, Ostrom, & Brock, 1981) views attitude change as a simple function of the number of favorable or unfavorable cognitive responses the individual has to a persuasive communication. Ajzen and Fishbein's (1980) theory of reasoned action holds that behavior follows in a straightforward, rational way from its perceived costs and benefits. Expectancy-value or subjective expected utility theories (e.g., Feather, 1982) view the individual as scanning different possible utilities and, using a simple statistical rule, combining them according to their probabilities of occurrence to produce a rational decision. In each case, thoughtful, deliberate, self-conscious, and thus rational processing is assumed along with such cognitive variables as expectancies or subjective probabilities.

Other contemporary work is equally cognitive, but it emphasizes "irrational" errors and biases, using such concepts as salience, availability, illusory correlation, misattribution, categorization, schemas, and mindlessness (see Fiske & Taylor, 1984; Kahneman, Slovic, & Tversky, 1982; Nisbett & Ross, 1980). This approach shares a focus on judgments that are erroneous from a normative standpont and biased as a result of cognitive processes; hence, it emphasizes both cognitive and irrational processes.

In short, I would argue that the emphasis in social psychology has shifted from irrational, affective, evaluative processes to cognitive processing with a renewed interest in rational models. To be sure, there remains a lively debate within the cognitive camp, pitting rational theories against biases in information processing. Some approaches encompass both (e.g., Kelley, 1967; Taylor & Fiske, 1978). But this very controversy yields a net shift away from the irrational. In all, social psychology's portrait of the human being has changed quite markedly: no longer driven by primary drives, unconscious motives, stale repetition of childhood learning, and blind conformity, but thinking, perceiving, remembering, aware, reasoning, and often reasonable.[10]

The Role of the Data Base

Why did these changes occur? In part, no doubt, for several reasons that have nothing at all to do with social psychology's unique data base. In recent years the pendulum of intellectual fashion throughout all the behavioral sciences has cycled away from emotion-laden theories of human irrationality, such as psychoanalytic theory and behaviorism, toward more cognitive and economically rational theories. Also, because of heightened ethical sensibilities and more extensive ethical monitoring systems, many investigators have no doubt shied away from research on emotion-laden, upsetting, "hot" processes and have been encouraged to do research on safer, less controversial and troublesome, "cool" cognitive processes.

Nevertheless, I would argue that the shift to more cognitive theories has been at least abetted by the increased dependence upon college students tested in the laboratory. Here the students' life stage is probably less relevant than their unusual cognitive skills. They have been carefully preselected for these, usually by some combination of prior performance at the cognitive tasks in high school courses and cognitive tests like the Scholastic Aptitude Test (SAT). As a result, information-processing skills of the kind emphasized on academiclike tests are considerably stronger among those

attending college. Similarly, the complex cognitive structures that are relevant to sociopolitical attitudes are much more common among persons with a college education (Converse, 1964).

Moreover, customary procedures in laboratory studies should produce a strongly cognitive set. Almost all studies are conducted in an actual classroom or in a rather artificial, sterile, official-seeming laboratory on a college campus. The student usually participates as a requirement for some college course. And the studies themselves resemble standard college tests, with paper-and-pencil question-and-answer formats and complex, authoritative directions. A college student in a testlike situation knows not to respond with simple evaluative preferences; rather, what is called for is paying close attention, dispassionate judgment, a search for the "right" answer, critical thinking, and close attention. Many studies use artificial or novel content, or role-playing techniques. Others have cover stories presenting them as studies of perception or learning, not of prejudice or idiosyncratic emotion. Social psychology's use of relatively well-educated subjects, selected for their superior cognitive skills, along with research sites, procedures, and tasks that promote dispassionate, academiclike information-processing, should help produce empirical evidence that portrays humans as dominated by cognitive processes, rather than by strong evaluative predispositions.

These same conditions seem to me likely to allow the cognitively oriented researcher to make a fairly strong case for either rational or biased processing, depending on theoretical proclivity. On the one hand, the conditions of most psychology experiments encourage "cognitive miser"-like behavior. The incentives for participating in experiments are minimal, and students generally try to get through the task as quickly and painlessly as possible. Haste and meager incentive are likely to produce shortcuts of all kinds, among them presumably cognitive errors and biases.

On the other hand, college students are selected for their ability to be rational. They are taught the habits of rational thought quite explicitly, to treat evidence objectively and to develop conclusions from it in a logical fashion.

---

[10] Perlman (1984) has presented data documenting these shifts, based on the Social Science Citation index and research citations in textbooks. There is a recent renewal of interest in affect (e.g., Clark & Fiske, 1982; Roseman, Abelson, & Ewing, 1986; Ross & Sicoly, 1979; Smith & Ellsworth, 1985; Weiner, 1982; Zajonc, 1980). Some of these are genuine exceptions to the dominant focus on cognition, whereas others analyze affect from a cognitive point of view.

Rational thinking is a prerequisite for success in the academic, grade-oriented world. So it should not be difficult to set up conditions in which students process information in a logical, rational way.

Some tests of the cognitive response, reasoned action, and expectancy-value theories adduce evidence of rationality from the reasons subjects give for their actions, before or after the behavior itself. But college students in particular have been exquisitely trained to rationalize conclusions when they can recall little or no real information. One of their most common tasks is to make up and write down plausible-sounding reasons for something they know they are supposed to believe but usually cannot remember in detail the reasons why. Indeed Nisbett and Wilson (1977) suggested that asking a person to give "reasons" may lead to a falsely rational portrait of the determinants of the decision because people provide the most available plausible causal schema for their behavior rather than the *real* reasons. Such highly trained confabulators would seem to provide a particularly apt subject population from which to gather data that demonstrate rational decision-making processes, or at least reasonable-sounding reasons for decisions.

EGOCENTRIC BIASES

Finally, late adolescents are considerably more egocentric and preoccupied with their own needs and desires, often overwhelmed by their own emotions, and less empathic with others than they are likely to be later in life. In parallel fashion, recent research has dramatically underlined the egocentricity of social perception. It is given to egocentric biases, such that both members of a dyad claim most responsibility for joint activities (Ross & Sicoly, 1979; Thompson & Kelley, 1981), and to self-based consensus or false consensus effects in which one's own behavior or attitudes are seen as typical of everyone else's (Ross, Greene, & House, 1977). It is possible that indeed these should be explained as cognitive biases on the grounds that the self is most salient and/or available in memory. On the other hand, virtually all this research has been done on college students

(see Mullen et al., 1985). Again, humans in general are described in terms that particularly characterize the late adolescent life stage.

CONCLUSIONS

The questions raised here are twofold: How heavily has research in social psychology relied on American college students tested in artificial laboratory settings during the past 25 years? And, to what extent might primary reliance on this particular data base have led to biased substantive conclusions about human social behavior? Does social psychology's portrait of human nature match American college student's behavior in a laboratory better than the general population's behavior in its natural habitats?

Social psychology has indeed, since about 1960, relied primarily on a very narrow data base: young American college students tested in the academic laboratory. This data base is unusual in a number of respects. Such students tend, among other things, to have incompletely formulated senses of self, rather uncrystallized sociopolitical attitudes, unusually strong cognitive skills, strong needs for peer approval, tendencies to be compliant to authority, quite unstable group relationships, little material self-interest in public affairs, and unusual egocentricity. The sociopsychological laboratory also has its idiosyncrasies, being a rather authoritative, academic, test-oriented setting that isolates subjects from their normal interpersonal relationships.

Some of the main emphases and conclusions of contemporary social psychology parallel these unusual features of its data base. Four examples have been presented above. First, modern social psychology tends, in a variety of respects, to view people in general as having a weak sense of their own preferences, emotions, and abilities: They have easily damaged self-esteem; they are quite compliant behaviorally; their attitudes and judgments are easily changed; their attitudes have a minor effect on their behavior; they are ignorant of or insensitive to their own true attitudes; and their long-standing personality predispositions are not important determinants of their sociopolitical attitudes. Second, material self-interest, group norms, reference group identification, and social support play little role in current research on attitudes and social cognition. Nor do stage-specific theories of attitudes, which assert that the individual's particular life stage may powerfully affect attitude formation and change. Third, contemporary social psychology views humans as dominated by cognitive rather than affective processes, especially emotionally based irrationalities. And, finally, sociopsychological theories tend to treat people as highly egocentric.

In all these respects, the idiosyncracies of social psychology's rather narrow data base parallel the portrait of human nature with which it emerges. To caricature the point, contemporary social psychology, on the basis of young students preselected for special cognitive skills and tested in isolation in an academic setting on academic tasks, presents the human race as composed of lone, bland, compliant wimps who specialize in paper-and-pencil tests. The human being of strong and irrational passions, of intractable prejudices, who is solidly embedded in tightly knit family and ethnic groups, who develops and matures with age, is not that of contemporary social psychology; it does not provide much room for such as Palestinian guerrillas, southern Italian peasants, Winston Churchill, Idi Amin, Florence Nightingale, Archie Bunker, Ma Joad, Clarence Darrow, or Martin Luther King.

The effects of this narrow data base on our portrait of human nature is nicely illustrated by Steele and Southwick's (1985) meta-analysis of the effects of alcohol consumption. They predicted, and found, that higher blood alcohol levels produced more impulsive social behavior (aggression, gambling, sexuality, etc.) when inhibitory conflict was strongest, presumably because intoxication's disinhibiting effect has its most potent effects when the individual is most conflicted about the behavior in question. But the strongest predictor of extremely impulsive behavior, after conflict and blood alcohol level, was subject type: Noncollege student populations produced larger alcohol effects. The difference was a major one: Conflict and blood alcohol level (and their interaction) accounted for 20% of the variance; subject type accounted

for 9% (the equivalent of a partial correlation of .30). This study reveals that subject effects are of the nature suggested above: College students in laboratory studies behave less emotionally and impulsively than the general population. And it indicates that the effects are potentially of major importance.

What is the recommendation? We have developed an impressive corpus of scientific knowledge and, indeed, have learned a great deal from studying college sophomores in the laboratory. But it may be appropriate to be somewhat more tentative about the portrait of human nature we have developed from this data base. The specific examples given in this article perhaps will serve to illustrate the point and raise the larger question and, in that way, point to a research agenda that might examine the question more directly.

Most obviously, a greater effort must be made to conduct research on persons from life stages other than late adolescence. But simply testing samples of a broader age range, in my view, would not by itself be sufficient. Other changes in our conventional methodologies would have to be made. Everyone has been to school, and I suspect that even middle-aged people, separated from family and friends and confronted with testlike materials on novel and artificial topics in an academic laboratory, would often behave like college students do. Any parents who have sat at their child's desk in a third-grade classroom on Parents-Back-to-School Night can testify to the power of that situation. However, that is not how a truck driver and his cronies behave at a Teamsters meeting. Even "genuine" courtroom judges behave in an artificially rational and normative manner when tested with artificial paper-and-pencil materials by a student doing a class project, as Ebbesen and Konecni (1975) have compellingly demonstrated. My suspicion is that the biases introduced by reliance on the college sophomore in the laboratory reflect a genuine interaction of subject characteristics with the many unusual features of the academic laboratory method. Very different people, in very different behavioral settings, would need to be studied.

On a cost-benefit basis, it would not pay to

convert all sociopsychological research to adult populations in more representative settings or to replicate all past findings on them. Rather, selective conversion and replication is called for, when there is reason to believe that the findings might be biased by our peculiar data base. Much is already known about the life-span trajectory of social processes, and knowledge is rapidly accumulating as various disciplines recognize the value of a life-span perspective. The question of the ecological representativeness of research behavior settings has been raised explicitly in developmental psychology, and analogous questions have been raised in cross-cultural and comparative psychology. Enough is known to allow some good guesses about where the laboratory study of college students is likely to mislead us and where it is likely not to. This article has offered a few examples, but a wider canvass, both of the life span and the full breadth of social psychology, would surely present a more complete picture.

This would require more vigilance to the possible limitations of student and/or laboratory-based data than most social psychologists have practiced in recent years. My guess, as developed above, is that such a strategy would open some of the more interesting developments of recent years to question, perhaps partly because their interest value is due to their contradicting our everyday experience (and perhaps, therefore, valid only within some rather narrow conditions). At the very least, it would lead to more complete and ecologically valid substantive conclusions. And, for the future, it might bring back into the purview of social psychology a broad range of important human phenomena, presently largely ignored, whose inclusion would allow social psychologists to speak with more authority to the full range of human social experience.

REFERENCES

Abelson, R. P., & Rosenberg, M. J. (1958). Symbolic psychologic: A model of attitudinal cognition. *Behavioral Science, 3*, 1–13.

Ackerman, N. W., & Jahoda, M. (1950). *Anti-Semitism and emotional disorder: A psychoanalytic interpretation*. New York: Harper.

Adorno, T. W., Frenkel-Brunswik, E., Levinson, D. J., & Sanford, R. N., (1950). *The authoritarian personality*. New York: Harper & Row.

Ajzen, I., & Fishbein, M. (1980). *Understanding attitudes and predicting social behavior*. Englewood Cliffs, NJ: Prentice-Hall.

Allport, G. W. (1954). *The nature of prejudice*. Garden City, NY: Doubleday Anchor.

Anderson, N. H. (1971). Integration theory and attitude change. *Psychological Review, 78*, 171–206.

Aronson, E. (Ed.). (1981). *Readings about the social animal* (3rd ed.). San Francisco: Freeman.

Atwater, E. (1983). *Adolescence*. Englewood Cliffs, NJ: Prentice-Hall.

Bem, D. J. (1972). Self-perception theory. In L. Berkowitz (Ed.), *Advances in experimental social psychology* (pp. 1–62). New York: Academic Press.

Berelson, B. R., Lazarsfeld, P. F., & McPhee, W. N. (1954). *Voting: A study of opinion formation in a presidential campaign*. Chicago: University of Chicago Press.

Berkowitz, L., & Donnerstein, E. (1982). External validity is more than skin deep: Some answers to criticisms of laboratory experiments. *American Psychologist, 37*, 245–257.

Bettelheim, B., & Janowitz, M. (1950). *Dynamics of prejudice*. New York: Harper.

Brigham, J. C., & Wrightsman, L. S. (Eds.). (1982). *Contemporary issues in social psychology* (4th ed.). Monterey, CA: Brooks/Cole.

Bronfenbrenner, U. (1977). Toward an experimental ecology of human development. *American Psychologist, 32*, 513–531.

Brown, T. (1981). On contextual change and partisan attitudes. *British Journal of Political Science, 11*, 427–447.

Brunswik, E. (1955). Representative design and probabilistic theory in a functional psychology. *Psychological Review, 62*, 193–217.

Byrne, D. (1971). *The attraction paradigm*. New York: Academic Press.

Cantril, H. (1940). *The invasion from Mars*. Princeton, NJ: Princeton University Press.

Carlsson, G., & Karlsson, K. (1970). Age, cohorts, and the generation of generations. *American Sociological Review, 35*, 710–718.

Cartwright, D. (1949). Some principles of mass persuasion: Selected findings of research on the sale of United States war bonds. *Human Relations, 2*, 253–267.

Chaiken, S., & Baldwin, M. W. (1981). Affective-cognitive consistency and the effect of salient behavioral information on the self-perception of attitudes. *Journal of Personality and Social Psychology, 41*, 1–12.

Christie, R. (1965). Some implications of research trends

in social psychology. In O. Klineberg & R. Christie (Eds.), *Perspectives in social psychology* (pp. 141–152). New York: Holt, Rinehart & Winston.

Clark, M. S., & Fiske, S. T. (Eds.). (1982). *Affect and cognition: The Seventeenth Annual Carnegie Symposium on Cognition.* Hillsdale, NJ: Erlbaum.

Coch, L., & French, J. R., Jr. (1948). Overcoming resistance to change. *Human Relations, 11,* 512–532.

Conger, T. (1977). *Adolescence and youth: Psychological development.* New York: Harper & Row.

Converse, P. E. (1964). The nature of belief systems in mass publics. In D. E. Apter (Ed.), *Ideology and discontent* (pp. 206–261). New York: Free Press of Glencoe.

Converse, P. E. (1970). Attitudes and non-attitudes: Continuation of a dialogue. In E. R. Tufte (Ed.), *The quantitative analysis of social problems* (pp. 168–189). Reading, MA: Addison-Wesley.

Converse, P. E. (1976). *The dynamics of party support: Cohort-analyzing party identification.* Beverly Hills, CA: Sage.

Converse, P. E., & Campbell, A. (1960). Political standards in secondary groups. In D. Cartwright & A. Zander (Eds.), *Group dynamics* (2nd ed., pp. 300–318). Evanston, IL: Row, Peterson.

Crutchfield, R. S. (1955). Conformity and character. *American Psychologist, 10,* 191–198.

Davidson, A. R., Yantis, S., Norwood, M., & Montano, D. E. (1985). Amount of information about the attitude object and attitude-behavior consistency. *Journal of Personality and Social Psychology, 49,* 1184–1198.

Deutsch, M., & Collins, M. E. (1951). *Interracial housing: A psychological evaluation of a social experiment.* Minneapolis: University of Minnesota Press.

Douvan, E., & Adelson, J. (1966). *The adolescent experience.* New York: Wiley.

Duval, S., & Wicklund, R. A. (1972). *A theory of objective self-awareness.* New York: Academic Press.

Ebbesen, E. B., & Konecni, V. J. (1975). Decision making and information integration in the courts: The setting of bail. *Journal of Personality and Social Psychology, 32,* 805–821.

Erikson, E. H. (1963). *Childhood and society* (2nd ed.). New York: Norton.

Fazio, R. H., & Zanna, M. P. (1981). Direct experience and attitude-behavior consistency. In L. Berkowitz (Ed.), *Advances in experimental social psychology* (Vol. 14). New York: Academic Press.

Feather, N. T. (Ed.). (1982). *Expectations and actions in expectancy-value models in psychology.* Hillsdale, NJ: Erlbaum.

Festinger, L. (1950). Informal social communication. *Psychological Review, 57,* 271–282.

Festinger, L. (1954). A theory of social comparison processes. *Human Relations, 7,* 117–140.

Festinger, L. (1957). *A theory of cognitive dissonance.* Evanston, IL: Row, Peterson.

Festinger, L., & Carlsmith, J. M. (1959). Cognitive consequences of forced compliance. *Journal of Abnormal and Social Psychology, 58,* 203–210.

Festinger, L., Schachter, S., & Back, K. (1950). *Social pressures in informal groups: A study of a housing project.* New York: Harper.

Findley, M., & Cooper, H. (1981). Introductory social psychology testbook citations: A comparison in five research areas. *Personality and Social Psychology Bulletin, 7,* 173–176.

Fiske, S., & Taylor, S. (1984). *Social cognition.* Reading, MA: Addison-Wesley.

Freedman, J. L., Carlsmith, J. M., & Sears, D. O. (Eds.). (1971). *Readings in social psychology.* Englewood Cliffs, NJ: Prentice-Hall.

Fried, S. B., Gumpper, D. C. & Allen, J. C. (1973). Ten years of social psychology: Is there a growing commitment to field research? *American Psychologist, 28,* 155–156.

Glenn, N. D. (1980). Values, attitudes, and beliefs. In O. G. Brim, Jr., & J. Kagan (Eds.), *Constancy and change in human development* (pp. 596–640). Cambridge, MA: Harvard University Press.

Higbee, K. L., Lott, W. J., & Graves, J. P. (1976). Experimentation and college students in social-personality research. *Personality and Social Psychology Bulletin, 2,* 239–241.

Higbee, K. L., Millard, R. J., & Folkman, J. R. (1982). Social psychology research during the 1970s: Predominance of experimentation and college students. *Personality and Social Psychology Bulletin, 8,* 180–183.

Higbee, K. L., & Wells, M. G. (1972). Some research trends in social psychology during the 1960s. *American Psychologist, 27,* 963–966.

Hovland, C. I. (1959). Reconciling conflicting results derived from experimental and survey studies of attitude change. *American Psychologist, 14,* 8–17.

Hovland, C. I., Janis, I. L., & Kelley, H. H. (1953). *Communication and persuasion.* New Haven, CT: Yale University Press.

Hovland, C. I., Lumsdaine, A. A., & Sheffield, F. D. (1949). *Experiments on mass communication.* Princeton, NJ: Princeton University Press.

Hyman, H. (1959). *Political socialization.* Glencoe, IL: Free Press.

Hyman, H. H., & Sheatsley, P. B. (1954). The authoritarian personality: A methodological critique. In R. Christie & M. Jahoda (Eds.), *Studies in the scope and method of the authoritarian personality* (pp. 50–122). Glencoe, IL: Free Press.

Jennings, M. K., & Markus, G. B. (1984). Partisan orientations over the long haul: Results from the three-wave political socialization panel study. *American Political Science Review, 78,* 1000–1018.

Jennings, M. K., & Niemi, R. G. (1981). *Generations and politics.* Princeton, NJ: Princeton University Press.

Kahneman, D., Slovic, P., & Tversky, A. (Eds.) (1982). *Judgment under uncertainty: Heuristics and biases.* New York: Cambridge University Press.

Katz, D. (1960). The functional approach to the study of attitudes. *Public Opinion Quarterly, 24,* 163–204.

Katz, D., Sarnoff, I., & McClintock, C. (1956). Ego defense and attitude change. *Human Relations, 9,* 27–46.

Kelley, H. H. (1955). Salience of membership and resistance to change of group-anchored attitudes. *Human Relations, 8,* 275–289,

Kelley, H. H. (1967). Attribution theory in social psychology. In D. Levine (Ed.), *Nebraska Symposium on Motivation* (pp. 192–238). Lincoln: University of Nebraska Press.

Kelley, S., Jr., & Mirer, T. W. (1974). The simple act of voting. *American Political Science Review, 68,* 572–591.

Kiesler, C. A., Collins, B. E., & Miller, N. (1969). *Attitude change: A critical analysis of theoretical approaches.* New York: Wiley.

Kinder, D. R., & Sears, D. O. (1985). Public opinion and political action. In G. Lindzey & E. Aronson (Eds.), *Handbook of social psychology* 3rd ed., pp. 659–741). New York: Random House.

Kirkpatrick, S. A. (1976). Aging effects and generational differences in social welfare attitude constraint in the mass public. *Western Political Quarterly, 29,* 43–58.

Kirscht, J. P., & Dillehay, R. C. (1967). *Dimensions of authoritarianism.* Lexington: University of Kentucky Press.

Lane, R. E. (1962). *Political ideology: Why the American common man believes what he does.* New York: Free Press.

Lazarsfeld, P. F., Berelson, B., & Gaudet, H. (1948). *The people's choice* (2nd ed.). New York: Columbia University Press.

Lewin, K. (1947). Group decision and social change. In T. M. Newcomb & E. L. Hartley (Eds.), *Readings in social psychology* (pp. 459–473). New York: Holt.

Lipset, S. M., & Raab, E. (1978). *The politics of unreason* (2nd ed.). Chicago: The University of Chicago Press.

Loewenberg, P. (1971). The psychohistorical origins of the Nazi youth cohort. *The American Historical Review, 76,* 1457–1502.

Markus, G. B. (1979). The political environment and the dynamics of public attitudes: A panel study. *American Journal of Political Science, 23,* 338–359.

McGuire, W. J. (1985). Attitudes and attitude change. In G. Lindzey & E. Aronson (Eds.), *Handbook of social psychology, Vol. II* (3rd ed., pp. 223–346). New York: Random House.

Merton, R. K., & Kitt, A. S. (1950). Contributions to the theory of reference-group behavior. In R. K. Merton & P. F. Lazarsfeld (Eds.), *Continuities in social research: Studies in the scope and method of "the American soldier"* (pp. 40–105). Glencoe, IL: Free Press.

Milgram, S. (1974). *Obedience to authority.* New York: Harper & Row.

Miller, J. G. (1984). Culture and the development of everyday social explanation. *Journal of Personality and Social Psychology, 46,* 961–978.

Mueller, J. E. (1973). *War, presidents, and public opinion,* New York: Wiley.

Mullen, B., Atkins, J. L., Champion, D. S. Edwards, D. H., Hardy, D., Story, J. E., & Vanderklok, M. (1985). The false consensus effect: A meta-analysis of 115 hypothesis tests. *Journal of Experimental Social Psychology, 21,* 262–283.

Newcomb, T. M. (1943). *Personality and social change.* New York: Dryden Press.

Newcomb, T. M., Koenig, K. E. Flacks, R., & Warwick, D. P. (1967). *Persistence and change: Bennington College and its students after 25 years.* New York: Wiley.

Nisbett, R., & Ross, L. (1980). *Human inference: Strategies and shortcomings of social judgment.* Englewood Cliffs, NJ: Prentice-Hall.

Nisbett, R. E., & Wilson, T. D. (1977). Telling more than we can know: Verbal reports on mental processes. *Psychological Review, 84,* 231–259.

Norman, R. (1975). Affective-cognitive consistency, attitudes, conformity, and behavior. *Journal of Personality and Social Psychology, 32,* 83–91.

Osgood, C. E., & Tannenbaum, P. (1955). The principle of congruity and the prediction of attitude change. *Psychological Reveiw, 62,* 42–55.

Perlman, D. (1984). Recent development in personality and social psychology: A citation analysis. *Personality and Social Psychology Bulletin, 10,* 493–501.

Petty, R. E., & Cacioppo, J. T. (1981). *Attitudes and persuasion: Classic and contemporary approaches.* Dubuque, IA: Wm. C. Brown.

Petty, R. E., Ostrom, T. M., & Brock, T. C. (1981). Historical foundations of the cognitive response approach to attitudes and persuasion. In R. E. Petty, T. M. Ostrom, & T. C. Brock (Eds.), *Cognitive responses in persuasion* (pp. 5–29), Hillsdale, NJ: Erlbaum.

Potter, J. (1981). The development of social psychology: Consensus, theory and methodology in the *British Journal of Social and Clinical Psychology. British Journal of Social Psychology, 20,* 249–258.

Proshansky, H. M. (1966). The development of intergroup attitudes. In L. W. Hoffman & M. L. Hoffman (Eds.), *Review of child development research* (Vol. 2, pp. 311–371). New York: Russell Sage Foundation.

Proshansky, H. M., & Seidenberg, B. (Eds.) (1965). *Basic studies in social psychology.* New York: Holt, Rinehart & Winston.

Roseman, I., Abelson, R. P., & Ewing, M. F. (1986). Emotion and politcal cognition: Emotional political communication. In R. R. Lau & D. O. Sears (Eds)., *Political cognition: The 19th Annual Carnegie Symposium on Cognition* (pp. 279–294). Hillsdale, NJ: Erlbaum.

Ross, L., Greene, D., & House, P. (1977). The "false

consensus effect": An egocentric bias in social perception and attribution processes. *Journal of Experimental Social Psychology, 13,* 279–301.

Ross, M., & Sicoly, F. (1979). Egocentric biases in availability and attribution. *Journal of Personality and Social Psychology, 37,* 322–336.

Rubenstein, C. (1983, July). Psychology's fruit flies. *Psychology Today,* pp. 83–84.

Sarnoff, I. (1960). Reaction formation and cynicism. *Journal of Personality, 28,* 129–143.

Schachter, S., & Singer, J. E. (1962). Cognitive, social and physiological determinants of emotional state. *Psychological Review, 69,* 379–399.

Schultz, D. D. (1969). The human subject in psychology research. *Psychological Bulletin, 72,* 214–228.

Schuman, H., & Johnson, M. P. (1976). Attitudes and behavior. *Annual Review of Sociology, 2,* 161–207.

Sears, D. O. (1969). Political behavior. In G. Lindzey & E. Aronson (Eds.), *Handbook of social psychology* (Vol. 5, rev. ed., pp. 315–458). Reading, MA: Addison-Wesley.

Sears, D. O. (1975). Political socialization. In F. I. Greenstein & N. W. Polsby (Eds.), *Handbook of political science* (Vol. 2, pp. 92–153). Reading, MA: Addison-Wesley.

Sears, D. O. (1981). Life stage effects upon attitude change, especially among the elderly. In S. B. Kiesler, J. N. Morgan, & V. K. Oppenheimer (Eds.), *Aging: Social change* (pp. 183–204). New York; Academic Press.

Sears, D. O. (1983). The persistence of early political predispositions: The roles of attitude object and life stage. In L. Wheeler & P. Shaver (Eds.), *Review of personality and social psychology* (Vol. 4, pp. 79–116). Beverly Hills, Sage.

Sears, D. O., & Allen, H. M., Jr. (1984). The trajectory of local desegregation controversies and whites' opposition to busing. In N. Miller & M. B. Brewer (Eds.), *Groups in contact: The psychology of desegregation* (pp. 123–151). Orlando, FL: Academic Press.

Sears, D. O., & Citrin, J. (1985). *Tax revolt: Something for nothing in California* (Enlarged ed.). Cambridge, MA: Harvard University Press.

Sears, D. O., Steck, L., Lau, R. R., & Gahart, M. T. (1983). *Attitudes of the post-Vietnam generation toward the draft and American military policy.* Paper presented at the annual meeting of the International Society of Political Psychology, Oxford, England.

Shanks, J. M., & Miller, W. E. (1985). *Policy direction and performance evaluation: Complementary explanations of the Reagan elections.* Paper presented at the annual meeting of the American Political Science Association, New Orleans, LA.

Sherif, M. (1936). *The psychology of social norms.* New York: Harper.

Shils, E. A., & Janowitz, M. (1948). Cohesion and disintegration in the Wehrmacht in World War II. *Public Opinion Quarterly, 12,* 280–315.

Sivacek, J., & Crano, W. D. (1982). Vested interest as a moderator of attitude-behavior consistency. *Journal of Personality and Social Psychology, 43,* 210–221.

Slovic, P., Fischhoff, B., & Lichtenstein, S. (1977). Behavioral decision theory. *Annual Review of Psychology, 28,* 1–39.

Smart, R. G. (1966). Subject selection bias in psychological research. *The Canadian Psychologist, 7a,* 115–121.

Smith, M. B., Bruner, J. S., & White, R. W. (1956). *Opinions and personality.* New York: Wiley.

Smith, C. A., & Ellsworth, P. C. (1985). Patterns of cognitive appraisal in emotion. *Journal of Personality and Social Psychology, 48,* 813–838.

Steele, C. M., & Southwick, L. (1985). Alcohol and social behavior I: The psychology of drunken excess. *Journal of Personality and Social Psychology, 48,* 18–34.

Steiner, I. D., & Fishbein, M. (Eds.), (1965). *Current studies in social psychology.* New York: Holt, Rinehart & Winston.

Stouffer, S. A., Suchman, E. A., DeVinney, L. C., Star, S. A., & Williams, R. M., Jr. (1949). *The American soldier: Adjustment during army life.* New York: Wiley.

Swanson, G. E., Newcomb, T. M., & Hartley, E. L. (Eds.). (1952). *Readings in social psychology* (rev. ed.). New York: Holt.

Taylor, S. E., & Fiske, S. T. (1978). Salience, attention, and attribution: Top of the head phenomena. In L. Berkowitz (Ed.), *Advances in experimental social psychology* (Vol. 11, pp. 249–288). New York: Academic Press.

Taylor, S. E. (1975). On inferring one's attitudes from one's behavior: Some delimiting conditions. *Journal of Personality and Social Psychology, 31,* 126–131.

Thompson, S. C., & Kelley, H. H. (1981). Judgments of responsibility for activities in close relationships. *Journal of Personality and Social Psychology, 41,* 469–477.

Weber, S. J., & Cook, T. D. (1972). Subject effects in laboratory research: An examination of subject roles, demand characteristics, and valid inferences. *Psychological Bulletin, 77,* 273–295.

Weiner, B. (1982). The emotional consequences of causal attributions. In M. S. Clark & W. T. Fiske (Eds.), *Affect and cognition: The Seventeenth Annual Carnegie Symposium on Cognition* (pp. 185–209). Hillsdale, NJ: Erlbaum.

Wood, W. (1982). Retrieval of attitude-relevant information from memory: Effects on susceptibility to persuasion and on intrinsic motivation. *Journal of Personality and Social Psychology, 42,* 798–810.

Wrightsman, L. S., & Brigham, J. C. (Eds.). (1973). *Contemporary issues in social psychology* (2nd ed.). Monterey, CA: Brooks/Cole.

Zajonc, R. B. (1980). Feeling and thinking: Preferences need no inferences. *American Psychologist, 35,* 151–175.